Passion and Prejudice

PASSION
and
PREJUDICE

A Family Memoir

•••

With a new Introduction

SALLIE BINGHAM

PASSION AND PREJUDICE
A Family Memoir

Copyright © 1989 by Sallie Bingham

PASSION AND PREJUDICE: What Came After

Copyright © 1991 by Sallie Bingham

Cover photograph from the author's private collection; hand-tinted by Sandra Fine. Jacket design by Elizabeth Koda-Callan. © 1989 Alfred A. Knopf, Inc.

Library of Congress Cataloging-in-Publication Data

Bingham, Sallie.
    Passion and prejudice : a family memoir / Sallie Bingham
       p.   cm.
    Includes bibliographical references.
    ISBN 1-55783-077-0 : $12.95
    1. Bingham, Sallie—Family. 2. Bingham family. 3. Upper classes—Kentucky—Louisville—Biography. 4. Louisville (Ky.)—Biography.
I. Title.
CT275.B5737A3   1991
976.9'44—dc20
[B]   90-48852
                                        CIP

Applause Books
211 West 71st Street
New York, New York 10023
(212) 595-4735

First Applause Printing, 1991

THIS MEMOIR IS DEDICATED TO THE PAST:

Lucy E. Cummings

AND TO THE FUTURE:

Barry Ellsworth, Christopher and William Iovenko

———

If I could have one wish for my sons, it is that they should have the courage of women.

Adrienne Rich

Every age and generation must be as free to act for itself, in all cases, as the age and generation which preceded it. . . . Man has no property in man; neither has any generation a property in the generations which are to follow.

Thomas Paine, *The Rights of Man*

The past is male. But the past is all we have. We must use it, in order that the future will speak of womanhood, a condition full of risk, and variety, and discovery: in short, human.

Carolyn Heilbrun, *Reinventing Womanhood*

Contents

Author's Note

In re-creating my past, I asked questions about the world that once encased me, questions I did not have the authority, or the audacity, to ask when I was still a part of that world. In attempting to answer some of those questions, I have relied almost entirely on the printed word: newspapers, magazines, letters and diaries, and especially books, which have illuminated some small part of the world of which I was once a member.

I did not interview the many people who were and are part of that world, and who formed it. Since they are bound by ties of loyalty and doctrine, love and fear, their replies would be, it seemed to me, defenses of past positions or explanations of past decisions. In a dynasty, maintaining power is more important than any individual, and ultimately more important than the truth.

Women have often been silenced in history, our voices discredited or blotted out. We have been silenced to preserve elements in the hierarchy, political or social, public or private, institutional or personal.

I chose to speak.

As a result of this choice and many other factors, the two daily newspapers that my father and his father had owned and run for seventy years were sold to the Gannett Company in May 1986 for $307 million. The television and radio stations, also owned by my father and grandfather, and several other companies were sold at the same time.

As a minority stockholder in all these companies, my share of the proceeds amounted to $62 million, before taxes, legal fees, and the expenses charged by accountants and advisers. Half of the remaining proceeds are tied up in trusts established by my father and grandfather.

I have used $10 million of my proceeds to fund a private foundation called the Kentucky Foundation for Women, which supports women in the arts in this state and publishes a literary quarterly called *The American Voice*.

Acknowledgments

I am grateful to Anne Tillinghast, Carson Thomas, Robert Kelley, David Chandler, Mary Chandler, Frederick Smock, Patricia Buster, Linda Norman, Michael Kirkhorn, Helena Stevens, and Thomas S. Kenan III.

I was much helped by Linda McCurdy of the Southern Historical Collection at the University of North Carolina, Chapel Hill; James J. Holmberg, Curator of Manuscripts at the Filson Club, Louisville, Kentucky; Charles Simmons, Director, and Joan Runkel, Curator, at the Flagler Museum in Palm Beach, Florida; and Betsy Parkin, Archivist, Special Collections and Archives Department, James Branch Cabell Library, Richmond, Virginia.

I have turned to books by Nina Auerbach, Carolyn G. Heilbrun, Ann Firor Scott, Carroll Smith-Rosenberg, Marilyn French, Mary Daly, Susan Gubar—and especially Adrienne Rich, whose father had been a cadet at the Bingham School. These women, through their books, accompanied me. Because of that companionship, I was spared some of the pain that resulted from the fact that I was a newcomer in Louisville, with only a handful of women friends.

This book could not have been begun or finished without the help of my editor, Vicky Wilson.

Much of the work was done at the MacDowell Colony and the Virginia Center for the Creative Arts.

PASSION AND PREJUDICE:
What Came After

<hr>

How does it feel?" people sometimes ask me. Not how does it feel to
write a memoir, or to live in Kentucky, or to continue on my path
as a writer, or to raise three sons, or start a foundation for feminist artists,
or co-edit a literary quarterly for feminist writers called *The American
Voice*—but "How does it feel to be attacked by your own family?"

I shudder when I remember: the sessions with lawyers, the accusations,
the tears—and finally the sale of the media companies controlled by the
men in my family for more than seventy years.

On "Sixty Minutes," my brother told Diane Sawyer that I am "unlovable."
My mother told the same reigning princess of network TV that I, her eldest
daughter, live in a dream world. How does that feel?

First of all—why does it matter? We are killing people, again, in the
Middle East, and young women who are afraid to ask for their parents'
permission are beginning to die, again, from botched abortions.

So who cares?

Everyone, apparently. We have made the American Family into an
institution holier than capitalism and the CIA—two institutions more important
to American life than Mom and apple pie. We insist on believing in family
love even when we know most women who are murdered are murdered in
their homes, by their "loved ones"; when child abuse is so prevalent in all
classes that we must recognize it as an institution, too—and anyone who
has tried to help a judge to understand that wife-beating and child abuse
matter knows how acceptable both these activities are to our male elite and
those who imitate them.

Is the American family an instrument of oppression?

We don't want to believe that. It would mean admitting that we must find our nourishment elsewhere, in friends, in self-help groups, in attempts at spiritual growth.

So the question "How does it feel?" does matter, and it deserves an answer.

At first, being publicly attacked brought on numbness—the shield of the survivor, and I have been a survivor for all of my fifty-four years.

And then laughter.

That's the way I felt about the television interviews, the newspaper hoopla—"King Lear in Kentucky"—and so forth.

But it was different when they attacked this book, an attack planned long before the book was written. When my mother told me she would not speak to me if I mentioned my step-grandmother in the yet unwritten manuscript, I knew some sort of "rebuttal" would emerge as soon as pirated copies of the uncorrected galleys could be secured.

I didn't anticipate the size, weight and expense of the eleven-pound attack on my book the family generated. A Louisville lawyer speculated that their campaign had cost half a million dollars, including the fee paid to the writer and the enormous mailing costs of sending the eleven-pound lump of a rebuttal to every magazine, newspaper and reviewer in the country—minus, of course, the feminist press, which does not exist as far as these people know.

One of the greatest pitfalls of the very rich is our ability to act out compulsions and fantasies. Cost is no factor and so anything, literally anything, can be done, especially if someone can be hired to do it so no direct confrontation is necessary. The money we give to charity would, I imagine, pale in comparison to the money we spend on lawyers, advisors, manipulators, publicity agents and other guns-for-hire who pursue our imaginary enemies and engage in endless vendettas.

Still, who in the world would believe that a newspaper "family" versed in first amendment lore (which should be translated as someone else's ox is always the ox being gored) would descend to commissioning an eleven-pound attack on a book written by one of their own? A critique, to dishonor the word, that included xeroxed pages from ancient telephone directories and squeals about nineteenth-century middle names and Civil War forts?

Unfortunately, we have seen this happen here, there and everywhere—in Cincinnati, where a gallery director faced a year in jail; in Washington, where war is declared (virtually—a fine word) while Congress and the President play golf, effectively stifling public outcry because there is no one to outcry to; in the performing arts, where Karen Findley (whom Louisville loved) is pilloried as an example of all that we, collectively, fear: the outspoken woman who dares to feel.

Annihilation—that is what my family's attack felt like, after the numbness wore off and the laughter died. Pain that still wakes me in the night like a jolt of electricity, panic that dries my throat, anxiety that kills my appetite and my dreams.

To attack my integrity as a writer endangers my survival. And it goes on. How many editors and book reviewers retain some vague memory of that mass of expensive material landing on their desks? "Where there's smoke, there's fire" and so forth, especially when the rich are doing the puffing.

Sure, there were some errors in the first edition, which have been corrected; for example, I reversed two digits on a date, and called a Civil War fort by the wrong name. That, of course, was not what the attack was about. It never is . . .

It was about guarding secrets, keeping lies intact, protecting the reputations of some pretty dubious men—one of whom, a former foreign correspondent, screamed so loud it must have been heard in Moscow. The attack was against the truth: against naming names, telling stories, and putting women back into the spotlight—dragging them back, if necessary, from early graves. It was one more attempt to cover up the cause, long successfully concealed, of my step-grandmother's death, and the miseries, which were not even worth concealing, of other women in my family. And it was an attack on the right of a woman—any woman—to tell the story of her own life.

I was frightened by this onslaught. Who would not be? At one point I even feared for my life. I was also mystified. All sensible people know the best way to keep a book afloat is to attack it.

And I remember having been taught, as a child, to tell the truth "and shame the devil." But the devils I was shaming were special, and the axiom, like most axioms, does not apply to them but to those who have no Character, no Reputation to Keep Up, no Position to Maintain. If I had written about a poor family, about women on welfare, no one would have minded; in fact I would have been praised for reinforcing useful stereotypes.

A lot of public people took sides with my family. The rule of thumb seemed to be that I could expect personal harassment from men, and some women, who were east-coast-big-media monsters; and of course from their hangers-on in publicity and covert doings, all closer than kissing cousins to the men who own the news.

Reviewers sometimes quoted some nasty little morsel from the eleven pounds. I've been a book editor too, and I know how easy it is to liven up a column or a review with a quote culled from the mail. And then, the lives of the people who govern us—especially the women's—are completely covered in stereotypes—Poor Little Rich Girl, etc.—and so any apparently "inside" information such as the eleven pound attack has an irresistible lure, as though the secrets of the tombs of the Pharaohs are finally to be revealed.

But most reviewers stood by their integrity, read the book and realized that the eleven pounds was a threat, a hoax, and a joke. The big-time papers did their usual balancing act, citing something from the eleven pounds (hamburger, as I came to call it) and from *Passion and Prejudice* and leaving the reader to make the dangerous decision about which one to believe— a balancing act done with a good deal of grace but not particularly to my satisfaction.

Then there was the man who runs an early morning radio talk show in North Carolina, who brightened with enthusiasm when we talked about *Passion and Prejudice*, and Studs Terkel in Chicago, who underlined whole pages and talked about Lillian Smith; and Larry King in Washington who asked an insulting caller whether he was connected to the Binghams (it turned out he was), and hundreds of readers all over the country who wrote me that they, too, had experienced "family life in the U.S.A.," whether with or without big money, and knew first hand about the connection between abuse, sexism, racism and the silencing of women.

The connections between the rich and powerful and a large group of what might charitably be called their supporters are long, old, and serpentine — like a *New Yorker* cartoon which showed a whole roomful of people connected by subterranean roots. So you never know where you will find someone who is a "close personal friend" of the great, who was "helped so much" by their benevolence, or who still hopes against hope to be invited to sit in a box at the Kentucky Derby.

Apparently, we need our rich—certainly we are willing to make sacrifices to support them, as our tax system shows. We need the myth that the Rich are Better Than You and Me—or they wouldn't be rich. The Horatio Alger story is still intact in 1991, especially because no women and no minorities need apply.

Perhaps the rich inhabit the vacuum formed in a society that excludes women.

Yet Americans need to transform rich women into witches, evil step-mothers, criminals convicted of no crime except that of using their money (or what they thought was their money before some man claimed it) in a public way.

The ends don't matter. Who notices the beautiful flowers in the lobby of the Plaza Hotel, and wonders who sees to them every day? Who crawled on their knees to the altar beside Imelda Marcos when she thanked the

Goddess for allowing the truth to prevail? Every newspaper hack who repeated the slogans that demeaned and degraded these two ladies should have been there on his knees, or even on hers—although the news room, as one remarkably boring New York columnist recently proved, still hopes to be perceived as a male preserve—complete, I assume, with rhinoceri.

The next question people ask me is, "So do you speak to your family?" The real question is whether they speak to me.

Yes, my poor dear mother, now eighty-four, did once send me a formal invitation and then instructed her secretary to write and explain that it had been sent by mistake. Yes, it is hard to see people in public who seem to want to be invisible, at least to my eyes. And yes, Louisville, although technically a city, is still a very small town.

It does make sense to me. My relatives are frightened people who have, at least in certain cases, lost something much more important than the enormous sums of money they received from the sale of "our" companies: they have lost the definition they depended upon as "That Family," ("Which one are you?"), "Those People": the Binghams.

We hate people who strip us of our identity, or who allow reality to intrude on a dream. Ibsen knew that. Reality, however, is not in my hands, or in anyone else's, and my hunch is that when my lively and intelligent sons and their cousins come into their own, they will enjoy (if they wish to) a few breaths of fresh air. Who, at twenty-two or twenty-three, wants to be "important?" And the money they hold because of the sale of my father's companies will enable them, if they wish, to change some sector of the world.

But that may be wishful thinking. We are formed by our families, and only by breaking away at an early age (preferably before eighteen), taking drastic action to learn a skill, and engaging in years of therapy of the most eclectic kind do we ever become whole and sane enough to seek those people, surely not blood-relatives, who can be our friends.

Certainly the best way to restore family harmony (if such a thing is possible, or even desirable: it usually depends on the silencing of all the women) is not to attack your daughter and sister, not to isolate her with a wall of silence, which is what has happened in the time since the first edition was published.

I run into my relatives here and there, and they are unfailingly polite. I love them, and I look with admiration on their children. But I know the wall must remain between me and those dear folk who fear the truth as I see it, and who will go to any lengths short of murder—and will certainly indulge in soul murder—to prevent me from speaking it.

Soul murder; yes. That's what can happen to a writer, especially a woman, who becomes isolated, loses her faith in herself, no longer believes she has anything worth saying.

It hasn't happened to me because my soul is a tough little seed that sprouts wherever there's a drop of kindness, and there are quite a few. And because I have my prized, my priceless connection to the women's community, both here in Kentucky (where it flourishes) and in the rest of the country, and one day, I hope, in the world.

We who never had a past are taking on the future: we will see change in our lifetimes, if the war machine doesn't grind it out. As state legislatures fail to make their anti-abortion legislation stick, we see the power of women (and even some men) united against oppression; as the economy falters, more attention will be focused on those who keep it going even in slack times — the hourly worker, the wage slaves, the "service people"—the women. We are essential, because the hospitals must be run and the houses cleaned even when the Wall Street guys are giving out.

We will see the ERA passed as soon as the women in my sons' generation—now in their twenties—understand how important it is. We don't have equal rights, except by special permission, in special situations (and this is true for rich women, too, as you see proved whenever one of us doesn't appear dressed for the part). And special permission can always be withdrawn, certainly as we grow older and lose the automatic, slight power of youth and beauty, the only power women of my generation believed was legitimate.

Power is the core of the dispute. To write is to have the impudence to claim that I have something worth saying. To write is to lay hands on the tools of the patriarchy, not the pretty plumed pens but the missiles— the adjectives and verbs and nouns that change minds and sometimes even change people.

That is impudence: it starts a tiny flare that attracts other flares, giving hope to women lost in the twists of so-called "family" businesses—nearly always run by father-son directorates.

I take credit for none of this. I am satisfied to say with Frieda Lawrence that what I write is the wind blowing through me. My single obligation is to be receptive to that wind.

I have been encouraged by the response *Passion and Prejudice* has received from readers who point out the connections between my story and theirs, or who remind me of women ancestors I was never able to find, or who seem to have been changed in some way by the experience of reading and reacting to the book.

I am most grateful to the people who have written me about their own struggles and their successes. Perhaps most poignant was the letter from a cousin-by-marriage in North Carolina, of whose existence I had been ignorant. He wrote to tell me that a woman whose life had been erased from my family's record was indeed his great-great aunt, and that he has a few of her letters and the plate-silver tea-set which was her only material reward for a quarter century of service to the military-school headmaster—my great-grandfather and her husband.

Somehow the chickens always do come home to roost. And the hens, at least, tend to sprout new tail feathers to replace those singed off by events—which is what my life, and this book, are all about.

Sallie Bingham
Prospect, Kentucky
January 1991

Passion and Prejudice

Prologue

Once upon a time, there lived a little girl. Her name was
Nanny. She was a sweet little girl, but for one thing. She
NEVER told the true.

From my diary, 1945

I began life on summer mornings. Wakened early by the rising sun, I would
get up and steal out of the big silent house.

At that hour, the hill on which the house stood seemed to have come
unmoored. It floated above the Ohio River, awash with trees. The tarmac
of the long driveway was cool under my bare feet as I ran down the hill,
past the tennis court, the entrance to Mother's garden, the place where the
road divided to go to the garage, and the mossy swimming pool.

Here and there sundials and statues from an earlier time marked the
green. Steps led down into a sunken garden, gravel paths circled a fountain
where a bronze boy crouched on a dragonfly's back. Beyond, at the rim of
the Place (as we five children called it), woods crowded out the view of more
ordinary houses, and the Ohio lay in the distance, blue or brown, with
Indiana on the other side.

Later, when I was seven or eight, walking outside alone in the early
morning, I realized that the world existed independently of me.

The maple trees swung their leaves whether I was looking or not. The
breeze had its own way. The sun kept its measured pace.

I felt an astonishing relief, knowing that the world, the beautiful, soft,
green world, turned on its axis with no reference to my small life.

During those years, the Place provided all the materials I needed to
entertain myself.

Beside the east terrace, a Japanese magnolia dropped its pink petals in
the spring. I arranged them into faces, which I pressed on a stone bench

under a piece of glass from the ruined greenhouse. I changed a magnolia petal into a pale, pained face, tinged with pink, with two bits of twigs for eyes. After a while the petals turned brown, but by then I would have gone on to something else.

I explored the Back Woods, a strip of trees and honeysuckle at the edge of the Place. Jack-in-the-pulpits grew there in spring, along a small stream that flowed through the concrete buttresses of the swimming pool. In the summer, we spent most of our days in the cool green water, which was full of leaves and spiders.

Sometimes I would go over to the barn, climb up into the hayloft, and listen to the pigeons whir and fly, or continue my efforts to sweep out the old cow shed we used for a playhouse. There were moss rose seeds (my nurse's favorite) to plant in a hollowed-out stump near the cow shed, or Captain Bud to watch as he nailed one of his windmills to the end of a pole.

Sometimes I would arrange imaginary tea parties in my log cabin, where the latch on the door could be pulled up with a string. Doll clothes in various stages of decay and a small iron stove that really worked made the cabin seemed inhabited.

Finally, there were animals to care for: spring lambs who grew too quickly into smelly sheep, ducks who laid their eggs in the concrete-lined pond my older brother Barry built, or horses who sometimes escaped their hilly pasture.

Always, in the Big House and on the Place, there was a sense of earlier times, of another cast of characters, some of whom could not be mentioned.

My grandfather the Judge's black patent-leather slippers with flat bows on the toes were still lying in the attic, with my second stepgrandmother's long dresses, which she had worn when she was Ambassadress to England. Massive pieces of furniture filled corners in the attic, waiting to be shipped off to an aunt or a cousin in New York, Virginia, or North Carolina. Other relatives, whose names I did not know, existed in the things they had left behind and in the almost visible presence of their childhood and adolescence, a generation before.

The past was also preserved in books in the dark green library. Victorian and Edwardian classics were there in rows, from which Father chose a novel for the evening reading-aloud.

A conveniently low shelf housed a collection of large art books. I had to protect myself against some of the plates, especially the terrifying green El Greco crucifixion. The Pre-Raphaelites' sleepy-eyed madonnas and the Botticelli maidens, so innocent and yet so knowing, attracted me more than the stiff little Infanta whose portrait hung in my bedroom. They had the underwater quality of untouchable heroines. Millais's openmouthed drowned Ophelia was more beautiful than any woman alive.

Words did not disturb those images, bound between covers or loose in the world. I could not read when I first found those books.

It seems to me, in memory, that silence bathed the Big House, at least its formal rooms. Silence lay along the wide, highly polished floors and slipped down the double stairs, where Father, as a child, had kept a sliding board, equipped with cushions which carried people all the way to the front door.

Silence lay in the glazed eyes of the two polar bear skins in the front hall, and the long windows, draped in split brocade left from my grandfather the Judge's time, gave onto reaches of tranquil outdoor quiet. Only the shouts of the black mule-team driver, cutting the grass, rang out in summertime, changing everything.

Into this silence, the five children of my generation were born.

Each of the first three births was marked by a dramatic event, according to our parents.

The eldest son, Worth, was born on May 7, 1932, on the eve of the Kentucky Derby, the social excitement of the season.

The next son, Barry Jr., was born on September 23, 1933, when a haystack caught fire on a neighbor's farm.

I was born on January 22, 1937, during the great Ohio River flood.

The last two children belonged to a different category, less dramatic in its outward forms.

Jonathan was born on June 1, 1942, during the Second World War.

The last child in the family, Eleanor, was born on July 7, 1946. "The fam," or "the tribe," as Worth called it, was complete.

Alone on the Place, we were a tribe, as isolated and peculiar in our habits as any group of Stone Age creatures in the forests of New Guinea. Although we lived only ten miles from Louisville, a Midwestern city with Southern pretensions, we were completely sealed up by our routine, and by the special position of our parents.

I knew at an early age that "the fam" represented something entirely different to outsiders—friends, relatives, and business associates of Father. He owned the only major newspapers in the state of Kentucky, as well as other enterprises.

I understood this whenever the Big House was being prepared for one of the great dinner parties that seemed to me as elegant and as mysterious as the celebrations in an enchanted palace.

When the big table had been set with gold plates and gold utensils, when the vases were filled with heavy-scented flowers from Mother's garden and all the candles were lit, I would wander around the dining room, scooping butter balls from the butter plates, imagining the company of immortals that would presently descend.

They hardly existed as individuals for me but rather as a kindly murmuring swarm from which occasionally a hand or a word would issue:

"You are so lucky to have these parents . . . this house . . . this life . . ."

The comment always surprised me. It meant that the golden dinner table was the sum of it, all that really counted.

Beginnings

I can only make direct statements, only "tell stories." Whether or not the stories are "true" is not the problem. The only question is whether what I tell is my fable, my truth.

Carl Jung, *Memories, Dreams, Reflections*

1

On mornings when I did not get up before the other dozen or so people in the house, Lizzie Baker, the oldest of the four black servants, would come in to wake me. Rocking across my room on short, bent feet, she would go to the windows and crank open the wooden shutters.

In wintertime, Lizzie would strike a match to the coal fire in my grate. Then I would lie for a few more minutes, listening to the crackle of burning paper and kindling, the sharp burst as a lump of coal split and caught.

Breakfast was served to the three older children in what had once been the servants' dining room, a small room, tall as a well, next to the kitchen. On one wall hung a ghostly picture of a female figure, barefooted and draped in green, sitting astride what appeared to be the world. She sat in an attitude of mourning, her head bowed on a lyre. Years later, I learned to my surprise that the picture, by Elihu Vedder, was titled "Hope."

Breakfast was large and hot. Sometimes there were steaming griddle cakes, corn cakes, or large, doughy pancakes with syrup, sometimes stiffening scrambled eggs, broiled tomatoes and sausages, or the dreaded white calf's brains. When brains were served, my brother Worth refused to eat them, which meant he had to sit at the table while the brains congealed on his plate. I later learned, with considerable awe, that he had disposed of the problem by dumping the brains into the table drawer.

After breakfast, I would go up to my parents' bedroom, at the end of a long corridor on the second floor. Mother would be sitting up in the bed with the dipping-swan headposts, wearing a lace-bedecked bed jacket, often one made by her mother, whom we called Munda, in Richmond, Virginia. The snowy blanket cover with its satin binding and broad satin monogram lay evenly over her legs and feet; the breakfast tray, beside her on the cover, was set with flowered linen and china and what seemed to be an abstemious feast: a boiled egg, quite runny, and a bit of toast.

Across the room, Father, wearing his city trousers, shirt, and shoes and a sort of loose at-home jacket, was consuming more substantial fare.

Each parent had a complete morning newspaper. I could tell from the way the sections were separated and the pages folded back that these newspapers were to be read, cover to cover, as it were, not merely glanced at and tossed aside. Almost before I learned to speak, I understood that we, as a family, were responsible for every word in those newspapers, including the comics and the advertisements.

After 1950, Father also owned a television station, one of the first to receive a license in this country. From his father, the Judge, he had inherited a radio station and a printing company. But these other enterprises were seldom mentioned when I was a child. Instead, the newspapers, but especially the morning *Courier-Journal,* were the topic of much intense and mysterious conversation. I did not understand that there had been a time when the family had not owned the state's only newspapers, a time of smaller, more private concerns. It seemed to me that we *were* the newspapers, collectively, and that our kinship to their pages was so close it could not be questioned or discussed.

I seldom understood the conversations I heard between my parents about the issues of the day; they seemed to speak in a foreign tongue, with shrugs and frowns and telling pauses. I did not dare to ask questions which would reveal my ignorance. I remember my acute embarrassment when I asked, at ten or eleven, for the meaning of "yellow-dog journalism"; no answer was forthcoming, only what I interpreted as shocked silence. How could any member of the family know so little about our parents' consuming passion?

For years, I associated the newspapers with those early-morning scenes in my parents' bedroom rather than with the building, which took up a block in Louisville, or with the staff or the readers, all of whom remained remote. People spent their lives working "downtown" for "us," but what they actually *did* remained elusive. The newspapers' readers were represented by the drunken Saturday-night callers who raised hell with Father about editorials they considered liberal or even radical—or about wedding announcements that omitted a crucial detail.

He never complained about these intrusions, always taking the calls himself and listening resignedly. It seemed to me that he and all of us were supposed to be teaching the people of our rural, impoverished state how they ought to think and be. We were all meant to provide shining examples.

In elementary school I provided no example at all. I was a clown, and not a very successful one. I was still trying to find my way between my parents' rules about correct behavior and my classmates' leisurely pursuit of pleasure: candy, ice cream, radio serials, ruffled dresses—all forbidden to me.

Coming home in the afternoon was coming back to silence and enchantment. Sometimes Curtis Madison, our carpenter, handyman, and chauffeur, would drive the station wagon full of little girls home. Once, we threw his black visored cap out of the window. He stopped the car without a word and went back to get it.

If one of the mothers was driving the children home, I studied the back of her neck, where pale or dark hair curled or twined. I did not understand why an adult would permit herself to be enslaved by such a routine; I could not imagine, though, what these women did with the rest of their time. Mother's life seemed far more interesting, if equally mysterious.

She was usually at home or traveling somewhere with Father. He was usually at work downtown at the newspapers or he was traveling, sometimes without Mother. I did not question what Father did; he was gone, like all other fathers, from early morning until evening. I wondered about Mother because she was present, yet slightly withdrawn, like a figure in the brocade.

At times, she would appear, vigorously and suddenly, in the middle of our lives; on our nurse's day off, she took over our routine until we were old enough to manage on our own. Sometimes she would read "Peter Rabbit" or sing folk songs, accompanying herself on the piano.

I see her now in several settings. One was her study at the top of the house, where she often sat at a desk heaped with papers—letters, bills, speeches. She had a filing system for her five children and could find report cards and test results quickly. The rest of her paperwork, I assumed, concerned the outside world. She had many projects and served on committees, and all of this meant mail and time spent dealing with it.

Later I learned that she believed passionately in improving education, both locally and nationally, and served on committees which strove to find ways to deal with the collapse of standards, the declining reading scores, the removal first of Latin and then of all foreign languages from our high school curriculum. She believed in reading as a moral force, a way to shape character, and felt that the world provided too many alternatives to good books, alternatives that came to include radio and television. Intent on getting books into the hands of the underprivileged, she organized Kentucky's first bookmobiles, which carried reading material into the remote Appalachian hollows. Later, she would turn her great energy to the cause of conservation, saving the beautiful green fields along the Ohio River from development. All of these concerns kept her desk piled high with mail, and the desk itself became, for me, one of her attributes—that and a spray of lilies.

In good weather, she spent the afternoon in her garden, a formal rectangle below the tennis court. Here her battle was unending with weeds, pests, disappointing perennials, moles, dogs, and the unhandy help of Luebell, the black man who worked outside. The garden seemed pesky and demanding, and I resented its intrusions, yet I also knew that she was possessed by it, delighted by it, and that she rendered up its fruits—the splendid bouquets that adorned the Big House—as proof of her individuality, her talent, and her bone-breaking labor.

I did not see the results of Father's work, except as they were represented by the newspapers. Nor did I expect to. Crises sometimes loomed behind the grown-ups' talk; sometimes Father would have to rush into town. But it was all, to me, insubstantial, imaginary. The real work of the world was done by Mother, in her garden, and by the five other people who tended our lives.

We called them the servants, yet they were never, by any stretch of the imagination, servants. They were sharply marked and to some extent unpredictable individuals who were spending their lives with us, for reasons that seemed to me to have more to do with companionship among themselves than with the fat envelopes of cash that were brought out from town every Friday. I was too young to be aware of their lack of choice. Instead, I noticed the dense, colorful fabric of their lives, which was only partly visible to me. They kept their secrets. In fact, they hoarded and delighted in them.

Cordie, in the kitchen, was taciturn about her special rituals. Her big black stove was always covered with boiling pots and pans, the ovens going full blast to prepare a company dinner. Before those occasions I would see her going over an elaborate recipe, her finger underlining the words, her lips moving. Sometimes, in the afternoons, she could be found half dozing in her big wooden armchair; her feet rose out of her flat slippers like loaves. I knew she had a family up the road and had lost one son to the river.

Ollie Madison, rake thin in her candy-striped uniform, took care of the upstairs. I would see her on her knees, scrubbing out one of the bathtubs, or jerking off sheets. Often I would hear her shouting for her husband, Curt, fighting the furnace in the bowels of the house.

Curt himself spent most of his time in the basement, where in winter he tended the enormous coal furnace; when he opened its door, a malevolent red eye of fire glared out. Near the furnace, he had set up a large, crowded workshop where he repaired broken furniture. He knew where each tool lay in the confusion. Once he copied an ornate French bureau for Mother, so perfectly no one could tell which was the original. I had heard that he had been a soldier in the First World War and had gone to France, but he never mentioned it.

The doyenne of the household was Lizzie Baker, who seemed unimaginably old to me. She still wore the white turban of an earlier age, the white uniform and long white apron. She had strong views on the family and now and then would let slip fascinating hints about our shared past. She had known Father as a child and claimed the special prerogative of that lost

The Big House, early 1930s.

One of several formal gardens on the Place, 1933.
We used to wade in the round pool on hot summer days.

LEFT:
The decorative pool
behind the Big House.

BELOW:
Mother's garden, 1933.
The tennis court is
on the left; Jonathan's
baptism was held
under the arbor.

Lizzie Baker and
Worth, 1932.

Curtis and Ollie Madison, 1930s.

Nursie (Lucy Cummings) and I, perhaps at Harmony Landing Farm,
Kentucky, 1939. One of the very few photographs of Nursie,
who didn't like to have her picture taken.

Easter party, Harmony Landing, 1942. I am in front on the left,
my brother Barry diagonally behind me, Worth next to him.

intimacy. She had known his older brother and sister, my Uncle Robert and Aunt Henrietta, too, and told stories about them with a submerged chuckle.

Our indoor life was organized and dominated by our nurse, who had been hired just before I was born. Her name was Lucy Cummings, but we called her Nursie (spelled in various ways by various children) and loved her devotedly. She was a large, firm woman who meted out judgments and affection impartially. My two older brothers were already nearly beyond her when I was born, and so she focused her love on me.

Nursie had fallen into a fire as a small child, and the lower half of her face was glazed with pinkish scars. A dent in her bottom lip was the result, she told me, of biting her mouth closed to keep out the flames. People stared at her, but we did not think she looked strange. Her square, strong hands, covered with freckles, could do everything. On one hand, she wore a braided gold friendship ring and a stout watch. She also proudly wore, when she dressed up, a small gold brooch from which hung a heart for each of us five children. Mother had given it to her.

Her sure sense of justice was the rock on which I leaned. There was a right and a wrong in every situation, as she viewed it, and she could usually come up with a proverb to support her position: "A stitch in time saves nine"; "Take care of the pennies and the pounds will take care of themselves"; "Pretty is as pretty does." Her hand could smack hard on an offender's rear end, but she always offered a lap, an embrace, a quick kiss at the end of the day, expressions of an affection never lessened by our bad behavior. She knew how to dip fall leaves in paraffin to preserve their colors, how to soak pine cones in a chemical that caused them to burn green when used as kindling, how to mend and iron doll clothes, cut out valentines, and dye Easter eggs.

Our birthday parties were her greatest accomplishment. The table would be decked with homemade baskets of candy, hats, and streamers; she even made costumes of crepe paper, covered with ruffles. One Halloween, she dressed up as a witch in Mother's old academic gown and allowed the little girls to be frightened of her. She was always with us, except on Thursdays, her day off, when she would sometimes take one of us into town to visit her mother, a gaunt, terrifying old countrywoman whose failing health was a problem we all shared.

Sometimes Nursie fell asleep in the evening when I was sitting on her lap. I had never before seen anyone exhausted from hard work. The black servants divided up their tasks among them and moved slowly, without urgency. But Nursie had no helper, unless she could dragoon one of us. I knew she was paid for her labor, but I also knew this was the least of it; she worked so hard because she loved us fiercely, yet with a sense, always, that we were not and would never be hers.

She taught us well, impressing on us the fact that life is hard, even for children of privilege.

When Worth hit me, she reported the matter to Mother; justice always came first. Once she took me to Mother and showed her the red mark Worth's hand had left on my behind. Nursie often stood between me and Worth's merciless teasing until I was able to take care of myself.

In those early days, before the births of the two younger children, my older brothers appeared to me as a pair, like Castor and Pollux, or Cain and Abel. From the beginning, Worth was treated with special deference. He had an electric quality, without moral or intellectual dimensions, like a bolt of lightning that struck at random. His temper was ferocious, and he used his muscle to get what he wanted, pushing and shoving Barry and me around. He was extravagantly emotional, angry and outraged at one moment, then rapidly calming and cooling and moving on to another interest. All his interests were obsessions: football, tennis, swimming, and, later, the pursuit of girls, gambling, and liquor. His blue eyes and dark hair were in dramatic contrast to Barry and me; we were both pale blonds. Worth's ability to get what he wanted, however, was the most compelling feature of his personality. I used to think that everyone was a little afraid of him, even the grown-ups. I do not remember that he was ever punished.

Barry was a sweet, docile little boy, always slightly overweight, who followed Worth around as often as he was allowed to do so. He was slow in school, although he worked hard, and it was years before his reading problem was diagnosed as a form of dyslexia. He seemed shy to me, quiet, inoffensive, the kind of child who does not protest. Perhaps he had learned early that his protests were ineffectual. Worth could reduce him to tears with a cruel taunt, usually about his weight, yet Barry was always loyal, following Worth and his friends around, trying to imitate his older brother's grandiosity.

Barry's subdued sweetness did contain a kernel of stubborn resistance. Now and then, pushed to the limit by Worth's teasing, he would break into sobs, or flail with his fists. No one had any use for his protests. Teasing, Mother explained, was usually the victim's fault. We could bring the teasing to an end by simply ignoring Worth, advice which proved hard to follow.

Looking back, it seems strange that Barry and I did not form a coalition against our tormentor. However, the family had a way of fanning competition among the children that prevented us from becoming allies. What mattered most was who could talk the fastest, tell the best jokes at Sunday lunch, or enter a room filled with grown-ups and shake hands without stuttering or blushing. When we failed at these tasks, we were not criticized but bathed in condescending silence.

These trials were even more important than our grades. Worth, who never did well in school, won all these private contests. He had the gall, the confidence—brittle as it may have been—the looks, the humor Barry and I both knew we lacked. Yet Barry would never make an ally of me, or me of him, because we knew we would lose every chance of shining if we linked up with a failure.

During those early years, neither Barry nor I could hold our own at the dinner table. Conversation was expected—children were not to sit with their faces buried in their plates—and our table manners were also on display; Mother spent most of those meals correcting our hands or our elbows, telling us to chew with our mouths closed or not to interrupt.

Yet the highest praise was reserved for the child who could dominate the table with a witty story or an apt description—something to provoke and amuse. Later the din was overwhelming as the five children's voices strove together, each outtelling and outlaughing the others, moving from exaggeration to exaggeration while Mother tried to calm us, Father laughed at our indiscretions, and the servants, passing platters of food, trembled with suppressed giggles. Sooner or later the conversation would descend into taunts and digs, both verbal and physical, and someone would be sent from the table in tears.

My early childhood ended when I realized that I could stop hearing what was said to me, simply blot it out.

It happened one day when I was eight or nine. We were riding in the station wagon. Worth had been repeating some gibe with me as the butt as we passed the gasoline station at Harrods Creek. I began to repeat those two words to myself—"gasoline station"—and, to my astonishment, they blotted out the gibes. I learned then that I could withdraw whenever I needed to behind that phrase, ceaselessly repeated. It was an impenetrable defense, maddening to attackers.

The ability to withdraw from combat, to seal my ears, had another effect. I began to separate myself from the family. As I did, I continued to observe them carefully. Gradually I realized that it was much safer not to tell, and perhaps not even to see, the "true." The family was anxiously guarding a hoard of secrets. So I learned not to notice, or at least not to comment—to cut out the offending true.

2

Before the Second World War, we lived in the Little House, across the lawn from the Big House. The Little House had been built for an energetic Louisville woman, on a bluff over the Ohio River, about ten miles from town. Using as her model a Tuscan villa, she designed a large cottage with stucco walls and an orange tile roof. By the time my father moved into it as a young bachelor, the original owner was spending most of her time in an apartment in Paris, where, in 1949, I came to know her.

The Little House reflected a wider imagination, a simpler and at the same time more sophisticated view of the world than the ostentatious and sometimes hideous mansions on the bluffs nearby. Light and proportion meant much more than grotesque, expensive detail; the windows opened onto a sweep of hillside and the distant river.

The children's nursery and sleeping porch were in the rear wing of the Little House, near our parents' bedroom. The large, sunny nursery was modeled on those in Edwardian children's books. There were painted scenes from *Alice in Wonderland* on the walls and, in winter, a coal fire. Next door were the bathroom and a small room which became Nursie's. On the other side of the nursery, a screened porch, built during the period when it was considered healthy for children to sleep in unheated rooms, housed Worth and Barry.

My parents had moved into the Little House shortly after their marriage in 1931. There Worth and Barry were born, in 1932 and 1933, and the family life was started which would be continued, on a different scale, in the Big House.

I was born in 1937. In later years, my mother sometimes mentioned that difficult pregnancy. She had felt unwell during the summer of 1936, when she and my father and his older sister, Henrietta, were spending time at a fishing camp in the Laurentians. The vacation, Mother said, had been nearly spoiled by rain, blackflies, and her pregnancy.

The Little House, where we lived before the war.
Our nursery was in the wing at the rear.

Worth and Barry, 1930s. The leather leggings
were a perpetual bother in cold weather.

Worth, 1930s.

Henrietta Bingham may have added to her discomfort. Henrietta was always surrounded by admirers. That summer she invited John Houseman, a lover from an earlier period, to visit the fishing camp. In Houseman's autobiography, *Run-through,* he described the scene:

"An hour out of Trois Rivières, on the river road, I passed a speeding black foreign convertible which seemed curiously familiar. At the Ritz-Carlton mail desk in Montreal there was . . . an unstamped note, left that morning, in a small, crabbed writing I had almost forgotten. That evening I went back to Trois Rivières, where Henrietta Bingham . . . was waiting to drive me to her brother's fishing camp in the mountains where she was spending the end of the summer.

"So this voyage which had begun as a nightmare ended in a strange holiday reunion beside a dark mountain lake high in the Laurentian hills. It was more than nine years since we had lost our virginity together in a hotel room overlooking the sea: we talked of the curious turn my own life had taken since then; she spoke of hers as an Ambassador's daughter in London. Certain things had not changed at all; the color of her eyes and skin, the warmth of her voice, the way she wore a tailored suit and her hands held the wheel of the car. But there was one major difference—I was no longer in love with her."

Although the affair was over, the atmosphere Henrietta usually created—exotic, strenuous, sexually and emotionally charged—could not have been easy for my pregnant mother. She hated gaining weight under any circumstances. Years later, when I was pregnant with my first child, she told me that she had always tried to wear something white near her face, when she was in that condition, to distract attention from her distended abdomen. She also told me with bitter amusement that a friend of Father's had once said she looked beautiful when she was pregnant. "How could he say that?" she had wondered.

Later, I wondered why she had chosen to have six children (one of whom died at birth). She was a fastidious woman who seemed to loathe the demands and frailties of the flesh. I could not imagine her choosing to be "overweight" six times, or facing the indignities of labor and delivery. She never discussed her reasons for having children; we seemed part of her role, like the golden plates on the company dinner table. Yet I always sensed a resistance, a distaste, under her acceptance of her duty. She had been meant for another kind of life, a life of the mind. She had borne us, it seemed to me, because it was what Father expected her to do, it was what her world expected her to do; but she was sickened by the task, even though she came to love her children, little by little, as we emerged from babyhood.

I would have carried out of childhood an impression of pregnancy as a disease had it not been for a random encounter when I was seven or eight.

Houseguests were arriving, as they so often were, in a whirl of opening doors, suitcases, and hurrying servants. I happened to be standing around when a woman appeared carrying an infant in her arms. She had beautiful red hair that hung to her waist, and she was on fire with her determination to nurse the baby. She hurried upstairs without the usual polite greetings, and I flew after her. I was closed out at the door to her bedroom; I did not see a woman nurse a baby until I was an adult. But I had caught a glimpse of a woman who passionately enjoyed being a mother. I never forgot.

The difficulties of Mother's third pregnancy were much compounded by the difficulties surrounding my birth.

The Little House on its bluff over the Ohio was always at the mercy of that big river. There was only one road into town, which was often flooded in the late winter and early spring.

December of 1936 was a peculiarly gloomy month, with much rain. By the second week in January, I was already, as Mother later told me, overdue. When the Ohio River began its steady rise, she worried about getting to the hospital, ten miles away in town. No one believed, however, that the river would rise high enough to seal the Place off completely.

It rained for a hundred straight hours from January 17 to January 21, the day before my birth. On the twenty-first, the floodwater was already cresting at forty-one feet, and the road to town was under water.

Stranded high on the hill, Mother called in Cordie for a conference. I can imagine from later scenes how Cordie must have stood, deferentially, just inside Mother's bedroom door. She may have worn an expression of anxiety which I never in later years saw on her face, for Mother was asking her if she knew how to deliver babies.

Cordie had many children of her own, but she told Mother that she could not deliver her baby. Perhaps an invisible barrier was approached when Mother asked for help. Cordie knew exactly where her limits lay. The terrible intimacy of childbirth could not be shared. As Mother recalled it, Cordie had seemed afraid.

Not afraid, I feel sure now, of her ability to handle a home birth, but afraid, as I saw many black people afraid during my childhood, of breaching that invisible barrier. Relations were considered good "between the races"; there was much humor, kindness, and mutual concern. But there were also barriers that could never be mentioned or touched. Black people were involved in many intimate and essential aspects of white life, bathing and feeding infants and the elderly, attending sickbeds, but there was a line that could not be crossed. Beyond it lay the terrifying intimacies of birth and death.

By the time Cordie had refused to cross that line, the Little House was cut off by water. At some point during that dismal afternoon, Mother went into labor.

An unpaved cart track ran out of the back of the Place, down a steep valley and up to a paved road. Now it was the only way out. Father summoned three men who were working on the Place and asked them to see if the stream at the bottom of the valley had washed out the track. Then he helped my mother into the car.

Legend here intervenes. Apparently the stream had washed out the track, but the men had no chance to warn Father, or else they realized that he would have to make it across somehow. So when the car approached the bottom of the valley, a makeshift bridge consisting of two planks was erected across the rushing stream. The planks were held in place by the three men, one of whom had a wooden leg. As Father later recounted, this man sank into the mud up to the top of his stump when the car thundered across the planks.

Hours later, Father's car reached the outskirts of town, threading unflooded streets and bypassing barricades. Mother's anxiety and suffering must have been acute. Finally, they were able to reach a hospital, which was not the one she had chosen for my brothers' births. By this time she was near delivery; she once told me (although it may have been a joke) that I was born in the hospital elevator.

I was a large baby, weighing almost ten pounds. My father cabled his father, the Judge, in London on the evening of the twenty-second: "Big Beautiful Girl born today. Mary doing splendidly." He had cabled Henrietta four minutes earlier: "Isn't it grand, biggest prettiest girl ever seen." No one recorded her reaction.

The Judge, in the American Ambassador's residence at 14 Prince's Gate in London, had been listening to news of the Kentucky flood with great alarm. By this time, the entire West End was underwater; there was a threat of epidemics because of burst sewers, and the mayor ordered all gasoline stations closed to conserve fuel. Father took Worth and Barry to stay with his Aunt Sadie in Asheville, North Carolina.

By the end of January, the floodwaters had subsided, and I was established in the nursery of the Little House with Nursie. According to the practices of the day, she took over my care and feeding, under Mother's supervision.

Like all young mothers, Mother tried to do what she was told was best for her babies. She said once that she used to wait until the scheduled time before picking up Worth, even when he was crying fiercely. I imagine her walking the floor by his crib, her eyes on the clock, subduing her own instincts in the interest of doing what the authorities said.

This rigid schedule apparently did not work well for me. I was a fretful and continuous crier. Finally someone—the doctor? an older woman? my nurse?—suggested giving me another bottle of formula. I had been hungry. When I was fed, my crying stopped.

But I was still an unsatisfactory baby. Years later, Nursie told me that Mother used to say I looked like a little Dutch girl, not like a member of the family.

Father loved having a pretty, agreeable, highly responsive little girl to dandle and caress. For years he picked me up at night and took me to the toilet, occasions I anticipated with a mixture of excitement and dread.

Often he would have been at a dinner party, and his breath would smell of bourbon while he gleamed dimly above me in the white and black of his dinner clothes. I felt both flattered and helpless, riding high in his arms.

In the spring of 1937, Munda, my Richmond grandmother, came to Louisville for a long visit so that my parents could go away on a vacation. She sent a description of life in the Little House to her Asheville counterpart, Aunt Sadie:

"Sarah was five months old as you may remember on June 22 and that day seemed definitely suddenly to spring forward in her development, chatting with us and making sounds that really sound like words, but as I always like to keep probability in view, I cannot quite agree with the adoring Miss Cummings [Nursie] that Sally has expressed her views coherently. Worth and Barry are a delight to me in every way. Of late they have developed along the line of fighting roosters, which all little boys do sooner or later, it's just a phase, and there is a total lack of animosity, and little carnage. We have such good times with books and stories, which I so delight in. . . . Barry has taught them yards of Shakespeare . . .

"The nurse Mary has now is a treasure. I take over Mary and Barry's room so as to be near the children, and I never hear anything that is not wise and kind, and her worship of Sally is almost pathetic. In fact the whole staff of servants functions just as if the mistress of the house were at home. As for Curtis, he is my guide philosopher and friend. The two day guards are splendid nurses, and I think a fine thing not only for the feeling of security it gives us all but a man's direction is robustly wholesome when boys reach that age. On rainy days, it amuses me to see these huge men playing nursery games, on the floor, a large revolver protruding from the hip pocket."

The three guards had been hired after a neighborhood kidnapping, following the Lindbergh kidnapping, frightened our parents. They installed an alarm system as well.

The alarm system was the first of its kind and it frequently malfunc-

Mother, with me on her lap, Long Island, 1939.

Sallie at Rock Creek Riding
Stable, Louisville, 1939.

ABOVE:
Barry (left) and Worth
in the pony cart
on the Place, 1930s
(before Barry's blond
curls were cut).

RIGHT:
Barry and Worth
outside the Little
House on the first
day of school.

tioned. Sometimes Worth and Barry set it off, either by accident or on purpose. Then the loud shrieks of the fire engine could be heard rushing up River Road. I imagine the hysterical laughter, the running out of doors as the engine raced up the long curving drive. A real fear, never discussed, was overlaid by much laughter. The alarm system and the guards, who were all former police captains, became material for years of family jokes.

All three captains became friends, especially Captain Bud, who was to spend the rest of his life with us. I do not remember the other two clearly. Someone described one of them sitting all night in the basement of the Little House, his revolver on the table in front of him. He may have been the same individual who, having had something to drink, shot at my parents when they were returning from a party, then fell into the box bushes and was retrieved by Father. (Father often retrieved the fallen on the Place; he was called upon once to cut down the body of a stableman who had hanged himself in the hayloft. Years later, Father said, "He looked like some kind of underground creature.")

One of the captains, too, was said to have shot the ear off a marble bust of the Judge, which he mistook for an invader.

The captains took over some of our hard-pressed nurse's duties, especially the supervision of our physical regimen, which was complex. As infants, we had had our ears taped back so they would grow close to our heads, and had worn odd stiffened mittens to prevent thumb sucking, nail biting, and other uncivilized activities. Now, to prevent fallen arches, we exercised our feet every day, picking up a certain number of marbles with our toes; the captains made a game of this.

In winter, we lay under a sunlamp every evening, to combat the colds to which we were all somewhat prone. I remember the delicious warmth of the sunlamp as I lay naked in my crib, while one of the captains read me a Babar story.

Before I was old enough to notice, Mother became pregnant again. Toward the end of her pregnancy, Munda arrived from Richmond for one of her extended visits. Later I noticed a reserve between the two women, as though too much had been said or done. Certainly too much was said during that visit in 1938 or 1939. Munda disapproved of the fact that Mother was still driving her car in an advanced state of pregnancy.

Mother insisted on continuing to drive; the car, after all, was her only link to life off the hill. Somehow she became involved in a minor accident. Later it was discovered that the baby she was carrying had died. Mother was advised to carry the dead baby to term and deliver it. It was a girl.

Nursie told me years later that she had hidden all the infant clothes before Mother returned from the hospital. As soon as possible, Father took her away on a long trip.

The dead baby was never mentioned, except by Nursie. I have often thought of the difference it would have made to me if that lost baby girl had survived, and of the difference it would have made to Mother.

Silence closes over areas of great pain. I was too young to understand. We went on.

3

I do not remember the events which led up to the family's departure for Washington in the summer of 1941. The United States had not yet joined the war in Europe, but Father's newspapers were advocating engagement. Later, Mother explained that Father had felt obliged to enlist in the Navy before Pearl Harbor because of the newspapers' stand. He was stationed in Washington for a few months before being sent to London.

With or without explanations, the move was exciting. The big steamer trunks, left from the Judge's peregrinations, were brought down; standing open, they displayed a rank of drawers, their little brass handles winking, faced by a hanging space covered with a flap of blue brocade. The lining of those trunks smelled of adventure.

Everything we might possibly need for an unlimited time away was packed, so that when the family moved, it moved as a world rather than as a group of individuals. Nursie accompanied us, as well as Cordie. We must have created an impression when we boarded the overnight train.

We were installed in an elegant old house in Georgetown. It was perpendicular rather than horizontal, unlike the Little House, which existed mainly on one level. The Georgetown house had staircases, landings, and window seats, all good observation points. That fall, the house hummed with mysterious activity; since I was four years old, I only picked up the hum.

In that hot Washington summer of 1941, friendships began that would influence our lives—with Adlai Stevenson, then assistant to the Secretary of the Navy; with Archibald MacLeish, who would, according to John Kenneth Galbraith, participate in the birth of the CIA (although, also according to Galbraith, the poet would soon realize his mistake and sever his connections); and with columnists like the Alsop brothers.

Some of these journalists and soldiers would find connections, or forge them, with the Office of Strategic Services, or OSS—"Oh So Social," according to its detractors—which preceded the CIA, and with intelligence gathering and propagandizing in wartime London and Washington.

The excitement, the happy buzz of those summer months surprises me when I remember it. After all, the country, so long isolationist, was about to be pulled into war. It was the sense of power passing into the hands of a few men that made that time so heady, as the aims of the New Deal were eclipsed by the demands of a wartime economy and the birth of a secret service that would long outlive the war.

In Washington I learned songs from the kitchen radio, and used to stand on a table to sing my selection to the admiring servants: "My Wife's a Corker, She's a New Yorker"; "This Is the Army, Mr. Jones"; and some Australian tunes from records Aunt Henrietta had brought. Their vocabulary baffled me, but I was too proud to ask for translations, and I butted my way triumphantly through "You'll Come A-Waltzing, Matilda, with Me," which seemed to contain an obscure threat.

The narrow city garden behind the house had a goldfish pond, perhaps two or three feet deep, which attracted my attention. The weather was hot, and so the pond was filled with water and I was allowed to paddle in it. I decided to try an experiment: I put the handle of a big tin bucket around my neck and jumped into the shallow water. I felt perfectly capable of dealing with the outcome. Even if the bucket had filled with water, I knew I could slip my head out from under the handle. But Cordie, who must have been watching from the kitchen window, saw me and rushed out. Terrified, she pulled me out of the pool. I had not realized before that I counted for so much.

After a few months, Nursie left to go back to Louisville because her mother was sick. She was replaced by a temporary nurse, a Mrs. Houlahan—"very difficult for Sallie to say," Mother commented in a letter to Nursie. She added that the temporary nurse "is very nice, but has too little iron in her soul to be able to deal effectively with all three children." It was understood that Nursie would return to us at Christmas, which we planned to spend back home in Kentucky at Aunt Henrietta's farm.

Early that December, within days of Pearl Harbor, we went to Richmond, Virginia, for the wedding of Mother's sister Harriette. We stayed at the Jefferson Hotel, where, Mother wrote to Nursie, the three children all rushed to desks and composed letters to her the minute they arrived. Worth's letter, neatly printed on hotel paper, announced, "I want to tell you that I am the second best boy in my grade!" He and Barry were attending schools in Washington, where Worth was already beginning to shine in sports.

Mother wrote that Worth was reading *The Prince and the Pauper* to Barry, but first extracting three pages of reading in his primer from Barry.

Worth himself thought of this method of forcing Barry to read, with no suggestions from her, Mother explained.

(A slightly later letter from Worth to Nursie reads, "When are you coming back? I hope soon because we are going to get a governess." Possibly this was a threat, used when the three of us were getting out of hand.)

Barry's letter to Nursie begins, "Wish you were here. I hope your mother is feeling better." He signed himself Barry Bingham.

My letter, scratched on a piece of notebook paper, expressed the futile hope that "you are here when I am in the wedding," reflecting my faith in the ability of grown-ups to appear or disappear at will. I was still spelling my name with a "y" in the usual way, rather than with the "ie" my parents used, and which I had inherited from my maternal great-grandmother, Sallie Montague Lefroy.

I was to be Aunt Harriette's flower girl. Dressed in a long pink dress, with a garland of rosebuds in my hair, I stepped into the hotel elevator with Mother. A man who was sharing the ride remarked that, with my blond hair, I looked just like the kind of female Hitler would appreciate. Mother bristled. I didn't understand why; a compliment of any kind was a highly valued commodity in my life. I had never heard of Hitler, and it was years before I understood the significance of this bizarre remark.

Meanwhile, the war was coming closer. I do not remember when Father left for England; if there was a dramatic departure scene, it has escaped me. Nor do I remember how we traveled from Washington back to Kentucky sometime in December of 1941. We spent that Christmas at Harmony Landing, Aunt Henrietta's farm outside of Louisville in the rolling Kentucky countryside. It marked a turning point: the dim, warm memories of life before the war were about to give way to the sharper, more ambiguous images from the war years.

The Harmony Landing farm had been a gift from the Judge to Henrietta. He had perhaps supposed the farm to be a safer setting than others in which she had figured. She loved horses and riding, and it made perfect sense—too perfect, as it turned out—for her to devote herself to breeding racehorses.

The house had been built a hundred years earlier by a riverboat captain. It was comfortable, even luxurious, with views over rolling fields to an octagonal barn.

There was a great air of festivity that Christmas, in spite of the war— open fires, big meals, and piles of presents. An attempt was being made, perhaps, to prevent us from missing Father. I do not remember noticing that he was gone, only that something inexplicable had changed—a gap had appeared in what had seemed to be a solid piece of fabric.

That Christmas, Henrietta, my beautiful, dark-haired aunt, with her terrifying blue eyes, surrounded herself with visitors from foreign parts. Women and men—but never married couples—hovered and buzzed around her. To me, they all seemed exquisite. They were forever mixing cocktails or dashing off to dinner parties. In the midst of the excitement, Nursie preserved some of the rituals of our old life; I always knew there would be a safe corner upstairs, where she would be sitting, doing some mending.

At Harmony Landing, I learned to enjoy my role as observer, living in my own world and, peripherally at least, the world of the adults. My pleasure was only slightly diminished by Aunt Henrietta's snapping temper.

I knew early on that she did not like me. She made it clear that she preferred my older brothers, especially Worth, who was said to look like her. While she was never unkind to me, she ignored me, which was a novel experience. Nursie neither liked nor trusted her, an opinion that did not need to be conveyed in words. She told me once that Henrietta—or Miss Henrietta, as we called her, imitating the servants—had appropriated a little antique tea set the Judge had sent back from England for me. I did not quite believe it at the time. Years later, the little blue-flowered tea set came back into my hands, cracked, pretty in an ordinary way, hardly the sort of antique that would have value for an adult. Henrietta had kept it for thirty years.

"I am the only Miss Bingham," she is said to have observed on several occasions.

Knowing that she disliked me, I avoided her, while watching her curiously from afar. With a child's fatalistic acceptance of grown-ups' ways, I did not hold her coldness against her. Her dislike did not seem to have anything to do with me.

In fact, Miss Henrietta's dislike made her more interesting. She seemed to choose her own way, unlike my mother's sisters, who were all affectionate, compliant women. As pretty as they were, with their lovely clothes and soft, lilting voices, the Caperton sisters did not have Miss Henrietta's dash and sparkle. They had married well-off men and were in the process of having children and arranging households, conventional exploits I sensed my other aunt would scorn. While Mother's sisters were careful and kind, Miss Henrietta was temperamental and explosive; she liked her liquor, her fine clothes, and her foreign cars, and she carried herself like a woman who had been part of a wider world.

Father adored her. His face would light up when she made an entrance, flipping the skirt of her beautifully tailored English suit or tossing a fur over her shoulder.

She was entrancingly wicked, it seemed to me, and Mother disliked her. Later in the war, when Miss Henrietta was drinking heavily at the farm, Mother would go and take away her liquor, delivering lectures that had little effect. Mother could not diminish Miss Henrietta's charm, which lay in the folds of her mysterious and highly unconventional past.

I knew nothing about her past during that Christmas of 1941 at Harmony Landing, but I found Miss Henrietta fascinating. The intensity of Father's attraction to her and the ambiguity of her response to him and to the other men and women around her taught me a peculiar lesson. Although Father rewarded Mother's goodness, her bearing of many children, her glorious dinner parties, with affection and consideration as well as with jewelry and beautiful clothes, the hot eye of his attention was directed at Miss Henrietta, who was unpredictable, addicted to drink, and of cloudy but challenging sexuality. I never forgot the lesson I learned when I watched that brother and sister together.

Many years later, after Miss Henrietta's death, I volunteered to clean out her New York apartment. By then alcoholism had sent her into a long decline. In one closet, among moldering underclothes and broken shoes, I found a group of framed black-and-white photographs of women dressed in the styles of the early forties. Although I could not identify them, I knew where I had seen their like before—that Christmas of 1941 at Harmony Landing. With sleek cropped heads and sibylline smiles, they looked out at a world that even now would not have a chance of amazing them.

4

In the late winter of 1942, Mother faced the task of moving her three young children into the Big House. Father was in England, and she made the move alone. The house had been closed since the Judge's death five years earlier.

On our first day, we three children raced up the double stairs, which bisected a front hall as big as a hotel lobby. We tried the creaking elevator, installed for our second stepgrandmother's invalid daughter; we peered into enormous mirrors and uncovered a secret compartment for jewelry behind a set of drawers. We were then allowed to choose our own bedrooms.

I knew even as I marveled at the size of the bedroom I had chosen that it was not suitable for a child. It was much too large and grand, with a marble fireplace and elaborate molding. Nothing in that house was really suitable for children. It had been created to frame adult life.

The house had been built thirty years earlier by one of a pair of brothers who had amassed a fortune in flour. Its neo-Georgian façade, decorated with enormous pillars, is forbidding even today when espaliered magnolias and urns of flowers have considerably brightened it. How gloomy it seemed that winter of 1942, with its heavy mahogany furniture, sun-streaked and tattered curtains, dark wainscoting and deep-green walls.

Mother was not able to make many improvements, due to the exigencies of wartime. Nor was she able to lead the elaborate formal life for which the house had been designed. In the Judge's day, a large staff had lived in the basement; there had been gardeners in the cottages scattered over the forty acres, a working greenhouse, a kennel for hunting dogs, a barn. All of this had fallen into decay; the greenhouse was completely smashed. Even the beautiful gardens, with their statues and fountains, were badly overgrown.

Nursie was ensconced in the Judge's study, with its mounted sailfish and yards of matching books. Cordie ruled in the huge kitchen. Lizzie was queen of the upstairs, doling out clean sheets and towels from a closet to which she alone had the key. Curtis moved silently through his chores, waxing and polishing the front-hall floor or shining the silver, which was kept in a safe.

After the dinner dishes were washed, the four black people would retreat to the third floor, Cordie and Lizzie riding the elevator because of their size and age, while Ollie and Curt made their way up the dark back stairs. I would hear their feet overhead as they prepared for bed, hear water running in the pipes and the distant drone of a radio.

During the war, Lizzie began to tell me some of the stories she had been hoarding since Father's childhood. She did not mention the Judge or his three wives. Instead, she told me about a monkey the Judge had once brought home. The monkey, according to Lizzie, was named Parpeetus.

Parpeetus was a wicked beast. He terrorized the inhabitants of the Big House with his tricks. He would go down to the kitchen at night, steal some eggs, and carry them up to the top of a tall cabinet. When the servants came to make breakfast, Parpeetus would bombard them. Or he would sit at the dressing table in one of the guest rooms to powder his "ugly old face" or climb into a parked car and mimic driving.

Lizzie also told me baffling tales about Father's older brother, Robert. She had a way of leaving out the most important parts, which whetted my imagination. Her stories did not match the enormous oil portrait of my uncle that hung on the front stairs. There he looked somber and manly, wearing the jodhpurlike britches and high boots of his First World War aviator's uniform.

Lizzie told me with much laughter about the time Uncle Robert, before going into town, had told her to be sure to find his missing bedroom slippers. Lizzie had spent the day scouring the house. Toward four o'clock, Uncle Robert had telephoned to tell her it was a joke; he had hidden the slippers himself.

Another time, she said, he had come home late from a party, as was his wont. Instead of parking in front of the house, he drove his car through the enormous double doors and parked in the front hall.

I never knew what to make of these stories. Nor was the mystery explained. Uncle Robert led a life furnished with few visible details. He had been a wild young man; he weathered into a seasoned alcoholic. Along the way, he married two women with similar first names. At the end of his life, he was living frugally in a ranch house in Reno, Nevada, raising roses in spite of the terrible heat. I saw him once or twice; he seemed a troubled, placating spirit, entirely dependent on Father, forlornly seeking an approval that would never be his. By then his charm and his good looks were gone.

Lizzie always spoke of Father with special affection. She never mentioned his mother's death, and I heard about it only much later. Mr. Barry and Miss Mary were at the top of Lizzie's world, and she would hoot and clap with excitement when they came home from a trip.

Lizzie was also excited when Miss Henrietta was expected; she would spend a long time getting the lavender guest room ready. Yet she knew that things were not quite what they appeared to be with this exotic stranger. Once, when our guest spent several days in bed, Lizzie explained that Miss Henrietta was very tired. Something about her life in New York made her liable to collapse when she came home. Nothing further needed to be said. Lizzie would shake her head, make a low clucking sound in her throat, and say, "Miss Henrietta just wore out." It was most convincing.

Lizzie Baker could not have been more than five feet tall, and she was as round as a barrel. Father recalled that she had been a pretty young woman when she first came to work for the family. He reflected once that her forebears had probably come from the Gold Coast, which was famous before the Civil War for the quality of its exports.

I never heard Lizzie mention her own family, although Father alleged that she had been married, briefly, to a man not thought to be worthy of her. She seemed to have sprung from the white family that loved and exploited her for her entire life.

Her rule over the other servants was absolute. Sometimes she would set her mouth and her eyes would flash. There was no need for words. The others called her Miss Lizzie and treated her with deference.

In hot weather, she would order Curt to descend into the basement and throw a hidden switch which activated the "coolers." These were large metal fans suspended over pans of water. The whole contraption was concealed under the tiered organdy petticoats of dressing tables. After Lizzie tucked up these petticoats, the coolers would breathe their long, languorous, and increasingly chilly sighs into our bedrooms.

Lizzie never kissed us. At best, she would give us a pat—a quick, light flip on the shoulder or arm. Ollie and Curt never touched us at all, and Cordie only watched us gravely from a distance. Once, however, when I had been spanked, Cordie whispered to me fiercely, "You always my baby."

I kissed them all when I was small, quickly, with a sense that perhaps they did not like it. Sometimes they would smile. I liked them so much that kissing seemed natural. Liking was only a part of it. I was fascinated by them.

At mealtimes Cordie's big kitchen table was surrounded by an assortment of kitchen stools and broken-backed chairs. From her huge stove, she would ladle greens and fatback, corn bread and stewed okra—food we never ate in the dining room—into mixing bowls. She placed the bowls in the middle of the table and the others helped themselves. Lizzie always sat at the head in a special wide chair. Curt and Ollie and whatever extra helper happened to be on hand ranged themselves along the sides. Cordie sat at the end. Sometimes she would pass plates of food out the back door to the men who worked outside.

They took their time eating. Even in hot weather, their plates were piled high. But it was not the food that fascinated me. It was the conversation. No sentence was ever finished—it did not need to be. There was much sly laughter. Ollie always covered her mouth with her hand when she giggled. Heads were shaken, shoulders were shrugged, a knee would bounce, a foot kick under the table. Grins and glances were passed along with the bowls of food. I could not tell what any of it meant. I was not meant to know. But I could guess.

Although I could not have put it into words at the time, I sensed that theirs was the silent language of rebellion. Their jokes surely had something to do with the grand white people in the house—the guests with their matched luggage and weird demands, the spoiled visiting children—if not the family itself. I learned something invaluable from what they left out. I learned that it is possible to communicate without words. Many years later, I began to have a sense of the oppressive conditions of their lives. By then, all four were dead.

Lizzie alone died in harness. Toward the end she was senile and waspish. Mother took care of her. One of her tasks was to cut Lizzie's long, hardened toenails. She had to sit the rebellious old woman on a chair in a bathtub until the water had softened her nails.

Finally Lizzie was afraid of everybody. "Call the police," she would advise on every occasion. But she always recognized Mr. Barry and Miss Mary, her twin stars.

Nursie's attitude toward the stars was ambiguous. Since she did not eat her meals in the kitchen, she did not share the wry exchanges which took place there, although sometimes I would see her standing in the kitchen doorway, arms akimbo, gossiping with the black people. She was on friendly terms with all of them—I sensed that she made an effort in their direction—yet she did not share their unspoken deference or their wordless irony. She neither adored our parents nor criticized them, although sometimes I thought I felt in her silences words she would never have dared to speak. When she ate with the youngest children in the servants' dining room off the kitchen, where the sad lady sat on the world, Nursie was our parents by extension; she fussed about our table manners. At other times, it seemed to me that she forgot those preoccupations, becoming a source of another kind of wisdom, tolerant, humorous, yet at the core a wisdom that insisted on respect.

During the war, Mother decided that in order to conserve rationed gas we would go into town only once a week, to church. Worth and Barry were not satisfied with this arrangement; they wanted to go into town to the movies. So they were told to take the Prospect bus, an old blue vehicle which lumbered along River Road, mostly for the convenience of black day workers. When, as sometimes happened, the boys missed the return trip, they had to walk back home. They did not seem to be any the worse for it.

I did not ride the bus. Although the boys were only four and five years older than I, they were already launched on an independent course. Worth was the center of a group of boys who seemed loud and hardy to me; they would gather after school to roller-skate down the long drive or rampage in the woods. I would have liked to follow them but Worth was expert at cutting me out. Following my brothers around was connected in my mind to one of the times I had embarrassed Mother.

Luebell, the yardman, who lived over the garage with a silent wife and various kin, kept rabbits in hutches out back. I used to inspect them when I made my rounds of the Place. One day in the fierce heat of summer, I saw a fat white rabbit lying on top of another. It looked highly uncomfortable to me. When I asked Mother, in front of my brothers' friends, what the rabbits were doing, she seemed shocked. I was at once sorry I had asked. Like skating too fast downhill or playing football, asking this question was inappropriate.

During that time I learned to ride a bike, under Curt's tutelage. It was the first great adventure of my life. Curt was a hard taskmaster; he made me get on again when I fell off, and he urged me to try going down the perilously long, steep drive. Once I had mastered that, I had the whole neighborhood to explore: the long, curving drives that led to silent houses, the back roads that ended at garages and barns.

Sometimes during the war Mother would take me into town, with the boys or alone, to see the latest newsreel. I found the experience both exciting and terrifying. Since I did not really understand where Father was, I thought I might see his face suddenly in one of the grim scenes. He had been gone so long, from my point of view, that I was afraid I would not recognize him.

He was in London during the Battle of Britain. One of his many letters described how, while shaving on a Sunday morning, he had looked out the window to see the Guards' Chapel blown up by a bomb. Mother read part of his letter out loud. They had made an agreement to report only cheerful news, and so I was perhaps unduly impressed by Father's social life in London. Even during the period when buzz bombs were destroying whole neighborhoods, Father was able to find friends to go out to dinner or put together a weekend tennis game. I was struck by a description in one of his letters of London burning, observed from a car as he drove back into town from a country weekend.

At Mother's suggestion, I began to send Father poems. I "wrote" the first of these during one of my naps as I lay looking at the patterns light made on the ceiling. When it was time to get up, I told Mother my poem. She wrote it down, making a few improvements, and sent it to Father. After the war, Father gave me a red leather book for my poems with gilt edges and my name (spelled in the approved way) in gold letters on the cover.

My early poems were full of doom. "God will, God will not / Bless the lamb that he has got," one began.

After I learned to write, I copied them carefully. Mother suggested tying the pages together with ribbon and sending them to Father. However, when she looked at my copies, something in my writing or spelling displeased her; she did not want me to send such faulty work, and she refused to help me find the ribbon. I went lamenting to Nursie, and eventually the poems were put together and mailed. But I had seen something flash out. I would see it again.

Words, their proper use and ownership, became one of my first preoccupations. First there was the distinction between written and spoken words. To speak correct English was enormously important to Mother as she raised her children in the midst of rural Kentucky voices, both black and white. Her own soft Virginia accent had been from time immemorial a "better" accent than the harsher Kentucky and Indiana twang. Her relatives had settled Kentucky, and one, Adam Caperton, had been killed by Indians at the battle of Estill's Defeat in 1782 near Mount Sterling. Mother maintained the patrician Virginia attitude toward the accents and habits of the western state that had been in her ancestors' times a wild and heathen country. She used to warn us, laughingly, about crossing the Ohio to Indiana, where even more frightful accents were in use, accents which might perhaps be caught, like the polio whose summer epidemics terrified the whole family.

As to the written word, the rules were even more complex. Mother's insistence on the correct writing of English derived from her knowledge of its Latin roots; she used to tell us where words came from, and I admired her arcane knowledge, having never met anyone before who knew where anything came from, much less airy words. It was easy to irritate her with ignorant mistakes—split infinitives, for instance, evoked her wrath.

When I first began to write, I imitated the voices around me, or else the readings from the Bible that fell like burning wax into my ears at church. The New Testament was a more acceptable model than the voices of poor blacks and whites. However, its range was larger and its tone heavier than I could accommodate, while the insipid language of popular children's books was clearly too light, too small.

After the war, when Father began reading aloud, the Victorian authors provided me with a tapestry, a jungle of prose, in which the truth seemed to hide like a mouse or a rabbit.

Father's letters provided an example of wit and sophisticated innuendo I found puzzling, yet highly attractive. Mother perhaps could crack their code. One Christmas Father sent us a more easily understood message: a snapshot of a little girl about my age, standing on a table heaped with presents, holding an enormous teddy bear.

The little girl had been unofficially adopted by Father and a group of American officers stationed in London; they had seen to it that she had an American Christmas with plenty of presents.

I had seen jealousy before, in Miss Henrietta's beautiful eyes, but I had never felt it until I looked at that photograph. It swept over me then like a hot flood. I hated the little girl. I wanted to snatch all those beautiful presents away from her. At the same time, I knew I should be ashamed of myself. I should have been glad, for her sake. But I was not glad. I would not pretend to be. That teddy bear should have been mine.

This was not proper behavior and Mother was shocked. My ability to shock her seemed to be growing, which frightened me. Like most small children, I wanted to please, but the way to please her seemed to elude me. I used to pray in church to be forgiven for sins I was committing unawares.

I liked going to Sunday service in the dark old Episcopal church downtown. I admired the languishing maidens in the stained-glass windows, which reminded me of the Botticelli prints at home. Kneeling, I would pray earnestly to be forgiven, hoping I could shed my sins even before I knew exactly what they were. Once a parishioner complimented Mother on my piety and I was delighted. The outward and visible signs were, I knew, very important, and would perhaps herald the birth of the invisible spirit of grace. I would get up from the hard dark red kneeler with a deep sigh, feeling that at least for a while I had thrown off an intolerable weight. But I knew that within minutes I would begin to sin again. The sin, it seemed to me, had to do with seeing.

Later in the war we stopped going to church. Instead Mother held a prayer service every Sunday morning in her room. We three children knelt on the rug—the design was a beautiful white magnolia—while she read morning prayers. Sometimes she would discuss ethical questions with us, to measure our growth.

There had recently been a disastrous fire in a big circus tent in Florida. People had trampled each other to death as they tried to flee. Mother asked each of us what we would do if we were caught in a circus tent fire. As a clue, she told us about a woman who had cut a hole with nail scissors in the canvas, dropping her children through to safety. Mother did not say whether the woman herself had survived.

My brothers answered that they would help the old ladies and the little children to escape. Although I knew it was the wrong answer, I told Mother I would do everything in my power to get out of the place alive.

She stared at me, horrified. She did not need to say a word.

I knew that right behavior depended first of all on self-control, from which sprang consideration for others. But I could not do what Mother expected. Surely even the God of the Old Testament would not expect a little girl to sacrifice her life for others. I did not at the time know the story of Abraham and Isaac.

Often my feelings burst through my fragile efforts to conform. That summer, Mother was shocked by my outburst of jealousy when she bought a pretty painted wooden gypsy wagon for my cousin. Without being aware of an interval between impulse and action, I smashed the gypsy wagon with my foot.

It never occurred to me then that there might be another mode of behavior that demanded less, allowing room for human frailty. I only knew that I was often wrong, both in the way I behaved and in my attitude toward the lessons Mother tried to teach.

Twice a week Mother put on a suit and a pair of high-heeled shoes, pinned on a small hat, took up her gloves, and went downtown to run the newspapers. At least that was what I thought she was doing. No one who looked as beautiful and as competent as she did could have been going to do something unimportant. And she was excited; I heard her excitement in the sharp click of her heels as she crossed the wide front hall. Then she was gone. I don't remember hearing her describe what she did during the days when she was "downtown."

Once she took us to visit the newspaper office, then in a small corner building in Louisville. The lobby was papered with big black-and-white news photographs from the war; the atmosphere was exhilarating, as though we were standing in the middle of the present. I noticed that everyone in the building treated Mother with great deference. People were always polite to her—it was hard to imagine anyone having the nerve to affront her—but this was different. Later it seemed to me that all those men were taking her seriously. After the war, she stopped working abruptly, along with thousands of American wives who had grown to love their jobs.

Her other source of companionship during the war was the pool of wives in our green and leafy neighborhood, young women with small children who were temporarily stranded while their men were overseas. With live-in servants and ample energy, they had both the time and the inclination to "get together." These gatherings were informal, impromptu, not centering, like later entertainments, on elaborate meals, but instead on chance meetings and sudden impulses. Often the children were involved.

I remember wandering around the back halls of large country houses, going down strange back stairs, and hearing the sound of women's voices in the distance, women's laughter. They looked beautiful to me, those young friends of Mother's with their carefully lipsticked mouths, their war work, their many children.

An extraordinary bird of passage named Nila Magidoff made a great impression in those country houses. She had come to the United States from Russia shortly after Pearl Harbor, leaving her husband, an American correspondent, behind; he was ordered to leave Russia in 1948 after his secretary charged that he had been directed to get secret atomic information there.

Nila was an outspoken woman whose accented English seemed a foreign language to me. She was sent around the country to help collect old clothes to be sent to our ally. I thought she was quite frightening, because I had never before seen a "foreign" woman who did not in the least aim to be a lady. As Mother's friend the writer Willie Snow Ethridge described her, Nila was an "impressive figure" when she first arrived at the train station in Louisville: "Wearing a short mink jacket, and a mink hat towering like a joint of stovepipe on her head, she strode through the railroad gates. Her big-boned peasant body was arrogantly erect."

Like the red-haired woman with her infant, Nila Magidoff, the mysterious Russian who could be described with such adjectives as "arrogant" and "erect," became for me an indication that there was another way.

Father came home on leave in the summer of 1942. I do not remember his return, although later I used to look at a snapshot taken of him and Mother and imagine that I had been a part of the scene. The snapshot showed them in dressing gowns, sitting outside, eating breakfast off trays. The summer was green and soft behind them, and they both looked relaxed, romantic, and happy.

While he was at home, Father gave the commencement address at Berea College in eastern Kentucky, where he was a trustee. The college had been established to offer an education to young people born in Appalachia; they worked to put themselves through, serving in the dining room and the gift shop.

Father called his speech "The Road to Total Victory." It sounded themes, with a trumpet's blast, which would affect our lives in the years to come.

He believed, he said, that total victory for mankind was "somehow" possible, especially for those who believed with a Christian faith in its achievement. He referred to the attempt in 1919 to establish a "system to prevent further conflicts"—the League of Nations, which the Judge had supported. But, Father said, people were not then ready to accept "such drastic measures," perhaps because they had not suffered the effects of total war. He compared America's lack of experience with the courage of village people he had met in England, one of whom had been trapped in a bombed house for 102 hours. He explained how the trapped woman had kept up her courage: "I sang all the hymns I could remember, and then all the nursery rhymes I knew when I was a child, and then I sang them all over again, and once in a while I gave them 'God Save the King.' "

Father expected Americans to learn courage from her example, but that alone would not be enough. After we had beaten "the Japs and the Nazis," we would have to battle the "human injustice that causes wars." To do so we would have to make common cause with "our fellow human beings of any race or color." It was a radical statement for the Kentucky mountains at that time or any other, but it was a cause that would later be lost in the panic of the Cold War.

After my brother Jonathan was born in June of 1942, things in the Big House seemed to change. Perhaps it was the demands of caring for yet another baby, a little son of whom Mother was always especially fond; perhaps it was my strange ways or the older boys' fighting.

Their fights must have frightened Mother, who had to deal with them alone. Captain Bud, the only remaining watchman, lived over the garage, next to Luebell, and had begun to drink. The Richmond relatives seldom visited during the war. Henrietta was sinking into lonely alcoholism at Harmony Landing. The black servants would not have dared to intervene, and even Nursie, stouthearted as always, may have quailed at the sight of the two boys at each other's throats.

They had always been compared with one another, and the comparisons were not kind to Barry. He had not outgrown his early difficulties with reading. Worth was spinning through the first grades at Ballard School; he considered himself a natural athlete and he was surrounded by friends. Blond, plump, and amiable, Barry had only his sense of humor to defend him.

They were an uneven couple. As tiny boys, looking at the evening sky, Barry had told Worth, "You can have the moon and all the stars except for the evening star. Leave that for me." Now it must have seemed that even the evening star was slipping from his grasp.

Probably the last and worst fight began because Worth was teasing Barry about his weight. Some knives Father had sent home as souvenirs were lying at hand. The boys fell on each other. They were not hurt, but we were all badly frightened.

Soon after that, they were preparing to leave home for a pre-boarding school in Massachusetts. They had been away to camp before; it was not the first parting.

At the same time, I found myself offending Mother unintentionally. She mistook my silence for sullenness, for some underground virulent rebellion. I was no longer affectionate. I needed to be prompted to kiss adults who expected me to kiss them—aunts, grandmother, even Mother at times. I did not like the way most adults smelled—the strong combination of cigarettes, alcohol, perfume, and sweat. And I was much too prone to tears, along with a feeling of emotional rawness that reminded me of the way my fingernails felt when they were first cut.

I was also beginning to have nightmares. I remember only heat, suffocation, frenzied despair. Apparently the nightmares were frequent for a while, frightening Mother and Nursie, who sometimes punished, sometimes tried to cajole me out of them. Then I began to walk in my sleep during my daytime nap. I remember waking up abruptly on the steps to the swimming pool, wearing only my white cotton "training pants."

Mother did not want me to be unhappy. She did not want me to have nightmares, to sleepwalk, to close myself up behind my face. She could not argue or persuade me out of my "moods." She may have been desperate with loneliness herself; on my averted face, she may have seen her own unhappiness. In any event, she was determined to cure me.

I refused to share my feelings with anyone. My feelings were the only things I owned that were not open to public scrutiny. So I resisted, fiercely, Mother's attempts to know them, to change their somber colors. And she fought, as fiercely, to establish her authority over my mind as it was already established over my body.

She decided that my moods came from constipation. Perhaps some medical text gave her the clue. She began to give me enemas.

I remember lying on my side on the faded pink bath mat in my bathroom, which was, incongruously, lined with enormous mirrors (it had been my second stepgrandmother's), lying in terror and silence while Mother filled and strung up the red rubber bag and connected the long black nozzle.

The flow of warm soapy water into my insides terrified me. I felt I might burst. I could not get up until I had taken all of it, and by that time my small stomach was distended. Then came the ignominy of rushing to the toilet, in full view, dripping water, and the loud, ignoble sounds of the ensuing bowel movement.

The scene may have terrified Mother as much as it terrified me, for she soon substituted laxatives for the enemas. For a while Nursie gave me Milk of Magnesia, silently, from a big spoon. I hated the taste. At Nursie's suggestion, mineral oil was substituted, with a garlic bud added to give it flavor.

I was still stubbornly withholding my feelings and my thoughts, spending as much time as I could alone, scouring the floor of the cow shed or sitting in my little log cabin. I must have seemed like a wild child, a little demon, entirely self-possessed, needing and wanting no one.

In my loneliness and despair, I raged against the family's pets, two big black poodles who were impossible to control. They barked and capered and whined, ran away, got lost, but were always welcomed home again with agitated affection. I would have liked to kill them, but they were far too large. However, one day a neighbor's little lapdog wandered into our play yard, and I came very near to choking it with a rope of doll's clothes.

After that I knew I was wicked. It seemed hopeless to try to conform. I was possessed by a demon that would force me to break out, interrupt, contradict, disobey, and any attempts I made at politeness were only temporary, a hopeless effort to restrain this primitive force. I remembered the church's teaching about Eve's fall and original sin, and believed I had been bad from the start.

A series of misdeeds I no longer remember led Mother to punish me. Earlier I had been corrected with an occasional harsh word or a smack when someone's patience was exhausted. These new punishments were different because they were planned.

When I came into conflict with Mother, she would tell me that she was going to have to spank me. She would order me to come to her bathroom later in the day. Since my misdeeds usually occurred in the morning, I had the whole day to contemplate my punishment. I used the time to steel myself. I did not question her right to punish me. Instead I made up my mind never to cry.

When the time came I presented myself in Mother's bathroom, a spotless white chamber through whose high window I could see the tops of trees. She took off her belt or picked up a slipper and told me to kneel down and lean over a low chair or the rim of the bathtub. The belt cut two or three times while I gritted my eyes closed and squeezed back tears. Then she would tell me that she had finished, adding that she hated to spank me but that she was doing it for my own good.

I would leave her bathroom without a word, holding back tears until I could creep into my hiding place under the skirts of my dressing table. There I cried, but with fury, not remorse. I was determined to resist her, although I scarcely understood what it was she wanted.

Aunt Helena, Mother's older sister, provided me with an unexpected relief. She used to appear in the middle of one of those hot summer afternoons, cool in her pastel linen dress, and carry me off in her convertible. The top was always back and the sky was always blue as we rode to the country club, where she would buy me a package of peppermint sticks. Then she would take me upstairs to visit my uncle—they lived for a time in an apartment at the club—and I would be allowed to order a lemonade. Aunt Helena taught me how to suck the lemonade through the hollow core of the peppermint stick, which added enormously to the treat.

Best of all, Aunt Helena didn't talk. Instead she would smoke, her tiny foot in its elegant high-heeled shoe pressing the accelerator. She never asked me how I was or commented on my growth. The relief was intense. During the bouts of bright chatter at home, I remembered Aunt Helena's silence, that peaceful place where nothing was expected. Here was yet another kind of silence: the silence of complete, yet confident withdrawal—the triumph of the noncombatant.

During the last years of the war, Mother was preoccupied with Jonathan, who was a fragile baby. I became afraid for him, too, as though his rashes and bouts of croup were my responsibility. Mother had written proudly to Munda that I showed no jealousy of my little brother, and I would have been ashamed to admit to any such feeling. Yet I did not know what to do for him, wrapped as he was in layers of attention: first the special "baby nurse" hired to care for him, then Nursie, then Mother. He was surrounded by paraphernalia—sheets and blankets, often pinned down to hold him in place at night, steaming croup kettles and trays of medicine. I would creep in to look at him through the bars of his crib, and note with horrified wonder his transparent eyelids through which I could see his roving eyeballs. Since there was nothing essential for me to do, I learned to crow over him, to hold out my finger so that he could grasp it in his tiny hand.

Around that time, Nursie began to take me on walks down the cart track over which, a few years earlier, Father had driven Mother to the hospital. Nursie always called it the Rocky Road to Dublin. Her family had Scotch and Irish roots, and she longed to visit the British Isles. I promised her that we would go there when I was grown, and we planned the trip in detail. Much later I realized how awkward it would have been for both of us to make that journey, and I was saddened.

As we walked along the back road, hand in hand, Nursie would sing in her clear soprano, "Oh, you take the high road and I'll take the low road, and I'll be in Scotland before you." The song still thrills me. She would stop to collect bits of leaves, stones, thistles, wildflowers, bird's eggs—anything with a hint of color or an odd shape. Later she helped me to arrange these "critters" in a special display box.

I loved her songs and the way she sharpened my eyes. I never would have noticed those bits of things lying along the way if she had not directed my attention to them. I can still see the blue shell of a robin's egg in the soft, lined palm of her extended hand.

5

Worth and Barry wrote many letters to Nursie during the fall of 1944, their first away at boarding school. They were twelve and eleven years old.

Barry was worried about his weight, which had become a family obsession, although he could hardly have been considered obese at one hundred and fifteen pounds. He had been embarrassed at being placed, without explanation, in the fourth grade rather than the fifth, but he wrote Nursie manfully that he planned to "get it straten out."

He began to express an interest in the brother and sister who were still at home, hoping that I was doing well in school and that Jonathan was not causing problems by waking up Nursie at four in the morning. It was Jonathan's turn to be tormented by the nightmares that had hounded me at the same age.

Worth wrote Nursie less frequently; he was very busy, and had joined the stamp club at school and started ski jumping. He was proud of his progress and wrote that his teacher said he was going to be a "top notch jumper."

By now, Father had been away from home for three years. Mother expected him to return, like so many other soldiers, after D-Day and the end of the war in Europe; instead, he went to the Pacific, to Guam, an island Mother looked up in our encyclopedia. The brief, outdated entry provided little information: the island was said to be home to a peculiar fungus that grew out of the inhabitants' ears.

Guam is believed by some to have been the home of American intelligence during the war in the Pacific. Cord Meyer, Jr., served there and lost his eye to a Japanese hand grenade. In 1950, Meyer went to work with the CIA and was assigned to the International Organizations Division, under Tom Braden.

Other friends were in the Pacific in 1945, preparing for the dropping of the atomic bomb on Hiroshima and the Japanese surrender. One of them, Benjamin Bradlee, was an ensign on a destroyer in the Pacific from 1942 through 1945. He would reappear in Father's life in 1949, in Paris, along with James Angleton and E. Howard Hunt, who would serve as liaison between the American Embassy, the Marshall Plan, and the Economic Cooperative Agency.

Years later, when I tried to recall the specifics of Father's naval career, I would connect both the glamour and the peculiar vagueness of his accounts—did he go into Normandy with the D-Day invasion, or not? Did he go to Guam in order to be present at the Japanese surrender, or for some other reason?—with his membership in organizations such as the Asia Foundation and the Committee for the Present Danger. Perhaps Mother's anger at his decision to go to the Pacific was fueled by her apprehension about the associations he had enjoyed in England, where his friend David Bruce had organized the Office of Strategic Services in 1941 (forerunner of the CIA), and where Father had shared exquisite weekends at the Astor estate, Cliveden, with pro-Fascists and counterintelligence agents of all stripes. Secrets, after all, were Father's obsession, and for the powerful there is little difference between public and private secrets. The important thing is to be the only one who knows.

In 1945, I was bewildered by his long absence, which seemed to have little to do with accounts I heard of the war. I studied a snapshot he had sent home that showed him swimming naked with other handsome young men in a tropical lagoon on Guam.

Finally, in the fall of 1945, we were told that he was coming, and Mother left for San Francisco to meet him. She wrote to Nursie that they would be home, after a short vacation, on October 6. He had been away four years.

Half my life had passed during his absence, and I did not know what to expect. I studied the portrait he had sent back from London, which showed a very young man in a blue uniform. He did not look to me like a father.

He had been pleased by our letters, sent to him regularly during the war; Mother had told him that she did not correct them, so he was amazed by how "entertaining" the letters were, as he wrote his Aunt Sadie in Asheville.

He went on to describe for Sadie Mother's summer routine at the Big House, after the servants had left for their annual two-week vacation. Father wrote that Cordie had roasted chickens and a ham before leaving for "the vacation season" in the tiny frame house she shared with her family on Harrods Creek. He said that he didn't like to think of Mother being in the kitchen in the heat, but he felt it was better for her than going to the office every day.

Years later, Mother would explain that Father had told her to go down to the newspapers to write editorials because she would know Father's stand on various issues better than anyone else. On at least one occasion she had expressed an independent point of view.

It occurred after she went with Mark Ethridge, the newspapers' publisher and my godfather, to the Democratic Convention in 1944. She was disappointed when Roosevelt eliminated Henry Wallace from the ticket, preferring Harry Truman for vice president. Mother wrote Eleanor Roosevelt that she would have trouble "fighting the good fight" without Wallace—a potent enough threat, given the power of the monopoly newspaper and its radio station, to result in an invitation to the White House.

Mother was overwhelmed by Roosevelt's charm and abandoned her position. Later, she agreed with Father that Wallace was a little crazy; Father distrusted Wallace's sympathy for the Russian people, which became a political liability during the Cold War.

Even now, after the Japanese surrender, Father seemed reluctant to come home, although he wrote Henrietta that Mark Ethridge had written in "the strongest terms" of the need for Father's presence at the newspapers. He said that he had almost decided to apply for inactive duty. Intelligence activities in the Pacific finally ended, for the time being, when President Truman signed an executive order in September.

On the way to San Francisco in October, Mother was making plans for a triumphant homecoming. She wrote Nursie, enclosing menus for Cordie, and asked her to suggest that the servants forgo their day off on the Sunday of Father's return. She needed to see the seamstress, Frances, in order to get her clothes ready for a trip to Asheville; they would be leaving to visit Aunt Sadie in a few days, and then would go to see Worth and Barry in boarding school. She asked Nursie to give the children at home her love.

I do not remember the long-anticipated day of Father's return. Instead, I recall a day the previous spring when I came into the Big House and found Mother listening to the radio in the living room—an uncommon occurrence. The announcer's voice crackled with unintelligible words. I looked at Mother. She was crying.

I had never seen her cry before. Her tears startled me, forcing me to revise what I thought I knew. She was so elegant, so firm, that tears seemed inappropriate. I had locked her into one means of expression—crisp, formal, unanswerable—as she had locked me into silence and moods. Now I saw tears on her cheeks.

She explained that President Roosevelt had just died.

At fifteen, I recalled this scene. "I think I first realized my mother was human when I saw her crying over President Roosevelt's death," I wrote. "It scared me then, sitting quite still listening to the news reporter. I could easily accept the man's death, but my mother's tears made me feel so cut off and mixed up. I was not sorry for her. I think tears seldom stir that rare feeling. It was as if the moon had suddenly decided not to shine, and I stood on this whirling earth looking up at her dark face and had no more power to understand or change her than a bug crawling up a tree trunk. I felt that it was a mistake for her to cry."

Mother had a deep affection for FDR, as she always called him, and she admired Mrs. Roosevelt, who had visited Louisville at the time of my birth. In 1938, in her newspaper column, "My Day," Mrs. Roosevelt commented on her visit to the Little House, adding that she had met "three charming children—two boys and a girl. She was born just at the time of the flood, so she will carry through life a constant reminder that she is a 'flood baby.' Her mother must have had a decidedly difficult experience."

After Roosevelt's death and the end of the war, Mother gave up her work at the newspapers. In the fifties, she began to edit the Sunday book page, but never went into the office again after Worth's death in 1966. It seems to me now that the vigor and intelligence she had exercised during the war years found no outlet when the period was over. Like all the other women of her class and generation, she went back to raising children, supporting good causes, and giving parties. But something was lost, both for her and for the newspapers, which became once again, as they had always been, a kingdom of men.

Willie Snow Ethridge, writer and publisher's wife, showed another way—a way Mother found amusing. Willie Snow was a wild-haired Georgia lady who used to joke that her husband had lured her out of a swamp with a peppermint stick. All during the war years and later, she wrote and published humorous books on her travels and her life in the suburbs, books in which she referred to her distinguished husband as "the roommate" and poked fun at his absorption in the daily details of the newspaper business.

Willie Snow loved parties, and would dragoon any man in the room, including Father, to dance with her until he or she dropped. Her spontaneity and her sense of humor shocked and attracted me. Willie Snow seemed to have little use for the influential role she might have played, through her husband, in the social and political life of Louisville. She had been one of a group of women who denounced the Ku Klux Klan in the thirties, but she had done that on her own.

Mother admired Eleanor Roosevelt, but her stand on civil rights was too liberal for the Judge's daughter-in-law. After Mrs. Roosevelt reportedly rode in a car with a black woman in the South, Mother's admiration cooled. Although she would jeer at the notion that "Eleanor Clubs" had been organized to persuade black women to abandon domestic work, she seldom rose to Mrs. Roosevelt's defense. A life based on the labor of poor black

people would remain for two more generations a serious problem for journalists attempting to cultivate a liberal point of view. Mother knew this
conflict at first hand.

After the war, she spoke firmly and often and with great insight when
matters of moment were to be decided at the newspapers, but she spoke only
to Father, and through him, and that inevitably changed her voice.

Life in the Big House picked up after Father's return. The war was over,
everyone was coming home, and a new round of gaiety began. Mother
redecorated those gloomy rooms; the dark green walls were painted white,
and new, bright curtains replaced the faded damask. The polar bear skins
in the front hall disappeared, and the house seemed lighter and brighter,
filled with flowers from Mother's garden.

Against this backdrop, the ceaseless, oceanlike flow of entertaining
began. There were weeklong visits from the Asheville relatives, Sadie and
her niece, Martha McKee. Munda continued to come for weeks every
spring. Several times a month, there were dinner parties, sometimes large
formal affairs for which the gold service was brought out from the vault in
the basement and extra hands laid on to serve. In addition, there were often
overnight guests, politicians and acquaintances and old friends from other
parts of the country. Their visits were carefully orchestrated; Mother used
to pin a list of the entertainments—dinner parties, cocktail parties, and
tennis—to the guest-room curtains.

Especially during the Derby, the annual horse-racing extravaganza, the
Big House would be full of dashing people from afar, and we children would
sometimes find our rooms requisitioned for Frank and Polly Wisner (he
went on to perfect what he called his "mighty Wurlitzer," a system of
CIA-controlled media all over the country); David Bruce and his beautiful,
intimidating wife; Marietta Tree (whose first husband, Desmond Fitzgerald,
was a CIA bureau chief); and the attractive young men Father had befriended in Washington and London. One of them beguiled me by falling
to his knees on the black-and-white tiles in the back hall and asking me to
"wait for him." I had no idea he was drunk, and I was upset when I
discovered, a few weeks later, a glossy black-and-white photograph of his
wedding.

Life in the Big House seemed complicated and remote, and I kept to
myself. I had already moved a little way off, beginning the separation that
would take so many years to complete.

Father may have noticed my distance. Perhaps he felt I needed more
attention. He began to spend time every evening reading aloud to me. The

On the side of the porch
of the Big House, 1945.
Left to right: Sallie,
Worth, Barry, Jonathan.

Summer on the Cape:
Sallie and Jonathan,
pretending.

Mother and Eleanor, Cape Cod, 1940s.

reading-aloud became a sacred ritual that was almost never interrupted, except when he was away from home. At one time we thought we would read all of Dickens, but I grew up first.

Earlier Father had given me the red leather book for my poetry, stamped with my name. The two gifts, the one of time, the other of possibility, prompted important changes in my life. Words were no longer internal and hidden, or external and relatively meaningless. They began to form a shining chain, a prophecy, a way out.

I began to write ghost stories that were full of haunted rooms and hilltop castles, writing in the fustian that was the nearest I could come to the prose of Victorian England.

I knew I could capture attention if I had something to read out loud. But how to imitate the atmosphere of threatening mystery that coiled in the Victorian novels Father read? What really was going on at the end of *Vanity Fair,* when Becky Sharp, whom Father grudgingly admired, appeared like an evil demon? What did the governess mean in *The Turn of the Screw* when she stared across the lake? Who could say what Catherine's ghost really wanted when she moaned outside the window at the opening of *Wuthering Heights?* The simplest of Dickens's plots contained twists of action and human motivation that were baffling, evil, not to be questioned or explained. So I lost myself in ghost stories where everything was bizarre, satisfied if I could make my audience laugh, and I continued to write sentimental poems in the red leather book, which I no longer read to anyone.

One evening in the spring of 1946, I was called into the living room for an important announcement. In this solemn setting, with the portrait of a curly-wigged ancestor over the mantel and the chariot-clock drawn by bronze steeds, Father told me that Mother was going to have another baby. She was lying on the couch during the announcement. I remember feeling only intense embarrassment, as though I had no business knowing their secret. To relieve my feelings, I rushed out to the kitchen to tell the servants. Their eyes told me that I was behaving foolishly; I returned to the living room. It was one of those familiar situations where it did not seem possible to do the right thing, or even to imagine what the right thing might be. To cap it, I realized that my parents might have been hurt by my sudden departure to spread the news in the kitchen.

I was nine years old when Eleanor, the last baby, arrived, and I played a larger role in her early childhood than I had in Jonathan's. Nursie was tired; when the baby nurse left, she had difficulty extending herself to take in even this quiet baby, who seemed to demand so little.

Mother was tired as well. One winter when Eleanor was still quite small, we had a snowfall, an unusual event in Kentucky. Mother pulled

Eleanor, called Missie at this time, on a sled up the Hill. But then she returned to the house, pale and exhausted. "I'm too old to have a child this young," she told me.

Eleanor began to trail along behind me almost as soon as she could walk. I was touched and flattered by her devotion.

Meanwhile Worth and Barry were moving into adolescence. They were sent to separate boarding schools and began to spend some of their vacations away from home. When they came back for the holidays, they seemed to be strangers. Worth was tall, loud, and forceful; Barry was quieter, more shadowy. I felt I had little in common with them.

Because I was the middle child in the family, I had at a younger age shared my older brothers' nursery routine. Now, as they moved into adolescence, a wall grew up between us. I was left suspended in the middle of the family, a perfect vantage point for observing.

I realized how early, and how sharply, Worth and Barry were directed toward running the family businesses. There was never any discussion of other careers, other directions they might take; their only divergent interests, in sports and music, were, after all, merely hobbies.

Father supervised their education from afar, and it lay along familiar lines. The men who govern this democracy have sometimes come from border states like Kentucky, but they have moved upward along a prescribed route: private boarding schools, almost certainly in the East, Ivy League colleges in New England, certain graduate schools and exchange programs, such as the Columbia School of Journalism and the Nieman Fellowships, entrance to which depends more on the connections, both political and social, their fathers have built and maintained than on the sons' talent or ability. Worth and Barry were both set on this course, which included summer jobs in the family companies.

I did not realize at the time that my parents' willingness to allow me to spend my elementary and high school years in a private school in Louisville, to avoid going to camp or boarding school, to remain sheltered, private, and alone, was consistent with their belief that the family businesses held no roles for women, as the world at large held no roles for women who were not wives of important men, hostesses, and mothers. Yet because I stayed at home, I learned the way the family worked, the way it fit at an odd angle into the life of the state. And I was taught by women, brilliant, dedicated women, until I graduated from high school.

As a child, I was not able to grant my oldest brother the special deference the rest of our little world accorded him as heir to an enormous fortune, a monopoly newspaper company, an increasingly lucrative television station, and so on. I remembered his teasing, and it continued even when we were both adults.

I had absorbed Father's condescending attitude toward Barry without realizing that along the way I had stifled a natural affection for a placid, pleasant little boy. I scorned Barry's compliance, even while I knew he had no other way to survive. I laughed at his slowness, his silence during the family's sparring matches, his quick blushes and far too easily provoked tears. I dreaded finding that my painful sensitivity was akin to his, dreaded finding that I, too, could be worsted in a verbal or physical battle. His few enthusiasms and pleasures in life seemed ridiculous to me, and they were treated as ridiculous by the rest of the family: his tooting away on the French horn in the back of the house, his dreaminess and abstraction, his tenderness toward all growing things, which led him to build me the concrete-lined pond for my ducks. Barry loved flowers and used to pick great globes of daffodils every spring. But his special qualities could not be appreciated in a family that valued only winning the game, only triumphing over opposition.

As Barry grew older, I saw the dreaminess disappear. As he lost weight, I saw the hard brittle musculature of a character built to order emerge. He lost his kindly, patient quality, and by the time he entered college, he was as driven, as ironic, and as desperate to succeed as he needed to be in order to earn Father's approval.

But it was too hard for him, and it came too late. Father never admired anything that was done with difficulty. Barry lost his sense of humor somewhere in the thickets of late adolescence; he lost his boyish charm, his naïveté. Father was not impressed by the hard-muscled, hard-driven ex-marine who emerged from college and the service. It all looked too dreary, too narrow, too elemental. Barry could never win in that contest; and although he maintained his close, unspoken relationship with Mother, she could not protect him.

By contrast, Worth did everything with ease. He possessed a physical recklessness that daunted and amazed both parents, who were both cautious and probably at heart rather timid. From the time he crashed into a stone wall on a sled through the endless series of nearly fatal car wrecks of his adolescence, his recklessness, while a source of worry, was also secretly admired. Conventional families often overvalue the black sheep in their midst, whose escapades reflect more conservative relatives' nightmares, or dreams. Worth rode this reckless streak to his death, and it was his primary, almost his only characteristic during the period I knew him.

He was very attractive to young men, who rhapsodized over his drinking, his gambling, his fast driving; he victimized young women, plucking virginities. None of us knew how to resist him, partly because he was so loud. He alone in the family seemed to possess the full range of his voice, shouting, growling, cursing without shame. He could easily move from the male vulgarities of boarding school to the polished, humorous eloquence of the young public man. Machines were his, and he rode and ruled them, while the rest of the family were helpless in the face of their demands.

Worth used to take Jonathan, as a little child, on long "ghost rides" at night. I myself had been on one and knew better than ever to subject myself to that torment again.

Worth would drive out to a remote country lane, turn off the head-lights, and speed up to eighty or ninety miles an hour, meanwhile telling ghoulish stories about victims of wrecks and their avenging spirits. Jona-than, who was easily terrified, must have been paralyzed as he sat, a small frail boy of seven or eight, in the front seat of the speeding, darkened car. But he never complained, knowing already that to complain courted not only Worth's wrath but our parents' silent scorn. He had to endure.

Jonathan's fears dominated his early childhood. He was subject, as I had been and as Eleanor would be, to nightmares that left him soaked with sweat, screaming. He was also terrified by seemingly innocuous events: the noise a car made passing over the metal "cattle guards" that prevented cows from crossing farm roads, for example. He would crouch on the floor of the car with his hands over his ears when we approached the guards. He seemed to me to exist in another sphere, neither brother to the two older boys nor sister to Eleanor and me. Later, he went through a version of the hardening process that turned Barry into a martinet. But Jonathan did not live long enough to complete the process. He never lost his frail, strange charm or his painful sensitivity, even when he had begun to adopt Worth's reckless-ness and Barry's military self-discipline.

The struggle to understand the past is never entirely successful. I have tried for years to piece together the childhood we all shared, especially to sift it for clues to Worth's and Jonathan's deaths. Our childhoods alone do not contain all the information that is needed for even a superficial under-standing.

All five children in my generation were crucially influenced, as were our parents before us, by the earlier life of the two families, the Binghams and the Capertons, especially those characteristics that were only partly con-scious. The families had produced many determined men, locked in battle with their relatives or with the limitations of life in the rural South. On both sides, there were mysteries, deaths that could not be mentioned or explained, moves and motivations that were never examined.

To understand these past lives that continued, and continue, to influ-ence my own, I began to piece together my mother's Virginia family and my father's family in North Carolina. Both families had grown and spread, Mother's into West Virginia, Kentucky, Tennessee, and Alabama; Father's from coastal to piedmont North Carolina, to the Blue Ridge, and then to

Kentucky. Mother's family was large and distinguished, including men who had fought in all this country's wars, who had served in state legislatures, had been lawyers and judges and large landowners, men who had sometimes been very rich, but who had possessed, with or without money, the assurance of the Shenandoah Valley and of the West Virginia coalfields. Father's small, tightly constructed family had not voyaged as far or done as well.

Gradually in nineteenth-century North Carolina the Bingham men had emerged as leaders in that landscape which could be dominated by a Presbyterian elder who was also headmaster of a small military school. In Virginia and West Virginia, Mother's family, the Capertons, which had early moved into prominence, did not continue to rise so quickly. The two families represented two sides of the emerging South: the elite Virginian going west to make his fortune and name the land, and the determined North Carolinian laboring to imitate his Southern rival's prosperity and assurance.

On both sides of the family, the roles of women were hidden yet crucial. They had borne the children and bound up the wounds, but their names and characters, their homely achievements and unimaginable endurance were largely unknown. Here and there women who were larger than their assigned roles emerged, such as Mother's ancestress who had been kidnapped by the Indians and survived for five years after seeing her husband murdered and her infant's brains dashed out against a tree. And there were others whose names and faces I began to find, coming upon them suddenly in the course of reading and remembering.

One of the most crucial of these women was my mother's mother, Helena Lefroy Caperton—Munda—a writer and spinner of tales, a determined matchmaker, and a passionate partisan of upward mobility.

Antecedents

Most of our families could not take these traumatic experiences. . . . There was too much. And their past life, their values, their beliefs, their mental habits had not prepared them for this kind of trouble. Insight was not a quality their culture valued; nor intellectual honesty; nor self-criticism; nor concern for human rights; nor could they laugh at themselves. With all their capacity for gaiety and wit, they had so little real humor. . . . All these planter families had was courage and anger, and it was not enough.

Lillian Smith, *Killers of the Dream*

6

My grandmother Munda, whose real name was Helena Lefroy Caperton, lived all her life in Richmond, Virginia, in the small house where she had raised her seven children. As I grew old enough to travel alone on the train, I was sometimes sent to spend a few days with her in an old-fashioned downtown neighborhood called the Fan.

Munda was a great storyteller. She said she had inherited the gift from her father's Irish nurse, Curtie, who had taken care of Munda during childhood trips to Ireland. Some of Munda's stories were versions of Irish fairy tales, with gypsies and ghosts and haunted castles. Other stories were more directly related to the facts and myths of her family background, to both my great-grandmother Sallie Montague's genteel Virginia people and to her husband Arthur Lefroy's grander Anglo-Irish family.

Munda sometimes showed me a closet where she kept a collection of mementos: the dagger a distant relative had seen used to kill his lover, who was a Chinese emperor's concubine, the handkerchief this same lady had embroidered before her dreadful demise, as well as dueling pistols, jewels of dubious worth, daguerreotypes and faded spidery letters.

My great-grandmother died in 1942, and I do not remember the old lady whose name, Sallie Watson Montague Lefroy, was to become, in part, my own.

Late in life, Sallie Lefroy wrote a memoir for her grandchildren. It is called *Autumn Garner.* Behind the conventional pieties of a woman writing for her beloved family lie myths and images that lead back into the labyrinth of the pre–Civil War South. Like the mementos in my grandmother's closet, these images attest to the unspoken aspect of the family's past: the Sealed Room, the Statue of General Wolfe, the Slave Who Had Fits, the Hanged Pirate . . .

When Sallie Watson Montague married Jeffry Arthur Lefroy in the 1870s the match must have seemed promising. Lefroy was a younger son of a well-placed Anglo-Irish family; he had come to Richmond looking for land to buy.

The time was propitious. Sallie had recently become conscious "of a slight spirit of anxiety for my future on the part of certain relatives, aunts, cousins, etc. They began to say that I must be heartless, that I did not seem to care for anyone, and greatly to my amusement, the dark shadow of an old maid in the family loomed before them! When my father sensed this he was indignant. He promptly took occasion to urge me never to consider marriage until someone arrived who should be absolutely essential to my happiness. Thus encouraged, I went serenely on my accustomed way until 'someone essential' did arrive."

Sallie had received more schooling than many women of her period—including her Irish sisters-in-law, as she later observed—but her education prepared her to assume only one role, that of the wife and mother of a prosperous upper-class family. Although the headmaster of her school in Richmond observed that after his experiences in the Civil War, he wanted to prepare the girls to "make a living in the higher walks of life," what these walks could have been Sallie does not indicate; perhaps teaching school or caring for children. She was the beautiful daughter of an adoring father. She was also, according to Mother, "a woman of vigorous intellect" who later in her life started the Richmond Women's Club. "Her gentle but persistent correction of our grammar" marked her interest in forming young minds—an interest that persisted in the family—forming them to avoid the mistakes that would have raised questions about their place in society.

In the South, then as now, certain accents as well as certain mistakes in grammar narrow the already perilously thin margin between those who consider themselves gentry and their neighbors, poor whites or poor blacks who may even be distantly related. Much of the South's snobbery developed as a desperate attempt to ignore the results of miscegenation.

On her first visit to her husband's family in Ireland, Sallie Lefroy was fascinated by tales of a sealed room in the big old house. The room "had its tragic story. Love, murder and a prisoner had shadowed its history. I was thrilled! 'Can't you have it opened for me?' I asked my [sister-in-law]. 'I am afraid not,' she said. 'A wall would have to be torn down, but if you are quite decided to explore it, it can be reached through a trap door in an upper room, down a flight of dark ladder-like steps.' I was hardly brave enough for such an adventure." The sealed room turned up in one of Munda's stories.

Sallie Lefroy was brave in all other respects—she was a great rider, and was on horseback shortly after her daughter's birth—but she did not want to descend into the sealed room. Too many secrets were hidden there. Sallie accepted certain versions of life in the South and discarded others; for example, she believed that during the Reconstruction period, Virginia had been "overrun by the very scum of the earth from the North." Whatever discomfort she may have felt on the subject of slavery was eased by stories about the amiable foolishness of black people and their dependence on their white masters.

Sallie substituted the word "servants" for "slaves" when she described the family's life before the Civil War:

"Mammy was definitely a Personage. She ruled with a fierce and abiding love which came to our generation from the day when my father first saw the light and was confided to her devoted ministrations. In those early days our servants in the South 'belonged,' and when my generation began my Grandmother made Mammy a welcome present to my parents. She reigned in our nursery and commanded her subordinate helpers until the day of her death."

The term "benign neglect," which turned up in Munda's theories on child raising, explained the treatment of "nerves." Munda believed that it was a mistake to encourage children to examine their own feelings. It was a useful philosophy. In raising children who were taught to look outward rather than inward, Munda, like her mother before her, achieved certain striking results: her children and grandchildren learned to keep their worries to themselves, and to ignore certain facts about life in the antebellum South. One of these facts was the passionate love white children often developed for their black nurses, who had raised and loved them from babyhood, an attachment that must be suppressed as the white child came into maturity, and finally replaced by humorous stories about devoted darkies.

In *Killers of the Dream,* Lillian Smith described the way she came to understand this truth: "I knew that my old nurse who had cared for me through long months of illness, who had given me refuge when a little sister took my place as the baby of the family, who soothed, fed me, delighted me with her stories and games, let me fall asleep on her deep warm breast, was not worthy of the passionate love I felt for her but must be given instead a half-smiled-at affection similar to that which one feels for one's dog—I learned to cheapen with tears and sentimental talk of 'my old mammy' one of the profound relationships of my life. I learned the bitterest thing a child can learn: that the human relations I valued most were held cheap by the world I lived in."

Smith's discovery is made by all children who are raised by servants, black or white, especially when the beloved and scorned caretaker dies.

When my great-grandmother Sallie's Mammy Polly died, her funeral, as Sallie described it, was a display of the mourning black people's ignorance: "the preacher prayed earnestly that we might all be 'reluctant to go to heaven,'" she reported in her memoir. "This evoked deep responses of

'Yes, Lord.' My father said that Mammy's highly ornate coffin was the envy of every darky in town."

Sallie's daughter Munda used to terrify me with an account of a black woman's funeral on a remote plantation in Virginia sometime before the Civil War. This black woman, unlike Mammy Polly, who was "tall, thin, very black, and stern of feature," had weighed three hundred pounds when she died. She had gained the last pounds to win a bet with her master, and she had gone to a cattle scale to be weighed to prove she had won. When she died, shortly thereafter, her white people had an especially large coffin built for her and accompanied it to the black church. During the long funeral service in the stifling church, the sides of the coffin began to swell, and a noxious liquid seeped out and ran down the chancel steps. As Munda described it, the black worshippers fell into a panic and began a stampede to the doors and windows. Eventually the white family departed as well, and the service was broken off. I wanted to know how the coffin was finally disposed of. "They had to throw chemicals at it through the windows," Munda told me. It was the sealed room again. Someone in that congregation had loved that black woman, probably a white "chile" she had raised. But her ignominious end could only be treated as a macabre joke.

According to Sallie, her mother always kept a "Dorcas basket" packed with clothing and food for the poor. But no amount of giving could relieve the feelings of women whose children preferred their nurses. Sallie's mother-in-law in Ireland, whose children had been raised by a nurse, commented, "I think I must have some good in me because I am not jealous of Curtie."

As a Christian, she could not afford to be; as a practical matter, she could not have done without Curtie's services. Rich women of that period and long afterwards could not provide their husbands with the companionship and the organized social life they expected without turning over their children to other women to raise. The quandary that is now distressing professional women was a quandary for rich women generations ago: when the children have to be cared for by someone else, what price is paid? The children are turned over to less educated women, black or white, who are paid a minimum wage to raise them. How, then, do the parents retain their children's trust and love, and how do they lead them to speak and think in their parents' mode, rather than in the words and terms they have learned from their nurses? What was once a heartrending problem for a few well-off women has become a problem for many women who have made the decision to work. It will remain a problem as long as child raising is felt to be suitable work only for the poor and the ignorant and is paid accordingly.

The accommodation was made silently in the South of Arthur Lefroy: the children were cared for adequately or more than adequately, and they learned something about human nature and love they could not have learned without their black nurses.

In her memoirs, Sallie remembered fondly the organized gaiety provided by one of the resorts in the Southern highlands, White Sulphur Springs: "A season at the White was the very cream and perfection of a young girl's belleship. The vast hotel with its immense dining and ball rooms, its vivid green lawn, and fine old shade trees surrounded on all sides by deeply wooded mountains is a picture of rare beauty and charm. In my young days the dear White was more a resort for Southern people than it has been of later years. We all knew one another more or less. Year after year friends from South Carolina, Louisiana and other Southern states greeted one another joyously each evening as the stages drew up under the long porticos . . ."

In "later years," strangers did come to the "White" and other Southern resorts. One of these strangers was a young Jewish girl. Munda recounted with bewilderment how this stranger came to the evening dances, apparently expecting that someone would dance with her. Of course no one did. After several evenings of public humiliation, however, General Robert E. Lee, then the president of Washington College, asked the young woman to dance. After that, other men felt obliged to ask her. As my grandmother said, only General Lee could have produced such an effect.

Sallie Montague spent a summer in the Adirondack Mountains with an aunt and uncle while her mother prepared for her "turning out" party at home, "ordering my first grown up dresses." When Sallie came home from her vacation, she was "burned brown as a berry." Sallie went on: "Care of the complexion was a rigid rule. Mammy often threatened to sew a sunbonnet on me if I didn't mind what she said. . . . I dreaded this, feeling that it would mean suffocation!

"When my Mother looked upon her sun-browned daughter she was truely shocked and indignant. She asked if I supposed she wanted to turn out a daughter who looked like a mulatto."

This is the only angry incident Sallie mentioned in her memoirs. The system demanded careful attention to its rules. Although she was an intelligent, determined woman, Sallie never questioned them.

Sallie was not the first woman in her family who was bright, observant, and noticeably courageous. She described her own mother as remarkably brave; during the Civil War, after the fall of Richmond, this lady drove back into the city, over a burning bridge, to reach her husband. Sallie described her daughter, my grandmother, as "fearless," "helping" sailors on an ocean crossing to hoist the sails when she was only two years old.

However, this personal courage had few outlets, except in mastering horses or in verbal exchanges within the family which could on occasion draw blood. Intellectually, these Southern women learned not to advance too far, not to develop their minds too deeply. Reading and writing were allowed as long as they did not become burning interests, intrude on the business concerns of husbands and fathers, or interfere with the round of social obligations required of upper-class women and girls.

Arthur Lefroy died of tuberculosis when his and Sallie's daughter, Helena, my grandmother Munda, was five. Left alone to raise her daughter, Sallie must have often dwelled on her short, romantic marriage. Early in the marriage, her husband had acted as her father, correcting her gently, nursing her when she was seasick on their frequent ocean crossings: "Arthur was a wonderful nurse. He should have been a physician . . ." But as he sickened with tuberculosis, she became the "wonderful nurse," especially during his long last illness when she cared for him in the South of France.

Sallie never remarried. Munda sometimes described the impression her mother had made as a beautiful young widow in Richmond; she had had many friendships with men. My favorite in the crowd was Buffalo Bill, who passed through Richmond performing with a troupe of displaced Indians in a sort of sideshow.

According to one of Munda's stories, Buffalo Bill had been invited by her grandfather to have a meal with the family. He had reciprocated by requesting that the women, including Munda, then a small girl, be allowed to ride in his show in the Dead Wood Coach, which had been the first mail carrier in the West. Munda was amazed and delighted when her grandfather gave his permission. She realized that Buffalo Bill was attracted to her mother; later he sent Sallie a silver-headed riding crop inscribed with her initials. Munda thought it would have been great fun to have Buffalo Bill for a stepfather.

Sallie's relationship with her only child was disturbed by the fear that Helena would somehow be "spoiled," a fear that touched all the women in the family when rearing girls. My mother shared this belief in the benefits of "toughening" girls, which was why she seldom intervened when my oldest brother was teasing me. Perhaps she had made a realistic appraisal of the life I was facing, a life in which I would be entirely dependent on husband or father for survival. Surely there was little point in training a girl to insist on justice when she would have to submit, later, to men who might freely and privately abuse her.

Stories of beaten and raped wives were of course never told at our dinner table, although Munda's stories often featured women who were mysteriously murdered. Mother sometimes told me unexpected stories about young girls who had committed suicide or about older women who had been given frontal lobotomies to make them more submissive. As a child, I met one such woman, a pliant, smiling creature, who seemed to me to have no more character than a carrot.

Munda was certainly no carrot. Seeming, from her stories, to have been her children's only parent, and raising a family of seven children on a limited income, she made pin money by writing articles for *The Ladies' Home Companion* and other magazines. One was called "The Care and Feeding of Sons-in-Law"; she described it as her most successful and amusing piece. In it she set down her "formula for the perfect son-in-law: a young woman should not look for wealth in a suitor but the ability to acquire it." This ability derived, she wrote, from "brains, good health, and ability to meet life gallantly; gentle birth and clean line, educational equipment for success in a definite profession or line of business, a sufficient degree of clean-cut good looks, tolerance, broadness of outlook, and humor—and the greatest of these is humor, for happiness in married life somewhat depends on the mutual conception of a joke."

The article itself was something of a joke; Munda was too intelligent to believe in formulas. But behind the "humor" that was so important in maintaining relationships, among the secrets in the sealed room, was the terrible recognition that pretty, bright women were entirely dependent on men—fathers or husbands.

"I had early learned that the pleasures of imagination were [Helena's] greatest delight," Sallie wrote. "When her Uncle George (who was Bishop of India) related weird incidents of his life in India, perilous contacts with its wild life, she would try to match his true stories with her glamorous experiences in Virginia. . . . I once exclaimed, 'Oh dear the child doesn't know truth from false.' My mother said, 'Never let her hear you say that! Just accept it as a fairy tale, and in time she will make the distinction.' "

The "distinction," however, obliterated much that the bright child had observed. Those tales of the imagination displayed truths that belonged only in the sealed room. In her fiction, Munda, in spite of everything that constrained her, touched lightly on matters the genteel South preferred to ignore. Like her mother before her, Munda was a truth teller. In both cases, however, the truths remained lodged in the unconscious, revealed only partially in the stories she told me and the fiction she wrote.

Munda dedicated her first book of stories, published in 1943, to her mother. The collection, *Like a Falcon Flying,* was prefaced by "A Few Words" written by Dorothy Parker: "These are curious tales to come from the pen of a gentle, pretty Richmond lady, the mother of a son and six daughters. . . . There is a wildness, a fierce rush of drama, a long spreading terror . . ."

All the stories are concerned with the central obsessive question of love:

will a young girl preserve herself and her chances of a decent life through marrying well? Other matters are minor compared to this question, which the author knew was the meat and gristle of female survival.

These are not happy stories. Even when the central figure succeeds in snaring her man, the outcome is clouded by sexual ambivalence. For example, in the title story, Diarmid and Zoe are finally reunited, but only after the death of the rich American to whom Diarmid had sold himself and his ancestral home, Castle Tandgregree. Their married life is haunted by her ghost. The quest for money is justified because the ancestral place must be preserved, and children born to carry on the name. The quest for personal power is much less easy to excuse, especially in women, and it is ominously touched by violence and eroticism. When Zoe drives Diarmid away because of his connection with the rich American, she kicks him in the mouth (she is on horseback at the time). She remembers long after "the feel of the flesh of his mouth against her booted foot."

Sexuality can only lead to trouble for women whose survival depends on husbands, fathers, and brothers. Black musicians and bold pirates represent terrible risks: in "Pirate Sapphires," the pirate is immediately more attractive to the young bride-to-be than her respectable fiancé. The pirate does not hesitate to give her the magnificent sapphires "bought with the lives of many men"; her fiancé rejects them outright. He is "shocked beyond measure by something he had never seen in her face or heard in her voice" when the pirate speaks. Desire is inappropriate for women, who must be either virginal or matronly.

The more dangerous the pirate is, of course, the more irresistible. In Munda's story, he is given supernatural powers: when the bride-to-be dies of the plague, he revives her with a magic potion. In the cabin of his ship, the pirate tears open her bodice, but the "pure chalice of her body" prevents any evil thought from forming in his mind.

Southern popular fiction like the tales Munda wrote and told echoes women's after-dinner gossip: wellborn white gentlemen often seemed lacking in drive. So the pirate, with his swarthy good looks and his ability to take action, remained a seductive image for women like my grandmother.

Even more seductive, and even more dangerous, was the image of the black man, not the meek old servant with his bows and scrapes, his humble worship of "Old Mistus," but that figure out of the Southern nightmare, the rebelling black man turned rapist and murderer.

That there were amazingly few incidents of slave revolt before what Munda called the War had little effect on the recurring Southern obsession with black violence and sexuality. This obsession justified and fueled the activities of the Ku Klux Klan, which my Bingham great-grandfather organized in North Carolina during Reconstruction. The obsession would scarcely be touched by law or public opinion until a group of wellborn Southern women formed the Association for the Prevention of Lynching in 1930. Willie Snow Ethridge, whom I remembered as a frivolous dancer, was one of its founding members.

This group repudiated "the crown of chivalry which has been pressed like a crown of thorns upon our heads." They wanted no part of the protection that justified lynching.

Munda must have drawn in with the air she breathed whispered myths of black sexual potency. This was too dangerous a topic for her to tackle in her romantic stories. But she touched on it in "Miss Angel Gabriel," in which a crippled black boy has a single transcendent experience: "He had looked upon an unclothed white woman. . . . He shook in terror and pure adoration." The result of this experience is, eventually, death for the black man who has unwittingly broken a taboo, even though the writer makes it clear that he never desires the white woman, seeing her instead as an angel in a stained-glass window.

By the time she wrote these tales, Munda had raised seven children. She knew all about the privations of genteel poverty: "a desperation of shabby gentility" marks the seamstress's house in "Miss Angel Gabriel" where "the oriflamme of struggle" is defined as "the odor of long forgotten meals and leaking gas." Even marriage to a wellborn man does not assure lifelong economic sufficiency.

When marriages are made primarily for security, love often must be ignored or denied. "How often do you women marry your true loves? Practically never," the worldly obstetrician in another story remarks. "First you give your hearts, then you bow to expediency."

Pride—of family, of class—keeps all Munda's ebullient, hopeful heroines in line, reinforcing their obedience to the male hierarchy. Yet the rewards of obedience are joyless: sexless marriages, a limited field of action, and subdued rage that can only be expressed in the kicking of "a little booted and spurred foot." There are no happy people in her stories, only survivors, more or less deformed by the price they have had to pay for their survival.

Munda was a limited writer; she could not afford to follow the clues she buried in her tales. If the secrets of women's unhappiness were revealed, the doctor in one story says, "then God help the state."

Nor could Munda resist adding dark hints about sexuality, which I accepted fearfully but without question. Something happened to women after they were married, she implied; they lost their spark, their fire. I associated her hints with her own overburdened life as a mother of seven children, without the money to buy all the help she needed. She did not describe her own marriage or the births of her seven children as the conclusion of a fairy tale. Instead, her own life had been grueling, a triumph over fearful obstacles, culminating in the marriage of all six daughters to socially acceptable men. But was that really all life offered a woman?

Munda managed to speak in a secret language to me, which perhaps had more in common with the kitchen language I listened to so eagerly than with the talk of the dinner table, where she often sat silent and isolated among my parents' friends. Although I grew to distrust her easy romanticism and her fairy tales, I never distrusted the other truth that she presented to me, silently, as the fruit of her own hard life and quick observation: in marriage, women lost more than they won. She would have been the first to object, outraged, to such a statement. Yet as she sat on the chaise longue in the lavender guest room at the Big House, propped up on lace pillows, her little feet free at last of her tight high-heeled shoes, she gave off an aura of wildness, of scarcely controlled rebellion, which interested me far more than her exquisite "hand work" or her tales of her six daughters' weddings. Like so many women I have known, she managed to hint at the truth as she had learned it during her own packed life even while she was telling me something entirely different.

In her tales, Munda mixed the language and images of antebellum Virginia with the colors of the Ireland she had known as a child when she visited her father's family. Those visits were richly embellished in a reminiscence she wrote late in life, *Recollections of an Ulster Childhood*.

She had collected images from that time much as I collected Elihu Vedder's "Hope," the Botticelli maidens, and the Velásquez Infanta. Munda remembered a picture, "Cherry Ripe," which had hung on the nursery wall in Ulster: "a touchingly grave child in a mob cap." She remembered the delight of being bathed by Curtie before a peat fire, then dressed in linen undergarments "woven in our village, the simple lace edging made for me in the thatched, white-washed cottages, whose occupants I knew and loved well." The education of an upper-class mother and wife had begun; in Munda's Ireland, there was no poverty, all the cottages were clean and decorated with flowers, and even the gypsies she met on her travels in a donkey cart were beautifully dressed and well fed.

Although she was carefully raised, learning the church catechism early and reciting it for "My Grandfather the Dean," Munda was given a great deal of liberty. She and her two "boy cousins" explored the Irish countryside in her donkey cart, stopping at pubs to drink Guinness's Dublin stout.

She adopted the icons of her large Irish family. On both sides of her family, she rejoiced in connections with important men, such as her ancestor Peter Montague, who had come to Virginia in 1621 with Sir Francis Wyatt and had served in the House of Burgesses.

Later the Montagues were reluctant hosts to Lord Cornwallis, the British general, who stopped at their plantation, White Chimneys, on the way to his encounter with the French and Continental soldiers at Yorktown. The family kept the table where he had sat to write and eat and play cards with his men. The ten-year-old son of the family, Nathaniel Price, had refused to join the soldiers when they drank to the King's health, saying, "I will drink to the health of George Washington, but not to that of the King of England." Yet Munda was also related to the Irish Trenches who had provided a lady-in-waiting to Queen Victoria; she was descended from Lady Mary Wortley Montagu, the outspoken traveler and writer of the eighteenth century, who had been held up to ridicule for her adventurous ways.

Mother seldom discussed her remarkable relation, perhaps because Lady Mary's character had been vilified by Pope and Walpole. As the wife of the Ambassador to Turkey, Lady Mary had begun a life of travel and writing that continued until, at the age of fifty, she left England forever to live in France.

Her letters have been praised for two and a half centuries, but even more amazing to me was the story of the way she inoculated her small son with smallpox in 1718. First she sent for "an old Greek woman," according to her account, who went to work on the six-year-old boy, but "so awkwardly by the shaking of her hand, and put the Child to so much Torture with her blunt and rusty Needle, that I pitied his Cries . . . and therefore Inoculated the other Arm with my own instrument, and with so little pain to him, that he did not in the least complain of it."

Lady Mary "engrafted" her son without asking her husband's permission, and reported to him a week later: "Your Son is as well as can be expected, and I hope past all manner of danger." This success helped to persuade the upper class in England to submit to inoculation, which eventually ended the scourge of smallpox.

When she married Clifford Randolph Caperton in 1897, Munda entered another family of Virginia gentlefolk who had been magistrates, judges, landowners, and people of substance since the colony was first settled. No one has ever described Clifford Caperton in my hearing; he died in 1939, and the cause of his death remains a mystery. Munda cast a discreet veil over her marriage when she talked about her earlier life, yet I detected a hint of reproach in her description of having seven children so close together that two were often in the baby carriage at once—and she had no twins. She bore seven children between 1898 and 1910.

In an article printed in *The Ladies' Home Journal,* written when her older daughters were already grown, Munda laid down her rules for raising girls. Since money was always an uncertain proposition, she believed, girls must learn how to support themselves. Through education both in the South and in the North—Munda thought the mixture was necessary—a girl could become at least marginally self-supporting as a secretary, librarian, "athletic dancer," or playground director. Of course, these were temporary jobs, not careers. For Munda believed that even an unsatisfactory marriage was better than no marriage, because marriage alone provided a secure place in life. She did not believe in divorce.

Munda depended on early training in "implicit obedience" to shape her daughters, and felt that they could be counted on after about the age of fifteen to behave themselves in any circumstances. At that age, she wrote, she gave them complete liberty of thought and action.

By then it was probably safe to assume that they would not take advantage of either liberty. Munda's discipline was highly effective because it was not punishment; it went deeper. She inculcated a sense of responsibility so powerful that once, when stung by a bee, a little daughter sobbed, "I stung myself."

Reading aloud to the girls from the time they were three was an essential part of their training. Munda believed that adults and children only do what is right to escape punishment; she held up as examples to her girls self-sacrificing Rebecca in *Ivanhoe* and meek Amelia in *Vanity Fair,* but also Florence Nightingale and Joan of Arc. She did not allow them to read the popular girls' serial novels of the period. Munda thought that these books were often badly written, and style was always more important to her than any other issue.

Style, after all, was what each of her charming but impecunious daughters had to offer. Munda considered charm the only really necessary skill for a woman. Logic was poison in a woman, but charming evasions and subterfuges would win the day. Wallis Simpson, who beguiled a king with her wit, was Munda's prime example.

Behind this well-thought-out scheme, two unresolved problems lay. One was the attitude of "Father." In several published articles, Munda referred to her husband's unwillingness to see his daughters marry, an unwillingness so pronounced she offered to excuse him from one wedding. She noted that his attitude had changed after she had told him that his daughters were the best stock in the world: Pretty Girls Preferred, which could be exchanged on the open market for money and advancement.

The bargain implied something "Father" could not accept, but it was a bargain Munda understood and even enjoyed. She realized that a Malthusian system existed in the marriage market: a girl who allowed "inferior" men to court her would not be attractive to "superior" suitors. Everything about a young woman's adolescence must be attended to with scrupulous care, from her looks and education to her deportment, clothes, ability to dance, and self-esteem. Munda understood that unwise marriages were often caused by a girl's having been starved for matrimony; she recounted how, as she tied on each baby girl's first bonnet, she always said, "You are the most beautiful thing in the world. Kiss me." A young woman who felt that she was attractive—that, after all, was the salient detail—would be less likely to marry the first man who paid her a compliment.

But the "thingness" of her daughters must have caused her some pain. Her bitterness, later in life, expressed in a brilliant wit, meant to me that Munda understood the kind of bargain she had succeeded in making. She knew about unhappiness, even violence, in marriage; she knew about suffering in childbirth, and the exhaustion of young mothers. That had to be explained away, because there was no other system that would guarantee financial security for her beloved girls. Here and there a trace of the real struggle is preserved, as when Mother, as a small child, given a new coat rather than a hand-me-down, asked wonderingly, "Do I really wear it before anyone else does?" or when Munda described the six weddings she had organized as "a pagan winding of chains with garlands."

But when one of her daughters came to her to complain about her husband, she sent her off to have a good time at the Kentucky Derby. When her husband behaved mulishly about a wedding, when he refused to believe that his daughters had grown up and took his men friends to look at them lying in their beds at night, Munda reflected that he had not been necessary to anyone for a long time; then he fought wearing spats at a wedding and had to be persuaded by one of his daughters sitting in his lap.

Munda wrote that she divided humankind into the caught, the uncaught, and those who think they are not caught, relegating herself to the last category. Her untamable spirit fanned the sparks of individuality that, in spite of her prescriptions, developed in all her daughters.

When she had married, Munda had taken on, along with the shadowy Clifford, a family full of heroes. His ancestor Adam Caperton was killed in 1782 by the Indians in Kentucky; another relative was shot by a renegade Yankee during the Civil War; and many others died in the Revolution, the Indian Wars, and the Civil War. Other male forebears bought and sold land in Monroe County, West Virginia, and owned and operated coal mines near Union. They were prosperous and adventurous men, sending forth many of their number to settle the West, one of whom ran afoul of Daniel Boone.

Of the women little remains, other than descriptions of the number of children they bore, many of whom died in childhood.

Clifford Caperton's sister Rose left a mark because of her strong and individualistic temperament. She lived and died on Wynderidge, a farm near Union in West Virginia, where her mother and father had lived before her. At her death in 1969, Rose was buried, as she had requested, in an unmarked grave in her barnyard, and her two collies were shot and buried beside her.

According to a newspaper account, "Miss Rose" "wrote a big, bold hand, and she was a big, fearless woman." "If her work shoes at Wynderidge were often decorated with animal manure it was also true that she had twice done the Grand tour of Europe, and there were Parisian wines in her cellar. She had been schooled in Richmond and New York City and was an avid reader," and she could "lead a two-year-old Hereford bull around a barn at 2 A.M. until the homesick animal stopped bawling. But she also liked white kid gloves and linen handkerchiefs and a beautiful fan for evening."

Miss Rose never married. She refused to be woven into the domestic tapestry. Perhaps she acknowledged her essential alienation from tradition when she insisted on being buried in an unmarked grave. I never met her, and it is impossible to invent her attitudes and thoughts now, long after her death. However, her life became a symbol to me of the independent and successful woman who made her own tradition, at some cost, in the midst of Caperton family lares and penates.

But she never married. That had to be included. It began to seem to me that all the women on Mother's side of the family had made a fearful compromise when they celebrated those grandly described weddings where silver candelabra, "great clusters of feathery white chrysanthemums, the green of tall palms, lace draperies and ferns" obscured the primitive nature of the exchange. On that altar, bright and extraordinarily well defined women traded their freedom for security.

7

My mother, Mary Clifford Caperton, was born in Richmond, Virginia, in 1904. She was the fifth child, following Arthur, Rose, Helena, and Sarah and followed by Harriette and Melinda. She was in many ways different from her sisters, more complex perhaps—certainly more cerebral.

Munda's six "girls" were educated at Miss Jenny Ellett's School in Richmond; two went away to boarding school, but they hated it and insisted on returning. Far more important than formal education, however, were the lessons in charm, self-discipline, and deportment they received at their mother's knee. She could be fierce even in old age in her battle to preserve the decencies. Her daughters learned early to be gracious, correct, and charming in all situations; they also showed small signs of independent spirit. Munda did not tolerate lapses in decorum. She once sent word to a Richmond movie theater to which Harriette had repaired wearing a pair of stockings borrowed without permission from a sister. The manager made an announcement over the public-address system, and the culprit hastened home to make amends.

Sets of anything evoke sentimental appreciation; this set of small blond Caperton girls was much admired when they made their appearance as debutantes in Richmond society. Their fates, however, were uncertain. The eldest, Rose, suffered through years of marriage to an alcoholic, raised five children, survived tragedy, and finally remarried.

Rose did not seem able to lay aside the partygoing propensities which had been the meat and marrow of her younger life. (Munda, in fact, noted approvingly that none of her girls "settled down" when they were married.) When, at seventeen, Mother announced that she wanted to go to Radcliffe instead of making her debut like her sisters, she was perhaps responding to what she had witnessed in Rose's early marriage, which was the first dramatic proof that the story was not ended when the girl was "given" by her reluctant father to another man.

Munda knew how to turn her talents to the family's advantage: she "ground out" many articles for *The Ladies' Home Journal* and other women's magazines, mixing romantic fiction with practical advice. She made enough money off her endeavors to help pay the bills, but at one point she went a step further: she took a job as hostess at a big new hotel in Richmond, using her tact and charm to provide guests with introductions that often inspired them to lengthen their stay. Rather uneasily, she noted that some of these new friends did not know she was being paid for her service. In fact, the energetic and pragmatic woman who had known so much hardship in her married life was, once again, saving the situation, using the skills she had learned in her grandfather's guest-filled house. Although she felt some scorn for the "Babbitt families" of the newly wealthy, she found something to like even there, and recounted with humor that one woman, threatened with a trip abroad, asked fearfully, "Is Europe hilly?"

If her expectations for me, many years later, were at all like her expectations for my mother, her "Star of the Sea," then a sketch Munda wrote about a visit to the Place in July 1937 indicates that we were both repositories for her sizable ambition. Although I was only six months old at the time, Munda created in her story a thirteen-year-old "beauty" with masterful charm and a sense of ruthless purpose who sneaked out at night to appear as Jean Harlow at a variety show, dressed in her mother's skintight white satin gown.

After Rose in the line of sisters came Helena, my favorite aunt, who lived for a while with William Lee Lyons, her husband, whom we called Uncle Billy, in an apartment in the Louisville Country Club and then in a series of charming flower-filled houses outside of Louisville. She was the soul of kindness to me.

Aunt Helena had no children; she was an excellent tennis player; she wore beautiful pastel linen dresses with her monogram on the breast, and carried matching linen bags, also monogrammed. Everything about her seemed quiet and kind and elegant. We seldom talked, or needed to. She had preserved some of the spontaneity and verve of her childhood, hidden under a careful veneer; she finally broke her hip in her seventies playing a furious game of tennis. She remarked with humor that the ambulance attendants carrying her away from the field of battle said, "It's some old fool, playing tennis . . ."

Uncle Billy created ripples on the smooth Bingham family surface. He was a self-confident man who had made a fortune before he married Helena; he had first appeared, like his Irish grandfather-in-law, driving a striking pair of horses. Like most of the well-off men of his generation, he was an outspoken racist who enjoyed venting his opinions at his brother-in-law's dinner table. As a small child, I was fascinated by the silences and awkward attempts at distraction that attended his pronouncements at Sunday lunches and holiday feasts.

Finally, one Christmas Eve in the late forties, Uncle Billy went "too far." We were celebrating Mother's birthday, as usual, with family dinner and a play for which I was responsible. Before the play, however, Uncle Billy insisted on reading a poem, based on "The Night before Christmas," which contained references to "kikes," a term I had never before heard. A great smoldering silence ensued. Uncle Billy was never invited to Christmas Eve dinner again.

I was proud of Father for refusing to tolerate Uncle Billy's genial anti-Semitism, an accepted part of upper-class Louisville life. Yet I sensed another motivation. Uncle Billy was simply too loud. He talked too much, and with irrepressible conviction. No one else dared bellow at Father's dinner table, interrupting more decorous voices with his coarse bray. It seemed to me that Uncle Billy's noxious prejudices were perhaps less unbearable than his defiant self-confidence.

Aunt Helena and Uncle Billy were the only married couple I knew who fought, loudly, even ostentatiously. I always believed that Aunt Helena, who was a foot shorter and a hundred pounds lighter than her husband, held her own in these verbal fracases. But I drew the line at Uncle Billy's discussion of their childlessness, which he blamed on my beloved aunt, proclaiming in stentorian tones that he was a "proven sire." He had been married before and had fathered two daughters.

Mother's immediately older sister was my godmother, Sarah, who lived in New York with her husband, Thomas Roderick Dew. I loved his name, and bestowed it on a pet canary Uncle Tom gave me when I was quite small; it seemed an eponymous name for a singer. When a rat killed Tom Dew in his cage, I was outraged. I could see in my mind's eye the fat black rat climbing the long stalk on which the cage hung, squeezing himself through the flimsy bars and cornering the terrified puff of feathers.

Like my canary, Aunt Sarah was ultimately a sad figure. She had one son, a redheaded boy, Roderick, whom I never knew well. Instead my attention was fixed on the relationship between his parents. Mysterious currents of rage ran between them; mysterious silences developed when we had lunch in New York. Even their carefully kept apartment on Park Avenue, the first city apartment I ever saw, seemed to hum with suppressed resentment. What its causes were, I never knew, and perhaps neither did they. They died together, crushed, I was told, by a falling kitchen cabinet. This death seemed to me as unlikely and as tragic as Aunt Sarah's life.

Next came Harriette of the long blond hair, a dancer whose humor and charm delighted me. She, too, had an only son, and a complex relationship with her husband, a handsome Scotsman I admired because he had read Colette in French. Something about him, however, offended my parents—perhaps it was that he had pretensions to a Scottish tartan. He was imperturbable, handsome, aloof, removed, it seemed to me, from the war raging around him. "They" said he scorned his wife's dancing and made fun of her one fling. But then "they" did not like this man who would not dip into the boiling cauldron of family politics. Perhaps after all he simply didn't care.

Youngest and cheeriest, Aunt Melinda was as pretty as her name. The humor and gaiety that was so striking in the blond Caperton sisters when they were young seemed to last longest in her, in spite of a difficult marriage. She married into a Virginia family, the Pages, with a lineage that awed even Munda. Thomas Nelson Page had written novels of Southern plantation life, such as *Two Little Confederates,* which had enjoyed a vogue in the early twentieth century. The novels were set on the Page family plantation, Oakland, outside of Richmond.

As a child, I listened to *Two Little Confederates* with delight, identifying easily with the brave little boys who watched the Union and Confederate armies pass by and through their home, and who were tended by loving and beloved black slaves. I longed to be as confident and as "manly" as those long-lost brothers of the Old South. Years later, I began to wonder about Page's point of view, and I was not entirely surprised when I read that "the greatest enemy of the late confederacy was certainly not Ulysses S. Grant, or even William T. Sherman. . . . Far more lasting damage was done it by men whom the south adores: at the head of the list Stephen Collins Foster. . . . Deceivers of the same kind were orators of Henry Grady's school and a long procession of literary gents beginning with John Pendleton Kennedy and culminating in Thomas Nelson Page."

Indeed, Page's influence on my family, although seemingly of small importance—by the 1920s he had been discredited as the school of literary realism arose—was actually profound. Page absolved Southerners like the Capertons and the Binghams of all guilt for their treatment of their black servants and slaves by creating a stereotyped happy old retainer.

He also introduced black dialect, now almost unreadable, into his stories. In purloining the speech of ex-slaves, Page and his ilk ignored the great majority of people in the South, the poor whites and tenant farmers who made up the bulk of the population, although they were seldom represented in state legislatures or in Washington. As Page ignored poor whites in the South, he ignored women who were individuals in their own right; he could not write about black women at all, and his white women never lived long, remaining as sickly as the romantic dream they represented.

Page's imagination was crippled by the Southern myth he was determined to justify, and he influenced a later generation of popular writers, especially Margaret Mitchell, whom my grandfather the Judge called "the greatest American writer that had ever lived."

I visited Oakland, site of *Two Little Confederates,* once, as a small child. I was enchanted by the bustle of life there—my three lively cousins vibrating inside their small house, the older relatives hidden away in the big house, the field of watermelons, and the constant activities of animals. Uncle Robert Page, Melinda's husband, in an act of kindness that amazed me, gave me a toy broom with a red handle, with which I vigorously swept the porch. Why the gift should have created such an impression, I do not know; perhaps it was because I had done nothing to earn it. Perhaps it was the smiling boyish face of this uncle, who, like all his brothers-in-law, was remarkably handsome, at least when I first knew him, before life began to exact its toll.

It seemed to me as a child that Mother's sisters had nothing to do. Their families were small; there was money for domestic help. There was no need or call for them to do more than generously and elaborately "entertain." But what in the end is the satisfaction for a woman who has spent days planning a dinner party? The results are so thin: kind thanks, friendly smiles, a boost to her husband's career, and a black woman in the kitchen wearily washing dishes. My mother's sisters, like my mother herself, seemed designed for something else, a role closer to the romantic and dangerous roles of the women in Munda's stories, who kicked their lovers in the mouth or chose the dashing pirate rather than the correct fiancé.

When they married, these six young women made the single most important decision of their lives. It was in fact their first and last decision, for it defined their roles as wives to well-off men of some charm. Their mother would never have tolerated a hint of scandal, or any talk of divorce; none of the marriages broke up before Munda's death, although two ended in divorce after she was gone.

Mother sometimes described the rigid social conventions of her childhood that excluded everyone who engaged in "trade." Once the sisters had been invited, as small children, to a party given by a Richmond candy king where there would be spun-sugar centerpieces and baskets of bonbons. The girls were not allowed to go. The candy king was "in trade."

The same rigid concern for the proprieties governed whom the girls could see during the precarious years between their "coming-out" parties (which their grandmother had called turning-out parties) and their marriages.

One daughter was pursued by a young man of whom Munda did not approve. When he came to the door to pick up his particular sister, he was met instead by her formidable mother. His heart must have quaked within him; although she was scarcely more than five feet tall, Munda had a majestic carriage, a solidness that seemed both physical and moral. When she planted her small feet, she took a stand that few would challenge. She told the young man to leave and never to call again.

As she told me, he gasped and grew pale. "What have I done, Mrs. Caperton?"

"You've done nothing," she replied. "But I don't know your people."

My mother, Mary, decided early that she did not belong in the blossom bunch of her partygoing sisters. She was a serious girl and a fine student. Through the influence of a teacher, she became interested in going away to college. Her grandmother's preoccupation with Latin and Greek, especially the symbolic search for the "roots" of words, took its own root in Mother's ambitions; she wanted to be a Greek scholar, a classicist, in the time-honored English tradition of the bluestocking, the brilliant, achieving, solitary woman. Certainly she had the necessary tools, the mind and the self-discipline, as well as her sisters' beauty and charm.

Munda expected all her daughters to be well read, at least in the English classics; she expected them to write a fine hand and to have some awareness of history. Beyond that lay the strange land of intellectual development where, as all Southerners know, students may begin to question the very truths on which they were raised.

Mother was not to be deterred. As a child, I felt the heat of her intense intellectual energy. It never surprised me that she had made her way out of the South in the 1920s; it never surprised me that she had obtained a scholarship to Radcliffe. It seemed to me that Mother could do anything she set out to do, especially if it involved books. Later I used to examine her college texts, interleaved with tissue-thin pages of notes. By then I could imagine the struggle she must have waged to prepare herself in that noisy, sociable family. As I grew older, I found Mother most sympathetic, most easily understood, in terms of her passionate interest in the Greek classics— her ability to translate a phrase of Greek (for example, "the tears of things") and relate it to present reality.

She told me a few stories about her escape from Richmond in 1924. A year earlier, she had moved out of the family house to stay with her teacher.

She moved out, she said, because it was impossible to study at home, with the endless in-and-out of partying girls. "There was nothing in the icebox but flowers," she would say, charmed, in spite of herself, by the memory of those five blond sisters, their suitors, their dramas, their dance dresses, their apparently gilded fate. She had chosen a harder path.

When Mother left for Cambridge in 1924, Munda was relieved. Her attention was taken up with the trials of marrying off the older girls and grooming the younger for their turns. Perhaps it was a consolation to have one daughter temporarily settled, in the grave atmosphere of the old Eastern university. Perhaps Munda, whose own mind was so sharp, whose curiosity was so wide, may even have been proud.

Mother seldom talked about her four years at college. Her memories had been obscured by the shine of her romance with Father, whom she had met almost at once. I extrapolated something from the quality of her reserve: those four years had changed everything. It could not have been easy for a quiet Southern girl to make her way in a university where male faculty left Harvard Yard every day to lecture their women students at Radcliffe. Cambridge was a lonely place for a Southern girl who knew only that she wanted to learn. Mother never mentioned the friends she had made there. However, she did talk, reverently, of several of her professors—the old Greek scholar at whose feet she had sat and the Shakespeare professor who had opened her mind to the beauties of the plays. She also took part in some undergraduate theatricals, where, in a play called *The Love of Three Oranges,* she first met Father. He helped her out of an orange shell.

Mother found at Harvard the perfect husband Munda could never have produced in Richmond. Southern gentlemen after the Civil War tended to be poor; the men who were wealthy had earned their money in dubious ways. At Harvard, Mother found a suitor who combined wealth and prestige, looks and charm, to a greater degree than any of his brothers-in-law. At their elaborate wedding in 1931 Munda must have been delighted.

Munda was not overly impressed, however, by the sudden prosperity of the Bingham family, which had begun just fourteen years earlier with Mary Lily Kenan Bingham's death. Munda knew she could not afford to buy the wedding silver that was traditionally the bride's mother's gift, but she did not hesitate to ask the groom's father, Judge Bingham, to buy the silver for her. It seemed an extraordinary story when she told me, and I was not sure whether or not Munda had invented it. However, invention or no, the tale told me something about the Richmond firebrand's refusal to be intimidated by her Kentucky relatives, even by the Judge, then at the height of his career as press lord in Kentucky.

Munda knew what counted in a family, and it was breeding, not money. In terms of breeding, the Virginia Capertons and Montagues and Lefroys had a good deal more to offer than the North Carolina Binghams. The knowledge stayed with Munda, and her self-confidence seemed to strain her relationship with her handsome new son-in-law. Munda was not to be intimidated by displays of wealth and power. In the Big House in Kentucky, Munda always held her own, even in old age, when she galvanized a large dinner party by suddenly calling out, in the middle of other conversations, "I don't care what you say, it's nothing but sex."

Before her marriage, Mother had worked for a time in publishing. She had also won a scholarship to study at the American Academy in Athens. It was a great honor and a great opportunity for a woman who had majored in classics, who was at home in both Greek and Latin. She left for Athens sometime after graduating from Radcliffe in 1928, planning to spend a semester there before going back to Richmond for a sister's wedding.

Athens was cold and gray that winter, and she found herself isolated at the academy by her liberal political views. Al Smith was running for President back home, and Mother espoused his cause. The faculty and students did not see things her way and some iciness interfered with the development of friendships.

The archaeology in which she was engaged, too, was not very rewarding; scratching about in the dust for shards, under the supervision of a cranky old scholar, did not hold many charms as the warm weather changed to cold and drizzle.

Father decided to go to Greece to escort Mother home for her sister's wedding, taking along as chaperone his lifetime friend Edie Callahan.

Edie's closeness to Father depended to a large degree on shared jokes. In a shorthand which reminded me of the kitchen shorthand at the Big House, they discussed various cousins, in-laws, and step-relations. A word would do it, a glance, a shrug, and my father's hearty laugh. Edie understood everything. She also adored my father.

A small woman enshrined in turbans and deafness by the time I knew her, Edie never married; her life was spent caring for her mother, playing the piano, and waiting to see Father. It was one of those delicately complex relationships that would never have endured the bright light of analysis. She was obviously the right chaperone to choose for the trip to Greece: one who would never intrude, would show no jealousy, and would contribute to the lighthearted gaiety which Father so much enjoyed—which, in fact, he required.

No one ever said exactly what happened in Athens. Perhaps there was a tearful reunion, although it is hard to imagine; perhaps Mother recounted her difficulties in her new surroundings; perhaps Father exaggerated her discomfort. In any event, they returned to the United States together, on a stormy winter crossing where the ship's orchestra often played to a deserted dining room.

Once or twice, someone in the family joked about the night my mother went up to the orchestra, sawing away to emptiness, and asked if she could play the violin. Apparently she had studied the violin as a young girl, although I never heard her mention it.

Perhaps she and Father and Edie had been drinking champagne, said to be a cure for seasickness; perhaps she was exhilarated at the prospect of the life opening in front of her even as another life closed behind. It is hard to imagine a woman who in later life valued circumspection so highly making a conspicuous display of herself. But she did. Imagining the scene, I remember how, very rarely, her cheeks would flush with merriment, or she would snap out a blazing criticism, rejoicing in the strength of words. Perhaps the same bright flush climbed her face as she took the borrowed violin and placed it under her chin.

"Sawing and screeching . . ."

That is hard to imagine. Everything my mother did was done perfectly.

Yet "sawing and screeching . . ." It is Father who speaks. He mimics, with dancing eyes, the violin propped under the chin, the precise, ridiculous arrangement of the hands.

Later someone said there was an old violin in the attic at the Big House, but I never saw it.

8

The antecedents of that marriage lay in a different place and a different time, when the eldest son of a family of Irish Presbyterians emigrated to the United States from Dromore, County Down, in Northern Ireland, just before the end of the eighteenth century.

Time has burnished the account of the original Reverend William Bingham's pilgrimage to the land of opportunity. He was the eldest son of James Bingham, an Ulster farmer who died young. James's great-great-grandmother, Cecily Martin, provided a link to the English de Binghams of Dorset that would be treasured by later generations. She was the first of many women to elevate the Binghams' status.

James Bingham's sons and his brothers belonged to the order of United Irishmen, organized by Wolfe Tone in Belfast in 1791. Tone's group united both Protestants and Catholics against English rule, "an improbable and remarkable amalgamation," according to one history.

Wolfe Tone set out for Paris in January 1796 to solicit help from the French (whose revolution had inspired the Irish), but the fleet of ships he assembled broke up in fog off the Irish coast. This failed insurrection led to the British reprisals that shook Protestant Ireland in 1798.

During this period, William Bingham, James's eldest son, perhaps foreseeing a future of endless trouble for Irish rebels, set sail for the United States. His uncles and brother had already left, one sealed up in a hogshead to escape the English soldiers. William may have lingered because, as eldest son, he would by the law of primogeniture inherit his father's farm and would get a classical education. Neither opportunity worked out as expected. He did not graduate from the University of Glasgow, where he had enrolled in 1774, nor did he inherit his father's farm, coming, like so many others, penniless to the New World. An obsession with inheritance would mark his male descendants for generations to come.

William left Ireland after meeting a group of men from Cape Fear in

North Carolina who offered him a position in a school there. His Atlantic crossing was rough, his landing was delayed, and when at last he set foot ashore, he was horrified to learn that through miscalculation or chicanery, he had been set down in Wilmington, Delaware, rather than Wilmington, North Carolina. With the determination that would drive his descendants, he set out to walk the Great Wagon Road, which ran through Delaware, Maryland, Virginia, and North Carolina.

As he walked, William's stick picked up something that flashed in the dust. It was a ring, set with a diamond. William sold the ring at the next village and bought himself a seat in a coach for the rest of the journey.

Family stories always contain an element of exaggeration. However, the diamond ring is harder to choke down than most of the embellished details. William may have fallen in with thieves; he may have been a reluctant witness to a murder; or perhaps he was given the ring as reward for a service he later wished to forget. His male descendants often saw their fortunes rise because of a rich woman: perhaps the diamond ring was the first fruit of those successful enterprises.

In the lost iconography of the Bingham women, the diamond ring occupies a special place. Symbol of engagement in recent times, it had no such connotation in the eighteenth century, yet when the story was repeated during the following one hundred and fifty years, wives and daughters must have made the association: love and money; money and love. The savage twins could not be separated; the diamond ring sealed their union.

William's sons' and grandsons' determination to accept the story of the windfall ring at face value marked their characters. It is better, according to this way of thinking, to accept a fact that seems dubious rather than to upset the mythology with awkward questions.

Eventually William arrived in Wilmington, North Carolina, a bustling little coastal town, to find that his post at the school had already been filled. However, he gave a Masonic sign while drinking a glass of water and was recognized as a member of that secret society. He was hired as a tutor in a private family until the head of the academy resigned, whereupon he took over the position.

His male descendants all belonged to secret societies, whether the Masons, the Ku Klux Klan, or the more informal group of powerful political supporters and secret agents.

For ambitious newcomers in a raw country where there were few clear avenues to advancement, membership in secret societies was perhaps more important in the struggle for wealth and power than political or religious convictions. The secret societies, of course, offered no places for women.

In 1799, William joined an even larger secret society when he made a highly advantageous marriage. His wife, Anna or Annie Jean Slingsby, was the only surviving child and therefore heir to Colonel John Slingsby, an officer in the British Army who had fought during the Revolution. Annie Jean inherited from her father an estate twelve miles outside of London called the Beverly Farm.

His wife's inheritance apparently caused William some consternation, according to one of his descendants, my grandfather the Judge, who had reason to understand William's hesitation: "The title to the property was unquestioned, and all that was necessary to secure great wealth was a voyage to England; but the anxieties inseparable from leaving their children and business for at least six months, if not longer, the dangers of a sea voyage, and the fear of ruining their children should they become rich, so oppressed husband and wife that they made a bonfire of the papers, and 'The Beverly Farm,' which is now part of the City of London, passed away from them and their heirs forever."

No one recorded Annie Jean's reaction to the destruction of her inheritance, if in fact it took place. But the Binghams' connection with the English, represented by Colonel Slingsby, did not burn in the blaze. The family always stressed its English and Scotch connections rather than its primitive and primal Irish root. In colonial North Carolina, the settlers who achieved prominence were most often of Scotch descent, like the men from Cape Fear, or James Hogg, a distant relative, who financed the exploration of Kentucky.

The little school at Wilmington prospered under William's leadership; for a while a school for girls was also offered. Annie would certainly have been in charge of the physical care of the pupils, the family, and its few slaves. She cooked and preserved, washed, ironed, mended, and provided medical care. Her nursing skill was especially important in an era when so many children died, both in the headmaster's house and in the school.

William soon moved the school from Wilmington to Pittsboro, in the higher, drier piedmont section of North Carolina, the first of many moves that would bring the headmaster and his school into the orbit of the recently founded University of North Carolina at Chapel Hill.

In the early 1800s, William was a professor of classics at the university, but soon returned to his own school because he found his students so badly prepared. He may also have encountered problems with the Kenans of Kenansville, North Carolina, who along with James Hogg were founders of the university. The conflict was the first phase in the Binghams' long rivalry with more powerful neighbors and relatives.

The Bingham School at Pittsboro, Hillsboro, Mount Repose, Oaks, and Mebane was a modest proposition, easily moved from place to place, entirely dependent for its success on the character and reputation of its headmaster. William taught Latin and Greek as the foundations for a gentleman's education. Henry James described such a school in *Sketches for the North American Review.* "The stock in trade required . . . is very slight. The education of others is the last recourse when all other means of livelihood have failed." It was a trade that reinforced certain characteristics in the Bingham men: gentility, genial charm, social connections, and an ability to rule adolescent boys.

The school also created a role for five generations of headmasters' wives, which they pursued with greater or less enthusiasm according to their temperaments, but always with unremitting toil. Certainly there were two or three slaves to help with the daily work, but no one except the mistress could devise the menus, make the invalids' broth, put up food for winter, cut out clothes, or make the soap for the weekly washday.

In addition to physical labor, the headmaster's wife was responsible for the students' health; she may have been aware of their emotional health as well. Homesick boys would have looked to her for comfort, and her sympathy might have caused the strife which lay concealed behind the period's disagreements on pedagogy.

Small boys were often taught by women who used love and praise as inducement to learn: the teacher would "stoop over and kiss me, on my low seat, when I was successful, and very pleasant were her 'good words' to my ear," according to a contemporary account. Later at a "man-school" the boys were taught with threats of physical violence as part of the "hardening process" that would make them "manly" and violence-prone themselves.

Like all the Bingham men, William was short, but he was a commanding presence both in and out of the schoolroom. He was described by a contemporary as "a terror to evil doers and a praise and glory to those who did well." An elder in the Presbyterian church, William taught the faith in hard work, self-discipline, and predestination that would have its most famous disciple in Woodrow Wilson. William died in 1826, having run the school for thirty-two years.

Immediately after his death, his widow, Annie Jean Slingsby Bingham, moved to Tennessee with all of her children except her eldest son, William II, who took over the school. Perhaps the first war for the succession began and ended in the months following the first William's death, before Annie Jean disappeared into a long life of bad health and meager resources in Tennessee.

In her will, Annie left everything to her surviving children and grandchildren in Tennessee. "To my son W. J. Bingham" (then running the school in North Carolina) "I do not leave anything as I well know his generous nature would not let him accept of it while his sisters and his brothers are so scantily provided for." In addition to "my Negro woman Caty and man

Cupid and Cupid's son, Virgil," Annie Jean left her Tennessee descendants "the profile of their dear Father," his Greek Testament, and "the little plate I have." Nothing else remained of the estate she had inherited from her father, the British colonel.

William II was as small and as determined as his father; he was known as "the Napoleon of Schoolmasters." At a young age, he married Eliza Alves Norwood, daughter of a judge; her mother, Robina Hogg, brought a much-cherished connection to the distinguished Hogg family. Robina's cousin was Walter Scott, with whom she had gone to school in Scotland. His novels became family icons.

The connection with James Hogg, co-founder of the Transylvania Company, was cherished for another reason. Hogg went to the legislature to request that his sons' names be changed to their mother's maiden name, Alves. The wish was granted. When asked why he did not have his daughters' names changed, he supposedly replied that if they did not marry, they could remain "damn Hoggs" all their lives. The girls' names were supposed to have been Sheesa, Ima, and Yura.

Of Mrs. Hogg, nothing is remembered except that an old slave, Aunt Polly, said she was called "Miss Papillo." Her maiden name would be carried on in her daughter Eliza Alves Norwood Bingham's family.

After their marriage, William II and Eliza lived with his father, William I, and were described in a contemporary's letter as being "both very young, almost children." Eliza bore seven children, four of whom died young. One died at birth, one at the age of ten, and two more in their mid-thirties, long before their mother's demise.

Slavery was a fact of life for Eliza, as it was for her husband. Like many Southerners of his period, William II lived uncomfortably with the theory of slavery, although he was dependent on the labor of slaves to maintain his way of life.

He belonged to one of the Southern societies that studied remedies for the situation. (Of the 130 abolitionist societies established before 1827, four-fifths were in the South.) In the 1850s, William II offered his children's "black mammy" a trip to Liberia, where he proposed to support her until she became self-sufficient. Not surprisingly, the old woman refused to go, preferring the ills she knew of to exile in an African country. After Nat Turner's rebellion, however, William II, like most slaveholders, no longer questioned the "sacred institution" and bitterly opposed criticism from the North. By 1861, he was a supporter of the Confederacy.

Before Emancipation, the Bingham women lived with ten to fourteen slaves, who took care of the house and the school and raised food for the cadets. While later versions of antebellum life emphasized the good relations between white mistress and house slave, women who left records of their sentiments tended to be bitter if secret critics of the system. The Bingham women, like others of their time and place, felt the oppression of slavery daily, in the constant presence of black people unwilling or unable to do the work they were required to do, in the oppressive atmosphere of latent violence, and in the sexual abuse of women slaves which was the bane of Southern women. Fanny Kemble in her diaries recorded that Southern women were fiercer than Harriet Beecher Stowe in their private denunciations of slavery.

The white mistresses in the Bingham family have disappeared into obscurity along with the black men and women who served them, all devoured by the silence that awaits the powerless. Perhaps one of the strongest secret bonds between these women and their slaves was that sense of powerlessness, of imminent and unavoidable obliteration in the slave graveyards, where wooden crosses soon rotted, and in the white family's plot, where fallen headstones preserve all that is left of the white women: their names, their birth dates, and their death dates.

In addition, for sensitive and intelligent men and women who owned slaves, there was the affliction of loving people whom society degraded. The rules governing relationships between the races left no room for the love a woman might feel for the black woman who raised her or who tended her children, or the affection which a white man might feel for his boyhood companion. As Lillian Smith wrote in *Killers of the Dream,* "The mother who taught me what I know of tenderness and love and compassion taught me also the bleak rituals of keeping Negroes in their 'place.' The father who rebuked me for an air of superiority towards schoolmates from the mill and rounded out his rebuke by gravely reminding me that 'all men are brothers,' trained me in the steel-rigid decorums I must demand of every colored male. They who so gravely taught me to split my body from my mind and both from my 'soul,' taught me also to split my conscience from my acts and Christianity from the southern tradition."

The attempt to justify slavery after the Civil War made it necessary for women who had noticed its terrible effects to keep silent. As Southern men reconstructed their history, glorying in Thomas Nelson Page's happy slaves, the women who remembered how it had really been rarely set pen to paper. As W. J. Cash explained in *The Mind of the South,* that determination to stamp out the memory of the horrors of slavery led to further attempts to stifle the inquiring mind. Lillian Smith wrote, "We defended the sins and sorrows of three hundred years as if each sin had been committed by us alone and each sorrow had cut across our heart." Cash added, "From the taboo on criticism of slavery, it was but an easy step to interpreting every criticism of the south on whatever score as disloyalty." In general, he went on, "criticism waxes feeble" in the face of these prescriptions, leading to "the savage ideal: whereunder dissent and variety are completely suppressed and men become, in all their attitudes, professions, and actions, virtual replicas of one another." This conformity placed outspoken women in the outer fringe with lunatics and children. In life as in death, these women shared the fringe with their slaves.

As the Bingham School grew larger, the role of the headmaster's wife changed. She no longer helped with the instruction of the boys, which fell to the headmaster's assistants. At the same time, the physical labor of cleaning and feeding increased, and even with the help of slaves, her life must have been extremely hard.

When the Civil War broke out, the current headmaster's wife, unlike many Southern women, did not find herself left in control of the enterprise. Robert, the younger of William II's two surviving sons, went off to join the Confederate Army, but his older brother, William, and their father remained behind to run the school. So the opportunity to prove herself competent to run the family business passed Eliza by, with important consequences for her descendants.

William II died at the close of the Civil War, of a broken heart, it was said. During the war, his older son, William III, consolidated his hold on the school, replacing the former William Bingham and Sons with a partnership that included his brother-in-law Stuart White and his cousin William Bingham Lynch. At the same time, he incorporated the school as a military academy. With this act, the women's roles were decided. They had no official part in the enterprise.

William III was a scholar and a disciplinarian. He received erring students on Saturdays in his study, a small room built onto the end of the family house in Mebane. On the wall hung two straps, which he called Mr. Brown and Mr. Black. The miscreant was allowed to choose which strap he wanted used for his beating, a choice with little meaning since the straps were the same size. The beatings, it was said, were never resented, being preferred to the other form of punishment: time spent in a cooplike building called "Mahogany," too small to lie down in unless one stretched one's feet into a sort of extension.

Eliza Alves must have listened to the boys cry out on Saturdays when her husband was meting out his discipline. She must have seen the same firm hand at work among her seven children. Perhaps, like Louis Gaylord Clark, writing in 1850, she wondered "why it is that parents and guardians do not more frequently and more cordially reciprocate the confidence of children" and use "the law of kindness" rather than the law of force. If she ventured to dissent, however, the record of that dissent is long lost.

In spite of the beatings, the students engaged in pranks that alarmed their neighbors, including burning a small building on the grounds. As a result, the village boardinghouses refused to house the Bingham pupils and William of necessity built barracks on his grounds. Infected by the spirit of the times, the school became increasingly militaristic; now the faculty were all majors.

In 1865, William III dispensed with his two partners, reserving for himself "the original and ultimate right of property in the name of the said school, pertaining to William Bingham as the representative of the name and reputation of the School."

When Robert returned from four years in the Confederate Army, he found that he was no longer on an equal footing with his older brother. Of the two ex-partners, one, William Bingham Lynch, eventually left the enterprise, moving to Florida, where he became superintendent of education in Orange County. Stuart White hung on, and would have a hand in later troubles.

William III had the glow of a brilliant man who would die young. When he graduated in 1856 from the University of North Carolina, he was described as "sedate beyond his years, grave with a tinge of melancholy in his countenance." Stuart White, another fine student, had been his closest friend at the university. Immediately after graduation, William married Stuart's sister Owen.

William III wrote and published texts which were widely used in schools throughout the South. They included *A Grammar of the Latin Language,* Caesar's *Commentaries on the Gallic War, A Grammar of the English Language,* and a *Latin Reader.* He was also a musician and a poet, as well as the headmaster responsible for the school's metamorphosis into a military academy.

In their use of discipline and their establishment of a military hierarchy, William III and Robert were responding to the Southern defeat as well as to the coltishness of male adolescents. During Reconstruction, their memories of lost military glory would ennoble the defeat, and their anger at the work of Northern "agitators" would help them to justify the emergence of the Ku Klux Klan.

The Bingham men were never plantation owners, yet like many other backcountry Southerners, they accepted without question the standards of the tiny plantation aristocracy. Defeat sealed this bond. From now on, the Southern myth reigned, encouraging the development of certain characteristics in the headmasters and their assistants: defensiveness, paramilitary ardor, and a smoldering resentment over the defeat which had robbed them of both political power and the goods of the world. This resentment gradually eroded their earlier Presbyterian piety. Like many dispossessed men in the Reconstruction period, the Bingham men became bitter, avid, and litigious.

Meanwhile the wives and daughters were playing an increasingly peripheral role in the military school. They could not lead cadets in uniform or threaten unruly students with Mr. Brown or Mr. Black. Instead they labored alongside two or three freed slaves or white hired workers, washing the clothes of the fifty or so cadets in the school, preparing the gargantuan meals, and attempting to repress whatever resentment they may have felt because of their endless work and limited influence. The greatest change in the lives of these women came when the village boardinghouses refused to keep the cadets, thrusting their physical care on the Colonel's wife, sisters, and daughters.

Like Woodrow Wilson, William and Robert "shared a Calvinistic belief, held in his day mainly by southern Presbyterians, in predestination—the absolute conviction that God had ordered the universe from the beginning . . . a sure sense of destiny, and a feeling of intimate connection with the sources of power."

This conviction held no place for women who lacked the vote, access to education, or an independent income—only a recent change in the law allowed them to inherit property. It was in the years following the Civil War that the family's defensive stance against women first developed, culminating in the Colonel's speeches against education for women at the turn of the century, and leading to his sons', his grandsons', and his great-grandsons' intransigence on this subject.

Other factors separated the Bingham men from the women. The long fight for possession of the little school in North Carolina which broke out in the 1880s would set brother-in-law against sister-in-law, brother against sister, and father against daughter.

All were reacting to the emergence on the national scene of the "strong-minded woman," whose example incited women to independent thought and action while it exacerbated the defensiveness of men. For the first time women were attending universities, even in the South, and Chapel Hill had admitted a few.

Another and more powerful movement was afoot that would limit the lives of the headmasters' wives and daughters at the military school. New studies in anatomy were revealing the hidden secrets of women's bodies, which were interpreted in a way that would influence opinion about women's ability. The ovaries were said by many doctors to govern every aspect of a woman's life, and puberty and menopause were both considered dangerous periods. A woman passing through these storms at either end of her "useful" reproductive life must guard against taxing intellectual work,

William Bingham
(the Colonel's brother),
who ran the Bingham
School during the
Civil War.

Owen White Bingham,
William's wife.
After her husband's
death, she ran the
school until her brother-
in-law, Colonel Robert
Bingham, filed a
lawsuit against her.

My great-grandfather
Colonel Robert Bingham,
at the Bingham School in
Mebane, North Carolina.
(Note the Bingham
School button.)

Home of the president of the Bingham School, Mebane. During my childhood,
Father's cousins Temple and Martha McKee lived in this house.

The Bingham School, Asheville, North Carolina, 1900.

Owen White Bingham (left) with her music class. She lost the battle
over the Bingham School in Mebane, North Carolina.

The arch that once spanned the entrance to the Bingham School in Mebane. After the school was closed because of lawsuits between the two branches of the family, it became for a time the Bingham Motor Court.

Highway marker near the site of the vanished Bingham School in Mebane.

physical exercise, or excitement; she should lead a restricted life, devoted to cooking, cleaning, and child rearing.

The same imagery which, a few years later, would color the Colonel's speeches on coeducation was invoked to explain the fragility of a woman's temperament: "How sensitive—how tremulous is now her nervous system!" a doctor of the period wrote.

An additional strain was placed on young women when their relationships with their mothers broke down during adolescence. Often this was ascribed to the mothers' inability to explain menstruation to their daughters, leaving them exposed to collapse and despair at the sudden appearance of the menses. Hard as it is to imagine that any physical process could have been hidden in the crowded confines of the Colonel's house, it must be conceded that the often-invoked modesty of the women of the period would have made it nearly impossible to refer to what women a hundred years later were still calling "down there." Yet if the Colonel's wife lost touch with her frightened daughter during this period, a crucial link was broken; only through an empathic understanding of her mother's choices could a daughter learn to seek another way.

When William III, the third headmaster, died in 1873 at the age of thirty-eight, he and Owen White Bingham had four surviving sons who ranged in age from infancy to mid-adolescence. A fifth son, Norwood, had died at the age of a year, but Owen had every reason to expect that she would raise the other four sons, as well as her youngest child, a daughter named Mary Stuart, afterwards called Isabelle. Someday, Owen must have believed, one of her sons would take over the running of their father's school at Mebane.

Perhaps she had even more ambitious aims. She was the first Bingham to educate her daughter, sending her to the Mary Baldwin Seminary in Virginia, where she became an accomplished pianist.

After her husband's death, Owen was left in charge of the school along with her brother-in-law, Colonel Robert Bingham. Together with the formidable job of tending to the cadets, Owen dealt with her brother-in-law's ambitions, already exacerbated by eight years of subservience to his older brother.

The Colonel and Owen set up a partnership of an informal sort, which apparently irritated at least one of them. In 1903, when he was organizing the succession once again, the Colonel wrote his son the Judge, "AS A ONE-MAN-POWER THE SCHOOL HAS SUCCEEDED, in my grandfather's day, in my father's, in my brother's during the war, and in mine. In the quasi partnership between Mrs. Wm. Bingham & myself, she got the money & I got the experience. She SAID that 'SHE furnished the money and I the brains.' "

This uncomfortable arrangement endured from William III's death in 1873 until 1891, with many turbulent episodes along the way.

Much of the turbulence was blamed, years later during the lawsuit that closed the school, on the evil influence of "the White gang." In addition to Owen's brother Stuart, who had been William III's classmate and friend, the "gang" contained Stuart's sister Mary, who, the Colonel threatened later to reveal to a jury, had been incestuously involved with her brother. William Lynch, the other partner, would remember that he and the Colonel "had to combine . . . to run her off the premises for incest."

If Owen discussed this episode with her daughter Mary, the two women might have agreed that incest was easy to understand in a tightly bound family like the Binghams. Traditionally, sons chose their wives from the families of their male friends, initially attracted to a young woman because she shared characteristics of mind or appearance with her brother.

The closest relationships of the period were between men, relationships that were nurtured at boarding schools, sporting events, fraternities, and universities, as well as in the clublike business enterprises of adulthood, where women never appeared. Therefore, when, as in Stuart White's case, his best friend's only sister was not available to him—she had left to be educated in Virginia—he would gravitate toward his own sister, who was part of the tight little circle of daily life. The scorn for outsiders that was such a marked characteristic of the Bingham family would have made it difficult for Stuart to fall in love with a woman who was not "one of us." One of the hideous realities in a family constrained by its own importance is incest, whether overt or repressed. As always, it was the woman who suffered the consequences. Stuart White would stay on at Mebane for ten more years before it was his turn to be expelled.

During this period, Colonel Robert's three surviving children and his sister-in-law Owen's five were growing up together. Robert Worth, my grandfather, later the Judge, carved his initials at child height on the siding of the old house in Mebane while his Aunt Owen cut her name with a diamond on the living-room windowpane. Robert's initials were his father's; Owen's first name was her own. While Robert's initials would be repeated in two succeeding generations, Owen's genderless first name would be replaced by the more familiar Marys and Sadies.

Owen Bingham left no written record. Her brother-in-law, the Colonel, is preserved both through his many actions over a long public life and in his written words.

Colonel Robert Bingham was the first of the Bingham men to appear slightly larger than life. Until then, the men had been backcountry school-teachers and Presbyterian elders. The Colonel moved onto a larger stage. He would become a politician and an orator, a spokesman for the defeated South.

The Colonel's experience during the Civil War set his character and influenced the character of the family and the school he eventually came to dominate.

After being defeated at the South Anna Bridge in 1863, the Colonel was sent to Fort Norfolk, where with sixteen other prisoners he was confined in "a room 17 feet square, with only one window. . . . There was no ceiling, and there was a slate roof over us. We passed the 4th of July, 1863, in this place of torment with a temperature of 140 degrees."

He was then sent to prison on Johnson's Island in Lake Erie. There he kept a diary on minute scraps of papers, which was smuggled home to his young wife, Dell, in North Carolina. In his diary he described the cold and hunger that reduced the prisoners to eating rats. He did not mention the presence in prison of two other Confederate officers from North Carolina, the Kenan brothers, whose ancestor had caused William I trouble at Chapel Hill.

The diary, which he wrote for "Dell" or "wifey," explained the Colonel's feelings when he had surrendered at South Anna Bridge—the event that would become the center of the family's myth. He emphasized the overwhelming Union force he had faced, which meant that he was "firmly convinced that he had no choice but to give in." He especially regretted turning over "a favorite revolver," a gift from his father, which meant more to him than his Confederate sword.

Defeat brought an end to the Colonel's belief in the invincibility of the South; it also affected his religious faith, which he questioned at each report of a Union victory.

When he was threatened with hanging as a reprisal for the execution of Union soldiers in the South, Robert's spirits sank, and the diary entries became "maudlin and melancholy."

At the same time, he was horrified to note that "Yankee women" were watching him and other soldiers as they bathed in a stream: "How different are northern females from ours!" he wrote. "They came out and looked at us, using opera glasses."

Finally the Colonel was saved by an "Angel of Mercy," a "ray of golden sunshine," Miss Linda Tarring.

Miss Tarring had come to Johnson's Island to nurse her wounded fiancé, who eventually died. She stayed on and frequently visited the other prisoners, especially the handsome young captain, Robert Bingham, who was spending his time reading Dickens and making gutta-percha jewelry.

Robert described Miss Tarring as "a beautiful girl of about twenty. . . . She relieved the wants of the needy and had a kind word and a beautiful smile for us all.

"As I was the only gutta percha workman among the prisoners, she came every day to my little work bench and I made trinkets for her . . . inlaying the rings, breastpins, earrings, etc. with Lake Erie shell showing most of the colors of the rainbow. She tried to press money on me; but I declined to receive it."

After almost a year in prison, Robert was finally released, "got to Richmond on the first of May, 1864, and was exchanged in time to be in ten pitched battles during the siege of Richmond and Petersburg. I was struck but once and my skin was not broken, and I had the great honor of being one of General Lee's 7,892 men at Appomattox Court House . . . at the surrender on April 8, 1865."

He did not mention the presence at the surrender of the two Kenan brothers, fellow officers from North Carolina.

Miss Tarring figured in stories my father told about his grandfather's imprisonment. He described her as a beautiful young Quakeress who had fallen in love with the handsome Confederate prisoner. She had brought him a long gray dress and bonnet for the purpose of escaping. In gratitude, he named his first daughter after his savior. In reality, Miss Tarring had to make do with the gutta-percha jewelry; but the image of the beautiful, self-sacrificing "angel" became part of the family mythology.

The Colonel's son Robert, my grandfather the Judge, saw women through a golden haze. Many years later, he wrote Margaret Mitchell, the author of *Gone With the Wind,* "My mother was Melanie to the last emotion, but very beautiful, outside as well as within. Melanie was beautiful, too. Even you must not deny me that. They were saints, both of them, my mother and Melanie."

In her reply, Margaret Mitchell complained that too many readers paid attention to Scarlett—whom the Judge never mentioned.

The Judge remembered another of his father's exploits at the battle of Petersburg, an exploit that was not repeated in the Colonel's official reminiscences: "He was at Petersburg, in command at the point where the explosion which formed the crater came. His men held the breach and killed over two thousand negro troops who had been made drunk and pushed into the crater by white Federal troops behind them. They rolled their bodies to the bottom of the crater, scraped a few inches of dirt over them and held that charnel house against all assaults for six week . . ."

Nearly a hundred years later, walking on the Boston Common, I stopped before the monument commemorating Colonel Robert Shaw and his black volunteers and wondered if these were the men the Colonel had ground under his heel.

Another curious incident from Colonel Bingham's war career was also enshrined in the family mythology. At the end of the war, when his regiment was about to be captured, a soldier took their flag, wrapped it around a stone, and threw it into the Appomattox River. Somehow a large scrap survived and was framed to hang in Father's office, a symbol of the sentimentalized past that would continue to influence the family.

The experience of the Colonel's young wife, Dell, pregnant immediately after their marriage, then bearing a child who died through lack of medical attention, has not been preserved. Dell Worth Bingham left behind only one souvenir of her existence, a letter written to her fiancé, the Colonel, in 1861: "Please accept my thanks for the copy of Reed's Lectures which you have been so kind as to send me. I read the lectures with interest and find it just the thing 'to rest profitably on.' "

After carefully explaining why she will not venture to comment on the lectures, Dell went on: "I can't imagine why you should think that I considered some of your themes 'slightly fanciful if not actually vagarious.' " Language as charm and disguise was already at work in the family as male orators tried out their "themes" on an admiring family audience. Such exhibitions were not for criticism, but for admiration and enthusiastic support. Dell must have been shocked that Robert thought she might have criticized.

Of Dell and Robert's five children, two, the oldest and the youngest boys, would die early, leaving a fateful triangle: two older daughters, Mary Kerr and Sadie Alves, and a younger son, my grandfather, Robert Worth Bingham.

They grew up next door to the school, described in a contemporary account as "a brick building about two hundred yards east of [the headmaster's] house. It has three very comfortable rooms, in a row from east to west, with a long piazza in front, supported by brick columns and extending the length of the building. He has fifty-four boys this session and an assistant who presides over the English department while the Latin-Greek lessons are recited to them."

As for the women: Walter Hines Page, the expatriate North Carolinian who graduated from the Bingham School and later co-founded the publishing house of Doubleday, Page & Co. and was Ambassador to Great Britain during the First World War, described in his "Study of an Old Southern Borough" (1881) the life they led. "Every effort is made to give to the girls all the current accomplishments of the society in which they move. The intellectual training that they receive is indeed insignificant and in the main worthless. They are never trained to think in good earnest, and they learn nothing thoroughly in literature, in art, or in science. The whole structure of society is opposed to their being made able to support themselves."

He went on: "Their home is their entire world. . . . They hear of men achieving wonderful things in learning away somewhere in the big world, which is so far off from their quiet life; they dream at once of a brother's or a son's going to form a part in this wonderful achievement. Thus many brothers and sons are induced to leave their legendary borough." The women, Page concluded sadly, are "virtuous if helpless."

By 1872, William III's health was deteriorating, and he left for warmer climes in hopes of recovery, leaving Robert and Owen in charge. William III died the following year, giving rise to the next war for the succession, which would continue until 1907.

Eliza's account of her brother's relinquishing the school does not fit another account of William's wishes, mentioned only once, in a letter from William Lynch. Lynch referred to the Colonel's promise to his brother to "care for and protect his helpless family"—Owen Bingham and her five young children. The promise would cause the Colonel some anguish during his lawsuit, which closed Owen's school for good. He would stop short, however, of dropping the suit to permit the widow and her children to survive.

In 1873, at the time of William III's death, the Colonel was not able to take over his brother's school. Instead he was obliged to enter into an uneasy alliance with his sister-in-law, Owen, and to countenance the continual presence of her brother Stuart, whose earlier behavior had caused the exile of Mary White. Stuart White was disliked by both the Colonel and William Lynch, who recalled years later that Stuart White was to blame for "the condition of rottenness in the boarding department." Lynch did not wish this "whole stinking concern" to be ventilated at the trial, fearing that it would hurt the Colonel's reputation.

During this period, Owen was raising her five children, expecting that one of her sons would eventually take over his father's school. A series of tragedies in the 1880s ended Owen's dream of continuity, as it would end the same dream in Kentucky a hundred years later.

Owen's son Walter Lenoir died in 1886 at the age of twenty-three of unknown causes. Two years later, another son, Willie, died at thirty-one, also of unknown causes. Her son Ernest was still at the school, but he was a deaf-mute who could have had little hope of taking over as headmaster, even before his brother-in-law attacked him with the chair.

Owen's only other surviving son, Herbert, her youngest, was eighteen in 1891 when his Uncle Robert, the Colonel, made a decision that would have many consequences. Perhaps Robert was sick of the fight with "the White gang"; perhaps he saw in the able and attractive Herbert, about to leave for college at Chapel Hill, a competitor who would win the fight for the school. Time was a-wasting; the Colonel's three surviving children were growing up. His son Robert, my grandfather the Judge, had recently enrolled at Chapel Hill, where he became a mythic hero.

Robert was described by a friend as being "at home anywhere, and I have seen him many times entertain a party of twenty or thirty after a dance and have the full attention of all. A social success always." In addition, Robert had founded yet another secret society, an undergraduate male club called the Order of Gimghouls, housed in an imitation castle. The members, whose rituals were shrouded in secrecy, upheld the ideals of chivalry, with a special emphasis on modesty.

Although he always referred to himself in later life as a member of the "class of 1891" at Chapel Hill, Robert never graduated. He left abruptly in 1890, as his father, the Colonel, was reaching his own decision to leave nearby Mebane.

Robert's reasons for leaving college are shrouded, but it may be that the qualities that led him to be a social success were not precisely the qualities needed to ensure academic achievement. Analysis and criticism would not have come easily to the delightful bon vivant and lady's man. Perhaps, like General Lee's son, who dropped out of Harvard during the same period, Robert found that "for a year at least he was the most popular and prominent man in his class, but then seemed to drop slowly into the background." Like General Lee's son, the Colonel's son Robert was "handsome, genial, with liberal . . . openness toward all he liked, and had also the habit of command . . . The habit of command was not enough."

Life at the Mebane school, with its scheming and private tyrannies, was not conducive to the development of an analytic mind. The children of the Colonel may have learned to grow deaf and mute, like their cousin Ernest, in order to avoid embroilment; but the very quality that saved them from family scuffles affected the development of their minds.

After leaving Chapel Hill, Robert went to the University of Virginia, where he enrolled for a year, leaving in 1891 without a degree. The University of Virginia may have been a more sympathetic setting than Chapel Hill; it was described by one historian as "a sort of fashionable club, propagating dueling, drinking and gambling."

Robert may have been motivated to leave Chapel Hill and the family home in Mebane by his father the Colonel's remarriage.

Dell Worth, who remains hidden from history, had died in 1886 and was buried, with many of her quarrelsome relatives, in the family plot in Oaklawn Cemetery. The date of her husband's remarriage is not recorded; at some time between 1886 and 1890, he married Elvira Woodward, about whom nothing is known, not even her birth or death dates.

His grown children—Mary, Sadie, and Robert—could not stand the stepmother my father always called with a shudder "Grandma Vi." She did not add to the family's luster, bringing a name that was not distinguished, but apparently she had other charms for her fifty-year-old husband.

Her stepchildren's hostility impelled the Colonel to make a decision that would affect them all. In 1891, he left the school at Mebane, moving to Asheville, where he built a far larger and more ambitious version of the Bingham School.

The move could not have been made without a new source of cash, which perhaps came into the family with the hated Elvira. The Colonel was able to buy 250 acres overlooking Asheville and the French Broad River at a time when Asheville was becoming popular as a health resort. The Vanderbilts were constructing their hideous castle, Biltmore, on the other side of the little mountain town, and various sanatoria and elaborate hotels, often serving the same clientele, were rising in the hills.

The one-story brick buildings the Colonel designed were intended to house 146 cadets, a sizable body compared to the 50 or so who had lived at Mebane. The school was not elaborate, except in comparison with its more primitive version in Mebane. There was a parade ground, a swimming lake, and schoolrooms and houses for the faculty, which now included the Colonel's two daughters' husbands, Major Grinnan and Major McKee. On the grounds, the Colonel built a house for himself and his second wife, Elvira, which would provide relief from the intolerable atmosphere in the old house at Mebane.

Thomas Wolfe left a portrait of Elvira in "The Battle of Hogwart Heights," a chapter in his posthumously published collection *The Hills Beyond.* According to a recent biography, *Look Homeward: A Life of Thomas Wolfe,* by David Herbert Donald, this material was not published during Wolfe's lifetime for fear of libel.

In *The Hills Beyond,* Wolfe described a retired Confederate general—a professional apologist for the Lost Cause, a "mummy," as Walter Hines Page called the Confederate officers who set the tone after the Civil War across the South and, as Page felt, impeded progress with their sentimental reverence for the past.

Wolfe implied that the Colonel's second wife was his equal in snobbery. Reigning over her military school on Hogwart Heights outside of Asheville, the imperious Mrs. Joyner, as Wolfe calls her, is the only person in Asheville who snubs Mrs. Willetts, wife of the Northern millionaire who has built a huge castle nearby. Finally Mrs. Willetts (modeled on Mrs. Vanderbilt) is reduced to driving up to Hogwart Heights to call on the only person who has not yet called on her. Mrs. Joyner meets her at the door with frigid politeness, and conversation is scanty until Mrs. Willetts reveals that she has aristocratic relatives in Virginia. Finally Mrs. Joyner melts.

In the same book, Wolfe pictured the son of the Confederate colonel, "Silk" Joyner, as a man who had little use for his father's Southern myth. He is bent on becoming a lawyer and leaving the mountains: "The world had been the mollusk of his desire since childhood."

Wolfe created other characters in his novels who are reminiscent of the Binghams, such as old "Bear" Joyner, whose two marriages had produced a schism in his family. The grown children of Bear's first marriage felt "superior" to their stepmother, who was a "hardshell Baptist."

Wolfe explained: "The Joyners, first to last, were a vainglorious folk. Even old William had his share of the defect." An acquaintance said of this progenitor, "Well, he KNOWED that he was good . . . He was remarkable, but he KNOWED that he was good."

The old man's first wife "was a special woman: she was a Creasman, and the Creasmans were 'good people' "—like Dell's family, the Worths. "She was a good wife, a quiet and hard-working mother, and a Presbyterian. This last fact, trifling as it seems, was all-important: for it bespeaks a kind of denominational snobbishness which is still more prevalent than the world may know, and which the Joyners of the first lot never lost."

Wolfe commented frequently on a characteristic of the large Joyner clan: "Of 'affection,' 'love,' 'devotion,' even 'clannishness'—as these terms are generally accepted—the family seems to have little. It is perfectly true that years have gone by when brothers have not seen or spoken to each other, even when they lived in the same town. It is also true that some have grown rich, indifferent to others who have struggled on in obscure poverty; that children have been born, and grown up, and gone away, scarcely familiar with the look of a cousin's face, the identity of a cousin's name . . . And yet, paradoxically, out of this very separateness came a deep and lasting sense of their own identity."

This coldness appeared in the Bingham family during the two lawsuits that finally divided the Asheville Binghams from their poor relations in central North Carolina.

When the young Confederate captain, later colonel, Robert Bingham returned from Johnson's Island, he had to borrow money from his wife Dell's family, the prosperous mill-owning Worths, to buy a new uniform. During the twenty years following the Civil War, the Worths, who had not suffered as heavily as had the Binghams, helped the Colonel and his children with money and influence.

When Dell's father, Dr. Worth, died in 1900, his will divided his large

estate equally among his eleven grandchildren, with no special gifts for the
Colonel's three children. The Colonel and his son challenged the will in
court, calling on Sadie Grinnan (Robert's sister) to testify that their grandfather had been senile when he wrote the will. Robert suggested that she imply
that other grandchildren had used undue influence to cause the old man to
rewrite an earlier version. Sadie, rebelling for the first and the last time,
refused to go along. The Bingham suit was unsuccessful, and the Worth
money went to all the grandchildren—a defeat the Colonel would remember
for years.

Eleven years later, in 1902, the Colonel wrote Robert a long letter
showing that the bitterness which had divided the family in Mebane had not
been forgotten.

The Colonel denied that he had lost his love for his daughters, Mary
McKee and Sadie, as Robert had implied in a conversation. Robert had
blamed their stepmother, Elvira, for this alienation of affection.

The quarrel, as always, was over inheritance. According to newly written North Carolina law, Elvira would automatically inherit a substantial
interest in the Asheville school at her husband's death as her dower right—
unless the Colonel could be persuaded to write her out of his will.

The Colonel announced that he was prepared to fight over this issue.
His children, he maintained, had no legal or moral claim to the school; in
fact, he would no longer permit them to visit unless they began to treat their
stepmother with conventional courtesy.

He recalled that at Mebane, the house belonged to his three children,
even though he himself controlled more than ninety percent of the stock in
the school—a result, perhaps, of conditions in Dell Worth Bingham's will.
As a result, the Colonel complained, he and Elvira asked for nothing—and
received nothing, except contempt.

With the revision of North Carolina laws on inheritance, however,
Elvira's legal position changed; now, she would inherit thirty-three percent
of the stock in her own home at Asheville, and the Colonel had given her
his proxy for his own sixty-six percent of the stock, leaving her, after his
death, in control of the school. This agreement may have reflected Elvira's
substantial contribution to the building of the school in Asheville.

The Colonel's children continued to treat their stepmother with active
dislike. Finally the Colonel, who had attempted to remain neutral in Mebane, had decided to take his wife's side. After the summer of 1890, he
declared, he became "so full of contempt for myself for my neutrality that
henceforth I will defend her against all comers."

Now, eleven years later, the Colonel was attempting to enlist his son's
support. He wanted to persuade Robert to exercise his considerable influence over his sisters. Sadie Grinnan, according to her father, was easily

swayed, and did not present much of a problem. But Mary Kerr McKee, the Colonel's older daughter, was a different kind of woman, "queenly" and "the danger center." The Colonel wanted the Judge to tell her that if she came to Asheville "under a flag of truce with war in her heart," he was prepared never to see her, or her children, again.

He wrote that turning his back on his daughter and her children would cause him pain, but would be even more harmful to Mary Kerr. She would lose Asheville as an escape from the heat and malaria of central North Carolina at a time when she could not afford a vacation retreat elsewhere. This was a powerful threat, since Mary Kerr's aunt, Owen White Bingham, had already lost one son and would soon lose another to disease in Mebane.

Sadie, who had rebelled only once, did not share equal blame with Mary Kerr for the continual hostilities. As often happens, the daughter who was the more independent was the more feared. Sadie did not side with Mary Kerr in the quarrels; for the rest of her life, she would support Robert and their father. Sadie stood to benefit materially and emotionally from her support of the Bingham men's causes. Perhaps she realized that she would have to sacrifice her relationship with her sister.

The Colonel felt that Mary Kerr's sense of superiority was an innate characteristic, which he had unwittingly encouraged when he made her his companion after her mother's death—a mistake his son Robert would repeat a generation later when his own daughter was left motherless.

Now the Colonel turned to the question of how his one remaining son could control his sisters. He wrote Robert that he could dominate their thinking, either by calming their anxieties or by adding fuel to the fire. The wisest course, he counseled, was to keep Sadie and Mary Kerr in total ignorance of family affairs by never discussing money or inheritance in their presence. Elvira, the Colonel added, was never included in such discussions.

As a reward, the Colonel was prepared to extend his hospitality to his son, but only if Robert's young children were taught to treat their step-grandmother as though she were a "blood grandmother." In that case, the Colonel wrote, Elvira might of her own free will resign her interest in her husband's estate in favor of Robert's son, since Elvira was much occupied with the question of which grandson would take over the school after the Colonel's death.

"YOU can COMMAND a lasting peace and nobody else can," the Colonel wrote, washing his hands of the situation he had created.

Then, growing angry at the thought of his son's unwillingness or failure to command their pesky womenfolk, the Colonel plunged his relationship with Robert and his children into the abyss. As though obeying a higher command, the Colonel wrote that he might be forced to lose the opportunity of seeing his son and his family, should Robert not prevail over his sisters.

Mournfully, the Colonel wrote that he had already lost two sons to early deaths, but that even those tragedies had been less bitter than his daughters' criticism.

"Fecit, et ditum est, et finitum est," the Colonel, son of the Latin scholar, ended his letter.

Perhaps Robert misunderstood the waving of flags, or perhaps he realized that his own financial security was at stake; he took three weeks to respond. He admired and loved his father, who was by now his partner in lawsuits and business ventures and his confidant, and who would become his beneficiary. But to stir the sleeping tigers of dependency in an adult son is always dangerous, and the tone of Robert's eventual reply was not conciliatory. The Colonel's heart must have sunk when he read Robert's references to "your wife." Robert never referred to Elvira as his stepmother.

He expressed amazement that his father wanted to argue, again, about a subject that had been settled long ago. However, Robert was prepared to bargain: if the Colonel would discipline his wife, Robert would coerce his sisters.

Robert refused to accept responsibility for charming Elvira into abandoning her dower rights. He wrote that it had never been known in the history of the world for a woman to give up her interest in an inheritance. Only the Colonel had the ability to persuade or pressure Elvira into assuring for herself a poverty-stricken widowhood.

Robert knew of a way to this end that depended on trickery rather than persuasion. Elvira could be defrauded of her dower rights quickly and easily, he wrote, and the maneuver would not even require her signature.

The Colonel's reply to this extraordinary suggestion has not been preserved, although events after his death, twenty-five years later, indicate that Elvira perhaps fell prey to this scheme.

Elvira's death date and place of burial are not known, nor is there a single scrap of evidence, other than the mention of her name, to prove that she lived. Yet she probably financed her husband's escape from Mebane, and his entry, as head of a large and flourishing military school, into North Carolina politics. For years Elvira was at the eye of the family storm, which then swept her away into oblivion.

She was not the first woman to bring money into the Bingham family. Annie Jean Slingsby, the British colonel's daughter, and Dell Worth, the wealthy mill owner's heir, had already contributed their share. Elvira, not being a first wife, was more completely obliterated than the women who came before her. Later stepmothers would be stripped and canceled in the same way.

Blood, as Southerners like to say, is thicker than water.

During the long period from the building of the Asheville school in 1890 to the Colonel's death in 1927, there is every reason to believe, from her husband's letters, that Elvira devoted herself body and soul to the Colonel's enterprises. She ran the school during his prolonged absences, when he traveled around the state making speeches in support of compulsory education for white males. She took care of the school's enormous correspondence, organized the cadets' routine, supervised the staff, and perhaps even doled out a little affection to the homesick boys. (One of them, the Colonel complained to his son, had been kidnapped from the school by his mother, and another, who was said to have suffered from a brain injury, hanged himself in the barracks.) Yet Elvira's labors left no trace behind. She remained an alien, a non-Bingham, until the end—and her husband, after his brief abandonment of "neutrality," did not protect her from her stepson's schemes.

Many years later, in a letter to his son, the Colonel mentioned visiting "Mother," who was recovering from a nervous breakdown in another state. Perhaps Elvira eventually earned the title, and with it some relief from her stepchildren's hostility. If so, the price she paid was very high.

The Bingham family pattern was set by 1900: a patriarch who loses two of his children early—in two generations, both the eldest and the youngest son—and who projects onto his remaining son all his ambition. Daughters and sisters lose in the endless warfare over money. And mothers, perhaps worn out by the family's contentiousness, die young, having contributed their labor and their inheritance to the family enterprise. They are replaced by despised stepmothers, who contribute even more.

Six years after these letters were written, Robert received a law degree from the University of Louisville, although he had never officially graduated from college. The Colonel and his son would become a formidable team in the hurly-burly of turn-of-the-century life, where rapid industrial growth, a migrating population, and a primitive system of communication would lead to many problems that could perhaps be more efficiently handled in the courts of law than through the older methods of discussion and compromise.

Beneath the struggle for ownership of the school lies the issue of Robert's departure for Louisville in 1896. A few years earlier, he had left the University of Virginia without graduating and had been teaching at his father's school in Mebane. Certainly he was expected eventually to take over the headmastership. Yet unlike four generations of Bingham men before him, Robert set out for the West and never returned. He was the first Bingham heir to leave his father's school rather than run it. Into the vacuum his departure created rushed others who believed themselves heirs: his two sisters, and his widowed aunt and her daughter.

But the Colonel would have none of these would-be inheritors. Being women, they were not Binghams, except for a brief period as unmarried girls, or on sufferance as wives. The essential ingredient in the Bingham character is gender.

After struggles which lasted nearly thirty years, and which left the family in Mebane emotionally and financially exhausted, the Colonel had his way: the old school closed after a court decreed that it could no longer use the Bingham name, which, as the Colonel pointed out, belonged to Owen only through marriage to the long-dead William Bingham. The barracks then became the Bingham Motor Lodge—the Colonel did not object to that use of his name.

The school in Asheville was now the only Bingham school—but the Colonel had no heirs. Robert was installed in Kentucky, and even the Colonel's pleas did not result in his dispatching his eldest son, Robert, back to be raised in Asheville. Sadie Bingham Grinnan had no children, and her sister, Mary Bingham McKee, had three—but only one son. This son, Bingham McKee, was not turning out as the Colonel wished; he was intent on having a good time. Nevertheless, in his will, the Colonel left him a loophole: should he decide to run the school, Bingham McKee must go to the legislature and reverse his names. Nobody but a Bingham could rule at Hogwart Heights.

By the end of his life, the Colonel was embittered in spite of his successes. The most important question, the question of the succession, was not and could not be settled. He dwelt more and more in the imaginary world "before the war," when there were always enough heirs to go around, and none of them rebelled.

"Thinking of a more ancient war, in which he had borne himself gallantly, Colonel James Buchanan Pettigrew, head of the Pedigrew Military Academy (Est. 1789), rode by in his open victoria, behind an old negro driver," Thomas Wolfe wrote in *Look Homeward, Angel.*

"Colonel Pettigrew was wrapped to his waist in a heavy rug, his shoulders were covered with a grey Confederate cape. . . . Muttering, his proud powerful old head turned shakily from side to side, darting fierce splintered glances at the drifting crowd. He was a very parfit gentil knight.

"In the crowd of loafing youngsters that stood across the threshold of Wood's pharmacy, Colonel Pettigrew's darting eyes saw two of his own cadets. They were pimply youths, with slack jaws and a sloppy carriage.

"He muttered in disgust. Not the same! Not the same! Nothing the same! In his proud youth, in the only war that mattered, Colonel Pettigrew had marched at the head of his own cadets. There were 117, sir, all under nineteen. They stepped forward to a man . . . until not a single commissioned officer was left . . . 36 came back . . . since 1789 . . . it must go on! 19, sir—all under one hundred and seventeen . . . must . . . go . . . on!"

A Pettigrew-like determination fueled the Colonel's drive to control the school's future. He wrote Robert, in Louisville, to propose a secret pact, which would defeat the joint stock company that Mary Kerr and Sadie were promoting. According to the Colonel's plan, Robert's son, "my first grandson and namesake," would buy out his cousins after the Colonel's death on terms to be settled by arbitration. If little Robert did not want to exercise this right, it would pass to Mary Kerr's son, Bingham McKee—who would have to reverse his names.

The Colonel added in a postscript that the pact might be considered unfair by some since it favored the only grandson who would be able to buy out his cousins.

Partnership with Sadie and Mary Kerr would have been impossible for the Colonel and his son. In a partnership, value would have to be assigned to the unpaid labor of the two women. In addition, their views would have to be considered, and a degree of flexibility and compromise used to arrive at a consensus. This was an impossible task for two men who believed that women were useful and occasionally charming inferiors to be dominated, for their own good and the good of the whole family, by their male kin. The Colonel sometimes worried that Sadie was exhausted because she took care of sick cadets and often stayed up all night, but her efforts did not mean that she could buy or inherit any part of the enterprise in which she had invested her life.

By now, Robert was the Colonel's last male heir, except for the increasingly discredited Bingham McKee. In 1897, in the foundering old school at Mebane, Herbert Bingham, Owen's last and youngest son, died of typhoid fever at the age of twenty-four. Typhoid was one of the scourges the Colonel had moved to Asheville to escape, and it was the reason the Mebane kin liked to visit Asheville in the summer.

Mary's family was racked by personal tragedies in the years that followed, as well as by economic hardship. One son, Preston's namesake, was thought to be insane, and was kept tied up with a cow chain, according to a neighbor. Another of their large brood, Herbert, cut his throat while shaving in the barracks. The parents became converts to Aimee Semple McPherson's International Church of the Foursquare Gospel, and were devotees of a neighborhood mystic, Sister Scott, who prayed over their afflicted son. Finally, the motor court failed (it had no running water), and the remaining members of the family drifted off to California and disappeared into obscurity.

Many years earlier, the Colonel had visited the Mebane family for the last time, in the midst of his lawsuit, and against Robert's firmly expressed advice. He had been invited to tea, and there had seen four of Mary and

Preston's children. The other two were already in bed. Mary invited her uncle to visit the sleeping babies, and the Colonel, ever sentimental about children, admired them in their cribs.

A note of doubt crept into his description of the scene; was there some way to prevent the ruin of this family? But the Colonel apparently never considered withdrawing his suit. As though the decision rested in other hands, he continued, in partnership with Robert, to press his claims until the old school was closed.

The successful suit against his sister-in-law, his niece, and her children was the first of many collaborations between the Colonel and his son.

9

The Binghams' future in North Carolina ended one day in 1895 when the Colonel's son Robert met a young woman from Louisville, Kentucky, named Eleanor Miller.

Eleanor's father, Samuel, had been sent to Asheville to seek medical help for melancholia and insomnia. During a visit to her father, Eleanor met Robert, perhaps at a social function in one of Asheville's mountain inns or when she went to see the view from the Bingham School. Robert took an instant liking to the attractive twenty-five year-old. He wrote her parents, "With Miss Miller's permission, I write to ask your consent to our engagement, or at least your acquiescence, until I leave to go to Louisville to see you. . . . I have resorted to a letter as the only means of communicating with you at present," since his teaching duties prevented him from leaving the school. Robert said he would discuss his feeling for Eleanor at a later date, when he would also reveal his financial situation.

The letter must have alarmed the Millers, a solidly established family who owned the United States Cast Iron Pipe and Foundry Company in Louisville, with connections to the L & N railroad and other enterprises, and substantial holdings in real estate. Eleanor's brother would become owner of a great estate outside Louisville called Bashford Manor, where he would breed racehorses that would win the Kentucky Derby. At her death in 1922, Eleanor's mother, Henrietta Miller, would leave an estate worth half a million dollars.

Before the issue of Robert's engagement to Eleanor could be resolved, tragedy intervened. In Asheville, Samuel Miller had begun to feel somewhat better; his doctor gave him permission to drive in a carriage with his son and grandson to the train station to meet his daughter. As the train roared into the station, Samuel Miller threw himself on the tracks and was instantly killed, in spite of his son's efforts to save him.

After her father's suicide, Eleanor returned with her mother to Louisville, and her relationship with Robert Bingham seemed for a while to have ended.

Robert was persistent, however. For the young man who had been a minor celebrity at Chapel Hill, life at the Asheville military school, surrounded by his contentious family, must have seemed limited. Eleanor Miller, with her prosperous family, with the opportunities for advancement which the rapidly growing city of Louisville offered, with Samuel Miller's large estate in his widow's hands, must have seemed an attractive proposition. A few months after Miller's suicide, Robert borrowed three hundred dollars and took a train over the mountains to be married.

After their wedding, in May 1896, Eleanor and Robert moved into her mother's comfortable Victorian house in Louisville, where they would live for the next eleven years.

Henrietta Miller and her daughter were close, often reading the same books—*Manon Lescaut, To Have and to Hold*—singing, playing the piano, going to the theater, and entertaining together.

The pattern of Eleanor's life did not change after her marriage. Robert's social life continued to center on his men friends, especially his classmates from Chapel Hill and the University of Virginia.

Hugh Young, who had been one of Robert's classmates in Virginia, recalled in his autobiography that Robert had been "a tall, handsome, dark athlete" who played right end on the Virginia football team.

Young went on to become a surgeon specializing in diseases of the urinary system; he invented several devices and procedures that were useful in treating cancer of the prostate gland, tumors of the bladder, and kidney problems. He was especially interested in what he called "Hermaphroditism: Those unfortunates who have the organs of both sexes."

He was best known for his development of a venereal disease program during the First World War. He was successful at treating syphilis with Salvarsan, produced only in Germany up until 1914 and available in the United States after a submarine bearing a cargo of Salvarsan "dived beneath the British warships guarding the entrance to the Chesapeake and made its way to Baltimore with its cargo."

After the war, Hugh Young practiced at Johns Hopkins Hospital in Baltimore. The Judge made his first appointment there in 1900, four years after his marriage. Thirty-seven years later, he would die at Johns Hopkins of a malady called in the newspaper account "abdominal Hodgkins."

In the intervening period, the Judge would return several times to Johns Hopkins. He would call for Dr. Young when he was named Roosevelt's Ambassador to England, at a time when the Judge's health was particularly fragile. In his autobiography Young described treating his old friend for various unspecified rashes and fevers.

Once, when they were at Pinelands, the Judge's hunting lodge in Georgia, Young wrote that the Judge's rash was so severe he could·not sit on a horse.

The initial uncertainties of Robert's position in his mother-in-law's house in Louisville are suggested in letters written in August 1896, four months after his marriage.

Robert had heard that someone had said that "Bingham is nothing more in Louisville than an ordinary drunkard," and he was fuming. His friends rallied to his support, and he received many letters repudiating the anonymous charge. His college friend W. W. Davies reported loyally that he had heard that Robert "was doing the great club and society act in Louisville," which is perhaps the other side of the coin. The amount of liquor consumed in Louisville was then (as it is now) astonishing, in spite of the efforts of the Women's Christian Temperance Union. The local breweries, just beginning to dominate the scene, peddled their products relentlessly, and no private entertainment could be offered which did not include enormous quantities of bourbon whiskey. Saloons, like clubs, were popular male retreats. Horse racing and gambling were also obsessions in the little world of ambitious lawyers, politicians, and businessmen. That male social world blended easily into the machine-controlled world of local Democratic politics.

The fact that men and women occupied different worlds at the turn of the century helped to preserve the sentimental illusion that wives were in charge of their husbands' spiritual and intellectual development. Robert wrote a friend a few years after his marriage that his wife had elevated his character in both departments, as, he implied, he had expected her to do. Based on the dualism that separated black from white, the damned from the saved, and the whore from the virgin in the antebellum South, this belief allowed husbands a certain amount of freedom, since it was their wives' duty to reform them slowly and gently over a period of time.

A husband was absolved of responsibility for his own behavior and development while his wife was elevated to the role of a domestic priestess, a keeper of the flame. Cookbooks of the period even preached that it was her responsibility to save her husband from alcoholism by tempting him home with nutritious meals.

If Robert was dependent on Eleanor, at least in theory, for his moral development, she was dependent on him for everything else.

At first Eleanor had her own bank account and paid her own bills, but Robert supervised, then took over her finances. In 1900, he wrote his partner asking him to take care of any of her overdrafts. In 1902, he wrote to the bank to close his wife's account, instructing them to send all future correspondence to him. At the same time, he took over his mother-in-law's extensive financial dealings, becoming her lawyer, rent collector, and trustee of a trust set up to receive mortgage payments on her various properties.

Around this period, Robert began to contribute to many local charities, especially the various church-run missions that gave aid to destitute women and blacks. He sought to hire a maid from one such establishment but was turned down. He occasionally sent a check to a charity in his wife's name, and he loaned large and small sums of money to friends who were in need. However, he wrote one such friend that Louisville was a poor place for an ambitious outsider because the people were old-fashioned and preferred old-fashioned ways.

In 1906, Robert composed a drinking song that expressed admiration for the Sultan because he had many wives; the song then extolled the Pope for being able to drink without the harassment of a wife; it concluded by celebrating the state of the single man, content with "my maid" and "Rhenish wine." At the same time, he noted that Babe (Eleanor was called both Babs and Babe) was not able to make her usual summer trip to Asheville because "the worry of preparation and the railroad journey seem to affect her badly and it will not be possible for her to go for a while yet, if at all. Poor Henrietta [their daughter] went under the bed and stayed there for an hour when she found that we were not going."

He added that Babe was "more nervous and more easily fatigued than I have ever known her." Their third and last child, my father, George Barry, had been born in February 1906, four months earlier.

Since she was still living in her mother's house, Babe would have had little authority over the menus, the servants, or the tone of the adults' conversations; instead, she devoted herself to her three small children. Her only surviving letters, tiny notes without dates or salutation, refer to making a costume for her eldest, Robert, the heir, and going to the theater with friends to see a production of Shakespeare.

Babe would have had the daily company not only of her mother but of her sisters, cousins, and aunts, who would have provided a highly organized life that revolved around the care of the children, teas, dinners, and cultural events. All of it was shaped by others; Babe remained, to some extent, a daughter in her mother's household, dependent on her husband and her family for money and for direction.

In return for her helplessness, Eleanor could count on the devoted support and admiration of her often absent husband. When a streetcar conductor refused to help Babe and her children off at their stop, Robert wrote furious letters to the company, intimating that he would have liked to settle the matter with a duel. The rewards of dependency in that time and place were conspicuous, and Babe may never have wondered why she had so little control over her life, or why her name, which had once been a queen's, had been reduced to an affectionate but demeaning nickname.

In 1899, Robert was dealing with problems at the Union Real Estate and Title Company, which he had started with two other men. Eventually one of the partners was bought out and the enterprise folded. Robert had by now obtained his law degree from the University of Louisville. He set up a law firm with his old friend from college W. W. Davies.

Not long after, Dave, as Robert always called him, married his fiancée, a Wyoming woman who showed herself keenly aware of the importance of the friendship between the two men. She insisted in a letter to Robert that she would never come between him and Dave, and profusely excused Dave for breaking an engagement with her because Rob "needed him." She mentioned her "constant dread that I should be the odd number in the circle," and pleaded with Robert not to judge her too harshly when they met. Later she complained that Dave had left her "a widow" for three days as soon as they returned from their wedding trip.

At the turn of the century, Louisville was entering a period of expansion as the largest tobacco market in the world, set on the banks of the Ohio River, a major trade route. The city was well served by the railroads, whose political favors were eagerly sought. A big hotel was being built and the first brewery was incorporated. The politics of the city were dominated by graft, with a thousand patronage jobs on the city payroll, which included all of the city's police officers. The Democratic machine was firmly in control.

When the Democrats ran for election in 1905, they were opposed for the first time by a reform slate called the Fusion ticket, made up of Republicans and some Democrats who were disgusted with the state of affairs. Joseph T. O'Neal was the Fusion candidate for mayor.

Mayhem broke out at the polls as the Democrats attempted to control the election, bringing in "repeaters" who were registered over and over, beating up voters, and stuffing ballot boxes. The Republicans replied by arming themselves with two hundred stout hickory walking sticks. According to a news story, the police beat up "leading professional men of the city" who were attempting to restore order, but apparently they did not attack Robert Bingham. He wrote to his father, the Colonel, "I was able to stop disturbances at three places today and I have got to stay and try to prevent any evil consequences from today's disturbances." He had been elected county attorney in 1903, a position, he wrote his father, which "will keep me constantly before the public" while not seriously interfering with his work as a lawyer.

Robert and his father had begun a long, shared involvement in investments which would bind them closer over the years. In 1899, the Colonel wrote to ask his son "to put me in on the ground floor in some investment that w'd be safe and that w'd bring returns," such as the Millers' pipe and foundry company. Robert was glad to comply, and for years afterwards their frequent letters dealt with the ups and downs of their stock. They also owned stock in a Kentucky zinc mine, which was less profitable.

A life combining politics and the law in a violence-prone, corrupt Midwestern city apparently convinced Robert to carry arms. Whenever he traveled, he carried a loaded pistol, which he occasionally left on the train. Robert sent his father a rifle with elaborate instructions on its use, adding, "I hope you will never need it, but if you do you will find this the best rifle for the purpose."

The violence surrounding the 1905 elections was not unusual for the time and place. The Democratic ticket won but the Fusion party challenged the election, and in 1907 the Kentucky Court of Appeals reversed an earlier decision and declared the election null and void. Newly elected Mayor Paul Barth committed suicide; I heard as a child that the last straw was a story in the *Courier-Journal* blaming him for feeding his horse at the public's expense.

The governor of Kentucky appointed Robert Worth Bingham to succeed Mayor Barth. The shrewdness that had served Robert so well during the family wars in North Carolina was to prove equally useful in the labyrinth of Kentucky politics. He called himself a Progressive Democrat. During his few months as mayor—he did not run for an elected term—Robert closed saloons and whorehouses in Louisville.

His interest in the question of prostitution was echoed in the work of another Louisvillian, the medical authority Abraham Flexner. In his autobiography, Flexner wrote that he had been asked by John D. Rockefeller in 1911 to study prostitution in Europe in order to make recommendations to a special grand jury studying New York prostitution and its connection with the police and organized crime.

In England, France, and Scandinavia, Flexner worked at night, interviewing streetwalkers. Flexner realized that the issue of prostitution was closely tied to middle-class marriage, as feminists had been insisting since the middle of the nineteenth century. Both were forms of economic exchange; both were examples of male dominance.

Mayor Bingham's brief campaign to end prostitution in Louisville may have been inspired by his sense of conflict. He accepted, as men of his time and class usually did, a dualism that condemned wives—the "Angels in the

House"—to frigidity, leaving lower-class women to carry the burden of the sensuality that intrigued and horrified middle-class men.

He would have had to believe, at that particular point, that venereal disease and sexual license were limited to the lower class.

Plagued for the past seven years by unexplained rashes and fevers, he would not have been able to take a Wassermann test—the first reliable test for syphilis—until 1906, when it was first developed. If he was suffering from the disease, the mayor would have been powerfully motivated to root out its cause: not a wellborn North Carolina lady, with whom he might have had a fling, but the poor black and white women in Louisville's red-light district. He would have had to believe that a chance encounter had caused his own infection, especially as his wife's health began to decline, leading her to visit the Louisville dermatologist Dr. Ravitch.

As mayor, Robert began to develop his gift for oratory at the same time that his father, the Colonel, was launching his speaking career in North Carolina. Robert wrote, "There is considerable difference in phraseology intended to reach the brain through the eye." He shared a rhetorical vocabulary with his father, who, writing to congratulate him on being appointed mayor, noted, "You will have to be a Sir Galahad."

The tendency to hyperbole that was an embellishment of the written language of the two men, father and son, had its counterpart in their temperamental tendency to sentimentality. Robert had been raised in an atmosphere of strenuous piety where the dictates of Presbyterianism were stretched to justify slavery and the rigid caste system of the Southern backcountry. He had been raised to believe that Bingham men were Sir Galahads even when necessity forced them to ride in disguise. In addition, his sense of timing was exact; unlike his father, he did not tie himself to lost political causes but was flexible enough to change when change was demanded. In closing saloons and prosecuting whores, he made a dramatic gesture that would be widely popular in white Louisville, especially among the women, but would cost him little. By refusing to run for an elected term, he avoided the threat of anticlimax. From 1906 on, he would appear before his public as his father had suggested, in shining armor, lance at the ready, striking quickly and moving on.

His daughter, Henrietta Worth, had been born in her grandmother's house in 1901, prompting a letter from an old friend who advised Robert that "a man can be the biggest fool over what? Your daughter." He added that fathers love daughters more than sons because daughters remain dependent for life, and finished with an outraged howl against his own daughter's beaux: "She don't give a damn for them!"

The Colonel in North Carolina continued to influence his son's family from afar. His career as a public speaker drew on the gift for words which had been a family strength for generations, and which a lowlier Irish immigrant would have dubbed "blarney."

According to an article in the Asheville *Citizen,* "Colonel Bingham not infrequently expressed a very warm and deep feeling of gratitude towards the north for freeing the southern states from a constantly enlarging and malignant cancer that had developed from an economic expedient brought into Southern ports by swift-sailing cutters that smelled rank of African jungles and New England rum." The Colonel believed that the Confederate states' defense of what he claimed was an issue of states' rights rather than slavery qualified them to lead the nation. But his political career was stunted by the split in the Democratic party during Reconstruction. He continued to speak, however, eloquently and persuasively, and eventually became a champion of public education.

Public education became essential to white supremacy during Reconstruction. There were forty black magistrates ruling in North Carolina district courts, deciding cases that sometimes involved white men. Black representatives sat in the state capitol, and their supporters, men and women from the North, had set up schools to educate a black electorate. After the establishment of the poll tax and literacy tests for voters, one poll watcher in the 1890s observed that blacks were more likely to pass the test than whites, due to the training given them by Northern "troublemakers." Far worse than the remote danger that women would take advantage of public education was the immediate threat of an educated, powerful black male electorate. White men must be assured of a more than adequate education in order to maintain their power.

By the time his granddaughter Henrietta was born, the Colonel had developed a seamless philosophy that included his theories about education, the relation between the races, and the role of women. Possessed of the eloquence of a Southerner raised on the Bible, with a commanding physical presence—unlike the other Bingham men, the Colonel was tall and broad and weighed almost two hundred pounds—with the glamour of a former Confederate captain, the Colonel made a formidable public speaker. His words would have an enormous influence on his son in Kentucky, reverberating down the generations.

In 1907, the Colonel read a paper on women at the Pen and Plate Club in Asheville, a gentlemen's club he had helped to found. In the paper, he tackled the problem of educating women, which had been introduced by the question of free public education:

"I would not deprive a woman of anything which tends to relieve her of the grievous burden which Nature has laid upon her, and which man, the stronger animal, has made more grievous by his selfishness, his cruelty and his lust. Men produce thought; but women produce men."

The Colonel was relying on opinions expressed by many educators and physicians of the period, whose conclusions were based on misinterpretation of new physiological studies.

These conclusions did not match the Colonel's own experience with the women in his family, except perhaps with his first wife, Dell Worth.

The Colonel's more recent experiences with his daughters, Sadie and Mary Kerr, and their warfare against his second wife, Elvira, as well as his sister-in-law Owen Bingham's fight to save her school in Mebane, abetted by her daughter Mary Gray—all these activities were causing the Colonel grief. Certainly these women were not fading flowers.

The Colonel was well aware of the power of women as mothers. His catalogue for his school warned against their insidious influence. Women "spoiled" their sons, listening to excuses, saving bad boys from the consequences of their misbehavior. The "queenship" of mothers was something the Colonel recognized, and feared; only in that role did women seize the authority as well as the regalia of that title.

His speech to the Pen and Plate Club continued: "The man's life history is in striking contrast to this often pathetic and often painful history of what may be called the partly submerged half of the world." Again his family life did not provide examples: nephews and sons who showed early promise were often blighted by death. In the case of his two remaining male heirs, his grandsons Robert and Mary Kerr McKee's son Bingham, neither was living up to the Colonel's expectations.

But the romanticized image of the Southern male, the Sir Galahad, obscured reality in the Colonel's mind. In his view, Southern upper-class white men were genetically endowed with all the attributes necessary for success. Gender was more important than character or training. Gender, in fact, was all. If male heirs failed, the failing would be attributed to an act of God or a cruel quirk of fate.

The Colonel concluded his speech with an argument current in his day: "Woman has one-fifth ounces of brain less than men," and she is plagued by "periodicity."

A corollary held that black brains were also smaller than white male brains; perhaps they were about the size of white women's. Eventually the Colonel would support a three-part system of public education in the South, which offered primitive instruction in reading and writing to blacks, a slightly more advanced program for white women, and a less than adequate classical education for white men. The South would never be able to afford such a system, which would ensure the eventual collapse of all three.

The Colonel spoke out strongly for discipline, which, he said, would prevent the "feminization of the incoming generation of men in the U.S. by their being trained very largely by women, most of them not even mothers"—that is, black nurses who might have even less commitment than white mothers to the status quo.

Discipline raised the question of "hazing" and other physical abuses which, the Colonel said, were prohibited at his school, although he could not resist adding that "the burning of witches yielded a higher and better civilization and religion."

Violence could be justified in some cases, especially when it was called for to prevent civil disturbances provoked by blacks. Stating that "more negroes are lynched in the north than in the south" at a time when lynching in the South was on the rise, the Colonel explained, "When we anticipate the law and put a negro to death for the new negro crime against white women, or for murder or arson, the violence, which never should have occurred, stops with the criminal."

This curious equivocation recalls the fact that the Colonel had been one of the organizers of the Ku Klux Klan during Reconstruction. Robert would remember years later that "my earliest memory is of clutching my mother's skirts in terror at a hooded apparition, and having my father raise his mask to relieve me. Then he went out in command of the Ku Klux in our district." Twenty years later, the Colonel did not repudiate his connection with the Klan. He simply buried it.

The Colonel said in another published speech, "A great mistake was made against the negro by arming him with the ballot while he was still an intellectual, moral and political infant. We are Teutons, God's kings of men. But every step towards the highest freedom was won in the best blood of our race."

As he wove his seamless web of misogyny and racism, his niece, Mary Bingham, was being educated at the Mary Baldwin Seminary in Virginia, and his daughters were attending Peace Institute in Raleigh, the first women in his family to receive a formal education.

Formerly all-male institutions like the University of North Carolina were admitting a handful of women, and independent colleges for women were being founded. But a strong opposition armed itself with the first studies in "hysteria" among educated women, as well as with a sentimental overevaluation of what Anna Freud at a later period called the principle of "altruistic surrender"—the abandonment of a woman's will in service to others, a self-sacrifice with religious and sexual overtones. The Colonel's patronizing attitude toward women would continue to have widespread support; together with hostility toward educating blacks, this attitude would prevent the South from developing.

C. Vann Woodward described education in the South as "a multitude of superfluous institutions" which hung on "in a dying condition"—private academies like the Bingham School competing with church-affiliated organizations, normal schools, industrial schools, black colleges, women's colleges, and state institutions. The South had neither the financial resources nor the teachers to support such a complex system. As late as 1913, bachelor's degrees given at thirty-eight women's colleges in the South were judged equivalent to one year of work at universities in the North. The Colonel's speeches did not fall on deaf ears.

Certainly they were read and discussed around the tea table at Mrs. Miller's house in Louisville. The pamphlets containing his speeches would have been spread on the cut-velvet cloth that covered the round table in the library, along with the latest editions of *Harper's* or *The Atlantic Monthly.* Perhaps Eleanor stopped to glance at one such pamphlet and was moved by the Colonel's eloquence and wondered what it all meant.

Eleanor was not seeking an education, or asking for the right to vote, and she probably felt little sympathy with the "New Woman's" demands for equality. She was a married woman, comfortably settled in her mother's house, bringing up her three children. Probably she had seldom come into contact with a woman who had graduated from college, especially since so many college graduates did not marry and so did not join the parade of middle-class social life. Eleanor had been born and bred to middle-class comfort and dependency. But she had once had a checking account of her own.

Perhaps Eleanor thought there was a risk in expanding educational opportunities for women and blacks, on even a limited basis. Eleanor might have felt that an educated electorate would eventually question the system of political favoritism, social elitism, and racial exclusion that once again dominated the South. Educated women, no matter how poorly prepared, would sooner or later demand the vote. Blacks given even a smattering of learning might fight against their disenfranchisement, might demand the places in the South's courts and legislatures that were snatched away during Reconstruction. Even Eleanor's North Carolina sisters-in-law, taking care of their children, their cadets, their black servants, their neighbors, and their eloquent men, may have realized that the seeds of change were being broadcast when their handsome progenitor rode up and down the land championing the cause of free public education—with reservations.

The Colonel's descendants would reap the whirlwind. One of the first private academies to close as free education became available would be the Bingham School. That, however, was only the most obvious consequence.

The Colonel's attitude toward the limited education deemed suitable for women was no longer acceptable as his son and grandson moved into a wider world. Ignorance could not be tolerated as the family became more sophisticated; "polish" must be applied to the daughters as well as the sons. The Colonel would certainly have blanched at the thought of his great-granddaughter's exposure to an alien breed at Radcliffe College in the 1950s. But by then the Bingham men were cornered by their ambitions. Eleanor's ability to make a fine syllabub and sing hymns was no longer enough. The Bingham women could not be relegated to a social and intellectual limbo shared with black servants and white sharecroppers, some of whom, if the truth were told, might be only too closely related.

The unimaginable became necessary as the family moved on from North Carolina to Kentucky, and then to Washington, New York, London, and Paris. Universities, however, do not offer courses in table manners. Academia is no place to learn how to dress. Once a young woman is handed a course catalogue, her future becomes problematical. There is no way to ensure that she will dwell in the realms of gold with poetry, music, and the literature of the Victorians. She may be lured into history or science, or even mathematics, once the family hold has been slightly loosened. Along the way she may begin to think of herself not merely as a charmer of men and a moral guide, but as a functioning mind somehow trapped inside a woman's body. The conflict set up is fearful. Out of it would come unpredictable results which, as my Richmond grandmother, Munda, knew, would have fearful consequences for "the state."

Charles D. McIver, a friend and contemporary of the Colonel's who also supported public education in North Carolina, believed that "the proper training of women is the strategic point in our culture," but his view did not prevail. Twenty years after the Colonel spoke, a historian noted, "In an attempt to busy themselves, women have built a complicated system of social rank to which they have become slaves." The history of women in the Bingham family is wedged between those two statements.

After 1905, the Bingham men became Southern liberals, cautious advocates of a degree of change at home and Wilsonian ambassadors of international cooperation. But the liberal creed was never a comfortable choice for a family steeped in primogeniture, misogyny, and racism. They were motivated by noblesse oblige rather than by understanding of or respect toward those they worked to "raise." Certain blacks, certain lower-class white men, and certain women were tapped for advancement and kept in line with favors.

The Colonel's son, Robert, now called the Judge, was the first man in the family who was not a Presbyterian elder and a schoolmaster. He was the first to call himself a progressive, an independent, and an Episcopalian, the first to achieve the wealth and power his father the Colonel so admired. Along the way, the Judge would change his political allegiance, perhaps as a result of his move to the bustling Midwestern city with its history of political graft, perhaps as evidence of his shrewdness, certainly as a result of his second marriage. As he moved from Southern conservatism to Southern progressivism—a distance no wider than a hair—the Judge began to revise his own history, writing that his father "advocated free public education for negroes in the dark days of Reconstruction, indicating a liberalism which may well have nourished the subsequent enlightened views of his son." Yet he also wrote that his first memory was the sight of his father dressed in the Ku Klux Klan's white sheet.

The Colonel's role in organizing the Klan in Alamance County, North Carolina, was an inconvenient detail, deleted when the family began to rewrite its history. But for at least one of the Colonel's descendants, the drive through the placid piedmont country into "bloody Alamance," with the old school appearing on the horizon, would produce a sickening sensation of responsibility avoided, of buried violence that defines a tradition purged of its essential elements.

As C. Vann Woodward noted, "Racism was conceived by some as the very foundation of Southern progressivism." Disfranchisement of the Negro, he added, quoting a Southern educator, promoted the growth of political and social solidarity among white males.

But learning through violence to "keep their place" was not reserved for ex-slaves alone. White women, middle-class women, petted women, revered women—they learned to keep their place as well, or suffer the consequences.

10

In Louisville, Eleanor had begun to talk about a house of her own around 1900, but Robert's financial resources were meager and they did not find a plot and build a house for six more years. Then Robert financed the move with a fifty-thousand-dollar gift from his mother-in-law, Henrietta Miller.

Robert's mother-in-law also bought a plot in a newly laid-out suburb at the eastern edge of Louisville, near Cherokee Park, and he began to build a house. He also began an acrimonious exchange with contractors, carpenters, plumbers, and electricians as the house, which was expensive in a period when most houses cost between five and ten thousand dollars, went up. Electric wires had to be strung and pipes laid; a telephone line was brought in and a telephone installed in the stable. Eleanor occasionally wrote to her decorator in Cleveland about wallpaper or rugs, but she bowed to his decision in everything, even to the changing of the rug in her three children's room. She was not able to move into her new house until 1907 and then there were many problems: there was no hot water, the toilets on the second floor refused to flush, screens failed to arrive for the windows, and the bills were pouring in faster than they could be paid.

Eleanor must have walked around her new domain, when at last the workmen were gone, astonished and a little frightened to find herself, at last, in charge. Her mother and other female relatives and friends would have called frequently, but Eleanor was the one who made the decisions about meals and help, about cleaning and child care that she had previously shared with her mother. The new house must have seemed lighter and airier than the old house on Fourth Street, even with its windows bundled up in brocades and its corners filled with darkly towering palms.

Her husband's life still centered on his law firm and his political aspirations. In 1906, after supervising the election of the man who would succeed

Eleanor Miller Bingham, 1900—the only portrait I ever
saw of her. It used to be on my father's bureau.

Father (left) with Henrietta,
Louisville, 1908.

Uncle Robert
(Robert Worth Bingham)
with kudzu at the
Bingham School in
Asheville, 1908.

him as mayor, Robert was appointed county attorney. For the rest of his life, he would be called the Judge.

His calendar was not lacking in cultural events. He attended a performance given by Sarah Bernhardt, heard Walter Pater lecture on John Paul Jones, commissioned an oil portrait of his son that cost seventy-five dollars, took German lessons and corresponded in German with a Louisville acquaintance. He also went to hear "Professor Washington" speak. Booker T. Washington's call for patience and moderation in race relations would have been acceptable to the Judge.

He organized expeditions with his men friends to Camp Kentuck in Canada. Eleanor went along once but stayed in the hotel, where her husband requested that they be given separate beds. At the same period, he began to visit Florida during the winter, first with Eleanor, later with friends. He perhaps made the acquaintance of the millionaire Henry Flagler, whose wife, Mary Lily Kenan, had been the Judge's sweetheart ten years earlier.

Their lives had been woven together at least since 1891, when the Judge had suddenly left Chapel Hill for the University of Virginia. It seems likely that he met Mary Lily at Chapel Hill, which was part of her family's kingdom; the Kenans' disapproval may explain his departure. However, years later Mary Lily would claim in an interview in the New York *Herald Tribune* that she had met the Judge in 1890 at the University of Virginia.

At some point during that period, the Judge had wanted to marry her, but Mary Lily's family had thought little of the penniless Confederate Colonel's son as a match for their attractive daughter. When their love affair ended, the Judge returned to Asheville, abandoning college for the second time without a degree—an odd action for an ambitious man—to teach in his father's school.

Perhaps there had been another reason for Mary Lily's resistance and for the Judge's retreat.

In 1891, Mary Lily met Henry Flagler at the house of friends, the Pembroke Joneses, in Newport. She became a friend of Alice Flagler. Later Mary Lily became Henry Flagler's lover, a relationship that continued while he rid himself of Alice. Henry and Mary Lily were finally married in 1901.

The proud and ambitious son of the Colonel might well have spent the next twelve years embellishing the image of the pretty woman who got away, whose family had always been better known and better heeled than the Binghams.

The Kenans had founded the University of North Carolina, of which the Bingham men longed to be a part. They had been trustees when William Bingham I, the Latin professor, was sent packing. During the Civil War, two Kenan officers had shared the Colonel's imprisonment on Johnson's Island, as they had shared the defeat at Appomattox; but no bonds had been formed. Perhaps the rivalry between the men scotched any attempt at friendship. The Kenans' history in North Carolina was both longer and more distinguished than the history of the Presbyterian ministers who had run the military school.

Class and breeding come by marriage and by marriage alone to young men making their way up in the hierarchy. The Judge had seen that in the case of his mother, Dell Worth, who had brought important connections to her husband's family. He would have known that Mary Lily had been his first and best chance. She remained his dream.

When Mary Lily married Flagler, one of the richest men in America, the Judge, who was beginning to feel the limits of his life in Louisville, must have been infuriated. Now she had given her attributes—grace, social breeding, a background—to a man who had made the kind of fortune the Judge planned and hoped to make—with increasing desperation.

Over the next twelve years, during ill health, the birth of his three children, social and political disappointments, and finally his wife's death, the Judge would continue to think of Mary Lily as the Prize.

The Prize that is won by another man, a tycoon who has already won all the other goods and services in the world.

Possibly all three were linked by syphilis, acquired by Flagler during the wild young days at Standard Oil, when all the men had mistresses, or passed along by the Judge after an undergraduate fling in a North Carolina bawdy house. Mary Lily, who may never have had children, suffered the consequences.

During his winter trips to Florida, while Eleanor stayed in Louisville with the children, the Judge saw not only Mary Lily but the life she led with Flagler: the marble palace, the entertaining, the private organist, the beautiful clothes and jewels, and the devotion of the people of Florida, to whom Flagler had brought hotels and railroads, tourists and dreams.

That was what the Judge wanted. That was what he had always wanted, under the protective coating of the Colonel's myth.

Henry and Mary Lily's palace, Whitehall, in Palm Beach, is far larger and grander than the house I grew up in on the Ohio River, the house the Judge bought and furnished after Mary Lily's death. But the details bear a resemblance that seems more than coincidental when I recall the way the Big House looked in the dark winter of 1942, with the Judge's imprint still upon it.

In Whitehall's baronial lobby, ten times larger than the Big House's front hall, the same Spanish-style armchairs, upholstered in faded needlepoint, are placed at regular intervals, as though awaiting the assembling of a company of knights. The same dark carved chests, which we used to hide in as children, stand forbiddingly around the walls. The same dark-hued, larger-than-life-sized family portraits hang from tasseled ropes in public rooms where it is so difficult, as it always was at the Big House, to imagine ordinary people finding a corner in which to sit. Mary Lily's wedding portrait (in which her hair appears to be gray because she told the painter she did not want to look younger than Flagler, as in fact she was) smiles down with the silken look of the portraits of my male relatives. In the great glass vitrines, the green-bordered porcelain service, the ornate silver center-pieces, including a pair of pheasants, and the vermeil place settings look like the objects I used to admire on the Big House dinner table when it was set for guests.

Of course, these two vast mansions share the style of their period, having been decorated less than twenty years apart; and it is possible that some of Mary Lily's possessions turned up, after her death, in the Big House pantry. But I retain a peculiar sense that the larger—and oddly, the more cheerful—of the two mansions influenced the decoration of the Kentucky house, bought with Flagler money and furnished to shine as his white palace shines even today.

But if the Judge copied Flagler's style, he ignored Mary Lily's influence. The second-floor suites at Whitehall, where Mary Lily housed her North Carolina relatives, are sunny and charming, each decorated to represent a historical period. Her presence even now, seventy years after her death, is palpable. She was a woman who loved people, who was outgoing, cheerful, animated—perhaps even a little silly.

It was not Mary Lily but the multimillionaire Henry Flagler whom the Judge admired. Flagler left behind the ugly business of Standard Oil when he moved to Florida; there he became a local philanthropist. His public works gradually dissolved the suspicion he had earned as John D. Rockefeller's first partner and the designer of the infamous Standard Oil Trust. Like Flagler, the Judge would in the last quarter of his life become a local philanthropist whose benevolence hid the facts of his rise.

Only Mary Lily, as it turned out, prevented the Judge from leaving behind an image as burnished as Flagler left to the people of Florida.

While Mary Lily entertained at Whitehall, the Judge was beginning to prosper in Louisville.

As the confusions and sorrows of his North Carolina past faded, the Judge attended reunions and commencements at Chapel Hill. He remarked in a letter that the Bingham men's association with the University of North Carolina was similar to the Adams men's association with Harvard, which showed the way his perception of his own life was changing. In 1908, he met

President Eliot of Harvard, and bought a jeweled dog collar for fifty dollars.

The Judge began to take his father and other relatives abroad during the summer, while Eleanor and the three children went to Asheville. On one of these tours, the Judge and the Colonel visited England, Ireland, Scotland, France, Germany, Austria, and Switzerland. Perhaps it was on this trip that the Judge met the German officer whom he later said he challenged to a duel. The man watched him at pistol practice and was so dismayed by the Judge's expertise that he fled at once.

In England and Scotland, he and the Colonel spent time refurbishing the family's past. Through Eliza Norwood, they claimed Sir Walter Scott as a "faraway cousin," and went to call on his descendant, a Lady. They also discovered a character in Hardy's *Tess of the D'Urbervilles* named Parson Tringham, who they believed was based on an ancestor. Hardy's parson was obsessed with genealogies, and his revelation of the D'Urbervilles' aristocratic lineage doomed Tess.

Back in Louisville, the Judge continued to manage Mrs. Miller's affairs as well as his wife's, to order her clothes from De Pinna in New York, to make speeches in "the oratorical style," and to drum up trade for his father's school. He interviewed likely candidates and passed out brochures, advising his father to improve the school's chances by adding such flourishes as a band and annual prizes. The Judge insisted that the school must begin to provide diplomas and a graduation exercise, no matter how simple. He helped to finance a clubhouse and a bathhouse, which were vandalized by some of the cadets. Then he advised his father how to get rid of the troublemakers, tactfully, by keeping them until the next vacation and then forbidding them to return.

Although he called Eleanor "the best and truest woman in the world," and said that she attended to his spiritual growth and moral education, the Judge continued to travel alone or with his men friends. His influence was spreading outside of the state. In 1908, Ansolan Buchanon of Oklahoma wrote to ask the Judge to support him for a local office, explaining, "Some little moral stamina as the country curator is needed" because a weak individual might be tempted to "pick up from 15 to 20 thousand a year from the Standard Oil crowd and land grafts." It was the first mention of an enterprise that would be of great importance to the Judge's future.

During this period, the Judge's three children, Robert, Henrietta, and Barry, were growing up. In photographs the handsome little Binghams appear with the paraphernalia of the rising middle class: ponies and sailor suits, lace baby dresses and hovering adults, both black and white. Robert, the eldest, was a daredevil and a scamp. Henrietta was a swimmer and a tennis player, a little beauty who knew her own mind. The youngest, Barry, was fair and pale with something dreamy about him. He wrote poems his father would later publish in a little book. Barry was his mother's darling. In one photograph, he sits leaning against her shoulder, his hand inside her hand.

The three children were being educated at a small private day school in Louisville. The headmistress wrote the Judge regularly to assure herself that he was satisfied with her program and would send the next child when the time came. In 1909, the Judge wrote his relatives at the Asheville school that he would probably send Robert to them in a year or so. Eleanor may have dreaded the separation. As the two boys grew older, their father took more interest in them, and their mother's influence waned.

A year later, in 1912, Eleanor paid a visit to her sister-in-law, Sadie Bingham Grinnan, in Asheville. She was devoted to the warm and loyal woman whose husband, Major Robert Temple Grinnan, was teaching at the school.

On the cool hilltop overlooking Asheville, Eleanor and Sadie may have walked arm in arm, as they had so often during Eleanor's summer visits. They may have taken tea together, or gone into town to shop; perhaps they discussed the succession, or the sad fact that there was no viable male heir living at the school. Bingham McKee was not "serious." Sadie may have then posed the question that her nephew Barry loved to repeat years later. She asked Eleanor whether something of an intimate nature was supposed to happen between husband and wife. Apparently it had never happened— whatever it was—between Sadie and Major Grinnan. They had no children.

Sadie drove Eleanor to the train station when the time came for her to return to Louisville. Perhaps both women fell silent as they approached the station where, many years before, Samuel Miller had killed himself on the track. The past always hung heavy in Asheville in words that no one could speak.

As Eleanor got down from the car, she is said to have turned to Sadie and asked, "Dear, would you take care of my children if something happened to me? Especially Barry. He's still delicate, and—"

"Don't be ridiculous," Sadie would have answered.

Yet Sadie, of course, promised; she loved Eleanor's children, especially Barry. Perhaps Eleanor had been stirred by a memory of her father's violent death; perhaps she had felt a touch of sadness, a hint of mortality, as she told Sadie goodbye.

Sadie never saw Eleanor again.

A few months later, Eleanor, Henrietta, and Barry visited Mrs. Miller's country place in Pewee Valley, a pleasant leafy suburb where Louisville's middle class retreated from the heat of the city. The Judge had to catch the train to Cincinnati, where he was litigating a case. Eleanor, her brother Dennis, who was driving, Henrietta, Barry, and a few other relatives squeezed into the big car to drive him to the station.

After dropping off the Judge, they turned around to go back to Mrs. Miller's house. Rain clouded Dennis's goggles; he stopped the car to clear them, then drove on. It was a cool spring day. The children were chattering, the adults looking forward to the good lunch at Mrs. Miller's house.

As he drove across the track, Dennis suddenly saw the interurban trolley from Louisville bearing down. There was no time to get off the track. The trolley, traveling fast, struck the car, flinging it off the track and into a telephone pole. Eighteen years earlier, the driver, Dennis Miller, had seen his f²ther die on the train track in Asheville.

᛫leanor was fatally injured in the accident, her skull crushed. Barry and Henri᛫ ᛫ ᛫ were slightly hurt. For a long time after the accident Barry did not spea᛫ ᛫bove a whisper and he walked on tiptoe. He was sent at once to Asheville to recuperate.

Eleanor was buried in the Miller family plot.

When as a child I first heard my grandmother Eleanor's death mentioned, it seemed to me that something was left out. She was my "real" grandmother, but I knew nothing about her. Because no one talked about her, I did not dare ask questions. She was the beautiful face on my father's chest of drawers. W₋o she was had not been open to discussion. How she had died could not even be imagined.

But imagine it I did. A grandparent's violent death is too frightening, and too interesting, to be dismissed. Who had she been, what had she thought and said? Father told me once that she used to sing around the house. She is nearly as invisible now as she was then, forty years ago, when I would glance at her face as I passed through my parents' bedroom. Her beautiful white shoulders slope in her pearl-and-lace-bedecked dress. How did she manage to hold her hands so serenely clasped? Was it pride that had persuaded her to wear no necklace around her perfect neck?

And what did she see as she looked out at me with dark, slightly smiling, quizzical eyes?

Many years later, I thought I recognized those eyes in a photograph in Henrietta's New York apartment. But was it the same woman, or another? Were the women in the family interchangeable, their characters matched like their expressions?

Later I took the photograph out of its frame, hoping that Eleanor's name would be written on the back. But there was only a square of dark blue paper which, when torn off, revealed nothing.

.   .   .

Half a century passed, and my grandmother seemed to have disappeared. Except for her stone in the family plot, which was inscribed "Beautiful and Most Beloved," she had left nothing: no clothes or books, no china or knickknacks or furniture, no friends or acquaintances, and, strangest of all, no stories. Even the servants in the Big House never mentioned her; there were no anecdotes. Something even darker than an accidental death, it seemed to me, had wiped out not only Eleanor's life, but the memory of her life.

Father could not mention her.

It began to seem to me that her death, like so many other essential facts, had been obscured by the family myth. There had been her trip to Asheville, and the Judge's lingering interest in Mary Lily; there had been the oddly neutralized marriage, which left no letters, no photographs, no mark that it had existed. There had been the Judge's health problems, possibly syphilis, and political scandals that never entirely went away. There was the long, bland future of a woman who "had everything" except her independence.

And there was her father's suicide, on the railroad tracks in Asheville, just before Eleanor's engagement.

Certain details about Eleanor's death continue to puzzle me. According to newspaper accounts, she lingered, hospitalized, in a coma, for two days, but my father apparently did not visit her. She had sustained a fatal injury but no one else in the car had been seriously hurt.

While some accounts said that the car had been struck by a train, others blamed the interurban trolley; but the trolley, which would have inflicted little damage on the big touring car, did not use the railroad track which still runs through Pewee Valley. All accounts state that Eleanor was fatally injured on the train track.

Had the car been struck by a steam engine, it seems to me, no one would have survived without serious injury. Eleanor was said in the news accounts to have been "thrown from the car" and killed by the impact, but that explanation is open to several interpretations.

No one will ever know what happened that rainy day in Pewee Valley— or even if it was raining. Perhaps my father's amnesia covers more than a terrible accident.

Children whose parents kill themselves may never be able to discuss, or even believe, that such a thing happened.

Perhaps Mrs. Miller's later hostility toward the Judge is explainable; perhaps the Millers' decision to bury Eleanor, at first, in their own family plot is also rooted in the reality of her death; perhaps the bond between Henrietta and Barry, two children who knew what had really happened that day when they were all in the car together, was forged by the secret they could never tell. Perhaps Dennis Miller wore a bandage on his head on the front porch in Louisville so that the neighbors would believe there had been an accident. Perhaps the emotional amnesia which crippled my father began that rainy day when the seven-year-old boy felt his mother push him off her lap before she sprang out of the car door.

It is only speculation. No one alive today can or will explain why Eleanor Miller Bingham vanished so completely.

The three years between Eleanor's death in 1913 and the Judge's remarriage in 1916 were an interregnum. The Judge was said to have been prostrated by the tragedy, unequipped to deal with his three children, who had been cared for entirely by their mother and other female relatives and servants.

Barry remained frighteningly frail, and was thought to be threatened with tuberculosis. It seemed best for him to continue to live at the Asheville school, where Sadie's care would help him mend. There he began to identify himself with the mythology of the family's past. Robert, at sixteen, was sent off to boarding schools, where he began a checkered career that would cause the Judge a good deal of trouble. Henrietta floated.

At home for vacations, Henrietta and Robert had the run of the house. Robert was handsome and charming, like all the Bingham men, already fulfilling the destiny his mother had laid out for him, years earlier, when she remarked that at a children's party Robert learned all the girls' names but not the boys'. Henrietta was enthroned as her father's hostess, as her Aunt Mary Kerr had been in the brief period between the Colonel's first and second marriages.

Soon after Eleanor's death, the Judge took stock of his financial situation. His relationship with his mother-in-law, Henrietta Miller, had deteriorated, and he was no longer her lawyer or trustee. A 1915 letter from the Judge to Mrs. Miller's new lawyer mentioned Robert's desire to possess a copy of "a trust . . . which was afterward terminated by the will of Eleanor Miller Bingham" and "a deed executed by Mrs. Bingham and myself to the Fidelity Trust Company, with a provision that it should not be put in the record." On January 8, the president of the Fidelity Trust, acting under Mrs. Miller's instructions, refused to return the deed to the Judge, reminding him that although the document covered "the residence property which Mrs. Miller gave to Mrs. Bingham," it had been superseded by Eleanor's will. Mrs. Miller, the letter said, was "opposed" to returning the original deed to her son-in-law, perhaps fearing his sharp legal eye. The Judge, in effect, was living in a house he did not own. He soon moved to a modest frame house on Burnett Street.

Six months later, the Judge was still trying to recover the deed, writing a pleading letter to Mrs. Miller's lawyer which was signed, unlike every

Father, 1918. This photograph was used as a study for the full-length
portrait that hung over the stairs at the Big House.

Henrietta Worth Bingham,
Louisville, 1910. She
was the first woman in
the family to become
a skilled athlete.

Robert Worth Bingham
(Uncle Robert), 1910.

other letter in his correspondence, "Ever your friend." The response came quickly: "I regret that the situation is such that an amicable agreement in regard to such matters does not exist between Mrs. Miller and yourself." Only a few years earlier, the Judge had addressed Mrs. Miller in letters as "My Dear Ma."

The process by which control of Mrs. Miller's finances had passed to her son-in-law was and is a familiar one. At some point, years earlier, Mrs. Miller may have complained of the tedium of dealing with bills, bank accounts, renters, and investments, and the Judge may have offered, sympathetically, to take some of the load onto his own shoulders. With relief, Mrs. Miller may have given him first some of the details to manage, then the more substantial question of investments, until at last the whole matter passed out of her hands and then out of her knowledge. The relief for a woman who had not been trained to manage her own affairs would have been great. Only later, years later, after her daughter's death, would she begin to question the whole process, to fear the results of her blissful ignorance. But what had triggered her alarm?

In November 1916, the Judge was asked to sign as trustee of a mortgage Mrs. Miller wished to foreclose. The Judge gave his permission for the foreclosure, adding, "I must further insist that a complete written record of every step of the transaction must be kept, and especially that when money is paid over to her [Mrs. Miller] receipts in duplicate must be executed by her, one of which shall be delivered to me." At the time, he was about to escape forever from financial dependence on Henrietta Miller.

After his wife's death, the Judge had found himself nearly one million dollars in debt, partly as a result of his political activities, which had included many kickbacks and other deals typical of Kentucky politics both then and now. The Judge's creditors, sensing his vulnerable position after Eleanor's death and the withdrawal of Mrs. Miller's patronage, insisted that he pay them what he owed.

According to a Louisville story, the creditors suggested that he go and visit a certain well-known widow in Florida. They even offered to buy the Judge a new suit and a train ticket.

No such inducements were needed.

Henry Flagler had died on May 20, 1913, having fallen down the stairs in his bathroom, some surmised, on February or March 15. He had never regained consciousness after the fall, and had spent his last days heavily drugged in a remote cottage on his estate in Florida.

Eleanor Miller Bingham had died less than a month earlier, on April 29.

There is some confusion about the date of Flagler's fall, as well as its cause. One biographer, Sidney Walter Martin, wrote that Flagler fell not in his bathroom but down the "long flight of marble stairs in Whitehall, which led from the second to the first floor. On the third step from the bottom, his leg gave way; and he plunged the remaining distance to the grand hall"—a distance of three steps.

A later biography by David Leon Chandler dates the fall as taking place on March 15, and implicates the automatic doors in Flagler's bathroom.

Both books agree that after the fall Flagler was taken from Whitehall to a remote beach cottage and kept heavily sedated. His estranged son, Harry Harkness Flagler, complained that the old man had been unable to recognize him because of the drugs he had been given. Mary Lily's cousin, Owen, was in charge of the situation, and Flagler was also guarded by two male nurses.

There is some disagreement about the state of Flagler's health before the fall. At eighty-two, he had never had a serious illness, and appears in photographs gaunt and white-haired but fit. Some accounts maintain that he was exhausted by the round of house parties Mary Lily so enjoyed, and that in the last years she curbed their entertaining. Yet the so-called secret staircase at Whitehall, which Flagler used to make his escape from dinner parties and balls, is an exceptionally long, steep flight of stairs, without a handrailing—impossible to climb for an infirm old man. It seems likely to me that Flagler was in good health for his age, before the mysterious fall.

In any event, the two deaths came conveniently together, releasing the Judge for more adventures and propelling Mary Lily into mourning—and independence. Perhaps it was during this time, when she became a director of Standard Oil and received an annual income of $100,000, that she learned the value of her money. Most of her assets, however, were tied up in a trust Flagler set up, which would not expire for at least five years.

Mary Lily was the eldest of four children from a prosperous and well-known North Carolina family. She had grown up in the old home, Liberty Hall, in Kenansville. She had attended Peace Institute in Raleigh for two years, at the same period when the Judge's older sisters, Sadie and Mary Kerr, were studying there. Like Mary Kerr, Mary Lily (or Lily, as her friends called her) had musical talent and became an accomplished singer and pianist. She was not enrolled in the regular academic curriculum at Peace but was a gifted music student who once sang in recital at the governor's mansion, down the street.

In 1891, Mary Lily met Henry Flagler. Her affair (as she called it later) with the Judge had begun several years earlier. That same year Mary Lily broke with the Judge.

When Robert withdrew from the scene, Mary Lily became Flagler's constant companion. In 1896, a daughter, Louise Wise, was born to Mary Lily's married sister. Gossip holds that Louise was in fact Mary Lily and

Henry's child, which would explain the central spot Louise occupied in Mary Lily's life; she later hung a portrait of the girl over the fireplace in her New York apartment, and she told reporters at the time of her marriage to the Judge that she intended to leave all her money to Louise.

Louise's birth may also explain the Kenan family's increasing pressure on Flagler, after 1896, to do something about Mary Lily, pressure that resulted in a gift of one million dollars in Standard Oil stock and, eventually, marriage.

This chain of events might also have been a precipitating factor in Robert's flight to Louisville and his marriage in 1896, the year Louise was born.

But if Louise Wise caused changes in other people's lives, she was no passive factor in her own. As an adult, she was an athlete of Olympic caliber and the first woman racing-car driver in the state of Florida.

By the time Henry Flagler met Mary Lily, he had already made one fortune. After 1891, he turned his attention to the development of Florida, bringing in the railroad that linked the Keys (at a cost of almost four hundred lives) and building the first great hotel. Flagler had been touched by scandal during his life, especially because of the way he rid himself of his second wife, Ida Alice. She had been the nurse of Flagler's first wife Mary Harkness. Harkness money had financed Flagler's first purchase of Standard Oil stock.

Henry's family repudiated Alice, who was a pretty, small woman with no intellectual or social pretensions. Henry's only son, Harry Harkness Flagler, who went on to have a distinguished career in New York music circles, said he resented his stepmother in spite of her efforts. Alice must have expected to have children of her own; she was eighteen years younger than Henry. But no children appeared, and she began to collect photographs of her friends' babies in a special album. She maintained her interest in fine clothes and big parties, but she was also said to have "a temper." Her first serious mistake was to take a party of friends on one of her husband's yachts and refuse to return to harbor when the weather became stormy.

After this incident, Henry moved to have her discredited. She was beginning to infringe on his freedom, behaving as though his money was her own. He leaned on the professional advice of two men: his Florida business partner, Dr. Andrew Anderson, from whom Henry had bought the land for his St. Augustine hotel, and Dr. George G. Shelton, a friend of the family.

In 1894, three years after Henry met Mary Lily, Alice Flagler began to complain to friends that Henry was unfaithful to her. At this point, according to one biography, "Shelton made it a point to place himself in her presence as often as possible; she was invited to his home and to his office for medical attention and advice. The unsuspecting Mrs. Flagler soon began to pour out her heart to the physician. She fell squarely into the trap he had laid for her."

According to Shelton, Mrs. Flagler had "delusions, one of which was in regard to her wealth." She gave a thousand dollars (another account makes it a thousand roses) to her manicurist and bought "a two thousand dollar cat's eye ring" (another book calls it a miniature) to send to the Czar of Russia.

Shelton and two other doctors descended on the Flagler house at Mamaroneck, New York, a great mansion called, appropriately, Satanstoe. One doctor had papers that would commit Alice to a mental asylum. When she saw them, she rushed upstairs and locked herself in her room with her maid. Later she sent the maid out to call a detective, presumably to make a record of the proceedings for her protection.

Alice Flagler had no family or friends to call on, and she knew that Henry, in spite of his sentimental protestations, wanted to get rid of her. Henry was in the position of the great king who does not need to tell his courtiers what he wants them to do. Absolving himself of all responsibility, he watched sadly from the sidelines.

Alice's maid was waylaid by the medical men. She told them that her mistress feared for her life. The maid was persuaded by whatever means proved effective to present one of the doctors to Alice as the detective.

Once inside her bedroom door, the doctor seized Alice and dragged her, as she screamed for her husband, down the stairs and into a waiting carriage. The carriage took her to Choate's Sanitarium in Pleasantville. There the doctors claimed that she was suffering from "delusionary insanity."

It was the beginning of the end for Alice Flagler.

She spent the next six months at Choate's, which she called "that hole." Meanwhile, Henry divided his time between Florida and New York. In Florida, he entertained Mary Lily; in New York, he was involved with a woman named Helen Long Foote, whose husband named him as a corespondent in his divorce.

In the spring, less than a year before Louise Wise's birth, Alice's doctor pronounced her cured and she went back to Satanstoe for a reunion with her husband. Soon, however, she was once again voicing her "delusions" about his infidelities. Shelton was called in. When Alice saw him, she tried to barricade herself in her room. Once more she was dragged off, screaming, and committed to an asylum where she would spend the rest of her life, complaining from time to time that she had been drugged and operated on, but growing quiet as the long years passed. She may have been victim of a frontal lobotomy. Henry said in court that the doctors prevented them from being together, and so they might as well be divorced.

Mary Lily Kenan's marriage to Henry Flagler, at her grandmother's house in Kenansville, North Carolina. The child is Mary Lily's niece, Louise Wise, to whom she later wanted to leave her estate.

Whitehall, West Palm Beach, Florida.
The marble palace Henry Flagler built for Mary Lily in 1901.

Mary Lily Kenan
Flagler, 1903.

Mary Lily and
Henry Flagler,
aboard his yacht
in 1912.

The doctors based their case on three points: Alice had threatened Henry with physical harm, according to his niece, Eliza Ashley; she was approaching menopause; and she was addicted to playing with a Ouija board, a fashionable game of the period, which pretended to reveal the future. In Alice's case the game was fatal: "within ten minutes her mental equilibrium was completely destroyed." She was committed for life, and Eugene M. Ashley, Eliza's husband, was put in charge of her fortune, worth more than two million dollars.

Ida Alice Flagler died twenty-nine years later, at the age of eighty-two, having spent almost half of her life in a madhouse.

Even before Alice's final commitment, Henry began to hear complaints from Mary Lily's family. Her grandmother told her that it was not the fact of her living in sin with Flagler that troubled her, but the embarrassment of the attendant publicity, which may have increased after Louise Wise's birth.

Now Henry faced the problem of his marriage to Alice, who no longer existed as far as he was concerned, but who did in fact exist and was an impediment to his plans. In New York State, adultery was the only grounds for divorce; Henry was not in a position to pursue that course because of his own behavior. Besides, he lacked clout in New York, but in Florida he was considered a great benefactor because of his development of the state. So he became a citizen of Florida, and immediately put pressure on the legislature to make insanity grounds for divorce.

The bill became law two and a half weeks after it was introduced. Florida newspapers claimed that bribes had greased its passage. Seventy years later, when researchers finally obtained access to Henry's Florida East Coast files, they found that he had paid a total of $125,000 for his bill, $15,000 to the governor of Florida.

Ten days after his divorce decree, Henry married Mary Lily at her family's house in Kenansville, North Carolina. It had been redecorated for the occasion. He gave her, her brother William, and her two sisters large portions of Standard Oil stock. At the wedding, Louise Wise was the only attendant.

Mary Lily's life at Whitehall was sumptuous, public, and highly satisfactory. Her bathroom held the first sunken tub in America, made of a single piece of rare yellow Carrara marble. Her bed was hung with gold cloth and panels of Cluny lace. Each of her fifteen guest suites had a bedroom, a drawing room, a dressing room, a bathroom, and a foyer. She gave splendid evening entertainments at which her guests dressed up in costume and received favors such as "sunflower pin cushions, brooches, gold cuff-buttons, and loving cups of silver having a souvenir of Whitehall on the outside . . ." Perhaps the Judge and the Colonel were present at these extravaganzas; a photograph at Whitehall appears to show the Colonel attending Mary Lily in her bath chair.

Later it would be claimed by her stepson, my father, that Mary Lily was drunk at these occasions and had to be sent upstairs by Flagler. But the scale of her entertaining and the publicity attending it makes it unlikely that the hostess was reeling.

Henry was growing old and deaf as the years passed, and according to Mary Lily's descendants, she was often restless and unhappy. However, she continued to sing at musicales and to entertain many guests, both in Florida and in New York.

In 1907, she hired an organist named Arthur Spalding to play at White-hall. His diary describes a life of constant entertainment, from "informal sings" to baseball games in which the teams were made up of the black employees of Flagler's hotels. Spalding liked Mary Lily, writing that "there is nothing snobbish about her. If you treat her well and don't appear to be using her for what you can get, you can't ask for better treatment than she will give you in return." He also noted her flirtatiousness.

Meanwhile, the charm that had made the Judge a social success at Chapel Hill had been polished to a high gloss by his recent life in the clubby atmosphere of Louisville. He was sharpened, too, by the anxiety of reaching his thirties without having achieved money or position; he was still largely dependent on his wife's family for support, although his law practice was growing—he was said to be a ruthless litigator—and he had made a stab at running for local office. The Judge was ready for more, he was prepared for more, and all the skills of his volatile and precarious existence would have been called into play during those entertainments at Whitehall.

Like all Bingham men, the Judge had the gift of implying everything and saying nothing. A glance, a quizzical smile, a turn of the head could be interpreted in a thousand ways, or none. There was never a trail of evidence: no letters, no statements to the press, no verbal promises which could be used against him at a later date. Brilliant, with the quicksilver charm of the great opportunist, he would have moved easily among the crowds at White-hall, chatting with people who did not really know him except as one of the charming Southerners who surrounded Mary Lily. But with her cousin Owen, the Judge would have maintained a tense reserve: they were inter-ested in the same woman.

Henry would have posed no problem: he was old and weak, and per-haps he reminded the Judge of the Colonel. It would have been easy to sympathize, even, with the old robber baron's complaints about his wife's social activities; had not the Judge learned to underline the differences between Elvira and his father? During the initial stages of this game, it was the bonds between the men which counted. Only later, when the final hand was about to be dealt, did the relationship to the woman at the center of it become paramount. And that time was not yet.

In April 1913, Eleanor Bingham died in Kentucky. In February or March, Henry Flagler had suffered the accident at Whitehall. He was alone in the house with Mary Lily and Owen Kenan. Owen, whom Henry's secretary described as "on the spot, in charge of Whitehall," spirited the old man away to a cottage by the sea.

Mary Lily stayed at Henry's bedside for the last nights, despite Owen's entreaties. Perhaps she guessed that someone had pushed Flagler down the steps, and was now waiting to take advantage of his weakened state. Or she may have escaped knowing: Henry was old and ill. Perhaps, simply, his time had come. Only Amassa Flagler, Henry's discredited cousin, would publicly question the way Flagler died.

He died on May 13, 1913, and was buried by the Reverend George Ward, who commented on "that cruel fall." Three years later in New York, Ward would marry Robert Bingham and Mary Lily Kenan Flagler.

11

Between 1913 and 1916, Mary Lily Kenan Flagler enjoyed her life as the richest woman in America. She had established her authority during Henry's long decline, when she had often ruled alone at Whitehall. Now she moved according to the season from one of her great houses to the other, followed by a retinue of servants and devoted friends. In spite of her wealth and her astonishing jewelry, Mary Lily was said to be modest and unassuming. Wealth had not made her aristocratic, although she enjoyed the admiration of the Florida "natives." However, her own family now deserted her, perhaps because they could not control the way she spent her money or persuade her to enrich them.

Since her trustees controlled the principal of Henry's estate, Mary Lily was dependent on their goodwill. The operations of Standard Oil were always conducted in the deepest secrecy, and as a director, she did not inquire into their practices. She had her brother Will to deal with as well, the engineer of whom even Henry Flagler stood in awe. Will had helped her along her path, as had her cousin Owen. To both these men she owed a peculiar and unstated deference.

When she went out in Palm Beach, wearing her collar of diamonds or her famous pearls, Mary Lily managed to maintain the discreet, ironic detachment from her wealth that is so important for a woman who has inherited a fortune. Something in her demeanor and her small stature conveyed the impression that she knew her prosperity was only on loan; she was still an example of Henry Flagler's shrewdness, a woman decorated for a man. But now there was no man, and the massive jewels seemed to take on a life of their own, glaring and flashing, signaling a dangerous change in ownership. To whom did they belong, to whom did she belong now that the old owner was gone?

In the summer of 1915, Mary Lily visited Asheville and spent some time in the Grove Park Inn. She saw a great deal of Robert Bingham, the widowed charmer from Kentucky. They had friends in common, as well as a romantic friendship which was now more than twenty years old. As Mary Lily pointed out, the Judge's oldest son, Robert, now at the University of Virginia, was exactly the age his father had been when she first met him.

As rumors of an engagement circulated, Mary Lily explained repeatedly that she had not seen the Judge since that interval in the nineties when, she told *The New York Times,* they had had "what you could call 'an affair.'"

The following summer, the Judge and Mary Lily met again at White Sulphur Springs, the elaborate mountain resort Munda's mother had called "the dear old White." Their romantic friendship continued, with tea and walks and genteel entertainments. At some point, the Colonel renewed his acquaintance with Mary Lily (he had met her when she was a student at Peace Academy with his daughters).

Another secret bloomed that summer. On July 7, in nearby Asheville, a baby girl was born. No one now living knows who her parents were, or how the infant happened to arrive, at the age of a few months, in Sadie Grinnan's house at the Bingham School. Local people remember that the baby was "given," without benefit of formal adoption, to a neighboring family. Sadie had been preparing for some time for the transfer, and had considered two women, but one of them had just given birth herself. The other woman took the little girl and raised her with her own children, naming her Sadie Ruth. That middle name had never appeared in the Bingham family. In the Bible, it belongs to a daughter who preferred her mother-in-law to all other people, and whose beautiful hymn of loyalty and affection is often used to describe a woman's allegiance to her husband. Ruth was a woman who lived in exile.

The Bingham School, like its counterpart in Mebane, had always been full of secrets. Now it was also full of adolescents: the cadets and the daughters of the establishment—Mary Kerr's two, Temple and Martha McKee, and the Judge's daughter, Henrietta. The combination was combustible.

Sadie Ruth's daughter remembered years later that as a child she had gone regularly with her parents to visit "Mrs. Grinnan," but she was never sure of the exact nature of the connection.

Had the child been a boy, the outcome might have been different. Perhaps a way would have been found to legitimize him, to fill the hole in the succession that so grieved the Colonel.

In New York that fall, Mary Lily turned aside reporters' questions with a deftness that bespoke long acquaintance with the press. She merely said, "I know Judge Bingham well; he is an estimable gentleman."

A few days later, she had made up her mind. She told the press that she and the Judge would be married soon. Mary Lily spoke of her plans with confidence; she said that after their wedding, they would live in Louisville for about a year. Then she would continue to divide her time between Palm Beach and New York, where she had purchased a block of real estate on the Upper East Side. She planned to build an enormous town house; she had even engaged the architect.

The wedding was held in the apartment of friends in New York. Mary Lily talked to reporters about her niece, Louise Wise, explaining that she was going to leave all of her money to the twenty-year-old, whom she described as "quite as capable as most men are, or more capable, of making money do the largest good." The Judge had already signed a premarital agreement which eliminated his dower right to fifty percent of Mary Lily's estate.

The Judge's three children were not at the wedding, nor was the Colonel. Only Sadie Grinnan, the good sister, was present in a small crowd that included many of Mary Lily's old friends from the Whitehall days.

In newspaper photographs, Mary Lily appears a forthright, pretty, young-looking woman (she was forty-nine, although she listed her age as forty-seven, splitting the four years' difference with the Judge). She was caught up in a dream of romance, which had for solid content a few meetings stretching over a number of years with a man who was a redoubtable charmer. She did not know his family, his children, or his life in Louisville, although apparently she did know that he was not considered a stunning success. She remarked that a friend of hers had observed, "Why, it's not a very brilliant match!" Mary Lily said she had replied, "It is from the heart, and what could be more brilliant than that?"

Immediately after the wedding, the Judge took Mary Lily back to Louisville on the overnight train. There was no honeymoon; he had urgent business at home. He installed her in a suite in the Seelbach Hotel and returned to his law office the next day.

The urgent business concerned the beginning of a rift between the owners of the local newspapers.

The Seelbach was chosen as their place of residence because the Cherokee Park house was no longer available, due to problems with Mrs. Miller and with Eleanor's estate. The small frame house on Burnett Street where the Judge had been living would hardly have been suitable for Mary Lily.

The Seelbach Hotel at that period was a monument to Louisville's commercial prosperity. It had been built a few years earlier, and had separate entrances for women and men and a well-known bar and roof garden; the lobby was decorated with murals, horse prints, and brass chandeliers. Women were not permitted in the public rooms.

Mary Lily had no friends in Louisville. She must have been often alone

Mary Lily Flagler in
demi-mourning, 1914.

THE HENRY M. FLAGLER MUSEUM, PALM BEACH, FLORIDA

The Judge, my grandfather
Robert Worth Bingham, 1914.

Mary Lily Flagler and Colonel Robert Bingham, Whitehall, 1912.
The carriage was called an Afromobile.

while the Judge began the first of his delicate and elaborate negotiations with the Haldeman brothers, who owned the newspapers.

Of course, it was only a temporary arrangement, and Mary Lily was looking forward to meeting her three stepchildren at Christmastime and to moving into a house of her own.

In December 1916, Mary Lily faced the closing in of winter in Louisville, a river town much afflicted with damp. The days were short, and the satin-shaded lamps in the Seelbach were turned on by four o'clock. Outside in the streets, pedestrians hurried by in the gritty dusk, and the little shops displayed a few wreaths or a handful of holly. Mary Lily spent a great deal of time searching for presents for her stepchildren; she received a few calls from friendly or curious women. But Louisville society prided itself on its Southern tone, and many of those who set that tone had become suspicious of the Judge, who had shifted from partnership to partnership and from clique to clique as he attempted to make a life for himself.

Mary Lily had not found herself in so small a world since her girlhood in North Carolina. She was used to organizing the elaborate court life of Henry's large estates, to planning entertainments and issuing invitations. In Palm Beach, she had given a *bal poudré* where the women had dressed in the fashion of Louis XIV, with powdered wigs decorated with rosebuds and velvet bows. In Louisville there were no *bals poudrés*. She was stranded in a little industrial town dominated by the intrigues of lawyers and business-men, railroad officials and the graft-riddled denizens of the Democratic party. Her husband's friends were the loyal steeds left from his earlier wars: W. W. Davies, Dr. Ravitch, the dermatologist who had tended Eleanor, and other obscure bureaucrats who had benefited, at one time or another, from the Judge's favors.

Mary Lily was prepared for her meeting with her stepchildren on December 22. Robert, the eldest and heir, was an entertainer and socialite who sometimes exceeded the limits. Henrietta was a beautiful adolescent who had just spent her first term, unwillingly, at a girls' school in Virginia. Barry, the youngest, had lived for the past three years with his grandfather and his aunt in Asheville. In anticipation of their arrival, Mary Lily covered the great marriage bed at the Seelbach with presents.

How shy, how silent these offspring of another woman and another world must have seemed when they were finally ushered into her presence. Mary Lily was anxious; the meeting was crucial, and she tried to charm the serious-faced young people, hanging back near the door with their father. She led them at once to the presents on the bed. But they were not to be so easily won. They knew a bribe when they saw one. The presents were opened with little enthusiasm and mechanical thanks. The beautiful cash-mere sweater she had bought for Robert was too small; the lace dress for

Henrietta was too large; and Barry felt himself too old to play with tops, even a glorious mechanical one.

Then a silence fell. What to do, what to say? There was no way to create intimacy and understanding with these three, who had little reason to welcome this woman's sudden intrusion into their lives. They feared yet another separation from their father, of whom they had seen little since their mother's death. Robert and Henrietta remembered his protracted warfare against their stepgrandmother, the hated "Grandma Vi," who had never become their "blood grandmother," in spite of the Colonel's entreaties. Was it possible that this newcomer, this alien might be rooted out as well?

Robert was the most approachable; but then, Robert was already in trouble, drinking too much and too openly, flaunting his affairs with women his father found unacceptable, floundering through his academic work as he tried to imitate the social and athletic successes his father had turned to such good purpose.

Perhaps Robert threw down the challenge. Perhaps he invited Mary Lily to have a drink, knowing that it was highly unsuitable. She was too keenly aware of the various ways in which she could be compromised to return his smile; she may have remembered, with regret, that she had once said that the son reminded her of the father.

Henrietta was implacable, a beautiful and determined fifteen-year-old. She must have looked at the interloper, with her elaborate clothes and shameless jewels, with the hatred of a young woman who is barely surviving, who knows that her future depends entirely on the favor of a man who has betrayed her often before and is betraying her now, every night.

Henrietta knew about jealousy; she had grown up in a family that tended it carefully and used its explosions for its own purposes. She must have glared at her father's new wife with her strange, enchanted navy-blue eyes.

Barry was only ten. His life had collapsed after his mother's death, and his struggle since had been to forget. He had planted himself in his Aunt Sadie's love, growing whole again in the little glass-enclosed bedroom she had added onto her house in Asheville for him. He had listened to her tales of his grandfather's exploits in the Civil War, of the South Anna Bridge, of Johnson's Island; he knew about chivalry, and honor, and the place that women occupy in that hierarchy. Above all, he had learned not to think too much, because it was unbearably painful; not to piece together motivations, or examine emotions, because it all led back to that terrible moment when he knew, suddenly, and out of nowhere, that his mother had died. He watched his older brother and sister, knowing that they would be angry with him if he went and sat on the pretty lady's knee. So he hung back, holding his sister's hand, wishing he was sitting by his aunt's cozy fire in North Carolina.

The Judge tried to smooth the awkward meeting, reminding Mary Lily that everything takes time and that the children were still suffering from their mother's death. He did not remind her of that other stepmother, the wretched Elvira. But this time, the Judge was not successful. Mary Lily was used to being loved, used to the flattery of those who were eager for her favors, but also to the love of her women friends, her sisters, her niece. She simply could not accept that her magic was not working with these three silent young people, all of whom wore variations of their father's face.

She cried. She sat down on the great bed with the torn-open boxes and screamed. The Judge, horrified by such a display, left her for a while "to get ahold of herself." Her maid was sent for a cup of tea. Meanwhile, in the lobby of the hotel, the Judge found his children waiting for him, read their faces, held up his hand. "Not now . . ." But they knew, at once. The first battle was won.

Later, or the next day, Mary Lily agreed that everything would improve in time, and turned her attention to another crucial matter: a house to fit the marriage. The house must be a symbol of solid achievement, wealth, and status; it must be chosen with care. But everything was so uncertain. The Judge had not yet told her when they would be leaving Louisville for good, and his business affairs made it difficult even to know when they could go down to open Whitehall for the winter season. So she made the decision to rent a suitable house, Lincliffe, a somber gray mansion overlooking the Ohio.

After Christmas, after the children had been dispatched, Mary Lily and the Judge went to Whitehall. The house was opened officially for the first time since Henry's death, and the Palm Beach newspapers rejoiced. Mary Lily introduced the Judge to her friends from the old days; now it was his turn to live in a marble palace designed by and for his predecessor.

In Louisville, the Judge had talked to one of the two Haldeman brothers, who owned, along with their sister, Isabelle, almost all of the stock in the two prosperous dailies, the *Courier-Journal* and the *Times.* The editor, Henry Watterson, owned a few shares as well. Watterson and the elder Haldeman brother, known in the family as Uncle Willy, had taken little hand of late in the running of the newspapers. The younger brother, Bruce, a hardworking middle-aged man, had shouldered most of the responsibility since his father's death many years before. It had seemed a reasonably workable arrangement: Watterson, who was a well-known orator and fiery spokesman for a variety of causes, spent a good deal of the year in Florida or Europe, cabling back his editorials, which Bruce sometimes refused to run. Uncle Willy amused himself abroad, and Isabelle led the encastled life of a Victorian daughter. She had turned her share of the newspapers' stock over to her brothers in return for assurances about her dividends.

The Judge knew that Bruce was increasingly dissatisfied with Watterson's high-handed ways. Watterson had insisted on printing a front-page editorial tying the new tax law, which the newspaper supported, to the question of Prohibition. Watterson had Uncle Willy's support, Isabelle was not a party to the discussions, and the hardworking Bruce felt more and more beleaguered.

Robert had noticed with interest when a new player entered the game: a former Confederate officer, almost as persuasive as the Colonel, who became Isabelle's lawyer. The vacuum had been filled. Colonel Bennett H. Young had been a great friend of Isabelle's father, and the Judge noticed that she took to him, as he would have said, like a duck to water.

These men all moved in the Judge's circle, frequenting the same clubs, telling the same jokes, married to cousins and classmates' sisters; they knew the same scandals, stopped repeating the same gossip when it became too pernicious, understood who was coming into power and who was on the wane. It was easy to slip a word, casually, into the conversation at the bar in the Seelbach, to stroll together in informal talk down Fourth Street, to meet in a lawyer's antechamber or find themselves sitting side by side on Sunday on the porch at the country club. Nothing needed to be said that was overt, brutal, or irritating. Simply the mildest expression of interest—"I hear they're giving you a little bit of trouble"—a brightening of eye or manner when the subject of the newspapers was raised. The Judge had resources now. Everyone knew it. When he took an interest in an enterprise, the owners noticed. He was no longer an outsider surviving by his wits.

It was especially easy to talk to Colonel Young. He and the Judge shared the saga of the Civil War—braver than the Greeks at Thermopylae; slate roof; one hundred and ten degrees; an angel of mercy, Miss Ida Tarring. They spoke the same language, shared the same nuances, dreamed of the same despoiled yet golden past in a time before blacks appeared in the legislatures and women started talking about the vote. Their shared chant led easily to the handshake, the pat on the shoulder. "Now, if it really gets to the point . . ." "Always interested in that kind of thing . . ." "Don't hesitate to let me know . . ."

So the Judge was preoccupied that winter in Palm Beach, sometimes sending cables back to Louisville, always so much less satisfactory than a conversation because they reduced what was best expressed with smiles and shrugs to a few, too-well-chosen words.

Mary Lily understood; she had seen Henry preoccupied, silent and absorbed, putting her off with a pat and a smile when she asked what was going on. Then she would kiss him and rustle off to another entertainment.

She was looking forward to Easter, when her three stepchildren were to come to Whitehall. She would put Robert in the medieval suite, give Henrietta the Marie Antoinette room, and delight Barry with the English country bedroom, where he could sleep in the small four-poster bed which had once been Harry Harkness Flagler's.

But the children did not want to come. They wanted to spend Easter in Louisville. The Judge, facing for the first time the dilemma of all remarried parents, chose his children over his wife. He left Mary Lily at Whitehall, going off to fetch Henrietta from her boarding school in Staunton, Virginia, and to collect Barry in Asheville before returning to Louisville.

In Virginia, the Judge found more trouble. Henrietta had grown increasingly rebellious. She argued with her teachers, smoked—which was absolutely forbidden—and made a mess of her room. The Judge was perhaps reminded of the scene he had survived when he came to Staunton the previous fall to tell Henrietta that he was about to marry again. She had torn up her room.

In the day coach to Asheville, the Judge perhaps appealed to Henrietta's better nature; he told her that he was embarrassed and surprised by her behavior. He expected her to cry—he even had his linen handkerchief ready to offer.

Instead she stared at him, then lifted her chin with a sharp gesture he had seen somewhere before. Was it Mary Kerr when she stubbornly refused to go along with the Worth lawsuit? Sadie when she insisted that her grandfather Worth had not been under "undue pressure" when he made his will? Aunt Owen in the old days when she had been a threat in Mebane, or Mary Gray, who claimed that she could run the Bingham School?

With that unmistakable look of defiance, Henrietta told her father that there was something he needed to know about his bride: she was a drug fiend.

The Judge knew that Mary Lily was not an addict. He had spent enough time with her to know her habits; in fact, she might have been easier to tolerate if she did take a glass of something or a little dose of laudanum every now and then. Her trouble was that she was too energetic, spirited, and determined. The sweet daze of the addict was not for her. He sighed and shook his head.

At the train station in Asheville, Barry ran to him with open arms, his pale, fair face flaming with pleasure. He adored his father and spent hours looking forward to their meetings. In his sweet, trustful way, he put his hand inside his father's hand. Sadie and the Colonel were waiting in the car.

That night, after the children were put to bed, the Judge told his sister and his father about his troubles. Mary Lily was proving to be a handful—she had her own wishes about everything, and she was stubborn. And then there was Henrietta. Her opposition to her stepmother seemed to be hardening. Robert merely laughed his devil's laugh when the Judge tried to find out what he thought of Mary Lily. Barry, of course, was too young to understand. The Judge felt that something must be done to reverse the trend of the situation, to get things, once more, firmly in hand.

The Colonel and Sadie were instantly alert. The marriage had been a good venture—they had both endorsed it—but no one was going to come between this man and his real family. No one was going to pose a threat to his primary loyalty to his children and his clan.

The next morning the Judge bundled Henrietta and Barry onto the train (Robert was going to Louisville separately) and rode over the mountains to Kentucky. Perhaps he was reminded of that first trip, twenty years earlier, when he had been a desperate young man hoping to find a place in life. Now he was nearly settled—nearly, if Mary Lily would cooperate and if his children would cease making problems.

They arrived in Louisville on Easter morning and went to the church where the Judge had married Eleanor.

After the holiday, Mary Lily came to Louisville and moved into the somber rented mansion, Lincliffe. There she planned a reception to be held in the early summer, a few days before Mary Lily's own birthday. She had heard that the girl liked parties.

The party went off flawlessly; the newspaper accounts were adulatory. Mary Lily made sure of every detail, from the card tables provided for the nondancers to the special trolleys that carried guests back and forth to the city. The Judge was in his element; his clothes and remarks were reported fully in the newspaper accounts, and Mary Lily found herself, for the first time, in the background. She was glad to see that the Judge was his usual charming self; she had been worrying about his mood since Easter, wondering if the income she had recently offered to him—fifty thousand a year—was really an insult, as he had called it when he told her he would only accept stocks—the principal—not the dividends. He needed collateral for a loan to purchase the newspapers.

After a trip to New York, where she bought herself another beautiful string of pearls for her birthday, Mary Lily decided to find a way to ease the lingering strain.

She had become used to the company of the Judge's men friends, who often came out for dinner and spent the night. Dave, particularly, made himself most agreeable, and was available during the day to go on drives. The days were very long on the bluff over the Ohio, and Mary Lily looked forward to the slight breeze along the river, and to Dave's kindly and respectful attitude; she felt that she could talk to him about anything.

One hot day in June, she told Dave that she had made up her mind to give the Judge a handsome present. He asked her what form it would take, and she said that she wanted him to draw up a codicil to her will, a separate document that would not be affected by anything in the will itself. She mentioned five million dollars. It was the amount she had originally planned to lay aside for the Judge, giving him only the income.

Dave went at once to his office and worked on a draft. He did not talk to the Judge; there was no need. Besides, the situation was delicate. He realized that it was important to get the wording exactly right and to have the paper ready to sign before Mary Lily changed her mind, or fell ill. She had been suffering from some undiagnosed complaint. The dermatologist Dr. Ravitch had been called several times to the house.

A few days later, Mary Lily called Dave from Dr. Ravitch's office, and sent her chauffeur to pick him up. Dave drew up the codicil on Dr. Ravitch's paper, and Mary Lily signed it. She was delighted with the secrecy they had been able to maintain; she did not want anyone to know about her gift, which she intended to present to the Judge herself.

She gave the Judge the codicil that night, after dinner, when they were sitting with their coffee on the terrace at Lincliffe. The Colonel was visiting, but he withdrew discreetly. It was dark, and she could not see the Judge's face, but he leaned across the table and kissed her hand. Then she asked him if they could leave for Mamaroneck the next week, before the terrible heat set in. He explained that he could not leave because the Haldeman case was about to come up in court. He had talked so little about it that Mary Lily had to ask him to start at the beginning and explain. All during his quick recital, the codicil lay on the glass-topped table, folded, under the Judge's hand.

Mary Lily did not really listen. She felt choked by the hot night around her. Why could she not leave, as she always had, when the climate took its regular turn for the worse? How was she going to survive all summer in that gloomy house over the miasmal Ohio?

The Judge told her it was simply out of the question. Bruce Haldeman was challenging his brother and Colonel Young's decision to form an executive committee; they wanted to snatch control of the newspapers out of Bruce's hands, and it looked as though the court would rule against him. The time was ripe; the Judge was needed in court, where his firm was representing Uncle Willy, Isabelle, Colonel Young, and Henry Watterson. In fact, the maid came in at that moment with a call from Colonel Young.

Mary Lily went upstairs, looked at her pearls, opened her closet and examined her dresses. The summer would pass, somehow. The children, at least, would not come to torment her; they had all gone to Asheville. As she looked at herself in the long mirror, she realized that she had given up.

After that it often did not seem worthwhile to dress when the day would be so long and hot. Dave did not mind seeing her in her dressing gown. After Dr. Ravitch came to give her one of his famous treatments—massage, a new lotion for her skin, occasionally a hypodermic to get her system working— she would spend the rest of the day in bed, drifting in and out of sleep. The Judge had explained that Dr. Ravitch had done wonders for poor Eleanor.

There really was no reason for Mary Lily to exert herself. The Judge often spent the evening in town, preparing himself for the next day's session in court. Mary Lily glanced at the headlines in the newspapers, but it was difficult to concentrate and she did not really grasp the complicated details of the Haldeman family vendetta. Usually she fell asleep before she had finished reading the article.

It grew hotter and hotter. Now in the mornings her maid did not even open the heavy wooden shutters that kept some of the glare away from her bedroom windows. Mary Lily drank tea, or lemonade, and sometimes she ate a cracker, but she had little appetite. Dr. Ravitch came and went, quietly, with his demure smile; she always felt better after he had gone.

Dr. Ravitch was coming every day now. One evening the Judge told her that he had suggested that Dr. Ravitch spend the night. It seemed that she was not well; when she tried to go to the bathroom, she fell, and the Judge had to help her back to bed. It was increasingly difficult to tell whether it was night or day, especially with the shutters closed. She asked the maid to open them, but she did not seem to hear. Then a new woman appeared, and Mary Lily would have protested, but her voice felt small. This woman was a nurse—at least she wore a nurse's uniform. She never left Mary Lily, except when Dr. Ravitch came. He always sent the nurse downstairs while he gave Mary Lily her treatments.

Her sisters came—she saw their faces, vaguely, as though through a screen—but by then Mary Lily could not tell them how surprised she was to see them. Perhaps they had decided to pay a visit, although it seemed unlikely in the heat.

The heat broke at night like great waves over the silent house; sometimes when she woke, Mary Lily would see the nurse watching her intently. She planned to get up, to go to the mirror, to call her maid and give her instructions, but every morning she had difficulty opening her eyes, and then Dr. Ravitch came—she felt his presence in the room before she saw him. At last she began to slip away altogether—she knew it was happening, she even formed the words: I am slipping away altogether. The sheets rested lightly on her body and the patch of ceiling over her head faded like a piece of the sky.

Jessie Kenan Wise vouched for the death certificate, signed by Dr.

Walter Fisk Bogges, a pediatrician, and   one time student of Dr. Solomon Steinberg. It said the woman on the bed had died of heart failure. She was fifty years old.

The Judge came and knelt by the bed and kissed the woman's hand. Then he looked at her face. She looked much younger now, with all that tension and confusion wiped away; she looked like the pretty young woman he had first known at Chapel Hill.

The Kenans were there, and they made preparations together for the funeral. The Judge had purchased a lot in Cave Hill Cemetery a week before; he liked to have things in order. But the Kenans objected. They wanted to take Mary Lily home. The Judge eventually agreed.

He was sorry now that he had written, on impulse, to the preacher George Morgan Ward, summering in Massachusetts, to complain about Mary Lily's behavior. Ward's reply had come a few days before: "It is almost as hard seeing it all happening to you two as it would be to be one of you. No, that is not true but I wish I could help." Ward had wanted to write Mary Lily a letter, but it was too late for all help now.

Now, even as the Judge prepared for the funeral, letters and cables began to arrive. He found them a torment. One, from a close friend of Mary Lily's, said that she had been terribly surprised at the news of her death. She had never known that Mary Lily was ill, and remembered her at her wedding, eight months before, beautiful and young.

The Judge was worried about the effect of all the commotion on his children. They seemed numb and dazed; even Henrietta was speechless. Barry was quiet—he did not really understand what was happening, as people came and went at all hours on all sorts of errands—and the Judge sent him back to Asheville to spare him.

At the funeral service in North Carolina, the Judge imagined that there was a good deal of whispering and meaningful looks, but he realized that he was likely to misinterpret almost anything. His skin felt as thin as air; he was haunted by something nameless. He kept turning over lost options in his mind: perhaps if he had taken her to Mamaroneck, as she had asked . . . perhaps if he had insisted on more doctors, specialists . . . Ravitch was an old friend and as discreet as the tomb, but perhaps he was not up on the latest treatments. And the two other doctors he had eventually called in were a pediatrician and a laboratory research assistant. But it was too late for any of that, too late to divide and share out the blame, if indeed there was any blame.

The niece, Louise, was the one who started the trouble. The Judge had never liked her. She seemed to be the kind of woman who would go on marrying men until there were none left. Already she had completely bested her young husband, who was eager to obey her every command. They came to stay at Lincliffe and then suddenly went away again, without even letting the Judge know that they were leaving. The Colonel, alarmed, asked if they had been approached by the servants, and the Judge remembered that they had been alone in the house with that foolish old cook, and the housekeeper, Ida, who was always up to no good.

Now, five weeks after the funeral, it seemed that the Kenan family could not accept the official account of Mary Lily's death. They accused the Judge of unspeakable things, and Louise Wise was at the head of the pack. It seemed to most sane people that these North Carolinians should be satisfied with the enormous amount of money they were about to receive—some said more than a hundred million—from Mary Lily's estate. But the Kenans insisted that it was not the money. They said they wanted to know how Mary Lily had died.

Men were seen in the North Carolina graveyard prodding the sod around her grave with their canes. A guard was set, but by that time it was too late; ghouls hired by the Kenans had come in during the night and dug Mary Lily out of her grave, lifting the concrete slabs that were laid over her and prying open the steel-plated coffin. When the Judge heard, he sat with his head in his hands; Mary Lily, so smooth and pretty, had been dragged out of her coffin where she had been laid to rest in peace, to be hacked open, her vital organs jerked out . . . It was unspeakable. People said that doctors had taken her heart and kidneys to New York in a box for examination at Bellevue Hospital.

The resulting autopsy was never made public, although it was said to have shown large quantities of morphine and traces of arsenic in poor Mary Lily's despoiled body. However, morphine had been in the embalming fluid, and perhaps Ravitch had used it to ease her final pain. Nobody knew for sure because burglars broke into Ravitch's office and stole Mary Lily's records. Ravitch himself went to Maine for a rest and was not available to testify in court.

The inquiry dragged and fizzled. Dave was on the stand day after day, the dear friend sweating in his three-piece suit in the early-autumn heat. Everyone said he had behaved like a trouper. The Judge was called, but he was not available. He had been campaigning for county commissioner, and afterwards he had driven off to Atlantic City in his new car for a vacation.

The scandalous news stories petered out. The Kenans still refused to reveal Mary Lily's autopsy. Finally her will was probated and the Judge was awarded his five million dollars in cash, just in time to make an offer to Uncle Willy and Colonel Bennett Young for the two newspapers. They accepted with pleasure, and Watterson agreed to stay on as editor. Bruce Haldeman still owned about thirty percent of the stock, but that would be dealt with in time. Isabelle paid Colonel Young a third of her proceeds as a consulting fee.

Standard Oil helped to bring things to a decent close. The stockholders hated publicity, and they knew that further disclosures about the Flagler estate might be damaging. They held a meeting in New York that fall and decided what to do about these quarrelsome Southerners. They knew who required what, where money would work its charm, where other forms of persuasion would be more effective.

The Judge was deep in mourning but he had no grave to visit. Finally he persuaded the Millers to allow him to move Eleanor to the plot he had bought for Mary Lily. He erected a headstone that said "Beautiful and Most Beloved."

The Judge let it be known that he did not welcome reference to the matters of the summer and fall. He was sick of descriptions of Mary Lily's wealth, especially her jewelry, the value always vastly inflated. After all, Mary Lily had given Sadie a pearl necklace that turned out, the Judge claimed, to be a worthless fake. Letters of condolence and sympathy continued to arrive from all quarters, expressing horror at the Judge's martyrdom. The Judge replied that he had been unjustly and cruelly accused—it was an example of the misuse of the press, of unbridled attacks a decent publisher would never tolerate. He did not like his three children to mention the stories or discuss their stepmother. He made a statement that he considered his newspapers a public trust.

In the next several years, silence obliterated almost every bit of evidence that Mary Lily had lived. Her papers, letters, and possessions disappeared, and the great gray house was finally stripped of her belongings. The inventory included gilded flatware—ice-cream spoons, orange spoons, berry and oyster knives. Then there was all that linen monogrammed MLK. They said her jewelry was worth half a million dollars—but the pearl necklace from Tiffany's had disappeared. The French gilded chairs were carted away along with silver inkstands, cologne bottles, clocks, lamps, laces, paintings, and a silver toilet set with twenty-eight pieces. Finally the house was empty.

The Judge went back a last time, to lock up. He stood in the entrance hall and looked up the staircase to where dusty windows let in a filtered light. A big oblong space on the wall marked where one of the oil paintings had hung; he could see the outline of the tasseled cord. He remembered the movers hunching to get the big oil on their backs the day he and Mary Lily had moved in, only a year before.

As he locked the door, the Judge must have felt relieved that the trouble was over. Certainly he was enjoying the prospect of running his morning and evening newspapers, with the expert guidance of two old friends, one of whom, Emmanuel Levi, would be called "Uncle Manny" by the Judge's children. It was a relief to know that no more scurrilous stories could be published in the state of Kentucky. The Judge now controlled the voice of the opposition, allowing it to speak only at certain times and in certain ways, through his monopoly press. At the same time, he would create a standard of journalistic objectivity and integrity for the reporting of all the news that did not directly concern him, and he would teach his son that "yellow journalists" like William Randolph Hearst were to be scorned because they were not gentlemen.

He may have believed that his children had weathered the scandal without much obvious harm. Barry, especially, had learned to pity his father during those years, and would always protect him from criticism. The Judge was thinking of bringing him home from Asheville.

As he walked out of Mary Lily's house, the Judge glanced once more at the steely Ohio between stripped winter trees. He believed he was putting the past behind him. Mary Lily was gone.

His chauffeur was waiting with the new Packard's door open, and the Judge climbed in for the ride back to town. After all, he thought, no matter what people believed, he had only killed Mary Lily with kindness. He had loved her to death. He had made her one flesh.

Later, Robert gave him some trouble—but that was Robert. He did not seem to appreciate the great Georgia plantation the Judge bought or the enormous Belknap place farther out on River Road or the summer trips to Europe. Perhaps Robert did not believe his father's statement of purpose for the newspapers: "I have always regarded the newspapers owned by me as a public trust and have endeavored so to conduct them as to render the greatest public service." Robert might have said he knew who would benefit from that public service: corrupt Democratic politicians, the railroad interests, and hypocrites like Franklin Roosevelt.

Robert was also drinking too much and making a fool of himself. One night he drove his automobile right into the front hall. The Judge began to fear that he would never amount to much, like Robert's cousin Bingham McKee, who had just been crowned king of the rhododendron festival in Asheville. These boys mistook sociability for the main thing.

Still, he did not expect Robert's last trick. On the evening of the Judge's birthday, when all the old hands were assembled at the big table set with the gold plate, Robert came down the stairs stark naked and presented his father with a flower box. It held horse manure.

Now the Judge set about consolidating his ownership of the newspapers—as his uncle, William, had seized control of the school in Mebane in 1865, as his father, the Colonel, had seized control in Asheville, squashing the "two-headed or triple-headed" ownership his two daughters advocated.

For a year, Bruce Haldeman remained in titular control. Henry Watter-

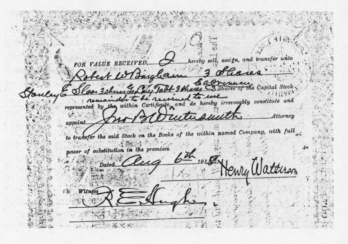

Following Henry Watterson's disagreement with the Judge over support of the League of Nations, Watterson asked that his name be taken off the newspaper's masthead. Soon after, the Judge bought Watterson's small share of Louisville *Times* stock.

The Ohio River from the terrace of the Big House, 1933.

son, the voice of an older South, whose bravado had created the *Courier*'s reputation, was still its itinerant editor.

Watterson (whose father had once given him a slave boy, later killed "fighting for his kind," as Watterson said, during the Civil War) was a complex, opinionated man who was used to having his way. He once called himself a free nigger.

Although he had been an early supporter of Woodrow Wilson, Watterson later turned against Wilson's anti-machine progressivism and called him "that crook from New Jersey." He castigated Prohibition and the League of Nations, calling the latter "a Utopian scheme to have the United States underwrite the combustions of Europe . . . I am amazed that any intelligent patriotic American should be misled by a fake so transparent." One who was so misled was the newspaper's new owner.

The Judge wrote Watterson, "I hope you will forgive me for asking you . . . not to request us to publish articles by you combatting the League of Nations, for I do not wish the paper to appear as assailing its distinguished Editor." This letter followed a special edition of the newspaper honoring Watterson, who was now called "editor emeritus." The honor did not prevent Watterson from seeing what was happening. He resigned at once.

Before Watterson's resignation, the *Courier-Journal* had for a while run editorials both attacking and supporting the League, which accurately reflected the Judge's ambiguous point of view. For the next five years, the Judge continued to vacillate. In 1922, he wrote Wilson a congratulatory note on his birthday, to which Wilson replied formally to "Major Bingham," which must have rankled. The same year, the Judge sent an admiring telegram to Calvin Coolidge, to which Coolidge replied from the White House that he was pleased to hear that the Judge, "a recognized leader of efforts along this line," understood the President's refusal to extend further federal relief to farmers who were suffering, in Kentucky and elsewhere, from a collapse in prices. Coolidge went on: "There is really very little demand for extreme, unsound, and uneconomic procedures in dealing with the present economic situation." A few years later, President Roosevelt's relief program would receive that label in some quarters at a time when the Judge had given Roosevelt his financial and political support.

The Judge's attitude toward Wilson was complicated. While Watterson hoped to use Wilson as a rallying point for anti-Bryan conservative Democrats in the South, the Judge expected Wilson's political liberalism to advance the cause of the weak Progressive party in Kentucky, to which he had at least in theory allied himself since his brief term as mayor in 1907. However, Wilson's refusal to give the fruits of patronage to members of the progressive group in Kentucky alienated the Judge and other Kentucky Democrats. Through the influence of his Postmaster General, the Texan

Albert S. Burleson, Wilson was persuaded to support the old conservative faction in the party. Control of patronage in Kentucky was turned over to Senator Ollie M. James, and only one "Wilson man" was named to federal office in the entire state. It was enough to discourage a local politician who expected any calls for "reform" to stop short of changes in the local system. After this period, the Judge began to call himself an Independent.

The questions of Prohibition and the vote for women caused the Judge deep private dismay. The state depended on its distilleries, which, with coal and tobacco, brought in the only capital Kentucky could command. The liquor lobby had long influenced Kentucky politics in an extensive way; personally, the Judge accepted the role of whiskey in the male world he had inhabited since coming over the mountains in 1896. So the passing of the Volstead Act, which had been vigorously supported by women's groups, signaled an ominous change in the temper of the country.

With the extension of suffrage to women in 1920, the change became even more alarming. That women should vote would have been an alien idea to the Judge, who saw women as helpmeets and civilizers who worked to improve the world through cooking, praying, and bringing up sons. What need did women have to vote when they were politically uneducated, prone to be censorious of necessary alliances, and unlikely to form powerful interest groups with other women? At best they would merely vote as their husbands did, which seemed a right hardly worth winning. The few women who took an independent stance might threaten the control of local machines whose workings were oiled by old-line politicians like the Judge.

The Judge, acutely tuned to political change, must have realized that the power of women, barely controlled in his personal life, was now breaking out on the public stage. As a dramatic example, his own daughter had abandoned conventional life as a Southern heiress to pursue adventure in London. Henrietta never held a political belief, yet her behavior was profoundly influenced by the newfound liberty for women symbolized by the extension of the vote.

Three days after Watterson's resignation, the Judge bought the remaining thirty percent of the newspapers' stock from Bruce Haldeman. Haldeman resigned a year later, leaving behind his life's work.

When he was first challenged by his older brother and Bennett Young, Haldeman had proclaimed in court that he had been "indecently treated" by his relatives. He went on to "apprise my friends that I am out of a position, and that I desire some business connection, as it is necessary for me to be at work to support my family." He never found that connection, and spent the rest of his life traveling.

Seventy years later, the Judge's grandson would resign with the same bitter complaint: the owner, he said, had built a mountain he could not climb. Both Bruce Haldeman and Barry Bingham, Jr., had put substantial portions of their lives into running newspapers they did not own.

Bruce Haldeman and his brother were enriched for life by the proceeds from the sale of their stock. Their sister Isabelle's fate was different. She paid nearly a third of her proceeds as a fee to her adviser and lawyer, the ex-Confederate officer Bennett H. Young. Then she placed the remaining cash in his hands to invest. By the time of Young's death, a few years later, Isabelle's fortune had disappeared.

An attempt was made to sue Young's estate for the squandered millions, but it was unsuccessful. Young's heirs were able to claim that he had merely made some mistakes in investing Isabelle's money. Her family believed that he had taken outrageous risks with her money, investing his own where her money had succeeded and leaving her to pay for his mistakes. She never understood what was happening, trained by lifelong compliance to accept a Confederate officer's word.

At the end of her long life, Isabelle was living in penury in a small apartment in Louisville. The bitterness in the family was still so intense, a half century after the sale, that Bruce Haldeman refused to contribute anything toward his sister's support. The two branches of the Haldeman family never spoke after the sale. Their children, growing up in the family compound in Florida, did not know who their neighbors were.

By 1918, the Judge controlled the most powerful private institution in Kentucky, which rivaled the state government for political clout. The newspapers were without competition inside the state. They were read far and wide, even in the western and eastern portions of the state which had little access to other news; the eastern mountains would be without television until the advent of cable. The newspapers' endorsements were crucial for state political candidates; the editor's decision on which news to report and where and in what detail would form the opinions and influence the voting of three generations of Kentuckians. In addition, the Judge need never again fear the kind of news stories which had embarrassed him during the Mary Lily scandal. He owned the voice of criticism.

Owning the press meant that continuing stories about Mary Lily's estate would not be read in Kentucky. It also meant owning the past. Seventy years later, newspaper, library, and historical society files in Louisville contained no reference to Mary Lily's existence beyond the announcement of her engagement to the Judge. No details about her death are contained in the information available to the public. Private papers stored in a safe at the newspapers' offices were removed when the newspapers were sold to the Gannett Company in 1986.

Control of the local press did not, of course, ensure control of newspapers in other states. Yet local control made it more difficult for the Judge and his son and grandson to countenance any criticism. If the critics could be dissuaded at home, why did they continue to rant abroad? Hearst and Lord Beaverbrook would become thorns in the publisher's side while he was Ambassador to England, and ire at their attacks would prevent the Judge from realizing that they were exercising the same power he exercised in Kentucky. Hearst was a disgraceful person, according to the Binghams, but Hearst shared many characteristics with Judge Bingham, especially in his unexamined use of power. The power was used for different ends, but the issue was not the ends, but the means. Voices of dissent, whether coming from the left or the right, would not be heard in a state where the only newspapers were controlled by one man.

Meanwhile, money brought its relief to the Judge. He bought Pinelands, a thousand-acre plantation in Georgia, where he gathered his men friends to shoot quail. There he would develop an interest in conservation that did not prevent him from hunting over baited fields, as his grandson would do half a century later; both men had excuses at hand. When he was Ambassador to England, the Judge was said to shoot as many as 250 pheasants in a single day. Both his son and his grandson admired and imitated the Judge's prowess with guns, which would deeply affect their political and personal creeds.

Honors and awards sweetened the ailing Judge's life in the 1930s, obscuring the past. For a while his old friend and personal physician, the venereal disease expert Dr. Hugh Young, kept at bay the rashes and fevers that had plagued the Judge since 1900. In England, the Judge was sheltered from the questions about his past that continued to be raised, from time to time, by the "yellow" press.

The Kenans still refused to reveal the autopsy done on Mary Lily's organs at Bellevue. They also concealed the long report from private detectives they had hired to investigate the causes of her death. As of this writing, these papers repose in an attic in central North Carolina. On the dusty lid, some long-dead relative scrawled, "Keep These Forever."

The Kenan family may have entered into an agreement with the Judge, but what that agreement was, and how it was paid for, may never be known.

Perhaps the agreement depended on the Judge's collusion in the court's decision that Mary Lily was a resident of Florida, not Kentucky. Since Florida had no income tax, the savings to Mary Lily's estate, savings passed along to the Kenans, her chief beneficiaries, were about five million dollars—almost exactly the sum the Judge received from the codicil to her will. When the Kenans did not pursue their case in court, the five million dollars passed to the Judge uncontested.

My grandfather Robert Worth Bingham (the Judge),
Pinelands Plantation, Georgia, 1929.

Father (center) with friends at the Judge's hunting lodge in Scotland, 1920s.

Father picnicking at the lodge, 1920s.

The loser was the state of Kentucky—and that more abstract entity, the truth.

The Kenans and their descendants were enriched for life with Standard Oil stock and shares in Flagler's railway and hotel system. One of the last bequests was for twenty thousand dollars, given to the little daughter of the New York architect Mary Lily had hired to design the Fifth Avenue mansion she did not live to build—across the street from the apartment where I lived in the 1960s.

Mary Lily's estate paid for the Judge's living expenses at Lincliffe, and even repaid him for flowers he had ordered for her funeral.

What actually happened to Mary Lily on those hot summer days at Lincliffe is no longer discoverable. The trail of evidence is gone, worn away by time or successfully hidden by Binghams and Kenans alike, who had the power to rewrite history. She died, like so many other women, rich and poor, of a combination of causes that included depression, neglect and medical incompetence, the failure of love, isolation, and a heart probably weakened by the syphilis she had contracted from the Judge in North Carolina or Virginia.

She also died because she would not, for a long time, give the man his money.

She made that clear in the message she prepared for reporters at the time of their marriage. All of Flagler's huge fortune would go, after her death, to her niece, Louise Wise—the young woman Mary Lily described as equal to any man in her ability to handle money and use it for the benefit of other people.

The Judge could hardly have welcomed the news that Louise Wise was to inherit everything he wanted. Perhaps some of Henrietta's dislike of her stepmother stemmed from jealousy of Louise, who was only a few years older.

But Mary Lily persisted. The money, she believed, was hers—not Henry Flagler's, not his first wives', not his son's, not the Kenans', who took a strong proprietary interest in it. All during the winter and spring of 1917, when the Judge was fiercely determined to raise one million dollars to buy the Louisville newspapers, Mary Lily resisted. According to a Louisville story, she paid off his debts and she offered to give him income from stocks she owned—but not the stocks themselves. It was the stocks the Judge needed, to finance his purchase of the newspapers, and her determination to control them herself must have maddened him even while he insisted that ladies—the Melanies he had invented all his life to replace the women he knew—simply did not behave as though they owned money.

She gave in at last, and drew up the codicil, probably with the help of the Colonel, who was visiting Lincliffe at the time. By then she was depressed and isolated—and it must have seemed the last chance she would have to redeem her relationship with her husband.

Her death, the scandal of the investigation, and the years of rewriting history affected her stepchildren and their children. The three young people who resisted her with the coldness and scorn that are so often the reward of a stepmother would benefit financially from her death; they would also create a nearly seamless myth to prevent their own children from knowing that the mother of it all had even existed.

Since scandal shrouded the source of Bingham money, even half a century after Mary Lily's death money could never be discussed. The questions all children ask—"Are we rich? Where did it come from?"—met a paralyzing silence.

One of Mary Lily's bequests changed the future of the University of North Carolina by establishing the Kenan Professorships.

The bequest was suggested by the Colonel during the summer of 1915, when Mary Lily was visiting Asheville in order to spend time with the Judge. Eager to curry favor with the man she hoped would soon be her father-in-law, Mary Lily listened to his suggestion.

The Colonel explained that bricks and mortar do not make a first-class university, but rather the quality of the professors, all of whom were men. He explained that universities like Chapel Hill could not compete with the salaries paid to academics in the North. The result, as the Colonel wrote gleefully on October 6, 1915, to President George Winston, was a bequest in Mary Lily's will of $75,000 annually. This allowed the university to establish the Weil Lectures on American Citizenship and to develop a school of commerce and business administration. Since the money was called the Bingham bequest, it finally created the bond with Chapel Hill the Colonel and his male relatives had wanted for so many years.

But Mary Lily was dead. Her wishes were no longer of any consequence.

While other rich families sometimes found ways to justify their accumulated money, relying on the American myth of hard work, native talent, and moral character to explain their success, the Binghams could make use of no such explanations. No Bingham man had worked hard to earn Mary Lily's five million, which started the empire. Like the idlest debutante, like the lily that does not toil or spin, the Judge had been showered with money and its attendant privileges and powers. Love had been the medium of exchange. Only a bland fatalism about ends and means could conceal such an unlikely, even grotesque event as the death of Mary Lily Kenan Flagler Bingham, especially in a family still singed by Southern Presbyterianism with its belief in hard work and spiritual election.

But if faith and not deeds formed the high moral character of the

Bingham men—faith in looks and charms and useful sociability—then they were in their own eyes worthy of whatever windfalls women bestowed on them, for they were, as the old Colonel himself believed, "kings of men."

The myth weathered and aged as the family grew more prosperous. It could no longer really cover the polite antagonism men felt toward the women they married, women who often possessed a large portion of the world's goods as well as wit and will. The same antagonism lay behind the family's condescension toward blacks, those subversive figures in every Southern landscape, totally powerless except for the power of observation, which sometimes leads to the telling of truths, even with a smile. Truth telling must be suppressed in women and in blacks by a family with so many secrets to shield. So the romantic notion was cultivated that women, like the best blacks, are submissive, gay, and useful, minions who make the gilded wheel of the day turn round.

Long before Mary Lily's death, a light but persistent breeze of hostility chilled relations between brother and sister, mother and daughter in the family, a hostility at home with conventional utterances about the beauty and grace of women and the sanctity of motherhood. Driven by that light wind, the perfect gentlemen the family continued to produce, replicas of the majors and captains and colonels of the old military school in North Carolina, married women who brought wealth and prestige into the family and who always promoted their husbands' ambitions.

The family has died out in North Carolina, the last generation producing no marriages and no children, as though every ounce of energy and imagination had been absorbed in the continuing battle for dominance—of the school, of the family, of life itself. In Kentucky, too, the name is now nearly extinct, having been passed only to one grandson. It is likely that after 150 years of secret turmoil that name, in its Southern manifestation, will disappear altogether.

The final characters, formed by years of strangled dispute, are bitter, avid, and litigious, like their ancestors in Reconstruction North Carolina who never forgot their humiliation at the hands of Union troops. Except for that myth, the family's past is too dangerous to contemplate; we are related, instead, to the vicar in Hardy's *Tess of the D'Urbervilles* and the imaginary de Binghams of a sanctified English history.

I never heard of Mary Lily Kenan Flagler Bingham until I was fifteen, when a stranger at a London luncheon told me that my grandfather had murdered his second wife. However, she deeply affected the family which rejected her. Her money started the empire; the scandal of her death formed its battlements. The newspapers were bought to answer a need to ferret out other people's secrets while closely guarding our own.

But journalism carried its own risks. For two generations, introverted men of great personal integrity embarked on careers in newspapers and television that demanded élan, publicity, and zeal—during which, inevitably, their pasts would be subjected to scrutiny. The Bingham men were perhaps poorly equipped to deal with the resulting strain.

In addition, men who have suffered terrible losses in early life need the unconditional love a wealthy family almost never provides. They come to fear their children's understanding because, in the old equation, understanding means the withdrawal of love. Such starved adults, clan-oriented to value their blood descendants more than their wives (who, after all, will never be "related"), lash their children close for a lifetime with secrets everyone knows about but no one can mention.

The increasing isolation money buys—the big "places" with their long drives and iron gates, the alarm systems, watchdogs, and security guards— makes it difficult for each generation to form friendships. And friends may pry into secrets. Only relatives can be counted on not to "bring it all up again." Minions, rather than equals, form the inner circle, servants and impoverished dependents, advisers and petitioners.

Women must be kept outside as well. For 150 years, Bingham women fell silent, died, or disappeared, from Annie Jean Slingsby, who departed for Tennessee after her husband's death, through Owen White Bingham's battle to keep her school, her daughter Mary's struggle and failure, Eleanor's death on the railroad tracks, and Mary Lily's death in the great gray mansion overlooking the Ohio River. The North Carolina women gradually disappeared as Sadie and her nieces declined into poverty and obscurity. Only the Judge's daughter, Henrietta, would remain onstage for a while.

In each generation, women (and the weaker men, like Ernest, the deaf-mute who fled to Duluth) lost out in the battle for inheritance, power, and money. They signed papers without understanding them, were parties to lawsuits aimed at disinheriting them, and turned what money they had over to their male relatives to invest. Yet in spite of all their disappointments, their loyalty remained to father and brother, thirdly to husband, and almost never to mother, sister, or daughter. Power was with the men. Perhaps not a single one of those lost women ever believed she owned any part of it. Perhaps gratitude for favors received was all they ever felt.

But I doubt it. In the trash burning that followed each woman's death, diaries and letters went up in smoke that told the other story: the passion and prejudice censored from the official documents. Here lay the expressions of anxiety, anger, and defiance, along with the account books that listed the women's meager personal resources, and photographs displaying a determined tilt of the chin. Nothing is left of these women's lives and so we will never know what it felt like to belong to one of the Bingham men: how that ownership defined the life of a piedmont North Carolina housewife before the Civil War, a Louisville matron between the two world wars, or an aging lesbian in New York in the 1950s. As Shakespeare said when re-creating the scene of another kind of battle, "On your imaginary forces work."

In the 1920s, the Judge was moving up through levels of prosperity and prominence. He had bought a big house on River Road, a house even grander than Mary Lily's nearby Lincliffe. It was called Brushy Hill, but the Judge renamed it Bingham's Melcombe, in honor of the prized connection with Dorset, the county seat of the English Binghams. He had his initials and the date set in the big wrought-iron gates. Here his three children, Robert, Henrietta, and Barry, came to spend their vacations from boarding school and college.

While his children gave parties (an elderly relative once had to poke through the shrubbery with her cane to dislodge late revelers), the Judge pursued the course that would finally carry him out of the South, and out of the past.

He helped the state's tobacco farmers form a cooperative to control their crop's wildly fluctuating prices. This is said to have brought him to the attention of Franklin Roosevelt. He made contributions to the local Democratic party.

He continued his interest in horse racing and appeared before the legislature in 1922 to argue for pari-mutuel betting. Later he separated himself from the ownership of Churchill Downs, the big Louisville racetrack where the annual Derby is run; it was controlled by remnants of the old Democratic machine the Judge had used and now wished to abandon.

In 1930 the Judge won the hearts of Kentuckians by guaranteeing fifty percent of the money in their Christmas accounts after a Louisville bank failed. Earlier he had refused to save the bank from going under; its head was an enemy from the old bad days.

The Judge became a director of the Louisville & Nashville Railroad, which had strangled the Progressive party in Kentucky. He was made trustee of two local colleges, and gave money to many good causes, while schooling his readers in a gentle Southern liberalism that left questions of inequality to one side. Moderation was all.

With Mary Lily's money, he made a substantial contribution to Franklin Roosevelt's first campaign for President. Through Colonel House, whose violent Texas background was so similar to his own, the Judge found connections first with President Wilson and then with President Roosevelt, connections sponsored by Cordell Hull and Louis Howe.

But the Judge never could stand Bernard Baruch—the financier with his brocade bathrobes and his sure sense of his own importance. Disagreements between these two men and their followers had an effect on the finagling at Versailles in 1919, on the failure of the League of Nations, and—through the collapse of the London Economic Conference in 1933—on the coming of the Second World War.

Perhaps if Baruch had been a little less self-assured . . .

The Judge spent almost no time in Kentucky during his last years. Abroad, he spoke as an internationalist and a detached critic of the United States. At home he created himself as a liberal Southerner who had put the hatred and the sectionalism of his father's world behind him. Roosevelt complimented the Judge in their first exchange of letters on understanding the importance of being "lifted above material things." Now he could afford it.

It is difficult to know how profound the change in the Judge's convictions was during the New Deal, when his native Southern conservatism would have limited his opportunities for political advancement. In Louisville, he supported the moderate Commission on Interracial Cooperation, which, unlike the more radical NAACP, sought to educate blacks to accept their inferior status. His newspapers praised the CIC for solving problems, and decided which blacks to single out as leaders. "Handling the Negro Problem" in this way led to the "polite racism" that became Kentucky's partial solution. Symbolically, the Judge helped finance the career of singer Roland Hayes, nephew of a headwaiter at the Judge's club. Half a century later, the Judge's grandson Worth would finance Cassius Clay's career. The attitude is the same.

A certain black man may be chosen for support and even for a limited kind of respect, while the more "difficult" and "rebellious" members of the race are quietly suppressed through a refusal to support their political activities or to report them in the newspapers. History was rewritten as the Judge and his newspapers tried to "gloss over racial discrimination and segregation and to speak in glowing terms about improvements in race relations," as George C. Wright described it in *Life Behind a Veil: Blacks in Louisville, Kentucky, 1865–1930.* This approach would lead to serious problems in the 1950s and 1960s when noblesse oblige and discreet control were no longer widely accepted.

Meanwhile, in the big house called Melcombe, the Judge's increasingly sophisticated life developed new rituals and attracted new celebrants. After Mary Lily's death, the young people, once again, were in command of the house and its considerable resources, including a staff of black servants, automobiles, guns, liquor, and a liberal supply of cash. The Judge was amused by his children's antics and did not seem especially concerned about the amount of liquor they were consuming; bourbon whiskey had long been a staple of his life. From this period came the stories Lizzie Baker, a generation later, loved to tell: the antics of Parpeetus the monkey, the parties that lasted all night, and the cruel practical jokes Robert played.

One guest from that period remembered, seventy years later, the atmosphere of a party at Melcombe, which she had attended as a girl:

It is late night. The Big House is full of young people, many of them drunk. Lights blaze from the French windows in the enormous ground-floor rooms; someone is pecking away on the piano, others are dancing in the hall, and one young man has removed his trousers, to sing and circle in drawers and tuxedo. There is a ceaseless flow of laughter and talk as the guests help themselves to drinks from the unattended bar, to food from the desecrated buffet. The black servants, both those who live in the house and those hired for the occasion, have finally given up and disappeared. They know these parties often continue until daylight, ending with a drunken breakfast "whipped up" in the enormous kitchen, where Parpeetus the monkey may throw eggs.

A woman who is a few years younger than most of the guests arrives at this point, on the arm of an older man who has offered to show her her first "wild party." She is a little shy at first, but she soon finds a friend, and they retreat to the gilded bathroom, reserved for the ladies, between the double front stairs.

The friend turns on the water in the basin to wash her hands. Suddenly the basin splits from the wall and crashes at their feet. Water surges out of holes in the wall where the golden spigots have torn off.

Horrified, the two young women snatch their wraps and flee. Water rushes out of the door behind them, into the front hall. They call for help. Several young men, more or less sober, arrive to survey the scene. No one can think what to do. Meanwhile the water is running out into the hall in a broad, increasing stream. People avoid it as best they can and continue to dance.

Finally, the young heir appears and organizes a group of men to go upstairs for towels. They return with armloads of thick white terry cloth, emblazoned with an enormous, almost royal-looking monogram. They begin to lay the great towels down in the flood of water, which rises over and submerges them.

The young heir goes upstairs for more towels.

While he is gone, the young man who had taken off his trousers descends to the cellar, where he threads a labyrinth of rooms and passages. He feels along the walls for light switches, finds them, and proceeds to the area directly under the ladies' bathroom. There he finds a set of pipes and knobs and turns off the one that controls the flow of water.

Upstairs, as though by magic, the water stops.

During all this time, the owner of the house has been sitting at a bridge table playing cards with his daughter, her lover, and a family confidante. They play hand after hand, laughing and chatting, excited by the tension that always exists between the Judge and his beautiful bisexual daughter.

At one point, the Judge glances at the commotion in the hall. The water has not yet reached his feet. Someone will deal with it. He goes back to his excellent hand.

The heir, too, turns away from the water. Someone will deal with it, in the morning. He returns to the music and the laughter.

It was a fine life, but limited by the barbarisms of the backcountry South and the Western frontier. The Judge wanted wider horizons for his three children. Nearly every summer, he took Robert, Henrietta, and Barry and their relatives and friends on a tour of the Continent and the British Isles.

The group usually disembarked at Calais ("Niggers begin at Calais" became a family joke, frowned on yet tolerated) but soon went to England, where the Judge was cultivating important friends. He hired a castle in Scotland, where he enjoyed both the hunting and his position as lord of the manor. The local people's reverence was balm to the wounds he had received during the Mary Lily scandal.

But the Judge's health was precarious, and he had several attacks, one of which was described as appendicitis. An English friend attributed his weakness to overwork in organizing the tobacco cooperative in Kentucky: "I asked him once why he had thus brought himself to the foothills of the Great Divide. In a low voice, much moved, he replied, 'I had read of men who died on the battle-field for a cause; I thought that here might be a cause for which it might be worth while to die, though not on a battle-field.' " The old Colonel died a few years later, in 1927, and the Bingham School in Asheville soon closed, but the voice, the oratory, and the emotional suasion of the Civil War officer continued to illuminate the family myth.

Robert, the Colonel's namesake, was drinking heavily; he sometimes picked up women the Judge found unsuitable. Eventually Robert contracted syphilis; the mercury treatment prescribed made the young man sterile. At one stroke, he was eliminated from the competition for Mary Lily's money and the newspapers. The Judge might countenance drinking; he might even tolerate a daughter-in-law who lacked the proper credentials, provided that she bore sons. Later, the Judge would explain the Prince of Wales's abdication as a blessing in disguise because the Prince was said to be sterile.

Now, he arranged his eldest son's abdication from the family competi-

Henrietta rode and hunted until an accident injured her leg in the 1930s.

Henrietta near her grandmother's house in Louisville. She and her brothers won city tournaments.

Henrietta and Father
(the woman at the left
is unidentified)
in England . . .

. . . and on the Riviera,
1920s.

tion. From now on there was no place for Robert except the place always reserved for the reprobate, the charming insouciant bon vivant who, with the passage of time, becomes the bewildered, dependent alcoholic. Only Barry and Henrietta were left to inherit the enterprise, which included three million dollars left from Mary Lily's codicil, the two thriving Louisville newspapers, and a radio station—the first in the area—as well as reflected glory from the honors and awards the Judge was assembling at home and abroad.

In 1924, the Judge married Aleen Muldoon Hilliard, a Louisville widow whose original family had grown rich off a funeral monument business, a fact her grown stepchildren found amusing. Her husband had left her handsomely enriched. She was received by her stepchildren with decided coolness; stepmothers were never welcome in the family, even those who, like Aleen, came with credentials and money. However, Aleen was a sophisticated woman who knew all about running a big house and maintaining an elaborate social life. In London, from 1933 till 1937, she would preside at social functions during the Ambassador's frequent illnesses, and she became a close friend of Anthony Eden.

In fact, she tempted the family demons by calling herself the Ambassadress, much to her stepchildren's chagrin. In a photograph from that period, Aleen smiles at the camera, poised and perfectly turned out in a trailing, embroidered dress; the Judge, small beside her, nervously stares off as though on the lookout for a taxi. He is wearing the court knee breeches he earlier wished to avoid and patent-leather slippers with flat bows.

Aleen made a special effort with her stepdaughter, Henrietta, as Mary Lily had in her time. Perhaps Aleen sensed that her marriage was connected in an odd way to her husband's relationship with his only daughter. Between the Judge's second and third marriages, Henrietta had once again sat at the head of his table and gone out with him as consort, admired and flattered, gilded by his adoration and the attention of his friends. Now she began, temporarily, to leave him, to depart on a life of her own.

In 1924, the English psychoanalyst James Strachey wrote to his wife, Alix, that London gossip held that "Judge Bingham married again to spite Henrietta because of her coldness towards him." The letter was written a month after the Judge married Aleen in Westminster Abbey.

Aleen's success with this beautiful daughter of turmoil was limited; Henrietta's ambiguous attachment to her father prevented a closer bond. In a photograph of the Judge, Aleen, and Henrietta, taken on a steamship deck, Henrietta's head has been torn off, presumably by its owner. She left her slender, beautifully clad body to stand beside her smiling father and stepmother. She did not stand between them.

During his excursions to Britain in the 1920s, the Judge was often called upon to make a speech, and some American newspapers resented his remarks. He was called "the prize ashamed American" for criticizing the failure of the American delegates at the Geneva Conference to understand England's need to rearm. During that decade, the Judge's alienation from the country that did not accept him on his own terms continued. He loved Scotland more than any other place in the world, he said, and especially appreciated its inhabitants' deference; later he would remark that the English made the best servants he had ever employed. At the same time, he said that he did not feel he had "earned" his privileged position in life. England, he believed, provided him with a fresh start, not Mary Lily's money. She was gone and forgotten, her memory a confused and confusing nightmare no one was free to mention. But the shadow she had cast made the Judge a more liberal and more complex man than the ambitious seeker who had crossed the North Carolina mountains a generation earlier to make his fortune in Kentucky.

"The Cinderella man," as an unfriendly newspaper called the Judge, never lost the shadow. Knowing Mary Lily, who not only was "queenly" in temperament (like the extinguished Mary Kerr) but also possessed a queen's power and fortune, complicated the Judge's view of the roles all women might be expected to play. The Judge attempted to still his unease by revising or smothering the past, using rhetoric to elevate the personal into myth. Now the Judge said in speeches that thirty-nine "men of my blood" had been slain by the Union soldiers; now he recalled his life-threatening battle on behalf of the Kentucky tobacco farmers; now he recited the tale of his duel with the officer in Munich.

Meanwhile, the Judge's children benefited from his prominence. Barry and Henrietta enjoyed the trips abroad, as, later, they would enjoy life at Prince's Gate in London. At Guthrie Castle, the rented hunting lodge in Scotland, they sometimes played a game called Tip the Table, foretelling the future, as the long-incarcerated Alice Flagler had teased prophecies out of her Ouija board. Barry was always the interpreter of the table's messages, as he interpreted his baffling brother and sister to their father, who was increasingly disillusioned with his two older children.

So much of success is the ability to imagine success: with his beautiful young wife, Mary—well educated, ambitious, eager for a role in life—young Barry found a confidence that helped him to seize opportunity. He loved his brother and sister, he understood their weaknesses—and with Mary, he helped his father to understand them, too.

As the Ambassador moved into the wider world of international proto-col, something spurred him to consider the heroic as it appears in women. In London, he ordered books by the yard for his library in the Big House in Kentucky. Among many other sets, he bought 337 volumes on the life of Joan of Arc.

His only daughter, Henrietta, had some of the qualities of that great female myth, but the eroticism of power kept her tied to her father until his death.

12

In 1918, Henrietta left the girls' boarding school in Virginia, Stuart Hall, where she had been sent before her father's marriage to Mary Lily. According to family legend, Henrietta had bitterly resented being sent away to make room for her new stepmother, yet the record she left at Stuart Hall shows that she was a lively and involved part of the community.

She was secretary and treasurer of her class, assistant business manager of the yearbook, and a member of twelve school clubs, including the Hobo Club, the Glee Club, the Tennis Club, and the Missionary Society, and she played on the basketball and volleyball teams. Yet she left before graduating.

Three years passed after leaving Stuart Hall before she went to college, years for which I could find no explanation until a chance question revealed that Henrietta had attended the same small girls' day school I had attended for nine years, the Louisville Collegiate School for Girls. I had seen Henrietta often during the years I was attending Collegiate, but she had never mentioned that we shared the same school.

School records reveal that Henrietta had first attended Collegiate in 1915, and had returned for the 1919–20 year, after her exile in Virginia was terminated by Mary Lily's death.

In 1915, when she was fourteen, Henrietta's grades ranged from the high 70s to the low 80s in subjects that included medieval history, Latin, French, German, and algebra, as well as English composition and reading. Her highest marks were in medieval history, Latin, and French.

Four tumultuous years later, when she was eighteen, Henrietta was earning grades of 80 or 90 in most of her subjects. Her highest grade—a perfect 100—was in spelling.

But in the "special" fourth term she took, as a nineteen-year-old, in the spring of 1919, her grades suddenly dropped; she failed algebra, and a handwritten note attests that she took the college entrance examinations "without recommendation of School."

Nevertheless, she was admitted to Smith College in 1920. Her preparation was probably similar to that of most well-off young women of her period: she had read Greek, Roman and medieval history, but not contemporary or American, she had some algebra and geometry, a basic knowledge of German (in which the Judge was fluent), and a substantial background in Latin grammar and composition. Like all her Bingham ancestors, she had read Cicero—she may have been the first woman in the family to do so.

Henrietta was the first woman in the Bingham family to go East to college. Her two aunts in North Carolina, Sadie and Mary, had attended the Peace Institute in Raleigh, as had Mary Lily, but it was a fashionable finishing school at the time, not a four-year liberal arts college.

Henrietta's grandfather the Colonel had somewhat modified his opposition to higher education for women after a trip to New England. He noted that educated women made useful teachers, a view that perhaps influenced his son's decision to send his daughter, in 1920, to college in Massachusetts.

In sending Henrietta to Smith, the Judge was preparing her for a larger public life as a daughter of an ambassador and heir to a newspaper monopoly, as well as great wealth. However, since her role might well prove to be purely decorative, as debutante, courtier, and consort, it was important that her education never induce her to question the status quo. So an inevitable conflict was initiated between the father's limited aims and the college's perhaps unlimited influence, at least as it would be expressed through its teachers and undergraduates. The way was opened to change.

By 1920, the first small group of women college graduates in the United States had cleared a path for their followers. The first group was highly motivated, tended to avoid marriage, and often entered the professions, working against strong opposition. The second group of women to enroll in colleges was larger and less well defined. Women undergraduates of this second wave were seen as floating or adrift, and both the recently introduced grading system and the expanded curriculum the women's colleges offered were to some degree responses to this change. However, many of the second wave, like the women of the first, had little or no educational preparation for college and, like Henrietta, arrived without a goal in view.

Smith College exposed Henrietta for the first time to educated women. Deprived of a mother since the age of twelve, Henrietta had known women who were severely constricted by their domestic roles—servants and aunts and grandmothers who spent their lives taking care of their male employers and relatives, losing out, as had happened in the fight over the Bingham School, in all disputes over inheritance, money, or property.

However fond she may have been of her female relatives, Henrietta could hardly have found their lives attractive. At Smith, Henrietta would see that there was another way: success in a world of women based on intellectual achievement.

She must have responded with excitement to the possibilities opening before her, although she had already learned to focus most of her energy on relationships and entertainment. Both were offered in abundance at Northampton.

According to Mary Van Kleech, a Smith graduate who became a social analyst and conducted a census of college women in 1915, the Eastern women's colleges at the time still disclaimed "any intention to give professional or vocational training." Sixty percent of the women faculty at these colleges were in the newly developed home economics departments.

Arriving in 1920, a proud, beautiful, intelligent, but largely unformed young Southerner who had known grievous disruptions in her life, Henrietta would have found herself in a stimulating world where much was unfamiliar. Her interest in sports would have been recognized; Smith undergraduates had pioneered in this area, even wearing short skirts in 1895 for a walking tour. Henrietta would also have appreciated the mania for mixed dancing that was sweeping through colleges at this period, following an earlier prohibition. "The forbidden waltz" had been danced at Smith as early as 1897, and by 1913, women and men undergraduates were dancing at college parties, although they were still closely chaperoned. By 1920, the social permissiveness that followed the end of the First World War had touched Smith, as well as the other women's colleges. Drinking (in spite of Prohibition) and flirtations, if not open affairs, were hardly unusual, although one report noted that freshmen women knew nothing about sex outside of the bare essentials of reproduction.

"Romantic friendships" had been tolerated at women's colleges for years, reflecting society's belief that crushes on a person of the same sex were a normal part of growing up. At an earlier period, elaborate rituals for "smashing" (crushes on women) existed at women's colleges; flowers, poems, and other presents were exchanged. This acceptance of loving relationships between women, whether erotic or not, disappeared in the 1920s, partly because of the rise of psychoanalysis and its emphasis on "mature" heterosexual love.

Henrietta came to Smith eager yet unprepared to make her own world. She was half educated, lonely, and while temperamentally independent, she lacked the means to prove her point of view or to support herself away from her family.

At such a juncture, she had the great good fortune to meet a brilliant young English instructor, Mina Kirstein (later Curtiss). Kirstein had graduated from Smith in 1918, returning soon after to teach freshman English; Henrietta was one of her students. Kirstein was becoming an authority on

Marcel Proust and was translating his letters. Later she would write biographies of Bizet, Anna Ivanovna, and Degas, as well as two memoirs. She came from a world far more intellectual than the world of intrigue Henrietta had left behind in the border South.

In her memoir, *Other People's Letters,* Mina Kirstein Curtiss described her childhood in terms of a single "traumatic episode" that resulted from her discovery of her parents' love letters. Her mother found her reading the letters in the attic, and "the rage she let loose at what she apparently regarded as an unforgivable invasion of privacy could not have been more violent had I sneaked into Paradise and caught Adam and Eve committing the pre-original sin. She took all the letters and burned them . . . I was permeated with guilt, shame and most of all curiosity as to the significance of my sin."

Mina's background was described by her brother Lincoln in an interview in *The New Yorker.* He and his sister grew up in Rochester and Boston in a family of wealthy and cultivated people. Through his association with the Boston department store Filene's, Kirstein Sr. became very well off and bought a large house in 1914 in Boston's Back Bay. The house was carefully decorated in the manner made famous in Isabelle Gardner's nearby establishment. Lincoln Kirstein was influenced by "beautiful Empire furniture and some very fine copies of large Venetian pictures, notably Titians and Tintorettos" at a period when the Judge had commissioned a decorator of New York hotels to fill his new house in Kentucky with matching suites of factory-produced mahogany furniture. Like the Judge, Kirstein Sr. was "particularly admiring of English workmanship, English craftsmanship, English tailoring. He made a kind of cult of the best suits, shirts, ties, shoes . . ."

At Harvard in 1926, Lincoln Kirstein noted that his classmates "were admired purely for their physical endowment, their looks, for their families. . . . They had no interest in anything except the immediate situation." He described his roommate, the nephew of the president of Harvard, as having no prejudices of any sort, and no curiosity. "The only people I knew were people of inherited wealth who had a certain kind of behavior, which I liked very much. . . . But then they were mindless, and they also drank a good deal, and that frightened me." His older sister at Smith would have met the daughters of the same tradition.

Henrietta, however, because of the turbulence of her early life, might have struck the Kirsteins as being among the "disinherited"—exotic wanderers on the fringes of wealthy families who were all "adventurers of a sort." If so, her strangeness would have established a link with the Kirsteins, who, as Jews, as intellectuals, and as newly rich, were, at least initially, outsiders. Lincoln Kirstein wrote, "I had no family; I had no dynasty," adding that his father had taught him that "nothing was possible for him but ANYTHING could be possible for me." His older sister had absorbed some of the same self-confidence, which would have made her a magnetic figure to Henrietta. For Henrietta and her brothers, it was the Judge who could do "anything"; their roles in life were less certain.

As a freshman in Mina Kirstein's class, Henrietta would have been among the most poorly prepared. As a Southerner with a noticeable accent, she would have been in a tiny minority. The intellectual seriousness Smith cultivated must have seemed strange to the Kentuckian. The anti-intellectualism of the South after the Civil War has been commented on by many historians, but they have not described the painful transition required for a son of that setting to become a dedicated student—a transition even more painful and unlikely for a daughter described entirely in terms of her looks.

Mina Kirstein was able to establish an atmosphere of intellectual and emotional freedom like the tone in London's Bloomsbury, which the English author Frances Partridge found so exhilarating: "It was as if a lot of doors had suddenly opened out of a stuffy room which I had been sitting in far too long."

Part of the sense of liberation was sexual. Henrietta would have had few illusions about heterosexual love after growing up in the fierce rough-and-tumble of life in Louisville and Asheville, subjected early to her father's bewildering combination of Calvinism and amatory adventures. She would have turned for affection to a safer source: to a woman who seemed humane, cultivated, and sensitive. A love affair with a brilliant woman might cast some of that woman's glow over the less qualified disciple; it might also bring to a starved adolescent the tenderness she had missed since her mother's death.

Henrietta might have continued at Smith and might even have graduated had Mina Kirstein stayed. However, in 1921, Mina took a year's leave of absence to go abroad. She had decided that she needed to discover the "living people" she had been treating as literary icons as she worked on translating Proust's letters. Some of his friends were still alive, and Kirstein wanted their reality to fill out her academic research. It was, she wrote later, a turning point. She invited Henrietta to go abroad with her.

Henrietta's family in Kentucky must have received the news of her departure from Smith with uncertainty. By this time the family traveled often to Europe in the summer, and perhaps Henrietta's trip seemed to fit that pattern. Certainly the Judge would approve of her connection with the Kirsteins, who possessed the worldliness he so admired; probably he was discreetly silent about the fact that they were Jews.

Research was not the motive that brought the two young women to London in the summer of 1921. According to several contemporary accounts and to Mina's memoir, she and Henrietta had come to be psychoanalyzed by Ernest Jones, Freud's preeminent British disciple.

Mina Kirstein would certainly have been exposed to discussion about the new "science" of psychoanalysis. Ernest Jones had visited Boston in 1908 to establish connections with an American disciple, Morton Prince. Jones became one of Freud's inner circle, and even wore the ring the Master designed for his seven Knights of the Round Table.

For Henrietta, the impulse to enter analysis may have come from her father's disapproval of her relationship with Mina.

According to an old friend, the Judge had accepted Mina as simply another of Henrietta's female chums. They had traveled abroad together, Mina perhaps almost hidden in the ranks of relatives and friends.

But Robert had noticed something, and he knew how to put his observation to good use in the family, where he was rapidly losing his hold.

During a stay at a European inn, Robert climbed the drainpipe to look in his sister's window. He saw her in bed with Mina, and promptly took the tale to the Judge.

This was too much for the Judge: the truth itself. He might have tolerated anything as long as the surface conventions were preserved, but now he was furious, mortified, and he told Henrietta that Mina was forever banished.

Mina disappeared from the Judge's environs, although not from Henrietta's life. Henrietta's fear of her father's anger, an anger that threatened to deprive her of her first positive relationship with a woman since her mother's death, may have sent her to Jones.

In 1921, Ernest Jones was in early middle age. He was coming into a period of success and relative financial security after an exceedingly troubled early life. Small, stubborn, and impetuous, he had nearly ruined his earlier career as a neurologist by becoming sexually involved with his women patients. Practicing in Toronto, he had barely survived the scandal when a patient accused him of a sexual relationship; Jones had silenced her with five hundred dollars, which he himself called blackmail. To exonerate himself, he explained to his mentor, Freud, that the woman was an active homosexual.

Jones's background was not unlike the Judge's. Both had risen from relative obscurity, and both had experienced problems with their domineering fathers and had expunged memories of their mothers, the Judge by deifying the long-dead Dell, the psychoanalyst by minimizing his mother's influence. Both men believed in the primary duty of women to nourish men emotionally and practically. In addition, they shared a fascination with the British aristocracy, Jones as a Welshman, the Judge as a Southerner. Both were small, intense, gifted, and combative men who were determined to leave their mark, and who lived in worlds defined by male cults and male concerns.

Jones was excited when he was approached by Mina Kirstein and Henrietta Bingham. He wrote to Freud, "My practice has once more improved; one has only to wait in bad times . . . Chance has brought me an unusual opportunity from which I hope to learn much. An actively homosexual girl came to be analyzed in December . . . Now her feminine partner who lives with her has come also. They are both well-educated and highly intelligent persons . . . so you may imagine that the analytic work is especially interesting."

The two young women were yet another link between Jones and Bloomsbury, from which Jones drew several of his clients. Henrietta and Mina had both come to know two of its denizens, David Garnett, who was running a bookstore in London, and his friend Frances Birrell. Garnett, an attractive, inquiring young man who would become a well-known author, dedicated a short novel, *The Man in the Zoo,* to "Henrietta Bingham and Mina Kirstein."

In her memoirs, Mina Curtiss referred somewhat coyly to her relationship with David Garnett, who was married, insisting that she was shocked by his behavior: "Our relationship, from his point of view, had certain limitations. He could not understand my puritanism, as he called it."

David wrote her, "I shall not say anything to you about love. It's much simpler than that. You make me happy." Mina commented in her memoirs that love is much more complicated.

Apparently Mina introduced Henrietta to David and his exotic friends at the bookstore, which was furnished with tables from Roger Fry's Omega Workshops and "cheap deal shelves" put up by a "young Quaker carpenter."

Mina must have been attracted to the shop's collection of eighteenth-century French books in addition to what Frances Partridge, who worked in the shop after her graduation from Newnham College in Cambridge in 1918, described as "modern French novels sitting on their haunches as French books will." The shop sold editions published by Virginia and Leonard Woolf's Hogarth Press (later Jones arranged to have Freud's books published there) and books written by the partners' parents—Augustine Birrell, Edward Garnett, and Constance Garnett. The bookshop must have provided a formidable introduction to the life of the mind for a young woman like Henrietta.

Mina was no casual customer. Henrietta, however, must have had difficulty navigating during conversations about Madame de Sévigné or Samuel Johnson, whose works she had not read. It was at this period that she developed the "silence" which seemed so "telling" to later observers, and which became her most attractive quality to these pretentious and loquacious intellectuals.

She relied for effect on her beauty and on music, singing black spirituals the Bloomsberries found exotic. John Houseman remembered Mina Kirstein talking to him about *The Education of Henry Adams* "while Henrietta—known in Bloomsbury as 'The Kentucky Heiress'—sat on top of a piano in a purple velvet dress and played the saxophone." She also played the guitar.

That Henrietta possessed a fine mind in addition to blue eyes may be deduced from her friendship with Mina, who would hardly have tolerated a stupid companion. Others rarely saw it. Playing the saxophone and wearing a purple velvet dress were attributes of a role that would gradually harden around Henrietta. Unable to compete intellectually in a group where the competition was particularly fierce, Henrietta retreated, again, to the display of charm, which seemed inevitably connected to a Southern accent and wealth. Perhaps Mina knew it was only a pose. But the pose was attractive, too attractive to drop.

Most contemporary accounts state that Henrietta was attracted to both men and women at this time. It would be more accurate to say that both men and women were attracted to her; she always displayed the essential coldness which Mina's brother, Lincoln Kirstein, described in another context as fundamental to success in life.

Two of the Bloomsberries who were attracted to Henrietta were the enigmatic, tragic painter Dora Carrington and the tormented sculptor Stephen Tomlin.

In 1922, when Henrietta arrived in London with Mina, Dora Carrington had been living for several years with Lytton Strachey. Their relationship was nonsexual after the first few months, but essential to both of them. Carrington had affairs with other men, as did Strachey, but the houses and the life they created together meant more than these alliances.

By 1924, Carrington and Strachey were in the process of moving into the last house they would share, Ham Spray, a mid-Victorian country house that looks rather like a smaller version of the flour-baron mansions in Kentucky.

Both Carrington and Strachey knew David Garnett and Stephen Tomlin. According to another intimate, Gerald Brenan, Henrietta "turned up" in the spring of 1924 with Tomlin at Ham Spray to help with the house painting. Brenan described her as "the daughter of Judge Bingham, a Kentucky millionaire who was said to have murdered his wife . . . Although she sometimes had affairs with men, as she was doing now, she was mainly a Lesbian."

Brenan went on: "Carrington was fascinated by Henrietta . . . some time that summer they had an affair. It was the only Lesbian affair of [Carrington's] life and it did not last long as Henrietta changed her lovers often."

Although he was in love with Carrington, Brenan wrote, "I did not feel jealous and not only offered them my room [in London] for their meetings, but said that I would give up my claim to seeing Carrington when she came up to town if that meant that she could spend time with her friend. What I did not then know was that Carrington was basically a Lesbian too and that her affair with Henrietta would affect her physical relations with me . . . I would pay dearly for her having met the American girl."

Brenan blamed Henrietta for turning Carrington against him, but Lytton Strachey told Garnett it was another man's "insensitive violence and clumsiness that made all physical love repulsive to Carrington, and he doubted if she would get over the repulsion it gave her."

Carrington, like Henrietta, paid for her independence, but Carrington's was an independence of mind as well as of behavior. In Aldous Huxley's acid novel, *Crome Yellow*, Carrington appears as a moon-faced girl with a golden bell of hair who is obsessed with birth control. While the houseguests admire a sow covered with suckling piglets, this young woman dares to discuss the problem of childbearing for women. Margaret Sanger was lecturing on birth control in the United States, and Carrington, like Henrietta, belonged to the first generation of women who would have the ability to limit their reproduction. Huxley was horrified.

When Carrington visited Brenan in Spain, long before she met Henrietta, she wrote that she was happier than during any other period of her life.

"You know my secret life is with you," she wrote Brenan, but "I am never quite certain of your affections," now that he had returned to the amatory circus in London. Clearly teasing him, she described her visit to Henrietta's "secret house" in Knightsbridge. "A house which nobody knew of except us. She had taken it for her friend who arrives tomorrow. But not a soul knew of it. We had a lovely tea in the kitchen, of biscuits and garlic sausage and tea with lemon. Then she drove me across the Park to Paddington. . . . I hope you will meet her soon. Perhaps it's all a delusion, she may of course be quite uninteresting inside. I hardly ever speak to her. We are the most silent of friends! But I feel sure she is very like her early Italian exterior. She also has a goodness that is unusual."

Ten days later, Henrietta was still being used to animate Brenan. "You mustn't think I don't realize how good you are," Carrington wrote him. "I do see it. And then I behave badly. I get carried away by Kentucky princesses who after all compared to my Amigo are not worth one half minute's thought."

Carrington's guilt over Brenan's anger brought on a black mood. "I cannot literally bear to let my mind think of [intercourse] again, or of my femaleness. It is partly because Ralph treats me not like a woman now that the strain has vanished between us. All of this became clear really last summer with Henrietta. Really I had more ecstasy with her and no feeling of shame afterwards. I think Henrietta, although she gave me nothing else, gave me a clue to my character. Probably if one was completely Sapphic it would be much easier. I wouldn't be interested in men at all, and wouldn't have these conflicts."

Carrington's ability to run a household, which attracted Strachey's friends, would have interested Henrietta. Here was a highly unconventional young woman who had made herself the center of an interesting life, creating at Ham Spray a retreat for writers and artists who came to depend on her caretaking.

At Ham Spray, Carrington painted walls, hung curtains, took on commissions for inn signs, and decorated trunks. She also continued work on her great portraits of Lady Strachey, Mrs. Box, Gerald Brenan, and Samuel Carrington. Although she complained of being merely a pair of dirty hands that emptied the houseguests' chamber pots, Carrington in fact was achieving her aim of becoming "a serious artist."

However, Carrington could not exist without the emotional and intellectual support Lytton Strachey provided. When he died, she killed herself, cutting short her life and her career. She is remembered only in the reminiscences of men who took her for a kind of housekeeper.

Henrietta would have found the atmosphere at Ham Spray oddly familiar. The inhabitants' determination to forgo jealousy would have seemed an attractive alternative to the repressions and storms of her adolescence. These writers were not rich but they had "just enough inherited wealth to go around." Although everyone worked, few worked as hard as Frances Partridge, who, during her years at the bookstore, called work her "compass and safety belt." Partridge was also the only one of the women to have been given early financial independence by her father, who settled a small amount of money on her when she went to college.

The weekends at Ham Spray were given up to cultivated leisure: reading aloud, games, walks, and the discussion and enjoyment of food and wine. But these were not the only similarities between life at Ham Spray and life during the interregnum in the Big House in Louisville. According to Michael Holroyd, sexual tension caused "a ceaseless pushing, pulling, quivering, throbbing commotion." The self-dramatizing antics of the owners and their guests created triangles and four-sided arrangements that were elaborately constructed, much discussed, and lasted until the next explosion—or indefinitely. Although Henrietta's Louisville family was more conventional in its behavior, sexual ambiguities always threatened the surface as Robert played his wild practical jokes and Henrietta moved back and forth between the Judge and her lovers.

Stephen Tomlin made a bust of Henrietta that shows her cool, enigmatic quality. Strachey wrote to Garnett that "I liked her more than before. She whitewashed amazingly and never said a word," but after the painting job was finished, she was not invited back to Ham Spray, perhaps because of her powerful effect on Carrington.

The following year, Carrington wrote, "I dream of her six times a week, dreams even my intelligence is appalled by, and I write letters, and tear them up, continually." Certainly Henrietta's relationships with Carrington and Tomlin, which overlapped, must have affected Mina Kirstein, who returned to Smith in August 1923 and married in less than a year. Mina did not mention Henrietta in her memoirs.

Henrietta stayed on in England. In September 1925, the English analyst James Strachey wrote his wife, Alix, that "the American woman (whose name I can't ever remember)—oh Henrietta—has a new lady friend and has thrown over Tommy [Stephen Tomlin] (and Carrington?). Tommy is in a terrible state, and Carrington is sending him to me for analysis—I don't think."

In November 1924, James had written Alix that "Henrietta is going to Jones for analysis; and had recently been persuading Tomlin (who was in a very gloomy state) to do the same."

In February 1925, Strachey described Carrington as still crushed by "this last Henrietta affair." Two months earlier, Carrington had had a last meeting with Henrietta "prior to the latter's final (?) return to the states." By then, Jones had already delivered his public lecture based on Henrietta's relationship with Carrington, in which, according to Strachey, Jones explained that the real reason why she threw over Carrington was that Carrington "wasn't a virgin."

Jones, like many psychiatrists since his time, performed functions which were not strictly professional. He advised the young John Houseman, who was about to take Henrietta away for the weekend, on the sexual techniques he should use—and on the method of birth control. Houseman had been chosen by Henrietta to relieve her of the burden of her virginity, he said. Young, in love, and inexperienced, Houseman went to talk to Dr. Jones while Henrietta drove around the block. Dr. Jones advised him in the ways of sexual love as years earlier Freud had advised Jones on his treatment of his wives and mistresses. The outcome, in a dreary seaside hotel, was not conducive to a long relationship; Houseman was in love with Henrietta, but she did not end her commitment to women. Later he would say that she was terrified of her father, and therefore wary of a man who had any strength of personality—which Houseman, at the time, thought he lacked. Yet he believed that she could only love a strong man.

Fortified by her intellectual abilities, Mina returned to Smith and to an interesting and more or less conventional life as a teacher, writer, and wife. Henrietta remained stranded between her lifelong wish to please the Judge and her longing for independence as expressed in her love for women.

Ernest Jones, who believed in pain as a way of forcing patients to change, based his conclusions about female sexuality on "his simultaneous analysis of five cases of manifest homosexuality in women. They were all deep analyses, three of which were completed and the other two taken to an advanced stage. Three patients were in their twenties, two in their thirties, and only two of the five were openly hostile towards men." He went on: "In all cases there was evidence of an unusually strong infantile fixation" on the mother which was "definitely connected with the oral stage." This was "always succeeded by a strong father fixation whether it was temporary or permanent in the unconscious."

In concluding, this paper ("The Early Development of Female Sexuality") made a statement that represented Jones's late and important reservations about the Freudian doctrine he had spent his life promulgating. Jones wrote that Freud's concept of castration fear as the most important factor in developing neuroses had "hindered our appreciation of the fundamental conflicts. We have here, in fact, an example of what Karen Horney had indicated as an unconscious bias in approaching such studies from the male point of view."

Rather than penis envy and fear of castration, Jones wrote, women's neuroses derive from fear of "aphanisis": "the total and, of course, permanent extinction of the capacity of sexual enjoyment." He felt aphanisis was caused by parents' prohibition of sexual pleasure—which the child perceives as permanent—and specifically by a prohibition against masturbation.

"Aphanisis" is derived from a Greek word that means total extinction. It was that sense of extinction, of powerful fires long ago put out, which fascinated me when I came to know my aunt, twenty years after her analysis with Ernest Jones.

Emotionally and intellectually starved during her adolescence, Henrietta came to Jones with a single relationship on which she could depend: her relationship with her teacher and mentor, Mina Kirstein. For Jones, the orthodox Freudian, Henrietta's lesbianism was a perversion, and he would have tried to "cure" her by any means. Jones believed that sixty percent of his patients were "cured" by their treatment.

Apparently Jones was able to convert Mina Kirstein to his phallocentric view; within a year of her analysis, she married. With Henrietta, the result was more ambiguous. He left Henrietta stranded in her dilemma, still drawn to women as well as to men, still financially and emotionally dependent on her father and subsequently on her brother, as she had been on Ernest Jones, who spoke their language and lived in their world.

Her younger brother, Barry, also visiting London, was intrigued by the magicianlike Jones. Barry went at least once to pick up Henrietta at Jones's Harley Street office. He said many years later that Jones had looked out the window and remarked to Henrietta that her brother had a very fine head—a remark that collapsed Freudian doctrine into the Colonel's belief in eugenics. The old regime and the new were not very different after all, since both defined the world only in male terms.

For the gifted and divided young woman who had seen her mother die on the train tracks and who had spent the following years desperately struggling to survive, questions of theory could have been of little importance. Dr. Jones represented the world of power, where she had floundered all her life. In accepting her as a patient, he committed himself to making her fit that world.

With Mina Kirstein, Henrietta had glimpsed a world not defined by her father or her brothers or Ernest Jones, a world where the "ecstasy" she had shared with Dora Carrington was available.

Perhaps for a brief moment Henrietta had hoped to break out of the Judge's sphere of influence when she entered analysis, or when she treated her father "coldly" in the summer of 1924. To punish her for her disloyalty, the Judge married for the third time. The price for even a moment of independence was very high.

13

When the Judge was appointed Ambassador to Great Britain in 1933, Henrietta once again joined his entourage. The attention paid to an ambassador's daughter who was beautiful and a fine horsewoman was more enticing than the trials of independence. Although she maintained a few friends from the period ten years earlier when she and Mina Kirstein had lived in London, Henrietta had by now moved officially into the Judge's orbit—as Dora Carrington might have predicted when she watched her enigmatic lover rush off to Scotland, "engulfed by her father and brothers."

The ambassadorship was a reward for the Judge's early support of Franklin Roosevelt, in the form of a sizable contribution to his first campaign. One historian described these early contributors, from whose ranks Roosevelt's cabinet and foreign diplomats were drawn, as "a strange assortment of old Harvard friends, city bosses, millionaires, Western radicals, Southern Bourbons, opportunistic Midwesterners who knew how to jump on the right bandwagon, Ku Kluxers, old Wilsonites, old Bryanites, professors, high-tariff men [and] low-tariff men . . ." The Judge would have found a comfortable niche in at least six of these groups.

As important as his financial contribution was, the Judge's political support through his newspapers and his radio station was even more valuable. The Judge had bought the radio station in 1922 for the "uplift" of Kentucky mountaineers, whom he imagined sitting on their porches listening to Beethoven. Roosevelt, the first politician to make use of radio's resources, would broadcast his Fireside Chats across a wide area, using the Louisville station, among many others. At night, its signal could be picked up as far west as Chicago.

The Judge had come to Roosevelt's attention through Colonel House. House's father had been another of the Southern officers who were confined at Johnson's Island with Colonel Bingham. By 1932, however, House's influence with Roosevelt was waning, due to his outmoded Wilsonian views—which the Judge had abandoned after Wilson's depiction of himself as an "uncompromising reformer" in 1911.

Memory must have agitated the Judge during Roosevelt's attempt at the 1932 convention to rescind the old two-thirds rule, which had assured Southern control of the Democratic party for years. The Colonel would certainly have been offended for both moral and political reasons by this last-minute shuffle, from which Roosevelt finally withdrew. But the Colonel had died in 1927, embittered by his failure to become an important spokesman for the New South.

The Judge's influence was felt at the 1932 convention when, in a compromise move, Kentuckian Alben Barkley was chosen to give the keynote address. Barkley used the opportunity for a two-hour display of Southern oratory. His selection as speaker ended the bickering between Kentucky governor Ruby Laffoon and the Judge. Kentuckians, hoping for better times than Hoover had provided, joined the landslide for Roosevelt.

In 1933, Roosevelt began to hand out foreign ambassadorships and cabinet posts according to the time-honored rule of patronage. He did not worry about his appointees' qualifications. Roosevelt liked to deal directly with heads of state, and he assumed that his ambassadors would limit themselves to ceremonial duties.

The President was apparently unaware of the storm caused by the Judge's earlier pro-British speeches, in which he had criticized the United States for its failure to support the rearming of the country that had become his second home. When the President sent the Judge's name to Congress, confirmation was held up for five days.

The reasons given for the delay vary with the giver. Some aver that the Judge's passionate pro-British stance alarmed an isolationist Senate, others that a disgruntled Kentucky congressman who had been attacked in the Judge's newspapers caused the problem. Ray Moley of Roosevelt's "brain trust" was given the task of pushing the confirmation through. A few years later, Moley would fault the Judge for failing to realize how hard Moley had to fight to quell the Congress's suspicions about Mary Lily's death.

The scandal, now almost two decades old, followed the Judge to England, but was apparently of little consequence there, where he became a beloved figure, comfortable with the British system and devoted to strengthening ties between the two countries.

Roosevelt's official letter introducing his ambassador to the King of England was couched in conventional terms. In a later note, he recommended the Judge to the King as an especially fine shot. Roosevelt's personal notes to the Judge emphasize the ceremonial and social side of his position, probably to the Judge's dismay; he failed to send the President a bit of historical trivia until the President wrote again to ask for it.

The Judge had undertaken his mission with zeal, determined to affect the future of relations between Britain and the United States. But he was out of step with President Roosevelt, who in the middle 1930s was more concerned with the problems of the American economy than with expanding alliances abroad.

The Economic Conference in London in June 1933 was viewed as an opportunity to stabilize currency and to prove that international cooperation was possible. The conference failed, due to Roosevelt's interference through Moley and to the ineptitude of the American delegation, headed by the Judge's friend Cordell Hull. The delegation included the drunken Senator Key Pittman, who shot out a few streetlights in London, and William C. Bullitt, Hull's special assistant, who insulted Ramsay MacDonald by inviting his secretary to dinner—interpreted by the British as an underhanded way to get inside information.

The Judge's gift for intrigue led to Moley's resignation. Irritated by the envoy's high-handed behavior at the embassy, the Judge waylaid one of Moley's secret notes to Roosevelt and gave it to Hull, who was outraged by the criticism it contained. When Hull complained to Roosevelt, the President asked for, and received, Moley's resignation. For the Judge, it was an important victory—another enemy was routed—but perhaps Roosevelt was not very pleased at having his hand forced.

As ambassador, the Judge was awarded many honors by the grateful British, and wrote to his sister Sadie in Asheville, "Good day on November 21 [1936] when I received my Oxford D.C.L. American papers had it 'Doctor of Literature.' It means 'Doctor of Civil Law.' Am the only ambassador who ever received degrees from both Oxford & Cambridge and the only individual who has ever had those and the Univ. of London in addition." He also instructed Sadie on the proper title and address to use on her letters to him.

But his outspoken pro-British statements earned him criticism at home, and one New York newspaper asked for his recall. After a speech criticizing Germany, he was condemned in the German press; the episode was embarrassing to Roosevelt, who had not yet made up his mind about either Hitler or Mussolini. The Judge had heard the cry of battle, and he was ready to rush into a world combat which the President still hoped to avoid. The old Colonel's voice must have been ringing in his son's ears as he imagined a European version of the siege of Richmond and even the gallant defeat at Appomattox.

The Judge remained true all his life to his North Carolina origins, unable to leave the myth of the Old South behind. Only a few Southerners, such as Walter Hines Page, were able to outgrow this sentimental addiction to the past. But Page, like earlier Wilson supporters William McCombs and

Walter McCorkle, was an exile from the South, exposed to a wider world while living in New York.

Now the Judge linked the Southern myth with the tradition of the British landed gentry, which had become his own when he visited the Binghams' Dorset manor house, Melcombe. He was becoming the consummate sportsman and landowner of British fiction, going over to his rented castle in Scotland to hunt, or taking his physician, Hugh Young, who was treating him for a series of unspecified maladies, to Pinelands in Georgia to kill birds by the hundreds. Young described in his memoirs how the Judge, irritated by the greater prowess of a British hunter, had ordered four metal stands constructed at Pinelands, from which "negroes" threw up birds as the Judge "marched" toward them and fired. The "negroes" had shields to hide behind. The result, according to Young, was that the Judge learned to outshoot his British rival.

Guns played an important role in the Judge's life. The violence of Kentucky politics had caused him to go about armed, and the railroad and tobacco wars would continue the pattern. William Goebel, campaigning for governor in 1899, had taken on the powerful Louisville & Nashville Railroad, threatening to increase its taxes as well as to clean up the railroad-dominated Democratic machine. After a violently contested election, during which the L & N imported a trainload of a thousand armed mountaineers, Goebel was shot dead on the steps of the state capitol.

While other Southern states continued to fight the railroad, Kentucky was controlled by its lobbyists for three more decades. By the time of his appointment as ambassador, the Judge was a director of the railroad which had put an end to the feeble progressive movement in Kentucky.

Although the Judge was a director of the L & N railroad for only one year (1931–32), it provided an important link. The L & N's parent company, the Atlantic Coast Line Railroad, was controlled by a closely knit group of Walters and Delanos. Lyman Delano, Franklin Roosevelt's first cousin, was chairman of the board of both the L & N and its parent company. The Judge would have understood the importance of legitimizing new money through such contacts, crucial in his case, where the money was perceived as tainted.

In England, he was sometimes asked about the racial problems at home, as when an English lady asked why blacks were lynched in the South. The Ambassador told her that "we would probably stop it when negroes stopped lynching white women and girls"—an excuse that had its origins in the terror in Alamance County, North Carolina, during Reconstruction.

It is worth noticing that Alamance County, where the Binghams lived, was noted for the ferocity of its Ku Klux Klan, supported by the Democratic newspaper in Raleigh as well as by many well-off white middle-class men like the Binghams. For a time in Alamance County, the Klan was able to murder blacks with almost no fear of reprisal. In 1868, a black woman and her five children were killed in nearby Moore County; the Klan usually dispatched men from neighboring counties to do the killing. According to a witness, a Klansman "killed one of the children by kicking out his brains with the heel of his boot."

Not a single rape of a white woman by a black man was recorded during this period in North Carolina, according to historian Allen W. Trelease. Yet "Alamance eclipsed the rest" in violence against blacks who dared to vote or run for office or demand representation on juries.

When Governor William Woods Holden finally declared a state of insurrection in Alamance and used federal troops to round up Klansmen, he was unable to secure the conviction of men who, according to trial records, were from "the local establishment and were well regarded." All those indicted were dismissed. Later they succeeded in impeaching Governor Holden, who became the first governor in the history of the country to leave office because of impeachment.

The Judge would write Margaret Mitchell, "I have always loved the negro and I shall never cease to love him. My father and mother reared seven children in a slave woman's lap. She loved us better than her life. We loved her next to our parents." The same mythmaking ability which had turned all women into Melanies, and which would extinguish those who did not fit, turned the black people the Colonel and his friends had persecuted into happy and beloved minions.

These ironies seldom mattered in London. In spite of his frustrations with American isolationism, the Judge enjoyed being ambassador. His three grown children also loved the life at Prince's Gate. Robert had married a Scotswoman, Dorothy Phyllis Fell Clark, in 1925, and Aleen presented her at court. Mary and Barry came to England twice to visit.

As for Henrietta, it was a long way from the untrammeled life at Ham Spray, and her former acquaintances must have read the news accounts with amusement. Now she was moving in a worldly society whose scandals were usually suppressed and which included, according to gossip, the Prince of Wales.

In 1936, at the commencement of Roosevelt's second campaign, the Judge sent ten thousand dollars to Louis Howe, the President's old confidant and adviser. The money disappeared into Howe's safe, which he carried to the hospital shortly thereafter. Howe had been discredited by his connection with a toilet-kit contract for the CCC camps; he was a pathetic leftover from an earlier period of Roosevelt's life.

When Howe went to the Naval Hospital in Bethesda with his safe, Roosevelt wrote, "I think one matter should be made perfectly clear. If your friends make loans to you to be used for education purposes, such as selling publications for public instruction through a non-partisan organization, all such loans to you should be kept separate and not put into your personal bank account. For your own protection you should get this straightened out, and if it is a loan it should be made perfectly clear that it is not a contribution." Howe had asked the Judge to write him that the ten thousand dollars was a "loan to a friend."

A few days later, Howe died. The Judge's contribution was presumably retrieved from his safe, but the fact that it had gone to Howe indicates the Judge's declining influence. Howe and, to some extent, House were mentors from the past. Now Roosevelt was ready to pass the British ambassadorship on to a big contributor who was also a fervent isolationist, Joseph P. Kennedy. The President wanted the Judge recalled early in 1938.

The Judge had left his Kentucky newspapers in the hands of his old law partner, Emmanuel Levi, and his own son Barry. Uncertain about his own future, interested in becoming a writer rather than a journalist, Barry eventually hired as editor Mark Ethridge, a respected Southern journalist who had been suggested by President Roosevelt.

Ethridge, who would become my godfather, set the tone of the newspapers during the forties and for many years afterwards. A Southern liberal, one of a group that included publisher Jonathan Daniels (who became my brother Jonathan's godfather) and university president Frank Graham, Ethridge disapproved of "radical" behavior. In 1942, the militant statements of some blacks, who questioned whether they should give their lives in another white man's war, caused Ethridge to say that "the white Southerner would never countenance the abolition of legal segregation." A year earlier, the same congenital fear of "radicalism" had prompted both Ethridge and my father to resign from the Southern Conference for Human Welfare because of its alleged Communist connections. In fact, Ethridge's "liberalism," like that of all the men in this group, was undermined by his experiences growing up in the South.

Ethridge, the editor who did so much to establish the newspapers as bastions of the status quo, struck me when I was a child as a complex, energetic, straightforward man who liked to tell jokes and sing Baptist hymns at Big House dinner parties—an unpretentious human being who told me frankly that he could teach me nothing about the church and hardly understood why he had been selected to be my godfather.

When a *Courier-Journal* editorial criticized Eleanor Roosevelt for riding in a car with a black woman during a visit to North Carolina, Mrs. Roosevelt appealed to the Judge in London. My father tried to resolve the dispute by writing to assure Mrs. Roosevelt that he knew such an incident could never have happened. In her reply, however, Mrs. Roosevelt made it clear that although this particular incident had not occurred, she would not

Henrietta and the Judge, c. 1930s.

ROBERT WORTH BINGHAM.

FOSTERED ENGLISH-AMERICAN RELATIONS.—The late Robert Worth Bingham who was President Roosevelt's ambassador to England, worked untiringly to bring about a thorough understanding of both countries. As early as 1935 he said in an address in London that "the foundation of hope of our world lies in whole-hearted concerted action between Great Britain and the allied States."

ABOVE:
The Judge and tennis champion
Helen Jacobs, England, 1920s.

LEFT:
The Judge's obituary in the
Charlotte *Observer,* 1937.

hesitate to ride in a car with a black woman if the occasion arose—at least outside the South. The Judge had to clear things up with the President.

By now, the Judge was more important to the President as a press lord than as ambassador. Roosevelt insisted that the Judge return to the United States during the 1936 campaign in order to control the Associated Press. The Judge obeyed, but he was eager to get back to London. He had found the adulation lacking in his earlier career.

Edward VIII's abdication gave the Judge an opportunity to pass the insider's version along to the White House: "The Duke of Windsor was surrounded by the pro-German cabal and many people here suspected Mrs. Simpson was actually in German pay. I think that it is unlikely and that her strong pro-German attitude was the result of flattering propaganda [during a period when she was being attacked in the British press]. However, the whole crowd has been cleared out. The Court has become respectable again, and the situation from the dynastic end is immeasurably improved."

The coronation of Edward's younger brother gave the Judge and his family a powerful whiff of ceremony. Henrietta was assigned to cover the event for the newspapers in Louisville. But the Judge was not well. A particularly bad attack had laid him low soon after his appointment to London, and Dr. Hugh Young had been called on to take him to a spa. In his reminiscences, Young referred to the complaint as a recurrent fever, which caused inflammation of the retina (for which the Judge had been treated in Louisville thirty years earlier), exhaustion, and skin rashes.

Terribly ill in the fall of 1937, the Judge denied all rumors that he was about to resign. In a painful incident, the appointment of Kennedy was mentioned in a column by Arthur Krock, although Roosevelt claimed that the word had not come from him. By now the Judge was too ill to return to the United States alone, and a staff doctor from Johns Hopkins was sent to bring him back.

An exploratory operation was performed, but the Judge lapsed into unconsciousness and died, only ten days after he finally sent the President his letter of resignation, naming a "recurrent fever" from which he expected to recover.

After an autopsy, the disease was reported in the newspapers as "abdominal Hodgkins," but the actual cause of death remained unclear. The fevers and rashes, recurring over a thirty-year period, and the attendance of Dr. Young would seem to indicate a virulent infection such as those men contracted on what was called "the open market of vice."

By the end of his life, the Judge had come far from his beginnings. The political adroitness that had guided him through the violence and corruption of Kentucky politics was not suited to his later career. He adopted a new standard of behavior, but he never outgrew his identification with the antebellum South as it was presented in the Colonel's tales and popular fiction. The Judge believed in an earlier Eden of happy slaves and beautiful women, none of whom questioned their subservience. In spite of his intelligence, the Judge remained until the end of his life unaware of his own deeply hidden motivations, creating a plausible and pleasing public personality that had little connection with his private beliefs and fears.

After the Mary Lily scandal, he never felt comfortable in the United States, where he believed he had been treated shamefully. The press, except perhaps in Kentucky, no longer accepted the word of a Southern gentleman, or even of a Sir Galahad. The Judge spent his happiest times in the pre–Civil War atmosphere of Pinelands, his vast hunting estate in Georgia, or in England, the home of the landed gentry, that sanctified class he longed so passionately to join.

If his development was limited by his adherence to the old Colonel's antebellum myth, it was also limited by his narrow conception of the role of women. The Judge knew few Melanies in his life; he was uncomfortably aware of several Scarletts. The powerful women's movement at the turn of the century, which eventually brought about Prohibition and universal suffrage, aroused fears the Judge could not address.

As mayor, he had attempted to clean up Louisville's gambling and prostitution, although the city rapidly reverted to its original identity as one of the roughest and wildest cities in the border South.

Secretly he would have sympathized with Grover Cleveland's hidden life, which produced a bastard and almost ended Cleveland's political career. The Judge would have been outraged that Lucy Stone dared to call Cleveland a "male prostitute." What connection could there be between a gentleman who sought relief from his heavy official duties in drinking and a little harmless flirtation and those fiendish denizens of Louisville's underworld who earned their living through debauchery? During the sanitary campaigns that improved health in the South in the 1920s, attention would be focused on hookworm in children rather than on the equally prevalent gonorrhea and syphilis. Hookworm came from poverty and ignorance; venereal diseases cut across all lines.

The need to guard secrets, and to place personal loyalty above all other virtues, would cause complex problems for the Judge and his heirs as owners of the state's only newspapers. If he and his family were protected from embarrassment by their press, did this mean that others of the Judge's sex and class could claim the same privilege? This came to be the case over a long period of time: the rich and powerful who had taken the old flour barons' places in Louisville society, business, and politics would not find their peccadilloes revealed in the local newspapers.

Yet a highly moral family would need to believe that the opposite was the case; how else could the important ethic of journalistic integrity be preserved? It was preserved on one level, in news reporting that concerned the poor and in the promulgation of national and international news. So the owner and his family could maintain a belief in their own integrity while at the same time suffering no anxiety about local exposure. It was a comfortable arrangement that led to peculiar evasions on a personal and a public level.

The Judge had made good use of his short association with the Fusionists in Kentucky, whose commitment to progressive social issues was as weak as their coalition. He would also support the New Deal. His son, my father, would attempt to tie together the same competing ideologies, to be at once patrician and liberal. He would be more successful than the older Bingham men at ignoring the inevitable contradictions. To be a Southern liberal meant, in the end, to endorse change as long as it came from the top. Change which was not influenced by labor, by militant blacks, or by women was acceptable, for it did not threaten the white male elite. An elite organized through secret societies was essential to the Bingham men, members of the Masons, the Gimghouls, and the Ku Klux Klan. Co-opting the feeble liberal movements of their periods was essential to the successes of the Judge and his son, and ownership of monopoly newspapers broadcast and legitimized their views. The Colonel was too staunch and undeviating a racist to make the necessary compromises with the twentieth century's attempts at progressivism, and he lacked, so to speak, an organ for his opinions.

All three men knew well that exclusion is essential to power.

After the Judge's death in December 1937, there remained the reading of his will. His three children had had their share of scandal after Mary Lily's death. If there were disappointments, even protests, no record was kept. By now the family had so many secrets to hide that any frank discussion was dangerous.

It may have come as something of a surprise to the two older children, Robert and Henrietta, that the controlling interest in the Louisville newspapers and the radio station was left to their younger brother, Barry. He had been called the "co-publisher" during the Judge's lifetime, but his future had been obscure; he had labored with difficulty under Manny Levi's rule, then accepted the leadership of Mark Ethridge. At a hidden point along this route, the Judge had made a critical decision: he had decided to leave the companies to his youngest son.

By then Barry's wife, Mary, had already borne two little boys. Henrietta and Robert were out of the dynastic race, not so much because of their at times embarrassing unconventionality (the Judge found their antics amusing) as because they would have no sons to whom the power and the money could eventually pass. Henrietta and Robert represented the end of the Bingham line.

The Judge, like the Colonel, knew that death could be cheated if the line of inheritance was kept intact.

Powerful men in America ensure their immortality through their inheritors. Everything except the frail male body will continue into perpetuity: the great estate will be saved by rigorous attention to inheritance taxes and discriminatory zoning; the piled-up fortune which conceals so many forms of wrongdoing will be saved from the Internal Revenue Service by the lifelong labors of devoted lawyers and accountants and by lobbyists in Washington who prevent tax reform. The family name will be engraved on a marble or granite cenotaph, and the prime mover's life will be cleaned up and presented in print by a journalist purchased for that task. Papers left to public and private archives will be made available only to approved researchers. Newspaper accounts that reveal too much will not be translated onto microfilm. The life of a woman who brought the wealth that started it all, but who also raised the demons of public suspicion, will be eradicated as though she never lived.

But the promise of immortality still depends on the presence of an heir who will have sons. Then there will be nothing to fear for two more generations, at least—more than a hundred years.

The Colonel, building his school in Asheville, said he "built for 100 years," but the school closed and its founder was deprived of immortality when his son, the Judge, defected. No grandsons returned to run the school, and outsiders and women were not tolerated. The Judge did not have to dread such an obliteration, although he must have worried when his two older children descended into sexual purgatory. He had his youngest son, and his youngest already had two little boys. Let the flesh fail; let the spirit give out. Immortality is assured, even for the faithless: the son and the eldest grandson will guard the flame.

Henrietta, of course, never really had a chance. She was not educated, after her brief time at Smith, and her considerable energies were wasted in sexual contests for the power and love that would never be hers. Had she borne a son before 1937, her fate would have been different. The same was true for Robert; he was a renegade, but even his wildness might have been forgiven had he not contracted syphilis and become sterile. The Judge had ordered the mercury treatment that left Robert sterile, treatment he had rejected in his own case. And he had kept Henrietta suspended in endless hope, endless excitement. He had in effect neutered two of his three heirs— the two who might have questioned the family myth. For they had felt the force of their father's power during the time when he was extricating himself from the Mary Lily scandal; they were not as likely to pity him as the younger son who had witnessed the Judge's life of near-poverty and apparent persecution in the little house on Burnett Street.

After the early 1930s, there was really no competition. The younger son, Barry, had won at the family game, because of special qualities of gentleness and sensitivity and unquestioning loyalty that his father prized. He was also, as a later and rougher relative would assert, "a proven sire." His wife, with her own dreams behind her, complied: she bore four children in the first nine years of their marriage, and two children later.

Beginning in 1937, and for the rest of their lives, Henrietta and Robert would depend on their younger brother for money. The Judge's will made Barry trustee of two trusts of which Henrietta and Robert were beneficiaries. Each trust contained three thousand shares of the newspapers' preferred stock. The rest went to the younger son. At best, Henrietta and Robert could try to forget their humiliating dependency and hope the checks would arrive in the mail. At worst, they could hector or complain, or sell their shares to their brother at a reduced rate. None of their actions were likely to end their dependency.

The Judge also left Henrietta two large pieces of real estate so that she could enter the world of the patrician landowner. She inherited the huge plantation in Georgia and the money to buy the farm in Kentucky, Harmony Landing. However, her income from her trust was severely limited, and in order to run the Kentucky farm she had to sell the Georgia plantation and most of its contents. She retreated to Harmony Landing to try that most quixotic of businesses, the breeding and raising of racehorses. In order for her to survive, the farm would have to show a profit.

Her younger brother, Barry, inherited the Big House and the Little House on the bluff over the Ohio River, a few miles from Mary Lily's gloomy Lincliffe; all three houses shared a melancholy grandeur. Barry also inherited the contents of the Big House, which had been closed since 1937, when the Judge died.

Robert was left nothing but the dividends from his three thousand shares of newspaper stock, in a trust controlled by his younger brother.

The Judge's will also revealed that he had had the foresight to sign a premarital agreement with his third wife, Aleen. She had relinquished all interest in his estate in return for a promise of one million dollars, of which she had already received seven hundred thousand. The remainder would not be completely repaid by the time of her death, almost twenty years later. Aleen had been outmaneuvered.

The Judge's estate outside of the companies was worth more than seven million dollars, some of it in Standard Oil shares. It included a note for the Bingham School, which had been closed for ten years.

The Big House, as described in the estate inventory, was the house I moved into as a small child in 1942. The inventory listed a motley collection of oriental rugs and tapestries, draperies in "bad condition," a portrait of "Lord Gray," a grand piano, and a white bear rug. There were twenty-four gold plates in the pantry, but the Big House was shabby, gloomy, and divested of life.

"I know the whole story of the negro," the Judge had written to Margaret Mitchell a few years earlier. "Most of ours would not leave us" after Emancipation. But the black servants who had run the great grim mansion were gone, along with those who had turned the daily wheel at Eleanor's house in Cherokee Park, now burned to the ground, or the "daily" who had attended the Judge and his son in the frame house on Burnett Street during the decay of their fortunes. The labor of all these people had once made the gloomy house on the Ohio River shine; their stories about the past would be the only connecting link between the Judge's life and his grandchildren's.

But they were gone. The great house was closed up and silent, and its memories and ghosts were buried.

Growing Up

We are judged by how hard we use what we have been given.

The Habit of Being: Letters by Flannery O'Connor

14

The family had no past, as far as I knew, when the huge front door was unlocked at the Big House in 1942 for the first time in five years and we three children rushed in. I had no idea who had lived there, even though I had sometimes peeked in the French windows when we were living in the cozy Little House across the lawn. When I discovered a secret compartment in my bathroom closet, I could not imagine why it had been constructed there; I did not know the long history of hidden or misvalued jewelry, the pearls and diamonds that had been given to or taken from the women in the family at important moments in its career. During the war, the hidden compartment was used to store baby-food coupons for my new little brother, Jonathan. As far as I knew, it had been designed for that purpose.

The family history continued to unwind around me, but I was unaware. North Carolina, which had been so important in the past, was for me merely the scene for delightful vacations. I knew nothing of the history of the Bingham School or of the struggle over the succession when we visited the elderly woman we called Zaddie (Father's Aunt Sadie) and her two nieces, Temple and Martha McKee, who lived in the ruins of the school.

We would drive to the Louisville & Nashville station on Friday afternoon and board the sleeper. Straws were drawn to see who would get the drawing room, with its plush-covered toilet and little tin basin where the tap water tinkled merrily. The losers would have to sleep out in "the car," behind swaying green curtains buttoned across the double-decker berths. Inset lights in the berths gave out a queer glow; the freshly starched white sheets still showed their fold lines. The pillows were thin yet somehow comforting. A net was slung across the wall of the berth, to hold shoes and purses. All night long, the blue night light in the corridor glowed while the train careened and bumped over the mountains.

If I drew a lower berth with a window, I would raise the shade in the middle of the night when the train stopped at some desolate mountain crossing. Looking out, I would see a single electric light bulb hanging over the concrete platform, and perhaps an empty baggage cart. Then the train would wheeze, jolt, and start. I never saw anyone get on or off. Someone said the train had to stop for water, which mystified me, as though, like a horse, the train had to drink at regular intervals.

Very early the next morning, we would be awakened by the porter's shouts: "Asheville! Garden City of the Universe!"

We would dress hurriedly and pack our suitcases. There was always a wait before we pulled into the station. The train halted, spewing puffs of steam, and the family tumbled out, helped down from the train by a porter who placed a metal stool beneath our feet.

Usually Martha McKee would meet us. She was a slender woman with a small, amused face. Sometimes she would have brought her sister, Temple. Temple was large. Her mouth beamed with lipstick. She kissed us all with a smacking sound.

Martha would drive us across the French Broad River, then up a hill. At the top, gates and a driveway led to the old school. The brick dormitories built by the Colonel still stood, their windows broken, their roofs caved in, kudzu surging up the walls. The sentry's round post box marked the top of the old parade ground. When I explored these ruins, I found desks and mildewed military manuals; the school appeared to have been abruptly abandoned. In fact, it had been closed for repairs after the Colonel's death and never reopened.

Martha and Temple McKee and their Aunt Sadie continued to live in two houses on the school grounds. The "girls'" house was chilly and slightly depressing; the past had died there. Aunt Sadie's house, however, was always cheerful with flowers and books and magazines, treats provided by Father.

She would be waiting for us, sitting on the patio in a wheelchair with a lap rug over her knees and a large picture hat on her white hair. When she saw Father coming, Aunt Sadie would clap her hands.

In the evenings, she and Father played a card game called snake-eyes. During the day, when it was warm enough, they sat in the courtyard and watched the birds. Father rarely left Aunt Sadie's side during the weekend, and the rest of us realized that here was a special love, sealed by events in a hidden past. I sensed that many lives had gone into that dark house, and many secrets were buried there.

One of the secrets, only half buried during my childhood, was Temple and Martha's brother, Bingham McKee. He was living on the second floor of Aunt Sadie's house. Occasionally while we were eating dinner he would appear in a doorway, wearing a robe, and pass through to the kitchen. Everyone spoke to him politely, but no explanations were made, and he

The front porch of the Big House.

Father reading aloud to Barry (left), Sallie, and Worth, 1945.
Father had recently returned from four years overseas.

ABOVE:
One of the few remaining
buildings of the Bingham
School in Asheville,
North Carolina, 1950s.

LEFT:
A "bed and breakfast"
in a former Bingham
School building, Mebane,
North Carolina.

disappeared upstairs again at once. I did not know who he was and his sudden appearance frightened me.

Many years later I learned that Bingham had been a very handsome man, like all his relatives. His looks had been his only accomplishment, however, and the high point of his career had come when he was crowned king of Asheville's rhododendron festival. At one point he had married, but it had been an ill-omened match, according to Father, who wrote to Henrietta about it in 1943, from London. He could not imagine why Bingham had decided to marry a woman when there was no "temptation of midnight feasts"—the family's name for sex—and no money to be gained. Father believed that Bingham would never move out of "the witchery of that second floor of his until the house is torn down around him." He was relieved that Aunt Sadie seemed "immunized" to the "incredible irritation" of having her incapacitated nephew as a constant guest. Father added that life on the hill in Asheville was stranger than any fiction.

Many years later, when all the Asheville relatives were dead and the old school had been sold and was about to be torn down, I visited Aunt Sadie's house for the last time. The rooms were empty and the doors and windows were hanging open, waiting for the bulldozers. But one room on the second floor was a foot deep in papers—bills, clippings, and many love letters written by a number of women to Bingham McKee.

Born to the "queenly" Mary Kerr and her husband, Major Reid McKee, Bingham (who was sometimes called Bing) had been a young man during the final struggle for the succession at the school.

He seemed to have spent his time meeting women at Asheville's resorts and they often wrote rhapsodically about their encounters. One remembered Bingham "sitting before an open fire, sipping a mint julep and gazing off into space." She described herself as "madly, beautifully, and completely in love" and remembered "that unforgettable night, your mountain top with the stars for our roof." Only a few months later, however, she complained that Bingham had not written, adding that "you are not thoughtful of such things, which is partly where your charm lies." Apparently he was at the core unattainable, perhaps because he knew he would never leave the old school.

A few years later, Bingham received many letters from a woman in Akron, Ohio, who wrote that "Father won't let me close my bedroom door because he likes to shout at me from his room. Always—'Tell about Bing!'"

In his beauty and inviolability, Bingham was a reverse image of the attractive yet virginal young woman whom the Bingham men admired and wished to acquire. The patriarchy creates in its male failures a clear and true vision of its female successes: eternally bound to family and birthplace, eternally seductive yet unseduced, Bingham was a fading flower from the old belle bouquet.

Inevitably his imitation of the female code revealed its terrible weaknesses. He could not support himself; he could not fight; he could not make an advantageous marriage. By the time I saw him in his bathrobe he had become a feared symbol of the ruin that threatened the Bingham men if they believed their own myth.

He shared the language of romance with his grandfather, the Colonel, as my father and Martha McKee shared yet another language, which they had invented during their childhood. I only learned a few words, and did not understand their meaning. "Boojum" (From Lewis Carroll's "Hunting of the Snark") seemed to be some kind of household demon; "bivens" was said to be the odor of exhaust fumes released by a bus, although I suspect it had a more human connotation. "ZooZoo," a useful word, meant a total failure.

Martha McKee, Bingham's sister, was slight and dry and quick; her charm was the adult sleight of hand that mystifies children. I did not understand the private jokes she and Father enjoyed. She took care of her sister, Temple, uncomplainingly for her entire life.

I never knew what was wrong with Temple. Sometimes I thought there was nothing wrong with her at all, that she was just a round, excitable, lipsticked, laughing person who didn't quite fit. But the stories I heard about her were disquieting.

I was rarely alone with Temple. She seemed to dodge about on the periphery of life. Once, I spent a night in the old unheated house on the school grounds which she shared with Martha. Temple was determined to make me comfortable—the house was very cold—and her good-humored offers of blankets and hot-water bottles caught my attention. Who was she when she was removed from her sister and their aunt? What kind of life did she lead in the ruined school?

There were no answers to my unasked questions until several years later. Then Mother revealed that Temple had suddenly fallen to the ground during a trip to Louisville, thrashing and foaming at the mouth. Father had explained, finally, that Temple suffered from epilepsy. Although she had medication, she did not always take it. Martha was so ashamed of what she viewed as a family failing that Temple's illness could never be mentioned.

Years later, after Aunt Sadie's death, as Martha grew old and frail, Temple's care became an unmanageable burden. In the fifties, Father decided to commit her to an institution, where she spent the last years of her life. Temple, with her big red face and her overhearty laugh, disappeared into the maelstrom, along with many other women who did not "suit." Zelda Fitzgerald, who had once claimed the nation's attention as F. Scott's bride, was committed to a series of institutions and died in a nursing-home fire just outside Asheville. Temple, whom no one knew, disappeared into a similar institution, and subsequently into death. She has left no mark.

Her grave in the little family plot overlooking Asheville is sinking dramatically. Temple lies in death, as she was in life, hemmed in by her sister, her brother, and her aunts. The plot is dominated by Colonel Bingham's marker with its menu of accomplishments. Beside it and behind it lie the small headstones of his nieces and his sisters. Only one husband's grave, Major Grinnan's, edges at an odd angle between the patriarch and his female troop.

There was another side to our Asheville visits in the forties and fifties, a side that was more ambiguous and also more interesting to me than the quiet life on the hill. Asheville was a rude mountain town where saloons and pool halls crowded the narrow streets. Closed in by the mountains, locked in a perpetual winter, it seemed to me a den of vice where gnarled-looking mountaineers prowled the shadowy streets in search of illegal entertainment.

Father sometimes drove down from the school to do an errand. Once we got out of the car and walked on those mean little streets. We shared a fascination with the untamable future, and enjoyed playing with the Ouija board. So when we saw a little hand-lettered sign in a curtained window that said that a fortune-teller plied her trade there, we were intrigued. However, for some reason Father did not go in, although he gave me the money to pay.

I must have been ten or eleven at the time, and as I went into the strange little shop, I was afraid. Nothing there seemed to indicate the presence of a sage who could foresee the future. It was a stranger's shabby bedroom. The woman sitting in an armchair seemed surprised when I asked her to tell my fortune. She went through a little constrained mumbo jumbo, and I paid her a dollar. Escaping, I realized that there had been some mistake. She was not a fortune-teller at all.

Father was secretly amused by the incident. He agreed that the little sign was probably misleading. Somehow he conveyed the impression that the place was a whorehouse.

I was fascinated by my close scrape with vice. It had never occurred to me that it would present itself as a tired middle-aged woman who had to pretend to tell a girl's fortune.

The ruined military school on the hill was connected by a way of thought to the grimy street of bars and poolrooms downtown. Thomas Wolfe understood the connection, but it would be many years before I realized that the big resort hotels and the Vanderbilts' egregious mansion had less to do with the old Bingham School than the tired woman who had looked at me with such surprise.

15

In 1943, I began first grade in a fieldstone building, named for one of the flour Ballards, which perched on a bluff over the river several miles from the Big House. It was a public elementary school that served the children of rich families living along the bluff and the children of poor families on the riverbank. Some of these families sold fishing worms. On the way to school, I read their hand-painted signs, some with a backwards "s" on "worms." I had learned to read the year before by piecing together newspaper headlines while sitting on the floor of my parents' bedroom.

Because of its proximity to the very rich and the very poor, Ballard School had a special atmosphere. In its classrooms the children of adults who would never share the same room came to know each other. The parents shared a simple objective: to send their children to a school within walking distance of home. The well-off parents also wanted their children to be "exposed"—a word much in vogue at the time—to good teachers, and so a fund was set up to supplement the teachers' pitiably low salaries. For a few years, Ballard School was a rare combination of upper-class idealism and Ohio River valley practicality.

This experiment made a great impression on me. It proved that I had a moral obligation to get along with all sorts.

I was dazzled by the vitality of the children. I remember standing on the steps leading from the school to what had once been a station on the old interurban trolley track, watching boys and girls race across a sunny meadow. I had never seen boys and girls play together, and I marveled at the bright independent spirit of those sturdy little girls who were equal to the boys in kick-the-can and capture-the-flag. Years later, they displayed the same confidence on the dance floor and the hockey field.

Even stranger were the children of the worm sellers. They spoke a language that seemed incomprehensible to me, the language of the rural, illiterate South.

Duke Appleton was a son of a family that sold worms. His older sister was in the third grade when I was in the first. Somehow she arrived at the idea that I was persecuting her little brother. Tall as a cornstalk, she cornered me on the school steps one day and threatened to strangle me if I didn't leave Duke alone. I thought she would do it and lived for a long time with guilt and dread.

Worth and Barry were both at Ballard School during those early years, and Duke became the generic boyfriend about whom Worth made his jokes. According to Worth, Duke was pining away, disconsolate, hoping for a glance from me, or he was cruelly encouraged by some aimless word or gesture, then cast down again by my indifference. Worth's elaborate tale baffled and enraged me. Even repeating the magic phrase "gasoline station" failed to blot out Worth's taunts. Finally, driven to fury, I found another way to stop him.

We were riding in the car, often the setting for our squabbles. In the car, we were packed together; there was an unavoidable, if brief, intimacy. That afternoon, we were coming home from dancing school. Worth began to invent another story about Duke's attempts to get my attention. Of course, Duke had long since dropped below the horizon. Worm sellers' sons were not included on social occasions. I knew it was useless to argue, and tears would only incite Worth further. Suddenly I turned around and scratched my tormentor's face.

Years later when Worth lay in his coffin, I saw that faint line running down his cheek.

At the time, he screamed and I laughed. Then I couldn't stop laughing. The hysterical release doubled me up. Mother, who was driving, did not say a word. When we arrived at the Big House, she took me upstairs and cut my fingernails down to the quick.

I was satisfied. I had paid a fair price for my victory. Worth never mentioned Duke Appleton again.

In second grade, I made my first friend, a small, merry boy who was the son of my parents' friends. Ted could read as well as I. We would sit together during math class and read from the same book, our heads meekly bowed so that the teacher would assume we were studying addition. I understood something about Ballard School when the teacher told us we could go on reading stories; math would come in its own time.

In the afternoons, I sometimes visited Ted in his peaceful white house, and went out to his mother's studio, where we were allowed to play with her paints. When it was time to go home, his mother drove us in the rumble seat of her car, or in a pony cart, rattling along River Road. I liked his mother because she seemed to enjoy her life.

Sometimes on the weekends I was invited to spend the night, and Ted and I slept in the same bed. We believed that the old white house was haunted, and we used to scare each other with ghost stories before falling asleep.

One night I woke up in the chilly dawn to see Ted's little brother dancing against his crib bars, several of which appeared to be broken. The baby was looking at a woman standing in the open door. She was wearing a long gray dress and she was staring at me. Terrified, I dove under the sheets and woke up Ted. But when he looked, she had vanished.

The material that separates the so-called real and the imaginary was a thin sheet of tissue when I was a child. The stories we heard were only another version of the world as we understood it. The big houses along the river bluff were shadowed by half-heard tales. Every family, it seemed to me, had something to hide, and these secrets bloomed at night. Perhaps that made it easier to bear my knowledge of secrets in my own family.

At the end of second grade, Mother decided that I was too old to spend the night with a boy. I was shocked by her decision; I did not understand what lay behind it, but I knew it was something bad. I felt ashamed. Ted and I continued to play in the afternoon.

Then Ted decided he was too old to play with girls. At least that is what I thought he decided. He was becoming a tease, like Worth.

One warm afternoon, Ted put me through a series of minor humiliations. First he locked me in his mother's bathroom, always a chamber of horrors, of odd-looking rubber paraphernalia and unidentified smells. Then he pushed me too hard on the swing.

Hurt soon developed into rage. I wanted to pay him back in kind. His father, who was overseas in the service, had sent home a little silver paper knife I assumed Ted prized. Before going home that day, I stole the knife.

It burned in my pocket. As soon as I could, I went outside the Big House and threw the knife into a group of tall pines.

Even now when I pass those pines, I think of the silver knife, buried in needles.

For weeks, I waited for someone to mention the knife. Either it was not missed or no one thought to connect me with its disappearance. I did not see Ted again for a long time.

A few days before Christmas, I was eating lunch in the pantry at the Big House, where our meals were served when we had missed the scheduled occasion. A huge warming table took up the center of the big room; my fork and plate and mug of milk looked small on the expanse. As I was sitting there, Ted suddenly appeared with a puppy in his arms.

He wanted to give me the puppy for a Christmas present. Dutifully, I went upstairs and asked Mother if I could it. I knew she would explain, reasonably and kindly, that we were not prepared to take on a dog that was not house-trained. Our big black poodles would surely hate the puppy, too. I went back down and told Ted he would have to take the puppy home.

I felt no resentment or disappointment. I knew my family too well to expect a different outcome. By that time, I was so deeply involved in life at the Big House that I felt rather superior to Ted. He simply did not understand.

Years later, one of my mother's five sisters told of having been given a puppy when she was traveling with her godmother, a rich woman of limited sympathies. The godmother indicated that she would not tolerate the puppy, and suggested that my aunt throw it overboard. My aunt retreated in furious tears, which aroused the interest of a fellow passenger, a naval officer of some standing. He took care of the puppy, and the story was given a happy ending.

I used to wonder at my aunt's persistence in wanting something her godmother did not want. In those days it seemed to me that my wishes were shaped by my parents' desires.

When I was eight or nine, Father began reading out loud every evening. Worth and Barry had gone off to boarding school, and the two younger children, Eleanor and Jonathan, were still sent to bed at twilight. I alone was of an age to eat dinner with our parents and to sit afterwards, rapt and silent, while Father read.

We had been weaned on the nineteenth-century British classics: Beatrix Potter, Charles Kingsley (Mother deleted his anti-Catholic tirades), George Macdonald, Lewis Carroll (I found *Alice in Wonderland* mystifying and somewhat repellent), and a few American oddities such as *Hitty: Her First Hundred Years,* the story of a mind encased in a wooden doll. Years later, looking at the illustration of Hitty floating face-up in a stream, I would be reminded of Millais's drowned Ophelia.

These children's books depended on a world of rigid rules, with terror just on the other side of the door. Beyond the placid riverbank in *The Wind in the Willows* lies the predatory nightmare of the Wild Wood. Goblins in mountain chambers threaten the children in *The Princess and Curdie.* The North Wind is as frightening as she is powerful in *At the Back of the North Wind.* Gnomes with poisonous fruit tempt the foolish sister in *Goblin Market.* These books prepared me for the family myth, for secrets, avoidance, and veiled eroticism. They also prepared me for Dickens.

The Colonel, imprisoned during the Civil War on Johnson's Island, had passed the time reading Dickens. My father had read most of his novels. So it was to Dickens we turned, adding Thackeray from time to time, and even George Eliot, who I assumed was a man.

Hour after hour, evening after evening, I sat on the footstool enjoying Father's voice, his evident delight in wit and melodrama and in the secrets with which the big Victorian novels abound. He seemed to guess the secrets long before I did, and would gleefully wait for me to "catch on." Sometimes it was the dark female figures, the Trilbys and Becky Sharps, who manufactured the secrets that hid their mysterious wrongdoing.

Power and evil existed together in these books, reinforcing each other in women. The traits generally admired in Southern girls reappeared in grotesque form in Dickens's conventional heroines, who often died young. But the monster women prevailed, fascinated, and destroyed. Father would read their stories until his gold pocket watch rang its tiny chime.

Later I became frightened of the power of these readings. I asked to hold the pocket watch so that I could see when it was time to go to bed. Then in my anxiety I began to pace the floor, the watch in my hand, while the reading continued. The magic was too strong. I did not know how to combat it.

The Big House would be very still. At first there would have been the sound of washing-up in the kitchen, and then the back-hall elevator would groan, carrying Cordie and Lizzie up to bed.

At last it would be time for me to go to bed, and Father would close the thick book, marking his place. Then I would kiss my parents good night and start upstairs, across the enormous front hall, lit by a single light. Shadows lay deep in the corners and curled in the long damask curtains; glints rode the surface of the gilt-framed mirrors. I put my hand on the cool ebony railing and started upstairs. On the landing, two long portraits faced each other in the dim light: Father as a pale young boy, dressed in black and surrounded by open books, and Uncle Robert in his First World War uniform. At the top of the steps, I would see the open door of my bedroom with lamplight shining out. I was safe.

Mother seldom read to me after I was eight or nine, but before that, she had introduced me to the classics of the antebellum period: *Uncle Remus*, written in a dialect she deplored; *Two Little Confederates*, which described the Virginia plantation where my cousins were growing up; *Diddie, Dumps, and Tot*, subtitled *A Plantation Child-Life*, published in 1882. This last dwelt on the special relationship between black slaves and white children, and the author stated (as the Colonel had said) that "no hireling can ever be to the children what their Mammies were." Love, not money, sealed the pact between powerless slave and powerless child.

Mother's respect for this tradition was tempered by her fear that illiterate servants would teach her children bad grammar or pass along "trashy" accents. She conveyed even while she read the treacle-sweet descriptions of life "before the war" that this kind of Southern romance was not something she admired. I knew she had not grown up in a "big white house on a plantation in Mississippi," like Diddie, Dumps, and Tot, but in a crowded little house in Richmond where she had had to fight for an education.

The stories she read us were not frightening. Father's often were. He particularly relished tales of supernatural intervention, in which Indian spirits preyed on innocent vacationers or a little girl was tormented by a demonic governess, as in *The Turn of the Screw*.

Perhaps Father, too, was terrified by tales that hinted at the horrors of his early life. But his relish seemed to mean that he did not feel fear, and in fact his favorite fairy tale was "The Boy Who Did Not Know How to Shudder." He controlled reality, it seemed to me, even the reality of the spirit world. Later I would wonder what numbness was disguised by his delight as he read "The Pit and the Pendulum" or "The Fall of the House of Usher." Worth, too, would seek again and again to feel fear, exposing himself to danger either because he believed he could not be hurt or because he could no longer feel.

Mother taught us early to behave like Christians. It was part of our training, along with manners. We repeated the Lord's Prayer at bedtime, knew the Ten Commandments, and went regularly to church. But religion seemed to have nothing to do with the rest of my life: the teasing, the remorseless competition, the horror of the secret past. Outside the Big House, innocent creatures suffered for no reason at all, in spite of the Bible teaching that God observes even the sparrow's fall. What malevolence caused the big spider to drown with all her babies in a corner of the swimming pool, where, years earlier, a little pony had also drowned? Why did the sheep abandon one of their twin lambs every spring on Aunt Henrietta's farm? What had really happened to the people who lurked around the edges of the family's life, either dead, exiled, or obliterated?

My school life at Ballard introduced me to injustices the Episcopal church seemed to ignore. No one in that congregation wore patched clothes or had the peculiar pale glow of the worm sellers' children. Yet the scriptures often spoke of the sufferings of the meek, while extending to them only the hope of a better life hereafter. That seemed unfair to me. Sometimes I wondered why all the coins and bills collected every Sunday did not go to the poor children who lived by the river. Those great silver plates, piled high with loot—sometimes one of the elegantly dressed ushers would have to press the bills down with his hand—began to sicken me, like the whiskey- and cigarette-loaded breaths of the adults around me.

Several years later, when I heard that two of the men who frequently ushered at church shared a wife—the lover spent one afternoon a week with her at the Brown Hotel—I was not surprised. That great white church on its hill seemed designed to ignore all the pain and injustice in the world around it. I stopped going to church as soon as I could persuade Mother that I was in no fit state to take communion.

The younger and the older children in the family escaped the reading-aloud, an expert and intoxicating introduction to the written word. Worth and Barry were spending most of their time at boarding school. Barry was working hard; Worth was less predictable. Now and then I became aware of tremors from the North, telephone calls, unexpected arrivals, hasty deci-sions and departures.

One day when I was ten or eleven I came downstairs and saw Mother standing in the front hall with her arms around Worth, whom I had not known was at home. He had been expelled for some infringement of school rules. Displays of affection were rare in the family, and I thought I had stumbled on something I was not supposed to see; I went back upstairs, embarrassed. Worth was dispatched immediately to another boarding school and nothing was said about the incident.

The scene remained fixed in my memory, disturbing, yet oddly attrac-tive. It seemed to prove that wrongdoing had its place in our highly con-trolled existence. I had often wondered about Aunt Henrietta's strange behavior, sealed up in isolation at Harmony Landing. Now it seemed to me that the black sheep in the family were at least tolerated if not actually admired.

Years later, when I was about to get my driver's license, Mother warned me that any infringement of the laws would end up on the front page of the newspaper, even if it was only a parking violation. I believed her and could even see the merit of avoiding accusations of favoritism in this way. It was a long time before I wondered why Worth's car accidents never appeared in print. It was even longer before I realized that many other stories were never seen in the newspapers.

When Worth was a much younger boy, away from home for the first time, he had written Nursie, "Today I got into serious trouble. My science teacher is Mr. Hogg, and I put in my science book, 'Please return to my room unless you want a wild Hogg after me.' He read it when he was correcting my book, and was about to turn it in to the Dean, but thought better of it when I apologized. I have to buy a new science book however and I have been broke and borrowing for two weeks."

Worth went on: "Barry has written me two letters. The last one had 53 spelling mistakes, but it was a nice long one. My braces are loose, my shoes need fixing and my clothes need sewing so I hope that money hurries . . ."

By the late 1940s, theater had begun to absorb me. I had seen several Shakespeare productions when road companies arrived to play for a day or two in the big auditorium downtown. These performances interrupted our routine; even on a school night, I was allowed to go to see Maurice Evans in *Hamlet.*

Near the Little House stands a Greek amphitheater the Judge caused to rise on the ruins of a burned house. The stage is backed by tall granite columns, topped with a frieze across which run the words TO HOLD AS 'TWERE A MIRROR UP TO NATURE. I was aware of nature but not of the mirror. Its exact location and purpose escaped me.

I harried my fourth-, fifth-, and sixth-grade classes into three summer productions in the amphitheater, choosing to do truncated versions of *Hamlet, Romeo and Juliet,* and *A Midsummer Night's Dream.* The productions were a reward for my improving grades, the only reward, one of my teachers noted, which persuaded me to work.

I had been transferred from Ballard to a small private girls' school in town, the Louisville Collegiate School. Mother was disillusioned, even angry with progressive education. Once I heard her criticizing John Dewey's theories while I was trailing after the grown-ups on a walk.

Mother believed in original sin, and her experience with her first three children had done nothing to change that conviction. School was a way of forcing lazy or recalcitrant children to learn. Anyone who thought that children were small human beings with interests and questions of their own, who would learn to read and write when those skills became necessary to them, was simply soft in the head.

The alarms and excursions from this pedagogical battle resounded through my childhood. Mother became a strong advocate of the phonetic method of teaching a child to read rather than the so-called look-say method. Dewey had found that "to make words by sounding during the first months of reading is likely to result in a fatal division of attention." His teachers used images, as vivid as possible, to help a child memorize words. The method has proved successful with dyslexic children.

Mother feared that children taught in this "permissive" way would never read at all. She found a strong ally in William J. Hutchins, president of the University of Chicago.

Such exercises as sitting in a circle and sharing personal experiences also aroused Mother's ire. Here school was impinging on a dangerous area. The family's secrets, even its everyday life, were not suitable material for a classroom discussion. Dewey emphasized the link between home and school, which was not acceptable to a family intent on keeping its distance. Our parents wanted children to acquire all the necessary skills at school, while maintaining an emotional separateness that would ensure their loyalty to the family.

The school to which I was transferred had been founded in 1916 to provide Louisville girls of good family with twelve years of education. Here were opportunities to acquire more than a smattering of English literature, some French, four years of Latin, and a grounding in science and math. Many entered the school at kindergarten and graduated thirteen years later, having spent the intervening years with one small group of girls and teachers. The school looks like a handsome suburban mansion, with its Georgian façade and neat lawn.

The atmosphere was warm and relaxed, especially in the lower grades. A good deal more feeling was aroused by hockey matches than by classroom activities. I began rather soon to be bored. I also felt safe for the first time from surprises.

By now I had become aware of family maxims: "No Bingham," male or female, was good at math or science; it was simply unheard of. On the other hand, "no Bingham" had difficulty learning to read or developing reading into a passion—which made life very difficult for Barry.

No one among us was "good with our hands." Anything that needed to be fixed would be fixed by someone hired for that purpose; mechanical ability was by its very nature lower-class. Boys and young men were adequate at team sports, but women needed to avoid becoming "muscle-bound" through such exertions, although we were all expected to play tennis well. Hobbies generally were a waste of time. Bridge, however, was a proper grown-up pastime, to which Barry and Worth were invited.

In short, we were to be cut to a very old pattern, one that had suited a generation of Southern aristocrats who had never existed. Our North Carolina and Virginia forebears had relied on the work of their hands as well as their heads. We were unsuited for practical life, although we did not know that in the magic kingdom on the hill, where the necessities were handled by Nursie and the five black servants.

I realized at an early age that drama—the ability to impersonate and to disguise—was an essential of family life. Exaggeration was highly valued, and it would have been "the kiss of death" to describe an event in literal, prosaic terms. Acting had brought our parents together; they had met in a college play, and a photograph from that period showed their classic, paired profiles, as beautiful and as icy as the Barrymores'.

Theater provided me with more than attention and the illusion of glamour. It allowed me to reinterpret reality. Playing the part of Titania meant dressing up as a fairy queen.

The Little House, 1930s.

The Place, 1950s.

The amphitheater at the Place. The façade is inscribed
"To hold as 'twere a mirror up to nature."

Captain Bud on the front porch
of the Big House, 1950s.

The old Colonel's Confederate sword reappeared, metaphorically, in a musical for which I supplied lyrics and plot when I was thirteen. Called *Out of the Fire,* it used Schubert lieder, which I had never heard before, for a Cinderella-like fairy tale.

Compared to the theatrics in the amphitheater, the school plays I acted in seemed bleak. I was uneasy, too, at being cast as a male because I was tall—or perhaps for other reasons I did not care to consider. My drama teacher remembered later that I loved to act, but I preferred directing, which made me feel less vulnerable. However, I had never heard of a woman director, and the authority I exercised over my classmates in that role disturbed me. After all, Worth often accused me of being "bossy" and called me "Miss Priss." Perhaps directing was another version of that unattractive behavior.

I cherished my time alone at home, exploring the Back Woods or riding my bike. When she was visiting us, Munda made me aware that this behavior was unsuitable for a young lady. Once she criticized me fiercely for not helping Mother arrange the flowers.

Inadvertently, Munda shed light on my relationship to Mother, which seemed oddly insubstantial. Our earlier difficulties had been surmounted—I no longer threw tantrums or had nightmares—but nothing had taken the place of the frightening old struggles. Mother seemed remote but not actively displeased. Munda, however, remembered a time when her own daughters' help had been essential to maintaining the appearance of a leisured life. But Mother did not need me; there were many other people to take care of things.

I knew that if I tried to help Mother, my efforts would not live up to her expectations. She was a perfectionist and her gleaming, beflowered house was her masterpiece. It was impossible to imitate her, for she did not share her secrets. Although she never cooked, she knew how to tell from a recipe whether a dish would be tasty, which seemed magical to me. When I decided later that I needed to learn to cook, I made watermelon-rind pickles, my only culinary accomplishment until I left home. Mother was not part of this experiment; Cordie, the cook, insisted on washing the pots.

The source of my nervousness was another secret. Sometimes I imagined that I was an orphan child whom my parents had adopted; it seemed to me they regretted traits in me that did not belong in the family. Perhaps I was a "sport," a sort of genetic mutation. I heard a good deal of discussion about genetic factors which produced inferior people, or revealed some genealogical scandal. The Kentucky mountaineers were said to be inferior because of years of inbreeding; Munda's story "Nigger Foot" (which she later retitled, carefully, "Negro Foot") showed the way a drop of black blood was revealed in the shape of a footprint. Perhaps I was a throwback to some earlier, worse version, a "bad seed" with hatred and rage planted in my genetic code. Nothing else explained my propensity to "moods" that continued to exasperate Mother. I was also aware that I could become angry and that sometimes I could not control myself.

Secrets were buried in my childhood, but curiosity, as Nursie said, killed the cat. For a long time, I managed to restrain my curiosity, even about my Raggedy Ann doll. A heart, labeled "Candy," was outlined on her cloth chest. We were seldom permitted sweets because of our teeth, and so my curiosity was partly the urge to eat something forbidden. But I also imagined that an essential secret was buried with Raggedy Ann's candy heart.

Finally, feeling as guilty as though I was committing a murder, I ripped open Raggedy Ann's chest with a pair of nail scissors. I took out a small red candy heart, covered with fuzz. I was wretchedly disappointed and ashamed, and my doll was ruined.

Raggedy Ann wore a print dress and a white apron called a pinafore. My clothes were more ordinary. By the time I was eleven, I was deeply aware of them. Clothes were the outward and visible sign of an inward and invisible grace. I loved shopping downtown with Mother, partly because of the serene and fragrant atmosphere of the big old department store. It was a haven for women. Nicely dressed middle-aged women served behind the counters, offering lipsticks, handkerchiefs, and conversation to shoppers who seemed to be their counterparts. There were floors of clothes to browse on—the special and esteemed pastime, almost the obligatory pastime, of well-off women. It was a relief to be involved in an activity that was almost never criticized. Years later, when I read Veblen in college, I thought he had partly misunderstood: "conspicuous consumption" would have been frowned on in Louisville; inconspicuous but perpetual consumption was what was expected.

Even now, when the old department store has fallen on hard times, with pillows and towels stacked haphazardly and sawhorses and sheets of plastic everywhere, I still go there to remember the comfortable middle-class assurance of that lost world, where ladies ate lunch in the Orchid Room and had their hair done in the vast pink beauty parlor. On one of these recent expeditions, the woman behind the cosmetics counter looked at me and asked, "Who did you used to be?"

When I went shopping with Mother, it never occurred to me to wonder where the black women I saw on the street shopped or ate a meal. In the 1940s a black woman could try on a hat in Louisville stores only if she first wrapped tissue paper around her head. She could not try on clothes at all, or use the bathrooms, or sit in the cafeterias. The stores finally changed their policies in the 1950s as a result of a black boycott called "No New Clothes for Easter."

When I was younger, Mother had ordered my striped and embroidered dresses from the Best and Company catalogue that arrived from New York twice a year. I would pore over the delicate pastel sketches, trying to imagine how the clothes would look on me.

Later I was given a monthly clothes allowance. One of my first independent purchases was a black-and-white polka-dot nylon blouse, also ordered from a catalogue—but not Best's. As soon as it arrived, I realized that the blouse was "tacky" and relegated it to my closet. Mother, seeing it hanging there, asked where in the world I had found such a thing.

My school uniform was a heavy blue wool skirt and long-sleeved white blouse with a Peter Pan collar for winter, and a navy-blue cotton jumper and short-sleeved white blouse for warmer weather, worn with a navy-blue cardigan, thick white socks, and laced-up brown leather oxfords. Although the uniform was particularly disfiguring, I did not object to it; it spared me anxious decisions about clothes, decisions that never seemed to result in my looking the way I thought I should.

Mother's beautiful clothes seemed to have grown on her. I was not aware of shopping trips or bills. Twice a year, our seamstress, Frances, would arrive and spread a white sheet on the floor of the sewing room. There she would fit Mother's new clothes, kneeling on the floor to adjust hems, her mouth full of straight pins. Frances seemed a magician who, under Mother's expert guidance, transformed "bought" dresses into queenly robes that never creased or stained.

Father's clothes seemed to have grown on him, too. Later, during summer trips to London, I realized that his wardrobe was the result of delicate and precise calculation, as had been the Judge's; the Judge was the first man in the family to order his suits tailor-made on Savile Row.

Father's outfits were always suited to the occasion, a feat I could not even manage with my dolls. His at-home clothes were soft, even luxuriant— a blue velvet smoking jacket with quilted lapels, creamy flannel shirts, muted tweed jackets. He never wore sweaters or overcoats or the kind of hats and gloves designed only for warmth. His "downtown" clothes were crisp, dark suits that seemed finer, more elegant than the clothes my friends' fathers wore.

His evening clothes were too dazzling to be seen in detail; he flashed out, black and white and brilliant. But best of all were his outdoor clothes: the soft, pale blue jeans and misty-colored corduroys, and the resplendent green jacket he wore for beagling, a curious sport in which human beings chase dogs who are chasing rabbits.

Beautiful clothes had no price, as far as I knew. Money was not to be discussed, and I died of shame when strangers asked how much something had cost. I believed that it was vulgar to mention prices; I also believed that, in spite of the evidence before our eyes, the family was living in straitened circumstances.

I often heard mention of the large debt we had undertaken when the newspapers' offices were built in the early 1950s. I thought this was a private debt that might affect our ability to go to the movies or eat a meal in a restaurant. It was a profound relief when the debt was finally paid off.

Both parents set us an example of abstemiousness. They drove small American cars and had no expensive tastes, other than for luxury hotels when they traveled, fine clothes, and fine wines. Mother wore no ostentatious jewelry. But I did not understand where the line lay between the exercise of good taste, which forbade extravagant display, and the fear of financial ruin, as palpable as it was unlikely. None of the five children learned to enjoy spending money, which made us perhaps peculiarly unsuited to inheriting large fortunes. However, it also prevented the growth of tastes and habits that would have further separated us from our friends.

We learned early the concept of noblesse oblige. Mother often spoke of our duty to the less fortunate; she also taught us that we should never feel superior to the poor black and poor white people around us. She did not want me to include Nursie or the black servants in this category. She used to reprimand me for sympathizing with them.

In this atmosphere, our allowances became the focus of much uneasy speculation. Did we deserve allowances, living as we did in the lap of luxury? Were our allowances, which were always small, in proportion to the family's wealth? Who decided on these small amounts, and what, if anything, were we expected to do to earn them? Since money was a forbidden topic, none of these questions could be asked.

We all learned early to count our pennies. I began in September to save for Christmas presents—I always had a long list that included both school friends and the people who worked on the Place. I shopped in the ten-cent store in order to stretch my savings. It was clearly inappropriate to give Nursie face powder, which she never used, or to offer bubble bath and cologne to Lizzie and Cordie, whom I could not imagine lying in bubble baths or spraying themselves with perfume. But I did not know what else to buy them. Rubber gloves and scrubbing brushes were obviously out of the question.

To supplement my allowance, I worked at small chores. Mother often needed someone to weed her garden and would pay half a cent a weed. She also asked me to debud her peonies in the spring, a job that had its perils.

My father, 1930's.

My mother (right)
and an unidentified
friend outside the
tennis court, 1930's.

Father, Mother, and George Norton, 1930s.

Mother, Worth, Barry, and Father, 1930s.

Lizzie Baker.

Eleanor and Sallie in Paris, 1949.
The white dress was probably handmade by Munda.

The sticky peony buds were swarming with ants, and as I broke off the secondary buds and dropped them into a bucket, the ants ran up my hands and arms. But I liked the logic of sacrificing the small buds to the growth of the main bloom, and enjoyed deciding which of the cluster promised the best show and should be preserved. The Darwinism of this project was, I realized later, peculiarly applicable to the family, in which lesser members were sometimes sacrificed to the growth and display of the central figures.

Mother's attitude toward money was influenced by her mother's cheerful insouciance, which disguised a determination to supply her six daughters with clothes and coming-out parties and vacations abroad she could not really afford. Munda used to describe how a young woman's presentation at the Court of St. James's in London could be, with skillful maneuvering, paid for almost entirely by the kindness of friends. In one of her stories, the narrator, one of six sisters, described her trip to be presented in London as a lucky adventure, carried off with enormous dash and optimism, paid for with wins at the racetrack, the subtle use of influence, and the exercise of charm. Such maneuvers would have embarrassed Mother.

Father's attitude toward money was also colored by early hardships, and I used to watch with interest when he carefully counted change at a restaurant, holding the coins and bills under the edge of the table. His early life had been affected by the Judge's mercurial fall and rise. After Mary Lily's death, money could never be discussed without the threat of revelations. Our wealth had the evaporating quality of money that is not earned: money that grows because of fortunate friendships and marriages but has little relation to more obvious forms of labor.

Unaware of these complexities, I made money raising chickens. I bought an old white hen with an ugly disposition and gave her twelve fertilized eggs. She haughtily obliged by sitting on them. When the chicks began to peek out from under her feathers, her temper turned even uglier, and she would peck fiercely, with sudden thrusts of her long neck, when I tried to touch the chicks. Eleven of the twelve turned out to be roosters. Aunt Helena bought them all from me, saving me from financial ruin. Luebell took over the task of chopping off their heads.

I then purchased some white ducks, in the hope that their eggs might prove acceptable in the Big House kitchen. Barry, home on vacation, took an interest in my farmyard project, and spent many hot days building a pond. He dug the hole, lined it with concrete, and filled it with water. The ducks plunged in happily, and proceeded to lay most of their eggs in the water. By the time I found them, bobbing up to the surface, they were too far advanced to sell.

All these activities came to an abrupt end in July of 1949. Mother and

Father told me in an early-morning conference in their bedroom that Father had been asked to go to Paris with the Marshall Plan. We were all going over.

I had been unaware of the flurry of events leading up to his appointment as one of a group of friends who had, as one historian described it, "strolled with their parents through Europe's Edwardian autumn."

These aristocrats shared a commitment to European civilization that did not, at first, include overt anti-Communism. Under the aegis of General Marshall, these old friends designed the European Recovery Plan, which was promoted by journalists who belonged to the same club, such as Walter Lippmann and the Alsop brothers. Henry Stimson, George Ball, Chip Bohlen, and Averell Harriman shared in the "intimacy of decision-making in Washington during the early postwar years," as Walter Isaacson and Evan Thomas described it in their history of the period. It was an intimacy flavored with the amenities of Big House living: cocktails flowed abundantly, jokes were proof of shared values, and women provided emotional support and never emerged from the cozy background they provided for their men. Father's appointment was mysterious to me only because I did not understand that he was a member of this particular club, although I knew that some of these people took over my bedroom at Derby time.

Unlike the League of Nations, the Marshall Plan was a pragmatic approach to Europe's problems which, while rebuilding the war-devastated economy, would supply trade outlets for the United States, including Kentucky coal and tobacco. Forty thousand tons of tobacco was shipped to Europe, although none was requested, and while the Schuman Plan was rehabilitating the French and German coal mines, American coal kept the steel factories running. Both would have been of major interest to Father.

But before Congress could be persuaded to support what some Republicans were calling an "International WPA," a war scare was needed to whip up anti-Russian feeling. This was provided by the Russian "clampdown" on Czechoslovakia in February 1948, when arrests and executions purged pro-Western politicians from the government in Prague. Americans believed that the last link with the West was broken when the Czech Foreign Minister, Jan Masaryk, who had worked earlier in an American foundry, was pushed or fell from a window in Prague. (As a child, I had met his lover, Marcia Davenport, who had Kentucky ties.) The Judge in London had received a congratulatory letter from Masaryk, complimenting him on his attempts to involve the United States, then fiercely isolationist, in European problems that were leading to the Second World War: "It is ethical leadership this world of ours craves and must have—Europe especially," Masaryk wrote.

Ethical leadership may have been what Father hoped to provide in

France, but in the context of the Marshall Plan, he was no longer a free agent. I noticed that his excitement about his appointment was tempered by reservations, which perhaps included an understanding of the secret maneuvering of the Cold War.

Truman's policy of "containment" of the Soviet threat was implemented by the covert activities of the late Frank G. Wisner, an OSS ("Oh So Social") veteran and New York lawyer who came back into government in 1948. He and his wife, Polly, were friends of my parents. Wisner organized what he called "my mighty Wurlitzer" to discredit Communism, using foundations, labor unions, book publishers, and the student movement. The services of the working press were essential to the Wurlitzer, and most of the members of Father's club looked upon cooperation with the CIA as their patriotic duty. Joseph Alsop considered his connection with the CIA an example of his commitment to his country.

For me the term "Cold War" had no meaning, and I was ashamed to ask for a definition of a term that had become, overnight, as common as mayonnaise.

I was too excited about the trip to wonder about Father's exact title or the ramifications of what appeared to be a glorious mission to help devastated France recover from the ruins of war, ruins that would become real to me when I saw bombed villas on the Normandy coast. Later I would wonder why I heard more about the ECA—another indecipherable code word—than about the Marshall Plan, and why Father's role remained as mysterious as his title. At one time, he called himself Chief of Mission to the Marshall Plan in France. Recently he told a reporter he had been an administrator of the Marshall Plan.

The Economic Cooperative Administration had been created by the Smith-Mundt Act of 1948 to promote the spread of cultural information. It also represented the aims of Cold War warriors to separate Western Europe from Russia. The Marshall Plan headquarters and the American Embassy in Paris were said to be the center from which CIA agents, posing as journalists, sallied forth to plant stories in European newspapers and incite "Communist" riots. It was assumed that the resulting anti-Communist backlash at home would create more popular support for the Marshall Plan. Benjamin Bradlee, who, like Father, had been an officer in Naval Intelligence, and Father's old friend the journalist Alfred Friendly were on the ECA staff.

ECA and the Marshall Plan attracted other men during this period who would later hold important posts in the CIA. Richard Bissell was assistant administrator of the Plan in Paris from 1948 to 1951; he became special assistant to the director of the CIA three years later. Franklin Lindsay, who did a feasibility study of the Marshall Plan and went to Paris with Averell

Harriman, is said to have been one of the CIA's founders. William Casey, later head of the CIA, was associate counsel during these years at the Marshall Plan's European headquarters. E. Howard Hunt, later one of the Watergate burglars, joined the CIA in 1949 and was sent to Paris, where his official job was as liaison between the American Embassy and the CIA. Hunt worked directly under Richard Bissell.

In France I sensed an undercurrent of tension that perhaps contributed to the social frenzy of my parents' lives, even more driven by prescribed entertainments than they had been at home.

I became aware, peripherally, of Clare Boothe Luce, who I heard was Ambassador to Rome; that a woman could be an ambassador amazed me. I did not know that Mrs. Luce was the wife of the publisher Henry Luce, or that she had written plays. I was bewildered by discussions of her problems with the Italian "Communists"—I was not sure what the label meant— but they seemed to match her weird fate: I was told that she had quit her job after being "poisoned" by flakes of lead-based paint falling from the ceiling of her bedroom. Mrs. Luce's adventures and the mysteries of American activities in France all seemed to belong in the same category. They could not be questioned or discussed, only commented on lightly, with irony.

Had Father elected at that time to explain the connections between the ECA and the CIA, when, like most of his journalist friends, he probably considered cooperation with intelligence to be a patriotic duty, the younger children in the family, at least, would have been easily persuaded. Fortunately for us, he left us to form later conclusions against a background of total obfuscation. Perhaps he realized that Worth, at seventeen, would have been difficult to persuade that such activities were part of a patriot-publisher's duty. Worth's sarcasm and simmering anger during that year in France may have been the result of his partial understanding of the situation. It was then Worth began to refer to various political doings as "dirty tricks." Later, the newspapers' connections with the CIA would cause serious problems for Father and Barry.

The early summer of 1949, before we sailed for France, was enlivened by farewell parties given by my school friends. I had already decided that I was "not a belle" because I was too tall and too shy. This brought considerable relief, as well as disappointment, since the role of a belle seemed to me as constricted as the role of a diplomat in a foreign capital. It meant, first and foremost, that a woman had a duty to entertain all comers, to be available in a charming way to everyone, while banking down what I later called "the mammalian fires." Spared that fate, I enjoyed the lunches and teas and especially the going-away presents, which included my first garter belt. A year later, I would try to persuade my friends to forgo lipstick and stockings until they were eighteen. Now I looked at the lace-and-elastic harness as a symbol of the power of female maturity.

The other signs of that power were hidden; it worked underground, and I was not yet sure of its aims or results. I had known since early childhood that the mysteries of Father's important life were supported by the meals and the flowers, the discreet black servants and the great house that seemed a stage for adult transactions. I would have recognized easily, although with a growing sense of dismay, the role played by wives in the world of the Marshall Plan.

16

France changed everything. It was the wider world.

Nursie was busy for weeks before we left, sorting and mending our clothes, then packing them in the steamer trunks, which would be placed in the *Mauretania*'s hold.

Father had gone on ahead, and so Nursie and Mother shepherded the five children onto the train to New York. "Nursie cried so did all the servants," I wrote in my diary. "It nearly killed old Lizzie when we left," Nursie wrote her mother.

Nursie wrote her mother a letter every day. She described our trip from Grand Central Station in New York City to the Cunard docks on the West Side: "There were 2 big cars waiting for us and we rode to the pier in grand style." In my diary I wrote, "We set sail at 4:45, amid cheers and tears."

"It is so wonderful!" my next day's entry begins, followed by a line from "The Ancient Mariner": "All, all alone on a wide, wide sea . . ." Now that I was too old to be spanked, I was given long epic poems to memorize for punishment. It was a great improvement.

This great trip into the future brought on my physical maturation. I began having sharp pains in my chest. Was I sick in some way? I hesitated to say anything to Mother because I suspected that there was something shameful going on in my childish body, something that I should have understood, like the Cold War. So I endured, and by the end of the voyage, the pains had stopped. Then I noticed that my breasts had begun to develop. I was surprised and not particularly pleased. Breasts did not mean anything to me but a closer connection with the dreaded "mammalian fires"—those instincts and impulses which, according to Munda, burned up a woman's creative gift.

Nursie had already made up her mind to return to Kentucky. "The thought of coming home has not changed except to grow stronger," she wrote to her mother. "No matter how I look at it I feel that it would be best for the children as well as myself. Their mother and father being who they are the children need a lot of fine manners and polish I can't give them."

She added, "I don't think I am homesick but I am mighty dam lonesome. With all the hungry people in the world I think it is a sin to waste so much food like it is wasted here on the boat. You have heard people say they had everything from soup to nuts well they really do here. I never saw as many different kinds of food and some of it so pretty. Not only do they have 3 meals but soup and crackers in the morning and tea and all sorts of sandwiches in the afternoon."

After five days, we docked at Cherbourg, and for the first time in my life I heard a language that was not English. Nursie wrote, "I have really had a day of jabber and strange to say even though I knew very little that they said yet I knew or could guess enough for the most part what they meant." As she rose to the challenge of this strangeness, I noticed and admired her courage.

Father met us at the dock, and he and Mother deposited Nursie and the three younger children in a seaside hotel at Cabourg, in Normandy. (In college, I realized with amazement that this had been Proust's memory-haunted town.) They went on to Paris with Worth and Barry to arrange for summer school and to rent a house.

My first view of the situation in Cabourg was decidedly dismal. Nursie said later that I had resented being left with the younger children while my parents went away "just to enjoy themselves." Cabourg seemed wrapped in melancholia on that gently raining summer day, the beach guarded by bombed villas and German gun emplacements. The hotel smelled of age and gentility. Its long corridors led to suites inhabited by other children and their nurses. Glamorous parents sometimes arrived on the weekend.

During the week, the French children were subjected to a rigorous routine, supervised by their English, French, and German nannies: gymnastics in a fenced area at the beach, big meals, naps, and country walks with tea at a neighboring farm. We began, shyly, to make friends, a good deal handicapped by the lack of a common language.

Nursie quickly picked up a few useful phrases, writing her mother, "The maid thanked me in french and when I said she was welcome back in french she said I was clever and when I said goodnight also in french she was so pleased. I never saw people try so hard to please. I feel that I have found a gold mine as the nurse next to our table can speak both french and english. I mean to make a list of words that I want to learn and get someone to help me so I won't feel so lost." She was excited rather than frightened, and I tried to imitate her élan.

Mother had organized daily French lessons for the three children, and we spent the rest of the time at the beach, where I observed, "I have noticed the french families are so much more closely knit than the Americans, they seem to love each other more." It had never occurred to me before to make such an observation, when the Big House had comprised my world.

On the weekends Mother came down from Paris to see us, and her arrival made a holiday. We went shopping in the village or picked sweet peas in a farm garden; even now the smell of sweet peas, full of rain, brings back those misty Normandy afternoons. Father was busy in Paris and we did not see much of him.

Mother energetically organized expeditions. She found a place to rent bicycles, and took us for long rides along the country roads. I was overwhelmed by the beauty of the gentle green landscape and the long rows of poplars. Jonathan had difficulty keeping up; at seven, he did not yet know how to ride a two-wheeler. Mother somehow procured small training wheels to attach to either side of his rear wheel.

The country roads were not paved, and Jonathan's training wheels would often slip into a rut. I would look back to see him pedaling away furiously, deeply mired in the dirt, his face as red as a beet. Then we would all have to wait until he finally got off and pushed his bike up to us. By then, he would be crying furiously.

The characteristics that had been amusing, perhaps, when Jonathan was small remained and became more problematical as he grew older. He often seemed to lack the specific skills needed in a situation, yet he was determined to do everything, to keep up, a determination fueled by enormous emotional intensity. It was as difficult for him to ask for help as it was for him to give up.

He suffered more than Eleanor or I from the change, deprived for the first time of Mother, who had given him affection as well as protection from the world. Now he was living entirely in a world of strangers, a subdued and highly ordered existence where the children in the glassed-in dining room whispered their requests in immaculate French, where the calmly admonishing mam'selles and fräuleins chastised their charges with a look. We were barbarians all, like American children abroad over the ages, but Jonathan seemed to feel particularly different.

As strangers in the seaside town, we were less protected than as inhabitants of the Big House. "A man tried to pull down my bathing suit today, just to be funny," I wrote. "The other rough men he was with all laughed." At home I had felt the eyes and the hands of strange men on the crowded downtown streets. I did not think there was anything to be done about it, although these unwelcome attentions frightened me. Pawing and pulling were facts of life, like Worth's teasing. Abuse of this kind could never be mentioned; Mother might assume I had invited it.

That summer, to my great surprise, Mother arranged to take me to

Paris for several days. I did not remember ever having been singled out for such a favor, and the trip remains vivid in my memory, almost forty years later.

Mother took me to the Louvre. The Victory of Samothrace, winging down from her pedestal on the great staircase, filled me with awe. The Louvre poured its treasures out for me—the dark medieval madonnas, the Botticelli graces I had first seen in the big art books at home.

At the Louvre, Mother granted me entrée into her splendid knowledge and love of the past, which had been limited before to her explanation of the origin of the egg-and-dart moldings at the Big House. During that visit, and later on Paris outings, I absorbed her love of beauty, not trivialized in table settings and flower arrangements. It was a delicate, intuitive enthusiasm that could not survive Father's more dramatic and assertive passion for language. Perhaps it was her love of beauty and order that had originally brought Mother to the classics; perhaps this was the gift which was squeezed to death when she took on managing a large household and disciplining five children.

Later, Father's refusal to discipline us forced Mother to become the hectoring arbitrary voice of convention, suppressing her ability to love life, to revel in visual beauty.

Years later, Eleanor offered to photograph one of Mother's extraordinary flower arrangements, assembled blossom by blossom from the bounty of her garden. Mother seemed flattered by the offer yet slightly embarrassed, as though Eleanor had volunteered to paint a portrait of a cake. By then the delicate sensuous appreciation Mother had taught me in the Louvre had been smothered by her determination to teach us the rules of the world.

Discipline is also connected with power, and Mother seemed as fascinated by power as I was when I stood staring up at the Victory of Samothrace. At the very least, the demanding adult can compel obedience from children and servants; expanded, that authority can become a useful weapon in political and social life. Mother's love of Greek and Latin seemed to me to be part of that pursuit of power. After all, a classical education had armed her male forebears, as it had armed the Presbyterian schoolteachers in North Carolina. But it seemed to me those weapons were tin compared to the mysterious arsenal Father commanded, as member in good standing of a club composed of politicians, journalists, diplomats, and members of the intelligence community who had little need for Greek or Latin. Later, I understood the irony when I learned that some slaves after Emancipation had asked to be taught those ancient tongues.

The return to Cabourg plunged me back into the narrow world of childhood. I began to read aloud to Jonathan, to pass the long evenings, and it occurred to me for the first time that something was different about the two younger children. They were quieter, more accepting, and, it seemed to me, sadder than Worth, Barry, or I had been. Neither Eleanor nor Jonathan received the attention we had received, as beneficiaries of our parents' faith in their own future: we were heirs to their belief in the family's blessedness. The younger two, who always seemed smaller, frailer, and less demanding, had no roles to play in that drama. They were extras.

The hotel in Cabourg began to empty as the end of summer approached. The weather grew gray and dismal, and finally we were the only guests left. Mother was having difficulty, she said, finding a house large enough for the eight of us in Paris; perhaps she and Father were also reluctant to bring their younger children into the turmoil of postwar Paris, where, as Phillip Knightley described it in *The Second Oldest Profession: Spies and Spying in the Twentieth Century,* the activities of the CIA included "money spent on bribes and subsidies to anti-communist trade unions, plus the secret funding of newspapers and magazines. . . . Covert action became the natural ally of the Marshall Plan because it was seen as a way of countering communist opposition to it." I continued to notice that Father seemed worried and preoccupied on his rare visits to Normandy.

We went to see the invasion beaches on one of those occasions, found a boot half buried in the sand, and saw landing craft still lying abandoned in the shallows. Father told us then that he had been part of the secret planning for the Normandy invasion, and explained how U.S. intelligence had persuaded the Germans that the invasion would take place at Calais rather than on the undefended beaches further south. When I read William Casey's autobiography in 1988, I realized that this secret mission had been the centerpiece of U.S. intelligence during the war in Europe; and I understood, once again, that Father's wartime activities had included excursions into covert endeavors. After all, espionage was an elite club, with ties to the British upper class the Judge so admired.

Finally Mother arrived in Cabourg to announce that she had found a house. "We won't have it till the last of September but we also have 3 maids, a rather dubious but good cook, and a butler. Mother still needs to find the 2nd man, who will drive the car and do odd jobs. I am sorry to hear Mother has gotten a governess so dear sweet Nursie is leaving as soon as we are settled in the house. It makes me miserable."

There was no discussion. The decision had been made. Nursie told us she had to go home to take care of her mother.

I did not dare to say that I loved Nursie too much to bear her leaving. I already knew that my love was out of proportion, embarrassing to the rest of the family. I had tried to believe that because Nursie was white, she was "different" from the black servants at home, but she was welded to them by her lack of education, her colorful country speech, and her unflinching vision. Now I must learn never to pity her, never to express the deep affection which, as Mother saw it, could only embarrass subordinates.

As her last gift to me, Nursie showed me how to put on a sanitary belt, after I had spent two days believing I was bleeding to death from a mysterious hemorrhage. By then I was pretending that I understood why she had to go.

I did understand: I had absorbed my parents' preoccupation with the right way. I knew what it felt like to be unable to speak the language used by the people around me, to find confusion in the setting of my place at a table—which fork? which glass?—to shiver with anxiety when faced with the prospect of being introduced to strangers. The big world demanded forms of expertise that seemed as arcane to me as Mother's Greek and Latin. How would I survive if I did not know that you don't drink out of finger bowls? The elaborate pavane of grown-up life was taking over; there were no Back Woods and Midwestern rivers here. Nursie was part of the old way, the country way—the safe way. She would have to go.

But in dividing myself from her, I divided from myself in a way that took years to heal.

We moved to Paris when the Cabourg hotel closed, but our house was not yet ready. So for several months we camped in a dark old hotel on the Rue de Rivoli, where for the first time in our lives we were crowded together. All of us but Worth went to the American School, my first experience in coeducation since Ballard.

"Today was very sad and strange," I wrote one grim November day. "Nursie left for Louisville at 5:00, but I saw her last when I went to school. She left, I believe, in tears, and Missie [Eleanor], who was the only one to see her off, cried too. Will things ever be the same as they were before? Jonathan asked where Nursie was when he got home and when told he just stood with his mouth hanging open and neither of the two has spoken of it since."

Eleanor and Jonathan never discussed how they felt when Nursie left. I believed that her disappearance after thirteen years scorched them in a way that was too private and painful to mention. Perhaps they eventually came to terms with it by pretending that they had never cared much for her—a pretense made easier by the family's new sense of self-importance. I made the accommodation, too.

In early winter, we left the hotel for a beautiful house on the edge of the Bois de Boulogne, where I was given a jewel-box boudoir close to our parents. Jonathan and Eleanor were housed on the third floor, which was accessible only by elevator.

Madame, the red-haired governess who had replaced Nursie, was said to have had a colorful past as wife of the commander of the French forces

in Africa. She spoke beautiful French, however, and Mother believed she
was a lady. I was suspicious. Sometimes when Mother came down in the
elevator after kissing Jonathan and Eleanor good night, I would hear them
crying. Madame seemed to me a force of nature, a whirlwind, and the two
little children were her prisoners.

Madame did not last the year. Her peculiarities became too exaggerated
to ignore. Some days she did not dress at all, and would flounce around the
house in a negligee, smoking and scattering ashes. I realized that Worth,
who was attending college classes at the Sorbonne, was taking a dangerous
interest in Madame, and she seemed to be responding. She left, after a
dramatic scene, to be replaced by one of the mam'selles we had met in
Cabourg, a small, self-contained German whose sense and stability made our
life infinitely more secure. She soon had us on a regime that included walks
and even roller skating.

At the American School, the girls were much more sophisticated than
I. They were already wearing cosmetics. The boys were uncivilized, or so
it seemed to me. A final scene revolted and terrified me: two boys fell to the
floor, fighting, and one pulled out a knife. The puddle of mucus and blood
they left on the floor was more than I could bear. I went to Mother and told
her I would go anywhere else.

She investigated, then told me that the only alternative was a French
convent school of the Sacred Heart on the Rue de Lubeck.

Together we went to talk to the Mother Superior. In her long robes
and starched white coif, she was the most beautiful and the most cerebral
of angels. She spoke only French, and it is possible that Mother misunderstood what she said. As she interpreted it, the Mother Superior had agreed
to admit me as a day student on the condition that I pretend to be a Roman
Catholic. This would be easier to put across, Mother explained, because the
French believed American Catholics were very lax and not likely to be up
on all the rituals.

The first great challenge of my life lay before me. Speaking no French,
and having never been in a Catholic church, I started at the new school.

The school's great dark bulk loomed over the neighboring streets. Baths
were provided once a week for the boarders, and for the first time I realized
that human beings smell.

The large classes were conducted entirely in French, and I understood
not a single word. Twice a day, we were herded into the chapel for services,
and I learned to genuflect and cross myself, to bow my head and mumble
something that would pass for Latin. This experience reinforced the belief
I had acquired earlier that religion was largely a matter of forms. Sanctity
depended on the equivalent of knowing which fork to use.

About to leave on summer trips abroad: Worth, Sallie, Father,
Mother, and Candida Mabon aboard the *Queen Mary,* 1952.

Making costumes and scenery for "Rumpelstiltskin," Paris, 1949:
Jonathan, Eleanor, Sallie, the "old Mam'selle" (she took the
governess's place on her day off), Barry, and Worth.

Although I wrote that "the nuns are like a drug" and suspected that they were trying to convert me, I was fascinated by these garbed figures from an unknown mythology. My fascination was somewhat diminished when I noticed that there were two orders of nuns: the beautiful teaching sisters, in their flowing habits, who had brought substantial dowries to the convent, and the coarsely garbed women who scrubbed the stone floors and ladled out the appalling food.

I do not remember when I understood French. It seemed to happen all at once, like learning to read, rather than as a slow process of accumulating grammar and vocabulary. One day I could speak and understand nothing. The next I was keeping my diary in French.

My new language was as clean and sharp as a new tooth. The fuzzy old associations were gone. I read the fables of La Fontaine, Victor Hugo, and Racine. What large certainties were there! Everything I read in French literature seemed edged and direct, like the orders French nannies gave to their charges. The world made sense for the first time, and its language was my own.

At first I was driven to school by the family chauffeur, who sometimes forgot to pick me up at the end of the afternoon. I would grow frantic with apprehension as I waited on the deeply shadowed side street with the convent closed and silent behind me. I knew I would never have the courage to knock for readmission.

After long deliberation, I asked Mother to allow me to go back and forth on the public bus. She gave her permission. Every day I faced the challenge of finding the right bus, paying the correct amount of money, and jumping off at my stop even when the bus only slowed down. I remembered Nursie grasping Jonathan's hand firmly as she asked a Cabourg shopkeeper for directions.

Worth saw me once, standing in the rain at a bus stop. He told me I looked like a fish, so pale and flat there in the crowd. I knew he found my determination ridiculous, but it did not matter. For the first time, I was speaking a language clean of the past, and I was getting around a great, terrifying city on my own. I was thirteen years old. Paris in the winter, dark at four o'clock, with its dour, shuffling crowds, gave me proof that I could survive.

Mother noticed my pale intensity, and arranged for me to be released from school earlier in the afternoon. Now and then she would take me with her to a fitting at Dior, where the New Look reigned, and I would sit in a corner of the dressing room, awed as though I was witnessing a religious rite. Mother's Dior evening dresses were great froths of crinoline in smoky pastel colors, with overblown roses hidden in the skirts. I had never seen anything so beautiful. One day she took me to a seamstress who sewed my first grown-up party dress with a discreet neckline and a jade-green belt. I have not seen its equal.

I saw the other side of those sessions at Dior when Mother and another woman wore the same elegant greenish suit on an expedition to the country. Mother was devastated, even when Father told her that her slim figure was shown to better advantage than the other woman's. I realized that her clothes were not just bought and worn for pleasure. They were signs of uniqueness. The signs concealed tense anxiety, even more tense than my determination to make my way around Paris alone. My mother and all the other beautiful intelligent women were replaceable. Their substitutes waited, smiling, at every embassy party, wearing the same beautiful Dior clothes.

That winter Mother included me for the first time in her life, taking me to the Left Bank to visit bookstalls and antique shops. She seemed less angry with me now that Father was completely preoccupied with his round of speeches and parties. Mother bought me my first "real" desk, a little Empire affair with brass knobs and a cracked mirror.

One afternoon she took me to visit the Kentucky expatriate on the Rue du Cherche-Midi who had lived years before in the Little House. This formidable Francophile made me a present of a gift certificate at Brentano's, where I bought a set of Modern Classics, covering each book with Florentine paper.

Mother seemed to be enjoying herself with women who loved the gaiety of diplomatic life in Paris. Their voices were louder and clearer, it seemed to me, their eyes flashed with a different light, and they wore beautiful clothes as though they had every right to them. Their relationships all seemed "amusing," as though, like Nancy Mitford heroines, they had shed the shackles of responsibility. No one "worked"; no one had children; no one mentioned material cares; and even their servants seemed independent and self-respecting, professionals who would leave at once if they were not satisfied with their treatment. Presbyterianism, even Episcopalianism, did not exist in those high airy drawing rooms. Here women amused themselves, appearing to toy with larger issues, turning somersaults over foreign affairs. I had never seen Mother as happy as she was that winter. She had found the perfect setting for her talents.

Every year we gave a play on Mother's birthday, which fell on Christmas Eve. The custom had been established before I was born, and as I grew older, I was given the onerous responsibility of organizing the evening. Often we presented a version of "A Christmas Carol" with Father as one of the ghosts, rattling tire chains in the Big House basement. In Paris, we chose to present

"Rumpelstiltskin" because Jonathan seemed perfect for the role of the mercurial dwarf.

This family entertainment became a public event in Paris when photographers from *Life* arrived. Later, looking at the pictures, I was disturbed. It seemed unlikely to me that other children fell as easily into dramatic gestures or lost themselves so completely in performance. Only Worth preserved his ironic detachment.

I was introduced to alcohol that winter in France. Alcohol was no stranger; the drink tray in the Big House living room was a shrine with its tinkling and glittering icons. Jonathan had once downed a whole bottle of bourbon, out of curiosity, but I knew whiskey did strange things to women. A friend of mine had scandalized our parents by drinking aspirin and Coca-Cola at dancing school; she had become talkative, even silly. The effects of the real thing would be far worse.

In late winter, Father was invited to dedicate a dam in the French Alps that had been built with Marshall Plan money. There were rumors of a "Communist" riot at the dam, which of course never came off. Barry and I went along for the ceremony, which included a large formal lunch.

Our parents were seated at the head table, and Barry and I were placed with a group of journalists. These young men took pleasure in refilling my wineglass and I in emptying it until I suddenly realized I could no longer function.

Earlier, I had made the mistake of telling these teases about Father's secret language. Now they insisted that I send an SOS to the head table. I knew only a few words, and these were hardly appropriate. I managed to scrawl them on a sheet of paper—and was horribly embarrassed when they turned up next day in the Paris *Herald Tribune*.

When it was time to leave the lunch, I could barely walk and had to be assisted to the official car. Father and Mother did not scold. I was too sick with nausea and shame to need further punishment. I spent the next day in bed with a vicious hangover, blinded by the bright light from the sun on the snow-covered Alps.

This was learning "the hard way," through public exposure and humiliation. A few years later when I smoked my first cigarette, I would suddenly realize that I looked silly; I never smoked again. This way of teaching depended on my sense of my own importance. Other people, especially young people, made fools of themselves and recovered from it. But we were public children. Everything we did reflected on our parents either a good or a bad light. The good light was dim and soft. The bad light was the harsh glaring searchlight of public humiliation.

Barry had watched me getting drunk at the journalists' table, but it would have been impossible for him to intervene. When women showed their frailty, men laughed; it was a strong bond. Later I heard stories of older brothers who actually protected sisters from exploitation, but I knew I did not want that shield. I preferred to learn, even the hard way, rather than to be obliged to my brothers for their protection. I did not realize that this meant a hardening of the heart between us.

A last lesson was needed in that year of multiple lessons and transfigurations. I had begun to be haunted by fantasies that shamed me, lurid sexual imaginings which I could not suppress. I would lie in bed, tormented by visions which flashed through my mind, rigid in the grip of hateful lust. I did not think anyone else had ever been gripped by those demons, and I longed to find a way to rid myself of them. The only way I could devise was to write out the fantasies, covering pages with a feverish scrawl. I was used to guarding myself from the intrusions of males who wanted something unnamed but clearly sexual. I had never had to protect myself from myself before.

The grip of those demons had not relaxed, however, when our parents took us to London for a visit. They had obligations of long standing there and were busily engaged with friends from the Judge's time. Usually we three "children," awkward adolescents all, were left to our own devices, but once we were included as guests at an elaborate lunch.

On that occasion, in a high sunny London dining room, a stranger seated next to me suddenly told me that my grandfather had murdered his wife. I was speechless with amazement and then I thought he must be mad. My stepgrandmother was living in Louisville, and I knew the story of my "real" grandmother's death. I had never heard of Mary Lily Kenan Flagler Bingham.

I tried to believe that I had not heard what the stranger said, and in memory he appears as a sort of dwarf or magician, beckoning the way to a goblin's market: "Come buy! Come buy!" If a woman had died, she had asked for it, I thought, by pursuing goblin men and sucking their fruit.

During the evenings in London, my brothers and I were often on our own. Worth and Barry sometimes made arrangements to meet other young Americans whom they had met at boarding school. I usually had dinner on a tray and sat at the hotel window, looking out at the bustle of life in the London streets, imagining lives for strangers.

One evening I had already gone to bed when the boys erupted into the sitting room, trailing several acquaintances. I shrank under the covers; their voices were very loud. A minute later, the door to my bedroom burst open and Worth and a young man I had never seen before lurched in. I jumped out of bed. They pushed me around the room, poking and pinching me. I tried whining and pleading, but nothing persuaded them to leave me alone.

Their poking and pinching grew more determined and I was desperately aware of the thinness of my "travel" nightgown. Finally I was able to slip into the bathroom, which had a lock on the door. I locked it before they could get their hands or feet in. Gasping for breath, I listened to them shout and bang until they lost interest and went away.

I did not dare to unlock the door. I spent the night in the bathtub. "The Lord preserve me," I wrote in my diary.

Mother noticed the next day that I looked pale and asked me what was wrong. I told her that Worth had frightened me, but she did not need to say that I was being ridiculous; I already knew. A brother's teasing was a realistic preparation for the world of hard knocks that lay ahead.

17

"Some day I'll write a book about these days and call it *The Five Roads*," I wrote in my diary after we returned from France in the summer of 1950. "We are a remarkably book-like family. Worth, dissipated and handsome, a veritable black sheep; Barry, quiet, almost angelic, loveable; me, undecided; Jonathan, sentimental, terrified, bordering on genius; Eleanor the only stable one, to hold us all together."

That fall, Mother bought two stalwart middle-aged horses for Barry and me, responding to our sense of boredom and emptiness now that we were back on the Place. I was eager to take up this new challenge. I remembered Henrietta in her beautiful riding clothes, full of laughter and determination. I also greatly admired my riding teacher, a slight, brisk woman who put me smartly through my paces. I began to spend every afternoon riding through the thin woods and up and down the ravines of the still-undeveloped river country.

For the next four years, riding became the way I tested myself. I grew strong and bold in the Kentucky woods. Gradually I came to rely on my own view of the world as I came to rely on my developing sense of direction to guide my horse home through the briary undergrowth.

Barry and I seldom rode together; each of us was intent on securing a private space for reflection. He was absorbed with worries about boarding school, where he was struggling to overcome his dyslexia. College loomed just ahead of him, and the dreadful prospect of not being accepted at Harvard. The Korean War had started, and both Worth and Barry joined the ROTC.

I was appalled by the raucous Kentucky accents on my first visit to the ten-cent store after returning from Paris. I saw the hideousness of the old industrial city and of the raw suburbs where Colonial and Tudor houses reflected an imaginary past. There were no museums to visit, other than one which had served as an attic for generations of rich people, and I seldom heard music or went to the theater. Worst of all, I was now different from the girls in my eighth-grade class, who were preoccupied with clothes, makeup, and boyfriends.

I had learned in Paris that I was responsible for my schoolwork; my parents had no access to that convent world. I had also seen that I could overcome a barrier that had seemed impassable until I learned French. From now on schoolwork would be easy and gratifying and I knew how to study hard when it was required. In ninth grade, I was extremely, if silently, proud of my B minus in algebra. I had learned that all that was required was concentration—a willing suspension of fantasy. The next year, I made an even higher grade in geometry, and began translating Latin. The following year, all my grades were A's.

Now and then, with great excitement, I went to a "mixed" party, and stood by the record player, wishing I could disappear, while other boys and girls danced. Their easy assurance amazed me. I felt like a crane, too tall and too strange to join a flotilla of ducks. Now and then a boy would ask me to dance, but my criticism was merciless: "I make myself dream of Richie's arms and am aware all the time of his poor, bepimpled face, his baggy, grown man's suits."

I was fond of the girls in my class, the little group of twelve or so I had known since third grade. Yet I seldom mentioned them in my diary. When I was fourteen, they were only links to boys, framers of stratagems, rivals.

Father and Mother said nothing about their expectations for my social life. As time passed, however, and I did not go out on dates, Father appeared concerned. He did not say anything directly to me; he never did. But his hidden language—sighs, headshakings, a worried yet quizzical look—told me everything I needed to know.

One evening when I was about fifteen, I was called from the dinner table to the telephone. A boy asked me to go to the movies. I accepted with alacrity, then rushed back into the dining room to tell Father, who cried, "At last!" A few minutes later, the telephone rang again. It had been a hoax, perpetrated by one of my school friends.

Mother seemed unconcerned about what was called my "popularity," or lack of it. However, she made it clear that "sex" was a serious threat to my future. "Sex" was an explosion with bad consequences for which a woman was responsible. I agreed with her; I knew all about the dangers, although I knew none of the details. A year earlier, with my connivance, she had scotched my first summer romance. I had been appalled by the intensity of my feelings for a young man who, too clearly, did not measure up.

Mother led me to understand that men did not marry women who were not virgins. She expected me to marry when the time came, and so preserving my virginity was important. There was no romance in the matter. An intact hymen was the medium of exchange.

I did not want to marry, had never wanted to marry, for as long as I could remember. There was something terrifying and degrading in the contract that confused love and money. I was going to be a writer—but I did not dare to tell anyone.

To plan to "be" anything seemed presumptuous in a world where women floated vaguely from one level of existence to another, working during wartime when work was applauded, then retreating to social lives that seemed even more laborious. Marriage meant to me obedience to that system, which decreed what a woman—or at least a lady—could and could not do. There was a deadly vagueness to the state, it seemed to me, as though married women walked in their sleep. They were said to be happy. Everyone insisted that they were happy. But something was wrong.

Mother, who had given me my most important opportunities—the Louvre, my desk, my horse—seemed preoccupied and unhappy to me. I excused everything she did because of that sensed unhappiness, which she would have furiously repudiated. When she forgot once to pick me up at school, I wrote piously in my diary, "Dear Mother, whom I cannot blame . . ."

Of course, I did not understand or forgive her, but I was ashamed to blame her for behavior that did not seem planned or intended. She wanted, so desperately, to do what was right, and she succeeded almost always in fulfilling every obligation. Now and then she would forget out of sheer exhaustion, and one of us would be left stranded. Then her remorse made it impossible to complain.

Father shared none of her responsibilities for the five children. He was for fun.

Perhaps she felt lost in the glitter and glamour of Father's relationship with children. Any child in the vicinity would flock to Father because of his wizardlike humor and fey charm. He would not scold, and our times with him were romps, physical or verbal. At the first hint of conflict he would melt away.

Mother may have dreaded that we would ignore her when Father was shedding sparks all around. And we did ignore her then. Yet there had been times when, alone with me, Mother had shown an understanding that made Father's charm seem superficial. In Paris, especially, I had felt her subtle intelligence come alive, her shy humor revive. But those occasions—the fittings, the visits to museums—were rare in Kentucky.

I noticed the change, and drew my own conclusions. It seemed to me that Mother had thrived on the attentions she had received in Paris as an intelligent, beautiful, well-dressed woman—and I had benefited. There her talents as hostess had found a setting worthy of their display; there she had learned another language, as I had. And, as in wartime Louisville, she had been surrounded by smart and independent women, wives who did not seem entirely defined or confined by their husbands and their husbands' roles.

They enjoyed themselves. There was no talk of noblesse oblige. Sometimes they did not even take their husbands, or their husbands' work, very seriously.

As our year in France receded, the isolation of our lives on the Place became, once more, almost impenetrable. The outside world made few intrusions.

Truman was President, and during his campaign in 1948, I had been the only girl in my class to support him against Dewey. I had found myself poorly equipped to argue, however, since the only thing I could say against Dewey was that he sported a cad's black mustache. It was one of many signs that the Eastern Republican was "not a gent." Unfortunately my classmates failed to understand this distinction.

Truman, the haberdasher who was the product of a Midwestern political machine, would hardly have been considered "a gent" either. But he was another of the small-town politicians who had been part of Father's boyhood, like the Kentucky governors and senators who might someday appear on the national ticket. The Colonel and the Judge would have understood Truman and his brash down-home style. Besides, any Democrat in the White House was good for the newspapers and the state they instructed. So Father stifled his condescension. Mother was less discreet.

In 1949, Senator Bilbo was urging "every red-blooded white man to use any means to keep niggers from the polls." My parents would have been horrified by his crudeness, although they would have understood his aims. We were living an imitation of antebellum plantation life, dependent on aging black servants. For many liberals who had supported the New Deal, black equality remained unacceptable.

The fearfulness that gripped liberals during the Cold War made my parents hesitate to repulse the old racial attacks. Any journalist with a liberal reputation was exposed to the powerful threat represented by Senator Joe McCarthy. I underestimated his power because, according to my parents' code, he was a little man of no distinction. The Colonel would not have made that mistake. McCarthy, like the Kingfish, Huey Long of Louisiana, was a legitimate descendant of the Colonel's "kings of men."

Kentuckians appeared to have the makings of their own small king in

"Happy" Chandler, who had showed no signs of being a gentleman during his time as governor of Kentucky. He had scandalized Father by calling Mrs. Chandler "Mama" and fighting with her in front of his chauffeur.

During this time I was puzzled by discussions I overheard of the Hiss case. Hiss, after all, was "one of ours," unlike the Rosenbergs. But the details of pumpkins and typewriters were beyond me, and I sensed with some dismay that Mother was losing this particular battle. For a while, she supported Hiss as once she had supported Henry Wallace.

Now John F. Kennedy, son of the Judge's successor in London, was running for office for the first time. Now the Kinsey Report, published in 1948, indicated that "95 percent of all males are sexually active by the age of 15," which should have raised questions for an adolescent girl. But I had tamed my demons. All these events passed unnoticed, part of adult conversation I no longer tried to understand.

I was interested in any direct explanation of events, and often telephoned Nursie, now taking care of a new baby, to ask her for her view. Mother, at times, was as direct as Nursie, especially when she was alone with me. Once, I remember, she recounted with rueful humor how she had been turned away at a neighbor's door, where she had gone to solicit a contribution to the Good Neighbor Policy—a national program to improve our relations with Latin America.

This neighbor was a parvenu, in Mother's eyes, who had recently bought a grotesque white castle on a neighboring hilltop. He bore a German name, was said to lack cultivation, and had induced Cordie to write what appeared to be "something dirty" on the kitchen message board. When our swimming pool was emptied, this neighbor's connecting stream and pond were affected, and so Mother always gave him warning. Once Cordie innocently relayed his message: "Miz Bingham, hold your water."

Yet Mother had not argued when this neighbor explained to her, in his doorway, why he would not make a contribution. Being a good neighbor begins at home, he said, and we had not treated him well.

For the most part, however, adults were still speaking in code. So much was left out that the remainder made no sense. How had important men come to power, and what was the role of women? Who attended to the grinding daily tasks, and how did wives stand sleeping with the same man every night? Who knew what went on when children were born, and why did so many children, and their mothers, seem so unhappy? None of this figured in grown-up talk, which remained my only source of information outside of books. I did not look at television because Mother considered it a destroyer of young minds; and the radio was only the source of the Hit Parade. I seldom read the newspapers. They, too, were written in code, and I was now too old for the Sunday comics Father used to read aloud.

Bilbo's fulminations, however, touched me in a way I did not at the time recognize.

Our black yardman, Luebell, had recently adopted his wife's nephew, a sturdy little boy named Luke who was about eight years old. Although Mother expressed respect for Luebell's kindness, she was also uneasy. None of the other servants on the Place had children, except for Cordie, and hers were grown, dead, or invisible.

Luke took to following me around. I described him in the terms I had absorbed long ago from *Diddie, Dumps, and Tot:*

"He was a little well shaped negro boy [I had crossed out "colored"], straight and slight, with sharp, iron filing fuzz all over his large head and great, wicked brown eyes. His clothes were always on the point of disintegration, grey undershirt tail hung out, shirt sloped over that and his unbuttoned blue jeans exhibited an even greyer expanse of drawers. Pulled down over his ears he invariably wore a cheap red and blue cap, the ear muffs tied up or let down according to the weather, the ragged visor concealing his eyes. Likewise, he always wore the remains of an expensive, little boy coat of Jonathan's, the velvet collar ridiculous under his face."

Luke often kept me company at the barn, where, late in the afternoon, I cleaned out my horse's stall and fed her. One evening "I opened a drawer in an old marble-topped bureau, and put my hand into a paper scrap nest of baby mice. They were bright pink and wriggling, with bodies like premature babies and skinned-over blue eyes. They were so disgusting I could hardly kill them, but managed to get a bucket of water, and with Luke watching terrified, threw them in with their nest. I think they must have died immediately. I feel as if I could never forget the startled color of their bloated little bodies."

Another afternoon "I was slabbing over-diluted whitewash on the tackroom wall. Luke watched me from the door. Somewhere in our disconnected, irritated conversation, I wondered whether he wished he were white. I launched into the usual bon mots about color making no difference.

" 'Yes,' he agreed, 'if you're light they don't think you're colored.' "

I could not discuss this subject with my parents, who insisted that we all believed in equality, and that the belief was more important than the reality around us. My classmates, many of whom had been raised by black women, did not discuss the issue. I, alone, it seemed, wondered why some people walked on others all their lives.

My parents prided themselves on their fair treatment of Negroes and Jews. I saw the first black woman I had ever met who was not a servant at a luncheon in the Big House. Both parents contributed to organizations that worked for "better relations," as had the Judge in his time. Yet I knew which of my friends were Jews before I knew anything else about them.

Blacks, I realized, were simply invisible to most white people, except as a pair of hands offering a drink on a silver tray. But I had lived close to them; I had seen the expressions on their faces. Now, as Lizzie and Cordie, Curtis and Ollie grew old and feeble, I remembered that they had spent their lives in our service. Had they ever had a choice?

It would be years before I recognized the spine that connects all prejudices: the condescension to black "friends" which was similar to the patronizing favors offered to "superior" women or "philanthropic" Jews. I sensed the connection before I could put it into words. My attempts to understand it were thwarted by my parents' liberal philosophy, which ignored the fact of prejudice entirely.

Prejudice had been revealed to me often. As a small child, I had hidden in a corner of the Big House living room while Mother fired a yardman, a tall, young black man with physical authority in every inch of his body. The young man did not say a word as she explained her reasons for dismissing him. He could not even "answer back."

I learned the lesson once more when Luke became a threat. At ten or eleven, he was said to be using "bad language" and he was interested in playing with Eleanor, who was about his age.

The result was predictable. I wrote in my diary, "They are going to send Luebell away, because Luke says Fuck. I have no power over them, nor enough to keep myself from crying."

I had to recognize Mother's logic, as years before I had understood why she sent away Luebell's older son, George. He had been Worth's companion until early adolescence, when one summer day he had gone down to the swimming pool with the white boys. We saw very little of George after that. Years later Mother explained that none of her friends would have allowed their sons to swim with Worth and Barry if Luebell's son had used the pool.

In Luke's case, there was the added threat: he had befriended a white girl. The forces of evil were abroad in the land, Mother believed, as they had been when the Colonel had donned his sheet. A black boy who knew how to say "fuck" might know other things as well.

Luke disappeared in a few days' time, along with Luebell and his wife. Mother found Luebell a job further out in the country. I never heard of Luke again.

I thought that Mother was right to put the interests of her own children, as she saw them, ahead of the interests of two black boys. I thought she was right to add up the column as she did and arrive at the foregone conclusion.

But I also knew the consequences, and they were hard to bear; they haunted me like the drowned baby mice. Many of the people I had loved all my life were powerless in the face of white authority, white fears, and illogical resentments. I could not forget that those who had loved me long and well might disappear at any time. There could be no real equality as long as they depended on us for survival.

Meanwhile, Nursie was surviving on her own. One afternoon I took Eleanor to visit her. "She lives in a house downtown, once white, but whose original red shows through, a long, narrow house with a baby crying on the other side of the partition, a covered bird cage, and a vase of premature green jonquils."

Nursie had given up working for families to become a registered nurse. She showed me her diploma and her little white cap with pride. She was taking care of old people, whose demands on her affections were less insistent than those of children. She loved her tiny apartment with its crochet throw, photographs and knickknacks, and a refrigerator full of her special treats: strawberry cake, bourbon balls. Her careful use of her scanty funds to piece out a decent life touched me deeply. She never complained. Once she told me that a clergyman she admired had invited her to tea and made her a piece of buttered toast.

18

A year later, Barry and Worth were taken to an English tailor in London for their first "tails," as I recounted jubilantly in a letter to Nursie. Father added more details when he wrote to thank Nursie for the Christmas presents she always sent for everyone in the family.

He described my two brothers starting off to a dance, looking "pretty handsome" in their new evening clothes. He said they went out to the kitchen to show themselves to Ollie and Curt, who admired them profusely.

When I appeared in my new evening dress, its neckline cut a little below my collar bone, Father wrote, "the boys yelled at her to go and put a towel around her shoulders." I wore the dress without the towel, but I was terrified by the implication: What harm might I unwittingly do when I exposed my neck?

At fifteen, I knew that Worth was my enemy, and that Barry could not be trusted because for his own survival he followed Worth's lead. I could deal with the teasing, although I was still humiliated when Worth railed about my clothes in front of other people or tripped me when I walked into a room. Much worse, my sleeping demons were roused by his ribaldry. Perhaps he was right to say that I wore an off-the-shoulder blouse, fashionable just then, to provoke young men to explore my breasts; perhaps I had chosen the straight skirt to force my "dates" to feel my behind. After all, Mother had always taught that sex was an explosion for which women must accept the consequences.

I learned to control myself rigidly and compulsively in order not to fly at Worth or to let the fears he aroused into consciousness. I hated the fact that he seemed to own me; my behavior was not my concern, but his. Mother, too, believed that what I did and said was a reflection, not of my choices, but of her success or failure to teach me how to behave.

With Worth, the connection was even more intimate. He owned my virginity. The passionate jealousy he had felt earlier was now matched by

a scathing overheated possessiveness. He had the world behind him when
he insisted that I alone had the power to humiliate him and ruin the family
name.

He was acting on an old directive, written in the genes of eldest sons.
Daughters in a rich family are always the vulnerable point. Emotionally
starved, we may respond to the first man who treats us with kindness.
Ignorant about our assets, we may give everything away—our virginity, our
love, our loyalty, and our shares—to a man the family dislikes. Sons can
raise their consorts to their level with a little intense teaching. Daughters
are less likely to be able to "form" their husbands, to teach them to submit
to the family's aims.

Worth watched me closely for the rest of our short life together. When
I arrived at a dance, he would careen or stagger by me, leering, growling,
reminding me that he was on guard. His friends stayed away from me as
though they had been warned.

The young men who took an interest in me were always, I knew,
inferior in Worth's eyes, "wonks" who wore the wrong tie or spoke with the
wrong accent. I realized years later that his bulldog proprietary passion
spared our parents many alarms. He was acting out, in crude terms, what
they quietly believed. Like the old fable of racial equality, this was a story
that existed on two levels, in the abstractions adults mouthed and in the
actions that reflected the way they felt. Worth was good at picking up their
cryptic communications and translating them into violence. It is one of the
skills of the heir.

At my day school I was safe in a world of women, but it was a world
I did not respect.

I began to be disturbed by the fact that all of our high school teachers
were women who appeared to have no life outside the school, and who were,
with one exception, unmarried. Although my history teacher was the first
adult to teach me something I did not want to learn—she told me my
grammar was faulty—I still could not credit these dedicated women with
control of their own lives. It seemed to me that some misfortune must have
set them down in the narrow confines of the girls' school. When I saw them
crossing the street after school to go to the apartment building where several
lived, I would feel suffocated.

Mrs. Alcorn, my English teacher, admired my writing and encouraged
me to enter various high school competitions, one of which I eventually won.
My story, "And the Band Played On," was printed by *The Atlantic Monthly*
in a pamphlet for students. Mrs. Alcorn also touched my attitude, an occurrence so rare I noted it in my diary.

"During class I looked down and across the street to where a man stood
leaning heavily on a cane. Then I saw Mrs. Alcorn cross the street quickly

and come to him. She came near, speaking hurriedly, and held out her hand. He took it and kissed it, then placed her in his arms where she stood close, suddenly silent. Then he clasped up her other hand and kissed her tired wrist and her face was expressionlessly sensual. I sat there horrified, wondering if she had seen him from her classroom window, or if he had called to her, standing there patient, but virile, and I was so afraid of telling, for I know the danger of words, not only to destroy the realness of a thing, but to endanger more tangible securities.

"A minute later, Mrs. Alcorn crossed back over, patting her hair, and walked quickly up to her classroom. She was careful not to look up at the blank inhabited building, yet I knew she wondered how many frightened eyes had watched her behaving like a human."

"Behaving like a human" carried a huge, unarticulated threat. It seemed to me that danger lay on the other side of all our rules and regula-tions: the family strictures about tact and self-discipline and good manners, which served to hide and protect all kinds of secrets, the school rules about homework and obedience and classroom decorum, the society's rules about ladylike behavior. Rules did not control and repress feeling: they replaced feeling.

It was an important rule in the family that we learn to notice, care about, and take responsibility for people less fortunate than we. However, we never discussed why certain people were in need of our help, or whether they deserved or had been forced into misery. And we were not to pity them, which might result in a degrading empathy—or a questioning of the system.

Volunteer work was expected of me all during my adolescence. I never asked why. My brothers had done no volunteer work, nor was Mother committed to what she called, at humorous moments, "flannel petticoat charity." All the girls in my class read to shut-ins and played with crippled children and even visited the terrifying wards of the public mental hospital, on the principle that we owed something—something undefined—to these people who were less "lucky" than we were. The assumption that we were "lucky" disturbed me. How did we know we were? And did we deserve it?

In my diary I wrote, "This morning Helen and I went to the Jewish Convalescent Home. The children there are so pitiful, they are clean and have food and a bed, but they are starving for affection and love. One little crippled girl told us her cat had died and she knew why, because cats always die with cripples."

The work made me feel desperate. There was so little I could do to relieve the hopelessness of these lives. It also made me wonder, in a confused way, about the structure of the society around me. Poor children in institu-tions looked, talked, and smelled differently from me, my family, and my friends, and at first it seemed that perhaps they had been "born wrong," born into a class that must forever labor in poverty and disease. Yet these children—and Luke and George—were also like me in many ways. Why were they condemned to suffer? Perhaps at the root of the world lay a tendency to injustice which sent these poor children to institutions but which sent us to the series of English governesses who replaced Nursie.

"Mother is sweet, but mothers love boys," I wrote in my diary. "Daddy's love is sometimes ample substitute, but Daddy is seldom here. I don't know where he is, but the usual answer is 'away making a speech.' And when he comes back, the new things come quickly in and invade my interests, so here I sit, stony and sorry for myself."

I was not always so resigned. When Munda came for her spring visit, the air in the Big House seemed to crackle. I wrote, "Across the table, through china flowers, I see my grandmother's face, and into the lines drawn so skillfully about eyes and mouth is forced all the pain and frustration with which she talked. . . .

"But Daddy—I have lost my yardstick of emotions and so can't tell if what I feel is nonsense or lostness. All I know is that I must be exaggerating, that with loving parents and 'all the advantages of life' such things don't happen. It's only the drunken, filthy, common mothers who don't love their children, it's only in miserable circumstances that misery is inflicted on the young.

"Yet here I sit, gulping down milk to strangle the great sob in my throat and completely unable to say what I want so badly to say; and all the time these two people sit at the other end of life—and don't seem to care at all."

Pride, and my determination to become emotionally independent, made me reject Mother's rare, timid advances. Once, on the train to Asheville, I realized how deeply I could hurt her. We were in the dining car and, due to the crowd, she had been placed at a table with Jonathan and me while Father and the others were seated elsewhere. Jonathan and I were both tongue-tied and listless and Mother worked hard to make conversation. It was close to Christmas, and she asked us what we had bought for Father. With instinctive resistance, we refused to tell her, insisting on our right to our own secrets.

After a moment, I looked at Mother. She was crying.

The last time had been at Roosevelt's death. Now what had we done? I felt a terrible pang of guilt and desolation, as I had when Luke left, or when I threw Curt's chauffeur's cap out the window. I could not blame Jonathan. He had only followed my lead.

That night I got out of my berth and stood on tiptoe to reach Jonathan in the upper berth. I told him fiercely that we must never again "do that" to Mother. I did not need to explain. He promised quickly. I wondered for the first time if Mother was as invulnerable as she seemed.

As I grew older, many things contradicted what I had been told to believe. The world seemed to exist in fragments that could not be forced to fit the moral and intellectual doctrines our parents preached. There were links and clues lying half hidden or obliterated, secrets which would have connected everything. Unfortunately I was aware of them. I would have been delighted to have been spared.

I knew that the secrets, whatever they were, were evil and dangerous. To seek them out, one would have to be a little animal or a genetic mutant like the child in a movie the family particularly enjoyed called *The Bad Seed*.

The fantasies that continued to haunt me and the stories and poems I buried in notebooks described the world of secrets—violent, melodramatic, like the moors in *Wuthering Heights* where human passions defined reality. I would have been horrified if anyone had discovered these stories. The distance between my life and my writing was too far to be crossed on foot. Yet I managed to hold both in balance, perhaps because as I spent more time away from the Place, visiting friends or at school, I realized that there was another way. How normal—if boring and pedestrian—the lives of my friends seemed when I spent a night in one of those girlish suburban bed-rooms, where a flock of stuffed animals coexisted with crinolines, boys' tokens, and a wasteland of makeup.

Often grown-ups would approach me in a fawning way to compliment my parents, even to compliment me for being their daughter. I could not explain to these strangers that nothing was as it appeared, that the two beautiful and intelligent aristocrats who represented, for Kentuckians, their closest approach to royalty spoke in a code I did not understand.

Friends sometimes asked me how many rooms there were in the Big House, which embarrassed me; well-bred people were not supposed to ask such questions. I wondered what they would think if they were present at the strenuous meals where we all strove to outspeak and outjoke each other, if they saw the tension and sadness on Mother's beautiful face, or noted how Father came and went, mysteriously, lightly, like an elfin king. My friends seldom sat at our dinner table, however, and their parents were not invited to my parents' parties, so the comparisons were not made.

I watched with interest the people who came to parties at the Big House, and noticed when a particular favorite, usually a bright young man, returned again and again. One of these young men disappeared abruptly in the early fifties. His name was never mentioned again; he seemed to have been expunged. Years later I learned that he had been exiled for stuffing the ballot box during his first political campaign, a practice the Judge would have understood.

As David Halberstam described him in *The Powers That Be,* this attractive young man, Ed Prichard, "had come from Kentucky by way of

Princeton and was a backcountry boy genius himself, funny, full of charm, country-slick and country-shrewd, sure to be a senator from Kentucky and perhaps more. It was clear to the other young men who knew him that Pritch was touched with greatness, that he was going to excel, not just in school but in life, that he was brilliant and funny and good with people."

Halberstam comments on the fact that both Philip Graham (who was publisher of the Washington *Post*) and Ed Prichard somehow lost track of their promise: "No two men seemed to have so brilliant a future. How tragic then that Ed Prichard would, as a still young man, his entire future in front of him, go to jail for ballot stuffing in Kentucky; and Phil Graham would, on the threshold of his best years, take his own life."

Many years later, after Pritch had been forgiven and had become the power behind the throne in Kentucky politics, I met him for the first time. He was blind, and standing behind his desk in Frankfort, he still exuded a terrifying charm. I had just emerged scathed from my first skirmish with Barry, and the old lion, who knew Kentucky so well, smiled devilishly at my description. "He won the fight but not the war," he said. I wondered then if Pritch had ever been reinstated at the Big House.

Pritch's mysterious disappearance reminded me of Father's ability to summon or to exile, to create or to destroy, an attribute of his political power and financial clout. Politicians hated and feared the power wielded by the only newspapers in the state—unless they were sure of their support. Social events and weddings were evaluated on our society pages, and death became real when it was listed in the obituaries. It sometimes seemed to me that Father's power was limitless, that he could create or destroy with a single gesture, a gesture that might even be unconscious.

19

Nearly every summer, the family spent August on Cape Cod, renting a series of ordinary, commodious houses in a little town called Chatham. Here we seemed to become just another big middle-class family at the beach. Here I first learned the smell of the ocean. We ate hot dogs at Howard Johnson and gorged on saltwater taffy, and I noticed the resplendent green of golf-course grass, and the many shades of hydrangeas, and the beautiful ordinariness of other people's lives.

My weekly telephone calls to Nursie were replaced by long letters. "We are having such a wonderful time here. Worth and Barry are teaching Toad [Jonathan] how to sail. Jonathan sails in races three times a week, but I am too heavy to sail in races except with a very heavy wind."

At this time, according to my diary, I was five feet seven inches tall and weighed 122 pounds. The family's fear of fatness had infected me, and I dieted constantly. I hated to look at myself in a mirror for fear I would note more stomach or behind than I thought I ought to have. For ten years I denied myself butter and sweets and wondered why my weight barely fluctuated. I was light for my height, but I had heard that the doctor's charts were based on women who were "big-boned," another term of opprobrium in the family. I did not think I was big-boned, but I was not sure.

Once after long agonizing I had asked Mother what I looked like. She replied, "You look distinguished." I was mystified.

My height, which seemed so unusual then, made it difficult for me to act the part of the Southern belle. I had broad shoulders and long, strong arms and legs, all considered "masculine." In spite of the agonies of self-consciousness I suffered, I knew that my failure to fit the feminine stereotype gave me some interesting options. I would never look "just right" in a crinoline and off-the-shoulder blouse, but I was strong, and I had by reason of my height a certain advantage over the delicate doll-like girls who fulfilled the ideal.

Worth took winning sailing races very seriously, and blamed losing on the boats we rented. Since we arrived late in the summer, we had to take whatever was left.

Once he permitted me to go along as crew because no one else was available.

It was a squally, overcast day, and the ocean was very rough when we put out in our small boat. Worth scolded me for various errors in putting up the sails. At last we left the buoy, and at once I knew I was in trouble. I was not strong enough to hold the mainsail sheet in such a heavy wind. Worth was at the tiller, oblivious to my distress. The boat heeled sharply as we flew along. My hands were skinless within minutes. I decided to wrap the line around a cleat to take some of the strain off my raw palms.

A minute later, we came about. The mainsail did not respond to Worth's tiller because the line was around the cleat, and the boat capsized.

I came up in icy water, out of sight of shore, with the boat's wooden hull floundering in the waves beside me. We had no life jackets.

Worth cursed me furiously for causing him to lose the race. I thought he would rather have seen me drown than lose. I was not certain how long I could survive in the rough, freezing water, and I concentrated on keeping a grip on the hull. Eventually someone came along in a motorboat and hauled us in. But I did not forget the lesson I had learned. No one could come between Worth and winning and escape without injury. I never went sailing with him again.

The whole family played tennis, and there again, winning was all. We were expected to take lessons at the little beach club in Chatham. I did not mind the lessons, but games with my brothers and parents were difficult. Worth's tantrums on the tennis court were not unusual, and I dreaded being the target of one if I played badly. There were always people watching as I awkwardly dove and darted to return the ball. Worth did not throw his racket as often as he did on the tennis court at home, but his language was colorful.

Although I was convinced that I was awkward and uncoordinated, the woman who taught gym at my school during that period had a different impression, as she told me many years later. As she tactfully put it, I did not have a great aptitude for team sports, but I "went along" with the enthusiasm of my classmates, who worked hard to beat the seniors at basketball that year. I remember the excitement of watching those tough and determined girls, not yet aware that ladies don't sweat. By senior year, many of them had abandoned athletics, but by then it seemed to me they had learned something important. I was sorry that my fear of making a fool of myself prevented me from trying hard. Years later, I finally learned to play tennis and to sail on my own.

I loved the cheerfulness of August life at Chatham as well as the crowding impressions: the smell of the brackish salt marshes, the damp skin of mushrooms we picked on the golf course, the splintery feel of the wooden bridge under bare feet. The world seemed to open on those long, desolate beaches where once during the war I had found a Japanese knife. When we left, after Labor Day, it seemed to me that we were going back into a closed world.

Vacations during the rest of the year were rare, except for annual trips over the mountains to Asheville. Now and then Father took Barry and Worth on hunting trips, more modest versions of the expeditions the Judge had made to Pinelands.

Barry looked forward to these trips, writing to Nursie, "We are going to hunt quail and I can hardly wait to go. I never knew Grandfather but I wish he had lived to teach me to shoot like he could. He really must have been a great man."

Handling a gun well became a source of fierce competition between the two brothers. As in everything he undertook, Worth proceeded with a fearlessness that sometimes led to accidents; once, as he was getting over a fence, his gun fired, barely missing Barry. Yet Worth was a fine shot and Father worried that once again he performed better than his younger brother.

For Barry, who learned from imitating his older brother, these contests took a toll. In the end he would become an excellent shot, but that was after years of working to outshine a brother who never seemed to care as much but who always learned quickly. Later, on a safari in Africa, the two brothers would seal their bond hunting big game. Barry wrote to Nursie that he hoped to get a "rogue" elephant in order to sell the ivory and pay for part of the trip. He added that the natives were beginning to call him an old ivory hunter.

Guns belonged to the male which I had no wish to penetrate. I was afraid of the impulsive violence associated with hunting. As a small child, I had watched my brothers shoot a squirrel out of a maple tree in front of the house; the squirrel fell to the road with a sickening, small whack, its soft body spewing open. A hardening was required to weld boys to guns, a hardening like the hardening of the heart that made relationships between the children in the family so harsh, so relentless. Why did boys need to shoot? Why was this so desperately important? In the Judge's former bedroom, now painted white and given to Eleanor, a glass-fronted gun case held her stuffed animals and dolls. That did not mean that guns and the memory of guns were gone from this house, although Mother had tried.

Lizzie Baker in her white cap and apron posed in front of that gun cabinet for the English fashion photographer Cecil Beaton. He said she had great style. Guns: black servants: style: there was a strange connection, going back to the black men who had crouched behind metal shields at Pinelands.

Except for those August vacations, the children in the family were spending more time apart. Worth and Barry were at boarding school, and then at Harvard; they spent most of their time when at home going to parties.

During his years in boarding school, Barry frequently wrote to Nursie, asking her to send him sweet potatoes to grow in his dormitory room, telling her that he had found an arbor of Concord grapes that reminded him of the ones he loved at home, commenting on news of Jonathan, who had started at a private school for boys in Louisville which Father had helped to organize. Barry had heard that Jonathan would not say a word about the school, but "everyone thinks he likes it. I certainly hope he does, since I would hate to see him start going away to school."

Jonathan was spared some of the rough-and-tumble life on the Place that had served to educate and to separate the three older children. He kept his secrets to himself. He was pale and somewhat slighter in build than his older brothers. His sudden passions caused the family to nickname him "Toad," after the fad-crazed animal in *The Wind in the Willows*.

About this time Jonathan became involved in the Boy Scouts. He developed a group of friends who enjoyed imaginary games: acting, photographing each other in costume, setting up dioramas and photographing them, digging tunnels and fortifications—creating an imaginary world on the Place. Jonathan seemed busy and absorbed. His life at home was far more intense and interesting than his life at school.

Worth was at Harvard in the early fifties, enjoying himself thoroughly, spending a great deal of time at his club and at debutante parties in Boston. College work seemed to mean little to him, but he passed all his courses with what were called at the time "gentleman's C's." No one expected anything more. It was the fact of being at Harvard that mattered, the development of friendships that would forward his interests in life and the construction of a social life with attractive young women. Going to Harvard was an essential first step. No one discussed the reasons; it was accepted that for bright young men from the South, Harvard was the place to get an education. Later, reading William Faulkner's *The Sound and the Fury,* I imagined how difficult the transition must have been for my three brothers. They were Southerners, hardly intellectuals, and, except for Worth, rather shy.

Worth knew how to navigate. He had learned a good deal from Henrietta, to whom he was devoted, spending time with her in her rented houses at the beach, drinking beer and discussing life. When he got into trouble, he went to her New York apartment for solace, and although Mother may have disapproved of the connection, it gave Worth a frame of reference.

By this time Henrietta was poor. The Harmony Landing farm had failed, and she had sold it after the war. She was living in a little apartment in New York, drinking, and remembering the past. Her candor and her cynicism attracted Worth. She had seen the other side of family life, the side that was complex, shadowed, sophisticated, where the ability to drive a car fast and hold your liquor was more important than academic honors or proper behavior. Henrietta must have smiled when she heard of some of Worth's escapades at Harvard, such as the time he displayed his watch on his penis at a Boston debutante party.

Several years later, when I was a freshman at Radcliffe, Worth once again became a factor in my life. He was a senior at the time, and had become something of a legend. Undergraduates looked at me with a peculiar glint in their eyes when they learned that I was "Worthless's" sister.

Timothy Leary was teaching at Harvard, and had put out word that he wanted to try a strange new substance, LSD, on a bunch of students. Ever ready for any risk, Worth rose to the bait. He never described his experience, but another student in the group walked into a subway tunnel after taking the LSD and was killed by a train.

Following a brief flurry that Father settled, Barry was admitted to Harvard and set about imitating Worth's career. When he was being considered for membership in Worth's club, Barry got drunk, lost control of himself, and ripped a telephone out of the wall. He was not accepted, and spent his undergraduate years in a quieter and less prestigious club where he made close friends.

By then the pattern had been set. Although in theory work and thought were important, in fact it was social behavior with all its glitter which roused Father's interest and appreciation. History had taught us that honors are bestowed on men who hew close to the male code, who learn that drinking together is more important than studying together, and that the secret society of clubs is of greater worth in making careers than academic honors.

Harvard's final clubs, of course, discriminated against women, blacks, and Jews. In 1954, I heard a "clubby" play a Nazi drinking song out of a window to torment a couple who ran a nearby eatery; they were refugees from the Holocaust. The avoidance that made racism acceptable in the South made anti-Semitism irrelevant at Harvard. What mattered was the bond, the secret society of men.

This group of sons of privilege depended for its cohesion on a misogyny that deeply influenced my brothers. To be united against people who are perceived as outsiders is a stronger bond than shared alcohol, shared sex, shared drugs, or shared danger. Outsiders were inevitably Jews, blacks, and women, who, for obvious reasons having to do with skin color, gender, and, in the case of Jews, an imagined profile, could never be mistaken for white upper-class males.

In 1985, the Harvard *Crimson* described Radcliffe students as "bitches," "ugly as sin and not nearly so tempting." A *Crimson* reporter wrote that Radcliffe students "learned everything by rote, spewed it forth on exams and got A's. Or rote learning failing, they would sidle up to an instructor, display a little leg and get an A."

In 1984, one Harvard club, Pi Eta, sent out an invitation describing women as "grateful heifers" for the sexual services of club men, leading, at long last, to the termination of ties between the university and its clubs. Those attitudes were part of the air Worth, Barry, and Jonathan breathed. The small number of women professors with tenure on the Harvard faculty (which continues) underlined and elaborated this misogyny.

The family's attitude toward all of this was confusing. Father had not belonged to a club when he was a Harvard undergraduate in the 1920s, and he sometimes seemed to hint that he would never have dreamed of joining. I realized later that the club system had so dominated Harvard life at that time that the answer could not have been so simple. Both Joseph Kennedy, Sr., and Franklin Roosevelt had been deeply hurt by their exclusion from the Harvard clubs; indeed Roosevelt called it, many years later, the biggest disappointment in his life.

By the time my brothers arrived in Cambridge, the house system had been created, but it had already achieved a set of snobberies that made the houses rather like the final clubs they had been designed to replace.

As John Kenneth Galbraith described it, "Each student's application for a house was charted on a large form. To the left was 'SP' for St. Paul's or 'SA' for St. Albans. Then 'M' for Middlesex or 'G' for Groton, and 'OP' for other private schools. Then religious preference . . . If 'Jewish' was checked, all the rest was irrelevant, for the Jews were still a class unto themselves." So were Southern boys who had not succeeded in graduating from the top Eastern boarding schools, in spite of their parents' efforts.

The effect of the clubs was still pronounced in the 1950s, and as an undergraduate I would note with wonder the amount of attention students paid to their largely colorless activities. It was considered an honor to be invited to eat the horrible food at one of the rare ladies' functions, which revealed to me dark rooms with heavy leather-covered furniture and gloomy portraits, like the state rooms at the Big House.

Harvard remained for the family, as the Judge would have understood, an escape from life on the Ohio River, a view of, and entry into, a larger world. The Judge had dreamed that the Bingham men might have an association with the University of North Carolina rivaling the Adams men's association with Harvard. By the 1930s, however, the family's connection with North Carolina was frayed, and in any event, the Southern universities do not confer the social standing Harvard grants its graduates.

Many years later when I was speaking at a small western Kentucky town, a young man who was mildly retarded had only one question to ask me: What was Harvard really like? In stuttering, faltering tones, he got the question out. That, as far as he was concerned, was all he needed to know—although it seemed likely that he would never leave Kentucky or even visit Cambridge as a tourist. So far has the mantle of honor been spread.

We all longed for that honor, wordlessly, and for the romance that Cambridge, oddly enough, suggested: our parents had met as undergraduates there, and a bartender in a Cambridge haunt had been the first to hear of their engagement. So there was an aura of romance and gentle endings in Cambridge, never detailed or described, which sweetened our expectations of college. Worth did not take advantage of the romance—he was not one for romances—and I was more dazzled by the myth of our parents' courtship than I realized at the time. Lesser mortals did not match the memory of those twin profiles, pale as alabaster, in the early photograph.

Cambridge and Chatham, the little town on Cape Cod, were the only real alternatives to Kentucky for "the fam." As alternatives they had enormous value for the older three children, who knew instinctively that some escape, no matter how brief, must be found. But neither Worth nor Barry thought of that escape as permanent. The younger children, too, never left the Ohio River for long.

By 1952, I knew I would have to leave as soon as I could, at seventeen, when I would graduate from high school. There was no other way. For a young woman, to "be" anything in Louisville—even to be a writer (that most ladylike and decorous occupation, which can even be conducted in a few leisure hours in a corner of a bedroom)—was not imaginable. Serious writing, like serious studying, requires sweat, effort, and tears.

Cambridge and Chatham: the sleek Charles River and the blue Atlantic waters. These were the northern boundaries of the family kingdom.

20

In June of 1952, when I was fifteen, I wrote, "I have learned that to dream too much is suicide to hopes."

"The dream" seemed so obvious I didn't describe it: I wanted someone to fall in love with me. I had watched Worth fascinate a series of girls, who did not seem the better for it, and I had watched the elaborate quadrille my parents had mastered. Neither of these forms seemed possible for me. I lacked Worth's sexual aggressiveness and our parents' ability to submerge their individual needs in the beautiful pattern of their relationship. Never to disagree seemed to me a noble objective, but I had no idea how to reach it, or how I would manage to be always freshly bathed and beautifully dressed as Mother was at the coming-home hour of men.

That June, our parents announced that their three older children (who were not children at all but adolescents aged fifteen through twenty) would be taken on another trip abroad.

"I can't wait for the trip!" I wrote. "It seems that the younger officers [on the ocean liner] dance with the 'extra' girls. There is a dance every night and, oh mercy! It COULD be so much fun. To arm myself, I have given in at last about dancing lessons."

The class was held on the second floor of a drab little building in Louisville. There I immediately faced a problem: I did not know what to do with my wallet. (I was not yet carrying a purse, which, like lipstick and high-heeled shoes, seemed a badge of servitude.) At the bottom of a long flight of stairs that led up to the studio, there was a large radiator. I hid my wallet under it.

The following day, I wrote, "What a ghastly, nightmarish day! I feel as though it happened a thousand years ago, yet the scratches on my pride are very fresh.

"I went at three. Mr. Jones danced with me for a few minutes. Then came Dit. Obviously he must have been suffering from a hangover, though to my innocent eyes he looked no more dissipated than usual. Poor man! Perhaps it was fear, not liquor, which made him bare tooth and claw. He took me into a small room, put on a record. The last straw came when I refused to dance close."

Dit and I had been arguing this point for several days. He maintained that he could not teach me to dance without shoulder-to-thigh contact; I was repelled and frightened.

I went on: "I have never felt hatred before. Dislike, yes, but not hatred from a man forcing me into movements with little, hard cold eyes close to mine.

"In short, he said, I would make him lose his job. I would never learn how to dance. All I did was fool. Either I do as he says or go get a new teacher. He paraded before me the cripples, idiots and babes in arms of whom he has made perfection. THEY tried. THEY danced close.

"There I stood, my eyes filled to the lashes, and my whole insides so dried-out my tongue was like a gardening glove."

After another lesson, I wrote, "Today when I went downstairs, my wallet was gone. I wish I could have gone out without a word, but a wild idea of a trick planned by someone who had seen me made me turn back.

"They gave me a dime to get home on. I left them standing at the foot of the stairs, wondering if I was insane or just stupid. It hurt."

The incident soon vanished in the tumult of summer at the Big House. I wrote, "Things go on in this house that no one knows, or even imagines.

"It is such a huge old house, rambling half way down the hill, and there are so many of us, seven in the family and six servants, each living his own secret life. We scarcely know each other, each bears a vague and varying label, the servants are seldom thought of as individuals, yet we are the most vital, energetic family I know.

"There are things which are rather queer—Worth, coming home drunk in the middle of the night and practicing piano scales; Barry, marooned in a little shell of hard work; me, alone in the silent house with Punch [the old poodle] pacing the hall and every breeze a hand on my neck; Jonathan, perhaps the most normal, kissing goodnight with the sexy passion and prolongation of a man; and Eleanor, screaming in the night with terror, till Mam'selle comes in, a stiff-lipped specter, and quiets her with an even larger measure of fears. It is only chance and love that threw us here together, we go along so selfishly, hating and lonely in the midst of relations. And in the kitchen, the servants quarreling and laughing by turns, and in the hall, the same thing, only carried on with more deadly purpose."

Because Mother had suggested various self-improvements, I blamed her for the mediocre outcome, writing, "Yes, Mother, I have taken dancing lessons, I have practiced my tennis, I have had my teeth straightened, and cut off my hair. I have followed all those unconquerable formulas for success you have thrust on me. But I am still the same, still an outsider, a lone one, stupid and unloved. For what have you done for my heart while you were putting braces on my teeth? What have you given me for self-reliance?"

I did not understand that Mother was obliged to teach me certain rules of behavior and deportment, lest I learn these lessons with greater pain on my own. I did not appreciate the degree to which, in teaching me, she was trying to protect me from a world which, in her experience, was merciless toward a naïve, romantic girl. I only sensed that I could never live up to her expectations, whatever they might be.

I did not know what to do to please Mother, or to please the world she so effectively represented. I did not know how to satisfy myself without her praise, which I sometimes sullenly repelled. I could not set my own standards, I felt, until I had satisfied the world around me. But the world around me was insatiable. Nothing I did would ever be enough.

Meanwhile, the world around me went on its way, with little attention to me or from me.

"So we may not be able to go to England," I wrote later that summer. "Barry, the good sheep, the white lamb, whose sweetness seems to draw calamity, may be drafted. I can't believe it, I can't be afraid yet he is so young, so naive in many ways, self-conscious at going to parties, how will he make out in a camp designed for tough older men as a private, beginning in the filth of the army, to struggle upwards, with his customary difficulty and his never failing efforts . . ." By one of those mysterious twists I did not understand, Barry was not sent to Korea: he went to Harvard in the fall.

I had scarcely been aware of the Korean War until the draft threatened Barry. It had begun in 1950 while we were in France. General MacArthur's landing at Inchon, the crossing of the 38th parallel, the phrase "paper tiger," and the death of 34,000 young Americans passed over my head.

Meanwhile Worth was fulfilling his NROTC obligations by serving during the summer on a warship in the Pacific, which caused Mother great alarm. Her fears for her two older sons did not diminish her support for U.S. aggression, which both Father and the newspapers saw as patriotic. Later, information about the role the CIA played in MacArthur's bungling would reveal that Korea was another of the exercises that had begun in the 1940s in London. But no one I knew in the early 1950s was talking about the CIA's covert actions, and so the Korean War had for me the same glow as the hand-to-hand combat of the Greeks and the Spartans—the glow so cherished by the Judge and the Colonel. Years later I would read that "the main reason for the Korean failure was not a lack of raw information, but the

CIA's obsession with covert actions and subversion which led the agency to ignore or misinterpret the information available to it." By then I would have changed my definition of patriotism.

It was formed by reverence for secrecy and for government by an elite, which was part of the air we breathed in the Big House. That a democracy is a democracy in theory only, and is in fact an aristocracy that allows underlings the vote—and that, in some states, was still severely compromised by the remnants of the poll tax, which I had heard Mother justify—was accepted without need for explanation. We saw all around us evidence that "the people" cannot govern because of ignorance, genetic limitations, and prejudice. Yet we, too, were ignorant, limited by privilege, and firmly if secretly prejudiced against blacks, poor whites, most women, and some Jews. This did not seem relevant when we defined the patriot: a white male of good family and education who through both open and covert means makes decisions that shape the lives of others. The CIA was the patriot's tool, as journalism was the tool of righteous men who wanted to control the flow of information.

At fifteen, I was far more concerned about my social success than I was about patriotism or democracy. That summer, I gave my first "mixed" party, on the big side terrace overlooking the river.

Awkward young people stood in clots on the sidelines until Father began to organize games. Later we heard snarls and groans from the front lawn; our two poodles, father and son, were at each other's throat. In front of the startled adolescents, the son stretched the father out dead on the grass. "It is the law of survival," I wrote later, "but somehow Punch's liquid eyes seem tortured by a fear civilization has put there."

The family's dogs reflected the family's peculiarities. The black standard-bred poodles became eccentric after a few years in the Big House. They darted to the front door with furious barks whenever Mother pressed the bell under the dining-room table to call for the next course, they chased cars down the drive until Worth dissuaded them with BB shots and buckets of cold water, and they got lost in the Back Woods and were found with their heads inside hollow trees. The dogs seemed to have replaced the eccentric relatives, who, by the early 1950s, were either dead or no longer in evidence.

We five children developed our own peculiarities. Eleanor had become excessively pliable, remote, and pleasing; Jonathan was silent at family gatherings, rarely hearing what was going on around him; I was compulsive, anxious, unsmiling; and Barry was imitating the white hunters he had admired on his African safari. Worth went his own way, imitating no one; but Worth was the heir.

Barry sometimes involved me in his rituals. I wrote, "On our last evening before the trip abroad, we went Bat Hunting. Barry, equipped in his Darkest Africa bush jacket, helmet and knee boots, climbed up the loft ladder. I, grasping a belt, stood on the ladder. Presently, a few bats, awakening with evening, glided around the hunter's head, showing the way to their nests, where hundreds of others still hung asleep. Barry fired into the melee, and several bats bit the dust. The rest, risking daylight rather than mass slaughter, burst out of the loft door. Lashing about with my belt, I hit one just as it flew up, when its wings like skeleton fingers stretched over with skin were over my face. It fell on the loft floor, its wings folded, looking like a legless mouse trying to get up. Barry came over and smashed it under his heel."

On July 29, 1952, Worth, Barry, our parents, and I boarded the overnight train for New York. "Here I am, sitting without any clothes on waiting for the cream on my face to dry," I wrote in the green-and-gilt travel diary Nursie had given me. "This is the beginning.

"Tonight in Ohio, tomorrow at sea . . . I feel as if I were coming to something new, and yet, I am still the same."

Sylvia, daughter of my parents' friends, was to cross the ocean with us. I was pleased to have her company; her quietness was a relief, in contrast to the constant word sallies of the family.

"We have spent the afternoon most profitably," I wrote the day after we sailed, "making remarks on people's appearance. So far we have found any number of buffoons, nightmares, and horrendous, puffy faced women, and three boys, between the age of 15 and 20. Two of the three, sized up as a gambler's son and a 'nice boy,' seem good. But the nice boy is too nice to make advances, and the gambler's son is complete."

Father enjoyed the sizing-up; he had a sharp eye for character, and could deduce a great deal from a certain way of walking or the cut of a suit. Very few young men withstood his scrutiny. He could devastate a stranger with a word. Always polite to acquaintances, he seemed to enjoy the relief of mercilessly imitating strangers. Yet he was eager for me to meet someone "suitable." The *Queen Mary* held little promise of that.

Every evening, Sylvia and I dressed in long evening gowns—a different one for each of the five nights, with the most elaborate saved for the last. After a large formal dinner, we would repair to one of the ship's lounges, where we would play Bingo or Horse Race. Finally, the older and younger people would depart, and the ship's small orchestra struck up. At that moment, alone at the table with Barry and Worth, I felt terrified that I would not be asked to dance, yet almost equally terrified of dancing with one of the "buffoons." The "younger officers" did not materialize. One evening Worth grew so desperate he agreed to dance with me himself, then held a five-dollar bill over my head to lure a partner. He was unsuccessful.

After debarking, we traveled by car through England, three adolescents crammed into the back seat along with maps, digestive biscuits, books, and other debris. We got along as well as we ever did, with an occasional outburst of cuffing or sarcasm. I loved the English countryside, which had been the backdrop of the stories I had read as a child.

Father's enthusiasm carried us. He was a tireless walker, a tireless enthusiast of local cider and even local food. The inns always seemed cozy to him, the landladies agreeable, the cottages we passed settings for rural romance. Even a gloomy adolescent was infected by his cheer. Nothing could be hopeless in a countryside dotted with hollyhocks. England remained for him the scene of the Judge's triumphs, Henrietta's adventures, his own wartime escapades, and the official rehabilitation of the family name.

Inevitably, we wore on each other. I wrote, "Take tonight for an example. I don't know about other families, but in ours the one really strong affection is between our parents. The rest of us have just been tossed together under one roof, harboring the same hatreds and selfishness of any individuals, almost untempered by love.

"If it were not for Daddy, we would rub each other to the bleeding point, but always when the sobs come up, and those hard little words start, he laughs and makes me remember how many similar pains we've faced and forgotten, or, if the case is more serious, stops the frightful pause which comes at the end of every cruel reprimand."

Later, I wrote, "When I have to kiss Mother I feel like a hypocrite. I know I unjustly dislike her, yet somehow we are death to each other. Just two women both loving one man, not drawn together by any bonds but those deadly ties of similarity."

One night we stayed in Yorkshire with friends of the family: "Lady F. is one of the most charming Englishwomen I have met. Her husband is mysteriously not here, instead Lord T. occupies a rather questionable position in the household. I cannot imagine anything more uncomfortable than entertaining such a guest while your husband is away. However this is all supposition."

Later I added, after this entry: "Ha ha!"

My hollow humor grew from Father's disclosure that Lord T. had been in love with Lady F. for twenty-five years. "The affair is accepted by everyone, for it is only because she is a Roman Catholic that she has not been divorced long ago and married him. Her husband, who is twenty years older, is a dismal old man, and the second of her daughters, who is excessively beautiful and nice, is thought to be Lord T.'s daughter. The older girl, who is hideously plain and a little neurotic, is miserably compared to this sister, who married at seventeen.

"Lord T. is the most eligible bachelor in the world," I went on, quoting Father. "All England is dying for him to be married, so that there may be an heir for the estate and title."

This was not my first exposure to the breeder attitude toward women. I had never questioned the listing of priorities for a married couple: an heir first, personal happiness later. Knit into the patterns of inherited wealth and power is an image of woman as the mother of sons. A woman who cannot bear a son to perpetuate her husband's name and inherit his fortune is of little use.

Although I could not have articulated it at the time, I resisted the view of woman's role as breeder of sons, and I began to say that even if I eventually married I would never have children—an unheard-of reservation in the 1950s. My parents seemed startled by my announcement but they did not argue with me; I was "serious," after all, and anything can be expected of a serious young girl—especially in view of the fact that she is sure to change her mind. And my link in the family tradition was not essential: my brothers' sons would carry on the name.

Later I realized that it works well when the daughters of wealth do not marry and do not have children. The male line is not endangered by the introduction of strangers, husbands who might challenge the patriarch's authority or weaken their wives' loyalty; and the sons of sons do not have to fear the competence of the sons of daughters.

With the prospect of breeding before me, I began to be fascinated by the young men who crossed my path. They had access to other futures, and like Mother before me, I was interested in annexing one of them. Fortunately I was too young to encounter men who had already laid hold of their futures—the male sages who are such a potent threat to unformed young women with no plans of their own.

Instead I watched and coveted the assurance even the least attractive young man seemed to possess. I began to cultivate my ability to identify, not with the now forgotten figure of Joan of Arc or the Victory of Samothrace, but with "dates"—they had a future.

On the liner returning to New York from our month abroad, I had a brief encounter with a nameless young man. He possessed assurance, if nothing else.

I wrote in my diary, "When his arm closed around me, and his head touched mine, I felt only comfort and certainty. He sighed, a sigh of happiness complete and physical which I will remember. It came through his throat into my head." Here was the complete physical identification I craved.

That summer Worth sometimes inveighed against women he called "nymphos," a term so common at the time it did not require definition. Although willing girls served his sexual purposes, Worth seemed to scorn and fear them, perhaps because they expected something in return. Yet women were always attracted to him, not only the Louisville debutantes but our parents' friends. I did not understand the contradiction.

At that point and for many years afterwards, I never met a woman who would discuss sex, or indicate in any way that she enjoyed it. My classmates were constrained by the fear that someone would discover that they had "gone all the way"—a fearful obloquy. Mother once spoke of the pleasures of sleeping together, which seemed innocuous enough to me. But where was the thrill?

In Paris a few years earlier, I had seen a production, in French, of *A Streetcar Named Desire,* with palm trees, half-naked black women, and a tom-tom in the background. I knew why Blanche ended as she did, in the madhouse: she had felt something sexual toward men. It all made sense, in a terrible and limited way: nymphos and virgins, sleeping together and identification with the male, surrender and destruction.

I thought I understood why a woman might "let herself go," as the phrase went, with a confident man. I did not think it had anything to do with enjoying sex, or with love. Violence was always a possibility, it seemed to me, in relations between men and women, and violence—or the possibility of violence—could be very convincing, more convincing even than the axiom that girls were responsible for restraining boys.

Beyond violence, there was the quest for identity. Perhaps "sleeping together" allowed that perfect melding, that taking on of a man's wishes and ambitions, that seemed to underlie our hungry search for "togetherness."

But what was the alternative?

21

"Louisville has, to my horror, gone on without me," I wrote when we returned from England. "The girls are preparing to 'marry' different boys than when I left, school has started, and I have no part in these last days."

That fall, one of Worth's friends was to be married, and I wrote, "I suppose it is no more strange to hear this than to hear of all these boys in antiaircraft bases in Korea, or submarines in the Pacific. A boy can perhaps do that, but marrying comes so close to maturity." Fighting, from what I had seen of it, did not.

My life still centered on the big barn on the Place, a run-down frame structure without electricity or running water.

"When I get home from school," I wrote later in the fall, "I spend the afternoon cleaning the stalls or doctoring [my horse] Miss Jane's infected foot. Dora [the daughter of the family that was renting the Little House] comes at the same time, and manfully pitchforks manure from her stall. Jonathan makes frequent trips to collect wood which is stored in one of the stalls, this he laboriously drags down the hill to the Duckyard where he is building a suspension bridge. Eleanor and Mam'selle are peacefully occupied in the Duckyard, except when Eleanor is allowed to come up to the barn to help. Mother, Dora's mother, and her brother Richard usually pass back and forth through the vegetable garden all afternoon.

"It takes nearly an hour to clean out the stable, and it gets dark so early now. Around four-thirty we light four candle ends and set them up on the ledges around the stall where we're working. Out in the half-dark passage the horses stand patiently or whinny when a load of hay goes by. The candles drip long fingers onto the ledges, and from outside the windows glow as if there was a dance within."

My social life revolved around meetings at church on Sunday evenings, where a group of adolescents talked and ate. "Perhaps it's the boys, here so consciously Kings, knowing that there will be twenty girls breathlessly awaiting them each Sunday. The worst is the ghastly motto, 'Together we will enjoy being Christians.' We are more likely to regret not being utter pagans."

If the existence of God did not explain the world, perhaps the explanation lay with the drives that seemed to control my own body. The myth of female periodicity that had haunted the Colonel when he spoke against advanced education for women had begun to torment me.

"I am nothing but an animal driven on by biological frenzy," I wrote that fall. "When the time for my period draws near, I cannot sleep for fumbling about with my limbs and having strange, lurid dreams. Nature struggles in me to reproduce before too late. She succeeds in nothing except making me think of all the boys I have known. The time comes: again a chance for life dies quietly. Thank goodness the cycle will have begun again by Saturday, and so I can want even Dennis Finn."

Dennis's attentions filled some of the void left at home when Father became absorbed in Adlai Stevenson's first campaign for the presidency.

I was not aware of the antecedents of their friendship, but when I met Stevenson at the Big House, I knew at once that he was "one of us." Articulate, well educated, definitely a "gent," he possessed a familiar ability to distance himself intellectually. Father resented the country's scorn for "the egghead," for it was this frail, wispy, cerebral charm that drew him to Stevenson. He appeared to me a vague if well-meaning presence, victimized by life.

Mother was often at home while Father was with Stevenson, and I noticed that she seemed exhausted, faced with the enormous house, her three younger children, and servants who needed constant supervision. She sometimes showed me her frustration, "crying out with her forehead all crinkled up that she is turning into a machine, a poor petty instrument which can only calculate the tiny measures of life." Her days were spent producing a perfect life; she was never without her lists.

That fall I was spending time with Eleanor and Jonathan, both at the barn and during the long evenings at home. "Down the hall the children are put to bed, shockingly late due to cookie making," I wrote. "Before them lies the whole agony of growing up."

Father's frequent absences that fall resulted in glorious homecomings; we shared Mother's delight in his return. But the evenings I had spent with her that fall, far from his gravitational pull, were also sweet: "Tonight as I sat making a catalogue of the endless, pathetic books which sit forever unread [in our library], I found a flat pressed telegram in the back of a first edition. It was dated May, 1929, two years before my parents were married. As I read it, and heard at the same time Mother's quiet voice, I bridged in one quick second all these years between the 'my darling' in the telegram, embarrassed by being read to an operator, and the present. They have neither changed, nor done anything extraordinary. Theirs is the most perfect marriage any one can dream of, yet I wonder how far marriage can carry life into fulfillment, and I wonder if I will ever think a wife is the only goal I will attain."

I began that Christmas to go to dances, which soon lost their appeal. "Dennis does not torment me, he merely wears and drags on my mind," I wrote under Mother's recipe for cooking Kentucky ham: "Soak the ham overnight. Wash it thoroughly. Put into a large pan, and cover completely with equal parts of cold water and cider . . ." The military school cadet alarmed me with his ostentatious car and his too brightly colored ties; Worth was making fun of him, and I could not help seeing his point.

We went to see a movie about the Civil War. "I had my head on Dennis' shoulder, wondering rather vaguely whether the hero was Confederate or Yankee at the present moment. I noticed that Dennis' heart was jarring in my head and neck, with an insistent note, like a child with a drum.

"Then he kissed me. All that I could feel was the suddenness of it. I knew that he had moved, and the next instant—I can't describe. I only know that he must have thought me as impassive as a cabbage, as he twice pressed his lips to mine—and I could not even be sure, half a minute later, that it had really happened.

"In the movies! I can only be thankful for my pride that he did not do it at the identical time as the hero and heroine."

I went on: "And so home—and a careful and cool goodbye (my eyes were red and my pimples obvious) and up to dance with hypocritical glee over the prey."

I was ashamed of my urgency, which had nothing to do with love, or even with sex. It would have been easier to accept that I was a "nympho," as Worth would have called it, than that I was entirely without feeling. My feelings seemed pared, numb; it was total identification I lusted for, the moment when it was not clear who was kissing and who was kissed, who was wearing the pink silk party dress with the crinoline petticoat and who was wearing the Confederate gray uniform.

22

O n my sixteenth birthday, "I felt the heat of the little candles burning
splotches on my face, and Daddy said in a toast those knockout words
which are saved up during a whole year of loneliness and self-pity, to almost
suffocate you on your birthday."

The "knockout words" certainly dealt with my appearance, which
people seemed to think was improving: an old family friend had remarked
that I was losing my "underwater quality," which meant, to me, my
similarity to the drowned Ophelia.

For my birthday dinner, the mahogany table would have been laid with
transparent organdy mats, rimmed with embroidery or appliqué, crisp linen
napkins folded so that the monogram was displayed, the flat silver my
parents had received at their wedding (the gold service, so like Mary Lily's,
was reserved for parties), and, for my milk, the battered silver coronation
mug the Judge had sent home in 1937. By now I had traced the lion's head
on its handle so often with my thumb I felt it in my grain.

Father would have offered me a drop of champagne—French, and very
dry, named, to my amazement, for a widow. But a drop was enough. I had
known since the disastrous lunch in the French Alps that I could not afford
to drink.

Turning sixteen meant becoming "a female animal," who was expected
to "emerge from the shadows of adolescence, waltz on village greens and
hang around by old mill streams."

To do these things, the female animal required a mate. I was receiving
letters from Dennis, now at school in the Deep South.

Dennis's letters touched me. "It was one of those letters which should
be called illiterate, because it stumbles so badly trying to express itself. It
makes me realize how isolated he is in a desert of monotones."

Having a serious "beau" gave me a link to the girls at school, yet I could
not make common cause with them without betraying my specialness.

I decided to go to the next "slumber party" to which I was invited, writing, "I have avoided [the girls] like poison for the last five years, due to my devotion to sleep, my horror of the haggard, drawn ferret face in the mirror next morning. But I feel like a scientist who has the opportunity to use a powerful microscope. I must go."

Sexual attraction between girls was unheard of; we never hugged or kissed, except to celebrate winning a hockey or basketball game. I wrote, "I have heard many allusions to homosexuality, but always so clouded with subtleties that I cannot really grasp the horrible meaning. That two women may be in love in terms of idealism, of seeing perfection in each other, I can understand as almost normal, but that it should proceed farther into those ill-concealed allusions is to me incomprehensible.

"If I were not afraid of myself, I would say that I am in love with Alice Taylor," I went on. "Immediately the phrase strikes me with its implications, yet I only mean that I see in her beauty crystallized."

Earlier in the year I had spent a night at Alice's house. We shared a big double bed. While we lay waiting to fall asleep, I regaled Alice with some of the "dirty stories," drawn from my own fantasies, which had impressed the other girls. She listened drowsily, without much interest. After a while I began to act out the part of the lover, stretching myself on top of Alice and grinding against her. She seemed neither pleased nor displeased. Finally I left her alone.

Next morning we got up and went to the kitchen without a word. Alice mixed up a pitcher of frozen orange juice concentrate, the first I had tasted; we had fresh-squeezed juice at home. The concentrate tasted delicious, yet it was associated in my mind with unspeakable vice. We never spent the night together again.

As Eleanor grew older and started going to school with me, I was astonished by her cheerful normalcy. She did not seem a member of the strange tribe that had in the old days lived on the Place. She understood the importance of friendships, outings, camp, and, later, boarding school. The magic web was broken, and she emerged a solid and trusting little citizen of an ordinary world. Running around with a gaggle of girls, organizing tea parties, with Jonathan and the new black butler as guests, riding horseback in the acknowledged way, with lessons and companions, she seemed better equipped than I to deal with reality.

The family maintained its hold over us through various routines: elaborate evening meals, church services, and long walks in all weathers.

"We walked for three hours in the rain—a thing no one but Binghams would do." Now that I had reached my full growth, I could keep up with the furious pace Father set. It was more difficult for Eleanor and Jonathan, who sometimes lagged behind and complained. In winter, we were often chilled, but Father was never cold, even in the light jacket that was his only concession to low temperatures. He would be brisk and glowing, exhilarated, when we were ready to collapse. I learned then that there is no mercy for the straggler. Mother almost ran to keep up, but she never complained about the pace or the cold.

That spring, "I began to dream again about a garden. I took my basket and went to pick glass out of the cold frame, to sort the riffraff of human debris from the rich, rank earth where I would grow a whole sanctuary of flowers.

"As I picked along in the drizzling rain, old Captain Bud came breathing liquor like a vat on fire. He stood on the path, repeating over and over, 'Don't get offended with me, I just like to watch you. Why does Barry wear that hat?' (His safari hat, which he often wore for outdoor chores.) 'I didn't know who it was. Grand boy, swell. Want me to do that, Miss Sallie? Don't cut your hands. They say I'm old, but I do my work, yes, I always do my work. Tell your mom, I'll finish this frame tomorrow. I got to go to bed when it's dark. I'm old. Don't get offended with me.' "

My parents had not yet recovered from their disappointment over Adlai Stevenson's defeat in 1952. Eisenhower, with his bland manner and his military deportment, was a successful version of a type they scorned.

Life changed abruptly in February, when Father left home again to visit Asia with Stevenson. "We drove Daddy to the airport," I wrote. "Three months is a long time. This was impressing itself carefully into each of us, until Mother gave a dramatic sigh.

"The plane took off. Mother fumbled in her purse for cigarettes, and Jonathan and Eleanor watched from the warmth of telephone boxes.

"Daddy had kissed Mother goodbye gently, and more. He said something to her, and I, half cruelly embarrassed, half hypnotized, wondered what there was left to say after so long, and so many tearful, cheerful departures."

The scene is emblematic: the mysterious departure, which no one questioned or explained, and the two younger children closed up in telephone booths, watching their parents. I was a slightly closer observer of events, physically at least. But I did not dare to ask what was going on, or why Father had decided to accompany Stevenson on his tour.

Father's absence re-created a world of women I remembered from wartime. Munda came for a long visit, and the governess of the moment, a kind, quiet woman, spent her evenings with the rest of us in the living room. During those long evenings, Mother would sew or mend, Miss Faye would have a book open on her knee, and Munda would vigorously stitch on one of the dresses she was making for her younger granddaughters. Munda also talked.

"When Munda talks," I wrote, "I feel progress for the first time, I realize the widening gap between past and present. They call us the material-istic age; it seems to me that we are, superficially at least, turning away from the security of money and realizing that the most terrible agony is worth paying for the few great and mysterious ideals."

Burning with nameless idealism, I entered a high school speaking con-test. The theme was "I Speak for Democracy," a theme which, in the increasingly rigid society of the Cold War, had connotations I did not understand. .

"I stood up to make my speech today," I wrote, "a half-hypocritical speech, bloated with youth and florid old expressions." To my surprise, the speech won first prize, and I was invited to read it over the radio.

According to the newspaper story, I said, "I speak for democracy because I speak for hope—a hope based on the one changeless thing in this world, the power of the individual." It was a dangerous theory.

It applied, I knew, only to certain members of my world. The black servants did not have the power of their individuality; they could not even have voted if Mother had not driven them to the polls.

Nor did the privileged girls I knew enjoy any power other than the power of being pretty. Even that led often to helplessness. Now and then one of my friends would report, with glazed eyes, that her "date" had fallen for her. Then she could count on a season in the sun, with dinners out and flowers, regular telephone calls, movies, and the luxury of affection. Almost at once, however, the horrible dilemma of sexual behavior would begin. We all knew we would be ruined if we "gave in," and we also knew we were responsible for setting and keeping the limits. We might allow our breasts to be caressed after a certain number of dates, but hands must never be allowed to forage below our waists. "Heavy petting" might cause a boy to ejaculate, creating embarrassing problems, but none of us knew that girls could have orgasms. Our sexuality was a dangerous bait, and we were in charge of making sure that it was used in the prescribed way.

The adult men I knew who owned, edited, and wrote the Louisville newspapers clearly had the power of their individuality and could express their viewpoints freely, in print and in conversation. It did not seem to matter much whether anyone agreed with them or not. In fact, their power was so great that readers or listeners who disagreed were assumed to be ignorant or benighted.

As liberals in a conservative state that became more conservative as a result of exposure to Father's newspapers, the family had the power of moral leadership. It was accompanied by a subterranean threat of violence, the violence ignorant people might use against us, their moral superiors, but also the violence we used on a daily basis against them. This was expressed in our denigration, in private, of our readers and the low-class politicians who represented them. It did not surprise me to read, years later, that Mrs. Hodding Carter, wife of the publisher of a well-known liberal newspaper in the Deep South, remarked, "Not a Saturday evening went by that someone in our circle didn't seriously consider killing Huey Long." Unlike Louisiana, Kentucky had no local rabble-rouser, but widespread "ignorance"—as we called it—aroused the murderous instincts of men who did not tolerate opposition easily. "Ignorant" people should not be allowed to exist.

Thoughts of this kind did not limit my enthusiasm when I "spoke for democracy" in front of a few people at the high school competition. My speech earned me a trophy and a television set. My parents felt that it would be wrong for me to accept the television, both because they disapproved of it and because we already had one. Their argument was familiar and acceptable. Material rewards were not what mattered, and I returned the television set without regrets.

I did not understand Father's relationship with Adlai Stevenson, although it colored my life in the early fifties when Stevenson ran twice for President on the Democratic ticket. Father was involved peripherally in 1952, offering advice, money, and encouragement; in 1956, he was co-chairman of the national Volunteers for Stevenson.

I did not understand, nor did I ask, nor was I even curious, although Father's long absences left me bleak and wan. By now the code my parents talked seemed unbreakable to me, and my earlier curiosity had seeped away along with my urge to interrupt the smooth flow of grown-up life around me.

Another reason closed my mouth: in all adult relationships, and most conspicuously in the relationships between powerful men, secrets shed shadows I could not explain although I felt their darkness. Secrets about mothers and wives and sisters, particularly: Father's friends were too young to have adult daughters, and they tended to wax romantic about little girls who were not yet old enough to cause them trouble. But grown women, divorced or banished, forgotten or denied, stood for events and feelings that must be repressed.

These shadows explained a great deal: the hesitancy with which these influential men sometimes acted or spoke, their reliance on a bright fabric of words, and the curious atmosphere of passivity that diluted even the most heated political revel, as though the men on whom the attention was so hotly focused expected a sudden revelation to blot it all out.

In the end, the presence of secrets gave men like Father and Stevenson a private excuse for failure, private rationalizations when the brass ring slipped by. It was this vulnerability that made them ultimately unapproachable, for it seemed that a touch might wound them intimately, revealing something which must be hidden. Their uneasiness with wives and children stemmed from their fear that those who knew them best might inadvertently make the crucial disclosure. Both men were called sensitive, perhaps too sensitive for politics, and both were living in the aftermath of dramas with women.

Adlai Stevenson's family had come from North Carolina and Kentucky. His grandfather had been Grover Cleveland's Vice President in 1892, and he was related to Kentucky's Ur-politician, Alben Barkley. Stevenson's father never found his niche in life, moving from one occupation to another, cultivating important friends; and his mother died of a mysterious fever complicated by "manic-depressive depression," according to the doctor's report. The cause of her death was vague enough to worry her son, and even more troubling was the memory of her restless life.

She had concentrated all her efforts on her home, defining her life in the terms acceptable in her day, yet she had been unhappy, ineffective—and angry. She and Stevenson's father had often quarreled and spent much of their married life apart. Over these facts an explanatory myth had grown: the family was so devoted that Stevenson and his sister had difficulty making their escape, and the phrase used in farewell telegrams, "There is no parting," must have had an ominous ring.

The myth covered important ambiguities about inherited money. Stevenson's sister received a trust fund only when she married, and he would spend the early part of his life dependent on "the old man."

Stevenson had a lifelong fascination with the press. His family's newspaper, the Bloomington, Illinois, *Pantagraph,* had been the subject of family battles and lawsuits. His later affair with Alicia Patterson, of the Chicago *Tribune* family, was perhaps heated by his feelings about the uncontrollable power of that conservative newspaper. Attractive to women yet repelled by intimacy, Stevenson, like Father, had an elusive quality that made him irresistible. Both men disliked television, the medium of the masses, which sometimes reveals too much. Both men had been formed by ambitious fathers and by Eastern universities, and their lives revolved around house parties, tennis, and talk. Reading aloud was their way of relating to their children, all of whom would in various ways disappoint them.

Part of Father's elusiveness depended on the hidden scandal of Mary Lily's death. Part of Stevenson's mystery was connected to his accidental shooting, when he was a boy, of a playmate. Both dramas were hushed up; both raised complex questions of responsibility. Did a boy who playfully aimed a gun at a girl and shot her dead deserve any form of blame? Did a man who profited from the fortune inherited from a woman who died in mysterious circumstances owe her memory any special attention?

The conventional philosophy of the final club, the officers' club, the CIA, and the club of Democratic politics offered no answers.

The accidental shooting was "discovered" by a *Time* reporter in 1952, the year Stevenson was finally persuaded to allow himself to be nominated. His recent divorce and his relationship with his ex-wife, the highly charged Ellen Borden Stevenson, was also discussed in the press. For Father, the dreaded intrusions of the past were equally alarming, and the resulting sadness and confusion led to instant sympathy. Both men were "misunderstood."

The two men had shared the excitement of Washington in 1941, when war was about to provide them with legitimate escapes from the claustrophobic world of home, an excitement that would continue in England.

As a very small child, I had felt this nameless excitement when the two families shared a weekend cabin on the Potomac River. After lunch, I climbed up to the loft to take a nap; the bees buzzing around the window seemed to mimic the tone of adult conversation downstairs. During that summer, Ellen Stevenson decided she wanted a divorce. She would say later that she "helped Stevenson become a success in those early years so she could leave him." It was also the summer that led to wartime friendships, the OSS, and eventually the CIA.

Later Stevenson's marriage would seem to me a point of contact with danger. Ellen Borden had been rich, attractive, and an ambitious poet when she married Adlai; her letters reveal her range, as well as her determination to manage her own finances and her writing—and an increasingly desperate flirtatiousness. She hated the life of a politician's wife. Her face did not seem capable of the expression of devout adoration that can be seen in all photographs which show the candidate speaking while his wife sits nearby, preferably with her arms full of squirming children.

After bearing three sons, Ellen divorced Adlai and descended into the maelstrom. The outspoken and unusually vivid young woman had lost her place in life. Her sons sided with their father—he had seen himself, and they saw him, as a helpless victim of her anger—and his political friends treated Ellen as a potential threat.

Years later, at a wedding of one of their sons, I became aware of a dark and troubling female presence of whom everyone was afraid. As in the case of Mary Lily, I was not certain who the woman was, but I knew she represented danger. By then, Ellen Stevenson had become the Other incarnate, an irrepressible force that must be kept forcibly on the outside of events and consciousness.

The obligation to forget united the two men, both of whom shared a reputation as liberals and as intellectuals, which was open to question. Stevenson had flunked out of Harvard Law School, and he was too uncomfortable with reflection and solitude to develop as a thinker. Father loved books but restlessness and an ultimate reserve about the truth limited his curiosity. They were liberals by temperament rather than by conviction, patricians whose sense of superiority propelled them into leadership.

Neither had any understanding of the needs of people who were not white and male. Stevenson was blandly anti-Semitic for years, finally laying the prejudice aside at the same time he learned that all blacks are not old family retainers. Father was never anti-Semitic—the Judge had depended heavily on his Jewish friends during the bad years—but like Stevenson, he thought of women and blacks as lovable servitors who did not really want to "rise."

When Stevenson visited Louisville to attend the Derby, I noticed only the fuss and confusion. The Duke and Duchess of Windsor were accepted as last-minute guests, much to Mother's chagrin, and all of Louisville seemed tiddly with excitement. Excitement always made me suspicious, for it revealed a slavishness in grown-ups that frightened me.

The Duke and the Duchess, who had arrived for the Derby in Robert Young's private railroad car, had not been invited to spend the night at a private house in Louisville. Mother was called on to entertain them because of her long-lost, and long-denied, connection with the Duchess, a connection Munda prized.

I was baffled by Mother's silence about the Duchess, who was, I found out much later, a distant cousin—although she does not appear in Caperton family genealogies. Munda had been openly fascinated by her, which perhaps explained Mother's reticence—she hated Munda's exuberant snobbery. But it seemed to me later that there was another reason for Mother's distaste—if that is what it was—for the rail-thin, elegantly gowned Southerner who had never been a belle. Wallis was said to have taken the young Edward in hand, curbing his passion for parties, making him "serious," even putting down persistent rumors about his sexual preference. She had, it seemed to me, formed him to be a king—but because Wallis was a commoner, the actor never found his role. Perhaps the inevitable comparisons made Mother uncomfortable, raising again the question of a strong woman's ambition and its effect on the vessel into which it is poured.

Mother's reservations were confirmed by the behavior of the Louisvillians who wanted to meet the so-called royal pair: the demand for invitations to dinner seemed extraordinary, and the frenzy to purchase new clothes and practice bows and curtsies astonished me.

Finally the pair arrived, and seemed to me small, withered—almost ordinary. The Duke sat down on one of the Judge's relics, an old velvet-upholstered sofa in the front hall, and rose to find himself covered with feathers. The aged material had split. Mother noticed with admiration that he was not in the least chagrined. Perhaps noblesse oblige also helped him to ignore the fact that one of the Louisville ladies, curtsying low before him, in her excitement peed on the floor.

Another curious incident remains from that visit: Father's oldest friend, Edie Callahan (who had been his chaperone on the bride-bringing trip from Greece), was not invited to the dinner. She came across the lawn that divided her small modern house from the Big House and peered in at the window, much amused by the antics displayed—as years earlier Father and Martha McKee had peered in a window in Asheville to laugh at the hated Grandma Vi.

In 1956, when Stevenson was defeated by Eisenhower, my parents' hurt was simple and serious. His defeat seemed to prove that a man of aristocratic background and intellectual pretensions was unacceptable to the American public. The same people who complained about the newspapers' liberal bias, who now even went so far as to call it "communistic," had defeated a potential "Great Man."

Yet the defeat did not come entirely as a surprise. After all, the Colonel had predicted that a Southerner would not be elected to national office until the 1960s; Stevenson was by temperament a Southerner, a man who did not question the answers provided by the past. The Judge, too, had been too much of a gentleman to engage in politics after his early grubbings in Kentucky. We were better than the people on whom we depended for votes and circulation.

23

"This morning my stepgrandmother, Aleen, died," I wrote that spring. "We won't be flying from here tomorrow to see the eastern colleges as planned. I'm so glad we're not going. For one thing, it will be escaping the eventual mold for a long while, for my choice has become so limited that I have already chained my future."

I did not know about the premarital agreement that had cut Aleen out of the Judge's estate. Anxieties about the amount of money still owed her rocked the family that spring. Only three hundred thousand of the million dollars the Judge had promised Aleen had been paid. Tension about the sum remaining perhaps accounted for the coldness I always sensed between the family and Aleen's son from her first marriage, the glamorous polo-playing Byron Hilliard.

The questions raised by Aleen's death were, once more, the questions of love and money. How much money had she been worth as the Judge's wife, the competent ambassadress who had run his social life in London? Was three hundred thousand enough—or too much? Had the Judge loved her, or did it matter? Aleen's daughter from her earlier marriage had died alone out West after Aleen went off to London. Was there a connection? These explosive issues were banked down at once, and their fire only glittered in my stepuncle's blue eyes.

I found solace from tension in the woods, and even tried to imagine "what would happen if I stayed several days in the woods completely alone."

I planned to leave Mother "a considerate note: 'I shall be home Thursday.' But now I know these woods are too close, too nervous. Now I have been planning a summer trip on one of those Mediterranean freighters which lounge from port to port, carrying eight or ten passengers. At night, when I don't care if sleep ever comes, I go through the details. But I know that if I do it on parents' money, I might as well be still attached to Mother's navel, their worn-out remonstrances would follow me all the way. I have to get away from here as soon as I'm educated and, please God, grown. If not, I know what will happen. I will stay on and on, pretending to support myself through some three-hour job got through Daddy's influence, until finally all channels of inspiration are fallen in, and waking one night in the middle of black terror, I force myself into love, and marry."

"Daddy came home today," I wrote in the spring of 1953, after Stevenson's Asian trip was over. "Just at that moment when Edie Callahan said 'I see him,' I was terribly afraid that he would be suddenly fat, or sick, afraid of seeing him kiss Mother, almost afraid that I would begin to scream and cry, and say, 'Why weren't you here before, when I needed you so badly?' But instead I only couldn't decide whether to run to him with Eleanor and Jonathan and Punch, his topknot full of red roses, or to stalk sedately along with Mother.

"He brought me a dress which is so close to a dream that I don't dare think about it too much, for how could a tangible thing be so beautiful? It is all silver and white.

"When Daddy kissed Mother, I hardly dared to look. Yet I know the way she stood leaning against him is exactly the way I lean against Dennis, and when I think that they will be doing it tonight, I want to know and yet I hate the forbidden knowledge."

My military school beau, Dennis, was back for spring vacation. He came for me almost every night in his parents' baby-blue Lincoln. The car was a torment to me; I had never ridden in such an ostentatious vehicle.

Early in June, I had to make a decision. "I have just rolled up my hair," I wrote that night, "having finished crying and making my speech for Mother. Dennis's ring is on my finger, cold and large and very unfamiliar.

"We came home [after a horse show]. Dennis put his arm around me, and I sat with my cheek on his rough jacket. I asked him to tell me what was on his mind. He said quietly, 'I want to ask you one thing. Will you wear my ring?' My mind was clear, I knew what I must say. I explained that I couldn't go steady, giving two valid reasons."

The reasons were so obvious I did not write them down. Now that I was older, Mother was more outspoken. She wanted me to go to the big dances which were given every winter and summer, to wear a crinoline-buoyed dress and pin a corsage over my breast. But my relationship to the "boys" who escorted me should be formal, confident, calm. They were unimportant as individuals, however important they might be as social functionaries. It would be a serious mistake to value one of them over the others, to sacrifice variety for the staleness of "going steady," a vulgar phrase she particularly deplored.

"He said, 'Will you wear my ring anyway?' I put my head down, and there was not even the smallest doubt quibbling in my mind. 'I'd love to,' and his ring, suddenly, was on my finger."

When I accepted Dennis's ring, I accepted his right to what were called "further intimacies."

"I used to think that many things were bad," I wrote that June, "but at least they were uncomplicated by a terrible measure of good . . ."

My sexual education had been limited to the facts in *The Stork Didn't Bring You,* with its emphasis on the lower forms, like bees. I did not really believe that boys were ravening beasts; they seemed frightened to me, confused—more likely to need leading than fending off. Besides, I was surrounded by a circle of fire as the daughter of power, and no one I knew would have dared to approach the flames.

"Parents are good watchdogs, but never sympathizers," I wrote as I began to stay out later in the evening with Dennis. "When I came in, Mother wisely scolded me for being late. I endlessly hear good-natured but galling criticisms of Dennis. I am in an entirely new experience, one which commands me to use every drop of wisdom when we are together."

Now that he officially belonged to me, Dennis seemed faded. I no longer wanted to become this boy who seemed shy, sensitive, overwhelmed by my attention. The male I longed to become was the violent, daring, cruel tease, the possessor of mythical power, not the kind young man who took me every evening to the movies. I could feel nothing at all for Dennis except a dreadful responsibility. After all, I had agreed to love him.

For the first time that summer I had a chance to work for pay, but it did not materialize. Instead, I worked as a volunteer in a Home for Incurables. "A spastic woman was my first task. She beat her hands so hard against the wall I was afraid she would hurt herself, yet I did not dare to comment. Sweat ran down her dark, wrinkled underarms, and she laughed hoarsely, showing heavily mended teeth. Yet above her writhing body her gray eyes were strangely calm and wise, almost as if they looked from some far-off vantage point at her miserable situation, and gave no pity. I held up pictures of her family, and she admired them; on seeing one of her husband, she made a long kissing noise. 'I love my Daddy . . .' "

These castoffs, buried for life in institutions where they received little treatment, seemed to me victims of a terrible injustice, which had left them maimed enough to need care but had not relieved them of consciousness. Sometimes in the shrewd eyes of these entombed women—"Mind you don't come here when you're old!" one of them warned me—I saw understanding of the condition we all shared. I remembered the woman I had met at a party, softly smiling, who had been lobotomized; I remembered tales of women who had been "put away" for a variety of eccentricities and infractions. I first heard women curse in that abominable Home, using words I had thought belonged to men.

Later I would wonder if Mary Lily had used "bad language," or if the second Mrs. Flagler had been in the habit of cursing. Father would comment on the fact, which I had also observed, that women in institutions used worse language than men. How did language finally explode out of the gilded net of rhetoric? Was it really the first and final sign of insanity when a woman said "damn"—or "fuck"? I was frightened by the obscenities I heard in the Home for Incurables, as later I would be frightened by the verbal violence of women inmates in a Massachusetts asylum. But I was also excited. This was the language my brothers used. It meant freedom: not the freedom of black Luke in his hand-me-down coat, now long gone into oblivion, but the freedom of the male heir in his element—a club, a bar, a speeding car—cursing the world he will dominate.

Dennis was still taking me out in the evening in the baby-blue Lincoln. I had never been able to tell him how much it embarrassed me. "I'm so terribly, terribly sad," I wrote one evening in July. "Barry drove up drunkenly behind us as we were sitting in the Lincoln in front of the Big House. He yelled and bumped into us. I had to leave Dennis before anything was satisfied or made sweet." The incident, or rather my failure to side with Dennis, killed our relationship, although it staggered on for a few more months.

"Tonight Dennis put his hand all the way down my dress, over my breast. If it had made me feel sensuous, the way clean sheets can, or the movement of his body against mine when we dance, I could soundly preach myself a sermon on giving rise to uncontrollable urges. But it was all so fruitless, just my rather small breast and his rather bored hand, each of us feeling that there ought to be some kind of huge thrill, like we once had in simple kisses.

"Dennis will go very quickly now, and there will be other things to wish on the star."

24

The songs played on the radio in 1953 brought back the memory of a brief summer romance: "Laura," the music from *The Band Wagon,* "Ebb Tide," "September Song." I was stronger than I had been before: "I have found my liberty. A year and a half of subtle entanglements, pretense, and a few granules of partnership is over."

The family's disconnectedness seemed a blessing now, because it protected my privacy.

Beyond high school commencement, my future was entirely vague. I was living on an allowance, in terms both of money and of my imagination; I had no idea where I was going.

"I rushed off downtown and spent the morning looking at things I couldn't afford, and forgetting the things I needed. The material beauty of things has a very high drawing power; some inanimate things are almost sensuous, like red velvet slippers, all embroidered, and fluffs of white nylon petticoats." I had no idea, and never asked, how I would afford to buy such luxuries, or even the necessities of life, once I was no longer on an allowance. Writing, I knew, did not make money. Serious writers did not expect to make more than three or four thousand dollars a year, and I did not think I would ever write a best-seller. The things I knew were special, secret.

The trip to visit colleges that had been canceled the previous spring was reinstated. Mother and I went to Bryn Mawr first. "Mother met me and we had a little dinner at the airport. In the mirror, we were so obviously from the same mold that it scared me terribly. Same cultured pearl necklaces and earrings, gloves, expressions, thoughts, everything stereotyped and carbon-copied from generation to generation. But there is a vast difference, under this reality, between us."

I went on: "In the train, there was a woman with pink plastic roses in her hair, such a welcome comparison to the low-slung, mousy college girls. The buildings here [at the college] are dark; we saw one girl in shorts squinting from the car light. This building is brown and yellow; we hauled our suitcases up two flights of stairs to a comfortable dormer room with the fire escape from the window. There is a feeling of objective depression here."

"Smith was huge, moneyed, and rather conventional. I felt the mold very clearly here, one it would be easy and unreprehensible to slip into; a hundred percent wool Bermuda shorts and knitting in a classroom full of giggles. Dress alike, girls, think alike, if you must think, and be sure you're married as quickly as is decently possible. The weird differences between the numerous dorm houses was wonderful, as well as the handsome girls in riding clothes and the echoing, rippling pool and the long, long list of courses to be chosen from, and the sunny rooms. But the place is full of niches." I did not know that Henrietta had spent a year at Smith, successfully avoiding niches.

Mother seemed irritated and silent during this trip, when, for the first time in years, we shared a room.

I wrote in my diary, "Tonight, sitting in complete and impenetrable silence with Mother in a little French restaurant, surrounded with half-drunk, immune college people, I felt again, or saw, that greyness of complete and terrible isolation that is neither past, nor present, but of all time. There was no hope of communicating with any living creature. In movies they picture castaways as the most terrified people in the world."

I sensed that Mother's time at Radcliffe had been enormously important to her, but I did not know how to ask her about it. Her life after graduation seemed to have obliterated her experience as a brilliant scholarship student. Perhaps she was silent with resentment as she watched me preparing to launch into what had once been her world. Perhaps she feared that I would learn at Radcliffe to avoid compromises.

Even when we visited Radcliffe together, she told me very little about her time there, and she did not seem to prefer it to the other women's colleges. Worth and Barry were both enrolled at Harvard, and their life made a greater impression on me than Mother's few memories. I lost, once again, the opportunity of making a connection with her.

More than thirty years later, I learned that Mother had worked after her graduation from college, in a publishing house in Boston. Three years had elapsed between her graduation and her marriage to the handsome young Kentuckian around whom she would make her life. I never knew what that experience had meant to her, or whether she had chosen to be independent for a while. I had seen wedding pictures, new-baby pictures, and pictures taken at sumptuous parties, but I had never seen a picture of

Mother during the time when she was working as an editorial assistant and living with a woman friend in a rented apartment.

No one talked about the decision I was facing, to maintain the fiction that no one particularly cared which college I chose. Worth found the charade amusing. "I didn't really get to talk to Sallie about which ones she liked," he wrote Nursie after our visit, "but I think it is between Bryn Mawr and Radcliffe. Don't tell her I said this, because for some reason no one is supposed to know what she thinks at all. She is supposed to have an absolutely free choice, I guess, though of course the fam wants her to come to Radcliffe."

The choice was not for Radcliffe or any other college, as far as I was concerned. The choice was for leaving home.

I knew that the chance to go away to college was the only escape from my endless dependency. But I had never lived away from home; I had never even gone to camp. I was peculiarly unsuited to collective living. I did not know how to "get along."

The fear of change, however, was less powerful than my sense of new possibilities. When I heard that I had been accepted at Radcliffe, I wrote, "The autumn is suddenly within reach; I feel as though I were about to be born."

Dissolution was in the air. The claustrophobic atmosphere of our childhood was about to lift and blow away. Worth and Barry went into the service as soon as they graduated from Harvard, Worth to enjoy a tour of duty in the Navy, Barry to grind himself down in the Marines. Afterwards they would both be groomed for the family business, Worth at newspapers in Minneapolis and San Francisco, Barry at CBS in New York. I knew nothing of these plans as I prepared to leave for college, but I felt that the family was loosening its hold.

My "real" life was so highly organized senior year that anything that broke my routine seemed dramatic. I wrote, "It happened tonight, one of those things that one thinks never happens to humans in your recognized sphere.

"Johnson came to get me at five-thirty. Tom, my blind date, seemed a nice, sincere sort of person. There were six of us in the car. Johnson's car is one of those old wrecks that is beloved and ratty and harmless. The funniest thing was that I have never felt in such a party mood.

"We were going up Zorn Avenue. I heard Johnson honk, and saw two close-set yellow lights on the right. I half saw them, rather, being wrapped in making an impression, half heard Johnson yell, and before I realized what was happening, a terrible crash that shattered the whole world, an immense folding-in of everything on top of me, and then silence and oblivion.

"In the stillness that followed so many sounds, out of the realization that I was still alive, 'Are they all dead?' There was a weight upon me, which I got out from under and stood up.

"Immediately I realized that Anne Moore was not there. With the necessity of finding her beating through the films of shock, I picked around the car for what seemed a long time, then saw a motionless bundle about twenty feet away on the grass. Next minute, Johnson was kneeling beside her. 'Anne! Anne! Speak!' And then cars were stopping, people circling around us, lights, confusion, women clutching my hand and obtruding their comfort, and in the midst of it all, Tom repeating, 'Sallie, Sallie,' with a little blood running into his collar. Then I began to cry, because Anne's face was silent with blood.

"The police were there, and put Anne in the car. She kept repeating, 'Don't tell my mother, promise me you won't tell my mother?' and 'Is there a scar?'

"I went to the hospital with her and the silent police. Whenever anyone looked me in the eyes I started to cry. And there was nothing wrong with me but a scraped nose and a cut lip. I sat in a dark room with Anne, she being groggy with novocaine.

"Anne went to have her face sewn up, alone, and I couldn't even sympathize, all I can realize is the poverty of human emotions, and the fact that had I died tonight, as I might have, I would never have lived at all."

Anne, who had once been my Hamlet, was scarred for life. Her beautiful, haunted face seemed after the surgery to have been sewn together like patches in a quilt.

I did not describe the way I had screamed at the news photographer from the *Courier-Journal* who had come to take a picture of my injured friend. It was the first time I had ever used the power of my name, and it frightened me. However, I had succeeded in preventing him from taking a picture of Anne as she lay bleeding on the grass.

During my last year at home, I had begun to avoid emotional entanglements, concentrating instead on schoolwork and writing. But it was not easy to "bank down the mammalian fires."

I connected celibacy with strength and purpose, and had since my convent days in Paris, believing that as a result of "this celibacy, or more likely as a result of growing toward the watery limits of my eventual character, I am more self-sufficient."

I rode my horse nearly every afternoon, connecting the secret risks I took, putting words on paper, with the risks of riding through the woods, forcing my skittish mare over streams and down banks.

As I approached the end of my life on the Place, I realized, "No one will ever know what riding has meant to me. I think it has been as vital a part of my education as all the thin hours I've spent in school, for it has been self-taught. I was given a horse, a saddle, a barn; with the first two, I plunged into quiet and far countries."

Although I was not aware of it, the first step toward the integration of the schools, which would convulse my world, took place that year when the Supreme Court outlawed segregated schools. There would be no local implementation of the order until, in 1956, the city school board dissolved itself and the county board adopted a desegregation plan that was widely hailed as a model. The real trouble would not come until I had been away from home for years.

The first tremors arrived with *Brown* v. *Board of Education* in 1954, although I was not aware of their source. For the first time in my life, I met a young black man who was theoretically my equal.

I went to a small gathering of local teenagers called "Youth Speaks Its Mind." A pleasant, well-dressed, confident young black man was in attendance. "This caused me to feel that democracy is, and that it ought to be. Also I realized that it is possible for me to fall in love with a Negro. That blank, hard statement almost frightens me. Could I really go to bed with him and, even more trying, wake up with him in the raw morning light? As easily as with anyone else."

In March, Mother told me that "Miss Henrietta has had a breakdown, has tried to commit suicide, and now is involved with a nightclub waiter. The facts are so brutal I cannot believe them, although I have never liked this aunt. I have never known why, or felt at all justified. Daddy has left for New York, and Mother told me the cause . . ."

Henrietta had become an infrequent visitor. The Bloomsbury beauty had turned into a stout, corseted matron with burst veins in her large red cheeks. Father continued to visit her in New York and to support her, for she had become a dependent, like all the rest.

Aunt Henrietta's tale, which had seemed a tragedy, ended in a comic vein. In spite of Father's remonstrances, she married the man who worked in an Asheville bar. He and his teenaged son moved into the comfortable house Aunt Henrietta had rented on the Connecticut shore. Mother said she was now pathetically grateful not to be Miss Bingham, and had her new initials stamped on everything she owned.

Like so many other family tales, this one came to an abrupt and bewildering end. In a few months Aunt Henrietta and her husband were separated and he was never heard from again. But she kept the use of her married name for the rest of her life. She moved into a small apartment in New York with a birdlike female companion.

Now that I know something about Aunt Henrietta's earlier life I realize that by marrying she had tried, one last time, to tempt and tease Father into playing the old family game. He was no longer alarmed by or even particularly interested in her changing women friends, some of whom she perhaps loved, but when she "took up" with the barkeep, Father was on hand at once. The class difference was important, of course, but the gender difference was paramount: a husband might demand money, compete for inheritance, file lawsuits if thwarted—while a woman lover, especially one out of the genteel Edwardian past, could be counted on to be grateful for handouts. Henrietta played the last card she held and it worked for a while: the family was in an uproar. But once the husband had vanished, Henrietta lost her ability to attract Father's attention.

At some point during those last years at home, I became aware of the shadow of another woman, although it was less distinct than the shadow cast by Aunt Henrietta.

Mother's sister Rose, the eldest of the siblings, had been responsible for Mother when she was small, according to Munda's system of making an older girl responsible for a younger one. Six years older than my mother, Rose had married John Wilson Brown III and had borne five children. The marriage had been difficult—Brown was said to drink—and Mother did not like the man who had taken her favorite sister. Although I never met Rose, her relationship with Mother had been so close that Mother had made her legal guardian of Eleanor and Jonathan for a while when they were very small.

Rose's divorce left her impoverished, and, according to family legend, only Mother's offer of support saved the children from being sent to an orphanage; the judge in Virginia who was deciding their fate supposedly called the Big House from the bench. Two of Rose's sons lived for a time with my Aunt Helena, and the daughters and their mother became entirely dependent on Mother's largesse.

They were very grateful for her support and tried to win her approval, but it was not forthcoming. However, when the eldest daughter, Austin, won a scholarship to Radcliffe, Mother offered to pay for her expenses, and the young woman went off to Cambridge, where she developed an interest in Slavic languages.

For two years, Austin did well in college. She was the kind of bright student Mother had been, but lacking Mother's determination to survive. Once Mother referred to her with compassion as a nearsighted bluestocking who bumped into the furniture on social occasions. The family did not like her to wear her glasses.

My grandmother Munda
(Helena Lefroy Caperton),
of Richmond, Virginia—
a spinner of tales and a
weaver of dreams.

The six "Caperton girls" (Mother and her sisters),
in a snapshot their brother, Arthur, carried in his wallet.

MY MOTHER AND HER SISTERS

Mary, 1920s.

Helena.

Harriette and her
dancing partner
Vernon Biddle, 1920s.

Rose, the first of the
"Caperton girls" to marry.

Sarah, who became
my godmother.

Mother disapproved of Austin's course of studies, which she did not believe would lead to a job. At the end of two years, she withdrew her financial support, and Austin dropped out of college. She went to work for the Voice of America.

After a few years, Austin became exhausted and discouraged; she wanted to go home for a vacation, and her superior at VOA asked her mother to let her return. By now Rose had remarried, and her husband was not eager to receive a stepdaughter on what might prove to be a long leave of absence. Austin's vacation was delayed.

She finally came home when her mother had gone into the hospital for an operation. Rose had been anesthetized by the time Austin arrived at the hospital, in a car driven by her brother. She insisted that she had to see her mother, right now, at once; no one understood her desperation. Frantic, she climbed out of the car and ran onto a railroad track, in front of a train.

Her VOA superiors said at the funeral that the kind of information Austin had been required to read had upset her. No one asked what kind of information it was. Rose's anger, like my mother's, was directed at the daughter who had survived. When Helena walked into her mother's bedroom, she realized from Rose's expression that she was disappointed, then outraged, that she was not Austin.

I did not hear the details of this death, but I felt that Austin had somehow deserved her fate. She was an awkward girl, like me, who had "something wrong with her eyes": she had to wear glasses, which spoiled her looks. Perhaps my clumsiness—which both Mother and Munda noted— and my glasses meant that I was like Austin: bright, maybe too bright, and not attractive enough to live.

Recognition raised my spirits that spring of 1954. Two stories I had submitted to *The Atlantic Monthly* high school writing contest pleased me, even though I did not win the prize, as I had the year before.

In June, I graduated with the rest of my class, wearing a long white dress and carrying a sheaf of sweetheart roses. As each graduate swam down the aisle to the violin's wailing, parents and relatives and boyfriends craned for a view. At the steps to the stage, each girl was handed up by a father, to be married in a crowd, it seemed, to an invisible groom. For many of us, I imagine, the "real thing" when it came seemed an imitation. On commencement day, we were brides in a bunch, spared the sense of enclosure which would darken our weddings. The boys sitting in the audience might take us to the prom that night, but we were all going on to college in other states; there was no entrapment in those long white dresses.

The intimacy of those nine years when we were all striving together, hiding our real aims and desires, does not penetrate the innocuous charm of my high school yearbook. There we are smiling, lipsticked, in strapless dresses, playing Scrabble with boyfriends. Our short, thick white socks and long skirts date us. Girls of the fifties, we flew apart as soon as we graduated. I seldom saw the others again.

25

"For a time I am living like a belle," I wrote in June.

I was beginning to go out in the evening, with boys I'd known for years but who had never paid attention to me before, and with an occasional maverick.

"Socially, I am suddenly a success . . ."

To be "a success" gave me a new view of life. Why I was accepted so suddenly remained unclear, but I was not eager to question my good luck. To swing from boy to boy on the dance floor, to be called to the telephone from deep sleep the following morning, to spend hours ironing dresses and washing out stockings—that was a life I had never imagined.

One of the young men who were taking me out revealed "the anti-Semitism in my own grain." I was embarrassed when he took me to the Jewish country club, so like its Gentile version I did not realize until afterwards why I had never been there before. "I kissed him," I wrote later that night, "telling myself that it was not because I feared he would otherwise think I did not want to kiss a Jew."

Degrees of difference existed among the young people I knew, subtle shadings I was only beginning to understand. Certain men were "gents," according to Mother, even though they wore tweeds polished from long use and drove shabby cars. Mother had little interest in the newly rich whose fortunes were derived from industries like coal. However, the scions of the bourbon families were different, and even tobacco heirs could be tolerated. Coal was ignorance; it was the strikers in eastern Kentucky who rolled boulders down on scabs. The strikers' wives were gross animals who smothered their numerous infants by rolling over on them in bed, according to the family prejudice.

Tobacco and whiskey, by contrast, were the entertainments of the upper class. In the 1950s, no one had yet connected smoking with lung cancer, and the only prohibition against cigarettes concerned young girls:

it was not considered ladylike to smoke in public, although many girls and women smoked in private.

Whiskey had already proved its connection with death. Every summer another young man, returning home from a debutante party, crashed into a bridge or a wall on River Road. Every summer the grown-ups shook their heads and murmured something about the problems of drink. But black waiters in Louisville's private clubs continued to serve imperious young men who shouted at the "boy" to bring them more. These young men had their fathers' example, and sometimes their mothers', although women tended to sip sherry in private. Not until the first lawsuits were brought in the late 1980s, lawsuits that threatened private clubs and hosts as well as the distillers, did the Louisville upper class begin to wonder about the price of our prime industry.

By then liquor was the foundation stone of that little world. Many of the rural Kentucky counties were "dry," controlled by Baptists. The sophisticated Episcopalians who were poised at the peak of Louisville society wanted nothing to do with that. Liquor and cigarettes, both of which I had already learned to avoid, remained the theme of upper-class life, and the big breweries and cigarette factories which crouched over the black West End were castles that did not need defense.

That summer I was staying out late nearly every evening, and Mother grew alarmed. I did not understand that she was trying to protect me from mistakes which would foreclose on my future. Although I was still a virgin, I was pushing the established limits further each evening. Yet I knew nothing about birth control. Pregnancy was a risk, perhaps the most threatening risk I could imagine, but it was far more frightening to imagine speaking to Mother about what was euphemistically called "protection," and I did not know how to go about finding a doctor on my own. To protect myself would have meant deciding to "go all the way," and I had no ability to make that decision. The "act" if it happened would have to be semi-conscious, unplanned.

This was the era when young girls passed out at parties and woke to find they had been raped by strangers. We did not, we could not protect ourselves in any way from the young men who pursued us without coming to a conscious understanding of our ambivalent feelings. To be admired, after all, was our highest goal, and had been so since we were infants, and we were admired most when we were most compliant. Girls trained to obey eventually obey everyone, even young men whose acts threaten their future.

That summer brought my first act of open rebellion. One night, "I told Mother good night, went back to the kitchen on the pretense of eating, crept down to the basement barefooted, and let myself out the back door. That was the best part, skipping free under a high, starred heaven, without the weary weight of Nathan. I met him under an oak; he was scared. We went over to the amphitheater.

"Finally I made him leave and walked back around the side of the house. Looking up at the second story I saw Mother's head silhouetted in the window, looking out. It was *The Turn of the Screw,* her watching me, silent and motionless and entirely alien. I let myself in and met her at the top of the darkened stairs. She was too even-tempered, and I could only agree with her."

The affection was not made of pasteboard, and it remained, complicating my life when we went to spend a month at a resort in Maine. Nathan soon wrote that he was planning to drive up to visit me, and I wrote him that I "almost fainted (with pleasure) at the breakfast table thinking that you would be able to drive all these thousands of miles to see me. I haven't had a chance to tell my parents yet, but there won't be any trouble from that direction."

I was wrong. Mother and Father told me that a Jewish visitor would never be permitted at our hotel.

"I've been trying to think of a decent way to break this news to you," I wrote Nathan the next day, "and have decided that the best way, in such a horrible situation, is to tell the truth, as I believe you would like me to do. I burn with shame to have to tell you that the owner of this hotel is violently anti-Semitic, and has said that no Jew will ever set foot on this damned piece of ground."

It did not occur to me to question my parents' pronouncement, or to wonder why they accepted the rules (if in fact these were the rules) of the resort.

Years later Nathan told me that anti-Semitism had been so well disguised in the Louisville of our childhood that he had never been aware of it. Overhearing his parents talking about avoiding certain places or situations had left him entirely baffled.

But I wondered; racism lay at the core of our lives, a racism so silent and pervasive that to an outsider it would not have seemed to exist. Jokes revealed it. The boys I knew used to pretend to run up scores based on the people they hit with their cars. Hitting a Jew meant scoring a certain number of points, a "nigger" counted for even more, but the highest score was reserved for pregnant women. This meant, I decided, that the jackpot would go to the boy who ran over a black Jewish woman who was pregnant. In that unlikely event, it all could be extinguished at once: the darkness that was part of blackness, part of Jewishness, and part of female nature.

That August in Maine, I took care of Eleanor for the last time. At eight, she was an undemanding companion. I typed short stories all evening while our parents went out to dinner parties and supervised Eleanor on the beach during the day, but I found the expensive resort "too stifling, too safe. I am barred from sailing, which makes it seem the only worthwhile pastime. I hate these brushed-up, grinning girls, too weak to get out on their own, as their brothers have done, but existing vapidly in these maleless haunts. This must be the last family vacation for me."

Back home, I danced "snakewise in the moonlight."

Nathan disappeared from my life as I began spending time with Kurt. He came to me from another life, a life I could hardly imagine.

Kurt had dropped out of college and was supporting himself by driving a cab; he was well read, articulate, and belligerent. He frightened me with his accurate assessment of the hypocrisy with which I was surrounded. He told me my parents disliked him because he was a Jew.

When I discovered that "Kurt wants me," I did not stop to wonder whether I wanted him. Mother had often said that no man would marry a girl who had been "used" by another man, but she had also taught me, by example, the importance of self-sacrifice. Kurt wanted me as passionately as other men wanted money and achievement and sons and good hot dinners. I had been trained to provide.

Kurt also offered me a less restricted life. "We went to the racetrack, and betted and cheered." We also went to a concert given by black musicians, taking our butler along as a guide.

Mother had remarked, "You're not in love with that boy," but had otherwise restricted herself to hard-eyed observing. Father seemed preoccupied, far away. Alone with the dilemma of my need for love, I tried in vain "to destroy all softness in my body, as well as in my mind. I am driven to run half miles, to play tennis in this cruel climate, to ride through these too luscious woods, until I am steaming like a pursued animal. And at night, I wake up dripping, halfway in a frightening dream of being with Kurt."

The last weeks of that last summer were wrapped in ominous silence. I was sleeping most of the day and out most of the night; the few hours left were devoted, as usual, to reading and writing, but my work now had no relation to what was happening. The link was broken.

One night when I came home with Kurt, I found a note on the front door: "Call under my window. Mother." We laughed and called. She came down and the minute I saw her face it was as if "I were a whimpering child again, seeing her unbuckle her belt." She ordered me off to bed.

The following evening "I ate a strained dinner with my loving parents. Afterwards they called me to their room; Eleanor followed and Daddy thrust her out as from an unclean place, locking the door. They sat facing me. First, horrible rumors concerning Kurt and me . . . Then they began.

Daddy, shocked and hurt, kept pleading that I think of my family and my future; Mother began by warning me that my future, highly desirable husband would not want me shopworn, and that my reputation was ruining her name. When I refused to accept her ten-commandment-blind morality, saying I had to find out for myself, she went into a harangue surpassing all others for brutality and selfishness, ending up by calling me a bitch in heat . . . I said nothing, I thought nothing, except that I must find out for myself, that I must see Kurt. Daddy put his hand on my shoulder with affection and pity, and I left, too far gone to cry."

Finally, and for the first time, Father took control of the situation.

"Daddy called Kurt this morning to come talk to him. I went downtown with Kurt, very clean in coat and tie, the seducer going to justice. But that's not just—I believe Daddy has my welfare at heart, as well as the family name. While Kurt was in conference, I shopped, miserable with anxiety, for Kurt has said he will not go against Daddy's command to stay away from me.

"Walking back I met Kurt with a root beer in his hand and collar open. He was a little tired. After the usual innuendoes Daddy had given him three alternatives. 1. Lay off all 'sexual' things—I don't know exactly what he means. 2. Stop seeing me. 3. Be chaperoned. All three would strike a death blow to our relationship."

Kurt agreed to keep everything "aboveboard" and to bring me home every night at one o'clock. He was only slightly intimidated by his appointment with the owner of the state's only newspapers, its leading citizen, and one of its few millionaires, presiding over our future from behind a big desk.

The agreement lasted several days.

Everything else was controllable. Everyone else could be soothed, threatened, or bought. But an angry young man finds through sheer persistence the one opening in the wall: the young girl who longs to be loved. I knew it was what I represented, rather than what I was, which my parents were determined to protect.

The outcome was inevitable, which frightened me but did not destroy the pleasure of what I called "the first feast of adulthood."

"Today I lost my virginity. I have not lost it, I have given a piece of myself for a piece of Kurt, I have fulfilled my love. This is how it happened. We drove up to Cincinnati to see Cinerama, both of us more excited than we could justify. I felt jealous of Kurt's eyes, his very enjoyment of the movie. Afterwards we walked rather somberly around Cincinnati. The alien aspect of so many strangers made us lonely, and we were both tired. Kurt said, 'I want to sleep with you,' and since we were sitting under the fountain reading a newspaper, I laughed, but I knew his words were only an echo of the premonition I had had early this morning when I put on a pair of pink pants.

"The next time he said it I assented, and we disentangled ourselves from the city, still somber and silent. I was nervous, not of the act, but of the circumstances surrounding it—motel superintendents, policemen, and so forth.

"We turned in at a long, low motel, and Kurt went into the office. I sat powdering, powdering my face, assuming the harsh mask of a dull wife; Kurt came back and the old colored man showed us to our room, unleering. There were two little boys in front, and I suddenly started talking to them with an adult's self-assurance; it perplexed me to feel so old. In the shaded, air-cooled room we undressed casually, and the radio played 'These Foolish Things.' "

A day later, sex seemed less important than "riding with Kurt through the slate-colored moonlight, cantering through such definite shade and clearing, or sitting afterwards in the kitchen while Barry, handsome, detached Barry with surgeon's hands, cleans a tiny dove, and two of his friends drink their after-party milk.

"Romance dwindles a little at such close quarters. I feel no guilt for what I did tonight in a ploughed field under a full moon, with the air congealing on my bare sides and the horses chomping nearby. It is a simple act, and expressive of the way I feel. My only dread is purely biological. I cannot face pregnancy. Sometimes in the mornings I wake up loaded with this dread." Kurt and I did not discuss birth control. I left matters entirely in his hands.

Sex as I understood it was entirely male, a question of relief and primitive satisfaction that had and could have no results. I had separated from my biological destiny, which had always felt like death. Taking care to avoid pregnancy meant accepting that destiny. I preferred to pretend that I was as free as Kurt, who was driven off the country club tennis courts because he was Jewish but who could swing from the chandelier in his parents' front hall and listen to them making love.

"And so ends summer, and childhood. I should feel inclined towards melancholia—this is such a bleak, definite ending—but there is no time or space for anything but hope."

On September 19, I wrote, "I left home for college. Kurt came and the lipstick remained on his lip the rest of the time I saw him. He laughed at my hat and my sadness . . . The hot air tore at me while he said that saying goodbye to things so emotionally is childish, since there are no permanent departures. He said I'd always come home again.

"At the train station there were many people I knew and I could hardly talk to Kurt. The train came. 'No passionate kisses,' he smiled, and I got aboard with the tears forcing themselves up. From the window I barely saw him waving and smiling from a life grown suddenly very empty."

Father accompanied me on the overnight train to New York, a rare treat that I considered an honor.

After dinner he told me with sadness and concern that "a reporter had seen us going to that motel. He asked me if there was a chance of pregnancy." He was prepared to take me to an abortionist in New York.

Now I understood why he had accompanied me. I also understood something about the function of reporters.

I managed to tell him that I was not pregnant, my breath rasping my throat. Then I retreated to my berth, too stunned to cry.

When Kurt came later in the fall to visit me at Radcliffe, I was horrified. Looking down at him from my dormitory window, I imagined that he had come to drag me back. I was determined to escape, I was escaping, but he was mired in Kentucky. I would never go back. The conversation on the train had revealed the extent of Father's power, which I had only guessed at before. It was the power of his world. There were no secrets there, no grimy little motels of the mind where a young woman could hide. Father, like most of the men he knew, had at hand the tools of dominance: friends, spies and reporters (the definitions overlapped), money and resolve, principles and principal, a communications network and a golden web of moral constraints from which I knew I would never escape.

Perhaps Father was remembering the fears that had swirled around Henrietta in 1916, when she had drifted through the Mary Lily scandal, moving from house to house, relative to relative, lighting most often at the Asheville school. There had been a rumor of a pregnancy, of a child hastily given away—but all of that was rewritten or wiped out. Perhaps it had never happened—no one could say. In any event, nothing had prevented Henrietta from enrolling at Smith, where, for a year, she had seemed to be safe.

The only safety for me lay in distance, measured in inches and then in miles. Once I had longed to kiss each inch of beautiful Kentucky farmland that separated the Place from Louisville. Now I longed to kiss each inch of railroad track between Kentucky and Massachusetts.

Kurt escaped, too, in time, as did Nathan. Other people I knew learned by sheer force of personality to break out of the net. But most, lions and mice together, lay down under the mesh. I needed twenty-three years to grow the necessary independence, and even then I knew I was risking my life when I went back to Kentucky.

Interlude

I spent my four years at Radcliffe gradually wearing away the ties that bound me to Kentucky. I also found my profession and realized at the same time that, as a writer, I would never be able to pay my way. I did not know about the trust funds, established by the Judge and by Father, which would support us for life.

Freshman year, 1954, was very difficult for me; I had never been away from home before, and I felt nearly as frightened as the six-year-old girl who had walked home in the dark rather than spend the night with a friend.

The big brick dormitory in Cambridge seemed comfortable to the other girls, most of whom were from the Northeast and had been to boarding school, but I was disturbed by the noise, the lack of privacy—even though I had a single room—the bitter New England cold, and the presence of Harvard boys, who outnumbered us fifteen to one.

I was also tormented by shyness and found it almost impossible to ask for help. On my first night in the dormitory, I went to bed at nightfall because I could not bring myself to ask for a light bulb.

My shyness made it difficult for me to speak in class, especially because my accent caused a ripple of amusement. Most of my classes were large lectures, but occasionally I would be assigned to a "section" where students were expected to participate. In one of these, a humanities course, the young instructor grew angry at my silence. Finally he made me climb up on the podium, sit at his desk, and "teach" the class—an experience that reduced me to tears. I had never been so bitterly humiliated, and I had to drive myself remorselessly to return to that class.

Those were the years when parietal rules still governed the dormitories at Harvard and Radcliffe, and we were only allowed to entertain boys in doorless sitting rooms on the ground floor. The Harvard boys surged in every evening, and I found myself overwhelmed by their attentions. Many of them seemed beguiled by my stories, and all of them wanted mothering.

I was confused and desperate as I tried to sort out their competing demands, and only my escapes on a bicycle to the countryside kept me sane. There were no guidelines; I had no friends; and the college administrators were distant figures.

After freshman year, I began to take writing classes and to publish regularly in the Harvard literary magazine, *The Advocate.* For the first time, I had an audience, both in writing class and in the readers of the magazine, and I was amazed and delighted to find that people responded to what had been, until then, secret stories. Classes with Albert Guérard and John Hawkes and Archibald MacLeish taught me little more than this: that some people seemed to want to hear what I had to say. I felt that I had nothing to learn from the awe-inspiring men who led these gatherings, or from the other Harvard professors, all men, and all, it seemed to me, remote, mysterious, and impressive.

At first I did not make many friends, but when I moved into a smaller, off-campus house I began to enjoy observing the lively goings-on of women who would become important friends. I realized that not everyone was as frightened and obedient as I had been as a freshman from the decent South, and that realization freed me to write about some of the central aspects of our lives as fifties coeds.

One of my stories, "Winter Term," described in depressing detail the dependency of a young college couple trapped in a clandestine, unhappy affair. What interested me was not the furtive sex but the emotional dependency that resulted. When the story was published in *The Advocate,* Harvard students called me on the telephone to solicit dates, which shamed me. I was as confused as they were about the difference between fact and fiction.

One of the Radcliffe deans was even more alarmed. She called me into her office; it was the first and the last time I saw a member of that hierarchy. My story was threatening alumnae giving, she said, because Radcliffe benefactors did not want to know about the students' sexual lives.

I had never intended to hurt the college that was teaching me what I wanted to do in life—if inadvertently. I accepted the dean's suggestions and deleted references to Cambridge in the story before it was published in *Mademoiselle.*

At home for vacations, I realized that the magic of the Place was wearing off at last. I had another world. It was a world I was more and more eager to reenter as the four years quickly passed.

But I knew I could not support myself after graduation, and by senior year this was a vivid preoccupation. Father offered to send me to London for a year, but I did not want to resume my dependency on his largesse. Meanwhile I had fallen in love with the gentle editor of *The Advocate,* and was somewhat surprised to find that his family matched my own family's

Sallie at nineteen.
A photograph by
Hal Phyfe, 1956.

Worth in his
early twenties.

Jonathan at
about eighteen.

Eleanor in the early 1980s.

sophistication and wealth. Marriage to a man who understood my ambition would allow me a measure of independence from Kentucky while I began my first novel. An editor at Houghton Mifflin had already expressed interest in reading it.

I graduated magna cum laude in 1958 and began my grown-up life shortly thereafter as a young writer, married and working hard, in Boston.

I believed I would never go home again.

The Middle Passage

Already it was evident from place to place, time to time, and setting to setting, the nature of our struggle was to be transformed and the questions reshaped. So it was on the ocean, as we moved further from the black shores into the agonies of the middle passage.

Vincent Harding, *There Is a River: The Black Struggle for Freedom in America*

26

During the 1960s and 1970s, I returned to the Place for brief visits, bringing home as the years passed two husbands and three sons. The little boys learned the geography of my childhood: the Back Woods, now surrounded by subdivisions, the wide marble terraces at the Big House, the shining floors, even the odd pastel chairs that covered the toilets, causing problems for children and inebriated guests.

Our stays were brief, but before leaving I would feel again the confinement of life on the Place. When my oldest son, Barry, hunted for Easter eggs on the terrace, I recognized the tension in the air: only one of the grandchildren would find the golden egg and win the prize money. When my second son, Chris, cried at a public occasion and I hurried him upstairs, I remembered what it felt like to "create a commotion," unforgivable no matter how young the child or how understandable the cause. When my youngest son, Will, asked his grandfather how much his new car had cost, I recognized the paralyzing silence that had always greeted questions about money. My three sons loved the magic of the Place and their kind and attentive relatives, but I was always in a hurry to leave.

On the surface, nothing seemed to change. The black servants grew old and feeble, but the grass was still smooth, the silver was still shined, and when I caught sight of myself in the gold-framed mirror in the front hall, I still looked like a child.

Death broke the pattern.

Jonathan, my youngest brother, dropped out of Harvard in the summer of 1963, after his junior year. He was twenty-one.

When he was at Harvard, I was living in Boston, and I saw a good deal of him. I was aware of strange currents in his life. His roommate was a close friend from Louisville, a brilliant, erratic boy who seemed to outshine Jonathan without trying. Jonathan was very intelligent, yet the promise he had shown at the boys' school in Louisville and later at boarding school in Massachusetts seemed to erode during his three years at Harvard.

Leaving Harvard, Jonathan told our parents, meant escape from an intense relationship with his roommate and with a Radcliffe student whom he had named after a character in a children's story.

Father was disturbed by Jonathan's decision to leave without graduating. In a long letter written in the summer of 1963, he urged Jonathan to join the Peace Corps or even the armed services, reminding him that he would no longer be exempt from the draft once he had stopped being a full-time student. But Jonathan had made up his mind during that summer's trip to Europe, from which he had returned wearing part of a suit of armor.

Both of our parents served as trustees and overseers and held places on visiting committees, which meant that they frequently appeared in Cambridge, taking their various children out to dinner or visiting class. Harvard also reflected in a larger mirror the values of the Place: self-restraint, hard work, ambition, success, patronage, as well as those values' qualifiers: emotional disturbance, volatility, avoidance, snobbery, and coercion.

Jonathan told me that he did not know how he would support himself out of college. Since he was about to turn twenty-one, I told him that the income from his trust fund might soon be available. I did not understand the factors that controlled the release of income from the trusts set up by Father and the Judge for our eventual benefit. It appeared likely to me that when Jonathan came of age legally he would come of age in the eyes of his trustees, who were Father and various colleagues from the corporations and their law firm. After all, I had begun to receive dividends when I married, at twenty-one. Jonathan was excited at the prospect of having money of his own, for the first time, and at once planned to go to Europe and perhaps spend a year there. However, when he telephoned Father, he was told that the trust fund income would not be available until he was either thirty years old or married—"too late," as he noted in his diary. He had made up his mind to leave college, but because he had no income, he went back to the Place rather than going abroad.

Jonathan and I shared a sense of confusion about our finances. Nothing was clear yet nothing could be questioned. In my case, checks arrived in the mail from time to time which represented quarterly dividends.

The arrival of the checks depended on our parents' secret assessment of our maturity. Fearful of the power of money, especially of the way it can buy independence, the trustees could withhold dividends, plowing them back into the trust, when they felt that their children were "out of hand." Getting married proved that we were in hand, at least for a while. There was hardly any other way to prove it.

I did not understand for many years the elaborate system of trusts, like an underwater mountain range, which had been piled up years before to avoid paying estate taxes. Little thought had been given to the effect on the next generation. There was an unspoken assumption that money should be passed along, like jewelry and antique furniture, yet underlying that facile assumption was a great anxiety about money and its mystifying uses, money and its perverse connection with love.

The Judge had begun the mountain range when he established Trust Number Nine—it sounded like a railroad engine, I thought—which had accumulated a large quantity of stock in the three corporations. The income from Number Nine went to our parents during their lifetimes, and the corpus would be distributed to their children, or their children's heirs, when both parents had died. That trust alone would eventually make each of us a millionaire several times over; but we did not know that.

Father had set up three smaller trusts on the same principle: his children would have the benefit of the income during their lifetimes, and the principal would go to our children after our deaths, making our children, as well, millionaires several times over. That decision was made before any of us were old enough to wonder whether we wanted our unborn children to become millionaires.

The primary purpose of the mountain range was to wall off the Internal Revenue Service, a highly acceptable practice in the world of the very rich. Death taxes were often mentioned by the family's lawyers as a threat to our way of life. The four trusts ensured that the estate that came to the Judge after Mary Lily's death, and which had been multiplied many times over, would remain in the family. Although we were taught that our obligations were large toward those less fortunate, we were never taught to question this accumulated fortune.

The mountain range of trusts lay in that deep underwater world where the big fish swam: lawyers and accountants who understood the territory but had little incentive to share their secret information. It would be many years before the beneficiaries of this mountain range understood that it existed, and many more years before I, at least, began to question inherited wealth. The mountain range walled us off from more than poverty.

Jonathan went back to the Place for good in the summer of 1963, after his trip to Europe. Father wrote in a letter that he was worried by his "nihilistic mood." Father knew it had a great deal to do with lovers and friends.

Jonathan's earlier connection with a little group of boys had been essential to him; in a photograph album, proudly printed with his name, he had collected snapshots of these boys making airplane models, setting up toy soldiers, digging tunnels at camp, dressing up as "the horrible hag" or "the ghost of Mr. Ballard"—the flour baron who was said to roam the Big House. As a child, Jonathan had lived at his own pace, in his own time, charmed and caught by the uses of his imagination. Even more than had been the case when I was young, his world was the magic world of the Place.

At Harvard, Jonathan was exposed for the first time to women students who were intellectually and socially his equals. At home and at boarding school, women had been mothers and sisters, nurses and maids. Although Jonathan had had several romantic friendships with young girls in Louisville, he could count on Mother to break up a tryst on the back porch. At college there was no such protection.

His relationship with the Radcliffe student he called Pooh soon began to overwhelm him. A shock of some kind shook Jonathan's faith in her. A few months later, he began to avoid Pooh. Jonathan believed his love for her was a bad habit that he needed to break.

Nearly every month that last spring in Cambridge, Jonathan had an impulsive overnight fling with an unexpected visitor, often a young girl from Louisville. It was the early sixties, and girls were behaving with a freedom which Jonathan would never have seen in the Big House. He was not ready to accept that freedom, at least not in the case of women. He was tormented by jealousy, especially when Pooh went out with other men. He did not see the connection between her flirtations and his overnight guests. Jealousy devoured his peace of mind.

Now and then a course would arouse his interest briefly and intensely. He became excited while listening to a Beethoven record, and believed that he could write music. He sketched an idea for the development of the poet as a sort of symphonic poem. But he also said that women plagued him more and more, and he received a C in his introductory music course.

B. F. Skinner's course on human development fascinated Jonathan during his last spring at Harvard. He went with classmates to visit Metropolitan State Hospital, outside of Boston; he found it enormous and depressing, and was surprised to hear that it was said to be one of the best in the country. He noted that perhaps sanity was worth it after all.

At the hospital, he observed experiments with patients using Skinner's Black Box. Closed up inside the boxes, the patients were tested on a schedule, and the timing of their reflexes served to determine their diagnosis: psychotics were slower to respond than other patients, for example.

Perhaps Jonathan found this approach to mental illness reassuring: if people were broken, they could be fixed by being put into boxes, like the broken typewriters which were cased up and taken into town to be repaired at the *Courier-Journal.* However, this logical, optimistic approach must have seemed remote as violent dreams began to torment him.

Both Worth and Jonathan, along with their classmates, were affected by the fads of the 1950s and the 1960s as they were promulgated at Harvard. For Worth, it was Timothy Leary's experiments with LSD, for which he had volunteered to serve as a guinea pig. Jonathan was introduced to the Black Box.

Harvard supported both Leary and Skinner as part of its commitment to the free discussion of ideas, much as the newspapers Harvard alumni own, write, edit, and read support freedom of speech. The question, of course, is: whose speech? Newspapers are not *in loco parentis,* whereas the great universities which house the children of privilege are, because of the peculiar immaturity of their students.

The phrase *in loco parentis,* or "in the place of parents," was given force in 1913 in a Kentucky lawsuit that judged that colleges had an obligation to nurture their students morally and intellectually as well as physically by shielding them from destructive influences. The philosophy was largely abandoned after the Second World War, when returning vets made it seem ridiculous; the turmoil of the sixties swept the last vestiges away. During that period no one addressed the vulnerability of young people who have always been protected, or the special obligations of the great universities which educate them and profit from them.

Not knowing how to change a car tire or a typewriter ribbon may seem a trivial matter to an august university. But the children of the rich who have never learned to deal with daily life are as handicapped as the children of the poor, who are sometimes taught in public schools or in the Army how to open a checking account or apply for a loan. Harvard undergraduates, like their counterparts at other Ivy League universities, may seem sophisticated by comparison, but it is a sophistication that depends on a retinue: servants, lawyers and accountants, psychologists, tutors, and advisers of all kinds. Harvard supplies no retinue. It assumes its students can survive alone.

When Jonathan decided to leave college, Father made an appointment for him with Dr. Dana Farnsworth, then Harvard's senior staff psychiatrist. Jonathan seemed concerned about what Father might have told the doctor. Dr. Farnsworth told Jonathan that Harvard was as good a place to flounder around in as any. The issue was treated simply as a question of whether or not to leave Harvard. All other issues were subsidiary.

Jonathan continued to see Pooh during his last spring at college, but he broke with her finally after she left a party with another young man. Jonathan said that he spat all the way down the stairs after seeing her French-kiss his rival. His revulsion reappeared after another young woman spent the night in his room: he opened all the windows to get rid of what he called her god-awful perfume.

Shortly after breaking up with Pooh, Jonathan descended into the pit.

While writing a paper for his English class, he said, he became so involved that he became violently depressed, to such a degree that he felt he wanted to kill someone. From 1 to 3 o'clock he could do nothing but imagine getting into a bloody fight over her with somebody, and breaking his brain out with a chair. All the time he was so filled with adrenaline that he could not stay still, and shivered with nervous excitement. He didn't remember being so totally homicidally depressed since the initial shock in the fall. He felt that if such a mood persisted, he might become dangerously ill.

He did not ask for help. Skinner's Black Boxes were for the patients at the public mental hospital, and Dr. Farnsworth was Father's friend.

There was nowhere else to turn. To the degree that Harvard is like a family—and that is to a very slight degree, for most undergraduates—it is like the cold, denying, unappeasable family of the very rich. I had noticed as an undergraduate ten years earlier that no human touch was available unless I went to the infirmary, no consolation, advice, or ready ear. My only visit with a member of the administration resulted in a reprimand, and I rarely saw a professor outside of his classroom. For Jonathan it was the same. Yet as Harvard became coeducational, it also became a crucible for young men like Jonathan who were raised in an unequal society.

The number of black students at Harvard in the 1960s was small, and Jonathan could have spent four years without encountering them. The number of Jews was likewise controlled by the use of secret quotas. On the faculty, women were and still are a tiny minority, seldom offered tenure. But the number of women undergraduates was growing all the time; it is now approaching fifty percent. Even in Jonathan's era, there were too many women in Harvard classrooms to be ignored.

Their presence, and their obvious confidence and ability, led to a flare-up of hostility on the part of some professors and students, like the hostility which followed the appearance of the New Woman at the turn of the century. Radcliffe undergraduates were the subjects of cruel jokes, and Harvard students believed or pretended to believe that these young women were beneath their contempt.

For Worth, that atmosphere was entirely sympathetic. He urged Barry and Jonathan to devour "a piece of ass" whenever a woman seemed to be sexually available. The expression was used as a matter of course by all three of my brothers.

At Radcliffe, however, the meat was walking around and talking. Jonathan said that two Radcliffe students brought him a raw piece of beef and grilled it over an improvised fire in his dormitory room—the piece of ass he said he wanted.

Liquor and drugs provided him with some relief. He often went to bed drunk, and the nights he spent with flitting girls were always fueled by alcohol. Drugs were available as a matter of course. Jonathan described parties where Radcliffe girls sat weeping and disoriented from the effects of various pills and potions.

One evening, after having dinner with our parents at a restaurant in Boston, Jonathan described how a friend brought the Freon air horn from his boat. The gas was mixed with ether and they had a marvelous time inhaling it.

He worried about his drinking and felt that he really knew nothing about himself. He described leaving Harvard as a choice between his room-mate and nothing.

This caustic and lively young man did not share Jonathan's ravaging uncertainties. He reminded me of the bright bachelors who often visited the Big House, naval officers, journalists, or theater directors who had avoided the limitations of matrimony. Both our parents enjoyed single men, who were considered the staple of amusing dinner parties—they gave their all to entertain. Their homosexuality was accepted as a matter of course: men were usually more attractive than women, and they shared their most important experiences in the military or at boarding schools. But homosexuality could never be discussed: it was another open secret.

That spring Jonathan struck on the region where, as Louise Bogan says, we are either keel or reef. Our parents disapproved of all open sexual behavior except what necessarily takes place in the marriage bed to produce heirs. Under this prudery lay a lurid zone where fantasies reigned, where young men's real or imagined exploits were the stuff of legend, elaborated and admired, especially the cunning required to seduce virgins and escape the unpleasant consequences.

Our parents supported the hoary tradition that values male sexual aggression to the point of rape while insisting on female abstinence. The connection between ruthlessness in business and ruthlessness in bed was too obvious to need mentioning. As a small boy, Jonathan had escaped this pattern of expectation: small boys and all females were exempt. Now that he was officially an adult male, however, he must enter the lists. His ability to seduce women would provide the first proof of his ability to succeed in the world. But he had been raised by women, by Mother and Nursie and all the mild little governesses; he had been placed by birth not between his brothers but between Eleanor and me. He could not quite convince himself that young women were pieces of meat.

Worth had shown him the way with drunken exhibits of male bravado. Jonathan did not have the heart to imitate him. Barry seemed to be failing the test: he was hardworking, severe, and withdrawn. There was no one else for Jonathan to learn from: Father had never offered an example to his youngest son.

Jonathan had been three years old when Father returned from the war in 1945. He had cried when he had been put into the arms of the dashing stranger, the young naval officer in full uniform. A certain reticence had always existed between them.

Once, years later, when Father was playing with some visiting children, sliding across the waxed front-hall floor, Jonathan had been shocked. He had never imagined Father doing such a thing. They had not shared the hunting expeditions and card games that had been part of the older brothers' childhoods, nor the reading-aloud and the trips abroad that had been part of mine. When Jonathan was small, Father had disappeared into the real world, and a friendly politeness developed between them.

In the English system of primogeniture, younger sons are extras who have no role in life unless their older brothers die. They must join the military or the church or make their living abroad.

I did not see much of Jonathan after he left Harvard in 1963. He seemed to me a gentle, increasingly vague spirit who would not compete in the family wars. It had become a joke that he often did not hear what was being said at the dinner table. We all gaily attributed his distraction to his similarity to Toad—his nickname—the bemused animal in *The Wind in the Willows* who rushes from one obsession to the next, from boats to gypsy wagons and from gypsy wagons to motorcars. But by now Jonathan had lost most of his obsessions.

He spent the fall and winter of 1963 in his old room at the Big House, off the sleeping porch where Worth and Barry had once heard owls at night. Jonathan was taking a chemistry course at the University of Louisville and learning to play the piano, bringing pretty girls home for supper with our parents and spending time with friends from his Boy Scout days.

I saw him for the last time at Christmas 1963. I had come to Louisville with my sons to spend the holiday, but Jonathan was more elusive than ever. At twenty-one, he was still entirely occupied with his childhood friends, and with a laboratory he had set up in the Big House basement.

On the last evening of my visit, I asked him what he did down in the basement, remembering when it had housed the older boys' chemistry sets and had been the scene of mysterious explosions. Jonathan seemed very serious about his purpose down there. He said he was discovering a cure for cancer.

More than twenty years later, one of his friends explained to me that Jonathan had told everyone who asked about his basement activities that he was discovering a cure for cancer. According to this friend, who had been part of Jonathan's little group, he had been making bombs in the basement, using explosives stolen from a military supply dump at Fort Knox, the big Army base outside of Louisville.

The telephone call came two months after that Christmas visit. My husband handed me the receiver, then brought a chair. Father was calling from Kentucky. He spoke calmly and clearly. It was a one-sided conversation. Jonathan had been killed that afternoon in an accident on the Place.

The Big House was in an uproar when we arrived. Flowers and casseroles were pouring in, the telephone was ringing wildly, and friends were stationed here and there, attempting to direct the chaos. Mother was upstairs in her bedroom. She had been given tranquilizers. Father had a pocketful, which he offered to all the women. But the family commitment to restraint was more powerful than any pill. Only Mother did not for the moment care about appearances.

Father quietly explained what had happened. Jonathan had been preparing for a party, a gathering of his old Boy Scout troop, in the barn where I had once stabled my horse. There had been no electricity in the barn for years; I had lighted my work there with candles.

Jonathan needed electricity for sound equipment for the party. He had completely wired the room he planned to use and was waiting for the electric company to make the final hookup. However, the electrician had not arrived and the party was imminent.

Jonathan asked Mother if she thought he could complete the job. Convinced by the work he had already done, ignorant of the risk, longing to believe in his competence, she told him that perhaps he could. He went into town and bought himself a linesman's outfit, complete with spurs.

That rainy March afternoon, Jonathan climbed the electric pole near the barn. A large gray metal transformer was fixed on top of the pole, with several heavy cables leading to the nearby garage. One of Jonathan's friends climbed the pole behind him, and the others congregated nearby on the ground. Mother and Father were also close by, taking a walk.

Jonathan climbed the pole and reached out to connect the electric line from the barn to the transformer. At contact, sparks exploded around him and the new line thrashed across the pasture like a snake. He had time to say, "I need help." The boy on the pole behind him tried to pull him free, but he was in danger of being electrocuted himself. Then Jonathan fell. He was dead when he hit the muddy ground.

Mother and Father heard the terrible cries and came running.

His death raised questions that could not be discussed. Tormented by guilt and sorrow, the family fled to silence. Any explanation would flay us with implications of wrongdoing.

Jonathan was behaving as his older brothers behaved, with the extra touch of recklessness which was his undoing. None of us had learned to fear consequences. We had lived in a world where, as children, we had been protected from consequences by money, servants, pride, and useful lies. To drive a car at a hundred miles an hour down a curving Kentucky road did not necessarily mean an accident; an accident did not necessarily mean bodily harm or financial loss or even public embarrassment. To climb an electric pole might be another way to fly, like Icarus, toward the sun.

All the Bingham men were risk takers—kings of men.

Where there are no consequences, reality seems muted. The ability to fear is perhaps essential in order to feel at all. It seems inevitable that the children of privilege search for risks that would seem ridiculous to other people, search for the limits that are always dissolving in front of us—search for the ability to shudder.

Jonathan was laid out in the ornate music room at the Big House. Tall candelabra stood at the corners of his coffin. Across the hall, in the dining room, the family gathered for supper the evening before the funeral.

At first we were all subdued, looking at our plates. But then someone made a remark, and we were off. The banter was shrill, the laughter was hysterical, and through it all Mother sat pale and silent at her end of the enormous table.

Paralysis seemed to grip us during the funeral, when it seemed more important to remember the names of the people who crowded into the mansion-church than to think of the young man who had died.

Mother wept. Afterwards she went at once to sort out Jonathan's clothes, planning to give them away to her sisters' sons, but she could not complete the task. She fled from his room in tears. Later, ashamed of her grief, she would go to the woods to cry where no one would be forced to commiserate.

I believed that Jonathan had been her favorite. His delicate unworldly quality had aroused her instinct to protect and preserve.

Back in New York after Jonathan's death, I began to wrestle with my own demons. Friends did not know how to deal with the fact of his dying; circles of silence widened around me when I mentioned it. We were all too young to know what to say.

In that terrible spring of 1964, I began to remember our childhood together:

"Wooden roses: I was made to take a nap every afternoon, no matter what, and in the summer, when it was hot, I dreaded it. I couldn't go to sleep, and I was frightened of lying for two hours alone, silent in my bed. At night I had the same trouble going to sleep. I would get up the prescribed number of times—six or seven—to go to the bathroom, to make sure I wouldn't wet the bed, and then I would have to get up again to be sure the tap was not dripping in the sink. Finally I would slip off into a kind of half-sleep, feverish, full of dreams.

"I had a horror of reaching up during this sleep and touching the wooden roses which were carved on the headboard of my bed. I was afraid I would touch them without knowing it. They were round wooden roses in high relief. There seems to be a connection between that and the canvas mittens I wore when I had poison ivy, to keep me from scratching myself, and the little cotton mittens which were put on the babies—Jonathan and Eleanor—to keep them from sucking their thumbs, and the strips of adhesive tape which held our ears back so they would grow flat to our heads. Nothing was said; simply, there were preventatives."

For the first time, I realized that there was a link between the mittens and the adhesive tape and the wooden roses and the rules we had learned about feelings: be quiet, stop crying, wipe that expression off your face . . . These elements were no longer separate, mysterious, floating, but connected. Original sin, unclean bodies, unhealthy desires; ignorant black people who were supposed to "smell," dark places of the body and dark places of the soul. Not talking about money meant not talking about pain; not noticing the exhaustion and the helplessness of the people who served us meant not noticing our own vulnerability. The silence that had closed over Mary Lily during those last months at Lincliffe had closed over us all, a golden shell shielding us from the truth. Money, and love; racism, and the fear of dark places; women, and evil, and the great white virtues of silence and self-control.

A few months after Jonathan's death, I went back to the Place for a visit, hoping to give or to receive some comfort. But "I found that his life is washed clean away. His ghost is laid. I would hesitate to mourn him here."

I had no idea what Mother was thinking. As I attempted to make sense of Jonathan's death, I wondered if it would have been a relief for Mother to admit that he had had difficulties. I knew that certain things had gone wrong, that certain things could have been done. I felt as though she was bearing the full burden of blame for what had happened to Jonathan, and yet it seemed to me there was little she could have done. I wondered if she was waking up at three in the morning, crying with terror.

Jonathan's relationship with Father seemed to have disappeared into the whirlpool of guilt, fear, and pain. No one mentioned it. I wondered if that relationship had existed only in formal terms, as an armistice between strangers.

The effect of his death never ended. His death was not understood, forgiven, or forgotten by anyone in the family, although it was sealed in silence. It became the base of our joint life. On it Mother built her philosophy, which matched that of the Greeks she had studied as a young woman: the highest tree is the one that is struck by lightning. She never mentioned the word "hubris," but I knew she believed that the tree's height caused its destruction.

Together Mother and I descended into the hubris of guilt. Guilt means refusing to allow another person to be responsible for his own destiny. Yet to refuse to feel guilt is to hurl the beloved child to his fate. Later, when Worth died and Barry's life was threatened, Mother perhaps expected me to connive once more with her in taking responsibility. But by then I had changed.

27

At Jonathan's funeral, I noticed for the first time the behavior of the black people in the Big House—noticed them as different from the white family and its tragedy.

That first day, I went upstairs to the bathroom I had used as a child, the peach-colored bathroom with its mirrors and the secret compartment that had hidden my second stepgrandmother's jewels. Frances, the black seamstress, was on her knees, scrubbing out the bathtub. She glanced up at me, then went on with her work. There was nothing to say and no sense in stopping.

I wondered if her tragic resignation had been there all along, disguised by jokes and silence. Frances had never really been a member of the family, although we had all pretended that she was. Now, for the first time, she refused to pretend. Jonathan's funeral would be held in the mansion-church where I had never seen a black face. Frances would not be there. Instead she would be doing the kind of work she was doing now: scrubbing out a bathtub so that it could be dirtied by a white guest.

I remembered her bent back and her stricken face for a long time before I understood why she did not stand up and commiserate with me about Jonathan.

In the years that followed his death, the five black people who had worked on the Place grew old. One by one, they retired, except for Lizzie Baker, who hung on until the end.

They all came back for a last visit to the Big House one spring in the 1960s when I, too, was visiting. For the first and the last time, they sat on the white iron chairs on the terrace and drank iced tea, embarrassed, smiling. Then Cordie, the old cook, went slowly and heavily back to the kitchen to look at it "one more time." She had spent her life there, coming into service thirty years earlier when my parents were married.

Everyone smiled and talked cheerfully of other visits, but we all knew it was the end. Shortly after that, these five people died.

I had long resisted feeling a special responsibility for the hired people who had cared for me since babyhood, as I had resisted responsibility for the slaves who had belonged to my great-great-grandfather. Both forms of responsibility were beyond my comprehension.

I did not go home for the funerals of the people who had raised me, although I read about them in my parents' letters. I was afraid that I would notice or feel things at those funerals which were best kept out of consciousness if I was to preserve my peace of mind.

Years later, during a visit to an island off the coast of South Carolina, I began to look for the graves of the slaves who had died there by the thousands and whose bodies had been consigned to the swamps. I still did not know where the black people who had lived and died for the white family in the Big House were buried, or whether their graves, too, had disappeared.

Unlike the South Carolina slaves, they had been paid for their work. They had been treated with respect, even affection. But what had been their choice? Under the dismal moss-draped trees that crowded the island's sand roads, I began to wonder for the first time.

By now the newspapers were filling with photographs and reports of violence in the South as schools were desegregated following the Supreme Court order. This violence lapped against Louisville, where, a few years earlier, school superintendent Omer Carmichael and newspaper editor Weldon James had written a self-congratulatory account called "The Louisville Story."

It described the success of the 1955 integration of the schools. Integration had been accomplished largely through redistricting, and the availability of transfers to all parents who did not want their children in mixed classrooms. Now, however, the Supreme Court had ordered busing to take inner-city black children to suburban white schools, and a white mob, infuriated by editorial support for the ruling, broke some of the newspapers' windows.

Perhaps these angry people had been lulled into believing that they were exempt from change. According to Carmichael and James, Louisville was a progressive city led by men who supported "a strong two-party system, a local tradition of public service, and an enlightened newspaper— they run things."

They did not, as it turned out, run things. The people who had believed in the invincibility of their leaders were disillusioned; they burned the mayor in effigy, and they broke the publisher's windows.

These angry people were the women and men from Shively and other city neighborhoods for whom the newspapers were said to be edited. I saw in their faces, in raw and hideous terms, things that had been subterranean, complex, carefully hidden. I began to remember images from my own past:

Cordie standing in the doorway of my parents' bedroom, just inside the frame, courteous, silent, as Mother explained the week's menus; Cordie later, in the kitchen, going slowly over the complicated recipes, underlining each word with her finger, her lips moving.

George's abrupt disappearance after he was caught swimming with Worth in the pool, and Luke, a few years later, vanishing with his family.

Mother coming back from the polls with the black servants in her station wagon, and the way they descended slowly, in their wide black coats, their big purses swinging from their arms.

Later it seemed to me that the window-breaking incident killed the family's ability to empathize with the people it had led and profited from for three generations.

That empathy had begun to die years earlier when publisher Mark Ethridge linked the racist Senator Eastland and the NAACP. Ethridge had remarked in a speech damning all extremists, "The reasonable people of the South are caught between two forces: one of them sitting down in the traces like a balky mule, the other trying to move it by setting firecrackers under its belly. Both attitudes are dangerous."

It should be noted, however, that the mule is only irritating. The people who plant the explosives are dangerous. The family was afraid of explosives—both verbal and chemical—and of people who used them, no matter what their purpose. Its sympathies were always with the stubborn but ultimately harmless mule.

"The reasonable people of the South"—leaders like Father and Ethridge—had always been threatened on an unconscious level by the dark presences who cooked and served their food and washed and ironed and mended their clothes. Ultimately the dependency of black people threatened the control of white masters, as the dependency of white women sometimes threatens the control of white men. A great deal of self-knowledge and self-control is required to prevent a master from taking advantage of such a situation, from striking, seducing or raping. Where there is darkness, there is always a threat to the light.

The black people who had lived on the top floor at the Big House had, willy-nilly, represented that threat, as I had felt when I tiptoed up those long dark stairs and, against all rules, rummaged the little rooms for signs of their being. Control is always at risk when personal power is without limits. Jonathan had felt that in the swirling confusion of Harvard in the 1960s, where the old controls no longer held.

Father was absent from these images out of the past, yet it seemed to me that he had always been behind the scenes, just out of the camera's line of vision. For him life on the Place was organized, to entertain his friends and maintain his position. He was often away, but when he returned, it was to the long green lawns and gardens, the sundials and the fountains, the amphitheater and the box hedges, the shining silver and the shining floors, the huge table set for twenty guests, the gold plates and the monogrammed linen. He relished each detail. His enjoyment of life was contagious. He did not question ways or means. He believed in ends.

Mother kept the Place going with her lists and telephone calls, her daily struggle with details. She had always treated the black servants with scrupulous kindness. Although she would have howled with derision at the thought, they had been her closest friends. She gave them fat envelopes of cash every Friday—but the cash arrived in a special car from Father's office. She took them to doctors and tried as they grew old to make the ends of their lives bearable. But at the end, they looked back on a life of servitude, essential to the maintenance of the family's position. Mother did not question that.

She could not afford to question, then or ever, the control exercised by Father and his newspapers. To question meant to recognize the darkness. We preserved and deserved our specialness as long as we represented a point of view more elevated, morally and intellectually, than the point of view of those we aspired to lead: white factory workers or farmers, black servants or laborers. When in the disintegration of the 1960s these attitudes fell into disrepute, when benevolence was seen as a form of condescension, "uplift" meant arrogance, and moral leadership was only authoritarian control, the family lost its excuses. By then it was inconceivable to live without money and power, and inconceivable to admit that we no more deserved our elevated position than we deserved the money that had come to us through Mary Lily's mysterious death.

To question is to let in darkness and chaos. Jonathan had felt the hot breath of that threat. Because he was not in line to succeed, he perhaps saw the situation clearly. Perhaps Mother had dreaded that one day he would ask her how it had all started, where it had all come from, and why he was not to benefit from the fruits. Because she loved him, his disenfranchisement would have been almost impossible to justify, but to question his lack of power would have meant to admit her own.

It was not only blacks who had lost their lives for the fantasy the Place represented. Women, white women of privilege as well as poor women, had given up their independence to maintain the illusion. Nursie had given the core of her life. Mother had abandoned something essential—her point of view? her love of the truth?—in order to work for the perpetuation of the myth. She had spent years of her life on the re-creation of a plantation world that had never existed, even in the antebellum South.

It was a world of darkness and light, of polarized male and female roles, of white goodness and black evil. There were no individuals in it, but caricatures of virtues and vices: Black Greed, Dark Sexuality, White Devotion, Crystal Love.

I had for a long time subscribed to the same legend. But a month before Jonathan died, I had gone to Atlanta to visit Robert Coles and his wife, Jane, who had been friends of mine at college. Bob was working on his first book about the effects of the civil rights struggle on the lives and minds of children.

During the visit, I heard the story of a pregnant black woman who had been lynched. The fetus had been cut out of her belly.

I had never heard much about lynchings, although they continued in the South, rising to a peak in the 1920s. I had never heard of Willie Snow Ethridge's group of Southern women who protested that they would no longer accept the excuse that lynching preserved white women's honor. I had never read of an incident of lynching in the Louisville newspapers, nor did I know that my great-grandfather, the Colonel, had been one of the organizers of the Ku Klux Klan in Reconstruction North Carolina.

I wrote Father about the Atlanta lynching and asked him to send a reporter to investigate the story, which had not been reported in Georgia newspapers. I never received an answer to my letter.

Father's silence did not surprise me. In fact, I was embarrassed to have asked: the question was clearly out of order. The world of the Louisville newspapers and of the news they reported was not my world. I knew how firmly Father and Mother were welded to the illusion of equality. In their view, lynching and other racist atrocities were simply aberrations, best ignored. There was nothing to be learned from the random violence of white males against black females.

The family, of course, would have condemned such behavior, yet our remoteness from it seemed part of our special destiny. In Kentucky, the family did not treat itself, nor was it treated, like any other family I had ever known. Father had become the eloquent voice of "social amelioration and uplift," as the Judge described it, and his many honors showed that his voice was appreciated: chairman of the board of Historic Homes Foundation, chairman of the board and trustee of Berea College, trustee of the Pine Mountain Settlement School, trustee and board member of the Rockefeller Foundation, overseer of the University of Louisville and of Harvard, director of the Asia Foundation, chairman of the International Press Institute, board member of the Committee on the Present Danger, recipient of seven honorary degrees . . . Everyone admired him. I alone had my doubts, which were painful. I began to fear that his eloquent voice was a tin trumpet, self-important and self-sanctifying.

A few years earlier, in 1954, I had waited in vain for that trumpet to sound. That year a pair of young white activists, Anne and Carl Braden, had bought a little house in Shively and deeded it over to a black couple, the Wades. Crosses had been burned in the yard, and eventually the little house was blown up.

During the trial, the Bradens themselves became the prime, and then the only, suspects, and much was made of such details as the presence in their library of college texts on Marx and Engels. It was the 1950s. The whole town was terrified. Rich white people in the suburbs began to comb their own shelves, throwing incriminating books at night into the Ohio River.

Carl Braden was a copy editor for the newspapers. He was suspended during the trial and fired when he was convicted of sedition, a conviction that was overturned after he had spent nearly a year in prison. No one ever found out who had bombed the little house, although Anne Braden believed at the time that the perpetrators had been connected with the police department, even now struggling to avoid revealing which of its officers belong to the Ku Klux Klan.

The newspapers' editorials during the Braden case were cautious. They expressed sympathy for the Shively residents, whose property values, they said, were bound to decrease, and they criticized the Bradens for being self-dramatizing martyrs. The time was simply not right for such a drastic action as buying a house for a black couple, and even had the time been right, the Bradens—young, labor-oriented, with few ties to the upper class—were not the designated leaders.

Without evidence, some people called them Communists, a charge that was not and could not have been proven. The label was applied, in the hysteria of the period, to everyone who refused to "go along," with almost no understanding of its larger meaning.

During her trial, Anne Braden had gone to Father, whom she admired, to ask if she should give up the fight, much as Mother, a generation earlier, had gone to consult President Roosevelt about her support of Henry Wallace. Both women were charmed, although only Mother was persuaded to desist.

Mrs. Braden told me years later that she felt that Father had encouraged her to continue the fight to prove her innocence, a fight for which he proposed to offer no support. But after all, she was a woman, and in the mythology of the Big House, women shoulder the responsibility for acting on matters of conscience—and take the consequences. It is not very important: our crusades always fail because we have no money, no allies, no power. But to try means that the system is once again justified, as it was justified when Mother drove the black servants to the voting booth.

There is another explanation for Father's friendly encouragement. The Braden case was persuading Louisville that it was host to a Communist cell, and although some might scoff at a group made up of two labor organizers, a retired riverboat captain, and several other fringe characters, others took their presence as proof that Communism was, indeed, the threat to democracy Senator McCarthy was decrying. For men who feel that covert action and the rooting out of Communism are proof of patriotism, it is important to keep the threat afloat. So Anne Braden served two purposes, and her courage was not only admirable, in Father's eyes, but useful to the propagation of his view of the world.

Mrs. Braden also talked to Mark Ethridge, the newspapers' publisher and my genial godfather. He told her that editorials would have very little effect on the angry people in Shively, no matter what they said. Again the "Shively housewife" made her appearance, representing all that is irrational, unreachable, and ultimately of no importance in the world of men.

Anne Braden reminded Ethridge that the newspapers "did have a great deal of influence with many liberal citizens in the community at large . . . These people would have influenced others and ultimately perhaps the influence would have reached deep into Shively. Instead the *Courier* provided for such people a reason for remaining silent." Silence, again, was the key.

The newspapers' stand on racial issues had begun to harden in 1941, when Father and Mark Ethridge had resigned from the Southern Conference for Human Welfare because of its alleged Communist connections. The same slur would explain their later repudiation of Henry Wallace. The Red scare was responsible for the flight of many Southern liberals, most of whom retained their positions of power and responsibility after they lost their ability to take risks. Fear of being labeled radical was as persuasive in their silencing as fear of being labeled Communist. The reaction was visceral: to white men from the upper class, radical behavior is exhibitionistic, hysterical, embarrassing—the way they believe women behave at our worst.

The newspapers' attitude raised many questions for me: the question of the rights and motivations of leaders, the question of the rights of those who, most willingly, are led, and the question of the influence of power and money on matters of conscience. Anne Braden's example as she continues to fight for equality illuminates, as well, the choices of a woman who renounces silence.

Silence had always been the choice of women in the Bingham family when faced with public issues, a silence that seemed to me to lead inevitably to covert manipulations, whether it was a case of the prosecution of lawsuits, the eliminating of political candidates, or the exiling of unruly family members. Words, and bitter words at that, were reserved for the failings of individuals who did not support the system. That silence, and those bitter words, had extended the power of the Bingham men and of their institutions.

The Braden case illustrated the collapse of Southern liberals (a term which is perhaps an oxymoron). It also threw light on the role the family women played in keeping the illusion of deserving leadership afloat.

Rhetoric has always been the tool of the Southern myth. It informs the rituals of the Episcopal Church.

After Jonathan's death, the family's kindly and concerned minister had made the only attempt I had witnessed at offering comfort. It had been fruitless although well-intentioned, like the polite phrases of sympathy offered sheepishly by old friends: "So sorry . . . So terribly sorry."

The minister had not been able to offer us a coherent explanation of Jonathan's death. He had nct suggested that we accept his death humbly as the will of God—who could have suggested such a thing to Binghams? He had not suggested that some hidden good would proceed from Jonathan's death, or that it was part of a design we could not comprehend. Would we have agreed to such a conclusion? He had been kind, and soothing, and I had felt his awkwardness and his pain as though he, too, sensed that our shared faith provided few answers, few sources of consolation for the children of pride.

Yet there was nowhere else to turn. During the funeral service, the grand old golden phrases I had heard all my life had a peculiarly tinny note.

By that time I had not been to church for many years. Mother and I had quarreled over it when I was an adolescent. Once she had forced me to attend Sunday service, and I had not been able to avoid taking communion even though I knew I was in a state of sin. I had hung suspended in a state of sin since childhood, guilty of nameless as well as named crimes, some of them connected to those feverish afternoon naps, the mittens, the adhesive tape, the enemas—the terrible physical facts of being female. For a long time I had not been able to ask for forgiveness for my state, since I did not see any alternative to being a daughter of Eve, condemned by gender to a life of darkness. When as an adolescent I took communion for the last time, consciously rebelling against the church's rules, I had half expected to be struck dead by a thunderbolt. Nothing happened, and I lost what little faith I had left in a Father and Son who seemed so like the fathers and sons in my own life.

After that religion became for me, literally, church: the dark old cathedral in Louisville where the Judge had married Eleanor Miller and where, during the war, I had prayed so intensely; the little frame black Baptist church in Harrods Creek where we had met informally during the war; and finally the enormous brick Colonial structure—the mansion-church—with its white trim and tall, slender white steeple. There I had first smelled on a Sunday morning the combination of bourbon, cigarettes, and perfume that had sickened me during the hymns and the prayers.

My beloved grandmother Munda had taught me many verses out of Ecclesiastes, and her delight in their verbal display had replaced my search for their meaning. Merely to mumble, "The pitcher is broken at the well . . . and man goeth to his long home, and the mourners go about in the street," induced a sleepy melancholy sense of fitness, as though life was shaped by those sonorous sounds, which cast their spell over Cordie dozing in her wooden chair on hot afternoons, or Nursie counting the pennies in her change purse, or Luke standing in the tack-room doorway, terrified, while I drowned the baby mice, or Jonathan stalking away down the darkened Big House hall. Munda and my parents loved the ritual and the magic of the King James version of the prayer book, which seemed to wall out change as it sanctified the elect.

When the prayer book was updated in the mid-1980s, Mother fought against the changes with passion and pain. She missed the magic of the old language, and the distance it had created between churchgoers in their pews. She was particularly appalled by an added ritual: at a certain point in the service, the parishioners now may turn and greet one another. In a letter to the newspapers' editor, Mother wrote in anticipation of a visit to a Kentucky church by Queen Elizabeth:

"At a point in the service when the 'Peace' is passed, it is now customary for members of the congregation to embrace everybody within reach, including perfect strangers. Indeed, I have been shrinkingly present when the priest, in an excess of bold and fervent zeal, advances down the aisle hugging and kissing all hapless, and accessible, parishioners. Will Majesty be thus affronted?"

This was no church for the poor and disenfranchised, nor was it a church that offered consolation in times of tragedy.

When I heard the New Testament quoted from the pulpit, I was dismayed. Many children have felt the first stirrings of discomfort during those bright Sunday mornings when a minister who is his congregation's favorite son reads from the Gospel: the rich man and the eye of the needle, the prophet who said, "Suffer little children," and made no mention of the obvious differences between black children and white, or who impudently told the rich man to give away all he had and "follow me."

This radical, incandescent message, of course, did not apply to us. No one mentioned the words of the scriptures outside of church, although everyone attended regularly and supported God's mansion with big contributions.

By the time of Jonathan's death, I thought I had left the church behind. No philosophy had come to take its place, however, and I did not yet have the authority to develop a philosophy of my own. So I made sense of what had happened with the materials I had at hand: the coded memories from our childhoods that had linked racism and repression, lies and silence, love and money.

28

In the early summer of 1966, I was living in New York, married for the second time.

Two years after Jonathan's death, on July 12, 1966, my oldest brother, Worth, was killed in an accident on Nantucket. He was thirty-four years old.

I felt blunt with shock when I heard the news. Worth was a stranger to me. During the years when he was being groomed to take over the newspapers, I had seen little of him.

This time the Big House was less chaotic. Everyone knew how to behave. A friend had brought a box of little black hats with veils for the women in the family to wear to the funeral, and I was shocked to notice how pretty they were, quivering on their nest of tissue paper.

All the other arrangements seemed equally discreet and attractive. Worth was laid out in the Little House, across the lawn from the Big House, the house where we had spent our early childhoods and where he had been living with his wife, Joan, and their two small children.

When I walked in the front door, I began to sob. This time I was more angry than grieved. A woman carrying a huge flower arrangement tried to distract me by asking where it should be placed. I could not give her any advice. It seemed to me that Worth's death might have been foreseen and prevented. He had given us plenty of warnings.

Six months before, at Christmas, he had seemed on the verge of collapse. During one evening meal at the Big House, he drank so much that he finally fell out of his chair and had to be helped upstairs by his wife. A terrible silence descended on the family as they departed. No one knew what to say. After a while the banter resumed.

Worth was popular at the newspapers and in the club life of Louisville; he had a leader's decisiveness and bold charm. He had taken over the responsibility for the operation of the newspapers after spending several years learning the ropes at newspapers in Minnesota and California. But he was also losing large sums of money in Reno and Las Vegas; Father said his love of gambling had begun when, as a small boy, he had hit the jackpot in a casino in Las Vegas and received a small rain of silver dollars.

Worth was drinking heavily, as he had since early adolescence. Several of his close friends had already been killed in automobile accidents late at night on River Road; he had served as pallbearer more frequently than is usual for someone of his age. That last Christmas, he had seemed to me black with anger, functioning successfully as always but more and more constricted inside the armor the family had designed for him.

He no longer seemed to enjoy the slavish admiration his role afforded him, or to accept Louisville's eagerness to see him as the hard-living, hard-drinking Southern journalist whose peccadilloes are grist for the gossip mill. He must have felt the narrowness of life at the top in a small Kentucky city, where he was known and recognized everywhere as the heir, the scion. It was a life composed of intertwined social and business obligations, with a wild spree every now and then to "let off steam." He had already spent years in the male world and he knew all about its rites of initiation: he had served in the Navy after graduating from Harvard, he had played poker and gone to the Derby, he had seduced women and shot big game in Africa. All that was left for him was a lifetime of fulfilling other people's expectations, which could include quite comfortably his excursions into recklessness.

I became aware of his vulnerability for the first time the night he fell out of his chair. I was visiting at the Big House, staying in my old bedroom, which was next to the guest room where Joan and Worth spent the night. As I was getting ready for bed, I heard them talking next door. Rather, Worth was talking. In a blurred, pleading voice, he was asking his wife to forgive him, using baby words I had not heard in years. I could hardly believe the crude monster of my childhood was talking baby talk. That frightened me more than his drunkenness at dinner, which was familiar behavior.

Six months later, Worth killed himself in an accident that seemed related to all his other accidents since the time he had plunged down the hill in front of the Big House on a sled, cutting his head open on a stone wall.

Father told me the details. Worth and his family had been taking a vacation on Nantucket. Worth had decided to try surfing; he bought a board and slung it behind the front seat of his small rented car, which had no partitions between the front- and the rear-door windows. The ends of the surfboard protruded from the windows on either side of the car. Then he jumped in and drove off, with his wife and child in the front seat beside him.

The roads on Nantucket are narrow, and when a car is parked on one side, they are nearly impassable. As Worth drove to the beach, one end of the surfboard protruding from his car window struck a parked car. The other end flew around and broke his neck.

The car rolled until his wife pulled on the emergency brake.

Later that day, our parents arrived in a private plane to take his body back to Kentucky. A generation earlier, Father had been in the car with his mother when she was killed; now Worth's wife and child had witnessed his death.

Before the funeral, I went over to the Little House. Once again, the family minister was present, and he attempted to say something consoling. Then he decided that the time had come to close the coffin. I looked at Worth's ashy face. The scratch I had inflicted as a child ran like a hairline crack down one cheek.

The minister lowered the coffin lid but he could not get it to catch. He leaned with all his weight on the lid to force it down. I felt that Worth was violently resisting this last attempt to seal him up as he had resisted all his life.

The funeral was larger and more public than Jonathan's had been, two years earlier. Friends from the big world were there in numbers, bright young men who were moving into top positions at newspapers all over the country. They seemed very young to me as they moved about slowly in the heavy rain. They were horribly shocked that Worth had died, as though they, too, believed in immortality.

During the funeral service, Barry sobbed. He was alone now, the last of the three brothers, and on his back would fall the whole weight of the succession.

As we drove back to the Place in the rented limousine, Barry's wife, Edie, remarked sadly that she had enjoyed living in their own house, had relished the relative obscurity of their existence while Barry was running Father's television and radio stations. Now, she knew, all of that was about to change.

Father offered Barry time to weigh the decision, but Barry needed no time. He told Father that he was prepared to step forward at once and assume Worth's position as assistant to the publisher.

He had never been prepared for such an eventuality. He was still a slow reader and he had become a passionate convert to television and the dream of a new technology. He had been prepared for his position at WHAS by working for several years at CBS in New York and at NBC in Washington D.C.; the Louisville station was an affiliate. There he had enjoyed making documentaries about Shakespeare and the Nile.

By temperament Barry was honest, thin-skinned, conservative, a private person who had conquered his early problems—a tendency to over-weight, by the family's standard, shyness, and lack of verbal ability—through extreme self-discipline, rowing on the crew at Harvard and becoming a devout marine.

Rowing at Harvard had been physically exhausting but it had given him moments of joy. He had described in letters to Nursie those times when the rhythm of the oars was perfectly coordinated and the narrow shell shot down the Charles River.

As an officer in the Marines in the years following his graduation from Harvard, he had found a congenial philosophy that matched his great-grandfather's belief in the transcendent heroism of the Confederate Army. Although Barry was slightly apologetic for his "gung ho" enthusiasm—an enthusiasm that was an easy mark for the family's humor—he had found a set of values which would govern his life.

The Marine dogma reinforced the lessons he had learned as the second son: duty first and foremost, unquestioning loyalty to the leader, a distrust of questions and the critical uses of the mind. The Marines taught him how to ennoble his inescapable obligation to the family, to remove every particle of self-pity, to turn devotion into a private religion: to settle for the evening star. That the religion required highly polished shoes, custom-tailored clothes, an automatic reverence for the chain of command, and remorseless physical fitness made it similar to the Colonel's faith. By now, however, the family had moved on, leaving the military school and its severe, romantic code far behind.

A new and subtler understanding of the uses of power had come into the family after the Judge was appointed mayor of Louisville in 1907. It was no longer enough simply to fight for the right, to put public duty above private gain. The game was more complicated and in order to win, the heir needed to combine cynicism with charm, to understand the uses of political and social manipulation.

Barry's sense of rectitude would lead him to scorn the compromises that had made success easier for his brother, his father, and his grandfather. He was closer in temperament to the ex-Confederate officer whose portrait hung over the Big House mantel—a beautiful young man, still strangely untouched by life, in the gray uniform of the Lost Cause.

Later I realized that Barry shared another characteristic with the Colonel: a tendency to lay blame. As the Colonel had blamed the Union Army for the death of his baby son, Barry blamed factors and people beyond his control for his problems at the newspapers. Perhaps the Colonel could not bear to think that it was his absence rather than the Union Army that had prevented his first son from receiving medical attention; the fury of Klan activities in Alamance County during Reconstruction seems to call for such a passionate blindness.

Perhaps for Barry it was intolerable to accept his own limitations, which were only human, his training to follow rather than to lead, as responsible in part for the newspapers' decline; his distrust of his relatives needed such a passionate blindness, especially in the case of Eleanor and me. The unexamined: the inevitable occurs again and again in the history of warrior men.

Barry did not know when he volunteered to raise the fallen standard that he would never own the majority share of the three companies' stocks. Perhaps he guessed that Father would always retain his office at the newspapers, just down the hall from the big corner office that eventually he would turn over to Barry. Like many of the prominent men of his generation, Father would resign at seventy-five in accordance with his companies' policy, but he would never resign as the prime mover, the beloved leader, the man who can do no wrong, particularly in retrospect. Even had he known that, Barry would still have stepped up to seize command, to raise the fallen standard.

The standard still hung on the wall in Father's office: the ragged remnant of the Confederate company flag that had somehow survived drowning in the Appomattox River. Like all relics, its provenance was somewhat mysterious, but not its effect. It had come across the mountains from North Carolina to Kentucky, surviving a dousing in the realities of the twentieth century.

Barry had heard the tales of the Old South, where duty was a passion, patriotism a religion, and the fathering of sons a holy mission. He did not understand that now the Confederate flag was just one of many icons.

Older and more experienced journalists were brought to Louisville to help him learn how to run the newspapers, but from the beginning Barry distrusted their advice: they were Father's colleagues.

So Barry was surrounded by Worth's friends, who in their mourning idealized him, and by Father's colleagues, who took to calling Barry "Junior."

He worked day and night to learn his new profession. But a successful publisher is something more than a hard worker. He has the charm of a local politician who has stumped the state and learned to work with the party hierarchy, the self-confidence of a small-town lawyer who knows everyone's first name. Those qualities seemed irrelevant to Barry, if not downright suspicious. Besides, he could not joke with his staff when he met them in the elevator or slap them on the back in the company cafeteria. He was not a public person.

His character had been shaped by his role as second son, the compliant follower who as a little boy had offered his big brother the sun and the moon and all the stars except the evening star.

Barry's wife, Edie, packed up and moved with their four children into the Big House, which they would finally buy just before Father's death, and which in the space of three generations had devoured so many loyal women.

After Worth's funeral I went back to New York. I was afraid I would be next. Fate seemed to be at work, cutting us down one by one. Mother believed we were the tallest trees in the forest, fatally attractive to lightning. After a while I realized she only meant her sons.

Worth's death did not lead me back into an examination of our shared past. I tried to put this new horror behind me, terrified of being infected by the fatal family virus.

My reaction was as stunted as my relationship with Worth. I had hardly known him as an adult.

I remembered the red mark his palm had made on my buttock when I was small. Nursie had taken me up to Mother's bedroom to show her, lifting my skirt and pulling down my underpants. I did not remember Mother's reaction. By then I had to a degree accepted her view that the victim invites her fate. I could not really hold Worth's teasing against him.

That these acts had continued into our adult life was a fact I could barely afford to bring into consciousness, now that Worth was dead. Only as I remembered the mark that violence had left on his own life could I begin to remember incidents which fit that pattern:

The hotel bathroom in London where I had crouched in the tub all night.

The bed in the summer house from which I had been evicted by one of his friends.

The letter that had been in my mailbox at Radcliffe one fall evening in 1954.

I had not recognized the handwriting on the letter. Worth had never written to me before. I unfolded a long letter, covered with an intense, knotted scrawl. When I saw the signature, I wondered what I had done to earn the honor of his attention. Father had paid Barry and Worth a fee to take me out to dinner once a week, but the deal had soon collapsed. Even money could not create a bond between us.

Worth's letter described in detail how to give myself an abortion.

He introduced his topic with a description of his shock and rage when friends in Louisville told him that I had been having an affair. Later I realized that he had probably been told by Father, who had been dissatisfied with our train talk and wanted to make another attempt to ensure that I was not pregnant.

Worth said that his good name had been besmirched: my sexual behavior was a direct reflection on him. As I read those fiery lines, I did not remember the humiliation I felt when a Harvard student recognized me as "Worthless's" sister—the gleam in the eye, the predatory smile. That did not seem relevant. My sexual behavior was the family's. Worth's was his own.

After warning me never to behave that way again, Worth gave me his advice. I must go to the dormitory bathroom at once and rid myself of the fetus by a method he described as foolproof. It involved hot water, bourbon, and violent exertion. He did not comment on its safety.

I was not pregnant but that fact, too, seemed irrelevant. I felt dazed as I tore up the letter. Later I went to the library and took out a book on prostitutes, which I read from cover to cover. It seemed to me that I had all the earmarks.

During the twelve years that followed his letter, I saw very little of Worth. I was afraid of him. He was living in other parts of the country, and I was glad to leave it at that.

In 1958, when I was married, I was surprised and touched that Worth came all the way back from an African safari for the occasion, paying his way himself, Mother told me. He and Barry had flipped a coin in some remote highland or veldt to decide which of them would return to Kentucky.

Worth was rambunctious at my wedding reception and again I was frightened. He and his friends, fueled by a day of drinking, seemed robust and ruthless seigneurs who might attempt to claim their feudal right. I was escaping a disaster when at last we drove away.

A few months later, at Christmas, my young husband and I came back for a visit to the Big House. As the family was opening presents, Worth handed my husband a wrapped package—Worth, who usually added his name at the last minute to the cards on presents Barry had bought. It seemed to me that everyone hushed and gathered as my husband tore open the paper.

Inside was a novel, published six months earlier, which described a college love affair. It was written by a friend of mine, a writing-class colleague at Harvard who had briefly been my lover. I had been flattered to recognize the ways his heroine resembled me, as I might have been seen through the eyes of a young, infatuated man.

The novel was considered candid, even shocking. It described the heroine as a greedy girl-child, impulsive and demanding, loving and unafraid.

I was a bride in the 1950s, when if a young woman was not a virgin at marriage she at least should pretend to be, and I had donned all the symbols of virginity: the white dress and veil, the sacrificial ceremonies of church and society. To preserve that illusion, I had asked my old friend the author to make several small changes in his manuscript, to dilute the comparison which would inevitably be made. After all, I had worn black stockings at Radcliffe before they were fashionable and had written stories about what was happening in the parked cars around Harvard Yard. That was ammunition for any battle. But I remembered the Radcliffe dean, and I was ashamed.

My husband had read the novel in galleys. Now he accepted Worth's present with a smile. I fled upstairs in tears, to the lavender guest room, where years before Munda had sat on the chaise longue, retailing her oddly bitter romantic stories and sewing a granddaughter's lace dress.

I wanted my husband to do something; in the style of the period, I could not imagine doing anything myself. What he should do remained unclear to both of us, although I would have found it gratifying if he had suggested a duel. Lacking that remedy, my husband went to talk to Barry. Worth had made himself scarce.

From the room that had once been my bedroom, I peered out at the two young men, striding around the circular driveway in front of the Big House. I had learned to ride a bicycle on that driveway. I was less in control of my life at that moment than I had been when I first started down the steep slope on a two-wheeler.

Barry and my husband arrived at some sort of agreement, which was passed along to Worth. I imagined his sardonic smile. The damage had already been done. The book was not to be mentioned again in my hearing. But I was deeply humiliated and deeply angry, still terrified of the damage Worth could do me almost without trying.

A few years later, he wrote me a warm, humorous letter—the second and last I ever received from him—announcing that he was about to be married. The letter ended with an anecdote about a young woman's "forty-yard douche" on water skis.

Now it seems to me that Worth proved himself on women. It was the one sure sign of masculinity, more certain and more conspicuous than success as a publisher or the esteem of friends or the luster of inherited money and position. All that, after all, was part of the system—inevitable, unearned. But young women possessed at least in theory the freedom to say no.

Again and again Worth had proved that he could have any woman he wanted. Once at the racetrack he had boasted that he had taken the "cherries" of every woman in the room. No one had contradicted him.

Like all of us, Worth had learned his lesson well, but his was written in mirror writing. At some moment with a woman, Worth became vulnerable, and it was perhaps that vulnerability he could not accept—the moment when the steel plates fall away. Worth possessed a sensitivity to others, a capacity to love and to be loved. But how could he value that aspect of himself—the vulnerability that exposed him to feeling, even to shame and regret? He had learned to feel out the soft spots in women, to penetrate them and possess them. Because of their softness, women were taken and abandoned. But what of the taker and the abandoner who feels his own softness, his fatal ability to love?

Worth was the heir, the chosen one. He was handsome and intelligent, educated and admired, poised to take over a little empire. But the clanking metal of male requirements drowned out the sweeter music.

The following year, on a spring visit to the Big House, I saw signs of the virulent disorder and despair that had entered the family. The myth of the tallest tree continued to cast its terrifying shadow. If we were no longer the luckiest family, perhaps we could hope to become the unluckiest.

The women were coping as best they could with the needs of their own truncated mourning and Worth's two small children.

I wrote, "The little girl's father is dead and her mother is in Aspen and her grandmother is determined to do something about her table manners: 'I will have dinner with her every night and light the candles.' The little girl reacts with passionate hostility to her grandmother's suggestions. The real structure is gone and we all try to replace it with something inessential yet defining. I tell her, 'You are my niece.' She tells Father, 'You are my Daddy, too.' The whole family seems to huddle under this cloud of destruction which has forced relationships and changed vacuums."

So much was needed—love and patience, courage and honesty. There was nothing for me to do. I went back to my own family in New York.

That summer I began to see something of Aunt Henrietta, who was living in a small apartment on Lexington Avenue.

On Sunday afternoons she would sometimes drop by for a visit. She would be zipped into a matronly miracle-fiber dress, ordered from a catalogue, and she always wore a few pieces of paste jewelry. The real ones had been pawned long ago. A tight hat held her head in its vise; underneath it her hair was still crow black. In winter, she draped over her shoulders the stone marten skins that had fascinated me when I was a child. Their glass eyes gleamed. She, too, was smiling, pleased to find an audience, but her voice had grown rusty and she often seemed to speak in code, referring to a shared past I did not understand. It no longer mattered. Cigarettes and liquor and memories furnished her life.

In the 1930s, when she was shuttling back and forth between London and New York, Henrietta had lived well at the Brevoort, driving a big car, entertaining, going to Harlem nightclubs, becoming acquainted with the black singer Florence Mills and with Tallulah Bankhead, even working for a while selling advertising for *Theatre Arts,* where one of her lovers, John Mason Brown, had introduced her.

But there was always the question of money: the Judge controlled her income, and she needed to wheedle and charm, insist and intrigue in order to keep the money flowing. Money and love . . .

Then the Judge had died, and the future had contracted to a farm in Kentucky, which had produced its own misery—and finally Henrietta was back in New York, without money, without hope, with the fragments of her charm.

She had married the North Carolina barkeep, but they had separated. Now she had lost most of her friends from earlier times, although now and then she would resurrect her silver and invite a few people to dinner.

I would notice the dust on the antiques she had bought in England during the time when she was serving the Judge as his aide and companion, the time, it seemed to me later, when she had finally abandoned hope for her own life. The alternative was so glamorous.

The Judge had told Henrietta that he would accept Roosevelt's appointment only if she went to London with him. He had implied that, although he had remarried, his third wife, Aleen, could not do for him what his daughter could do in the embassy at Prince's Gate.

For the last time, Henrietta became her father's consort. She had been elevated once before, in 1917, when Mary Lily was out of the way. Now, at the end of his life, the Judge invited his daughter to share his throne. When he died, five years later, it was too late for Henrietta to make a life of her own.

Her friends were dim presences from other lives, but I would sometimes catch the faintest scent of intrigue, as though there was still something slightly mysterious about the fat old woman who called herself, with pride, Mrs. McKenzie. Gone were the days when she had announced, "There is only one Miss Bingham."

The money she had inherited from the Judge had long ago been spent or wasted in ill-advised investments, supervised by her cousin the genial Lawrence Callahan. Now she was entirely dependent on Father's generosity, as the Asheville women had been.

During those last years in New York, Henrietta looked forward with excitement to Father's visits. He brought jokes and affection, checks and little treats, and a gleeful understanding of the coded past. For a while, Henrietta's life would be improved; she would go on a little trip or buy herself some new clothes.

Gratitude had never been one of her most conspicuous characteristics when I was a child. Then Henrietta had appeared to take it for granted that she would always be beautifully dressed and housed, attended by admiring friends, empowered by the mysterious erotic charm John Houseman described as a combination of mirth and melancholy.

During the war, Houseman had on impulse visited Henrietta at Harmony Landing, her farm in Kentucky, on a cross-country trip with the composer Virgil Thomson. Houseman and Thomson had "pitched hay in the morning, and after lunch I drove around the farm with Henrietta as she proudly showed me the colts she had bred. We all drank bourbon in the evening. She had as her houseguest a celebrated female tennis champion of whom she seemed to be tiring." When the two men left, Henrietta went with them.

Houseman described Henrietta in his memoir *Front and Center* as "a handsome woman in her early forties with a strong, graceful body (a little heavier now), her face shining and flushed from the wind and the sun (and from the bourbon in the long silver flask I remembered from Prohibition days) and the violet-blue eyes the memory of which, during our endless separations, used to turn my bowels to water and send me into orgasms of uncontrollable, delicious weeping."

He wrote that they "slept together and made love rather predictably in a motel in Missouri," but the magic was gone. Although he was "seized with a spasm of yearning" when he watched "her slender, strong hands on the wheel and the way her lips parted in a half-smile when she was going over eighty," Houseman knew he was "riding with a ghost." What the ghost thought or felt was not recorded. She had always existed most vividly in the imaginations of other people.

The Harmony Landing life had ended abruptly after Henrietta fell in love with her farm manager's daughter. The scandal, which had electrified Louisville at the end of the war, had led to the sale of the farm, and had justified Mother's fear and dislike of her outlaw sister-in-law.

The pattern was familiar: Henrietta liked her farm manager, who advised her in a fatherly way, and that liking led her inevitably to his daughter. Incestuous love was the only love that really counted, because it linked daughters and fathers.

Back in New York, out of money, Henrietta had begun to drink and to grow fat. Father lamented the death of her beauty, as though it was his most prized possession which had been rudely snatched away.

In June 1968, Henrietta died suddenly in her apartment. Years of alcohol and pills took brutal effect that Sunday morning when she was getting out of bed. A stroke felled her. Her body was sent back to Kentucky to be buried next to her older brother, Robert, who had spent the last years of his life trying to grow roses in the desert sand outside of his little house in Reno.

Someone had to clean out Henrietta's dark warren of an apartment on Lexington Avenue. It was the beginning of a hot New York summer and no one in Kentucky wanted to come up to confront the grimy chaos of those cluttered rooms. I volunteered to do the job.

An angry black woman who had cooked and cleaned for my aunt met me at the door. Reluctantly she let me in. The living room was dark, full of the roar of traffic from the avenue.

Big sideboards and massive upholstered furniture hulked in the shadows. The curtains hung in shreds, the venetian blinds clattered in the hot wind from the street, and a thick layer of oily New York City dirt lay on the surface of the dark mahogany. Hunting prints and photographs of strangers could hardly be seen through their fogged glass. The china figurines Henrietta had collected in England were disappearing as shadowy friends dropped by to stake their claims. I was glad to let them go. There was still too much left.

The pots in the kitchen were thick with grease, and when I opened a closet, clothes and old photographs and newspapers tumbled out. Long rows of Henrietta's narrow shoes sat on the closet floor, but the shoes had been cracked and burst by her swollen feet. Rubber girdles, mangled stockings, bits of old lace underwear from her frivolous time were mixed with receipts from the sale of horses and dogs and letters from her investment adviser.

There were few personal letters; Henrietta's companion had already picked through the debris. She had left a group of black-and-white photographs that showed the pale, sleek faces of the women I had seen once, long ago, during Christmas at Harmony Landing. There were no names.

There was little real jewelry in the shambles, other than a pair of cuff links enameled with the pennant from the Judge's yacht. I had never known about the yacht, and I was amazed to discover that he had kept it for a while at the New York Yacht Club.

Years before, at my graduation from college, Henrietta had presented me with an elaborate matched set: necklace, bracelets, earrings, and brooch, which appeared to be made of diamonds and sapphires. I had never seen anything like it.

Father had quickly explained that it was a paste replica of the real jewelry, a gift from the Judge, which Henrietta had pawned years earlier.

The set joined the parade of fakes with Mary Lily's pearls and the necklace she had given to Sadie Grinnan in Asheville.

Now, in a drawer, I found one remaining piece from the original set, a large sapphire-and-diamond brooch. It was real. To Father's dismay, I claimed it as payment for the work of cleaning out Henrietta's apartment.

The contents were appraised as being worth less than ten thousand dollars.

In the jumble of her papers, which included several copies of her will, there was a description of the Lucan coat of arms the Judge had ordered a generation earlier: "arms Quarterly, azure, a bend, colised, between six crosses patte orr . . ."

Henrietta's collapsing finances were represented by a sheaf of letters from the Chicago investment firm where her cousin Lawrence Callahan had worked. A letter written in 1946 indicated that her balance was a little more than $31,000, nine years after the Judge had died. An analysis was included of the sharp decline in the value of her securities: "The statement shows a loss of $16,876.41 for the securities if they were sold at the present market"— a decline of almost fifty percent.

The previous year, she had sent Callahan $85,000 to invest. Her dividends for the year amounted to less than $8,000. She had already begun to invade her small remaining capital, withdrawing $8,000 to pay for a new roof on the Harmony Landing barn.

She had worked for the war effort, raising hemp, which was needed for naval supplies. Father had written that he was proud to hear that she was being called in Kentucky "the civic-minded Henrietta Bingham." He assured her that she was in a position to perform a very useful service on her farm.

A little group of women friends had visited Henrietta from time to time during the war, or she had taken the train to visit them in New York or Virginia.

But some of the women were defecting, including the tennis player who had visited during Houseman's stay. A mutual friend wrote Henrietta, "You know Helen so well and can tell me what you really think. She never writes anymore, perhaps one letter a month. I think I will give up writing to her."

Another woman wrote to urge Henrietta to see a doctor; apparently the inroads of alcoholism had become conspicuous, and I remembered the visits Mother had paid Henrietta during the war to get rid of her bottles. But this friend also saw a future where she and Henrietta and another woman would form a powerful triumvirate, blessed with good spirits and natural efficiency.

This friend looked forward to horses bred at Harmony Landing that would be famous at racetracks all over the world, as would the flowers and dogs she proposed to raise on her own farm in Kentucky. She anticipated throwing "historic, brilliant parties," and added that she would be Henrietta's farm manager when she needed one (the letter was written after the scandal which provoked his departure), "and put you to sleep when you need that, too . . . We can be happy and proud together, darling."

She went on: "But even if you don't like the plan, I am beside you, behind you, and on top of you (if you want—!). You can do and say nothing to stop the constant flow of deep and growing love that goes out to you from my heart every time I look at you."

People repaid Henrietta lavishly for their moments of ecstasy; the Judge even dangled the promise of the newspapers before her. But the only prize she really wanted was to be her father's mistress, to rule his great mansions and his great enterprises.

When Henrietta could no longer arouse other people to feeling, she was lost. Perhaps she had always been numb, since her mother's death on the railroad tracks, since her exile from the kingdom when her father remarried.

At last she reached the state which Ernest Jones had described as aphanisis: the loss of all feeling. She seemed when I knew her oddly peaceful. At least there was no longer any pain.

A few days before she died, Henrietta helped my little son Barry to pry a plastic monster out of a mold. With shy pride, she drew a long pin out of her hat and used the tip to poke the creature out.

Barry was nearly as delighted as she was. Once more, perhaps for the last time, she had caused a response. Perhaps she remembered his beautiful blue eyes and his big smile as the last in a series of faces that had been lit, momentarily, by her charm.

A fourth death closed the sixties. When Nursie began to shrivel and weaken, she faced her illness with courage. She had cancer of the uterus, she who had mothered so many lost children but had never borne a baby herself.

The chemotherapy treatments caused her to lose her hair, but she said she enjoyed choosing wigs. When she was alone in her tiny apartment in Louisville, she wore a little cap, like the one her grandmother would have worn on a farm out in the state.

Close friends, women she had known and loved for years, helped her with cooking and shopping, and she was still able to go to church.

Over the months, her dear old face, still scarred from her childhood burning, grew skull-like, and her body seemed to lose both flesh and bone. Finally she left her beloved apartment, the symbol of her independence, for the last time and went to the Home for Incurables where I had worked as a girl.

My brother Barry's wife, Edie, a devoutly kind woman, called me in New York to tell me that Nursie was dying. Once more, this time alone, I flew down to Kentucky.

It was a beautiful fall day, and the ugly little city seemed balmy and secure, the trees Nursie loved still in full leaf, the gardens full of her flowers: moss roses and hollyhocks. Even the dismal Home with its highly waxed floors and its smell of sickness and death was full of air and light that day.

Nursie was lying in bed in a room with several other patients. She had shrunk even further, into one of the cornhusk dolls she had sometimes bought me when I was a child.

She was happy to see me, and talked for a while in a whisper. When she needed to urinate, she asked the nurse to help her to get onto the portable toilet. She was proud that she did not yet have to use the bedpan. Her legs under the crinkled hospital gown were dark with veins and very thin, but she was still wearing her braided gold friendship ring and I knew her stout watch and the brooch with our five names on five little hearts were put away carefully somewhere.

We talked a while. Her voice was light, and it was an effort for her to keep up the conversation. At last I stood up to go. I knew I would never see her again.

As I leaned down to kiss her cool, waxy cheek, I saw her brown eyes, as lively as they had been when I had sat on her lap as a child.

I looked back from the door. She had told me that she would not watch me leave. She lay on her side with her back turned to me, but she was waving, over her shoulder, her thin fingers which had governed my world fluttering as softly as feathers.

She died a few days later, as soon as Mother, who had been away, was able to get home. We all knew Nursie had waited to say goodbye to the woman whose five children she had loved.

Mother had recognized and honored that love. It had saved our lives. In giving us a woman who could love us unconditionally, Mother sacrificed herself as her mother and grandmother had done.

I did not go back to Kentucky for Nursie's funeral, and so I did not learn where she was buried: whether in the grand section of Cave Hill Cemetery where the Victorian angels look down from their tall columns, where Jonathan and Worth lie below Henrietta, Robert, the Judge, and Eleanor Miller, in the smaller, more cramped and crowded section, or in the other graveyards, provided for various denominations and classes and colors, which appear now and then in the midst of a grimy Louisville neighborhood.

I knew someday I would find her grave and take the flowers she had loved the most: the yellow jonquils that cover the long hill below the Big House every year at springtime.

Was it fate that was jettisoning bodies during the 1960s, when the Colonel's world, and the Judge's, and Father's, was shaken by a cold wind?

Or was the family once again purifying itself, as it had long ago in North Carolina, eliminating its weaker members in order to continue its relentless march?

Resolution

Feminism means finally that we renounce our obedience
to the fathers.

Adrienne Rich

29

On June 4, 1986, the last all-female class graduated from my Louisville high school. That evening in a church downtown, Angela Davis addressed a group planning to protest the resegregating of the Louisville public schools. She called it "part of a national plan to roll back the victories of blacks in the last several years."

These two events—the death of the all-girl private school and the apparent death of integration—marked the end of changes that had begun thirty-two years earlier when I left Kentucky to go to college.

The program for the 1986 high school commencement was the one I remembered. Red-faced daddies with tears in their eyes watched their daughters, dressed in long white gowns, as they walked slowly down the gymnasium aisle to the Processional March, squeaked out on piano and violin. The Kipling hymn I remembered with its mention of "lesser breeds without the law" had been abandoned along with the name of my athletic team, the Amazons.

At the steps to the stage, two daddies waited to help each graduating senior up. The girls were handicapped by long skirts, high-heeled shoes, and armloads of red roses. With their blond hair and their long backs, already tanned from backyard sunning, they looked like the girls I remembered. In the audience, an old black nurse was still the only representative of the "lesser breeds" who were listening to Angela Davis downtown.

In the front row, little boys and girls who were called honor guards and flower girls twisted restlessly during the speeches. Yet one six-year-old sent the speaker a note saying that she expected these graduates to be in the audience in eleven years when she in turn donned her long white dress. I did not see any of my classmates from 1954, yet the theme of continuity, of the shared, golden past seamlessly joined to the present and the future, was filling many eyes with tears.

The school chorus sang about sprouting wings and flying away, which caused more handkerchiefs to come out. Winged with hope, these white graduates might fly away altogether, leaving behind the notably dry-eyed faculty, the relatives snapping pictures, even the healthy young blond suitors in the audience.

The roses and the white dresses were part of a ceremony still celebrated at many female institutions in the South—for example, at Peace College in Raleigh, North Carolina, which my great-aunts and Mary Lily had attended in the 1880s. But the graduates' shout as they finally erupted into the parking lot seemed to challenge that dream of ritual and continuity. We had been through the sixties, Vietnam, the proliferation of nuclear weapons, the women's movement, black liberation—but what mattered that day were the long white dresses and the red roses and the sweet odor of stability.

These beautiful young women who won silver bowls for such qualities as "Good Sportsmanship" and "Noteworthy Thoughtfulness, Kindness, and Courtesy" were wrapped in privilege as they were wrapped in linen and organdy. But their favorite teacher spoke of Dr. Martin Luther King and a pluralist society; perhaps I was too much persuaded by the ruffles and the tears. Besides, did they need to fly away in order to thrive?

In the suburbs nearby, the same comfortable houses waited where I had gone to slumber parties, learning to suppress untoward urges. The same country clubs offered restricted access to swimming pools and tennis courts and June moons. The same mansion-church blessed weddings and baptisms, confirmations and funerals. As Kurt, my first lover, had said of me and of all of us sheltered girls who cried easily and browned our backs in the sun: "You'll always come home again."

I had come home in 1977, twenty-three years after the day I carried my own red roses down the aisle.

The call had come a few months earlier on a Sunday morning in Manhattan, where I had been living for fifteen years. The weekends were difficult for me because for the first time I was alone. I had recently divorced my second husband, and my three sons from both marriages often spent the weekends with their fathers. Since I had not cultivated a life of my own during the long years of writing and raising sons, I usually spent those blank weekends working, walking, visiting museums, even going to church.

That desolate Sunday morning, Father telephoned to tell me that there was a new house for sale in a subdivision near the Place. The house was sure to be snapped up at once because of its desirable location. Father wanted me to fly down the next day and inspect it. I went.

I had visited before, at Easter, with two of my three sons, and the little boys had seemed delighted by the beauties of the Place. My youngest had been given a ride on a tractor, and when it was time to leave for New York, his eyes had filled with tears. Perhaps, I thought, the old dream of family still held some magic, some cure for the isolation of a woman alone in a big city.

In Louisville, the ranch house I inspected smelled of new paint; the doors were very thin. Outside, however, the old trees and the rough meadows of my childhood stretched to the Big House woods. I knew there would be jack-in-the-pulpits there in the spring. My sons needed family, more family than I could provide. And on the dance floor in New York, a man whose name I did not know had put his hand all the way up the back of my blouse. In short, I was tired, and I was afraid.

By 1977, Jonathan and Worth had been dead for more than ten years. The family seldom mentioned them; the pain and the guilt were too great. Barry, my only remaining brother, had nearly died of Hodgkin's disease several years before. The disease had been far advanced when it was discovered in a routine checkup; apparently Barry had accepted the extreme fatigue induced by the disease as natural. No one expected the devastated young man to recover. His iron will saved his life. But chemotherapy had reduced him to a skeleton, and he had become anxious, thin-skinned, hardpressed. Neither of our parents seemed to be satisfied with him or with his wife, Edie, although their dissatisfaction appeared unimportant to me, as though it was limited to the subjects they mentioned: dinner parties, food, the upkeep of the Place.

Within a day or two of my visit, I had signed a contract for the ranch house, borrowing money from Father to pay for it. I went back to New York to pack, already feeling the strong pull of the unexamined—the inevitable. I had been out of the family for a long time. I no longer remembered all the complicated moves. Now the players seemed stalemated, sitting frozen around the board, as on rainy days in Chatham Worth and Barry had sat hunched over an interminable game of Monopoly. In the old days, Worth would have knocked the board aside, declaring that it wasn't worth playing, or that someone had cheated, and the game would have broken up in laughter and accusations.

Dreams continued to warn me: "I dreamed of two mines: the one in back belongs to me. Through aggressive questioning (I am enjoying myself) I find that my mine has been taken over by the others. I ask, 'Where is the boss?' and am shown to a group seated on the grass. There is my father! As I begin, 'This mine belongs to me,' he says, 'Well, perhaps in trust.' I am completely deflated and subdued. Later we are playing Scrabble and my mother chides me for not joining in. I tell her I can't be expected to play a game which is nearly over." But of course I could be—and I was.

During my inspection tour of the ranch house, Father had offered me two additional lures. He and several others had started a repertory theater in Louisville which, among other things, produced new plays. I was a new playwright, cracking the veneer of short fiction, and Father thought my plays might find an audience at his theater. He also mentioned the *Courier-Journal*'s Sunday book page, which Mother had edited until Worth's death. After his funeral, she never went back to her office, and her assistant became editor.

When Father offered me these lures, I found myself for the first time included in the ranks of maimed dependents, like Henrietta in the dark apartment in New York—dependent not only on cash and presents but on Father's assurance that I counted, Father's essential affection, which alone made life supportable.

I had to admit that both the theater and the book page tantalized me. Life on my own had been difficult. It always is.

My two younger sons and I left New York in July 1977, after packing all our possessions into a moving van: the curly tables from the old school in Asheville, the pine desk from Pinelands in Georgia, the canopy bed Mother had bought for me in England, my sons' baby clothes, my manuscripts and books and a trunk of diaries. The flat silver marked with my first husband's initials went, as well as the silver that had come at my second wedding and the mint-julep cups my godfather had given me every year when I was a child. Henrietta's paste jewelry was wrapped with the real brooch from her Lexington Avenue apartment and the necklace my husband had given me when my first son was born. In a worn green shoe box from Penney's, the family letters Nursie had given me before she died lay neatly folded, and Jonathan's diary and scrapbook were underneath. We traveled light, by air, leaving the past to trundle slowly after us on the interstates leading south.

The flight was ordinary until we met the exploding air currents of the Ohio Valley, where a storm had been brewing all afternoon. As the big plane was tossed around, people in the back rows started to scream, and the pilot's silence seemed to me like the silence of God before he puts out the light. When lightning flashed silver blades through the cabin, I was terrified. Worth and Jonathan had been killed in accidents, Barry had nearly died of cancer, and now the lightning was coming through the cabin. Nothing stood between me and the impersonal wrath that had never agreed to allow me to leave Kentucky in the first place and had done nothing to indicate it approved of my return.

The moving van arrived soon after we did and was unpacked, and Barry and Edie gave a party for me at the Big House. It was like the June parties I remembered: black waiters in white jackets passed trays of drinks and people moved slowly and gracefully through the big open rooms where the Judge had once played bridge and Father had slid on a cushion all the way down the stairs. Moths flapped against the lights and the trees outside sang with katydids. But now I was an adult woman and a writer with two children asleep in the house on the other side of the Back Woods. Now the single men who had been invited to meet me were less interesting than the women who had stayed in Louisville all their lives. Their pretty, carefully made-up faces reminded me of Mother and her friends, alone in their big country houses during the war.

As the first of many favors, the family offered me the services of a black housekeeper. She was one of a group of dayworkers who shuttled back and forth between the Big House and the Little House, replacing the people, now long dead, who had taken care of us when we were children. But these new workers were a little more independent: they had their own homes. Katy also had the look in her eyes I remembered: the look of stored secrets.

When I drove her home, I penetrated Louisville's West End, the largest black community in Kentucky. I had never been there before. Neat bungalows alternated with flimsy frame houses; wild lots where stores and movie palaces had been torn down stood between public housing projects, cut off from the white downtown by new thruways and chain link fences. I remembered hearing as a child that the people who lived in the first public housing projects stored their coal in their bathtubs—a statement I had found bewildering. Coal? For what? What did it mean?

Now these same projects had proliferated, but the old downtown had been nearly abandoned. Its main shopping street had been converted into a pedestrian mall, but white people lived in the suburbs and came downtown only to work in offices, not to shop. One of my son's friends had advised me to lock all our car doors when we went "in." Only black people shopped on the downtown mall and were held responsible for its wig shops and general desolation.

I wanted to believe that I could find a connection with Katy, and with the other people who lived in her neighborhood, different from the connection Mother had had with the black women who had served her all their lives. I wrote a short story about a white woman who, driving through a black ghetto, sees a woman knocking dirt off her child's boots on the front porch. The gesture reminds her of the years when she was at home with small children, before her husband made the money which allowed her to hire a maid. But the connection, obviously, was tenuous. I was once again a part of the old world.

In that old world, the power structure was unchanged: the monopoly newspapers Father owned and the Democratic party still controlled most aspects of public life. The turmoil of the sixties seemed to have passed Louisville by, as had, a century earlier, the turmoil of Emancipation and Reconstruction. The decline of the state's three industries, coal, whiskey, and tobacco, seemed likely to continue as concerns about health and conservation eroded their profits. Kentucky's unemployment rate was always higher than the national average and reached thirty percent in one of the mountain counties, but the atmosphere in Louisville was determinedly optimistic.

The boosterism once limited to the Chamber of Commerce had begun to appear in newspaper stories that boasted about high-rise buildings and new shopping centers built on the ruins of the black community. Fifty percent of the state's population did not graduate from high school, and generations of poverty and illiteracy had taken their toll. But at first I was more aware of the obduracy of social conventions among the upper class: when I tried to buy a ticket for a benefit, I was told they were sold only in pairs.

30

An earlier move in the family game had caught my attention even before I returned to Kentucky.

Shortly after Worth's death, Father asked me to serve as a director of his three companies: the two newspapers, the radio and television stations, and the gravure printing plant. I was so remote from the situation that I could not even express my amazement at his suggestion. It never occurred to me that he was attempting to replace his lost sons.

I was no longer a part of Father's world, and had not been for more than two decades. I hardly knew the history of the companies of which he now wanted me to be a part.

The Judge had established the AM radio station in 1922, hoping to provide "uplift" for rural Kentuckians; in an interview at the time, he imagined a mountaineer sitting on the front porch of his cabin, listening to classical music brought over the wire from the big cities to the north.

Whether or not mountaineers had ever listened to Beethoven, the station had been highly profitable for years, serving as a conduit for President Roosevelt's Fireside Chats in the 1930s, retailing farm information, and linking the state together.

As for the FM station, Barry had pursued the Judge's dream by using it for classical music, until revenue losses forced him to change the format.

The television station, a CBS affiliate and the top of its market in Louisville, had been established by Father in 1950. WHAS was a foreign kingdom to most of the Binghams, who professed scorn for the drivel served up on the screen; Barry and Eleanor were the only two family members who both understood and enjoyed television.

Father took great pride in the station's annual crusade for crippled children, which had not been influenced by changing attitudes toward the handicapped. Pretty little girls in braces were the prime attraction. The show was organized by one of Father's protégés, a woman who had once had other dreams.

Under Barry's direction, before Worth's death, WHAS was run competitively by an efficient, even ruthless team that seemed to set little store by the Bingham myth, which, in any event, could hardly be applied to commercial television. That the team included the only woman executive at any of the companies was perhaps one reason for its success.

The Judge had started the rotogravure plant, Standard Gravure, in the 1920s to print the newspapers' sepia Sunday section, as well as its comics. The plant was first expanded to produce circus posters, and over the years it became successful as the printer of Sunday magazine sections, at one time producing magazines for twenty-five newspapers.

As a child, I had been taken to see the big presses rolling as they printed the *Courier-Journal*'s Sunday comics in color, always a great favorite of Father's. Those noisy and antiquated presses, however, were not able to compete with the new offset presses which, by the early 1980s, were taking business away from Standard at an alarming rate. Expensive changes came too late.

The plant was heavily unionized and therefore less influenced by the plantation mentality that seemed to set the tone next door at the newspaper offices. A general distrust of blue-collar workers seemed to unite Standard's management and its owners, and frequent problems with strikes or threatened strikes discouraged benevolence at the top.

During the years when it was highly profitable, "the girls"—Eleanor and I—had been given large blocks of Standard Gravure nonvoting stock in trust. Its relatively high dividends, at that time, were to provide for us for life, and since it was in the family's eyes an unappetizing business, it must have seemed unlikely that either of "the girls" would interfere with its management.

The process of printing was considered dirty at the very least, if not actively dangerous, and the attitude of blue-collar men—Standard employed only a few women, as secretaries to the management—would have made the company a particularly alien environment for women owners. Or at least that was the supposition. "The girls," after all, were only interested in dividends, Father believed, and so it seemed safe to allow us, together, to own half of the printing company's shares. By the time we became aware of the potential power of our ownership, however, the company was about to fail.

The three companies shared a block in Louisville and were more interdependent, financially, than I realized. For example, the newspapers struggled with the printing plant over questions of quality and consistency. As

Standard began to print separate advertising sections, called preprints, to make up for its loss of Sunday magazines, other serious problems arose. Advertisers turned from the newspapers' pages to the preprints, where rates were lower.

The fates of the companies were intertwined in a way no one in the family seemed to understand, just as the fates of the twenty-two hundred employees of the three companies were interdependent in spite of the barriers raised by obsessions with gender and class.

When Father asked me to serve as director of these companies, I felt a flash of panic. Since the days when, as a small child, I had been driven into town to have lunch with Father in the company cafeteria, I had known the place was a foreign land.

I remembered how he had moved through the line at the steam table, with his children in tow, greeting employees who had seemed to me startlingly obsequious. They, of course, did not know us—a little bunch of children, carefully dressed and largely silent—and we were uneasy when presented with plates of food that would never have been tolerated at the Big House: sauerkraut and sausages, kale and fried fish.

Father was comfortable in that atmosphere, but it was not a place for his nameless children. I had been embarrassed by his employees' stares, knowing that they had no idea "which one I was": I was the anonymous little girl in a yellow sunsuit who appeared in the lobby mural.

As an adult, I would have hesitated to walk in off the street to use the ladies' room. I could not have imagined any other reason for going inside the big bow-fronted building on the corner of Sixth and Broadway.

As for the television and radio stations, I had been inside them only once, in the 1960s, when I had been interviewed on the occasion of the publication of one of my books.

The interconnectedness of these companies, and their mysteriousness, was represented by the way Father and later Barry moved between them, on a secret route that took them through the pressroom—later, I would nearly be crushed there by a falling roll of newsprint—and then through a labyrinth of passages that led to the television station. It was not a route anyone else could find unaided, and at times it seemed the only way in.

Physically as well as politically, the three buildings dominated downtown Louisville until a hospital chain built its headquarters there in the 1980s. Sixth and Broadway seems to terminate in the pale limestone newspaper building with its curving green glass windows, once broken by the anti-busing mob, and its relief of heroic pioneers looking skyward.

Just beyond, the ghetto begins. Farther down Broadway, the big distilleries and tobacco companies, whose success is so important to the city and its newspapers, crouch in the midst of poverty-stricken black streets.

The physical differences between the companies' buildings would have seemed slight to an observer, although they had been built at different periods. It is their solid mass which impresses, and the curious way they are connected by lots and fences, chutes and loading docks, internal passages and open sidewalks. For a long time, a honky-tonk bar, much frequented by the staff, held on to one corner of the block; Father viewed its continued existence with irritation. Finally even it succumbed, was sold to the companies, torn down, and replaced by an unused basketball court. The consolidation was complete.

There was no place for me on that square block, other than in the lobby mural, and I wanted to refuse Father's invitation to be a director. I knew I could not escape easily. He so seldom made a direct request that I had never learned how to refuse; his ways were usually more subtle. I was flattered, yet terribly frightened.

Quickly I thought of a substitute to throw into the ring: my husband.

Father agreed to the substitution at once, which proved to me that he was merely looking for a digit to add to his broken column. For the little time that remained before our divorce, my husband flew down to Louisville four times a year, returning with brief summaries.

The other women in the family were invited to serve as directors at about the same time: Mother, Eleanor, and Barry's wife, Edie. They all accepted.

Joan Bingham, Worth's widow, occupied an ambiguous position I never understood. As trustee for her two children, who had inherited their father's share of the companies, she would seem to have qualified as a director. However, although she often appeared at board meetings, she was never officially a director, which may have been a result of her keen understanding of the dangers involved. Besides, she was living in Washington, which provided an excuse.

I was enormously relieved not to participate except at second hand, in the acknowledged way, through my husband. I knew that on closer acquaintance I might see the gap between myth and reality that had always disturbed me in Kentucky—the difference between rhetoric and plain prose.

Over the elevators in the newspapers' lobby, the Judge's declaration of intent was engraved: "I have always regarded the newspapers owned by me as a public trust, and have endeavored so to conduct them as to render the greatest public service."

None of these large terms had ever been defined, and their weight alone seemed likely to bend fragile human spirits. What had the Judge meant by "public trust" and "public service"? The reiteration of the word "public" especially bewildered me. Of what public had the Judge been a part? From what position had he observed and judged that distant and mysterious public?

During the New Deal days, when Father had supported Roosevelt, there had perhaps been a perceived congruence between the aims of the governing and the wishes of the governed, but events in the past thirty years had widened the gap I had always felt between the well-intending and those on whom their intentions fall.

In the years since the anti-busing riots of 1974–75, the newspapers had changed, although I had not been aware of it. The riot had shown for the first time, and vividly, that the people the newspapers claimed to lead and inform were no longer willing to be passive recipients of this benevolent guidance.

In the early 1980s, Michael Kirkhorn, then a professor of journalism at the University of Kentucky, wrote an article in a Louisville magazine that touched on the effects of the anti-busing riot. "No one seems quite able to estimate the damage done to morale by the angry reaction to C-J coverage, which eventually won, ironically, the Roy W. Howard public service award, the Sigma Delta Chi public service award, and a Pulitzer Prize for photography," he wrote.

An employee told Kirkhorn it had been "the hardest period I've ever been through as a newspaperman. It was physically draining. . . . It was a story which would not go away. It went on and on and you never knew what an inordinate amount of time would be given to thought about underplaying or overplaying stories. . . . Ultimately it took its toll on all of us from a morale standpoint."

George Gill, president of the newspaper, told Kirkhorn, "I'm sure busing coverage had some lasting effect but I don't know how to measure it."

Kirkhorn himself felt that loss of control was the central issue, as Anne Braden had observed twenty years earlier. Kirkhorn wrote, "Most reporters and editors thoroughly dislike and fear disorder. To be confronted by enraged readers is one of the most disquieting experiences a journalist can have. . . . A newspaper will vibrate for some time from a shock that severe."

He went on to note two results of the unfortunate disturbance: a curious flatness in news coverage in the late seventies and eighties, and problems with leadership; for five years, the *Courier-Journal* lost a managing editor every year, beginning with the disaster that overtook Carol Sutton, reducing her to an assistant to the executive editor, and continuing with the departure of Michael Davies, Paul Janensch (who later returned), and Robert Clark.

Clark quit after eight years as executive editor because he did not want to be consigned, as Sutton would be, to overseeing the ombudsman—a recent and much-hailed attempt to deal with readers' criticism.

Editors whose services were no longer desired tended to find themselves in charge of reader complaints, questions of professional ethics, and quibbles about journalistic style—all serviceable smoke screens for more serious issues.

By the mid-1980s, there were other worries. Circulation was slowly but steadily declining. Small neighborhood weeklies and suburban "shoppers" were considered a serious threat, more dangerous than the potentially influential chain newspaper in Lexington, Kentucky's second-largest city, eighty miles away.

The newspapers' pretax profit sank to three percent, unheard of for a monopoly operation. The other companies were more profitable—until Standard Gravure began its decline—but the other companies had no symbolic value for the family.

Meanwhile, and probably most distressing to Father, the newspapers' right to lead was being questioned. Local politicians sometimes wondered out loud if the newspapers' editorial support helped or harmed them.

In the case of Harvey Sloane, a rich young outsider who had been elected mayor of Louisville in 1981, it sometimes seemed that the newspapers' admiring editorials had separated him from his first constituency, blacks whose respect he had earned when he operated a clinic in Louisville's ghetto. Later, Barry's successful battle to wrest control of this situation from Father and to reverse the newspapers' support for Sloane would further damage the mayor's political career.

As soon as I arrived in Louisville, I noticed the complicated and intense relationship among Harvey Sloane, his wife, Kathy, my parents, and Barry and Edie.

The Sloanes, an intelligent and attractive young couple who could still be defined, it seemed to me, as a unit, possessed the charm and the political ambitions Barry and Edie lacked.

Sloane's family were old friends of Father, and it may have been at his invitation that Harvey left the East Coast for the Kentucky hinterland, much as Jay Rockefeller had come down to West Virginia—to fill a perceived vacuum in native leadership.

Eventually Sloane became for me a symbol of Father's disillusionment with the poor and backward state where he had spent his life. Sloane brought with him a touch of the glamour of the big world.

Like Jay Rockefeller, Sloane arrived with a private fortune, obvious intelligence, and a well-developed sense of noblesse oblige. He brought the charm of the patrician to a state hamstrung by the quarrels of the local

Democratic party and the entrenched interests of coal mining, liquor, and tobacco.

He also brought a handsome wife who was overqualified for the traditional role of political helpmeet.

Father saw all the possibilities. He was excited at the prospect of coaching and supporting a young Democratic contender, as he had been years earlier in the case of Adlai Stevenson.

Perhaps he hoped that Sloane would one day represent Kentucky in Congress, where, with one notable exception, we had been served by men who were not patricians. Perhaps he even hoped for greater things. In any event, he chose to ignore Barry's increasingly jaundiced view of the relationship. As Nursie would have put it, Barry was "eaten up by the green-eyed monster."

That was perfectly understandable. There was never enough to go around in the Bingham family.

Barry depended on Father's goodwill to survive in his position as publisher, since Barry owned only a little more than fifteen percent of the newspapers' stock.

He soon became suspicious of the Sloanes, who seemed to be operating with all the guile and intelligence of those "politicians" Barry had begun to despise—smart and crafty manipulators who run off with all the prizes.

The Sloanes, in turn, complained bitterly when Barry tried to separate them from their patrons.

After Sloane was elected mayor of Louisville, Barry used the newspapers' Byzantine conflict-of-interest policy—of which I would learn more later—to excuse a cruel social break.

He decreed, and Edie carried out, an official edict: elected politicians were not welcome at the Big House, which for three generations had been the scene of endless political planning and celebration.

They were not welcome for fear that their presence might somehow contaminate the reporting of news and the editorial page—a fear which was of course real. They did, and do. But the mayor's presence at the Big House is not necessary for that result.

The Big House, however, was Barry's fortress—a fortress he never owned—and he could control access to its high iron gates. He could not control the revolving doors at Sixth and Broadway.

Father shook his head and sighed when the Sloanes were discussed—not, of course, in Barry's presence. Once again he was faced with Barry's stiff-necked propriety, which Father could not challenge without revealing his own compromises. Perhaps Barry's sense of propriety reminded Father of the Colonel's view of the fitness of things, or even the Judge's rectitude in the last years of his life, when the battles had been won.

Barry believed religiously in the family myth and interpreted it literally. He did not understand that it was only a myth, an elaborate justification, not a plan for daily behavior.

As soon as I returned to Kentucky, I noticed that the daily grind seemed to be wearing Barry down. He spent long hours at the newspapers, but in spite of a speed-reading course and an attempt at hypnosis, his reading remained painfully slow, and his many detractors would say that it took him two hours every morning to get through the morning newspaper.

He arrived at the office before most of his staff and secreted himself behind closed doors. After the riots, he installed bulletproof glass in his office windows and a button under his desk to summon the police.

The honors that had rained on Father and on his newspapers, which included seven Pulitzer Prizes, had declined to a drizzle by the early 1980s. Honors in journalism follow the lines of old alliances, and Barry's only alliances were with television.

He had never had access to Father's connections, many of whom went back to the old OSS days in London at the start of the Second World War.

It seemed to me that Barry had insisted on cutting himself off from that network, which included journalists and politicians, CIA agents and the owners of newspapers, when he refused to ask his old college roommate and friend Nicholas Daniloff to come to Kentucky as his assistant and adviser after Worth's death.

Daniloff had been Barry's friend in the Paris days; they had attended school in Paris and college together, where they had been roommates. But Daniloff's subsequent career in journalism led him elsewhere, and in 1986 he would be picked up in Moscow accused by the KGB of being an American spy.

It seemed to me that Barry was becoming a victim of the ruthless system that promotes nepotism yet degrades those who profit from it.

An older myth than the family myth decrees that males in America must make it on their own, and for men raised in privilege that rule both saps confidence and destroys outside support.

It takes an almost superhuman talent and self-confidence to justify, day by day, inherited power and money. Barry had neither the talent nor the self-confidence, and he was increasingly deprived of support. He was not a star, not even the evening star, and Father and his friends who depended on the myth of the star could not accept his limitations or see the strength of his virtues: his dedication and his probity.

Barry had always been close to Mother. When he was sick with Hodgkin's disease, he would eat only the broths and junkets prepared at the Little House. He admired and loved Mother and worked for her approval.

Eventually Barry became as angry as the Colonel, wrapped in his Confederate cape, glaring at the pimply Bingham School cadets outside the Asheville drugstore.

Like the Colonel, Barry believed in righteousness. He believed in a world where right was clearly divided from wrong, where devoted soldiers fought the enemy to the death. There were a few shadows on that landscape, cast by women who could not be fitted into the recognized categories of mother or sister, secretary or wife, nurse, cook, or maid. In Barry's world of male boarding schools, clubs and universities, hunting expeditions and safaris, the old view seemed to hold. But in Louisville in the 1980s—even inside the glass ball imposed by privilege—the old view was no longer adequate. There was a new reality, although it was very feeble. It depended on the emergence of a small black middle class and a handful of black politicians and on the presence of professional women.

In his position as publisher, Barry put into words the family myth. He filtered the changes in Father's view through his own political conservatism, giving voice to Father's disillusionment with what had happened to his world since the 1960s.

Father had taken the protests of the Vietnam years as a personal affront: the long hair and dirty clothes—often only too like his grandchildren's clothes and hair—the outrageous black leaders who were not interested in advice and moderation, the new young white leaders who were not part of the old system of Ivy League colleges and clubs, political patronage and the CIA, and who did not even aspire to belong.

Both black and white radicals represented the terrible threat of loss of control, of individual power free of a system that had allowed certain leaders to rise but had suppressed others entirely—especially when those others were poor, or black, or female.

Herbert Agar, who had been editor of the newspaper before the Second World War, had said, "The Truth that makes men [sic] free is for the most part the truth which men prefer not to hear."

Now those who had never been included in Agar's imagination—blacks, young people, women—were setting up their own Truth, refusing to hear the Truth as the newspapers preached it. It was one thing to run an interview with Oriana Fallaci above the fold on the newspapers' front page—few people in Kentucky knew who she was or cared about the issue. It was another to confront problems that had been part of Kentucky since long before the Judge came over the mountains.

It had seemed for a long time that Kentucky, which had once operated the largest slave market in the South, was safe from radical change. Integration had been "handled," and no effective black leadership had risen to dispute the control of white Democrats.

As the upper class abandoned the old city neighborhoods and its schools, where Father and his mother had been born and raised, physical separation from the problems of the decaying city made a cloying optimism acceptable. The same detachment and hope had produced the illusion of progress that had promoted a "New South" during Reconstruction.

In his book *Life Behind a Veil: Blacks in Louisville, Kentucky, 1865–1930*, George Wright described the "polite racism" which has flourished in Kentucky since Reconstruction. In 1891, a black reporter had remarked that in Louisville the "races get along nicely—like oil and water—the whites at the top and the Negroes at the bottom."

Wright added that this form of racism, with few overt incidents of violence or prejudice, would continue "as long as Afro-Americans willingly accepted 'their place,' which, of course, was at the bottom."

The amelioration societies the Judge and Father supported, such as the Commission on Interracial Cooperation or the Fellowship of Christians and Jews, publicized acts that showed interracial goodwill rather than attacking injustices. Well-funded white-controlled groups, in Wright's view, "attempted to control the black civil rights movement." For many years the attempt had succeeded. Only the emergence of militant blacks on the national scene threatened its continued success.

Its success involved blindness to the facts of racism in Kentucky, where in 1875 Henry Watterson, venerated as the *Courier-Journal*'s best-known editor, had called the Federal Civil Rights Act "an insult to the white people of the southern states."

Blindness cut out the sight of violence against blacks, which occurred in Kentucky as it did elsewhere in the South. Arthur Krock, who grew up in a small town in south-central Kentucky, recorded in his memoirs how he and another small boy had slipped into a shed to watch a lynching: "Then the mob hanged the Negro from a tree in front of the jail." He added, "It was a traumatic experience, and luckily I never saw, nor in our town was there, another"—a conclusion easily reached by men who believe in controlled change. But in 1988, a young black man was shot dead on a Louisville street; no suspects have been found.

There had never been a black mayor of a Kentucky city, or a black governor of the state, or a black U.S. senator or congressman since Reconstruction. The few blacks in the state legislature were controlled by gerrymandered political districts, and because they represented only eleven percent of the state's population, they were not powerful enough to force a change.

But the status quo had been weakened by changes on the national scene; there were new challengers, and the wire services and television sometimes reported their activities.

Most alarming, the newspapers continued to lose circulation. As one managing editor said a few years ago, "The people are voting out there every day, and it's going against us."

The changes since the sixties alarmed Barry. He was direct in expressing his concern. He was reflecting Father's increasing conservatism, but Father did not want the reflection to be so obvious. In putting Father's feelings into words, Barry was breaking an important, unspoken rule. These conservative ideas should have remained as private as the references to female "meat" that were staples in the family's repertoire.

What remained of the newspapers' liberal energy was spent in the 1980s supporting First Amendment issues, which were essential to continued control of the news. The newspapers seldom spoke editorially for equality now that equality was a right that blacks and women and other "minorities" were demanding rather than a favor handed down by the white leadership.

These changes, like other issues of power and money, could not be discussed within the family for fear of the contradictions that would be revealed. So Father could not explain why he wanted his female relatives to serve on the company boards. He needed us to right the balance, which was tipping dangerously toward Barry and his management. Father perhaps assumed that "his" women would act, unconsciously, as counterweights.

The unexamined—the inevitable.

Mother, too, was worried about changes in the old order. She had learned to work successfully in that world. She knew whom to speak to in order to get things done, and she knew who owed her a favor. Invitations to dinner at the Little House were the coin of the realm, and it was a coin which had great value.

The amenities could be preserved, the conventional view of woman as the protector of hearth and home could be supported when women used their dinner tables to raise and settle political issues, when the polite chat over coffee or drinks included tacit trade-offs. None of this, of course, could be described. For this the Big House, as well as the Little House, had been built, decorated, and maintained, and Mother's criticism of Edie perhaps stemmed from her anger that the big stage was not being used for important displays of skill and power. Edie tended to be more informal, more human—in Mother's terms, less political.

Mother's way was a highly successful one of causing things to happen without arousing the sleeping demons of male hostility. No one can criticize when power is used with such grace, along with a silver Georgian coffeepot and a tiny spoon.

Mother belonged, it seemed to me, to that "special group of women" which columnist Georgie Anne Geyer described so well: "They are almost all professional 'wives,' many of them having given up their own careers to marry rich and successful men. Many of the women are Hollywood-brittle, predictably coiffed and often similarly and expensively gowned—but they are also very bright women and they have the common sense their ambitious and limited husbands do not have. In a sense, one feels that these women are so strong that they have allowed their husbands to remain the eternal boys they indeed are."

I often had the same thought about Mother.

Whatever she abandoned to marry, it was not her intelligence or her ambition. Perhaps the prospect of teaching the classics or writing an important text on Greek drama or the elaborations of Latin grammar did not compare with the prospect of being the wife of a young man who, with her help and encouragement, would become the master of a big political galleon.

The fair young man Mother married, who was uncertain whether he wanted to be a poet, a novelist, or a publisher, was not the man who turned his monopoly newspapers into a state symbol. Something happened in between to harden his resolve, something that convinced the Judge, at the end, to give over the game that had kept Henrietta occupied for so many years, to cut her out, to cut his elder son out, and leave the companies to Father.

Of course, the Judge never seriously considered leaving this power in a woman's hands, but he used the long delay to shape and harden his younger son, and the tools he used certainly included both his daughter and his daughter-in-law. In matters of inheritance, family relationships become blunt instruments.

Soon after I moved back to Louisville, I saw how Mother worked at one of the ladies' luncheons she occasionally gave at the Little House. Father and Mother had moved back there after Barry became publisher in 1971; the wheel, it seemed, had come full circle.

The beautiful table on the terrace overlooking the river was set with embroidered linens and cut flowers. This was a scene where things were going to happen, not just the low-calorie salads and personal confidences of ordinary women's lunches.

As Mother talked to the mayor's wife, I noticed the subterranean communication between these two bright, energetic, and determined women, to whom direct action had been shown to be impossible.

Nothing needed to be said. It was all a question of hints and smiles, dangling sentences and raised eyebrows. These two women, although separated by a generation, understood each other perfectly. Scores had been settled, plans laid for the future.

Watching that delicate interplay, I realized for the first time that my presence at that scene, and at board meetings, would be seen as a threat. I spoke directly and even wrote things down.

I had forgotten the family code. Like Barry, I might find myself one day translating the unspeakable into words, turning our parents' secret reservations, their passions and prejudices, into bald statements. I, too, might be drawn into the vacuum created by their evasions. The unexamined, I knew, tended to become the inevitable. It was time to begin to notice.

31

By 1978, what I saw bewildered me.

My first board meetings were terrifying. I knew the extent of my own ignorance. I did not know the roles or the personalities of the dark-suited men—managers, lawyers, other directors—who sat around the big tables in the company boardrooms.

A few I remembered from childhood, old family friends like Wilson Wyatt, who had been mayor of Louisville during the war and had later managed Adlai Stevenson's campaign, or Lisle Baker, longtime business manager of the companies, whose family had lived in a big house near the Place. But even these men had known me, and I had known them, only when I was a child, thirty years earlier. They were survivors from that period, and their relationship with Barry seemed ambiguous.

Most of the other directors had been hired to manage the companies during the years when I was living in New York. Their positions in the hierarchy were hard to define, as were their personalities, under the bland and pleasant superficiality doing business in the South seems to require.

Of the power of one of these men, however, there could be no question. Paul Janensch, Barry's managing editor, had returned to the newspapers after having been expelled, a few years earlier, for general cussedness, I gathered. His forceful, humorless presence, his silence, and his dogged loyalty to his boss, whom all the other men called Junior, were conspicuous even at those first sessions.

The board meetings were held every three months. Each time, with considerable dread, I laid aside my own work and went to sit in those windowless and airless rooms, exempt from the play of weather and light. It is no coincidence that a recent book on the difficulties women face on newspaper staffs is called *A Room with No View*: the sealed rooms of modern newspapers seem to contribute to the inhibition and isolation of women.

The furniture in these rooms was heavily functional: a vast table and chairs as intimidating as the thrones at King Arthur's court. But this table clearly had a head, where Barry sat. The placement of the twenty or so other men represented mysterious alliances: lawyers sometimes sat with each other but more often at the elbow of a family member, managers from each company clustered protectively together, and Father, displaying his subtle use of symbols, often placed himself midway along one side of the table, next to one of "the girls."

Mother sometimes arrived breathless and a few minutes late, which gave Father an excuse to joke about the general tardiness of women, and the difficulty we supposedly had finding our way around town, a comment that seemed surprisingly inappropriate when he applied it to Worth's widow, Joan Bingham, who had lived and traveled all over the world.

Mother would place herself close to Barry at the huge table, while Eleanor, Barry's wife Edie, and I, perhaps less sure of our associations, plumped down wherever there was a vacant seat.

Barry, resolutely silent during the entire proceedings—a silence that matched Father's, but without his wordless dialogue of looks and sighs—sat at the head of it all with his yellow pad, on which he took careful notes. Near him would be Paul Janensch, also enclosed in cryptic silence, except when he issued his short report on the state of the newspapers.

The agenda would have been mailed out only a few days before the meeting, and its language seemed as arcane as the language of the meetings themselves. It was tempting to drop into a state of paralyzed boredom, especially when the lights were turned out and blurred figures flashed across a screen. I noted that these financial reports, that included data on circulation, advertising revenue, and profit, were offered with offhand casualness on machines that sometimes malfunctioned. The figures sped across the screen as though someone had assumed that this particular audience was neither interested in them nor capable of deciphering them—and indeed several years later Barry would complain that his female relatives did not know how to read a balance sheet.

When the lights came on again, I sometimes glanced at the portraits hung at odd intervals on the tan walls: the Judge, somber in academic robes that displayed a flash of scarlet, or "Marse Henry" Watterson, the fiery old editor. I also noticed a small picture of his wife, a nameless woman in spectacles with a book open on her knee.

The contrast between Mrs. Watterson's world of books and the world of print journalism seemed stark to me, and I marveled that Mother, in her days as book-page editor, had successfully, even brilliantly, put the two together. She had called her book page "The World of Books," and had seen to it that it was printed in the editorial section.

My talent and experience as a writer had no place in the world of the newspaper business. Here again the contrast between rhetoric and plain prose, between the dream represented by the myth and the reality of political intrigue and public events, seemed especially marked.

I had begun to teach writing at the University of Louisville, which had forced me to sharpen my use of terms; it was not possible to palm off abstractions on a classroom full of shrewd, undereducated, and determined people. I realized that the terms neither defined nor questioned in the company boardrooms would have been picked to shreds in the classrooms of the city university: terms such as "journalistic objectivity," "professional standards," "no sacred cows" . . .

At board meetings for the television and radio stations, terms the whole family appeared to find incomprehensible leapt into being, and we would murmur and titter as the new technology was paraded in front of us, veiled in a language more mysterious than that used in the Big House kitchen. Only Eleanor and Barry understood what these terms meant, yet the rest of us voted, with only a few sighs, for vast capital expenditures whose purpose remained obscure. I was struck by the family's unwillingness to ask awkward questions, as though we were not owners at all, but ignorant bystanders herded in for a display of magic.

The old half-friendly rivalry with the Norton family, which owned the television station rated just below ours, was also put to useful purpose. If they made an acquisition, it was a foregone conclusion that we must match them or go one better. If they bowed to the fad for traffic helicopters, then we must have one, too. The rivalry often seemed childish, and the issue was seldom the improvement of the "product." Prestige was involved, and when prestige was the issue, nothing else mattered.

In the same way, the ratings given our newscasts in a system that seemed to me open to manipulation were used to decide whether or not we were winning our war with the Nortons. Of course, advertising was the issue here, a critical one for the station, but that hardly seemed as important as the rivalry between the two families. A few years later, when the Nortons sold their television station, WHAS seemed to lose its only way of gauging success.

The expertness of the television station staff, and especially of the general manager, a saturnine man with whom Eleanor eventually became embroiled, was useful in intimidating the owners into silence. They knew and we did not, and they seemed less impressed by their easily cowed shareholders than the management of the newspapers or the printing company. Perhaps the general manager was aware that the television and radio properties were given little respect by owners who considered them the exclusive province of the Shively housewife. But his companies were making money.

A well-intentioned but undefined mandate to "diversify" had caused the purchase of several subsidiary operations that were only marginally successful. The managers of one such subsidiary, a company which produced television commercials, seemed particularly interested in new toys. One such wonder was proposed, voted for, and bought, with Barry's enthusiastic endorsement: a satellite uplink transmitter he hoped would be used by Kentucky corporations to woo their customers. "Teleconferencing" would be cheaper and more efficient than actually traveling to New York or Los Angeles.

I wondered out loud whether the big tobacco and liquor companies would choose to forgo the trips that provided their executives with so many treats: stays in expensive hotels, meals charged to the company's expense, flirtations with stewardesses, and so on. No one took my quibble seriously.

Five years and many uncounted dollars later, the staff promoter, now working for another company, admitted that the uplink had been a total failure. He said in an interview printed in the *Courier-Journal* that most executives preferred actually meeting their clients rather than conferring with them on a screen. No one had bothered to ask them before the uplink was purchased.

The same process was repeated many times during the next seven years. No proposal from a company manager was ever voted down by the board, and my questions were met with indifference, except in the case of the purchase of a license for so-called cellular radios. I felt that these car telephones might have a limited market in a poor, largely rural state like Kentucky; besides, there was heavy competition for the licenses and many had already been sold. There was some reason to worry, too, about the attitude of the FCC toward this extension of our monopoly.

In this instance, the vice president in charge of this purchase took the time to answer my questions, and although he could not persuade me of the viability of the project, his willingness to talk proved to me that such exchanges were not impossible. Eventually this project failed and the license was sold; the cost of the debacle was half a million dollars.

Generally, a subsidiary existed because of the determination of one man who was able to pursue his idea thanks to the family's bewilderment and management's implied belief that spending, or indeed losing money, was not a matter we took seriously. We would all have been ashamed to ask questions about our dividends, since we had learned from childhood that questions about money were vulgar and likely to be interpreted as displays of ugly greed.

Since the shareholders never asked why their dividends remained at a low level, or even declined, and since the executives did not own stock, there was no need for them to worry about the amounts of money they wasted on ill-conceived projects. No one asked what happened to these projects when they disappeared from the agendas, or how much money had been lost; that would have raised the dread issue of "accountability," which would have been viewed as a rude attack on the loyalty of our employees.

The board meetings at Standard Gravure had a different flavor, due to the greater age of the management and the vast gulf that divided their operation from the family.

The printing company had been considered a "money cow" for many years, and there was little interest in its operation. In fact Barry and Father seemed both amazed and appalled when union demands became a problem, a problem the management could not solve.

The printers were spoken of as wild men who resorted to sabotage when thwarted, and many stories were told about the vandalism that was said to increase the expenses of the operation. The blame was laid not on our inability to keep up with technological changes but on a recalcitrant union leadership. I first noticed the anti-labor prejudice that had come into the family since the New Deal days when those union leaders were described as irritating representatives of a class of which the family knew, and wished to know, nothing. It seemed likely to me that they were doing a good job of protecting their workers.

The tortured relation between white Southern liberals and the labor unions is far too complex to describe here. However, it is worth noting that while, as Morton Sosna wrote in *In Search of the Silent South: Southern Liberals and the Race Issue,* "racism and the willingness of employers to hire Negroes [sic] as strikebreakers traditionally had stifled the growth of labor unions in the South," progress had been made during the New Deal years, especially through the influence of native Southerners such as Katherine Du Pre Lumpkin of Georgia and Lucy Randolph Mason of Virginia, both of whom became executives in Southern offices of the CIO.

The North Carolina educator Frank P. Graham was also an effective voice for labor when, as president of the University of North Carolina, he defended labor organizers as well as denounced discrimination, with the able support of Josephus Daniels (whose descendant Jonathan Daniels would become my younger brother's godfather). But by the 1980s, these remnants of an earlier reconciliation appeared to have been destroyed by the South's ruling class. So we readily blamed company problems on the foolishness or the stubbornness of organized labor. At the newspapers and the broadcasting companies, union organizing was minimal or nonexistent, and so these problems did not, as the family saw it, arise. There "the plantation system," as newspaper employees called it, could be counted on to take care of any grievances.

The men in those boardrooms treated me with friendly politeness but had difficulty remembering which one I was. Perhaps shareholders all look alike, at least to the eye of management, as all black people or all Asians are said to look alike to their white observers.

The women in the Bingham family are blond, an example of the long underground life of the Colonel's faith in eugenics. In a bunch we must have looked like a small flock of birds, as alike in coloring and plumage as we were supposed to be in point of view. The company managers could not have known that we had been raised to live abstemiously; we probably would have been more embarrassed by conspicuous consumption than most of their wives. Money was not to be enjoyed but to be used for an undefined higher purpose—a family tradition that was seldom expressed directly and that would have been difficult for many of these managers to believe.

Barry's wife, Edie, often worked on a piece of needlepoint during board meetings, which gave her a distinguishing characteristic. I envied her the activity; perhaps it made daylong silence a little more bearable. In the same way, college girls in the 1950s had knitted their way through lectures given by male professors who were not likely to be interested in their female students' opinions. At one woman's college, I had heard, a professor stopped the clacking of the needles by telling his students that knitting was comparable to masturbation—an attack based on a misuse of Freudian doctrine, often a convenient way to dismay women.

Neither Eleanor nor I was yet at the point where we would begin to avail ourselves of the yellow legal pads and the nicely sharpened pencils, bought from the American Indians, which were laid out at our places. Later we would begin to make notes, but in the early years neither she nor I would have felt comfortable taking anything down.

Mother always looked pale and beautiful in her city suits, and she was treated with marked respect by the men around the table. Now and then she would ask a piercing question, often prefacing it with "I know this is a stupid question, but . . ." It was never a stupid question. She had known the companies thoroughly for fifty years, although at second hand, and she had her interests: conservation—a program to recycle newsprint was one of her causes—and the proper use of English. She abhorred faddish changes and bad grammar, and seemed, as her mother and grandmother had before her, to connect good usage with good morals.

Eleanor and I wore the feathers and flew with the flock. No one had any idea what we were thinking, although occasionally Father would whisper a question or a comment. Meeting between sessions in the ladies' room, Eleanor and I would sometimes sigh or laugh, but the curtain was going up again, we were wanted on the stage, and there was hardly time to dab on lipstick and comb our hair.

The atmosphere would change after lunch and drinks were served, still in the windowless room, by uniformed young women who seemed to know that they, too, were there on trial. Sometimes I would look at one of these unnamed servers as she poured the coffee or took my plate away, feeling the cruel separation that has long prevented rich women from identifying with women who work. I feared that to these women I seemed as alien as did the men, and I wished there was a way to tell them that I, too, poured coffee and took away plates and wondered if I had any business in a room flavored with the strong tobacco smell of power and money.

In the afternoon, the agendas would come out again, and any questions would seem impulsive, even rude interruptions of the schedule, of the smooth flow. This continued for two days, four times a year, without apparent effect on either the companies or their management.

After a year, I knew it would be impossible for me to remain silent forever. When I voted for an enormous outlay of money whose purposes I only partly understood, I felt queasy, sickened, as though I had signed my name to a forged check. When managing editors abruptly disappeared, with few or no explanations, to be replaced by men who seemed at least outwardly similar, I wondered what executions were going on behind the scene. There was something hostile to my existence in my continued silence. I was trying, once again, to fit in. I could tell from the somber suits I chose, which I never would have worn for any other occasion, that I was disguising and deforming myself in order to remain invisible.

Institutions create their own atmosphere, which grows dense over a period of half a century: in the atmosphere of those boardrooms, it was impossible to ask why there were no women in management, other than one woman executive at WHAS, impossible to ask why there were no blacks at all. To ask those questions would have been as ridiculous as to rise up at a country club dance and demand to know why there were no Jews. Yet the lack of outsiders, as they were labeled in that realm, isolated and weakened the Bingham women, who, after all, were perceived as outsiders, too. The sense of humor and the sense of reality outsiders sometimes share would have reinforced our right to be there. Instead we were surrounded by men, many of whom had known women only as wives and mothers, daughters and sisters, secretaries, cooks, nurses, and waitresses. Not until these men's daughters grew up would changes in women's roles appear in Kentucky which had become commonplace in the world outside.

Even more destructive to my sense of my own authority was the unwritten agreement signed by everyone who enters the corporate world. By sitting around one of those enormous tables, an individual agrees, tacitly, to support a system that excludes her most important values, a system openly or covertly endorsing racism, homophobia, an exaggerated deference to the upper class, and misogyny. These attitudes may never appear in writing, but they are sure to color the jokes and stories that are passed after drinks have been served.

A lone woman—or a lone black—at those vast tables is no threat at all. No one can be expected to take on the system single-handedly, especially since it is, after all, a club which one must agree to join in order to participate. Too often, the invitation is seen as a compliment: you are better than those others whose gender or color you share who would never be asked to join.

Father's role at those board meetings remained mysterious to me. Clearly he enjoyed the company of "his" women. He seemed to like to see the four of us, dressed up and attentive, sitting around the table as we had once sat around the dinner table in the Big House. The family did not spend much time together, except at board meetings; our differences lay just below the surface, differences that were serious. Questions of child rearing, of education and advancement, of the responsibilities and rights of individuals, were strewn like broken glass in our casual encounters. So the board meetings, where nothing "personal" could be discussed—although, of course, everything that was discussed was to a degree personal—gradually replaced the picnics and visits which, two years earlier, I had imagined.

Ideological differences were fed by old rivalries, by the anger of adult children who feel that there is never enough to go around and who are ashamed that they still miss the love they know will never be available. "Family Hold Back" was a motto from the poor South of Reconstruction, when there was not enough food for both guests and children. "Family Hold Back" was still the motto of our shared emotional life, when guests and friends, colleagues and advisers, seemed to have a surer place at the feast than more or less disappointing offspring. Lawyers knew their place there, managers felt that at least a hamburger was their fair share, but the adult children, rich and educated and, as Mother would later angrily assert, "all beautiful," were still not sure of the crumbs: "I am unworthy so much as to gather up the crumbs under Thy table," as the Episcopalian liturgy says. But whose was the table? Who was the host who might bestow the crumbs?

The silence which Barry and Father shared, which seemed to show deference, even condescension, to their employees, held the answer. But the answer was expressed ambiguously, in Barry's strained terseness and in Father's signs and whispers. We had all learned, as children, to earn attention, even admiration, by expressing what our parents did not express. Now it seemed we had a new and terrible secret to reveal. Father was letting it be known, without words, that he doubted Barry's ability to run the companies. He often mentioned Barry's exhaustion with anxious concern, shaking his head, as though he had realized too late that the son raised to be a follower would break his heart trying to be a leader. And there was no one else.

Father appeared not to like Paul Janensch, who was neither easily intimidated nor a fool. There seemed, in fact, to be nothing Paul wanted, which made him dangerous. He was an outsider, although he had been incorporated into the system and had burrowed to its heart. He had neither grace, smoothness, nor tact—the weapons of the upper class. He seemed stubborn, bad-tempered, and ambitious to me, and he knew all of Barry's secret fears.

Father, it seemed to me, preferred George Gill, the CEO, who had worked his way up from the bottom in the accepted journalistic way, beginning as a poor boy from Indianapolis who dreamed, as he later told me, of one day running the monolith at Sixth and Broadway. Gill seemed to me as tough as Janensch, with whom he was locked in secret combat, but far more intelligent, far smoother, and more direct. Paul had the temerity of the schoolyard bully who knows when threats are more effective than fists. George knew how to bring things to a head decisively, without bullying or evasions. Neither was cut from the cloth that had supplied characters like the Colonel, the Judge, or Father. But Father knew his man. Gill would appear to listen, then go his own way, and his own way would work. Janensch would cloud up and threaten, then go his own way, and his own way would fail.

Later I noticed differences between these men's relationships with their wives, which would have important consequences for me. Janensch's wife had been a reporter at the *Courier-Journal* when they met, and had been fired or "let go" because the conflict-of-interest policy prohibited hiring a married couple. She had tried valiantly to make an independent life for herself, but I felt that she had been harmed somewhere along the way. She was savagely criticized by the family because of her hair and clothes. In contrast, George Gill's wife, an outwardly more conventional and well-dressed woman, had with her husband's encouragement started a career late in life which she seemed to enjoy. Gill had been raised by what he called "an executive mom."

Father was pleased by one detail: the Gills wanted to join the Louisville Country Club, and he could arrange that. This meant a measure of control.

During those first years, I sometimes felt that Barry was on trial, as was Janensch, and that they both knew it, which explained their tense silence during board meetings. Gill was not on trial. He had the support of the man who owned the companies. This allowed him to be freer and friendlier.

I thought that Barry knew about our parents' criticism although he probably never heard a word of it. Privately Mother complained about Edie's parties: they were not brilliant enough, she felt. Father complained about a similar lack of *joie de vivre*; he seemed disappointed that Barry had to work so hard. Later, when I read a description of President Franklin Roosevelt's first hundred days in the White House, I would note the same emphasis on geniality and charm. It was upper-class, it was casual, it was the method of ruling least likely to cause dissent.

Perhaps Barry associated this muted criticism with the reappearance of his two younger sisters. In that world, women are nearly always genial and charming, and men can appear to be mere drudges by comparison. Women sometimes cause trouble, because of our ability to act on impulse, to turn the unspoken directives of men into action.

Barry probably knew that Father would never bring himself to make an ugly break, to discredit the son he loved but could not admire. So, from the beginning, Barry distrusted the uses to which his sisters might be put, and he displayed an iron resistance to our presence in his boardroom, a resistance partly disguised by his habitual good manners. He was glad to see us in the old familiar surroundings of the Place, where we were sisters and daughters, mothers and wives—or, more alarmingly, ex-wives. But he did not want us in his world at Sixth and Broadway, blurting out what might otherwise be left unsaid. His resistance stiffened his shoulders and back, engraved his silence, sharpened the flick of his wrist when he looked at his watch.

I knew that all the old forces were at work. I could feel the strong pull of the vacuum—the unexamined: the inevitable. Sometimes Father would glance at me meaningfully; very occasionally, he would whisper a word or two, usually in the form of a joke, but which indicated some half-smiling reservation about the business at hand. He had persuaded himself that he must not speak at board meetings since his son did not—both seemed to have agreed that management must not be embarrassed by questions—but Father had many things to say. He had not run the companies for a lifetime without accumulating a quantity of information and prejudices, opinions and fears. It seemed to me that I understood him far too well. I could almost taste his words in my mouth. Yet I knew if I summoned the courage to question him directly, he would deny all knowledge of discontent.

The studied formality of those first board meetings had been touched by a ray of brightness: Barry had presented a series of slides that showed company outings and award ceremonies, even including some shots of his daughters riding horseback. The slide shows were short, and Barry seemed to enjoy commenting on them as he stood behind the projector. After all, he had produced documentaries when he had worked at CBS in New York, a talent for which he no longer had an outlet. But I noticed that his managers smiled when they mentioned "Junior's Horse and Pony Show." They did not know that since childhood Barry had been detailed to make home movies and take snapshots; it was a role he felt comfortable in assuming, since it allowed him to scrutinize his exasperating family at a safe remove, through a long-distance lens.

Shortly after the women appeared at board meetings, these slide shows abruptly stopped. I did not wonder at the time what had happened. Later it seemed to me that our presence had forced Barry to guard himself. He saw himself now as the heir among challengers, rather than as the champion who had picked up the fallen standard. He could no longer afford the little indulgences, like the slide show, which might expose him to ridicule.

Finally, after more than two years of board meetings, I began to ask questions. The answers, when they came, were perfunctory. But I was pleased by my ability to ask at all—to risk words.

The atmosphere at the board meetings changed as Eleanor and Edie began to ask questions, too, often prefacing them with Mother's ingratiating remark: "I know this is a stupid question, but . . ." Although we lacked Mother's years of experience, none of our questions seemed stupid to me. Late learners, but not slow learners, we brought the experience of women who had worked and written, borne children and raised children, to questions which were often practical or value-laden, two areas in which we were expert.

Barry would flip up his watch and comment that we were already running twenty minutes late. Before the arrival of the women, board meetings had been accomplished in a matter of hours—a real rubber stamp, one of the old hands told me. Decisions were made at weekly "Dipnoan" meetings, named by Barry for a fish that can breathe both on land and in the water. They were held at the shabby private club on River Road that excluded Jews, blacks, and most single women. (Father sometimes persuaded the board to accept the widows of his friends, and to my embarrassment, Barry arranged a membership for me when I returned to Kentucky.)

There, served by black waiters in white jackets, with a view of the Ohio, the real decisions were made by Barry, Paul Janensch, George Gill, and a handful of other executives. Dipnoan meetings, of course, made the board meetings irrelevant, and explained some of Barry's irritation with the long-drawn-out proceedings, lengthened by discussion of issues that had already been settled. I did not understand until later the role of the fish that can breathe both on land and in the water.

Soon after I became a director, Father asked me if I felt that the board meetings should be longer, in order to allow time for more questions. I thought it was a fine idea. There was no further discussion, and soon the board meetings were taking two full days rather than a single morning. We began to see more slides, more graphs and charts, and to hear more presentations by company managers. There was still little time to ask questions, however. The business of the board meetings had simply been expanded to fill the allotted time, which increased my irritation and sense of futility.

By 1980, there was a touch of something electric in the air, like the flickering heat lightning before a summer storm.

32

The next move in the family game took me completely by surprise, for it had to do with the city. Louisville, a bustling industrial town during my childhood, had begun to die in the late 1950s.

The main shopping street was now a desolate mall, with empty concrete planters and tawdry shops that catered to the blacks marooned in the central city. The segregation of neighborhoods that had preserved the status quo had also drained the city of its mixed and lively population as middle-class whites moved to the suburbs. The connections between whites and blacks living downtown had been destroyed. Now the border between black Louisville and white Louisville was symbolized by graffiti on a wall at Eighth and Main: black to the west of the crossing, white to the east.

The blackening of downtown brought consternation to the owners of the newspapers. The afternoon *Times* had once depended on street-corner sales, and although that was no longer the case, it was still a city newspaper. As it lost circulation, because its white readers no longer lived in town, the need to whiten the city became acute—although not as acute as it would become when sales of the *Times* actually dropped below sales of the *Courier* in the metro area, a disaster curtailed by the closing of the *Times* in 1987.

Apparently no one considered attempting to attract black readers and advertisers by giving more coverage to "black" news and hiring black editors and reporters. That would have meant admitting that we were no longer serving our readers, which would have contradicted the family myth of public service.

By the late 1970s, however, preventative action was needed, and Father and his friends in business were encouraging commercial development downtown. White workers and shoppers and conventioneers might help to bring the old city back to life. A hideous riverside hotel was the first fruit of these efforts; its builder, who had also designed the hotel, was angered by criticism of its looks. Next Father commissioned a local sculptor to design a huge clock for the mall, where wooden racehorses sometimes pranced creakingly around a track, but the clock often malfunctioned and even at its best it did not attract crowds. Recently yet another gadget has been bought by the city to enliven its mall, a "trolley"—actually a bus with designs on its sides—which will cost taxpayers more than five million dollars. Its purpose is to ferry shoppers up and down the mall, since its length and desolate appearance make it forbidding to pedestrians. The newspaper, now owned by Gannett, christened the gadget "the boondoggle trolley," perhaps reflecting a less obsequious attitude toward downtown programs than that of the former owners.

Aside from its potential effect on the *Times*'s circulation, the death of the old downtown showed that the system was no longer working. Concrete planters and mechanical clocks could not reverse the effects of continuing segregation. The barriers that were keeping the city schools "unmixed" to a certain degree, even after busing, depended on "magnet" schools, easily obtained transfers, and gerrymandered school districts. However, the success of this effort was also preventing Louisville's whites from brushing elbows with people who looked different from their neighbors in the all-white suburbs. The distancing would lead to many problems, as whites began to imagine that every black figure represented robbery, rape, and murder. In the old days, when the downtown sidewalks were crowded with black workers, white shoppers, and rowdy soldiers from nearby Fort Knox, prejudice had had less opportunity to flourish than it had in the vacuum continuing segregation created.

Father and his friends decided that a downtown shopping center was the answer, one that had been applied with varying degrees of success in other failing cities. The hollow boosterism of the newspapers' editorials in support of this frayed solution astonished me. They were sometimes contradicted by the explicit, well-articulated criticism of the columnist who wrote in the *Courier-Journal* on local architecture. At the same time, an ex-mayor, a leading liberal in his day, suggested that fronts be erected to cover the many vacant lots downtown, where old buildings had been torn down. This would have created a Potemkin village to greet the thousands of guests who descend on Louisville every May at Derby time. Fortunately the suggestion was not accepted.

A determined group of "preservationists," as they were called, without ironic intention, were opposed to the destruction of late-nineteenth-century commercial buildings. They now rallied to defeat the latest plan, which called for the demolition of the Will Sales Building, a small and grimy structure with an interesting façade, to make way for the shopping center. The Will Sales Building had housed the *Courier-Journal* forty years earlier.

Barry's wife, Edie, devoted her considerable energies to this battle, which at once pitted the Chamber of Commerce, the newspapers, and local businesses against activists and volunteers. Edie had worked for The American Institute of Architects in Washington, D.C., and she brought to the contest an understanding of architectural aesthetics, as well as the energy of a young woman penned up in the suburbs.

Will Morgan, the newspaper columnist who wrote on architecture, supported the preservationists, and there was even talk of volunteers lying down in front of the bulldozers. Meanwhile the developers of the shopping center and their local backers were threatening to drop the project.

I did not know that Mother had championed the shopping center until a letter to the editor she had written appeared in the *Courier-Journal*. In it Mother sharply disassociated herself from her daughter-in-law, Edie, and criticized her campaign as shortsighted and destructive. I was horrified by the harsh tone of the letter, which would be read by many people who knew both women—and by many more people who, since they did not know them, would be baffled by the hostility the letter revealed. Mother later told an interviewer that she had been persuaded to write the letter by the chairman of a local bank, who had told her that the shopping center was at stake. Without it, Mother believed, "the desuetude and decay of Fourth Street [will be] permanently insured."

The language Mother used, both in her letter and in the interview, was the sharply defined, elegant English I had come to associate with the King James version of the Episcopalian prayer book, descriptions of character in Dickens's novels, and the cautionary tales of my childhood. For women who adopt this rhetoric of the upper-class male world, as I had tried to do in Harvard writing classes in the 1950s, the lash of language draws no blood: it is an exercise of the intellect, a fireworks display of detachment and erudition. But Edie felt the words as a lash, not as a display of rhetoric. Women in the Colonel's audience might have felt the same sting when he described them as the "partly submerged half of creation," a phrase he probably enjoyed for its sound and shimmer, ignoring its ability to draw blood.

Edie was hurt by the letter. She and Mother had lunch after it was published, as Edie later told an interviewer, but the occasion was painful, and Edie said that nothing had been resolved. She may not have realized that what bothered Mother most was her daughter-in-law's use of power.

Edie organized other people effectively and strengthened her own conviction with the support of well-informed friends and colleagues, and she was outspoken. Mother acted indirectly. She criticized direct action on the part of women as a misuse of the authority which was only on loan to them because of their husbands' importance. So Edie's way was by its nature a repudiation of the old velvet-glove approach, and although Edie was unaware of it, the success her group nearly achieved and the attention they were given marked the limitations of Mother's way.

Finally the old buildings on Fourth Street were torn down, and the Will Sales façade was stored for some vague future use. It was a victory for Mother, and for an older way of doing business. But it had been a close call.

The results, however, were not what Mother anticipated. The new shopping center blocked off Fourth Street and so it is considered a public space. Since the downtown area is patronized largely by the black people who live nearby, the shopping center became their territory. Security guards were hired to drive away what the newspaper described in headlines as "rowdy youths," inevitably black. The American Civil Liberties Union intervened, but young people who are black are still looked upon with great suspicion in the glass palace where the wares of the middle class—expensive soap, letter paper, lingerie, and knickknacks—seem to have lost their admirers.

Adrienne Rich wrote, "When we think of an institution, we can usually see it embodied as a building: the Vatican, the Pentagon, the Sorbonne . . . What we cannot see, until we become close students of the institution, are the ways in which power is maintained and transferred behind the walls and beneath the domes, the invisible understandings which guarantee that it will reside in certain hands but not in others, that information shall be transmitted to this one but not to that one, the hidden collusions and connections with other institutions of which it is supposedly independent . . . When we think of the institution of motherhood, no symbolic architecture comes to mind, no visible embodiment of authority, power, or of potential or actual violence . . . We do not think of the power stolen from us and of the power withheld from us, in the name of the institution of motherhood."

For years Mother had been "a close student of the institution" in Louisville; she knew how to use its energies for her own ends. Powerless as a mother, and once again powerless as a mother-in-law who could not control Edie although she had given her her house and her position as publisher's wife, Mother found her challenge to the old way insupportable. The destruction of the buildings on the mall, trivial in themselves and rapidly reduced to a pile of rubble, represented Mother's implacable commitment to power: as wife of the chairman of the board, mother of the publisher, and hostess to the town's businessmen and politicians, as well as to emissaries from the wider world. The institution of motherhood, had it existed, would have seemed by comparison only a shack.

The younger women in the family, however, had not learned Mother's system. She had not passed along its rules, any more than she had passed

along hints for making perfect beaten biscuits. Her secrets remained her
secrets in a system that inevitably pits women against each other. The
margin for activity is so narrow, there at the edge of the men's world, that
no more than one woman can get a foothold, and she must maintain it by
knocking off contenders.

Edie, Eleanor, and I tended to form political alliances with our contem-
poraries, young men striving to make their way up in the hierarchy, not yet
tightly strapped down by political and social ties. There were even a few
young women who were potential allies, such as my lawyer, Rebecca Westerfield, or the women who taught in the Women's Studies Department at
the University of Louisville, or the few women in state and city government.
These women were not dangerous, because they were not yet powerful. The
young men to whom we turned, however, were potentially quite dangerous:
managers and executives who might use our enthusiasms to advance their
own aims, or to enrage Barry, when that was useful, or to discredit the
causes we were supporting. Mother would never have made the mistake of
confiding in ambitious young men who were not yet recipients of seats in
a box at the finish line at the Derby or invitations to dinner at the Little
House. They were still outside the system and their loyalties were fluid.

In terms of our futures at the family companies, our ignorance would
cost us dear. It was impossible for us to know, as new directors, who was
currying favor with Barry, or combining with other men for other purposes.
Local politicians were part of the same elaborate mechanism, as I had
learned with Harvey Sloane. Yet we younger women in the family were
placed by inheritance at the bald spot where all systems meet, where money
and power are found, willy-nilly, in the hands of women.

My younger sister Eleanor had come back to Louisville in the summer
of 1978, encouraged by my reports; she soon began working at WHAS. For
nine months, she was a special researcher for the general manager, an
ambitious and talented man who had Barry's ear. In March 1979, Eleanor
became director of corporate services, a position created for her, to manage
all the departments in which the radio and television stations were jointly
involved: art, promotion, special programming, community relations, and,
much more important, the companies' moribund affirmative action program. I worried that a job especially created for a family member would lay
her open to attack. At the same time, I was impressed by Eleanor's energy
and courage as she moved quickly around town, talking at meetings called
to address issues of interest to various neighborhoods, serving as a sort of
ambassadress from the fortress on Chestnut Street.

Although she has never called herself a feminist, Eleanor was probably
the only woman in her family to have many close women friends. She had
been spared the automatic discounting of women that had been current in

the 1950s when I came of age. In fact, it had seemed to me that as a child she escaped the isolation of life on the Place by surrounding herself with friends who shared some of her enthusiasms. During the 1960s, she had known women who were not mothers, sisters, and wives, who functioned in a different world. So, almost as a matter of course, after she had been at WHAS for some time, Eleanor called a meeting of all the women in the "Bingham companies," as they were often called.

For the first time, at least in my experience, all the women Father employed came together in one room to discuss their shared concerns. I did not realize until I walked into that room the sheer number of women who worked for Father. No statistics were available, but it was my guess that at least a third of the companies' twenty-two hundred employees were women, and the figure probably was closer to fifty percent. Most were clustered in the lowest-paid and most vulnerable jobs, as secretaries, maintenance workers, cafeteria employees, mail-room personnel, and telephone solicitors.

The potential power in that crowded room was impressive. I realized that if these women acted together, anything might happen. Unfortunately there were no other meetings of the women. When, a few years later, I tried to resurrect the group, Barry vetoed the suggestion. Women who were surviving in the companies told me that an earlier attempt had met the same fate, and advised me to let sleeping dogs lie. Nothing is more alarming to men in positions of authority than the sight of a room full of women.

Now I realized that Eleanor, once the little girl I had helped to raise in the 1940s and early 1950s, had become almost a stranger to me during the years when I had lived in New York. I had felt that I had done all I could for the quiet, undemanding child Eleanor had been, who had learned to look for attention outside the family, combining the personal and the political in the style of the sixties, when she came of age. But she was the youngest of five children, and her appetite for recognition and love was sharp. Inevitably she would find, as I had, that the urge to be loved and appreciated was aroused by living in the haunts and among the figures of our childhood.

I had not followed Eleanor's activities between the time when she graduated from a girls' boarding school, Concord Academy, outside of Boston, in 1964 and her return to Louisville in 1978. She had gone for a while to the University of North Carolina, which the family still referred to as the Judge's alma mater. Mother had commented in a letter that it seemed odd to be sending a child South rather than East for an education. After a while, Eleanor had left North Carolina and had gone to England, where she had attended the University of Sussex in Brighton. Her later life in London, as she had described it to me, reminded me of Henrietta's vivid experiences in the 1920s and 1930s.

For a while, Eleanor had worked for a fashion designer on Carnaby

Street. She later told an interviewer that Mick Jagger had been among her clients and that she had asked him back again and again for fittings. Then she went to Spain, to an island off Barcelona where she and several friends bought a house. Somehow she turned up in Israel in 1967 during the Six-Day War and had an experience that reminded me of the Colonel's at Appomattox. In an interview, she described shrapnel rattling through the trees and Israeli soldiers throwing her and her friends to the ground and lying on top of them "so we would be saved and they would be shot if it was an all-out attack." She had grown up with the Bingham family myth, which embroidered heroics and quasi-military adventures, and she had been affected by it, as I had been. She was saved from a worship of the solitary hero of the Lost Cause by her involvement with a world where women's roles were changing.

But the questions remained for her, as they did for me. How does a woman who inherits wealth and position justify herself? And what is the role of glamour, magic, and excitement in privileged white upper-class life? There were no easy answers.

In the late 60's, Eleanor went to Egypt with the Grateful Dead, along with some members of the Jefferson Starship, who tried to find the chords to raise the spaceship which, according to a myth of the time, was buried under the Great Sphinx. Her account reminded me of the tale of our great-great-great-grandfather William's discovery of a diamond ring on a cart track leading south.

In 1971, Eleanor returned to the United States and went to work for a friend of Barry's who was starting a public-access community television station in Aspen, Colorado. Either in Aspen or earlier in Spain, Eleanor came across one of the first cheap, portable black-and-white television cameras, which interested her, she later said, in making documentaries. She began teaching workshops in New York and Los Angeles, and producing and editing films in partnership with a friend named Leslie Shatz. This young man was scorched by the family's attitude during a visit to Louisville in the late 1970s and he subsequently disappeared from view.

Before that, however, he and Eleanor made a documentary on the Ku Klux Klan called *Heritage of Hate*. To film it, Eleanor assumed a pseudonym, reassuring the "new klansmen" she interviewed that she was not antagonistic to their views. Eleanor asked Father to narrate the film, and his voice with its eloquent sweetness seemed to resolve hidden problems: the role played by the Colonel in the formation of the Ku Klux Klan in North Carolina, the role played by the invisible filmmakers, and the absence of a point of view about the activities of the modern Klan. The film was highly accomplished, and it won the John Grierson Award at the New York Film Festival in 1978 and was invited to the 1978 Cannes Film Festival as the only

American documentary shown that year. It was a strange sprout from the family myth.

During her time at WHAS, Eleanor seemed to me to avoid most of the traps laid for her by a management that saw her presence as an opportunity to demonstrate its loyalty to Barry. In the end, however, something happened which she did not discuss with me, and she left WHAS, it seemed, under a cloud. She was about to be married to a young Louisville architect, and that was the highly acceptable reason given. However, the role of the saturnine general manager remained obscure. As so often happened, the facts were veiled by embarrassment, chagrin, and swirling antagonisms, and I never knew the real story.

The pleasure Eleanor and I took in each other's company those first years in Kentucky was very sweet. We had not spent time together since the late 1950s, and I had forgotten her humor and her charm. As sisters, although separated by ten years, we shared a common language of illusion and allusion, hints and innuendos. We could nearly always understand each other, and our memories of life on the Place often matched, although Eleanor was somewhat more amused by the eccentricities of that life than I was. Years earlier, she had written me a letter describing a summer evening's expedition to cut flowers, which involved mosquitoes and misunderstandings, a bucket with a hole in it and the bemusement of several guests; the scene, which she had found entertaining, would have left me gasping for a breath of reality.

Eleanor had benefited in one way from her later birth: by the time she graduated from boarding school, the family had realized that women are sometimes allowed into the professions. Although she had never been encouraged to prepare herself for a career, Eleanor had been given an opportunity to work one summer as an intern for the *Courier-Journal,* an opportunity that would be provided to both the young women and the young men of our children's generation.

It was always easy to discredit any Bingham who came to work at the companies, since nepotism implies that its beneficiary is incompetent. Many years later, in an interview, Eleanor's city-room supervisor claimed that she had asked for the afternoon off because "I'm tired, and my name is Bingham." I did not believe the story. Eleanor and I had learned early that we would be punished for pulling rank. Employees of the companies could not be expected to know or to believe that. They were aware of too many instances when pulling rank had helped men in the companies to survive.

Eleanor was close to Mother and always had been. Father's remoteness had helped her relationship with Mother, who did not have to compete with his overwhelming charm. Eleanor knew more about Mother's early years, when, coming from Virginia as a bride, she had seen the Big House as a place where the dogs slept on the chairs and hunting boots steamed in front of the fire, almost a wilderness to the young scholar from Richmond and Radcliffe—a wilderness she soon settled, as Virginians, historically, had settled Kentucky, bringing their aristocratic ways and their finer accents to the wilds of the West.

Eleanor had a slightly different view of the life we had shared as children, due to having been born fourteen years after Worth. She and Jonathan had belonged to a different family from that of the older three children. She had been devoted to Jonathan, and I remembered her stunned look at his death, when she had been only eighteen. She had scarcely known Worth, who had died when she was twenty, but she seemed to admire Barry. She longed for his praise and shared many of his interests, as well as his belief in the future of television. Yet Barry seemed unaware of her, at best, or alarmed if she intruded into his view.

Eleanor's feeling about me was influenced by the family myth that imposed a dangerous dualism: The Bad Sister and the Good Sister. Rose Red and Snow White. Mary Bingham McKee, the queenly Bad Sister, and Sadie Bingham Grinnan, the mild Good Sister, were the most recent examples. The Good Sister was defined by her loyalty to father and brothers, which often made marriage impossible; the Bad Sister by her independence, which was called greed. That dualism produced the name later given to a business deal financed by loans from Barry, Eleanor, and me. It was called BGS: Barry and his Good Sisters. But where there is a Good, unfortunately, there must eventually be a Bad. That black-and-white view would threaten our relationship during the coming struggle.

Eleanor and I came to know each other better in 1979 when we talked to a reporter who was writing an article on "the girls" for a Louisville magazine. Michael Kirkhorn saw through our *folie à deux*—the shared humorous exaggeration through which we were filtering our memories. Eleanor told Kirkhorn, "For the youngest child in the family—by the time they get around to you they're exhausted—all they care is that you should have the basic skills—walk, talk, and feed yourself." Her attitude seemed to me appropriate for a survivor, a cheerful and determined young woman who would make her own way. Yet I knew she had been given even less of the little there was to go around: Family Hold Back. And that would eventually have its effect.

Eleanor and I both worried about reaction to Kirkhorn's article, which was called "The Bingham Black Sheep." It was headlined: "Sisters Eleanor and Sallie Bingham are making waves in their family's male-dominated dynasty." That shocked me into thought. I had my own life to live, as a writer and a mother, and the idea of "making waves" frightened me: what would be the result? I was particularly uneasy about Mother's reaction. Like all women in America who have borne children, Mother had long since learned that she was solely responsible for us, from the day of our birth until the day of our death, or hers. If questions were raised about us, she was immediately exposed to criticism, or felt that she was—which was the same thing. Many years earlier I had heard the slogan: "Women should appear in print only three times in their lives: when they are born, when they are married, and when they die." Perhaps that slogan provides a mother's only protection.

To my amazement, neither Mother nor anyone else in the family mentioned "The Bingham Black Sheep," although Kirkhorn told me years later that Barry said that "the girls" had "misremembered" things about our childhood. Perhaps the family was simply too stunned to comment. However, I suspect there was another reason: silence is at times a more effective threat than words. When silence is the weapon, there is always the worry that at some point far in the future the silence will be broken. The subject is never broached, the air is never cleared—and so the anxiety lingers.

Every night during that time, when I stood at my kitchen sink washing dishes, I looked across the Back Woods to the Big House's massive chimney. I was trying to live outside of its shadow, writing, teaching, raising my sons. But the shadow stretched to touch me whether I willed it or not.

33

In 1980, success honed my nerve, and time away from Kentucky reminded me that there was another world. I went to New York that winter for the production of my first play, at the Women's Project.

A year earlier, I had begun work in a wild rush of energy on a play I eventually called *Milk of Paradise,* from a line in "Kubla Khan," by Samuel Taylor Coleridge, which Father had read out loud years before.

The milk of Paradise represented privilege to me, and its magical isolation; Coleridge's poem seemed to describe the atmosphere of the Place as I remembered it through the haze of more than thirty years. The play was based on that world.

I was fired by a sure sense of success as I wrote the play in three weeks of long days at my desk. I showed the play to Father, reverting to an old habit: as a child, I had sometimes shown him what I wrote.

A few days after giving him a copy of the play, I went to the Little House for one of the family dinners that brought us together several times a year, usually to celebrate a birthday. During the elaborate meal, with flowers and candles and gold-rimmed plates all blazing on the marble table, Father slipped me a note. Too curious to wait, I excused myself and went to read it in the peach-colored guest bathroom.

Father was asking for certain changes in my script. He did not want people in the audience to identify the play's setting for fear that they would infer connections between the characters and Mother and Father—especially Mother.

He did not object to what he called the incestuous relationship between the father and his sister in the play, realizing that it was central to the theme, which contrasted illusion and reality: the reality of heterosexual married love and the illusion of imagined incest.

Father was worried about Mother's reaction, which followed an old pattern of behavior: she was the one who was easily hurt, he believed, although she would not have agreed. To shield her, he wanted me to alter the character of the wife in the play, removing the suggestion of what he called "sexual inadequacy." He also wanted me to emphasize the drinking problem of the character of the aunt, which, I felt, would discredit her on the stage, as Henrietta had been discredited by the imputation of alcoholism during her life.

I tried to understand whether in some way I had solicited this unwelcome interference, assuming, as I often did in those days, that I was somehow to blame. Of course, when a writer shows her work, any result is possible. I was not wounded by Father's suggestions—there was nothing hostile in the tone of his note—but I was disturbed by his assumption that the play existed solely in terms of its effect on the family. Mother would inevitably be offended by anything I wrote; she told me several years later that she disliked all my writing, perhaps because it revealed areas of feeling and behavior she felt ought to remain concealed. But I had lived with her displeasure for a long time, and it was too late for me to attempt to alter it by altering my work.

I tried rather unsuccessfully to explain my point of view to Father. He seemed to understand, on a cerebral level, but he still clung to the notion that I should change the play in order to avoid angering Mother. It seemed to me that we were both afraid of her anger, not her pain—but she was never asked. I wondered how often Father had warned other people not to say or do something Mother might find offensive. I also wondered if he was protecting his own feelings rather than hers. She was walled up in an isolation I did not dare to breach, which meant that other people could interpret her reactions as they desired.

I did not change the play. I had revised to please a censor for the last time at Radcliffe in 1956, when one of the deans had asked me to delete the place names from "Winter Term."

But my language remained Father's, and the Judge's, and the Colonel's. I had learned it at Father's knee, along with the rich rhythms of Victorian prose and poetry. The language I had learned from Mother was associated with behavior, not with invention: the harsh warnings in "Slovenly Peter," for example, or the humorous hints in "The Goops and How to Be Them": "They spill their broth on the tablecloth, oh they lead disgusting lives . . ." My writing had been formed by the language I had inherited from Father and the men in the Bingham family, easily twisted into rhetoric or oratory. The other language—Nursie's maxims, the black people's dangling phrases—was not mine: I was rich and white.

In writing *Milk of Paradise,* I had used the mother tongue—the kitchen talk, the expression of experiences essentially female that I had once believed not worthy of literature.

During rehearsals I collaborated for the first time with other people, especially the women in the cast, the director, Joan Vail Thorne, and the producer, Julia Miles. The process undid the last vestiges of fear and distrust of women that remained from my childhood. It seemed to me that these talented people gave themselves to me and to the play, but with a professional reserve that prevented the cruel grinding of family intimacy.

One night someone in the audience complained that the play dealt in Southern stereotypes: all the black characters were servants. Teresa Wright, who played the cook, rose from her chair, a commanding presence in her buttoned raincoat, to announce, "I don't act in Tom plays." There was nothing more to be said.

Toward the end of the run, my parents came to see a performance. I was not there. But a friend recognized them and told me that, before the play started, Father had taken out a little blue leather engagement book to go over plans for their next European trip. Then the lights went down and the play opened with a scene in which the father and mother discuss their plans for a trip abroad. It did not surprise me that neither Mother nor Father ever mentioned the play to me.

I noted a quote from Isak Dinesen: "Any sorrow is bearable if you make a story out of it or about it."

Harold Clurman came one night in a broad black hat and cloak. His review in *The Nation* said my play showed "an honest sensibility, an ear for true speech and a delicacy of sentiment." The women in the audience were gasping and laughing. That was what I wanted.

A few months before *Milk of Paradise* opened in New York, a family meeting was held on the terrace at the Big House. It was a beautiful day; the marble floor of the porch gleamed, and the white iron furniture was decked with fresh chintz pillows. Planters of flowers stood here and there, and the silver coffee service and delicate porcelain cups had been set out.

The men who joined us, lawyers from the firm that had always handled both family and company business, were dressed in sober dark suits; the family women, in brighter plumage, darted back and forth between them, carrying coffee, sugar, and cream. For everyone, it was a rare treat to be sipping dark strong coffee from porcelain cups on a marble terrace overlooking the Ohio. I imagined that the men might regale their wives with a description of the scene that evening.

Perfunctory matters were transacted to the tinkling of silver spoons. Then sets of photocopied papers were given to each family member. A lawyer explained that this was a routine matter, requiring all our signatures. He explained that the paper was called "a buy-back agreement"—a term I had never heard—and that it was intended to preserve family control of the companies.

I hastily scanned the pages of technical language and realized at once that I did not understand the implications of signing it. Meanwhile pens were being passed around and a sense of haste was developing. Really there was no need to hesitate over such a routine matter; there were other issues that needed discussing, and soon. Mother, Father, Barry, Edie, and Eleanor had already signed and passed their papers back, like good pupils in a grade school classroom.

I knew that I was on the edge of a divide. Either I could sign, on faith, and hope that the agreement was relatively unimportant, or I could, alone, refuse.

The little incident shows how firmly entrenched the notion is that women can easily be fooled. It is a notion that does not take into account a woman's individual characteristics: her education, for example, her intelligence, or her experience. It is tied firmly to gender. It would have been easy to prepare us with an explanation, or to spend a few minutes, beforehand, discussing the issues. But that would have meant entertaining the assumption that women, even rich women, even inheritors, need to be treated as rational human beings, if only to ensure their cooperation. Such an assumption did not fit the family myth.

I was frightened, but I remembered other experiences I had had as a single mother. Car salesmen, insurance agents, and realtors were always in a hurry to get me to sign papers before I had had a chance to read them, always eager to insist, "This is just routine, there's really no need to read all that fine print." The way the buy-back agreement was being presented seemed a genteel version of the same old rush and bustle.

"I want to show this to a lawyer before I sign it," I said.

The silver spoons stopped their clinking. The people on the porch grew very still.

"The room is full of lawyers," Mother said in her crispest tone.

"Yes, but not my lawyer."

Things moved on after that. No one commented on my outrageous act, which according to some views prevented the buy-back agreement from taking effect. I have never felt so alone in my life, but that provided a useful lesson: I could survive alone, even among the geraniums and the silver coffeepot and the tinkling spoons of my childhood.

In fact, I had no lawyer I trusted. I realized that I would have to choose one from outside the Louisville establishment, where, as elsewhere, the prestigious firms are closely tied to corporate interests.

I began to look for a lawyer who would, first of all, not remind me of the calm, kindly, but ultimately and unconsciously patronizing men who had instructed me in legal and financial matters for years. These men all knew each other, and their manner and their minds had been formed in the same schools: Eastern colleges (Kentucky universities, except for the University of Kentucky, were discredited in these circles), a few years of legal experience outside Louisville, and then a return to a firm where an uncle or a father was a senior partner. It was too much to expect that the men who looked so pleased when I saw them at the Big House Derby breakfast would offer me independent advice. It was equally unlikely that any middle-aged man born and bred in the South would be able to avoid "guiding" a woman client in a way that would ensure she never really understood what was going on.

I needed a woman lawyer, one who would be unlikely to fall into the father-daughter relationship and who by gender was excluded from the inner circles. I needed an outsider, and not an outsider who hoped one day to be let in.

I chose Rebecca Westerfield, a young woman who was born and raised in a small town in Kentucky, who attended a Kentucky university and had been active in the civil rights wars. She had known great losses early in life, and she is an unapologetic fighter with a sense of humor, which is perhaps more important than anything else. Later, her partner, a spirited warrior named Jon Goldberg, helped me to win the battle that began on that marble terrace overlooking the Ohio.

Women often fear isolation and its accompanying emotional pain, not because we are cowards (any woman who has borne a child is a hero), but because we sometimes depend on acceptance for our sense of authenticity. That day, the Bingham women flitted from man to man on the terrace, cajoling and serving, offering compliments and cream, just as their earlier counterparts, the women who had worked in the military school in North Carolina, had nursed and cajoled the cadets. An onlooker would not have believed that any of the women on the terrace actually owned stock in the businesses. In previous generations they had not, although they had contributed lifetimes of labor.

That morning on the terrace I had not thought of selling my approximately fifteen percent share in the three companies. I enjoy learning, and I hoped to take a more active role as director as I became better informed. I did not realize then that Barry was expecting some kind of betrayal. I will never know how his distrust started, although it seems likely that his managing editor, Paul Janensch, exacerbated Barry's fears.

The tinder was already in place, and only a spark was needed: Barry had been aware for years, it seems to me now, that Father was not satisfied with his performance—the phrase Jonathan used to describe both sex and skiing. Appearance was what mattered, not content, and Barry, driven, perfectionistic, totally devoted, was not superficially glamorous. Nor was he entirely compliant.

As I became aware of Barry's fear, through watching him closely, I decided that it was caused by the fact that he scarcely knew me. It seemed to me that he needed to know me better in order to trust me, rather than relying on a signed paper. Trust creates trustworthiness. To act with distrust, to use legal means to coerce cooperation, seemed to me the poorest way to go about ensuring the continuation of Father's empire.

When my lawyer advised me that signing the buy-back agreement would severely limit if not destroy my options should I one day decide to sell, I knew I had been right not to sign. My own future, and my sons', seemed precarious, and I was not ready to commit myself to a lifetime of supporting the empire.

By not signing, I knew I was giving other people what they would assume was proof of my bad intentions. Other people would exaggerate the danger, for their own purposes. How had we come so far along the road without my being aware of it? Who stood to gain from mistrust inside the family? I will never know the answer.

Shortly thereafter, at another family meeting held in a windowless "banquet room" downtown—surely the most cheerless of all settings for a festivity—one of the family lawyers called me a maverick, and I realized that a threat was taking shape. It was necessary to honor the label, to cherish it as a badge of worth rather than as a condemnation.

Perhaps Barry had begun to grow afraid at a board meeting some months earlier when he had announced that he was cutting back on state circulation of the *Courier-Journal,* at a time when gasoline prices were very high (a result, as we now know, of international oil manipulations). The cut was a fait accompli, decided at the Dipnoan meeting, and Barry assumed that all the directors would agree. It was costing too much to send trucks out to the distant eastern and western sections of the state, to small towns where only a few copies were sold.

I was still a believer in the myth, in the Judge's words inscribed over the elevators in the lobby. The newspapers had an obligation, it seemed to me, to serve everyone, which flowed from the fact that they were the only newspapers in the state. (The Lexington newspaper, owned by Knight-Ridder, had just begun to make its inroads.) The Judge, with his belief in "uplift" for mountaineers, would surely have opposed depriving readers of their only source of news, especially in counties so mountainous television signals were difficult to receive.

Advertisers had little interest, however, in the counties outside of the metropolitan area. An effective and outgoing executive who was in charge of the business side of the newspapers had persuasively made the case for carrying the newspaper only to those subscribers who were of interest to our advertisers. Newspapers have always existed, first and foremost, to carry advertising.

But the profit motive was never discussed in the family. The term itself would have been considered grammatically questionable and in terrible taste, reminiscent of such phrases as "the moneylenders in the temple . . ." To make money off "our papers," the family seemed to believe, should be only a fortuitous by-product of excellence. This, of course, was a naïve expression of the myth, which had little effect on daily decisions and operations.

"The myth of newspaper poverty," as Ben Bagdikian calls it, here coincided with the family's difficulty in believing in its own wealth. Delivering newspapers to rural Kentucky was expensive, but curtailing delivery meant that local librarians, schoolteachers, politicians, and ministers, the leaders of small towns, would have no access to what I had always assumed was a corrective point of view.

So I spoke up sharply and without premeditation, spurred by my old belief in the family myth. After all, "the girls" had been told for years that our dividends stayed at the same low level because the money the newspapers earned was "plowed back in" to improve an elusive and undefined "quality." Yet now the gas needed for delivery trucks was considered too expensive to justify. What, then, was "quality"? Who was it for? And how did profits improve it?

Of course, the decision to cut back state circulation had already been made, and so my criticism was worse than useless: it angered and frightened Barry, who always felt particularly vulnerable in front of his employees. (Years later, a friend would remark that one of Barry's editors used to ask him if he was willing to be "castrated" by his sisters.)

The circulation cuts were made. Soon our letters-to-the-editor column began to be filled with heartbreaking complaints from readers who had been subscribers for twenty or thirty years, and who were willing to pay almost any price to continue receiving the *Courier-Journal*. For me, as for Paul Janensch, those letters were "a nail in the heart." I began to realize that the family myth was only a myth, and that "the profit motive," as well as many other, more mysterious motives, controlled the newspapers. We were not so very different after all.

At the time, I needed the myth to justify the inherited money and power of which I was the still somewhat embarrassed beneficiary. That inheritance seemed to me at odds with the concept of democracy.

Another factor influenced the decision (which was reversed a few years later when gasoline prices fell). It was increasingly difficult for the family and its managers to imagine readers who were different from us—not urban, not educated, not attuned to the sophisticated interests of New York and Boston and London. Noblesse oblige was no longer thick or wide enough to bridge the gap between rich people who were educated at private schools in the East and spent their vacations in Europe and the middle- or lower-class black and white readers on whom we depended. So the ideal of service disappeared at last into the widening gulf between the class interests of the owners and their executives and those of their readers and blue-collar employees.

Inevitably, those employees would begin to look out for their own interests, as they realized that the plantation system benefited only the people in the Big House. Inevitably, service to readers who were unimaginably poor and rural would not be worth the cost.

The Shively housewife was not only female. She was "country."

Kentucky is a deeply divided state. The bluegrass region around Lexington shares some of the charm, the myth, and the history of the plantation South, while the western and eastern counties are rock-ribbed, poor, fundamentalist, "dry," and subjected to the vagaries of the coal industry. Tales from my childhood reminded me of the family's fear of the mountains, home of organized labor, prominent in the history of coal, and of illiteracy, which removes whole groups from the edifying influence of reading. Mountain Kentucky was a foreign land where violent strikebreakers or union men rolled rocks down on vehicles and moonshiners shot at revenue agents. In the fifties, when I worked for a few weeks at the Frontier Nursing Service, a private health organization for mountain families started by Mary Breckinridge, I had been warned to sing in the woods so that the moonshiners would know I was a woman and hold their fire. The terrible dark side of the Southern myth—its violence and rampant individualism, its racism and vigilante-style justice—was supposed to be acted out in the highlands. The myth did not fit the reality, but that was not important.

The historical "orneriness" and independence of the poor people of Kentucky was also a frightful omen of change to the privileged owners of the media in Louisville. That "orneriness" was especially marked in mountain women, as they were described in family anecdotes. Although horribly poor, they kept their pride, and that was the worst that could be said of them. They did not seem to be suitable objects for noblesse oblige.

In addition, the mountaineers were said to suffer from inbreeding, which raised the specter of incest. No taboo has more dramatic meaning for the families of the very rich, who rarely find that outsiders "measure up" and so turn, in secret, to their own kind. Besides, "our women" are "ours," like silver punch bowls and Aubusson rugs. The most recent example was provided by the biography of Seward Johnson, founder of Johnson & Johnson, who sexually abused his eldest daughter. Whenever the story of the very rich is told, incest is revealed, along with the family's surprise that such behavior is termed abuse.

In high school, I had read a study of mountain families that regularly produced idiots because of intermarriage. This was a dangerous idea for a family in which first cousins had often married, as in the case of earlier Binghams and in my Richmond grandmother's case, but also an important proof of the Social Darwinism so necessary to an elite.

The mountaineers were poor, they were ignorant, and they were supposed to be genetically inferior as well. They had once suffered from the diseases of the poverty-stricken South, pellagra and hookworm, which had replaced the even more widely spread venereal diseases as targets for social reformers in the 1920s. But if inbreeding reinforced these people's genetic weaknesses, might it not, in very different circumstances, magnify the genetic strengths of the elite? Fascist Germany had had some thoughts on this matter.

When the family lawyer called me a maverick in that windowless "banquet room," I was frightened. I was sitting alone at one end of the long table, and the family and its lawyer was grouped at the other end. I realized that I would have to find a source of strength to sustain me in that uncomfortable situation. I was still a newcomer to Louisville, a single parent, and a congenital outsider. I turned, as I had so often in the past, to books for help.

Four books helped me. In *Killers of the Dream,* Lillian Smith analyzed the failures of good Southerners, liberal Southerners ("a weak term at best," as one later commentator observed), to rise above their inherited views. She connected sexual repression of upper-class white women and oppression of blacks. Both forms of violence grew from the same root. It seemed to me that she had known the world of the Judge and the Colonel.

In her book *The Wall Between,* about the 1954 bombing of a house in Shively deeded to a black couple, Anne Braden talked about the failure of Louisville liberals to take the lead in denouncing this outrage. She understood that men like Father were used to controlling the rate of social change and were angry when activists, especially activists who were black or female, took control out of their hands.

In *In Search of the Silent South,* Morton Sosna described the failure of Southern liberals to resist the anxiety aroused by Communist participation in groups such as the Southern Conference for Human Welfare, from which both Father and Mark Ethridge had withdrawn in the 1940s, causing

Walter White to say that "the highest casualty rate of the war seems to be that of Southern White Liberals."

One more book helped to light the way. In *An American Dilemma,* Gunnar Myrdal described what seemed to me the family's attitude, as personal as it was political: "the absorbing interest in the form of a matter; the indirectness of approach to a person, a subject, or a policy, the training to circumvent sore points and touchy complexes . . . Grace becomes the supreme virtue."

One day Mother saw the Myrdal book in my car and said she thought it was out of date. I would have agreed with her before the morning on the terrace. Now it seemed to me that the past was still very much with us. Mother, who believed devoutly in grace—in its literal and its spiritual interpretation—would soon become my sharpest critic.

At the next round of board meetings, I continued to ask questions. Sometimes I would see a small grimace of irritation cross my brother's face, as though a not quite harmless insect, a spider perhaps, had crawled up onto the gleaming surface of the conference table. Then Father would sigh and gaze away resignedly, Edie would bend over her needlepoint, and Eleanor would correct her notes. Mother would gaze straight ahead. The men in the room would tense, except for one, an outspoken lawyer who said to me that there might be safety in numbers; he was not on good terms with Barry, for obscure reasons that probably had to do with this man's constitutional independence.

Now Eleanor asked questions of her own at board meetings. She sometimes supported my inquiries, but not always; she had her own point of view, and was both far better informed about television and far more conservative politically than I. Mother and Edie asked questions, too, but they were both opposed on principle to outspokenness. Even Edie, who was so kind, once advised me to save my questions for a Junior League meeting, although I told her with some heat that it was unlikely Bingham company issues would be raised there—and besides, I did not belong.

Yet I knew I could not afford to bluster and grow grand. My situation was complex and ambiguous. I had to weigh loyalty to the family and its myth against my autonomy, their love against my money, and that was a dangerous weighing. It called into question a major assumption about a woman's role: that a woman should be, first and foremost, a nurturing wife, mother, daughter, and sister, placing human relations far above questions of money or justice.

I was helped by the companionship of the man I later married, who aroused all the problems women must face when they share the warmth of male strength. Tim Peters had grown up knowing how hard Americans have to work just to survive. He had fallen in love with the military, and had become disillusioned, and he could understand why the sight of his old uniforms hanging in the attic of the house we shared aroused such complex feelings. He was raising his two sons, as I had once believed and hoped men would, without depending on the unremitting labor and interpretations of mothers.

When I moved with my two younger sons into Tim's house in the spring of 1981, none of us knew what to expect. But Tim was and is a fighter; his slogan was: "No guts, no glory"—a slogan he acted upon when he fell in love with a woman who was about to become embroiled with the power structure of a small Southern city. His life would suffer, his business would suffer, and the lives of our five sons would be irredeemably altered; yet the hardest task for him would be, not to continue to encourage me, but to learn to resist fighting the fight himself.

Two other incidents, unplanned and at first unexamined, widened the split in the family that had begun as a hairline crack in the marble that morning on the Big House terrace when I did not sign the buy-back agreement.

Both newspapers had endorsed Democratic candidates since Henry Watterson's day, although Kentucky Republicans had emerged as a force during the Eisenhower campaigns in the 1950s. I had no great enthusiasm for the Democratic party in Kentucky; it seemed mired in an ancient system of patronage, still stuck in a rut between the suspicions of the rural counties and the superficial sophistication of Louisville, still a prey to petty scandals as it had been in the Judge's time. But at least Democratic candidates were usually not overt racists, though they lived in an entirely white section of their society and employed black servants and sent their children to all-white private schools. They tended to support, tepidly, the public education they felt was far too mediocre for their own children, and to voice concern for the state's poor, unemployed, and illiterate citizens.

The Republicans had of late spent much time talking about running the state like a business, which, from what I knew of business, held little appeal for me.

In the 1980 mayoral race, the newspapers, to my surprise, endorsed the Republican candidate, George Clark, over the Democrat, Father's protégé, Harvey Sloane.

I knew almost nothing about Clark, who was a newcomer to politics, except that he aspired to run the state like a franchise of Kentucky Fried

Chicken, of which he was an executive. I took Barry's editorial in support of Clark as evidence of the increasingly conservative stance of the newspapers and of their submission to the interests of business. Later I realized that the editorial had an altogether different, personal meaning: Barry was tormented by the threat Harvey Sloane represented as an outsider who had found his way into Father's heart. That his intelligent and attractive wife had apparently won both parents was an additional blow, since Edie, who tried so hard, had been excluded.

The day the editorial ran, Kathy Sloane asked me to come and see her at once. She sounded desperate, and I went. In a little upstairs study, which gradually darkened as night fell, the mayor's wife sat listlessly, debilitated by weeping. She told me that her husband's career was being ruined by Barry's jealousy. The mayor himself did not make an appearance, but I was used to that: it is the way of power. I was moved by Kathy's unhappiness; her own life depended at that point on her husband's success, which gave her a role to play. Like so many women of my generation, she was far too intelligent to be satisfied with home life, no matter how luxurious, and she needed the forum provided by her husband's political success.

She told me about the letter Edie had written breaking off social relations between the two couples, using the newspapers' elaborate conflict-of-interest policy as an excuse. I was caught, I realized, in a war between two small kingdoms.

I went home and wrote a letter to the editor criticizing Barry's support for the Republican as a betrayal of the newspapers' ideals—that myth I was still attempting to believe.

Clark was defeated at the polls, but my letter was hard for Barry to forget. I was again seen as a threat to the status quo as it existed at Sixth and Broadway, and the Sloanes mistook me for a petitioner.

Eleanor had been something of a supporter of George Clark, as had her husband, and she had no quarrel with Barry's editorial. However, she was angry when he shortly afterwards fired the newspapers' architectural critic, Will Morgan, whose Mencken-like bite had annoyed Mother during the downtown shopping center controversy. Morgan had written harsh and amusing evaluations of various builders' atrocities, and the developers were writhing under his lash. Now Father had begun to raise several million dollars to supplement state revenues for an enormous arts center, the necessary complement to the shopping center and the riverside hotel in a society where the arts are another form of tourist attraction or consumer commodity. Perhaps Father had sighed at the thought of the lambasting the great hulking arts center might eventually receive at the hands of his architectural critic. If so, there was someone close at hand to interpret his sigh and arrange for his relief. Will Morgan was "let go."

Eleanor and I wrote letters to Barry protesting Morgan's ousting and asking that someone be appointed to his position. Mother countered with a letter in which, with her usual delight in words, she called Morgan "a chronic sourpuss."

Barry retorted angrily that we were trying to placate the critics we met at cocktail parties, which amused me, since I did not go to cocktail parties. In fact, Eleanor and I were exercising the only power we had as owners who did not cast nay votes: the power of words. We were also providing Barry's managing editor with more ammunition.

Barry had begun to seem terribly vulnerable to me, fearful of anything that might approach criticism. I did not understand why he felt so precarious, since I had not seen the effect of Father's lack of enthusiasm for him as publisher. But I knew that Barry seemed driven, deeply unhappy, facing monstrous enemies of his imagination. I planned a strategic retreat.

It was clear that I was accomplishing nothing at board meetings, where, except for Eleanor, I had no allies. Neither she nor I could bring ourselves to cast nay votes, even in the case of decisions we questioned; to do so, it seemed, would have been to invite a dose of disapproval so strong neither of us could survive it. I was twisted tight in the atmosphere of those windowless rooms, twisted tighter and tighter as I felt the pull of power and the old assumption of powerlessness. Finally I suggested to Father that he cut the length of the board meetings down again, to match the brief time accorded them in the old rubber-stamp days. After all, we were rubber stamps still, and it was intolerable to remain for days on end in that position.

Father listened to the suggestion, but did not respond. He was following his own line, and the tight atmosphere, for him, was not a problem.

I could not face the next series of board meetings, where my letter to the editor in support of Harvey Sloane and my refusal to sign the buy-back agreement would subject me to increased hostility. I stayed at home.

Writing to Barry to explain my absence, I said, "When I first moved down, I hoped to be both helpful and influential as a member of the boards. It's an ambiguous position. I felt that I was interested, and fairly well informed, and that my opinion on various issues would be fresh. However, it seems to me that I am neither helpful nor influential, and therefore the long two-day board sessions are painful. On the one hand, I feel that it irritates you and Paul Janensch to hear criticism—and who likes to hear criticism! However, agreement, or silence, is not particularly easy for me.

"Your job is difficult, I know, and it is not really possible for me to add to your difficulties by criticism. However, it is not possible for me to be

My husband Tim Peters and I lived here with our four sons for three years.

Tim, 1986.

My brother Barry and Father in the pressroom of the Louisville *Courier-Journal.* They were known as the "Mr. Clean's of journalism."

silent—and so, at best, I can stand one-day board meetings. I hope this is a clarification.

"I need to add that the general failure of the family is reflected at board meetings. By this I mean our shared failure to help or understand each other. It seems inappropriate to air these differences at the meetings—but inevitably, that happens.

"You and I have both known this family for a long time now, and we know how unlikely it is to change. With that in view, I think my best position is to be a restrained witness at short board meetings—which I gather we will have in June [1980].

"One more remark: I do hope you will go ahead and drop the subject of the buy-back agreement—at least as far as I'm concerned. I am not likely ever to sign it."

I wanted to explain my reasons to Barry in the hope of persuading him that I was a friend rather than a foe. My position, as minority stockholder and director, felt very precarious, and I did not want to limit my options should the time come when I would decide to sell. The buy-back, which would have given the companies a chance to match any offer from an outsider, would have severely crimped any attempt on my side to procure such an offer. In addition, I did not think that signing a paper would make Barry trust me. That would happen only if he came to know me—not as a threat, a gossiped-about outsider, but as a woman he had not spent time with since our childhoods.

Barry suggested a meeting to talk about the buy-back, with lawyers present. I asked him not to include lawyers, since they tended to inhibit discussion. The meeting never took place.

Later, many people would ask me why the family never "talked," why the disaster—as some saw it—of the sale of the companies was allowed to happen without an attempt to untangle personal motives, "to go out and have a cup of coffee and talk things over," as one friend described it. The lack of any real basis for communication in the family made such an informal "get-together" unimaginable. We had not spent time together in more than twenty years, except at what seemed to me state functions—anniversaries, Christmases, birthdays, nearly all staged, in the old way, at the huge table at the Big House or the icy marble slab at the Little House. We were not used to the rough-and-tumble of open discussion, and none of us had any ability to survive confrontation. Perhaps it is one of the peculiarities of the rich that we have been so blanketed by privilege that the first hint of disagreement arouses extreme panic. The people who wait on us and serve us seldom challenge anything we say, and our intimate relations are governed by the same reserve.

I knew that this inability to deal with disagreement meant that my future, as sister and daughter and director, was severely compromised. I wrote, "Some real despair yesterday over the failure of my efforts here: the family fatalism remains in full force. I've given up breaking through to Barry; my independent sons cause some friction with my parents, and the boys are not benefiting from their grandparents," who were usually too busy to see them. "WORK, that's all," I wrote.

It was at this point that Paul Janensch happened to find me one morning having coffee in the company cafeteria. I had been visiting the book-page editor, who occasionally invited me to write a review.

Janensch approached me warily, but clearly with some purpose in mind. After a little polite talk, he asked me "if I would fight," I noted later in my diary. I did not understand what he meant, although it seems to me now that Paul was seeking an ally in his battle with the CEO, George Gill, for control of the newspapers.

I replied to Paul's question that "I would fight if what I have to offer is crucial." I thought perhaps Paul was referring to Barry's health, and to the need he might have of support and reinforcements in his continuing, subterranean struggle with Father. Perhaps Paul realized, as I had, that Hodgkin's disease had changed Barry, making him angry and vulnerable, increasing both his sensitivity to Father's implied distrust and Father's reasons for doubting that Barry could ever become in fact what he was in theory—the next publisher, the inheritor finally of the majority of the companies' stock.

Perhaps Paul interpreted my answer to mean that I would not help him triumph over George Gill. After that bewildering exchange Paul seemed to assume that I was the enemy.

The vagueness of this exchange seems incredible to me now, in view of the importance of the issues at stake. However, when I remember the atmosphere of the board meetings, the swirling undercurrents, jealousies, and alliances which I did not understand because they were never explained, the conversation with Paul Janensch fits in neatly. Because goals for the companies were unclear—did the family even care about profits? and what exactly did "public service" mean?—the scheming in the ranks had become endemic. Only a few executives, it seemed to me, held themselves remote from the gossip and the manipulations.

The companies had become a series of small fiefdoms, each controlled by an ambitious man who viewed his rivals with disdain. There was no open discussion of aims because no one understood what the aims were—and the family, as a unit, was certainly not going to explain, because none of us, as individuals, could have agreed. So the rivalries that always attend a gross concentration of power grew and multiplied; there was no one to weed the garden, except perhaps the owner himself, and he was not yet ready.

34

I was startled and dismayed when, at the next board meeting in 1980, we were told that dividends from our Standard Gravure stock would be cut by fifty percent. While the cuts would not seriously affect other people in the family, they meant a severe decline in income for Eleanor and me.

I asked what was happening, and why, and when we might hope to see the dividends back at their usual low level. I was surprised by the casualness of the answers. No one seemed concerned. Standard was doing poorly, for reasons outside of anyone's control, and that was that. Perhaps things would improve when our new printing plant was built in a right-to-work state, Tennessee. This move seemed at best insensitive to me, since the newspapers' editorials sometimes attacked other companies for going out of state. The move was seen by some readers as proof of the newspapers' hypocrisy.

Father noticed my dismay, and within a few weeks, money from another source appeared to make up for the dividend cut. I was relieved, but the gesture seemed as arbitrary as the one that had taken our dividends away. Could shareholders be rewarded or punished in such a summary fashion? Were our dividends connected to the actual performance of the three companies?

Later Paul Janensch would remark to an interviewer that when Barry Bingham, Sr., went to London, he wanted to be known as the leader of a great newspaper, not necessarily of a greatly profitable newspaper. But it seemed to me that the connections between the quality of the "product" and its ability to make money, as well as the question of the companies' responsibility to their shareholders, needed to be considered, in spite of Father's patrician point of view. After all, during the Depression, the Judge had managed to maintain his newspapers' profits, and no one claimed that had been done through a sacrifice of quality.

However, the old paralysis that greets questions of money gripped me: as an inheritor, I felt that I really had no right to complain. The money that came to me was not really mine, and therefore I was embarrassed to speak up when it dwindled. It was terribly easy for managers at the three companies to shame me with a look or a smile: I was easy to shame because I knew I had no right to profit from their work. The problem remained, however. I depended on dividends to pay my bills, since my work as a writer and a teacher produced an income of less than five thousand dollars a year, and my only other income was a modest amount of child support for my two youngest sons.

To ask questions about profits would have seemed an attack on the loyal managers who oversaw the audits, ground out the agendas, drew up the budgets, and worked themselves to the edge of exhaustion to keep the companies going. It was not their loyalty or their probity I wanted to question, but the force behind the "facts," the uncontrolled and perhaps uncontrollable power of a monopoly owner who was accountable to no one except the federal government and who had able legal advice to outwit the government as well, if that was so indicated.

Eleanor had recently introduced the concept of accountability, and it had been received without enthusiasm. The word itself was considered illegitimate. The concept was at odds with the myth of dynasty. It ran counter to the notion of noblesse oblige. We Americans worship dynasty, and we do not seek to hold it accountable. We believe in the leadership of an elite, and we do not scrutinize the elite's motives.

I noticed that Kentuckians often viewed the Bingham family as a dynasty and worshipped it as such—an attitude that has a way of justifying autocratic abuses. In this, Kentuckians are no different from the rest of the country. Americans accepted and even admired the so-called dynasty of the Shah of Iran, which did not even have the excuse of longevity: it had been established in 1921, four years after the Judge established his dynasty at Mary Lily's death.

Father still held the controlling interest in the three companies, a fact I grasped for the first time during a grim discussion of his will. I do not know who initiated the discussion, which seemed dangerous to me. To reveal a will is an invitation to the disputes that generally take place only after the prime mover is gone.

Once more we were all called to a meeting at the Big House, where we found various charts and diagrams awaiting us. They presented designs for dividing up the Place, with areas reserved for tasteful condominiums, and other areas for trees and grass. A well-known architect had come up with this proposal, although it was not clear who had asked for it. I looked on, amazed, as he showed our parents, who seemed bemused, how their privacy might be preserved in the midst of this high-class residential development. As far as I knew, no one was in acute financial distress, which would seem to be the only motivation for such a drastic change. Finally the development idea evaporated. I heard later that Barry had said that he would have nothing to do with it.

The same sense of misunderstanding and paralysis pervaded the meetings called to discuss Father's will. The meetings seemed to spring, mushroomlike, from statements both parents were making about their determination to treat their three remaining children fairly.

I remembered a similar occasion years before, when both Worth and Jonathan were still alive. After the lawyers had presented us with a summary of the trust funds that would enrich our generation and our children for life, Worth had spoken up angrily. He was appalled to find that the two younger children, Eleanor and Jonathan, would have more money in their trust funds when they were dispersed than he would, because the trusts would have been accumulating income over a longer period of time. I had been shocked by Worth's anger, which seemed to have little to do with money; after all, we would all be rich. Perhaps he saw in the larger amounts coming to Eleanor and Jonathan a slight or threat, as though the two younger children were better loved.

Later I would remember Worth's anger with admiration. He had dared to speak up. For a moment, the connection between love and money had been revealed in a glaring light, before embarrassment brought the silence down again.

Father's will showed that he had followed several basic rules in the division of his accumulated wealth. The control of the three companies would pass to Barry, who would inherit the majority of the voting stock. However, "the girls" would receive nonvoting stock in the three companies, which would ensure a large income, without power. Eleanor and I would also receive a summer cottage.

In addition, there were possessions to be divided up, and Mother suggested a sort of Monopoly game. She would give us play money, which would represent our shares. Then we would all "bid" on our parents' possessions. This macabre arrangement with its potential for injury dissolved when no one could agree on an estimate of the possessions.

"The girls" were also to be allowed to buy two lots, at a price set by Barry, on the Place. He would be left the Big House and its contents.

I went away from those meetings feeling chilled and sad. I knew that Father believed that "the girls" only wanted money, as doubtless he had believed that Henrietta only wanted money, for clothes and jewels.

Yet I was glad that the will had been revealed, since it freed me from false expectations. But the will cast a harsh light on Father's view of fairness. He had a perfect right, I felt, to leave his companies to anyone he chose. After all, they were his. However, to structure the will so that control of the three companies, as well as the Place itself, passed to Barry, and then to insist that this was fair, was hard to accept. The concept of fairness in fact had no place here. Yet Mother, as always voicing Father's silent wishes, was insisting that we agree that this arrangement was fair. Silence was no escape. We must validate their choices. This led to a general sense of injury.

Power Corrupts was the title of the play I was planning in the spring of 1981: "Power corrupts and destroys children; the scene last night, my terrible sense of injury when Father asked me to move from Barry's chair at the dinner table, where by accident I had sat; Barry's toast to his daughter— 'More successful than the children of acquaintances'; ruthless insensitivity of the rich and powerful even to their own kind, connected to the lunch where the daughters are told to shut up at board meetings."

The lunch referred to was an opportunity, I thought, to get to know three of the company executives, whom I never saw except at board meetings. I had been flattered by their invitation.

Eleanor and I met the three men at a restaurant downtown. After the usual civilities had been passed, along with the drinks, we were told the reason for the lunch: we were talking too much at board meetings. The warning was crisp and clear. Shut up, or face terrible, although undescribed, consequences. I was hurt almost to the point of tears. For the first time, I realized that Eleanor and I were vulnerable to attack, not only from Barry and our parents but from the managers of the companies. The charmed circle was broken: these men, too, seemed to see us as the enemy.

Later I realized that Barry was preparing to launch a new and radical proposition—the so-called electronic newspaper. He did not want to face opposition. It was around this time that he began in speeches to refer to the Louisville newspapers as "the last dinosaur in the swamp."

Barry found the idea of the electronic newspaper as exciting as it was untried. By replacing the two newspapers with a signal received on a computer screen, Barry would eliminate at one fell swoop his problems with the increasing price of newsprint, with gasoline prices and truck drivers, and with the complaints of some people in Louisville that newsprint ink came off on their hands. (Mother once talked of a sort of coverlet that could be put over the bed so that the newspaper could be read without soiling linen sheets.)

The disagreeable luncheon, however, did not have the desired result. If anything, it hardened my resolve. So when Barry raised his proposal for the electronic newspaper, I was not silent. His arguments avoided, it seemed to me, important issues connected to the myth of our service to the public.

In a state as poor as Kentucky, home computers would never be widely available to our readers outside of the city, or to our readers in the West End. I agreed with George Gill when he said that the concept of the electronic newspaper threatens democracy by limiting information to the well-off few, the same few, of course, whom the advertisers were interested in cultivating.

No one opposed Barry's idea at the board meeting, and this stunned me: Was Father, who disliked mechanical gadgets, resigned to receiving the news on his television screen? The limpness of the discussion at those meetings is hard to believe, even now, except in light of a larger plan about which I knew nothing, a plan that would make the electronic newspaper and all other forms of nonsense of no importance at all.

Perhaps there was more opposition behind the scenes. Soon Barry announced that he was planning to take a year's sabbatical, during which he would study the idea of the electronic newspaper.

In the spring of 1981, I was "living off my hump." I tried to heal myself "with the help of God: to depend on work, prayer, and the blessedness of the world."

The old Episcopal church in Louisville where the Judge had married Eleanor Miller became, briefly, a haven for me. Green and gold light filtered through the stained-glass windows where Blessed Damozels like the Rossetti maidens from my childhood leaned out with armloads of lilies. Finally the sense of guilt that the service had once exacerbated was leaving me. I no longer believed I had been born to suffer, although suffering had certainly been a part of my life. Original sin was not my meat, and I learned to take communion with something approaching joy, rather than with the fear that I would be struck down by a Jehovah who would never be satisfied that I was, by his definition, in a state of grace.

My sense of guilt diminished as I struggled to take control of my life: to speak up, to say what I meant, to leave the green and gold glints of the sentimental and cruel past behind.

My first reading of Jung's works brought me to a new understanding: "Nursie's death: the loss of one of two mothers, the mother of instinct, of darkness, warmth, sexuality, and birth (rebirth?). Need to incorporate these aspects of the mother when she dies. To know where she is buried, to honor her name."

Meanwhile my life with my sons, now aged thirteen and eleven, and my work as a teacher and writer were a source of great joy to me. In spite of the struggles of raising children alone, and in spite of the fact that my parents had little time for their grandsons, I found that together the three of us were creating a life of sunshine: walks in the country around our house, Saturday-afternoon trips to the movies and the shopping mall—the ordinary sweetness of existence for a woman with two delightful boys, each a developing individual in his own right, each beginning to venture out into the world as their older brother, living in New York with his father, had done at the same age. Will, the youngest, on his bike in the long suburban twilights, or confabulating with neighborhood children under our kitchen window; Christopher finding a turtle in the long grass on a nearby hill—these were the pleasures that convinced me I had not been wrong to bring my boys to Kentucky.

At the same time, I was beginning to write short stories about life in this central part of the country, writing about people and places and situations which, twenty years earlier, I had believed I must abandon because as a rich white woman, a member of a tiny, alienated minority, I had no right to penetrate the lives of so-called ordinary people.

I began to question the role of inherited money in society, as well as in the family. A newspaper that descends only through the sons was modeled on the old English system of primogeniture. This system, which ensures that money and power go automatically to the eldest son, and if he falls, to the next eldest, is at odds with the egalitarian principles of a democracy. How does an individual resign himself or herself to being governed by gender and birth placement alone? How does a society that considers itself a meritocracy justify the automatic inheritance of accumulated wealth and money by eldest sons?

No one was asking these questions. Now and then, a letter to the editor in the newspapers would make fun of Barry for hunting doves over a baited field, or for some other mild eccentricity of the very rich. But no one seemed to notice the contrast between the rule of inherited money and the rule of the majority.

Father's extraordinary philanthropy and general friendliness made such criticism seem ungrateful. The ugly old city of Louisville was being improved by his tireless fund raising—the new arts center was opened to a burst of local pride—and when my sons and I had lunch with him at a cafeteria, Father knew the names of the people in the food line as well as he knew the names of his suburban neighbors or of his staff. Perfect paternal benevolence seems to stifle all questions.

Yet no benevolent patriarch can really know the people he leads, it seemed to me; the acquaintance is too superficial, filtered through old perceptions, especially when the acquaintances are so meek in the presence of power. Father spoke a language that could not be understood by most of his subjects: women, blacks, children, the very poor. It was not simply a question of vocabulary. It was a difference in point of view.

That point of view excluded many experiences. Puberty, with its terrible trials and uncertainties; rape and love, so similar in violence and danger; childbirth with its darkness and its light; age in a society that values only young women: how were these experiences to find a vocabulary in a world controlled by a few powerful men? Public life and thought, I had seen, was deep-dyed with the emotions and the prejudices of private life as it was lived by these men: the rivalries and jealousies, the passion of war, of male friendships and approval. Women had no public life, and our private life was discredited.

Such a peace with the powerful was not worth keeping. I realized that if I broke it, I would have to count on allies who were not at that point visible, and who might not exist. Even my sister's support was not certain, and I knew my mother would be a potent antagonist.

I was aware of the dangers: "Much too excited and angry to make a decision, no matter how trivial. This is the time to function simply, with careful restraints on impulse, compulsiveness, fantasy."

In spite of my own advice, I fell prey to one grandiose scheme. Two Victorian houses in Louisville, down the street from the site of the house where Eleanor Miller and the Judge had lived with Mrs. Miller, were to be torn down to make way for a parking lot. Mayor Sloane and his wife and other people who lived in that neighborhood were looking for someone to buy the deteriorating houses.

Impulsively, I agreed to come up with the money for a down payment, which fortunately was a modest sum, since the houses were far gone. It seemed that they could be converted to apartments and resold. However, the old houses proved obdurate, and after spending a good deal of money on exterior renovation, I was out of cash. Eventually I sold them to a developer.

The experience was not wasted. The contractor who refurbished those gaunt Victorian façades was Tim Peters, whom I would later marry. We scrambled through the upper floors together, upsetting roosting pigeons and ghosts from my grandmother's past. Just down the block, her brother, seventy years ago, had sat on the front porch with a bandage around his head after Eleanor's death on the track in Pewee Valley.

35

In the spring of 1981, I saw a young woman with two children outside of the Spouse Abuse Center in Louisville. I noticed the woman's shabbiness and desperation first, then the practicality of her solution to having too much to carry: she put the nipple of the baby's bottle between her teeth, leaving her hands free for the children. I realized that I had something in common with that woman, perhaps more than I shared with my sister, my mother, or my grandmother. She was going to other women for help.

I remembered Mother's one story about her stepmother-in-law, the formidable Ambassadress, who many years earlier had asked what dress Mother's new diamond clips had come on. That unsheathed rivalry was perhaps what Mother expected, even from me.

The little story contained a clue, explained when I read an English diarist had said the same thing about the Duchess of Windsor's jewels: they must be "dressmaker jewelry"—the stones were too large to be real.

Perhaps I was connected in Mother's mind to this uncomfortable subject: rivalry between women, as it is displayed most vividly in *Gammer Gurton's Needle,* the sixteenth-century play Mother had acted in at Radcliffe. In that ancient play, two formidable females batter each other physically and verbally over a needle, which the troublemaking prankster, Diccon the Bedlam, at last reveals in the seat of a male servant's pants. Their bad temper is a source of delight and mischief for the interfering, elusive prankster.

I remembered women who had resembled Gammer Gurton and Dame Chat: Munda, opinionated and fiery-tempered, the Ambassadress, Henrietta before life drained her of energy, Sallie Montague with her silver-headed riding crop, and that determined ghost, Mary Lily Kenan Flagler Bingham. All had feared and fought other women for that ultimate prize: a father, a husband—a status-conferring, handsome, wellborn man.

For five generations, the family myth had prevailed. Enmity between women who might have been allies had seen to that.

The next play in the family game involved a misuse of the potential sympathy between women.

We were informed by letter that a couple who advised women stockholders in family-owned businesses had been hired by the companies to come to Louisville. According to their books, they try to analyze personal relationships within families, then issuing their decision about whether or not we were serving a useful purpose on the company boards.

We were given copies of the book the couple had written and published themselves. It was called *From the Other Side of the Bed* and contained chapters with titles such as "A Boss We All Sleep With" and "We Make Lousy Directors."

When Eleanor handed me the book, I burst out laughing. It seemed incredible that an audience could be found, in the 1980s, for such chatter. But it immediately became clear that my hilarity was inappropriate. The book's authors were coming to see us, they were being paid a large sum to offer us their advice, and no matter how laughable we might find their point of view, there was no seemly way to avoid them.

I could not imagine spending a day of my life with this couple, and I said as much, expecting a storm of criticism. It arrived in due course. I was not displaying the obedience that had been my grandmother's cardinal rule for her daughters.

It still amazes me that anyone in the highly intelligent, combative, and articulate Bingham family could have endorsed the use of a blunt instrument like *From the Other Side of the Bed*.

Families that cannot talk are vulnerable to the manipulation of authorities—lawyers, accountants, psychiatrists, tutors, and consultants of every kind, especially if they write books. *From the Other Side of the Bed* reminded me of *The Stork Didn't Bring You,* a book Mother had given me when I was a child, in which gauzy pink-and-blue illustrations strove to blunt the impact of brutal sexual facts. Once more, the "facts of life," so called, were being presented in a pastel package, tied up by an authority on the subject.

Barry was furious when I refused to see the authors, and his anger revealed that they were part of a plan. Mother was furious because I had refused to accept the family's dictate. Eleanor thought the couple absurd but spent time with them because it was expected. Father remained silent on the subject, having realized, perhaps, that the ploy was unnecessary.

After a few weeks, the authors delivered their verdict, I was told: all the women should resign from the company boards.

It was the first time this solution had been mentioned, and yet I realized as soon as I heard it that the idea had been present, as a shapeless threat, for some time. Barry was too angry to continue in a situation where he felt beset by demons. Father's disillusionment with his son, and with newspaper business in general, had found a means of expression.

As was usually the case, the bad feelings resulting from this visit were never discussed, and the couple's recommendation appeared for a time to have been forgotten. But I knew, now, it was only a question of time. At every board meeting, Barry was signaling that he had been pressed to the limit of his endurance. It was in the set of his shoulders and the grimness of his mouth.

And at every board meeting, we—the four women, the unqualified, the outsiders—were learning more.

As long as the workings of the three companies and their subsidiaries remained mysterious, it was easy to convince the women in the family to accept an edict from the publisher, such as the one I had accepted since childhood: that all profits were "plowed back into" the companies rather than distributed as dividends.

Now the mysteries were evaporating fast. The board meetings showed the usual struggles between men with different goals, the usual subdued clash between the intelligent and the less intelligent, the eager and the meek, the secretive and that rare director, the one who is outspoken. Perhaps they had all been more outspoken in the club atmosphere that had reigned before the women appeared.

When I went to work for the *Courier-Journal* in the spring of 1981, the last patch of that necessary mystery dissolved.

Although Mother had been book editor in the 1950s, stopping abruptly after Worth's death in 1966, she had never discussed the job with me, and I had prevented myself from thinking about Father's offer four years earlier.

In the meantime I had become acquainted with the book editor, who had been Mother's assistant. She had invited me to review a book for her from time to time. When she asked me to take over for a couple of months while she had an operation, I was delighted.

The *Courier-Journal* was still a place of awe and majesty to me, and I longed to become one of its familiars.

I was timid at first, and terrified of learning to compose and edit on a computer terminal, but I found my colleagues friendly and helpful after the first wonder passed. They were curious about me as a new apple of nepotism, and they liked to gossip as they picked through the bright review copies that crowded my shelf. The feeling of camaraderie was nourished by the fact that many in the Sunday department were refugees from other departments, writers and editors who for obscure reasons had ended up in charge of entertainment news.

The section we produced was the most widely read in the newspaper, but it carried no special prestige since it printed the information that formerly appeared in the Woman's Section: recipes and household hints, as well as movie and theater reviews, book reviews, and evaluations of the local ballet, opera, and symphony, on whose boards Father and Barry served.

I loved the flood of new books coming in to be reviewed; they reunited me with the publishing world in New York. Barry looked on those free books with alarm, and had insisted for a while that the newspaper must pay the publishers for them, an unwieldy suggestion the publishers had repudiated. Traditionally, newspapers do not pay for books sent for review. His stringency was mentioned in an article in *The Wall Street Journal* which called Father and Barry the Mr. Cleans of the newspaper industry, a sobriquet more appealing to Barry than it was to Father.

Barry was still devoted to the family myth, and he was determined to eliminate the influences that had formed the newspapers since Henry Watterson's time: the efforts of local politicians and corporations, lobbying groups and special interests, to obtain flattering coverage. The book page might seem of little interest in this context, but Barry seemed to believe that it, and I, were susceptible to cronyism.

Once when I sent Barry two review copies—paperbacks—on Africa as a gift, he responded with a note thanking me but mentioning that he would be obliged to send a check to their publisher. All this was part of the Byzantine conflict-of-interest policy through which Barry tried to control the small doings of his staff while the larger doings of his executives continued to elude his supervision.

An especially disliked provision of this policy attempted to control the activities of wives—as they almost invariably were—of the newspapers' employees. Even Ben Bradlee at the Washington *Post* had despaired of maintaining that line: in 1979, Bradlee told Ben Bagdikian, "We tell reporters not to march in a demonstration. But what can you do when their wives march in demonstrations?" The cruel answer appears to be that a publisher can do a great deal to chill enthusiasms all too easily chilled in this society, if not to outlaw participation.

Over the years, the conflict-of-interest policy, which was seldom challenged, had served to divide our reporters and editors from their community and to deprive the city of intelligent volunteers. At first it seemed to have little effect on me, except in terms of the free review copies.

Finding reviewers opened the city to me. Hidden away at the university or in the interstices of old neighborhoods were experts who knew some portion of the wider world. In a society as constricted as Louisville's, there are no opportunities for people who are not part of the establishment to be heard. The book page provided one of the few open forums of opinion, in addition to the letters to the editor. I had little respect for acknowledged "authorities," who often turned out to have business, political, or social ties to the authors they wanted to review. I preferred the unknown.

My little office was behind the ladies' room, and all day I listened to the flushing of the toilets (which had driven the regular book editor almost to distraction). The only visible change associated with my time there occurred in that dreary bathroom. Painters suddenly appeared, and an interior decorator dropped by with samples. I was mildly surprised.

However, the change did affect the women who ate their lunch in the lounge area adjoining the bathroom. I was too new to realize how important it is for women to escape, if only for a few minutes, to sit down quietly and read a book while eating a homemade sandwich. Now at least there were a table and chairs, a few posters, and even a couch.

I noticed that the women who ate their sandwiches in the lounge belonged to a large group. Most of them worked in the lowest-paid categories as mail-room clerks, telephone solicitors, and cafeteria workers, as they do at newspapers all over the country, where the attempt to hire more women and move them up into executive positions has largely collapsed.

Several years earlier, the companies had drawn up an Affirmative Action Plan, and at every board meeting we were told that its limited objectives had been reached. The plan's aim was to hire a number of blacks to reflect about one-half of the percentage living in the metropolitan area—that is, about five and a half percent of our total employees—and to attempt to hire and promote women. Since I could not reconcile what I was told at board meetings with what I was observing as a newspaper employee, I asked the manager who was in charge of affirmative action to explain the discrepancy.

Over a period of time, and at considerable risk, she showed me the graphs and statistics that were not displayed at board meetings. They revealed that women were hired in large numbers but were contained at the lowest levels in all three companies. Blacks, too, were frequently brought in at entry level or as part-time workers with no benefits, but were infrequently promoted and were often laid off. This matched what I was seeing every day at work. Only in the newsroom had some progress been made, due to the efforts of Paul Janensch.

There was no on-the-job training; instead there were workshops in "stress management." Employees with problems were sent to the staff psychologist, who, it appeared to me, was successful at persuading his largely female clientele that all their problems were personal. The posting of job opportunities was meaningless since male managers were usually successful in promoting their protégés. As a result, most of the women in the three companies were low-paid, fearful of losing their jobs, and lacked any sense of a common bond. The few women who had risen were afraid of offending their male superiors by championing the cause of other women. It would be several years before the first suit was brought against the companies, and by then the woman who gave me the information would have lost her job and her position would have been eliminated.

The family's failure to insist on change justified the lies we were told—lies of omission, if not of commission. Mother frequently complained that affirmative action meant that incompetent blacks and/or women were promoted, to the detriment of the organization; she seemed to speak for Father. Eleanor and I were unsuccessful when we attempted, during the next year, to raise questions about both the goals of the affirmative action policy and the information we were receiving. No one wanted change, certainly not the owners, who had spent their lives reinforcing the status quo.

In my department, there were several women who were copy editors, and the assistant managing editor was also a woman, yet the atmosphere was dominated by the men who joked and gossiped around the terminals. The women were usually quiet, or spoke softly to one another; but the men, enjoying their friendships, filled the air with observations that reflected the preoccupations of their society: political misdeeds on a petty level, violent crime, sports, and the vague and threatening sexuality of women, especially as it is represented by actresses and victims of crime. Not all the men joined in these gregarious exchanges, but the ones who worked in silence had as little effect on the others as had the women.

The most outrageous sexist and racist jokes were curtailed, but the mood that produces those jokes was the mood most of my colleagues appeared to find comfortable. It was an entirely familiar mood to me, for it had shaped the atmosphere at the Big House, and the pleasant cheerfulness of its perpetrators made it difficult to criticize. After all, they were "just talking," and they were nice people, pleasant people, whom I liked.

This atmosphere governed the choice of wire service copy, the writing of headlines and cutlines, and the placement of stories on the page—all crucial in forming readers' attitudes.

I began to wonder if the pleasant plantation atmosphere everyone enjoyed had destroyed our ability to think. Or, over the years, had the thinkers fought, lost, and moved on?

My editor took the time to get to know me, in spite of what appeared to be profound reservations about my competence to do my job. No one knew that I was a published writer. Some wondered out loud if I could type.

My editor decided after a suitable interval that I was competent. In fact, she taught me a great deal about the way the newspapers worked and the personalities of the men who ran them, whom she knew as friends and peers. She had been the protégée of Carol Sutton, whose face had appeared, several years earlier, on the cover of *Time* as the first woman managing editor at an American newspaper.

Carol Sutton's fate seemed tragic and symbolic to me. She had traveled a great deal during her single year as managing editor of the *Courier-Journal,* speaking about the bright promise she represented for women in journalism. Since she was away so much, she had little opportunity to learn her new job, and no support from the men who resented her prominence. She was brought down by their complaints, demoted with a suitable explanation, and remained till her early death from cancer a sort of assistant to the publisher, in charge of readers' complaints, the conflict-of-interest policy, and other ambiguous issues.

The three months I spent as temporary replacement for the book editor flashed by, leaving me with an appetite for more. Yet when I left my tiny office for the last time, I realized that I was stepping out of the line of fire. Already women who worked at the lowest levels in the company were coming to me for advice, sympathy, or support—the distinction was not always clear.

When women complained to me, easing in my open door and whispering nervously, I was flattered, but I soon realized that there was almost nothing I could do. When the cafeteria staff, older women with a variety of health problems, were laid off with the excuse that the facility was to be renovated, I could not help them although some had worked for the company for many years. They were replaced by pretty young women in suggestive uniforms.

The mail-room clerks who brought around my books were young women, some of them black, who had the gleam of hope still in their eyes. Perhaps they had read the stories of "girl" reporters, published in the 1970s, which had told of bright young women working their way up from the bottom. But these clerks never stayed long at the newspaper.

The fashion editor, who had been imported from another newspaper, found her life in Louisville difficult: because she was black, she was turned away at the door of one of the benefit balls she had been sent to cover. Other women who were actively courted to work on the editorial pages of both newspapers seldom lasted more than a year.

There were exceptions, women who had worked their way up and were extraordinarily capable, such as my editor, who is still the highest-ranking woman at the newspaper. She never complained, nor did the women who were copy editors, even the young woman who spent all nine months of her pregnancy in front of a computer terminal. Her problems did not cease with her child's birth, since the companies provided no day care.

I did not know how to translate my concerns for the women in the companies into action. Yet I could not ignore them.

The board meetings had never been shortened, and since the failure of the *From the Other Side of the Bed* offensive, Barry seemed even more uneasy.

I was pained and thwarted by the lack of progress toward any degree of understanding: "Resisting two days of board meetings for the first time. I have been trying to earn love by agreeing. No use. Must be prepared, now, to pay the price: the family may abandon me. A small price to pay."

Sometimes in the long, hot evenings of the summer of 1981, I would walk over to the Place, passing along the back road where I had once collected "critter bits" with Nursie, where the man with the wooden leg had held up the bridge for Mother to drive over on her way to the hospital where I was born.

Mother was sometimes in her garden, and when I saw her basket of flowers, I would approach her tentatively. She tried once to explain why Barry should be protected from criticism, but I was confused by her scorn: although she pitied Barry, she also seemed angry at him. She had been at her best with us when we were sick, and now it seemed that Barry had claimed that devotion—but at a price. Even in the garden, I could hear the hum of her anger. He had disappointed her in a way I could not imagine. Now she blamed me for revealing his weaknesses, the hesitations and uncertainties she had pledged herself to hide.

Mother had a curious habit of calling me by her sisters' names when she was distracted, usually running through the whole list, in descending order. Her relationship with her three surviving sisters, now in their sixties and seventies, seemed to affect her relationship with me. Mother was unfailingly generous with her sisters, who as old age approached and husbands died, found it difficult to survive. Yet there seemed a lack of connection, a correctness, rather than affection between these women, as though, once again, pity had developed late, taking the place of other feelings. Mother's life had been, outwardly, much more successful than her sisters', in terms of money and prestige, and perhaps there was a sting in the inevitable comparisons. Yet they retained the spark that had been Munda's gift, the remorseless joy in life she had shared with all her daughters.

Mother had stopped calling me by her sisters' names, however, and I realized that I was coming sharply into focus. Perhaps too sharply. Still, I was astonished when, a few months after I had left the newspapers, she and Father telephoned to ask me to return, permanently, to edit the book page.

I was excited by their proposal although I knew it was hardly decent. The book editor, who was my friend, had no intention of resigning; she enjoyed her job, and although my parents felt that her work was not entirely satisfactory, she had never heard their complaints.

I admitted that I was both flattered and interested, but asked that the book editor be given a chance to improve her performance. It was agreed that she would be told what she needed to do; it was a question of the timeliness of her reviews and the small number of local reviewers she used. I said that if after six months she was still found to be unsatisfactory, I would accept her job, if she was given another. In hindsight, of course, this attempt on my part was entirely ineffective.

Six months later, the book editor became a features writer and I went down to the newspapers, again, as a $22,000-a-year employee. I planned to stay two years.

As suitable penance, every day I had to face the woman I had replaced—in the elevator, the halls, the bathroom, or the cafeteria. She never spoke to me again. I could hardly blame her.

A few weeks before I went back to the newspaper, Mother telephoned to tell me that Barry was very upset because I had taken the job. I had not realized until then that he had not been consulted. Although Barry said later that he did not object to my working at the newspapers, it was easy for me to understand why he would object, violently, to the high-handed way I had been hired. Almost inevitably, he would see my presence in his territory as an act of sabotage.

Perhaps he saw my employment as another proof that Father was still very much in control.

Father's office was down the hall from Barry's, and Father's charm, and the memory of his charm, was everywhere in the big shabby building. The newspapers' staff still told stories about Father's uncanny ability to remember names, in cruel contrast to Barry. Perhaps for a few years after Worth's death, Barry had believed that Father would eventually retire and leave the scene; he had retired, but he had never left. He could not leave. Like other men of his generation and his background, Father could not imagine a life in Louisville separate from his companies.

Eugene Meyer, owner of the Washington *Post,* had suffered from the same problem when his son-in-law, Philip L. Graham, became publisher. Meyer abruptly resigned from the World Bank in 1946, six months after he had made Graham publisher, and returned to the *Post.* But the outcome was different. Meyer let his son-in-law know that he was available for consultation, calling himself "just the old man called chairman of the board," but Graham called Meyer "an irascible old man" and threatened to return to practicing law if his father-in-law interfered with the running of the newspaper. Finally the old man sold the *Post* to Graham and his wife, Katharine, and this ended the dispute.

It would have been inconceivable for Barry, throttled by the problems of nepotism, to challenge the prime mover in this way. Rudeness was not his strong suit, and he was heavily aware of what he owed his father. So the long-drawn-out struggle for control of the newspapers—and of the other companies, although they were of minor importance—continued for a decade, with unspoken rages and rivalries, and a bitter sense of personal betrayal on the part of both men, who when they had lunch together seemed to attempt to say the unsayable. But it remained unsayable.

There had been a time, years earlier, when Father had been given an opportunity to choose another life. He had been secretly offered the Ambassadorship to England, as a reward for his support of Jimmy Carter's presidential campaign. I had been surprised when he turned the offer down, with the excuse that Mother could not face the social responsibilities involved. As usual, I did not know what Mother felt, although certainly she was supremely suited to the art of high-level entertaining, with its important political consequences, as she had proved during our year in Paris.

Later it seemed to me that Father might have dreaded that the confirmation procedure would, as it had in the Judge's case, recall the Mary Lily scandal, or induce some other revelation. Mary Lily's death had been handled during the 1933 confirmation hearings by Raymond Moley, Franklin Roosevelt's first brain truster, who had later reflected, "That first-class sonofabitch Bingham . . . whom I'd helped during his confirmation hearings when it was rumored he had poisoned his second wife (who was the widow of Flagler of Standard Oil), inheriting $5 million, with which he bought the Louisville *Courier.*" Moley's complaint had followed the Judge's successful attempt to discredit him in Roosevelt's eyes during the London Economic Conference.

After turning down the ambassadorship, Father perhaps realized that the newspapers would remain his primary field of endeavor for the rest of his life. During the 1970s, a power struggle became inevitable as Barry tried to exert his authority as publisher, as it would have become inevitable had Worth lived.

The struggle was wreathed in mysteries that had begun in the late forties, when the CIA was created on the foundation provided by the OSS and wartime intelligence activities in London, where Father had been stationed as a young naval officer.

The men who formed the OSS and later the CIA shared Father's background: Princeton, Yale, or Harvard, membership in prestigious clubs, both official and unofficial, and a belief in noblesse oblige and government by a white male elite. Their families shared one characteristic: a commitment to privacy that was nearly a passion, especially important in families where women, and relations with women, are often complicated by money and all the attendant half-hidden scandals.

The thread that connects covert activities to like-minded members of the government and the press has been proved many times over. Covert activity, after all, is simply another tool of leadership, whether it is the covert activity of the Ku Klux Klan or of the CIA.

Father may not have been aware of the ways in which the Marshall Plan was used as a screen for covert operations in Europe (although perhaps his unwillingness to spend more than a year in Paris is proof that he was uneasy about the connection). He did know that the Asia Foundation, of which he was a director, had been criticized as "heavily subsidized by the CIA"—in the amount of $8 million a year—since the information was widely reported in news articles in the 1970s.

Father and many of his journalist friends shared a point of view that justifies the use of covert activities to ensure the supremacy of the United States abroad. Newspaper publishers, reporters, and columnists have long supplied information to the CIA, with the same justification.

There is a connection, it seems to me, between a belief in secret activities on the national and international level and the preservation of secrets in a family. In both instances, the importance of control is the justification given: chaos would follow, for the family women as for the subject countries of Latin America, if the controlling faction's secrets were revealed. The potential for abuse of the powerless is the same in both cases.

The preservation of family secrets also ensured the supremacy of the family's position in Kentucky.

However, the uses the CIA made of the press in the 1960s provided an opportunity for a display of independence on Barry's part. In 1967, only a year after Worth's death, when Barry was beginning to chafe under the tutelage of the executive editor at the time, Norman E. Isaacs (who had been hired to groom Worth), Barry ran a story on the Senate Intelligence Committee, which was investigating ties between the CIA and American newspapers.

The story ran on the front page of the *Courier-Journal,* below the fold, on March 27, 1976. The reporter, James Herzog, wrote that the Senate investigation had revealed that, three years earlier, the *Courier-Journal* had hired Robert H. Campbell, a CIA agent, as a general reporter. Campbell had worked at the *Courier-Journal* for about a year, although he had no skills and no experience; his main assignment had been an article on drugstore Indians, Herzog wrote, which, understandably, never ran.

Other reporters at the *Courier* had commented on Campbell's lack of skill—he could not even type, a requirement even for my job as book editor—and his file contained no background references other than a note stating that Isaacs knew about him.

Although Campbell had been paid only $125 a week, other reporters had noted that he was able to fly around the country frequently; he was, meantime, living at the Louisville YMCA.

According to Herzog, Isaacs when questioned said that he no longer remembered Campbell or anything about him; Father claimed ignorance, too.

The same issue of the *Courier-Journal* that ran the story about Campbell also ran a notice that William E. Colby, then director of the CIA, was to speak at the University of Louisville, where Father had financed a chair for visiting speakers. Colby had earlier told the Senate committee, according to Carl Bernstein in an article in *Rolling Stone,* that leading publishers in the United States "had allowed themselves and their organizations to become handmaidens to the intelligence service."

Colby said that twenty-five news organizations (the same number Bernstein later cited) had been or were being used as covers for agents, men who, according to the director, "looked like they belong to the Yale Club." Colby added that newspaper publishers seemed "highly susceptible to intrigue," as well as extraordinarily reliant on their social relationships with important men who "were often schoolmates or social friends and who could be trusted to grasp nuance and exercise discretion"—as "the Washington elite [who] often spoke through a small band of like-minded reporters and columnists" has been described.

Worth had been a member of this informal club, which included highly esteemed publishers, columnists, and CIA agents, men who relied heavily on liquor, poker, banter, and their wives' social skills. Barry had never been invited to join, partly because of a change in the times and partly because of his grave demeanor, his probity, and his aversion to alcohol.

Whatever Father's role had been in the hiring of Campbell, or in other cooperative ventures with the CIA, he would not have been pleased to see Herzog's story on the front page. Although embarrassing peccadilloes sometimes received front-page coverage, to the wondering admiration of readers (Mark Ethridge's arrest for drunken driving, years before, had been accorded that celebrity), serious revelations that might undermine the newspapers' authority, or the power of its allies, were usually given short shrift.

Worth, people believed, had supported the kind of hard-hitting investigative journalism that reached its brief climax after the Watergate scandal. He had died too soon to prove the extent of his commitment, although when I recall his sardonic amusement at expressions of pious public sentiment, and the way he called his own forays into drunken displays and practical jokes "dirty tricks," I sometimes wonder if he knew of the newspapers' less obvious connections.

Barry, in turn, shared Worth's commitment to the truth, but he lacked the cynicism and the ability to form alliances Worth had learned early. Barry would have supported a reporter who had something damaging to write, and in fact all during his tenure as publisher he had the respect of his newsroom because they knew they could trust him.

Perhaps Father realized, when he saw the Herzog story, that something was changing at Sixth and Broadway.

The Colonel's concept of the gentleman enters here, as it did all during our childhoods, when Mother warned that certain targets were inappropriate for the unrestrained mirth of the Big House dinner table. Episcopalian divines and Democratic candidates who were gentlemen to boot, by birth and behavior, were not to be criticized; they were pillars of the structure, after all.

Sometimes one of us would make a mistake, since not all powerful men appear to be wellborn. Mother would remind us quickly: "He's a gent." Nothing more needed to be said. Her respect had been learned at Munda's knee, as Father had learned it from the Judge and the Colonel. It follows that if a spy is a gentleman, or vouched for by a gentleman, no other questions need to be asked, especially when secret activities are accepted as a way of running a family, a way of running a state, and a way of running the world.

Several months before I returned to Kentucky in 1977, a front-page story with embarrassing implications was printed in the *Courier-Journal*. It referred to the buying of prison records by a *Courier-Journal* reporter who was looking for proof of wrongdoing for a story.

An investigation by the Democratic governor, Julian Carroll, quickly bogged down, and the *Courier-Journal* reporter who had "broken" this story to another journalist at a small newspaper in western Kentucky was subsequently demoted to copy editor—for plagiarism, Father told me. The punishment seemed as odd as the accusation.

These two lapses may have alerted Father to the possibility that the newspapers were slipping out of his grasp.

Paul Janensch's bulldog devotion to an undefined idea of integrity may have alarmed him, too. Janensch had little reason to imitate the men of the club. His reporters knew they had his backing, for Janensch supported Barry's commitment to an old-fashioned, Old Testament morality. Both men appeared to believe in a white world of heroic male endeavor pursued and shadowed by a black world of impulse, only too often represented by the untoward thoughts and activities of women and blacks.

Like Janensch, Barry did not cultivate the fruits of influence, and so he did not receive the journalistic accolades that had rained on Father. In fact, it seemed likely to me that when the *Courier-Journal* finally stopped winning Pulitzer Prizes, in the mid-1980s, and was dropped from *Time*'s list of the nation's greatest newspapers, Barry's social limitations, rather than the newspaper's quality—which had by then been declining for years—was the cause of the humiliation. Membership in the club is more important, finally, than the quality of the "product," a quality that is, in any event, largely a subjective notion based on a sentimental reverence for the past.

If Barry resisted the uses of influence (and even his conflict-of-interest policy was a bemused attempt to forestall influence peddling), then he was at once a danger to the myth. It depended, and had depended for more than half a century, on keeping secrets. Secrets are kept by insiders, members of an order which endorses any action that maintains control.

Now I began to understand Barry's interest in the electronic newspaper, which had seemed so unlikely—a sad dream. As the pressures which Father had initiated, and which the women in the family were now doubling, made Barry's life difficult, he may have yearned to escape to a world where we would not know the rules. In a family where changing a car tire seemed an insurmountable problem, the challenge of somehow eliciting a newspaper from a computer terminal would have been, to say the least, terrifying—to everyone but Barry.

The Judge and the Colonel would surely have been all thumbs faced with the confusing intricacies of a computer keyboard. They might have looked on Barry as a sort of magician. Father, as owner and chairman of the board, would have been daunted, too, and would have found his role drastically reduced, if not eliminated altogether, when he would not operate the medium of his message.

Mother might eventually have supported a technique that spared linen sheets, although she would have shuddered at the thought of taking a computer to bed.

Nothing came of it, however. George Gill was opposed to the plan, for important reasons. Barry left Louisville for a year, and when he returned, he had found another way to escape the power of the chairman of the board.

36

By the spring of 1981, teaching students to write poetry, short stories, and plays at the University of Louisville had freed me finally from my old fear of speaking in public.

Although almost without exception my students came from poverty, although they had been maimed by years in a public school system the Binghams had done little to support, they nearly all appeared to be devout admirers of my family, and the admiration sometimes intruded on discussions of writing technique. This happened more frequently after the building where I taught was renamed to honor my parents, who were supporters of the university.

Meanwhile Tim and I had consolidated our two families, bringing four boys together in Tim's Victorian frame house in an old Louisville neighorhood. I was too afraid of making another mistake to risk marriage yet, although I realized that our unorthodox arrangement would cause comment.

Leaving my suburban house, with its view of the Big House chimney, did not increase my emotional distance from the family companies or the family tempest. Father made a conscious effort to include my new family by coming once a week to read aloud to the four assembled boys. His favorite author was John Buchanan.

The quarterly board meetings continued to provide me with issues I could not avoid addressing.

The next one was raised at the television station board meeting, where usually I found that I could leave most of the questions to Eleanor, who understood the business better than I.

I had long ago accepted that the family's undefined commitment to public service had only one outlet at the television station: the annual fund drive for crippled children, which often raised more than a million dollars. Other than that, the station, like all other television affiliates, was solely dedicated to making a profit, which it succeeded in doing handsomely. This profit was reflected not in an increase in our dividends but in vast capital expenditures for equipment.

To expect more would have seemed ridiculous, since the highly competent staff felt that there was no way to change the formula handed down by the network and the ratings. Canned shows disappeared when they lost their audience, and local shows—one had been produced during Eleanor's brief tenure at the station—seemed no more than pallid copies of network fare. I had largely given up questioning the way the station was run, since, in terms of profits at least, it was clearly achieving all that was expected.

At one of the 1981 board meetings, however, I was astonished to hear that our new anchorwoman, hired from the West Coast to boost our ratings, was to receive not only a large salary but an apartment building, bought by the company for her boyfriend to manage. My dismay was received with annoyance. In fact, the general manager intimated that he was proving his feminist credentials by providing the boyfriend with an occupation.

Eleanor, too, had questioned the practicality, as well as the probity, of this arrangement. But a few weeks later, she invited me to a party for the new anchorwoman and her friend. I reminded myself of the way we had both learned to get by, the way we would at crucial moments still bend and weave, flirt and cajole. I thought that Eleanor was still hoping to win the approval of the general manager, who, a little earlier, had helped to engineer her dismissal from her job.

She could display more courage than I, however, as she proved when she asked to be invited to the companies' Dingo meetings, now named for Kipling's yellow dog. Dipnoan had been replaced by Dingo, the dumb fish by the clever dog.

(Kentucky men are attached to their clubs, whatever their names. The chief executive of a car-assembly plant, lured with great effort from Japan, was refused membership in 1987 in the Frankfort country club, as was the black president of Kentucky's black college. Neither the governor, who was an honorary member of the club, nor the Democratic candidate running to replace her felt called upon to resign, nor did the newspapers suggest it in editorials. After a few weeks, under political pressure, the Democratic candidate announced that he would attend no more functions at the club.)

Eleanor told me afterwards that the atmosphere exuded by the men at the Dingo meeting was so frigid she did not dare to open her mouth. But she had been there.

One of a director's first lessons is that business is conducted independently of corporate boards. Directors' appointments are purely honorary. Yet a family myth held that the voice of the minority is legitimate, and should be represented in the decision-making process. Often it was the voice of a minority that the newspapers sought to protect in their vigorous defense of local First Amendment issues. But the "minority" in those cases was usually a white, middle-class reporter seeking access to court records for a story.

We had been raised since childhood to shoulder the responsibility of privilege. Nothing in our education had prepared us for the facts of the corporate structure, which evades responsibility on all levels, to its board of directors, to its shareholders, and to its constituency. Men who have held power for many years are seldom interested in dissent, and their defense of First Amendment issues reinforces their right to interpret reality.

The spring of 1982 was full of potent changes. I went back to work as book editor at the *Courier-Journal*. I did not aim to balance my reviews: opinion, it seemed to me, was more interesting when it was stated without equivocations. No one protested except my editor, who was in charge of teaching me the harsh ways of journalism. My poor spelling called down her wrath almost as frequently as my choice of books and reviewers.

The best part of the job was the actual design of the page, which was supervised by a brilliant man who devoted time and imagination to the weekly task. This collaboration reassured me that cooperation can sometimes work, and I looked forward to the design he would choose to surprise me every Sunday at the top of my column.

I also found that I was learning fast and furiously from my demanding editor, as I had learned in high school from temperamental teachers who inspired my respect. This woman knew, it seemed to me, everything that I needed to know about the mechanics of journalism, and I was determined to absorb it all as swiftly as possible.

As always, other factors intervened.

After we moved into Louisville from the ranch house in the suburbs, my two younger sons began to attend the city public schools, largely abandoned by the white middle class after integration. I wanted my sons to be a part of the real world, although I was not at the time aware of the cost, to them, of this change from the sheltered life. Now they were going to school with the children of the Shively housewife, who did not have enough money to pay for private education, and with black children from Louisville's West End.

The smoldering city schools seemed to me a funeral pyre where the ideals of the sixties were consumed. Teachers, most of whom were women, taught classes of as many as thirty-five children, many of whom had been neglected or abandoned by the system. I saw displays of heroism on the part of exhausted, underpaid women who were determined to pass along some of their enthusiasm for ideas. Unfortunately, control was the issue, over and over again, and the pursuit of control at all costs led to the limitation of freedom. No one working in the school system could be blamed for the result, which was largely the responsibility, it seemed to me, of wealthy white adults who refused to become involved in state education.

In the spring of 1982, a group of parents and other concerned people put together a committee to persuade voters to support a proposed tax for public education. Kentuckians are particularly obdurate on the subject of taxes, and people who have no children in the public schools are the most obdurate of all. Although money was not the only answer to a set of complex problems, it was a needed first step.

When I read a news story about the committee, I wanted to help. I volunteered to join the committee.

Big events are often in themselves quite trivial, until the uproar arrives. My telephone call was received with a manifest lack of interest. I carefully spelled my name, wondering if someone would find a role for me to play.

When I had started work as book editor, I had been shown a massive sheaf of much-amended papers called the conflict-of-interest policy, some of it the work of the woman who had been demoted from managing editor. The policy seemed to represent, in crude form, the fears Barry did not put into words at board meetings. Every conceivable kind of private activity, from having a drink with a source to working as a volunteer for a political candidate, was forbidden, in language that seemed oddly confused and contradictory, like the language we use with children when we are uncertain of our own motivations.

So many areas of life were covered and in such detail that I knew the policy was bound to cause trouble, if only because of inevitable confusion. The policy did not address the executives and owners of the newspapers who served on the boards of various arts organizations the newspaper reviewed and of downtown development groups whose projects we supported editorially, nor did it deal with the problem of the support, both financial and moral, which the owners gave to various political candidates.

It seemed to me that no self-respecting employee would agree to sign such a document, with its infringement of personal rights. We were not asked to sign it, of course; reading it was assumed to stand for agreement to its terms and restrictions. That agreement was in a sense broader than one procured by signing a legally binding document, since it included tacit acceptance of a certain mode of thinking—fearful, restrictive, punitive toward individual initiative—that could never have been put into words.

The conflict-of-interest policy seemed to me a way of controlling attitude as well as behavior. It hinted at dark and dangerous forces at work outside the big building at Sixth and Broadway, justifying the cynicism and laziness of those journalists who preferred to stay safely inside.

Yet I was surprised to find that people at the newspapers never grumbled about these restrictions, which in effect increased their isolation. However, to be involved, to care about issues, seemed at the time unfashionable, even sophomoric. This attitude was possibly a result of living on good terms with the plantation system. Few people were ever fired; instead they were shuffled off into other, less crucial jobs. Benefits were good, and our pension plan was overfunded to the tune of thirty million dollars. So why complain?

The plantation system perhaps explained the peculiar fortresslike atmosphere of the newspaper offices. Although passersby circulated freely on the first floor, and security guards were not much in evidence even on the floors above, there was an atmosphere of almost clublike privacy. Reporters seemed to live cozily in the newsroom, which the two newspapers shared. It seemed that the outside world might be largely a source of threat to the point of view—comfortable, moderate, satisfied—the newspapers conveyed. Although it was often maintained, with pride, that we had no "sacred cows," it seemed to me that reality had become the biggest sacred cow of all.

Kentucky seemed a particularly unlikely place for a patriarchal institution like these newspapers to flourish. Yet the state's poverty and sense of unimportance, on a national level, helped to prevent self-criticism, which was seen as a threat, as had been true all over the area since the partisans of the New South had boasted of imagined improvements in the chaotic period after Reconstruction.

Presently my name appeared as a member of the committee working for passage of the school tax. The next day, I was visited in turn by one of the newspapers' executives and by an editor. Both men seemed a little sheepish as they took the extra chair in my office. In fact, the wife of the editor was also on the committee, and had been asked to resign.

Their message was clear: I must resign from the committee because membership was forbidden by the conflict-of-interest policy.

I explained that since I did not report on education, there was really no way my work as book editor could be compromised by my support of the public schools. There was no answer to this argument, but the demand remained. Barry, his emissaries told me, would not tolerate an action he perceived as being a conflict of interest. As always, the perception was what mattered, not the reality. But in one way Barry's perception matched reality: I was using the Bingham name, for the first time, to support a cause with which the rest of the family had little sympathy.

Nervously, I went downstairs to talk to Barry in his office, where skins from his safaris and life-sized pictures of the next generation, including my three sons, contributed to an atmosphere at once enclosed and threatening.

I asked him to make an exception in my case, which angered him. How often, I later realized, other members of the family must have asked him to make exceptions to his rules. It was the worst argument I could have chosen, since it seemed to prove that I, too, meant only to challenge his authority. He brusquely refused my request.

Then I talked to the former managing editor who was in charge, it seemed, of the conflict-of-interest policy. Again, my ignorance of the long and troubled history behind this document led me into difficulties. I asked to be allowed to collaborate with her on the refining of the document, which was cumbersome and confusing, but she, too, saw in my suggestion simply a challenge to the tiny portion of authority she had been given after her demotion.

I realized there was no chance that we could make common cause. I was further weakened, of course, by the fact that no one else among the people affected by the conflict-of-interest policy seemed to support my position. I learned a lesson then and there about the difficulties, both practical and psychological, of having no allies.

I did not realize at the time how helpless Barry must have felt in his attempt to control the far more important, and far more insidious, connections the newspapers had forged since 1917—connections with other important newspapers and their owners, with columnists and power brokers, intelligence officers and members of the government, who had been involved at so many points in our history.

All newspaper publishers use their properties to support and advance their groups and causes, to benefit socially and politically as well as financially from owning a point of view. But our peculiar tradition—a commitment to service rather than to personal gain—made it difficult for my generation to accept this cliché.

The appearance of my name on the committee working for the school tax had the weight of half a century of owner interference behind it. Reacting to that past rather than to the present situation, Barry now sent word to me that I must either resign from the committee or lose my job as book editor.

Astonished at the size of the storm, I took a few days to think. I had been book editor for about six weeks, and I loved the job. I told Father about Barry's edict, and he sighed and shook his head. He had spoken to Barry about it, he said, but he had been too late to influence him. There was nothing more Father could do.

I found myself trying to understand Barry's point of view. I remembered how pale and drained he had looked when I asked him to make an exception to his rule, as though this was only one of a series of confrontations. What, in fact, were the constraints that seemed to make his life as publisher so difficult? Why did he only enjoy himself when, on weekends, he worked outdoors on the Place? It occurred to me that even Barry's dyslexia—exaggerated by rumor, perhaps—might not be as debilitating as the presence of the prime mover just down the hall.

I remembered how Barry's big desk had looked, empty as a continent, and how the huge photographs of the next generation seemed to imprison him in a limitless commitment to their future. The animal skins from his safaris, too, had lent a peculiar air of dead ferocity. The atmosphere around him seemed macabre. Where was freedom for this beleaguered last son? Father's smaller office was bright with awards and citations, displayed around the Colonel's Confederate flag, but Barry's office was hung only with reminders of the outlawed past and the threatening future.

Finally I decided to resign from the committee. I wanted to keep my job.

The choices were out of balance: I had not even been to a meeting of the school-tax committee, which gave weight to the attempt of one of my co-workers to support me. "I bet you never even wanted to be on that old committee," she said kindly. Unlike me, this woman and many others would never have the luxury of choice. They depended on their paychecks to survive.

My prickly editor saw the situation clearly. "So you caved in," she said, with satisfaction.

"Yes," I told her, "but I won't next time."

After I resigned from the committee, I continued to question the system that had forced my resignation: "Two days of board meetings raise all kinds of questions: why should a family run a newspaper? These connections which are largely financial are meant to replace the failed emotional ties. Love, and money . . . Yet a wide audience is affected by matters which most people would define as personal."

I began to see the threat that the continuation of the dynasty posed to my own sons, the same threat that had destroyed their uncles' lives. What price would my boys have to pay for acceptance at the chilly marble table in the Little House, or to sit in one of the executive offices at Sixth and Broadway?

Father, Mother, and Barry frequently spoke eloquently about their determination to pass the companies along to the next generation, which now included Worth's son and daughter, Barry's two daughters (his step-sons, Edie's sons, had been sent away after failing to live up to the family's implacable standards), Eleanor's two sons, and my three sons. No one asked my opinion about the wisdom of passing along wealth and prestige; it was assumed that we would all applaud this solution to our children's futures. Indeed it was a highly acceptable solution, it appeared, to Edie, Joan, and Eleanor. I had my doubts.

All "the grandchildren," as they were referred to, which eliminated their parents' generation, seemed bright and independent to me, ranging in age from Eleanor's infants to my oldest son, now graduated from college and continuing his own life in New York. Why did they need the safeguard of an assured income and profession? And were those safeguards really being offered to the granddaughters?

Since our society assumes that mothers live through their children, especially through their sons, our parents perhaps assumed that "the girls" (Eleanor and I) would be beguiled by the prospect of our sons' assured success. But success can never be assured. Besides, the complications of inheritance would produce an uneven distribution of the companies' stock. This, too, was unmentionable, since it called into question our parents' commitment to fairness.

Both Eleanor and I realized that since Barry would inherit the companies, his daughters would be likely to inherit them from him. There was nothing wrong with that, and in fact I took some pleasure in the thought that these two intelligent young women would one day, perhaps, be in charge. However, it was a fact which none of the grandchildren understood, and which ensured disillusionment later on.

I knew how important it had been to me, as a young woman starting her career as a writer, to find a publisher on my own, without my parents' help or interference. I had seen the same increased resolve and self-confidence as my oldest son started his own life. Why should the others be deprived of contact with the real world, of the inevitable pains and pleasures of making it on one's own? This had always been the American dream, and it seemed to me still a more creditable myth than the myth of dynasty.

Inevitably, however, the whole issue was one of control, of that need to prevent the unforeseeable that is a characteristic of the powerful. My own attempt to free my sons was also an aspect of the passion for control: even freedom cannot be given. So it would seem inevitable that my sons would resent my interference in their grandparents' generous plans, especially after they had been given a taste of that generosity during summer internships at the companies.

Thanksgiving, which as usual we celebrated at the Little House, seemed to give the tight atmosphere another twist. I noticed that my youngest son's eyes filled with tears during the meal when he was ignored. I remembered the power of ignoring—Munda had called it "benign neglect"—which is even more effective than criticism or punishment. Being ignored means that one ceases to exist. I had seen the technique used effectively, in the old days, with black servants, especially during a discussion they were not supposed to overhear. Ignoring people has always been used to preserve the white family's privacy, for it fends off everyone who is perceived as being an outsider—servants, children, dogs, black people in general, and often women. There is no arguing with being ignored, because the ignorer will insist that is not what he is doing.

I decided to concentrate on the board meetings, which were the only field left open to me. I felt that I was becoming more articulate as a spokeswoman for unpopular views; I knew I had no allies.

"More and more, Father's determination to pass all this on seems tragic: children burdened with lives they didn't choose, responsibilities, money, to keep the family name alive through another generation. The narcissistic determination to outwit mortality is paid for in the flesh of children."

When I saw the Colonel's Confederate flag in its place of honor in Father's office, I heard his voice thundering through the din of the half-century since his death: "We are kings of men." The worship of eugenics, which justified misogyny and anti-Semitism, posed a terrible threat even to those considered "wellborn." Kings demand a sacrifice, and it is often paid by their inheritors.

The people I worked with every day perhaps imagined the glories of that kingdom, which they would never enter. I was impressed by the dedication, and the weariness, of the editors and writers in my department; many of the editors had spent a large portion of their lives at the newspapers. They no longer tried to change any aspect of their working day; nor did they complain about the many inconveniences and hazards associated with the use of computers: glaring lights, faulty displays, broken chairs, shortage of terminals, overcrowded work spaces—all seemed accepted as part of the job.

Yet these men, and the few women, were the stuff of the enterprise. On their well-being, their sense of autonomy and of importance to the organization, the newspapers ultimately depended. It seemed to me that too many had been crushed by the system, losing heart after many unrecorded struggles with management and ownership. They would surely not have agreed with me, and would perhaps have interpreted my concern as merely another form of the condescension that provided them with a swimming pool and a basketball court but with no child care, no flexible work time, and little hope of advancement.

Women who had once worked at the newspapers occasionally asked me to talk with them, conspiratorially, at nearby restaurants. They were frightened yet angry as they reported years of struggle against discrimination, which had prevented them from moving up in the hierarchy.

At the same time, the token women, hired and fired each year by the *Courier*'s editorial board, came to me to complain. Their problem was with a certain editor who was gifted at undermining women who often appeared to have been hired because of their intelligence and their lack of self-confidence. As each one resigned, I realized that the practice would continue as long as women were available who could be discredited. Barry promised to prevent his editor from wreaking this havoc, but nothing changed until after I had left the newspaper.

That Christmas, life at the Big House seemed a little brighter, as it always did when all the children were at home. I wrote, "After five years, the thaw: it took us that long to begin to know each other. I had assumed that the old familiarity would hold, but it did not. Now, in the Big House library, I see the books I grew up with, the atlas my first husband gave my parents, its colors faded. I see the lights, mirrors, furniture, and realize that this continuity, over four generations, is a miracle, paid for in individual blood."

I remembered the other books on those shelves, where Pre-Raphaelite paintings of Blessed Damozels and drowning Ophelias were preserved; their influence continued. I sometimes thought about the mother of it all, Mary Lily Kenan Flagler Bingham, and wondered how she had used her money.

I knew that she had once bought herself a string of expensive pearls at Tiffany's. Father always claimed that she had been cheated—the pearls had been fake. Had she been stupid, then? It seemed unlikely that a woman whose life to a great extent was devoted to adornment would have known nothing about jewelry. Father went a step further: he said she had given those pearls, or another strand, to his Aunt Sadie in Asheville. Sadie had been embarrassed to discover, when she had to sell them, that these pearls, too, were fakes. Later, when I read the account of the inquiry that followed Mary Lily's death, I would realize that the pearls had to be fake, for the sake of the myth, because they had disappeared from her estate before it was probated.

Yet somehow this easily deceived woman, who had been, when the Judge married her, the richest woman in America, had managed to buy several houses, to entertain and to travel—to fulfill conventional expectations. I wondered how she could have managed such an active, public life if she was, as I had always believed, "a drug fiend."

Later I learned that she had contributed to some of Henry Flagler's charities, and had even left bequests for several women. But as I began to understand the power of money, it seemed to me that Mary Lily had never used it, or attempted to use it, to change the male world that eventually crushed her.

She had been frivolous, apparently; she had bought paintings and cars. Was it her acceptable frivolity that had prevented her from exercising the power of Flagler's money? Or was the money so safely sealed up in trusts controlled by men that she had access only to the income—to buy fake jewelry?

It seemed to me that Mary Lily might not have died at fifty if she had refused to accept her world's, and my world's, definition of femininity: to be pretty and pleasant, and to spend all the money available on fraudulent treats.

For the first time, I began to imagine what I could do with my fifteen percent of the three companies if the money was freed from Father's control.

I did not yet have the courage to act. I poured my energy into my job at the book page, enjoying the fact that my colleagues now seemed to accept me as another ordinary human being.

In the spring, I heard of a woman in Cambridge, Massachusetts, who taught women how to be more effective on corporate boards. She had written several books, and when I read one, I was impressed by her analysis of the difficulties women face in boardrooms. She implied that we had a right to be there, and that we also had a right, and an obligation, to become more effective. I made an appointment to talk to her—or rather, to listen.

The talk gave me the courage to act. I saw short-term goals and long-term goals outlined on large sheets of paper, and took down notes on each step in the process. The practical instruction was helpful, but the inspiration derived from the fact that the instruction existed. Perhaps my goal—to be a more effective director—was legitimate after all.

One of the first steps toward the short-term goal of getting to know the other directors involved asking each of these men to lunch. This was a bold move in a Southern city where women usually wait to be invited. But I was curious. Clearly these directors, most of whom were executives at the companies, knew a great deal, and they might be willing to share their information.

I invited Eleanor to go with me, and she agreed. It would prove to be one of the last projects we shared.

We began by inviting one of the oldest of the directors, Lisle Baker, who had been a member of the triumvirate, along with Father and Mark Ethridge, which had run the newspapers in the 1940s, 1950s, and early 1960s.

Eleanor and I did not know that Lisle was then a sick man who would die less than a year later. He seemed to me the same courteous, gentle, and deeply loyal man I remembered from my childhood; he asked wistfully about Barry, and wondered if he had any special advisers. Perhaps Lisle missed the close cooperation he had enjoyed with Father years before, when as head of the business side of the newspapers he had cultivated a fascination with politics.

He beguiled us with stories of how he first got printer's ink on his fingers and never got it off again. He had been director of the State National Bank in Frankfort in the 1930s when he had received a call to come to Louisville to be interviewed by Father and the Judge. He was hired as chairman of the finance committee at the companies, which at the time included only the two newspapers and Standard Gravure; later he became business manager and director of all three companies, serving for thirty-two years.

Like his wife, Lisle had been active politically all his life. He had argued vigorously for American disengagement in Vietnam, and said that an editor, Weldon James, had left because of Lisle's stand. At another point, he told us, the newspapers came out for a gubernatorial candidate whom Lisle did not support; he offered to resign, but instead Mark Ethridge gave him half of the editorial page to endorse his candidate.

Lisle reminded me that once there had been a golden time at the newspapers for the men involved in management and ownership, a time when the little club was still protected from the buffets of reality, and when loyalty to the boss was a lifelong passion, the only thing that really mattered. It was interesting to learn that differences of opinion had been tolerated inside a system based on personal loyalty.

The golden time had seen the newspapers grow until they were read all over the state, "jumping over" Lexington to reach eastern Kentucky by mail—approximately fifty thousand copies had been sold there, Lisle said. Single copies of the afternoon paper had been sold at trolley stops and factory gates, accounting for a large part of its healthy circulation.

At other lunches that summer and fall, I began to notice that the directors who were also self-made men had a certain perspective on the companies I found sympathetic. They were in the process of formulating goals that seemed more realistic than the Judge's axioms or the family's noblesse oblige.

Bernard Block, who had been a vice president since 1972, was an example. A cheerful, lively middle-aged man, Bernie told us that he had worked for eight years as a newspaper delivery boy and in circulation but had been refused a job at the companies after he graduated from college in Indiana. He spent the next eleven years working at General Electric in accounting, and was finally asked to run the newspapers' accounting department in 1970. His reasons for the transfer were, it seemed to me, the reasons many of our employees might have given: Total security: nobody is ever fired. Good benefits. Pride stemming from being part of companies well known in the city and the state.

Bernie had established several of the subsidiary companies about which I had had reservations, and he had been the only director to attempt to answer my questions. I enjoyed his honesty, his directness, and his accessibility, and felt that "he is depended on by everyone for major decisions because of his energy, enthusiasm, and lack of doubt or conflict. Essentially

a loyal follower catapulted into a leadership position." I would find that this
had happened in several instances, with ambiguous results.

The general manager of the newspapers since 1978, Maurice Buchart,
Jr., a bluff, handsome man, seemed to handle with ease his responsibilities
for advertising, circulation, production, new technology, and promotion.
His first job at the newspaper had been collecting bills for small advertisements run by residents of Louisville's black ghetto, suitable training for a
remorseless and charming businessman.

He seemed to me to have developed to meet the demands of his far-
reaching activities, making decisions that had implications beyond the advertising department.

As always, the subject proved on closer observation to defy generaliza-
tions. "He seems to feel that he is running the newspapers," I noted.
"Clearly, a man who is getting by on the force of his personality, looks,
voice, demeanor, etc. A small man filling a large vacuum."

The pattern was becoming clear.

As we moved on to the newspaper management, I began to note a few
shared goals. David Hawpe, then a managing editor but now, under Gannett, the newspaper's publisher, impressed me when he commented that
Louisville's thruway system had somehow failed to provide for the residents
of one neighborhood, the blue-collar South End. David said that it was
easier to drive fifty miles to the east than ten miles to the south, because of
the way money for the thruways had been allocated—the same thruways
that had devastated the old black neighborhood.

David and my immediate supervisor, assistant editor Irene Nolan,
talked a good deal about their concerns over cuts in space for news; the
news hole was constantly reduced because its size depended on advertising, which was declining, due in part to competition from the preprinted
advertising sections, offering lower rates, which were Standard Gravure's
way of surviving.

Irene and David worried that with reductions in the news hole, the
newspapers would hardly be able to do justice both to the 1984 session of
the state legislature and to the Olympics, which they saw as competing for
attention. These were concerns I later raised at board meetings, although I
found no support there.

David shared some of my concerns about our afternoon newspaper, the
Louisville *Times,* which had a separate news staff and was presented as being
in competition with our morning newspaper. David seemed to feel that the
competition between two newspapers owned by the same family was largely
a delusion, and that the state could support only one "great" newspaper. His
opinion turned out to be prophetic.

Both Irene and David were educated, intelligent members of my generation with whom it was easy for me to sympathize. It was also easy, unfortunately for me, to imagine that they were allies. In fact, they could not afford to be. My attempt to champion their causes would lead me into no end of trouble, especially with Mother, who bitterly resented my talking to "employees" about company matters she felt should be reserved for the family.

These meetings were curtailed after a lunch Eleanor and I had in the fall of 1983 with the outspoken lawyer Gordon Davidson, who had been one of the very few directors to challenge Barry at board meetings. His law firm had represented both the companies and the family for many years, and perhaps his boldness derived from that fact. But I felt it was his personal confidence and conviction that caused him difficulties with Barry. Gordon perhaps sensed a kinship with me; once, after we had both been worsted in some discussion, he wrote in answer to my sympathy note that perhaps if we hung together, they would not be able to hang us separately, and permanently.

Because of his position as family lawyer, Gordon was the first to hear of the debacle that would presently overtake us.

Eleanor and I were enjoying our lunch with this genial person when he suddenly—or so it seems to me in memory—blurted out that we should both be prepared for a terrible event. I was dumbfounded, and Eleanor could not imagine either what Gordon was implying. Was someone in the family sick, or dying? Were we about to go bankrupt?

No, it was not that, he assured us, but an event equally catastrophic, with the direst consequences for the two of us. He could not tell us any details and had, he intimated, taken some risk in passing along the hint.

It was early September, a season of bright, hot days in Kentucky, when the sky is still a summer blue and the sidewalks are inked with long shadows in the late afternoon. Walking back to the newspaper building, I tried to imagine what misfortune was about to befall us. I did not dare to ask; the truth would be, I felt sure, more terrible than the anticipation.

Eleanor, who was more adept at confrontation than I, decided to ask Father what was going on, but she reported that he was only willing to say that it was something terrible and that he would tell us about it after Thanksgiving—still two months away.

He did not want to spoil our Thanksgiving by telling us earlier, he said.

After that announcement, I lost faith in getting to know the other directors, although I did have lunch with George Gill, the handsome, competent, and assertive CEO who had reduced me to tears two years earlier when he told me not to talk at board meetings.

It was a little harder to reduce me to tears now, and George and I enjoyed our conversation, as I always enjoyed times spent with tough survivors who have some notion of the subtleties involved in winning the game.

Like several other directors, George had worked his way up from the bottom, and he told me candidly that he had, as a very young man, vowed to run the companies someday. He surprised me by discussing his wife and his grown children—a topic never before raised at these lunches—and also surprised me with his energy and honesty. "He is not a listener, and never will be," I wrote. But he had understood enough about the owners to realize that our inability to communicate was frustrating all our attempts; he made it clear that he could offer no solutions. I noticed that he seemed to have a more realistic view of the companies, as profit-oriented and entirely business-minded, than I found in the family. Stubborn, determined, and proud, he was the first leader, in the traditional sense, I had met in that context, and liable therefore to rouse Barry's deepest anxieties.

And, as Mother would have said, George was not a gent, which was a positive quality in my book. I had had enough of gentlemen and their schemes.

"A potential ally, due to his smartness about people," I wrote, but added, fortunately for my survival, "However, he is unreliable in a crisis because he does not share my system of values."

His was, perhaps, more realistic. I did not think he had ever spent a great deal of time worrying about the Judge's homilies.

As that uneasy fall progressed, I talked once more to Paul Janensch, Barry's right-hand man, who had been viewing me, I felt, with increasing alarm. This time, however, I was aware not only of his ambition but of his curiosity about me as a potential ally.

The bewildering exchange in the newspaper cafeteria months earlier was at last clear. Paul was looking for allies in the event that Barry did not return from his sabbatical, an outcome that seemed, to some people at the newspaper, quite likely, due to Barry's evident unhappiness as publisher.

I did not know how to answer Paul's question, so I said nothing. At that point I had difficulty imagining a publisher who was not a male Bingham. Later, it would become a little easier to envision a leader "from outside."

Although I had decided to drop the other lunches because of the threat hanging over us, I continued to work on another project that had grown out of my trip to Cambridge. Writing letters to the various management men about concerns as they developed had been suggested to me as a way to continue to learn between board meetings. My letters, which perhaps numbered six or seven, later appeared on Barry's grievance list. At the time, however, responses from his management indicated that they did not resent my inquiries.

I raised questions with Paul about the exclusion of addresses from cutlines under news photographs—an attempt to spare people obscene or threatening telephone calls, Paul said; about columns harshly critical of Martha Layne Collins, Kentucky's new governor, which began to appear as soon as she had taken office—Paul admitted that some of the columns were sarcastic; and about the decision to start a new printing company in Tennessee rather than Kentucky—to avoid the unions. Apparently a trade-off had been achieved with union leaders in Louisville, who had agreed not to protest the new plant if rotogravure presses, which would directly compete with the Louisville company, were not installed. Since the new plant was to have offset presses, this demand was easily met.

Other executives were equally gracious in replying to my notes. One of them even urged me to just holler anytime I had a question or comment.

I tried always to balance criticism with praise, which was easy to do as I came to know these men. All of them were trying hard, some with little support and few natural endowments. Most of them, it seemed to me, were attempting to fill the vacuum created by Barry's reticence, pessimism, and distrust.

They could not be blamed for not entirely succeeding.

Two other men were of major importance to the functioning of the companies: the treasurer, Leon Tallichet, who had become a good friend during numerous discussions of my complex finances, and Cy MacKinnon, who had been brought from Chicago after Worth's death to help Barry to run the newspapers.

During the next two years, Leon would impress me as the only one of the management "team" (as it was called) who was able to avoid personalizing the oncoming conflict within the family. A natural grace and kindliness allowed him to maintain his good relations with all factions, to see, it seemed to me, beyond the unreasoning jealousies and suspicions that would presently consume the rest of us. Such a quality is perhaps innate, or perhaps it has something to do with music: Leon, like Worth, played the saxophone.

Cyrus MacKinnon, or Cy, as most people called him, played a role I never understood. He was the "outsider" on the boards, an accomplished, well-read man who could be called an intellectual, certainly in Kentucky, with a large and interesting family and an understanding of life beyond the state boundaries and the state obsessions. Perhaps for all those reasons, Barry seemed to distrust him most of all. Cy was, after all, superior in the real sense, because of the quality of his mind, and that was a rare commodity at the newspapers.

In addition, Cy was "a gent," even by Mother's definition, which made him harder to ignore.

Barry's distrust had limited Cy's effectiveness, it seemed to me. Even

Father appeared to have withdrawn his support from the man he had handpicked to groom his son. By the fall of 1983, Cy seemed to have little influence at Sixth and Broadway, and I sometimes sensed beneath his geniality a heavy disappointment. The heir was failing, with or without his help, and I doubt if Cy drew much satisfaction from the fact that apparently it was without him.

37

That fall I felt paralyzed at the thought of the coming crisis, whatever it might be. It would clearly not improve life for either Eleanor or me.

I was reminded of the appointments I had been given, as a child, to appear in Mother's bathroom for a whipping. Then, I had waited several hours. Now, I was to wait several months. The result was the same: I hardened my resolve as, years earlier, I had made up my mind not to cry.

Finally the date was advanced by a day. We were summoned to meet at the Little House on the Wednesday before Thanksgiving, 1983.

The living room in the Little House had been our parents' bedroom during the years before the Second World War when Worth, Barry, and I were small children. It still retained the sweet smell of mystery—the mystery that had cloaked our beautiful parents.

The room was decorated with icons from the past. Many photographs hung on the walls, including my favorite, a portrait taken in the 1920s of the six "Caperton girls," my mother midway in the line—six pretty blond young women, each of whom had a distinct trait, a telling characteristic, which shone in the midst of their similarity.

Eleanor and her husband, Rowland Miller, Tim and I, and our parents gathered around the fireplace in the darkening room. It was late afternoon; tea and sherry were served, and the usual banter was passed around with the tiny glasses and the porcelain cups.

The atmosphere was so familiar and comfortable I was seized by the wild idea that the disaster had been an illusion, or that it had, somehow, drifted off—like a dark cloud.

It almost seemed that Father would take a leather-bound Dickens novel from the bookcase behind him and distract us by reading aloud.

Instead he announced bleakly that he had a message to convey from Barry, who was nowhere to be seen.

Father's face was haunted as he told us what Barry wanted, but he spoke without hesitation: the four women in the family must resign from all the company boards or Barry would resign as publisher.

We must resign before the annual meeting in April, five months away.

I looked at my sister and her husband, who seemed stunned. Tim and I, too, had had no idea of what to expect, although I had imagined it would have something to do with the so-called sabbatical Barry was planning to take in the spring.

Now we were all speechless. The fatalism that had afflicted us since Jonathan's and Worth's deaths made questions seem irrelevant. Perhaps this latest irrational act was the way fate worked in this peculiar family.

But when I glanced out the window at the wintry trees and the gray gleam of the Ohio in the distance, I knew that out in the world beyond my parents' box hedges and fountain figurines and Doric columns, Barry's ultimatum would seem perverse if not ridiculous.

I looked at Father's gaunt face and then at Mother's burning eyes. And once more I began to ask questions. My words wove around the two people who knew what was happening but who seemed to have little to say about it: Father, leaning far back in his deep armchair, his hands on his knees in an attitude of helplessness, and Mother, sitting forward tensely, already prepared to defend her only son.

When had Barry made this strange decision? What were his reasons?

No one dared to ask what role Father had played in the drama. Perhaps I was the only one who sensed how bored he had become in the limited world he had constructed for himself, how he longed, at the end of his life, for a little air to breathe.

Father told us solemnly that Barry had come to him during the summer, when they were vacationing together on Cape Cod, to give him the ultimatum. I imagined the scene: sun, and white curtains lifted by a gentle breeze, and the two men conferring together about a subject of the greatest interest to them both: the maintaining of control.

Father said that Barry had not explained why he could no longer function with his female relatives in the boardroom. Barry had said that he was only trying to do what Father had succeeded in doing after the Judge's death when he had consolidated power in his own hands, pushing his sister and brother to the margin.

I understood the attraction of this easy answer for Father, the attraction that perhaps caused him, against his better judgment, his keen understanding of the situation and the people involved, to "go along with" Barry's demand. If it was possible to maintain control, still, in the 1980s, to eliminate dissent at the most intimate level, to forget the rights of women and the rights of minority shareholders, then perhaps the old golden way could be re-created: the small band of like-minded men who had for a while controlled the world.

I remembered the glamorous young naval officer, the camaraderie in Washington at the start of the war, the tales of international intrigue and the good intentions of the New Deal—the idealism of the old elite, which always depends on exclusion.

Seduced by that memory, Father did not question or criticize Barry's pronouncement. It would lead to a re-creation of the past, or it would lead to the end. Either way seemed better to Father than the equivocal present.

Now I realized that our positions as directors, like the dividend checks that arrived in the mail, were favors that could be withdrawn, with no explanation needed. We had no rights of ownership because in that system we do not own. We are loaned money and position and privilege to use until the owner wants some or all of it back.

I remembered scenes from childhood when Mother had criticized or scolded until I was on the verge of tears. Then, too, Father shook his head and sighed. Sometimes he had looked at me with sympathy, as he was doing now, or reached to pat my arm. He believed that he was helpless, and he expected us to accept his belief. Once more, we would simply have to "cope," as best we could, with what the gods had ordained.

His was a powerful position, which supported the rights of the heir while making criticism difficult. We could hardly attack Father if he was helpless, if in fact he could do nothing about Barry or his demand.

I did not believe, then or later, that Father was helpless. Powerful men in difficult situations often choose that role.

Mother now came to Father's defense. She grew angry at the thought that our questions implied criticism or lack of respect for authority. We were to obey, as once she had obeyed Munda's dictums.

Mother was acting as she often did when she felt that Father was beleaguered. But I knew she could not take responsibility for Barry's decision, even though she might have wanted to assume it in order to spare Father. He had been involved in this crisis from the beginning, it seemed to me, although he did not believe that he had played a role.

It was easy to imagine the scene in the pretty summer cottage on Cape Cod, several months earlier, when Barry, apparently, had presented his ultimatum: the sighs, the throwing up of hands, the air of fatalistic acceptance among the chintz and the flowers.

None of us was able to challenge the illusion of helplessness Father had cultivated for so many years, perhaps from the time when he had been, indeed, a helpless, heartbroken, and abandoned child.

Rowland and Eleanor shared Thanksgiving lunch the next day with

Tim and me, the first time the family had been split into two camps since the old days of the forgotten Mebane-Asheville war.

Eleanor and I discussed combining forces, for the first and last time. Through cumulative voting, we could manage to hold on to a single seat on the boards of WHAS and the *Courier*—if we pooled our votes.

We also talked of a leveraged buyout of both companies, which would have left Eleanor in charge of WHAS and me in charge of the newspapers. I felt sure that we could arrange the financing, but we were both afraid of other costs. Eleanor was also not sure that we could raise the money; like me, she underestimated the power of her position and the value of her stock, having been raised to underestimate both.

We agreed on one thing: we would be excoriated not only by the family but by Father's loyal employees if we chose such a bold, unladylike option. Perhaps we would find that the companies simply could not be run because of revolt in the ranks. And we would both be saddled, eternally, with the burdens of nepotism.

Finally we agreed to wait and see what would happen next. Barry had told Father that he would meet with us to answer our questions.

A few days later, again in the Little House living room, we gathered—but this time there was no way to ameliorate the sense of crisis. Barry looked tense and exhausted, as though he expected a terrible display of hostility.

Tentatively, Eleanor and I questioned him about his motives, and he answered abruptly, as though gasping for breath. I too had felt that panic and almost intolerable pain when confronted with situations I could not control—with angry husbands, punitive lawyers, furious children, alienated friends.

Barry told us that he simply could not continue to run the companies if his mother, his two sisters, and his wife were directors. He simply could not do it.

It was not possible for him to explain his reasons, and his distress made it difficult to press him. He had reached the end.

Mother rushed to his defense. With tears in her eyes, she challenged us: why couldn't we be happy, when we were all rich, intelligent, and, as she said, beautiful?

The challenge did not seem connected to the matter at hand. We were arguing about money and power, not personal happiness. Later I realized that she felt condemned, as a mother, by our dispute. She should have taught us better manners.

We began to discuss alternatives. Was Barry interested in using his leave to explore other avenues, perhaps returning to run the television station, or to branch out in business on his own? In that event, someone else might be found to run the newspapers, to relieve him from what seemed to me to have become an overwhelming burden.

Barry seemed for a moment to brighten. I will never forget his eyes as he said, looking at me, "Yes, an outside publisher . . ." Perhaps he was thinking of his friend and ally, Paul Janensch.

Later I went to Father's office at the newspaper to discuss this possibility and saw for the first time the brittle determination that was usually masked by his charm. Sitting in the petitioner's chair, at an angle to Father's big desk, I suggested that we might find someone "from outside" to run the newspapers for a while.

Father's blue eyes were cold. He told me that he would never consider such a possibility. I realized that he did not want a solution that would leave the situation essentially unchanged.

I went to several other meetings, both in his office and in Barry's. Once, among the animal skins and the enormous photographs of "the grand-children," I tried to tell Barry that I was not his enemy. I thought perhaps he was looking for a way out of a situation he hated: an avenue of escape for a proud and decent man.

But he was bitterly offended by my suggestion, and seemed to interpret it as an attempt at manipulation. I went away from that meeting haunted by the memory of his white, grim face.

The winter wore on, and one by one, the other three women proffered their resignations.

My sister-in-law, Edie, never questioned the correctness of doing what her husband wanted.

Although I suspected that Mother had reservations about giving up a position she had enjoyed, and used well, she, too, resigned without a murmur.

Eleanor held out until after Christmas, but then she complied, telling me that she felt compelled to give Barry a chance to show that he could improve the companies' financial performance. He had told her he believed the newspapers' dwindling circulation would rise if the women were off the boards.

Now I was alone. The others soon realized from the seriousness of my reservations that I was not likely to resign, and their pressure on me became intense. Mother led the attack. She defended Barry so ably that he seldom needed to explain himself, and she knew my weak points.

At one of the last gatherings, in the gloomy library at the Little House, I realized that the family was uniting against me. As always, it is easier to pursue a dubious path if there is someone to blame. By now Tim was staying away from the meetings because he and I both knew that I had to deal with the situation without his protection.

Mother told me angrily that I was trying to destroy Barry by refusing to resign, and when I expostulated, she ordered me to go to my room. Disoriented, I felt for a terrible moment that I was again a teenager in that house, with a canopy bed nearby and a leather diary locked with a tiny key.

Gathering my shreds of dignity, I left the house of my young childhood, knowing that I would probably never return.

Only my sister-in-law, Edie, understood my distress, because she, too, had felt the edge of Mother's tongue. She knew how frightening it was to be cut out—but her own position was too precarious for her to offer assistance. However, she did offer me her understanding.

Eleanor and Rowland were upset by the turmoil. Recently married, with one small son and another child on the way, they were exposed to the threats and the embarrassment of a family quarrel. I knew that ten years earlier I would not have been able to stand the heat, especially at a time when I believed that my parents were important sources of love for my children. I was older; that made it easier. But it was saddening, nonetheless, to realize that Eleanor was slowly separating herself from me.

By Christmastime, I was exhausted. In a moment of despair, I asked Tim to go to talk to Barry.

Tim sat down with Barry in the library at the Big House to discuss the situation. Tim liked Barry, with whom he had sometimes shared war stories. A year before, Tim had given Barry a Christmas present of four hours of work, and together they had taken the chain saw into the Back Woods to cut up wood for Big House fires.

As Tim recounted it, he and Barry sat in the library, where an ancestor hangs over the fireplace and a gilded chariot with a clock in its wheel patrols the mantel.

When Tim asked Barry why he was insisting on the women resigning, Barry repeated that he could not run the companies if we were on the boards. Tim appealed to him to make allies of his two sisters, trying to persuade him that we might actually want to help rather than hinder him. Barry said such cooperation was impossible. When Tim pressed him for a reason, Barry said that I was "crazy" and that my writing proved it. Tim gently replied that he thought perhaps Barry was in need of help, to which Barry, in speechless agony, appeared to agree.

Tim left his meeting, he told me, feeling discouraged. What could be done to relieve Barry's anxiety? What connected that anxiety to "the girls"—or, it now appeared, only to me?

There was no answer.

Letters and notes began to flow back and forth between us, to supplement or replace the agonizing meetings. In one, Eleanor asked Barry to pass along a list of things I had done that he did not like. By this time, everyone was assuming I was the cause of his discontent. Barry replied in a note that to make such a list would require too much time and research, because my misdeeds were beyond counting.

These notes replaced notes we had once written about the companies to Barry, Janensch, and other executives. Those notes were Barry's most bitter complaint, the one he would always refer to later when asked for his reasons for eliminating us. I had written seven or eight, Eleanor possibly as many. Mother had written letters, too, but somehow that was different— perhaps because Barry knew she supported his position, as son and heir, no matter what she thought of his performance.

The letters maddened Barry because their writers did not respect what he called the chain of command.

Six months earlier, my attempts to raise issues with the people who were directly in charge of the companies had been at least partially successful. Both Janensch and Bernie Block had replied carefully and at length when I wrote to them.

A few months earlier, I had written a letter to the editor protesting the newspapers' support for the Republican candidate for mayor of Louisville, rather than Harvey Sloane. Now Mayor Sloane sent word that he was composing a letter to the editor criticizing Barry's attempt to oust all the women from his boards. I was mildly surprised.

The final result had its humorous side. The mayor's limousine was dispatched one day to bring me the three blocks from my office at the *Courier-Journal* to City Hall. I found myself wondering what I had done to earn this honor.

I noticed with delight the number of women who held positions inside City Hall. All of them smiled and waved me on into the inner sanctum. There, after a few pleasantries, the mayor told me that he had been forced to reconsider his offer. Various influential men had told him that a letter to the editor criticizing Barry's ultimatum would make things more difficult for me. They were already so difficult that I did not see how an expression of support could hurt.

I realized as I sensed the mayor's pain and embarrassment that of course this was not the issue. The powers had spoken, and an elected official who felt that he was at their mercy could only obey. I left City Hall feeling saddened that again a decent human being had been caught in the toils of the system. I was uncomfortable, too, with the mayor's assumption that I had counted on this quid pro quo. I had written the letter because I wanted to write it, not in hope of a favor, but that was not the way business was done in Louisville.

Father maintained all winter that he was helpless to influence Barry. But behind his resignation, I sometimes thought I saw a glint of his old devilish humor. It was part of the harsh dynastic vision that sees all heirs as specimens of genetic decay—chinless, no-neck monsters cast adrift on the sea of privilege.

Father would throw up his hands when the discussion was heated, as though to cry, "A plague on both your houses!" Yet the gesture was rather like the gesture of welcome I remembered from years before, when Aunt Sadie, waiting for Father on her patio in Asheville, had thrown up her hands.

It seemed to me that the shifting alliances in the family and the dominance they expressed were subtly sexual: the flirtations of our childhood had been replaced with flirtatious threats. The tone was not light, but then, the tone had never been light, merely unconsidered.

I was aware of odd undercurrents of affection, attraction, dominance, and destructive impulse.

This impression, enforced by Father's disillusionment, helped me to continue to question the system we had inherited. Money and privilege were the rewards that system gave to heirs who conformed. But compliance was valueless in Father's eyes; what he wanted was spontaneity, bravado, originality—like Worth, like Henrietta—not the bought agreement of dependent offspring.

In *The Tender Passion,* Peter Gay's study of love and the Victorians, I noted that "society manufactures its deviates by defining normality and then ascribing abnormality to the minorities who act out what more inhibited individuals only sublimate, dream about, or wholly repress."

Henrietta and Worth had both fulfilled that function, earning hatred and love, admiration and scorn, and a tie to the family they could never break. They had lived their lives as dependents. I did not intend to fall into that category.

Father might have understood a verse from Ecclesiastes that Munda never gave me to memorize: "So I came to hate all my labor and toil here under the sun, since I would have to leave it to my successor."

The greatest danger to me that winter was not Father's disillusionment but Mother's rage.

For a woman who has been taught, almost from birth, that displays of anger are wrong, who has been confined in ladyhood as once she was confined in the organdy bonnets Munda tied under all her little girls' chins ("You are the most beautiful thing in the world. Kiss me"), it is impossible to forgo a legitimate opportunity to express rage.

I was frightened. I knew that in Mother's world I now stood for the frightful forces of female power that overturn order, reveal secrets, explode myths.

I had resigned once before, to save my job, when Barry had demanded it, and I had decided then that I would not "cave in" again. I could not resign from the boards without understanding why I should take such an action, and the reasons given were no reasons at all.

I did not know it, but I was not alone in my opposition to Barry's demand. Several of his executives had tried to dissuade him. But they had failed. They did not believe that I was the cause of complex problems ranging from falling circulation to the breakdown of antiquated presses. I had never cast a nay vote at board meetings, although I had written notes and asked questions.

At the same time, I knew that on another level I had become for Barry the symbol of his unhappiness, the face of the Other—that dark presence, invariably female, which intervenes between a man and control of the world.

While accepting my unwitting function as a symbol on an unconscious level, I could not accept the translation of that symbol into reality.

I knew that we were all being drawn into the whirlpool of family history, where rivalries and jealousies, schemes and manipulations, had brought about crises having to do with power and money.

By early 1984, my options, few to begin with, were narrowing down to a single choice: resign or be forced off the boards at the annual meeting in April.

Since I owned only about four percent of the voting stock in the companies, I could not reelect myself through cumulative voting, a device designed to protect the rights of minority shareholders.

Eleanor finally decided that she would not vote for me at the *Courier-Journal,* in exchange for which I had offered to give her my votes at WHAS. To join forces with the Bad Sister was too threatening, and would certainly have caused her grief, as well as continuing her struggle with Barry indefinitely.

She knew such an action would endanger her relationship with our parents, who often turned to her now for emotional support. Never before had Eleanor been in the position of the favorite child, and now it was within her grasp.

Eleanor wanted the dynasty to continue for her two young sons, believing that they would define themselves best in terms of the Bingham myth: service, rather than other uses of power and money.

Like Joan Bingham, Worth's widow—who lived in Washington, D.C., and was able to stay largely outside of the fray at this point—Eleanor identified with the men in the family.

Barry continued to insist that all the women must go. He did not know about the years of strategic delays and strategic advancements that had preceded the reading of the Judge's will in 1937. He only knew that Father's brother and sister had disappeared at that point—with a puff of smoke, into the blue. Barry wanted the same general clearing of the decks, the same elimination of the sister whom he saw as a rival. His sense of family history and his sense of justice coincided. In each generation, the women schemed and flirted, ran away and returned, hoped and believed. But in the end they were always eliminated.

38

Early in the spring of 1984, the women in the family were informed that "outside" directors were to be appointed to take their seats after the annual meeting in April. Two of the proposed directors were women, one of whom was black; the third was a black man. None of them hailed from Kentucky.

I learned later that Barry's executives were concerned about public reaction to the elimination of all the women from the company boards. Perhaps they were also concerned about the companies' failure to represent its black constituency in Louisville's West End. Or perhaps they were only reacting to the boardroom joke that in a quota system a woman who is black equals two rather than one.

Father made this announcement proudly, as though it should solve all the remaining problems. Women would still be present at the quarterly meetings, and these particular women had impressive credentials: they operated businesses in Chicago and Boston.

I agreed that it was high time to secure the advice of outsiders—this had been one of Barry's aims from the beginning. But the appointment of outside directors had little bearing on my status. After all, the boards could simply have been expanded.

I also said that I did not feel anyone represented my point of view, except me.

Two years later, one of the women who had become an "outside" director wrote to assure me that she had never felt like a token two-fer. I was glad to hear that she had enjoyed her brief time as a director of the Bingham companies, yet the question remained: should women enable a chairman of the board to dispose of other women?

When women replace others, strife is created among individuals who might, in another context, provide each other with support. It is a familiar strategy, dangerous to women. It works because the few who manage to make their way to the top of hierarchies sometimes become convinced that other women could do it, too, discounting their own special aptitudes, luck, and bone-breaking labor.

From that assumption, based on lack of self-esteem, it is a small step to the scorn and alienation that has so often, and so tragically, divided successful women from those who are still struggling.

As Mother and Father realized that I was not going to withdraw gracefully, their attempts to persuade me became more obvious.

Father warned me that Barry had written a letter blaming his resignation on me. Father said the letter was full of dreadful accusations, which he could not bring himself to describe. He said Barry was prepared to publish this letter in the newspapers and then resign, if I forced him to do it by remaining on the boards. Whether the letter existed or not, I had no way of knowing, and the shamefulness of the maneuver prevented me from asking Barry about it.

I knew that endless accusations could be made, full of half-truths and imaginary stories, some of which will certainly be published in other accounts of these events. But none of them, it seemed to me, could hurt me. That had already been done.

Father then warned me that, of course, I would be fired as book editor if I persisted. I told him I had been expecting that for a long time.

Finally he presented his most terrifying threat. He told Eleanor, who passed the word along to me, that Barry might kill himself if I did not resign.

For six years, I had watched Barry's unhappiness grow without understanding all of its causes. Later I realized that we had both been suffering from interference.

I had watched him grow tense and grave, as I had grown tense and grave, more suspicious of everyone, as I was becoming more suspicious. I guessed that Barry had lost the support of both of our parents, even though most of their criticism was directed at Edie. Barry had been abandoned long before I entered the game, for reasons too complex to discern.

Yet I knew that if a tragedy took place, I would be blamed for it, no matter what other factors were involved. The blame would be justified. No issue is worth the loss of a life. I would have no excuses to offer, to myself, or to my children.

At some point in that terrible time, Mother suddenly asked me why, as a child, I had thrown Barry's cat in the fire. I was dumbfounded. I reminded her that we had never had cats, because Father was allergic to them.

In a newspaper interview, Barry acknowledged that the cat burning was a fabrication. This reassured me. If he knew that the cat story was a fable, he was still in touch with the life we had shared. We had never been enemies. We were not enemies now.

It was a tiny piece of evidence, fragile as a weed stem, on which to hang my heavy decision not to resign. But it was enough. If Barry remembered our shared past, he might still recognize the true dimensions of our present and realize that he had been betrayed not by me but by the excessive expectations of those who are kings of men. Neither Barry nor I was heir to the tradition, finally, nor to its necessary myths and lies.

That Father's threat was plausible reminded me of the terrible price Barry had paid for being the heir. I could not bear to think of the same price being extracted from my sons.

Children who are born to power and money must learn, and learn well, several fierce lessons. They must give up most evidences of independence or originality that conflict with the family's view of itself, whether it is the long hair and shabby clothes of the adolescent army, or the vocabulary and accent of poverty and rage, or the questions born of acute observation or the ideas that challenge the status quo.

To some extent, the same kind of compliance is demanded by middle-class white society, but in that case, the rewards are easily seen: respectability, an education, a job, a possibly unthreatened way of life.

In a gender-addicted family, however, compliance brings only the relatively cheap rewards: a dim appreciation, an admission that this particular dependent understands what is expected. Compliance is not highly valued in males, and since males are the designated heirs, an inevitable conflict results.

By the cruel reversal central to the rich-family game, the boy who conforms is secretly discounted.

Money, privilege, and isolation breed a certain romanticism, which the Colonel expressed in his love of war. His descendants' real admiration goes to the ragged remnant of a lost army: the outsider, the romantic rebel, the prodigal son. I always remembered the scene I had witnessed as a child after Worth had been expelled from boarding school: in the front hall of the Big House—that dismal cavern—Mother stood rocking him in her arms.

The romantic tradition of male brigandage, which justifies the victimization of women, flourishes alongside the tradition of noblesse oblige, a later development.

Noblesse oblige functions in an increasingly crippled way as the rich lose touch with those they aspire to help. But the romantic dream of brigandage grows wiry and many-branched in the land where the rich reign. We have always worshipped the individual, the ruthless aspiring male—the robber baron. Nothing has discredited him.

The trouble is that he is not a gentleman.

The family had already produced one man who, in his smaller world, rivaled Henry Flagler and John D. Rockefeller in ruthlessness and ambition. It was not the Judge's fault that his effect was limited. His desire was not.

Barry had worked all his life to do what was expected. He had learned his role well, first as second son, then as heir. But he had not understood that, in the end, working hard only proves that a man is merely human and not a hero; not a Sir Galahad entering Kentucky politics on a shining white steed, like the Judge, nor a Confederate officer, like the Colonel, fighting hand to hand with the forces of evil.

A different fate awaits the women. Around great men always circle those small sad planets, the dependents who are "their" women—mistresses, daughters, sisters, wives. Perhaps we have more in common with the women who cook and mend, polish and sew, type letters and take dictation for greatness; but we seldom recognize the painful similarity. Rather, we often hope to gain, through service to the man and his myth, the love that cannot be earned.

Instead, there is the money: Mary Lily's pearls—real or fake; Henrietta's diamonds and sapphires—sometimes rhinestones, sometimes priceless. Women and money: women and love. The shares in the men's businesses we sometimes own, almost by chance, are another form of decoration, like the coral-and-seed-pearl bracelet I had worn in infancy. The coral-and-seed-pearl string lay broken and scattered in its little red wooden box. My ownership in the companies might break and scatter, too, now that I was out of favor, or be replaced by the paste equivalent.

As I began to read the scraps that remained about Mary Lily—old news accounts of her engagement to the Judge, of her houses and parties—I realized that she had for a while earned approval by keeping a distance from her wealth. She was often described as modest and ironic about Flagler's money. Munda and the six daughters she had raised also knew how easy it is to lose male patronage, and with it the means to survive. Perhaps the quickest way to lose it is to treat a man's money as though it is ours.

Nursie had counted the coins in her change purse—but she had earned them. She had often told us that it was wrong to be an "Indian giver"—to snatch back what has been given because of a change of heart. But life is full of Indian givers. Most of them are men who are not constrained to support or tolerate women they fear.

Perhaps even Mary Lily's life had been on loan to the men who kept her supplied with jewelry.

In that context, it was outrageous for me to claim that I actually owned a small part of companies that belonged to men to whom I was a real or imagined threat.

Tim and I knew that my recalcitrance might lead to a maneuver that would destroy my holdings, such as a recall of the companies' stock. We calculated that we could live and raise our four boys without my dividends. I would go back to teaching, full-time, and Tim would continue to run his construction company.

We could survive—but the dividends were mine, and I planned to protect them for as long as possible.

My determination weakened when I faced Mother. All my old fears were aroused. I knew that she would blame me for any and all consequences. Once again she was confronting the stubborn little girl who would not cry when she was whipped.

Mother needed me to agree with her reasons for resigning—reasons that seemed so obvious she never expressed them. All her life, she had overruled her own rebellious impulses, stifled her independence, and learned to speak only through Father, to allow him to use and change her voice. Their handwriting by now was nearly identical.

How could she tolerate a daughter who made the other choice, who continued to function, painfully, as an individual, who spoke for herself? Indeed, the question of speaking was, as always, central; several years later, one of Mother's friends would ask me with asperity why I had not hired some authority to speak for me at interviews.

Here was my connection with other women who had been silenced in other battles: finally we must take possession of our own voices.

Mother freed me at last to take the action she abhorred. During one of those last, strained meetings, she asked me with blazing directness, "Don't you care what we think about you?"

It was an honest question, and it deserved an honest answer.

"No, Mother," I said. "I don't care."

For the first time in my life, it was true.

Two weeks before the annual meeting, my parents made a last attempt to persuade me to resign.

Again I went to the Little House, where the present seemed finally to have eclipsed the past. Again light banter was passed with the sherry and the tea as afternoon shadows suffused the room where I had once sat on a stool at Father's knee. This time I knew there was no chance that he would take down a volume of Dickens and enchant us all with his mellifluous voice.

Instead, he offered me several small incentives to resign, since threats had been ineffectual. They were very small, in comparison with the threats: a minor donation to the Women's Project in New York and a benefit for a local theater company. I was reminded of the small size of the bribes the family feared would buy their reporters: a hamburger or a beer.

We seemed to be getting nowhere and I stood up to go home. Father stopped me from leaving with a discussion about the new outside directors. Then, in a monologue full of mysterious twists, Father first said that all the women would stay on the boards and then that all of them had resigned except me.

I told him again that I would not resign but that Barry, of course, could force me off. Father did not care for the expression, and dreaded that the few executives who had not already heard it would hear it at the annual meeting. I repeated that Barry could, and presumably would, force me off.

After a brief hesitation—Father perhaps wondered if I was still ignorant of the facts of ownership—he said that Barry could not do that without his support.

"I assume he has your support," I said. "You want him to have what he is asking for."

The next seconds passed in a blaze of accusations. I was breaking up the family, forcing them to choose between their children. I told them that was not my aim. I was trying to protect my investment in the companies.

Father asked me what possible use I would serve as a "lone voice" at board meetings, after the other family women were gone. He assumed that the two outside directors who were women would not support my interests, an assumption that was certainly correct.

Father had never mentioned the fact that he was, of course, staying on as director; nor had Barry. It was a foregone conclusion.

I admitted that I would probably have little effect.

Again I was told that I would, of course, lose my job, although Father praised me for doing well as book editor, and for being liked at the newspaper. The rush of emotion in his voice revealed the keen edge of his disappointment with Barry.

I repeated that I had always known my job was "extremely precarious." Then he tried to find a way to persuade me to resign from my job, saying he did not see how I could go on at the newspaper in the present chaotic state of affairs.

By now, not only the management of the companies but the twenty-two hundred people who worked for Father knew that change was in the air. Some of them were angry and frightened, and some of them, of course, blamed me. The plantation system was showing its holes.

I said that I would continue to do my job. I was not prepared to spare Father the embarrassment of firing me.

I felt, for the first time, that Barry was almost irrelevant, almost as irrelevant as I. Without being aware of the fact, Mother and Father seemed to have decided to end the myth. It had become ponderous, unattractive—unreal: the notion of leading and teaching readers who were alien, young, black, ignorant, rural—lacking in charm.

As the beautiful Kentucky spring unfurled, I was afraid of the consequences of my stubbornness. Sometimes, as I drove along the Ohio River, I imagined a larger vehicle pursuing me, pushing my little car into the water. Every day I passed within sight of the great gray house where Mary Lily had lost her life. She had been only a temporary and partial obstruction to the Judge.

I was almost fifty years old. Mary Lily had been fifty when she died.

I had known since childhood that Father's power inside Kentucky was limitless. I also knew that he had minions who were eager to do his bidding, who would need nothing more than a sigh. Father would not have to be aware of what was happening. Men who possess absolute power, in a small sphere, do not always have to recognize the actions of their underlings.

Later I would think of Henry Flagler, crying out in court that the doctors were preventing him from seeing his wife, and so she might as well be institutionalized for life.

My fears were exaggerated by my isolation, which became almost complete after the family signed an agreement not to discuss what was happening.

Before that, I had taken satisfaction in talking to reporters from other newspapers who did not understand my point of view but who sometimes printed it. After their stories appeared, I received letters from women all over the country who had survived wars in family businesses. Their letters meant more to me than the ones that vilified me for not fulfilling a woman's destiny.

Those angry letters from strangers—nearly always women—reminded me, often with verses from scripture, that we are supposed to take care of people, especially men. Women do not challenge corporations. Women do not cause discomfort to millionaires. Women do not threaten the security of twenty-two hundred employees, many of whom were now in full howl against me.

I had other resources: my sons, who were confused and frightened by the outcry, but who listened to me. I depended on Tim's strong arms and strong heart. I sat talking for long hours with my women friends, in the little restaurants where intimacy seems to thrive along with the french fries and the crumpled paper napkins; they told me about their own battles, many of which had been more brutal than mine. I read everything I could lay my hands on about women and money and power, especially Marilyn French's *Beyond Power,* which legitimized what I was trying to do. I went often to talk with my lawyer, who had become a close friend, and together we planned what I would need to say at the annual meeting in April, now only a few days away.

I did not sleep very much, and I shed a lot of tears. But I knew there were worse things than losing one's birth family: illness and accident and death. I was particularly grateful that my children were whole and well and close at hand, and that I could continue, if somewhat sporadically, to write.

By the end of March, I was prepared for the last skirmish. I knew what a minority stockholder could do—which was very little—to protect her rights. But my heart was torn in two. My belief in the myth—the family dream—was gone.

39

The annual meeting took place in April 1984 in one of those window-less rooms where it sometimes seemed to me I had spent most of my life.

The family was herded in by a young factotum who seemed to dread the ugly business he had been chosen to oversee.

None of us looked at or spoke to one another as we began the process of dividing up and casting our votes for directors on the company boards. The young factotum flew around the room to answer questions and super-vise our progress as my family cast its votes for the men on the slate, all longtime directors.

Aware of the potential for future legal problems, our adviser helped us make certain that no votes were left unaccounted for or miscast. Since "no Bingham" understands math, he played the role of an elementary school instructor, helping with addition and subtraction.

I cast the four percent of the total voting stock I owned for myself, remembering high school elections when overambitious candidates were criticized for putting their own names in the shoe box.

My relatives cast their votes automatically, it seemed to me, as though they were responding to orders issued by a higher authority. But who was the higher authority? Perhaps it was our young adviser, who in flying around the cramped room struck a large television set a glancing blow. It fell with a crash. The patriarchy itself seemed to thunder in that fall.

After we had voted, we went through our last board meetings without speaking to one another. I looked at the faces of the men I had come to know and like over the past seven years and wondered if I would ever see them again. I did not see them again in that context.

As I left at the end of the day, I wondered if Paul Janensch, who had once asked me about my aims, believed he was getting rid of an enemy.

I did not take my exclusion from the boards as a personal matter. For a long time I had felt that I represented to the family an idea or cluster of emotions that terrified them. The idea or cluster was attached to me in some way, but it had grown in all directions on its own. When the family unit as a whole refused to look at me, it was because they did not want to see that I was, after all, only a daughter or a sister they had known for a very long time, and not a magnified, impersonal threat.

I did not take their behavior personally; it hardly seemed rational, which of course did not weaken its force. The process by which I had been converted from a living woman into a threat is a process familiar to any woman who has spoken up.

It was independent thought my relatives were trying to eliminate when they voted me off the boards. But independence is hydra-headed. Where one head is lopped off, another grows. There is no way to stop the process, which is bringing women and others who represent threat and change into the hierarchy of business and politics in this country. With outsiders come the ideas of outsiders, which sometimes have an effect.

As spring turned into summer, I knew I would have to make another decision.

My income still depended on dividends from companies whose practices I could no longer monitor. Certainly I was not welcome as an owner. I needed no further proof of that.

I did not feel that I could trust my income to the subjective processes I had seen at work in the companies, processes that sometimes frustrated the attempts of competent managers. If I had been cast out, so would other critics. The companies would eventually suffer from a lack of internal criticism, especially as they grew more and more isolated from the outside world. To avoid change, after all, is largely a negative aim.

Eleanor and I had often asked for a definition of the companies' aims, both in financial terms and in less easily measurable goals. There had been no agreement and little discussion of aims, other than the dynastic aim of passing it all along. The three percent pretax profit level of the newspapers had been challenged and subsequently was elevated to almost twelve percent. But other matters remained undefined. It seemed to me that the Judge's words about public service had been replaced by a commitment to enrich succeeding generations, on into eternity.

Father had told me several months before the annual meeting that Barry would buy my stock at any time. Barry had raised the same issue with me during one of our two meetings in his office. He had said that he would buy me out at any time—at MPI rates, referring to an analysis of the companies' worth made several years before for estate-planning purposes.

Certainly both men had given me every reason to believe that they would be relieved if I was finally out of the way. But I was still afraid of cutting myself loose from the past, casting off in my small rowboat from the great stalled steamship of the companies and the man who owned them. I decided to wait.

The day after she voted me off the company boards, Mother telephoned to ask me and Tim to join her and Father at the movies. I was dumbfounded. It seemed to me that she did not recognize the connection between the way she had cast her votes and her relationship with me. The voting had occurred in the sphere where authority reigned, and that explained and excused it. Her relationship with me existed in another world where there were flowers and good food, pleasant talk and family affection—and movies.

I could not accept that division.

I told Mother that we needed to talk about what had happened, rather than go to the movies. I should perhaps have been willing to accept the opportunity she offered, but I knew it would lead only to more evasions. I would not have the courage to burst through the old restrictions once I was riding in the back seat of Father's car on the way to the show.

Mother was angry, and she took my refusal to go to the movies as a final rebuff. She wrote a few days later that she reluctantly agreed with something I had not said: that we must, like two foreign powers, break off communications. In the language of codes and flags, she was telling me that to discuss issues of power and money was too dangerous. If I insisted, she would not see me again.

She went on to say that she had attempted to mediate the issues between Barry and me in what she thought had been a series of "hate-filled confrontations"—which had never taken place. My few meetings alone with Barry had been constrained and painful for us both.

Mother added that she had been within her rights in criticizing me for refusing to meet with the *From the Other Side of the Bed* authors, and for scolding me for not signing the buy-back agreement. I did not think that was the issue. The issue was the "implicit, unquestioning obedience" to authority Munda had required.

Mother chose to support the structure on which she had depended all her life, a choice which is ultimately necessary for all women who stay inside the hierarchy.

Mothers have often sacrificed their daughters to the system, whether it is the plantation system or the social system, the rule of an autocrat or the rule of necessity. Sometimes mothers have resisted: I thought of Demeter descending into Hades to search for her daughter Persephone.

Mother's rejection was particularly sad because she and I had shared a good deal: a commitment, at least in theory, to the life of the mind, and a consciousness, however muted, of the difficulties women face as we try to make our way in the world. Mother had felt those difficulties herself when she left the house in Richmond where there was nothing in the icebox but flowers.

Now, however, the beautiful woman who had so often reminded me of a delicate Demeter as she worked in her garden had chosen to stay on the surface of the earth. Perhaps no daughter is worth a descent into that Hades where women must oppose the men who support and love them.

Father did not seem angry with me. Perhaps I had been useful to him, and I remembered *Iphigenia in Aulis* and the sacrifice of the daughter. But I no longer feared the pull of the unexamined: the inevitable. Other women had gone my way and faced my choices. But most women do not have the freedom I had to challenge the system.

I was still living in what I called "the hot eye of the power struggle."

It was time to cut the last link. In June, I made the decision to sell my stock. I felt that I had a moral obligation to offer the stock to Father first, even though I had not signed the buy-back agreement. After all, the companies were his.

No one seemed in the least surprised by my decision.

As the summer passed and we saw nothing of my family, I felt my exclusion keenly, as did my sons. I was going to church regularly, kneeling down to ask for forgiveness in the dark old downtown church where Eleanor Miller Bingham's marriage and funeral had been held. I was also going to Alanon meetings, "to give me some perspective on the way I aggrandize my own misery. It's important now to clear my mind of brooding and blaming so the work can go forward."

I wanted to return a little of the money that had come to the Judge from Mary Lily's estate to women who had also been deprived of opportunity. Mary Lily had been deprived and finally extinguished by a society that mutilates the wives of rich men as it mutilates the wives of poor men and single women, but at least she had had her pearls. I began to study what little I could find of Mary Lily's past and the past of other women in the family whose influence seemed remarkably dim.

I visited the old graveyard in North Carolina where my great-aunts and cousins and great-grandmother were buried. These were the women who had spent their lives working in the Bingham School and who had been caught up in the Mebane-Asheville war.

I had not heard their names before I read them on those headstones, many broken off and lying face-up on the ground.

40

The company executives received my offer to sell my stock with the same equanimity Barry and Father had displayed. They had been expecting it for some time.

Barry and Edie had left to spend their year in Massachusetts, and the negotiations were handled by two men from the newspaper management and a lawyer who was also a company director. Father, of course, was in control.

As a first step, we agreed to look for a new evaluation of the companies, since all agreed that the study Barry had mentioned when he suggested buying me out was out of date and useless as an objective assessment of value.

That fall, we began to interview teams of smiling young people from the New York investment houses, teams which, at my insistence, always included a woman—although often it seemed to me that she might have been snatched up from the lower echelons for the occasion.

I was entering an elaborate dance, with many participants and changes of partner and an undisclosed end. It was like a portentous version of musical chairs. Although Father did not appear at the meetings, I knew he was in charge of the music and could cut it off at an arbitrary moment, leaving some of us abruptly stranded.

Father's team and I agreed without any difficulty to hire Lehman Brothers, a New York investment firm. At once the woman who had appeared at the initial interviews disappeared from sight. I felt a slight sense of foreboding, as I did when the companies announced that they would pay Lehman's fee. I had expected to pay part of it.

Now more meetings took place. The young men from New York would come rushing in, their dark suits and briefcases gleaming, fresh from the only remaining morning nonstop flight from New York. They hardly had time to glance at the Ohio River, spread out beneath the conference-room windows, or to observe the workmen on the scaffolding surrounding the high-rise monument a private hospital chain was erecting next door. Instead their attention was directed to the great bound sets of papers that laid out the companies' financial condition in detail.

For information, these men depended on their mentors, the three company men who had been chosen by Father to represent his interests. They guided the bankers through the intricacies of the companies' finances as they guided them on their tours of the buildings. It seemed to me that a good deal of worthwhile information might be filtered out along the way, but the atmosphere was so convivial I sometimes found myself imagining that my best interests were being served. It was a comforting fiction.

My indulgence in the fiction was limited by my lawyer's attitude. She knew that more was at stake here than met my eye. Energetic, positive, and outspoken, Rebecca Westerfield seized the attention of the men with unhesitating conviction. For the first time in my life, I saw a woman direct the flow of male conversation, not only through sheer force of personality but because she knew more.

The men from New York were not only less well informed about the business at hand, they were less interested. They appeared to have been boxed and delivered to Louisville, along with their heavy folders of information, which had, along the way, passed through the hands of many nameless women—the clerks and secretaries who ran the computers and edited and copied and bound the endless reports, as well as the wives and friends who had fixed these men their breakfasts and seen them off, with encouragement, at the front door.

My tendency to slide back into compliance was finally curbed that fall. Pleasant surfaces nearly always concealed something less pleasant, although the friendliness of the three men on Father's team was not deceptive. They wanted to settle the issue by buying me out, and they made their eagerness to cooperate apparent. It was not their lack of effort but the family myth that eventually frustrated our aims.

Finally the bankers delivered their report, and I realized why they had seemed so lackadaisical during its preparation. The companies were valued at only a slightly higher amount than had been offered by the earlier firm hired for estate-planning purposes.

They placed the total value of the three companies and their subsidiaries at $210 to $240 million, nearly a third less than they would command when they were sold a year later.

They priced my fifteen percent share in the total at between $22 and $29 million, almost half of what I would eventually receive. This included, they explained amiably, a twenty to twenty-five percent discount for minority ownership. The low evaluation included a variety of half-expressed assumptions, such as that more money would be paid only by a buyer I would not want to sell to, for unspecified reasons.

They added that the companies' subsidiaries were practically without value, and that the pension plan, which had accumulated $30 million, should not be treated as an asset, although it was greatly overfunded.

They also contended that the television station, still at the top of its market, would sell for less than the Nortons' less profitable station had commanded a few years earlier.

To say they contended is a misstatement. They calmly, almost flaccidly commented. These issues were of little importance to them; nor were my complaints of interest. The valuation, I finally realized, was a foregone conclusion. Somewhere along the way, they had been persuaded that I would accept whatever price Father offered. Perhaps they knew that over the years I had bought most of my clothes on sale.

These young men had not bothered to prepare answers for my questions or for my lawyer's. They closed their briefcases and went back to New York, and I decided to seek an independent opinion.

Barry's intransigence probably began when he accepted as gospel this low valuation. Perhaps he felt that was really all Father's companies were worth.

I knew better than to accept the first opinion of any authority. Several years before, a Louisville gynecologist had told me before he examined me that I needed a hysterectomy, basing his opinion solely on my age. As far as I was concerned, Lehman Brothers acted with the same arrogance and, like the gynecologist, clearly underrated my intelligence.

My surmises gained weight after I met with these same bankers in New York. It had seemed to me that they might be more interested in my point of view away from the deadening civilities of Louisville. They were not. One young man told me he felt I was certain to settle with the family for whatever amount was offered. They were not interested in such a limited horizon, and they did not know me well enough to realize that I was not interested either.

A few weeks later, I went to New York again with my lawyer and her partner, Jon Goldberg, who helped to add fire to the fight. I wanted another evaluation.

Together we interviewed teams of bored young men at well-known investment banks who seemed almost too weary to sit up straight in their chairs. Their lack of enthusiasm was now easy for me to understand. The highly prestigious investment houses are linked through social relations and shared values to big corporations and law firms and newspapers; they are not interested in compromising their connections by advising minority shareholders. All across America, the men who run businesses and the men who run banks know each other intimately, even if they have never met. Only people who know that they will never be inside the system—mavericks, foreigners, the plucky and the shady—are willing to take on the system rather than work to preserve it.

The status quo provides many rewards for its servants, even for those who only batten on the fringes. These batteners are of little use to women trying to protect their rights.

The most cheerful of this dismal lot was an outsider named Christopher Shaw, whose firm specializes in media acquisitions. Shaw was not weary, and he seemed convinced that my fifteen percent share of the companies was worth a substantial amount of money. He was prepared to begin putting together his own evaluations, which turned out to be amazingly accurate. Best of all, Shaw had the gall to inform me that I should enjoy the whole process. The choice was an easy one to make.

Shaw showed how well he understood the psychological factors involved when he brought in a team of gifted women to design a public relations campaign. Now the story—my story—began to be seen and read everywhere.

The exposure was not painful. It was exciting. Too many women who are noticed soon disappear, intimidated by exposure, lacking financial support, robbed of good legal advice, alone in small towns and cities across this country with men who have never understood that some women cannot be bribed or coerced. I hope some of them read my story, and persisted.

Having finally learned to speak in public, I shed my seven veils—the fear, guilt, self-absorption, confusion, loyalty, loneliness, and amiability that cover up so many middle-class white women. I was delighted to dance.

Shaw and his associate, Richard Cohen, put together a new analysis of the companies and their subsidiaries. They reckoned my fifteen percent share as being worth more than $60 million.

This analysis was presented to Father and his team, but no offer was forthcoming.

In February, with no offer from Father on the table, I decided to make the first move. After endless consultations with my lawyers, accountants, and advisers, I asked him for $42 million for my shares. We felt the companies could easily afford this sum..

Through his lawyers, Father turned down my offer in March, and immediately formed a voting trust, through which he controlled ninety-five percent of the companies' stock. This device is sometimes called a "shark repellent," since it discourages hostile takeovers.

I had been anticipating this move for a long time. I was surprised that

Eleanor signed the voting trust, but by that time she and I were pursuing different goals.

In the past, we had relied on each other for support. Now I avoided all meetings with the family because I knew their hostility might undermine my determination to sell. This left Eleanor exposed to a refocusing of their anger, which had to find a target.

In addition, it seemed to me Eleanor was no longer sure that she wanted to separate from the companies or from the man who owned them. She still hoped to return to her work at WHAS, and she enjoyed her increasingly close and confidential role with our parents.

From the outset, Christopher Shaw had said that an outside buyer for my shares or for the companies as a whole would be relatively easy to find, now that, as he put it, the genie was out of the bottle. I had hoped that Father would buy me out and spare me from making this decision. The prospect of soliciting an outside buyer was daunting, for I knew it would end my relationship with my family. Selling my shares to Father would have preserved the vestiges, at least, of precious connections. But it appeared that he was not eager to buy.

I wrote down several reasons for seeking an outside offer as the months passed and Father expressed no further interest in buying me out:

1. The "real" value of my holdings cannot be ascertained without an outside offer due to automatic discounting—twenty to twenty-five percent—on the theory that no one is interested.
2. I have no safeguards against the future sale of the companies at a greatly inflated price. Yet Barry is on leave, and may not return.
3. There are no clear family aims which might justify continued ownership. How can ownership be maintained without them? Simply to talk about "passing it all on" avoids the problems involved.
4. If Barry does not return, and some sort of "regency operation" under Paul Janensch continues, it seems likely that there will be a further decline in quality and profits.
5. Should the companies be passed along to my children's generation, they will bring with them a multitude of problems which will crush the new owners.

As I thought about the possibility of looking for a buyer outside the family, I knew that it was time to leave my job as book editor. It would be too difficult to deal on a daily basis with people who felt I was threatening their livelihood. Any change looks frightening to people who have benefited, or believe they have benefited, from the plantation system of private ownership.

By late winter, I was thinking about the uses of the money I would make from the sale of my stock.

I had thought of setting up a foundation to benefit Kentucky women, who often seem remote from the changes in American law and custom that have benefited women on the East and West coasts.

We had certainly not carried out, as media-monopoly owners, our responsibility to educate women about our rights, any more than we had taken seriously our obligation to represent and inform Kentucky's black population. Education appeared to be the first great problem.

Bingham money, a percentage of pretax profits from the companies, as well as private gifts, had supported certain kinds of endeavors in Louisville: the theater and the orchestra, urban beautification, mental health research, and, of course, a seventy-year-long list of Democratic candidates. But our money, which spread its golden glow over the family while it prevented many from asking questions, had not touched the state's basic problem. Thirty percent of Kentuckians over the age of twenty-five have less than eight years of formal education. Fifty percent never finish high school. As a result, four hundred thousand adult Kentuckians lack the basic skills to find employment, even if the jobs were available.

The state's poverty and illiteracy inevitably increased the power of its ruling family. We were badly needed, if only as proof that Kentucky could produce an aristocracy.

Illiteracy, racism, and high unemployment were making it difficult for women to survive in Kentucky, but I knew I would not have enough money to replace the federal, city, and county agencies whose budgets were being cut.

It seemed to me that the foundation might be able, instead, to attack the stereotypes that limited women's conception of ourselves, making us dependent on the false images offered by newspapers and television. We have not yet developed another set of images or visions to remind us that the chorus girls and sirens, the victims and witches in the news are not the women we are or the women we know.

Artists have a chance to alter attitudes because color and music, movement and words reach below the resistance set up by the conscious mind. I had felt the effect of images: the rare women in hard hats who work on Kentucky's roads always caused me to catch my breath.

One image was worth a thousand lectures, it seemed to me. So I decided to devote the foundation, when I could establish it, to women artists in Kentucky.

Long resistance leads to weariness and grandiosity. I had to remind myself that out in the real world stockholders sell out all the time. Here my action appeared to be a form of insanity, because of the misused word "family": I had been part of that family, part of the companies the family was supposed to own.

That the companies in fact belonged to Father, that the rest of the family, including Barry, were minority shareholders subject to his will, never occurred to anyone.

41

In July 1984, Father, through his lawyers, turned down my asking price of $42 million for my fifteen percent share of his companies. It had taken him six months to make the decision.

Through his team, he presented me with a counteroffer of $25 million. It was based on the evaluation of the companies made for estate-tax purposes years before, the same study Barry had mentioned, twelve months earlier, when he had said he wanted to buy me out. The work that had been done to establish a new valuation had had no effect on the owner's thinking.

The difference between the $42 million I had asked for and the $25 million Father was willing to pay was too great to be taken seriously. No one accepts such a sizable discount, except perhaps for a broken-down car. What I was selling was no rusted sedan but a fifteen percent interest in companies for which there existed an almost universal appetite. Shaw was stirring up interest, and stories in newspapers all over the country attested to a ravenous curiosity about these properties. Why was Father still under-estimating my knowledge of their value and my determination to sell?

I turned his offer down.

If he underestimated my determination, others did not. The reaction to a story in the *Courier-Journal* about his offer was powerful. Twenty-five million dollars seemed to many in Kentucky an enormous sum to "give" to an interfering woman. Some well-wishers told me that I should be grateful for such an offer and accept it at once. After all, no outside buyer had raised his head, in spite of Shaw's efforts. Perhaps there was no market for my stock.

There was another result of the publicity. For the first time, questions were being asked about the value of the monopoly to the community on which it had dined for years. These questions were few, and they were muted, because the questioners were of no importance to the system. Open disagreement allows people who have long been silent to ask a question or two, and that is always dangerous to monopoly ownership.

There was much disagreement about the value of my holdings, that did not, it seemed to me, depend on my personal weaknesses or strengths.

Others saw it differently. The stock had a certain value that depended on the companies' financial performance and reputation rather than on the reputation of the stockholder. Yet it seemed that my fifteen percent was like the secondhand fur coat sold at a discount because everyone knows the first owner was not a lady. The skins may be good but ownership has marred them. What an odd concept this would be in the wider world, where all stocks would face a precipitous decline in value if they were judged according to their owners' characters.

Another factor entered here: it was difficult for some people, inside and outside the family, to believe that I actually owned my fifteen percent. The fur coat is always a gift, and as a gift it can always be taken back.

Ownership implies authority, and that had never been conferred on the women in the family. Being women, we had no natural authority, in terms of the myth. Without it, possessions—whether pearls or fur coats or stock certificates—are simply gifts or loans. Everyone knows that such gifts can be reclaimed if the woman no longer satisfies.

It had happened before, most dramatically when part of Mary Lily's fortune was claimed by the Judge. Of course, she had died first: but that was likely to happen to women who resisted.

During the next six months, many meetings and negotiations took place of which I was not a part, although I occasionally heard something about them. It was almost impossible to avoid hearing "the latest," reports that often proved, in hindsight, to have been remarkably accurate. The gossip mills in Louisville were grinding night and day. Nothing so substantial had been fed into them since Louisville played host to the Duke and Duchess of Windsor and local gentlemen and ladies practiced their bows and curtsies.

By now I had decided not to attempt to influence Eleanor. She owned the same kinds and amounts of stock as I did in the three companies, and so the arrangements she made, either to sell to the family or to continue as an owner, offered an important standard of comparison.

If she "held out," as the saying goes, for money or for some recognition of her role, if she received concessions, either financial or in some other coin, I would feel the impact. Nevertheless, the fact remained that her goal was different from mine, and there seemed to be no way, at the moment, for us to cooperate. That we were able to preserve at least a part of our relationship proves that women can, among other things, respect each other's differences.

Eleanor was interested in running Father's television station. She had the nerve and the intelligence, it seemed to me, and perhaps would make the television station an example of what can be done when a talented, independent woman is in control. (No CBS affiliates are controlled by women executives, as a CBS anchorwoman recently pointed out.) After all, during her term there Eleanor had initiated the only local production, other than news, I had seen on WHAS: an evening "entertainment" show, which had not lasted long but which had seemed to indicate that WHAS might have an identity separate from its function of carrying syndicated shows.

But owning WHAS would mean that Eleanor remained within the family constellation, subject to its weather. She would have to find a way to deal with the station manager who, it seemed to me, had engineered her sudden retirement a few years earlier. She would have to find a way to cooperate with Barry because of the interdependence between the newspapers and the television station. I did not think he would welcome her as a partner. He had no experience in such an undertaking.

A few weeks later, I read in the *Courier-Journal* that Eleanor and Barry were working on a "stock swap" that would place her in charge of WHAS while he remained in charge of the newspapers. The failing printing company would then be sold to buy me out. This seemed ideal from my point of view.

Problems arose from the fact that shares in the television station were less valuable than shares in the newspaper companies. A straight swap, share for share, would be unfair to Eleanor, yet any attempt to make up the difference in cash would call into question the value of the companies. Barry had not yet, it seemed to me, begun to realize that the study made years before for estate-planning purposes was not acceptable as a yardstick. Father, apparently, was doing nothing to help Barry to change his mind. The only hope, for Eleanor, lay in finding a way to equalize her position with Barry's, which did not depend on valuations of the companies. That would be difficult to achieve.

Perhaps the time had finally come to weigh money in the scales with love.

I seldom saw my family that fall. Now and then we would run into each other at a public event or in a restaurant. Our upbringing would never have permitted a show of ill-feeling. Barry was always careful to shake hands, and although he looked grim and pale, I never felt—and indeed that remained true until the end—the slightest animosity. In fact, Barry now seemed more cheerful and relaxed, perhaps because of his leave in New England. While there he had decided to abandon the electronic newspaper.

After much consultation I decided to make a counteroffer to Father. It showed a precipitous decline in my expectations: I would accept $32 million rather than the $42 million I had asked for months earlier. Once again, I began to wait for Father's answer.

Meanwhile, I read in the newspaper that, as I noted, "Eleanor will be 'given' WHAS. I have had some difficulty with this, but am reassured, on the rational level, by the fact that she is winning by the rules of the white male world, which she knows so well, and which will always cause her some pain, like my stepgrandmother, married for her dead husband's money, like my other stepgrandmother, the Ambassadress, like my aunt, beloved in penury, living on handouts. I can't afford to hate Eleanor for succeeding at a game I refuse to play. The choices are different."

The sharp pain I felt, however, on reading the announcement warned me that I had not yet extricated myself from the rivalries of my childhood.

In fact, Eleanor was not being "given" anything. Months passed in protracted negotiations which, had they been successful, would have left her in charge of WHAS. However, she was now encountering Barry's refusal to consider realistic valuations for the companies, which in the end killed all efforts to resolve the crisis.

Behind Barry's stubbornness, it seemed to me, lay another aspect of the Bingham myth. While their executives sometimes joked about various maneuvers, "perfectly legal, of course," which lowered corporate taxes or sheltered our incomes from the government, such shenanigans clearly had no place in the moral universe ruled by kings of men.

Therefore it was simply not possible that a valuation made to reduce inheritance taxes should be seen for what it was. Seeing it in that light would mean admitting that the family was conniving to cheat the government, like the lowliest scoundrel pursued on the newspapers' front pages. Therefore the estimate that had been ordered specifically for estate-planning purposes must be seen by Barry to reflect the real value of the companies.

In the early fall, Barry offered Eleanor an elaborate stratagem that would, in theory, have left her in control of WHAS. But the stratagem, as I heard it described, was so elaborate and so binding—among other things, it set a ceiling on the amount of money she could borrow—I was afraid it would cripple her endeavor. I had seen women placed in positions of some power with factors built into the situation which assured their failure. I did not want to see this happen to Eleanor.

Eleanor apparently also saw the problems in this arrangement.

In the late fall, Barry offered another plan. By now the situation was becoming desperate, as Father issued edicts that conveyed his frustration. He was leaving the outcome of the negotiations entirely up to Eleanor and Barry, leaving them, as Munda might have said, "to fight it out between themselves."

This seemed to me to place them both in impossible positions, since in fact neither of them controlled the outcome of the struggle. Only Father could decide whether the stock-swap effort would succeed, since he owned the majority of the stock in both companies, and would make the final decision.

Now and then Eleanor would describe one of their conferences, and I would realize, uncomfortably, that she was exposed to the rage that had been directed against me. She seemed to survive it well, although she was at the same time burdened with heavy responsibilities to her own family, which now included two small sons.

She seemed to lose heart as her position was undermined, however, and eventually perhaps decided—although I will never know for sure—that she did not want the television station after all.

By early winter Father was warning Barry and Eleanor that if they could not agree he would sell everything. In fact, they did not have the power to make an agreement. That power was his.

42

In September 1985, I had realized that no one was interested in buying my fifteen percent interest in the Bingham companies.

Father had not met my price, now lowered to $32 million from my original $42 million, and there seemed little hope that he would do so. Christopher Shaw had talked with clients who were interested in the companies as a whole but not in my small portion.

Shaw now tried to turn this interest into written offers, but he was not successful.

Some of the men to whom Shaw introduced me seemed afraid of offending Father. Few were personal friends. They were impressed by an aura, an unspoken claim to a pinnacle of prestige in their world. To suggest buying Father's newspapers would be, it seemed, an act of impoliteness.

In theory Father could turn down any offer since he controlled ninety-five percent of the companies' stock through his voting trust.

However, the case was not quite so simple, as everyone knew. Father's responsibility as trustee for the many trusts set up for his children and grandchildren would hamper him in turning down big offers for the companies. His fiduciary duty meant that he would have to consider the best interests of the twenty or so people, many of them very young, who depended on his judgment. He had recently removed himself and his directors as trustees from the trusts that had been set up to benefit me, but he was still in control of trusts that benefited his other offspring.

As the months passed in this stalemate, I began to hope that we would find an outsider, a maverick, who would make an offer for one of the companies.

This person did not exist. The men who controlled capital sufficient for such an enterprise were interested in social possibilities, it seemed to me. They wanted to earn or keep the owner's goodwill, and perhaps eventually to be invited to sit in his box at the Derby.

This was as true of the young entrepreneur as it was of the old media owner. All had grown up in the same school or outside of it, wistfully looking in. Of course, there were no women or blacks at this level of enterprise, nor were there any representatives of classes or groups that did not define success as acceptance by a social elite.

I was reminded of the way the CIA had preserved its access to publishers because the agents, as Colby had said years earlier, looked as though they had been to Yale.

I slowly realized that our supposedly outspoken and fiercely independent newspapers had established a network that made them exempt from the threat of a takeover. The network, of course, limited their independence.

As I realized the weakness of my position, I wondered if all women who inherit money, and with it the illusion of power, are similarly handicapped. It began to seem to me that we have never overcome the prejudice that keeps women helpless or nearly so—at all levels of society. Without money, we lack clout. With money, we are hog-tied by our allegiance to powerful men, without whom we cannot exercise the power that money confers.

I continued to receive letters from strangers. Many blamed me for not acting as women are supposed to act: healing wounds, bridging gaps, interpreting, soothing, explaining. Letters to the editor in both newspapers attacked me for being a feminist and for not being a feminist, for being ambitious and for being misled, for having bad teeth and for craving expensive luxuries.

Sadly, many of the letters came from women. I did not know any of them, but I wondered if they had made painful compromises with their husbands and fathers in order to survive.

Many cited religion as their comfort and inspiration, quoting passages from the Old Testament that have been interpreted to prove that woman, as Eve, brought evil into the world and is therefore responsible for eradicating it. I remembered the sense of sin that had crushed me in the old downtown church, and was glad, finally, to be rid of it.

A retired schoolteacher wrote that she was a feminist (a rara avis in Kentucky) but that she had learned the good of the family and of the community was more important than feminism, which she considered a personal foible, like a taste for chocolates.

A man who had learned to read as a child by staring at the *Courier-Journal*'s headlines believed that the newspaper's magical quality was conferred on it by the Bingham men, and that I should make all necessary sacrifices to ensure that they retained their magic.

A woman whose mother had died the night before urged me to be a peacemaker and a healer. Being right is lonely, she wrote. That was true.

Other letters from strangers described situations that always shared several characteristics. A woman had inherited an interest, usually quite small, in a business controlled by her father and her brothers. Now she was trying to extricate herself, and she was being successfully opposed.

These women, who lived all over the country, had realized as I had that their ownership meant nothing. They had neither the money nor the power of their male relatives. Some had given up the struggle, overwhelmed by family hostility and legal fees. Some were still trying to get their money out of businesses whose owners scorned them. A few would go on trying. All of them needed independent legal advice, which they had trouble finding.

Now I decided to arm myself with a New York lawyer, to shore up my stance. Kentuckians often seem to be intimidated by the mere thought of a New York lawyer, as though he represents a freedom of thought and action that cannot be found outside of Manhattan. I realized how devoted I was to my Louisville team, however, when I contemplated telling them about this addition. I was relieved when they told me they had been anticipating this move for a long time.

That fall, for the first time, matters my parents considered private were becoming public: there was no way to control or delete the news stories which were being written, as later there would be no way to control or delete interviews on television. I decided my best bet was to speak for myself.

Old connections, of course, proved helpful, as I believe they were in the case of several misleading articles in *Editor & Publisher,* in the case of CBS's version of the story on *60 Minutes,* and in the case of National Public Radio's account, narrated by an angry and threatened ex-Kentuckian who had grown up admiring "the Binghams."

Editor & Publisher is a house organ of establishment newspapers, WHAS is a CBS affiliate, and a young man who has grown up in Shively and respects authority is likely to admire the Binghams. After all, he was never a Shively housewife.

Other interviewers, including several reporters in Louisville, were less susceptible to that combination of private grief and public nobility that is so seductive for journalists.

Always in the past it had been possible for the family to avoid embarrassing disclosures, or to remove them from memory, as Mary Lily had been removed, because the family's control was complete in the small world of Kentucky. Now, however, the big world was interested, and it was not possible to influence, persuade, embarrass, or intimidate everyone in that big world.

But Father was not deterred by the failure of these methods, as would be seen when, several years later, he used the same methods to attempt to discredit David Chandler's book about the Judge.

Father's attitude, vigorously expressed by Mother, is of course not unusual. Perhaps its most dramatic success was achieved several years ago when Pierre du Pont was able to suppress a book written about his family, the Du Pont family: *Behind the Nylon Curtain.*

There is nothing surprising about the attempt to protect privilege from the pain of public disclosure. What is surprising, it seems to me, is that so many people who stand to gain little from it support and even admire this use of power. Sometimes these are the same people who admire what they call "hard-hitting, investigative journalism"—as long as they, their families, their business associates, and their friends are not the target.

Staff cuts at the newspapers were beginning to be made, in preparation for the closing of the afternoon newspaper, the venerable Louisville *Times.*

When my youngest son and I were guests on a radio talk show, a caller asked what it felt like to be hated by twenty-two hundred people—the total number of workers at Father's companies. Fortunately it does not "feel." Hate is personal, and it cannot be felt by a woman who has been placed for purposes of convenience across the legitimate target. But as I told my son, it is worth remembering that the hate is there.

A friend told me excitedly that at a bar near the newspapers my photograph was being used as a dart board. For a hectic moment, I thought I would go down and see if it was so. But reason prevailed. Perhaps, I thought, I could now begin to manufacture my own mythology, as the Colonel had begun to make his during Reconstruction. But the materials were not at hand; I could not really believe that I was being persecuted. Again, I represented a cluster of emotions and ideas to people who did not know me but who were terrified of change.

Meanwhile my lawyers continued to talk with Father's team. In the late fall, it seemed that another offer from Father was about to be made. It appeared that this offer would be at least two or three million dollars higher than the $25 million I had turned down in the summer. I thought that agreement was coming.

In October, another meeting with the management team supported this impression. I wrote, "They seemed pleased with Don Siekman's impressive presentation. [Siekman was my accountant, another energetic and positive force.] His presentation asked for $8 million in 'up-front' money, the rest [of the $32 million] to be paid over a period of time with money and notes."

I began to realize that these executives were working hard to produce a better offer, but they were frustrated by Father's reluctance to end the stalemate and by Barry's commitment to an unrealistic valuation of the companies.

Matters were now out of my hands. I did not know what Eleanor and Barry were doing.

According to a story published later in the *Courier-Journal,* Eleanor told Father on November 19 that she was not interested in taking over WHAS after all.

I could understand her reservations about stepping into a situation that seemed full of traps. Later she told a reporter she did not want all her assets to be in a single company in a single industry in a single community. Now she wanted to sell all the companies.

At that point, Barry, who had garnered Joan Bingham's support, put forward something called the "Wednesday Plan," because that was the day of the week it was proposed. I learned about the plan much later.

According to this plan, both WHAS and the printing company would be sold, and the proceeds used to buy Eleanor and me out. By a mysterious calculation, we would be offered about $37 million each, five million more than I was asking. Then the newspapers would be given to Barry and Joan, and eventually to their children.

Perhaps realizing that the power in the situation was shifting again, Eleanor said she would rather keep WHAS than see it sold.

She wanted Barry to make me a better offer, but that he would not do for fear of plunging the companies into debt. Someone had figured that if I was paid $28 million for my shares, the companies would have to borrow $45 million. This would mean the companies' credit rating would drop for three years. Barry found that unacceptable.

Now Eleanor attempted to connect Father's next and last offer to me to her own arrangement to trade her newspaper stock for Barry's shares in the television station.

Later Eleanor described one of the many meetings that took place that winter. The dialogue sounded as though it were issuing from the House of Atreus.

Mother had said they would never have given Eleanor stock if they had known she planned to use it to destroy her brother.

Father had thrown up his hands, declaring that the blood should now be allowed to flow in the scuppers—which sent us all scurrying to our dictionaries.

I was surprised when I learned, indirectly, that Eleanor had called Christopher Shaw. I hoped this meant she was thinking of selling her fifteen percent to an outside buyer, which would, of course, considerably strengthen my position.

However, she was bound by the voting trust, as well as by her complicated loyalty to Father. Nothing came of the call.

The offer I had been waiting for since July arrived on December 12: Barry was now willing to pay me $26.3 million for my fifteen percent of the companies.

It had taken six months to raise his initial offer by $1.3 million. Most of that increase had already been consumed by fees.

Father and Barry still believed that I would give up and accept an amount that was almost exactly half what my stock was worth.

All the words and all the tears shed in the last year and a half had had no effect on the myth. I was still seen as a descendant of invisible women who had always placed their men's interests above their own.

The myth made idols of women, or erased them entirely. The women who became idols were like the image of the stiff little dressed-up Infanta that had hung in my bedroom when I was a child. Her attendant dwarfs and duennas were not in the reproduction I had learned by heart, nor did the reproduction show the reflected image of the Infanta's parents, the king and queen of Spain, in a mirror on the wall. The Infanta stood alone, in her elaborate dress, "pretty as a picture" and powerless as a picture, trapped by invisible attendants.

I turned down the $26.3 million.

Several of Barry's executives had argued that I would not accept such a low offer, but Barry had not been moved. He had convinced himself that any additional money would plunge the companies into debt, from which they might never recover. Some had tried to persuade him to increase the amount to $28 million, they later told me—a sum they had reason to believe I might accept. But Barry had made up his mind. Reasoning had nothing to do with it. I was worth $26.3 million, and that was that.

I did not know what role Father had played in Barry's decision, although clearly there was one role he had not chosen. He had not taken charge of the situation. As owner of the majority of the stock in his three companies, in total control through his voting trust, the chairman of the board could have insisted that I must be bought out, for a price I would have accepted, which would not have wrecked the companies. Barry might have threatened to resign, but that was no reason to hesitate; he had threatened it often before.

Father did not act because preserving family ownership was not his aim. His aim was to bring it all to an end.

.   .   .

A few days before Christmas, Father left a pile of presents on our front porch, and we managed to convey gifts to my family on the Place without actually seeing them.

In January, Eleanor decided to return to an earlier version of the stock-swap plan, adding a new provision: I was to be bought out for around $28 million before she would conclude her deal with Barry.

I learned of this new twist in a letter Eleanor wrote me asking if I would accept $28 million for my holdings. She said that this could be done by increasing the value per share of my WHAS stock, which would ensure that her stock, too, was valued at a higher rate. This would solve the problem of valuation that had prevented her from trading her *Courier-Journal* stock for Barry's WHAS stock months earlier.

The deal seemed acceptable to me, although I was somewhat disturbed at Eleanor's proviso that the biggest trust of all, the one I had always thought of as Engine Number Nine, would have to be "reformed" as well.

In her letter, Eleanor asked me to consider this option for her sake, implying that her arrangement with Barry would collapse if I did not go along.

It appeared to me, however, that I was not the crucial factor. Barry's low valuation of all the company stock was the real problem, and Father's refusal to force his hand. Again, I was being put into a position to receive the blame should I turn down this suggestion.

A few days after I got her letter, Eleanor and I met for the first time in several months at a small motel outside of Louisville.

As I drove up to the motel, I remembered a beautiful fall day nearly thirty years earlier when my first husband's family had been installed there on the afternoon before our wedding. Then Eleanor had been a little girl in a bridesmaid's dress; now she was an exhausted and frightened young wife who looked almost frail in the brilliant sunshine.

She had become the go-between, which was painful to me, although I understood the attraction of that position. The family was sending her to ask me what I would accept, as a compromise sum, for my stock. She mentioned $27 million, which seemed outrageously low to me, hardly more than the amount I had turned down months earlier. I noticed that she seemed startled by my refusal, as though she had perhaps persuaded herself that she could "bring me around."

When we parted on the doorstep, I felt the pull of our long shared past. She was still the little sister I had helped to raise, now pressed into a service that was likely to injure our relationship. A cold breeze passed between us. I wondered if she would always belong to the family now.

.   .   .

On January 10, 1986, I had lunch with two close women friends in a restaurant in Louisville that reminded me of the eateries on Lexington Avenue in New York, although this one had no ferns.

We were sitting by the window over hamburgers when a waitress called me to the telephone.

Over the telephone, a reporter at the *Courier-Journal* read me two long statements, one from Father, the other from Barry. They had just been posted in the newsroom.

Father said that he had decided to sell all his companies because of financial problems and family disagreements. Barry, in a yell of pain, called Father's decision a betrayal.

I did not know about the decision. Later I heard that Father had attempted to call all his grandchildren the night before, to warn them about what was coming; apparently he did not reach my sons. When I went to my office that afternoon, I found a message that he had called me in the morning. Months later, Mother told a reporter that she, too, had left a message and that I had "ignored her call."

When I called Father that afternoon, neither of us had much to say. He asked me if I had heard the news, and I said I had, and that although I realized the decision must have been very painful, I felt he had done the right thing. It was time to let the myth go and to liberate the living from its clutch—if that was possible.

A few weeks later, Father wrote a letter to his grandchildren and sent me a copy. It explained his reasons for deciding to sell.

He wrote that since both Barry and Eleanor had insisted that he and Mother were the ones to take responsibility for the decision to sell, he had assumed they would agree with his action. He had been horrified by Barry's reaction, and felt that he had deeply hurt his "well-loved" son, who was ready to sacrifice the rest of his life to running the newspapers.

Father did not want to permit that sacrifice, in the face of changes in the newspaper business that limited the opportunities he had once had, as publisher, to influence public affairs. He did not believe the role of publisher would ever again be so rewarding, partly because he felt that the public no longer accepted the kind of benevolent paternalism he had practiced.

He mentioned that Barry had refused to offer me more than $26.3 million for my shares, although Father had believed a somewhat higher figure would have been accepted. He did not discuss his reasons for allowing Barry to make this final decision, which Father called a value judgment.

Motivations seemed meaningless now. Change, with its own momentum, had begun. Another investment bank was called in to organize the offers that were already being made for the newspapers—starting the process which would end with the sale of all the companies.

The sale reflected a weakness in the structure of power. Corporations that had seemed pillars of the community were instead as fragile as cobwebs, because the people who ran them and who owned them did not understand each other, seldom communicated, and shared few goals.

During the next months, executives and shareholders who would soon make important decisions about appraisals, prices, and buyers did not talk to each other, or did so only with constraint and embarrassment.

A monolithic concentration of money and power had molded the family. Both the family and the companies were stranded, bogged down in misunderstanding and silence. There was no mode for communication, no method for dealing with disagreement, no way to decide what was personal and what was political.

Interviewers began to call me a catalyst, kindly, as though it was a substitute for something worse. A catalyst is a "substance" which "causes the speeding up of a chemical reaction." The "substance itself undergoes no permanent chemical change."

A catalyst acts without intention. It causes change as a spilled glass of red wine stains a white tablecloth. I had acted for conscious reasons: to achieve my separation from the family myth.

For others, my actions may have served a variety of purposes, as they certainly did for Father. To him, perhaps, I was, as I had been from the beginning, a substance that can be used to cause change. But I no longer felt the pull of the unexamined, the inevitable, which had attracted me five years before. I had acted, and I would continue to act, on my own. I was prepared to take the consequences.

Epilogue

In December 1986, I asked Mother to have lunch with me; I had not seen her since the previous spring. I hoped we might be able to resolve our differences now that the companies had been sold.

I planned to tell her about this book, in which I was describing the lives of Sallie Watson Montague Lefroy and Helena Lefroy Caperton, Mother's grandmother and mother. I had sensed that Mother resented the fact that her side—so wellborn, in spite of their genteel Virginia poverty, in comparison with the upstart North Carolina Binghams—was neglected when we talked about the family. A few years earlier, she had sent me many family documents, including her grandmother's reminiscences and a book about the Caperton family.

In spite of our differences, I thought Mother might understand my loyalty to the women who had contributed labor and imagination or money to the Bingham family—as she had contributed—often without recognition.

But I was uneasy.

Around that time, the Queen of England was visiting the Kentucky horse farms, and news accounts had informed us that she planned to go to Sunday service at an Episcopal church in Lexington.

Mother had written a letter to the editor, published in the *Courier-Journal,* deploring the fact that the Queen would be exposed to the hoi polloi during the Passing of the Peace. As I helped her into my car, I felt the chilly hauteur which reduced me to the humblest member of the congregation pressing forward rudely to paw at the Queen's hand.

How beautiful she looked, perfectly costumed in her autumn tweeds, pale, almost ethereal, with the authority of her age and of her intelligence still intact. She seemed to me sheathed and bright, and I feared that we would not get through the lunch without seeing the blade of her intellect, and her hostility, flash out.

We went to a restaurant by the river—the sweeping pale brown Ohio, where the big coal barges pass on their way to the locks at Louisville, the river that had cut off Mother's access to help the day I was born.

We talked about the details familiar to all women: food and sickness, vacations and outings, weather and children. Mother told me about her new projects—purchase of stock in a conservative textbook publishing company, involvement in the choice of the new state superintendent of education.

We were both uneasy, I realized. We had not talked since the angry confrontations, a year earlier, that had seemed to sear our mouths, sealing up the past. Still, we managed a little humor: she apologized, laughingly, for talking so much about her cook—her true friend, I felt, although Mother would have scorned the suggestion.

But she had been charged with a mission. Now and then during the meal, she glanced at me sharply, and I realized that she was waiting for an opportunity to speak her mind. I longed to avoid providing her with that opportunity, but I had promised myself to try at least once to explain why I was writing this book. I knew that would give her her chance.

Finally, on the drive home, I told her about the difficulties I had encountered when I searched the past for traces of our female ancestors. I asked about Munda and Sallie Montague, the two Richmond ladies, her mother and grandmother. She told me where their papers were kept.

Then, as we drove past the cornfields that skirt the Ohio, she told me that she and Father (and how often, I realized, she had spoken for him) wanted to heal the breach between us. I told her that I wanted to heal it, too. She said everything depended on the way I treated my stepgrand-mother, Mary Lily Kenan Flagler Bingham, in my book.

The flat cornfields, harvested down to the stubble, floated past as I explained that I had not planned to spend a great deal of time on Mary Lily; she remained mysterious to me, and I had not yet embarked on the research and the thinking that would make her real.

Mother was not satisfied. She told me she and Father would never have what she called a normal relationship with me if I implicated the Judge in Mary Lily's death—something I had not yet considered doing. She said— and again I heard flat echoes from the long past—that to mention such a possibility would break Father's heart.

By now we were parked in front of the Little House, where I had spent my early childhood, and she was talking quickly.

I was lost in the whirlpool of fear and despair her rapid words always induced. I finally summoned the courage to say that there was such a thing as the truth, and that I could not promise to withhold the truth about Mary Lily's death if I came upon it.

This infuriated her, since she realized that I recognized the situation: the use of emotional blackmail to prevent investigation—the bane of journalists, subject of countless of Father's editorials.

She quickly said that she only wanted me to see the issue from another point of view. The other point of view would be provided by the family's law firm, which was conducting research into the question of Mary Lily's death.

She repeated several times, "You know nothing. You were only six months old when your grandfather died," and I realized that she must have taken comfort from that over a long period of time: as though all I could ever know was limited to firsthand observation—as though I had no access to the past.

By now I was struggling to control my tears, and she was about to get out of the car. I asked her why the scandal surrounding Mary Lily's death, more than seventy years earlier, was more important to her than her relationship with me.

She replied that it was a question of honor, and got out of the car. She added that they would not see me until after my book was published.

I felt nearly obliterated by pain. It brought in its wake feelings of helplessness and terror that must have been familiar to an infant girl crying for food and love. For a while it seemed as though I could not survive the isolation Mother was imposing; nor could I expose myself to another attempt, which would inevitably, I believed, bring rejection and hours of weeping and despair.

I was not angry at Mother. It seemed to me that she had sacrificed her vision and some of her identity to Father's truth.

The Bible commands, "If thine own eye offends thee, pluck it out." Or thy daughter's eye.

I began to understand her definition of honor: to place Father's myth above all other values, all other affections, all other bonds.

Money came into the family through Mary Lily's death. That fact could not be denied. It tarnished the image of earned power and prestige that enabled the family to avoid guilt.

Since Mary Lily's death had made her five million dollars available to the Judge, her death must be ignored, then forgotten. She must be ignored, then forgotten.

No one may raise questions about the lives of kings.

I often think of Mother's word: honor. How often in the South has honor been called upon to justify dishonorable acts.

After a few days, my terror wore off. The world, after all, is changing. If I survive, if I succeed, as I plan to do—write, publish, raise my sons, preserve my marriage and my friendships, use my money—it means that perhaps the old way is changing.

They cannot write me out, as Mary Lily was written out, silence me, or reward me into compliance.

It is the loss of power that is most frightening for people like my parents. It means that reality is cresting, about to burst their limits.

What is love, compared to that fearful flood?

Father wrote me a note in the early winter of 1986 to tell me that he had what he called a malignant brain tumor and was going to Boston for treatment.

When I called him, he sounded relieved, even exhilarated, as though he knew exactly what to expect, had known, perhaps, from the moment when he had stumbled on the tennis court during his weekly game with three other men his age.

Before he left, he sent me a Christmas present: a letter and a photograph of Vita Sackville-West. It came wrapped in brown paper.

During his first week in the hospital, he told me he enjoyed watching the moon rise over the Charles River. He delighted in the visit of his grandchildren, but Mother was still angrily guarding the door; she told me they did not want to speak to me since a newspaper article on David Chandler's book about the Judge, which Father had tried to suppress, had reminded her of my role in that battle.

For my birthday, in January, Father sent me a novel of Sackville-West's, which I searched for clues before realizing that he meant only to remind me of the wider world, always represented by Bloomsbury and Henrietta.

His signature, on my birthday card, had a little jog in it. His writing had never shown a disruption before.

At first, Father was determined to fight. "Hope has returned," he told me, after his doctors advised chemotherapy.

He was not prepared for what followed. After a while he begged to be allowed to die. He said he wanted to go to heaven, with the simple, passionate faith of his North Carolina family. It was not permitted.

In the spring, he came home and was established in the room in the Little House that had been our nursery and later our parents' bedroom. The matrimonial bed with the dipping swan posts was replaced by the plain paraphernalia of sickness. By then he could not walk or speak.

The last time I saw him, he was lying in that room. I had already said goodbye to him six months earlier in Boston, when he seemed to be fighting his way vigorously toward the heaven he had imagined. Now, he was peaceful, comatose, relieved of responsibility for his own dying and our reactions to it.

The Alice in Wonderland illustrations I remembered on the walls were covered by half a century's worth of white paint, but the window seat where I had kept my toys and books still looked out on a tangle of forsythia, once as wild and fascinating as the Amazonian jungle.

I felt I had said goodbye to him the first time I stepped out into that tiny wilderness. My life has been a way of saying goodbye to the world he loved, the kindly Southern world that contains so much cruelty.

His body was slowly undoing itself, in the natural order of things, and he had been allowed to turn back into the peaceful, good little boy his mother had adored. He was coddled now by nurses, his wife, his daughter and granddaughters, as in the old Asheville days he was tenderly cared for by his aunt Sadie and his cousins Martha and Temple.

Sitting by him, I felt the relief of his helplessness—he to whom everyone attributed power, but who seemed strained and stretched to fit his role. Perhaps the reason no one believed he controlled his companies and decided their fate was that he never wanted the responsibility, longing instead for the world of childhood, the fantasy and sweetness of the half-remembered Southern past, which depended on secrets.

He had grown up, as he now was ending, in a household of women: his widowed grandmother, his mother, who seemed closer to her children than to her husband, and all the Miller and Callahan cousins and aunts, as well as the cooks and nurses, black and white. He had to leave that world in adolescence, and had to forget it, later, in order to become The Publisher, the charming, manipulative public man. Now he was claiming it again.

The violence done him in the hospital, the tube down his throat, the radiation, had produced a long, slow, painless decline into the earth, rather than the abrupt, brutal blooming of the uncontrolled brain tumor. The doctors had provided him with a long death rather than a short one. He had wanted a short one. Perhaps the lingering was merciful. I remembered his sunniness, when he was freed of demands.

I spoke to him but he did not respond, and it seemed best not to disturb him. I felt that he was already far away. Tim and I sat for a while, enjoying the summer sunlight, the flowers, the attentive presence of the nurse seated just out of sight. Everything seemed controlled, beautiful, even serene. I felt I was witnessing Mother's masterpiece.

We stood up to leave, and I leaned down to kiss Father's forehead. He opened his eyes and stared at me. There was no shadow of recognition, of pleasure or pain, interest or intention.

I felt relieved and even joyous. For the first time, he was looking at me without seeing the construction he had created to replace me. He was looking at me as he had often looked at me, without seeing me at all. I was reminded of my sons, in the days before they learned my face, when they stared at me as they stared at the mobiles hanging over their cribs.

His stare was smooth and pure as a washed stone. His extraordinary blue eyes, bright yet pale, registered me only as light. It was as it should be, for both of us. We were free.

Later, of course, came the grotesque public rituals: the great state funeral, recorded for television, the frail elderly personages called from faraway places to witness his official departure, the crowds of "plain people" who had been taught by Father's newspapers and his philanthropy and his kind, charmed presence to worship, with affection and awe.

As we stood at the side of the grave—hardly recognizable as a grave, since the dirt was covered with a sort of carpet—a crowd of onlookers moved forward, with a rustling sound, to hear the clergyman's last words. That sound had something primeval in it, like wind, or water.

What remains when a powerful man dies is the habit of worship. That habit had separated us finally and permanently, long before Father's death. That need dictated his will, in which he left my portion to my sons, because he did not approve of the way I give my money, to women.

I am grateful to him for that last gesture, which reminded me of his priorities. Acknowledged love flows along the lines of inheritance.

He was a true American patriarch, devoted to the achievement and institutionalization of power, which is best obtained by an idealist who knows that all forms of power are illusory.

He leaves me bereft of illusions, yet an inheritor of his ability to imagine a world—but an inheritor who knows that, for a woman, this ability arouses much hostility.

Hate distorts, but so does adulation. Under the flowers and the grass-green carpet and the Episcopal church's great white satin banner, Father was more than buried; he was elevated. Lost in that tumult of words and music was the child who had seen his mother die and had survived the experience, the boy who had blinded himself to his father's doings, the adult who had known that what he called "foolishness" was the adulation he required.

I felt great sadness when I remembered the father I had lost many years ago, who had played in the block maze with the china pig, the father who had painted my face for my role in *A Midsummer Night's Dream,* and had been delighted with the improvement, the father who had wanted to read all of Dickens's novels to me, while I sat on a stool at his feet with his gold pocket watch in my hand.

·   ·   ·

Sometime later, I found Nursie's grave.

She is buried beside her mother, the cranky old countrywoman I knew as Mom, in a section of Cave Hill Cemetery that looks like a field. The monuments that give the cemetery its peculiar theatricality—a sphinx and a temple of love, headless angels, and a woman with water pouring from her hands—do not appear in this field. Here the dead are marked by flat bronze plaques.

Nursie bought the plot for her mother and planted a magnolia tree over her grave. The tree is sturdy, rounded, fifteen feet tall. It had dropped a pair of seed pods, crossed, just at the top of Mom's marker—the seed pods whose tough, pointed chambers I used for eyes in petal faces on a stone bench outside the Big House long ago. Mom's marker reads: MILLIE A. CUMMINGS 1890–1963.

Nursie's plaque matches her mother's: a rectangle with three open roses in the top left-hand corner. It reads: LUCY E. CUMMINGS 1908–1976. She was born when her mother was eighteen.

The orange clay around the plaque was still bare. Wild violets, which had pressed up close to Mom's, had not yet reached Nursie's.

The little plot would have been expensive for Nursie, even there on the fringe of the graveyard, half a mile from the hillside where the Judge and his family lie, grand in life, undiminished in death.

The fragile haze of the October day veiled the sun.

Nursie had a way of standing with her freckled arms firmly crossed on her stomach. Standing like that, often in a doorway, she would tell me the way things were. Her pronouncements were simple: "Pretty is as pretty does." "You have to eat a peck of dirt before you die." "A stitch in time saves nine."

She knew there were other ways—complex, indecipherable. That did not matter. When she stood with her arms folded, she saw the world as one: united, revealed, true.

Although I argued with her—how could anyone be so certain?—I remember the way she pressed her lips together, looking at me with interest, knowing that one day I would understand.

Bibliography

Ascher, Carol, Louise De Salvo, and Sara Ruddick, eds. *Between Women: Biographers, Novelists, Critics, Teachers and Artists Write about Their Work on Women.* Boston: Beacon Press, 1984.

Bingham, James Barry, comp. *Descendants of James Bingham of County Down, Northern Ireland.* Mill Valley, Calif.: Gateway Press, 1980.

Blakey, George T. *Hard Times and New Deal in Kentucky, 1929–1938.* Lexington: University Press of Kentucky, 1986.

Bottigheimer, Karl. *Ireland and the Irish: A Short History.* New York: Columbia University Press, 1982.

Braden, Anne. *The Wall Between.* New York: Monthly Review Press, 1958.

Brenan, Gerald A. *Personal Record, 1920–1972.* New York: Alfred A. Knopf, 1975.

Brendon, Piers. *Ike: His Life and Times.* New York: Harper & Row, 1986.

Brome, Vincent. *Ernest Jones: Freud's Alter Ego.* New York: W. W. Norton, 1983.

Carmichael, Omer, and Weldon James. *The Louisville Story.* New York: Simon and Schuster, 1957.

Carrington, Dora. *Carrington: Letters and Extracts from Her Diaries.* Edited by David Carrington. London: Jonathan Cape, 1970.

Chandler, David Leon. *The Binghams of Louisville: The Dark History Behind One of the Country's Great Fortunes.* New York: Macmillan, 1987.

——. *Henry Flagler: The Astonishing Life and Times of the Visionary Robber Baron Who Founded Florida.* New York: Macmillan, 1986.

Chesler, Phyllis. *Women and Madness.* Garden City, N.Y.: Doubleday, 1972.

Clinton, Catherine. *The Plantation Mistress: Woman's World in the Old South.* New York: Pantheon Books, 1982.

Cooper, John Milton, Jr. *Walter Hines Page: The Southerner as American, 1855–1918.* Chapel Hill: University of North Carolina Press, 1977.

Curtiss, Mina. *Other People's Letters: A Memoir.* Boston: Houghton Mifflin, 1978.

Davis, Kenneth S. *FDR, The New Deal Years, 1933–1937: A History.* New York: Random House, 1986.

Dijkstra, Bram. *Idols of Perversity: Fantasies of Feminine Evil in Fin-de-Siècle Culture.* New York: Oxford University Press, 1986.

Donald, David Herbert. *Look Homeward: A Life of Thomas Wolfe.* Boston: Little, Brown, 1987.

Downs, Robert B. *Books That Changed the South.* Chapel Hill: University of North Carolina Press, 1977.

Ellis, William E. "The Bingham Family: From the Old South to the New South and Beyond." *The Filson Club History Quarterly,* vol. 61 (January 1987), pp. 5–33.

Ethridge, Willie Snow. *Nila: Her Story.* New York: Simon and Schuster, 1956.

Garnett, David. *The Familiar Faces.* New York: Harcourt, Brace, 1962.

———. *The Flowers of the Forest.* New York: Harcourt, Brace, 1955.

———. *Lady into Fox.* New York: Alfred A. Knopf, 1923.

———. *A Man in the Zoo.* New York: Alfred A. Knopf, 1924.

Gay, Peter. *The Bourgeois Experience: Victoria to Freud.* Vol. 2, *The Tender Passion.* New York: Oxford University Press, 1986.

Heilbrun, Carolyn G. *Reinventing Womanhood.* New York: W. W. Norton, 1979.

Houseman, John. *Front and Center.* New York: Simon and Schuster, 1979.

———. *Run-through.* New York: Simon and Schuster, 1972.

Howe, Florence. *Myths of Coeducation: Selected Essays, 1964–1983.* Bloomington: Indiana University Press, 1985.

Isaacson, Walter, and Evan Thomas. *The Wise Men: Architects of the American Century.* New York: Simon and Schuster, 1986.

Kozol, Jonathan. *The Fume of Poppies.* Boston: Houghton Mifflin, 1958.

Krock, Arthur. *Memoirs: Sixty Years on the Firing Line.* New York: Funk & Wagnalls, 1968.

Kwitny, Jonathan. *Endless Enemies: The Making of an Unfriendly World.* New York: Congdon & Weed, 1984.

Lash, Joseph P. *Eleanor and Franklin: The Story of Their Relationship Based on Eleanor Roosevelt's Private Papers.* New York: W. W. Norton, 1971.

Link, Arthur Stanley. *Woodrow Wilson and the Progressive Era, 1910–1917.* New York: Harper & Row, 1954.

Loveland, Anne C. *Lillian Smith: A Southerner Confronting the South.* Baton Rouge: Louisiana State University Press, 1986.

Marchetti, Victor, and John D. Marks. *The CIA and the Cult of Intelligence.* New York: Alfred A. Knopf, 1974.

Martin, Sidney Walter. *Florida's Flagler.* Athens: University of Georgia Press, 1949.

Meisel, Perry, and Walter Kendrick, eds. *Bloomsbury/Freud: The Letters of James and Alix Strachey, 1924–1925.* New York: Basic Books, 1985.

Morgan, Ted. *FDR.* New York: Simon and Schuster, 1985.

Paletz, David L., and Robert M. Entman. *Media Power Politics.* New York: Macmillan, Free Press, 1981.

Parenti, Michael. *Inventing Reality: The Politics of the Mass Media.* New York: St. Martin's Press, 1986.

Partridge, Frances. *Love in Bloomsbury.* Boston: Little, Brown, 1981.

Pearson, Carol, and Katherine Pope. *The Female Hero in American and British Literature.* New York: R. R. Bowker, 1981.

Rich, Adrienne. *Of Woman Born: Motherhood as Experience and Institution.* New York: W. W. Norton, 1976.

———. *On Lies, Secrets and Silence: Selected Prose, 1966–1978.* New York: W. W. Norton, 1979.

Roark, James L. *Slaves Without Masters: Southern Planters in the Civil War and Reconstruction.* New York: W. W. Norton, 1977.

Roazen, Paul. *Freud and His Followers.* New York: Alfred A. Knopf, 1974.

Shapiro, Laura. *Perfection Salad: Women and Cooking at the Turn of the Century.* New York: Farrar, Straus & Giroux, 1986.

Simons, Irving, M.D. *Unto the Fourth Generation: Gonorrhea and Syphilis: What the Layman Should Know.* New York: E. P. Dutton, 1940.

Smith, Lillian. *Killers of the Dream.* Rev. ed. New York: W. W. Norton, 1961.

Smith-Rosenberg, Carroll. *Disorderly Conduct: Visions of Gender in Victorian America.* New York: Alfred A. Knopf, 1985.

Solomon, Barbara Miller. *In the Company of Educated Women: A History of Women and Higher Education in America.* New Haven: Yale University Press, 1985.

Sosna, Morton. *In Search of the Silent South: Southern Liberals and the Race Issue.* New York: Columbia University Press, 1977.

Tuchman, Gaye, Arlene Kaplan Daniels, and James Benet. *Hearth and Home: Images of Women in the Mass Media.* New York: Oxford University Press, 1978.

Ward, Joe. "The Binghams: Twilight of a Tradition." *The* [Louisville] *Courier-Journal Magazine,* April 20, 1986.

Watterson, Henry. *"Marse Henry": An Autobiography.* 1919. Reprint. Woodstock, N.Y.: Beekman Publishers, 1974.

Westkott, Marcia. *The Feminist Legacy of Karen Horney.* New Haven: Yale University Press, 1986.

Wilson, Louis R. *The University of North Carolina, 1900–1930: The Making of a Modern University.* Chapel Hill: University of North Carolina Press, 1957.

Wolfe, Thomas. *The Hills Beyond.* New York: Charles Scribner's Sons, 1941.

———. *Look Homeward, Angel.* New York: Charles Scribner's Sons, 1929.

Woodward, C. Vann. *Origins of the New South, 1877–1913.* Baton Rouge: Louisiana State University Press, 1951.

———. *The Strange Career of Jim Crow.* 2nd ed. New York: Oxford University Press, 1966.

Wright, George C. *Life Behind a Veil: Blacks in Louisville, Kentucky, 1865–1930.* Baton Rouge: Louisiana State University Press, 1985.

Wyatt, Wilson W. *Whistle Stops: Adventures in Public Life.* Lexington: University Press of Kentucky, 1985.

Young, Hugh. *Hugh Young: A Surgeon's Autobiography.* New York: Harcourt, Brace, 1940.